Handbook of Criminal Investigation

Handbook of Criminal Investigation

Edited by

Tim Newburn, Tom Williamson and Alan Wright

Routledge
Taylor & Francis Group

LONDON AND NEW YORK

First published by Willan Publishing 2007
This edition published by Routledge 2011
2 Park Square, Milton Park, Abingdon, Oxon OX14 4RN
711 Third Avenue, New York, NY 10017

Routledge is an imprint of the Taylor & Francis Group

© Willan Publishing Ltd 2007

Hardback
ISBN-978-1-84392-188-2
Paperback
ISBN-978-1-84392-187-5

British Library Cataloguing-in-Publication Data

A catalogue record for this book is available from the British Library

Project management by Deer Park Productions, Tavistock, Devon
Typeset by GCS, Leighton Buzzard, Beds

Contents

List of abbreviations

ABI	Association of British Investigators
ACPO	Association of Chief Police Officers
AGMA	Association of Greater Manchester Authorities
AIM	Active Investigation Management
APA	Association of Police Authorities/American Psychological Association
APPRO	Association of Police Public Relations Officers
ARS	alternative remittance system
BCS	British Crime Survey
BCU	basic command unit
BI	best information
BIA	behavioural investigative adviser
BKA	BundesKriminalamt
BPS	British Psychological Society
BSU	behavioural science unit
BVR	Best Value Review
CAD	computer-aided dispatch
CAPE	Community and Police Enforcement (initiative)
CDRP	Crime and Disorder Reduction Partnership
CHIS	covert human intelligence source
CIA	community impact assessment
CID	criminal investigation department
CJ&PA	Criminal Justice and Police Act 2001
CJPOA	Criminal Justice and Public Order Act 1994
CMA	Crime Mapping Analysis
CNI	Critical National Infrastructure
CoE	Council of Europe
CPIA	Criminal Procedure and Investigations Act 1996
CPS	Crown Prosecution Service

CRFP	Council for Registration of Forensic Practitioners
CSI	crime scene investigator
DHS	(US) Department of Homeland Security
DPP	Director of Public Prosecutions
DSU	dedicated source unit
EAW	European arrest warrant
ECHR	European Convention on Human Rights
ECtHR	European Court of Human Rights
EJN	European Judicial Network
ELO	Europol liaison officer
EU	European Union
FATF	Financial Action Task Force
FBI	Federal Bureau of Investigation
FLO	family liaison officer
FME	forensic medical examiner (police surgeon)
FPN	fixed penalty notice
FSS	Forensic Science Service
FSSoc	Forensic Science Society
GI	geographic information
GIS	geographic information systems
GMAC	Greater Manchester Against Crime
GMAC PBM	Greater Manchester Against Crime Partnership Business Model
GMP	Greater Manchester Police
HMCPSI	Her Majesty's Crown Prosecution Service Inspectorate
HMIC	Her Majesty's Inspectorate of Constabulary
HMICA	Her Majesty's Inspectorate of Courts Administration
HMIP	Her Majesty's Inspectorate of Probation
HMRC	HM Revenue and Customs (formerly Her Majesty's Customs and Excise)
HOLMES	Home Office Large Major Enquiry System
HRA	Human Rights Act 1998
IAG	independent advisory group
ICAC	(Hong Kong) Independent Commission Against Corruption
ICPC	International Criminal Police Commission
ICPO	International Criminal Police Organization
INSPIRE	Infrastructure for Spatial Information in Europe
IPCC	Independent Police Complaints Commission
IPI	Institute of Professional Investigators
IQ	intelligence quotient
LGC	Laboratory of the Government Chemist
LPT	local policing team

MAG	Media Advisory Group
MAPS	Mapping and Analysis for Public Safety
MIRSAP	*Major Incident Room Standardised Administrative Procedures* (manual)
MIM	*Murder Investigation Manual*
MO	modus operandi
MPS	Metropolitan Police Service
NAFIS	National Automated Fingerprint Identification Service
NCIS	National Criminal Intelligence Service
NCOF	National Crime and Operations Facility
NCPE	National Centre for Policing Excellence
NCS	National Crime Squad
NDIU	National Drugs Intelligence Unit
NDNAD	National DNA Database
NFIU	National Football Intelligence Unit
NIM	National Intelligence Model
NOS	National Occupational Standards
NPIA	National Policing Improvement Agency
NPM	new public management
NSAC	National Security Advice Centre
NTAC	National Technical Assistance Centre
NTC	National Training Centre (for Scientific Support to Crime Investigation)
NYPD	New York Police Department
OBTJ	offences brought to justice
OLAF	European Union Anti-fraud Office
OS	Ordnance Survey
PACE	Police and Criminal Evidence Act 1984
PBG	Partnership Business Group
PDR	professional development review
PIP	Professionalizing Investigation Programme
PITO	Police Information and Technology Organization
POP	problem-oriented policing
PPAF	Police Performance Assessment Framework
PSI	public sector information
PSNI	Police Service of Northern Ireland
PSSO	Police Sector Skills Organization
PSTS	Police Science and Technology Strategy
PSU	Police Standards Unit
RCCP	Royal Commission on Criminal Procedure
RCS	regional crime squad
RDS	(Home Office) Research, Development and Statistics (Directorate)
RIA	regulatory impact assessment

RIPA	Regulation of Investigatory Powers Act 2000
ROP	Repeat Offender Project
SAPC	strategic analytical partnership co-ordinators
SCAS	Serious Crime Analysis Section
SDI	spatial data infrastructure
SEMTA	Science, Engineering and Mathematics Alliance
SERE	Survival, Evasion, Resistance and Escape
SIA	Security Industry Authority
SIO	senior investigating officer
SIS	Schengen Information System
SIU	special investigative unit
SOCA	Serious and Organized Crime Agency
SOCO	scenes of crime officer
SOC&PA	Serious Organized Crime and Police Act 2005
SSD	scientific support department
SSM	scientific support manager
SSU	scientific support unit
TA	Terrorism Act 2000
TCE	Tackling Crime Effectively (initiative)
TCG	Tasking and Co-ordinating Group
TIC	taken into consideration/time of conviction
TIM	tactical interview manager
TSA	(US) Transport Security Administration
TTB	traditional trait-based (profiling)
UN	United Nations
VCSE	volume crime scene examiner
VIW	vulnerable and intimidated witness
WTO	World Trade Organization

Notes on contributors

Laurence Alison is the Academic Director of the Centre for Critical Incident Research at the University of Liverpool. He has published in leading international journals and has spoken at conferences on social cognition and the processes by which individuals make sense of ambiguous, complex or contradictory information. He has evaluated so-called 'offender profiles' and researched decision-making and leadership processes in critical incidents. He has contributed to a number of major police inquiries, to particularly complex and controversial investigations (including *R* v. *Stagg*), to a review of the behavioural information provided in the Dowler Inquiry, and he has been key psychological adviser in over 40 major debriefs, including the recent London bombings.

Louise Almond is a research assistant at the Centre for Critical Incident Research, the School of Psychology, University of Liverpool. Louise's work has focused on behavioural patterns among juvenile sex offenders. More recently she has been examining the cognitive processes that underpin the interpretation of complex investigative information – specifically, offender profiles and behavioural investigative advice.

David Ashby completed his PhD at UCL, which explored 'The spatial analysis of crime and policing in England and Wales'. Co-sponsored by the Police Foundation, and including collaborations with the Audit Commission, the National Reassurance Policing Programme and a variety of police forces, his research has been widely published and has generated much interest from central and local government alike, including the Cabinet Office and the Home Office. His research interests lie in the use of geographic information in developing more efficient and effective public services (particularly the use of geodemographics and advanced spatial analysis). David also has an MSc in geography from the University of Toronto and a first-class honours degree from the University of Nottingham. He currently works as a business manager for Geospatial Technology UCL Business – the commercial and outreach arm of University College London.

A.P.A. (Ton) Broeders obtained an MA in English linguistics from the University of Nijmegen and a PhD from the University of Leiden for a dissertation on the interpretation of forensic evidence. In 1988 he joined the Netherlands Forensic Institute in The Hague, where he currently holds the position of Chief Scientist. In 2004 he was appointed Professor of Criminalistics at the University of Leiden. In addition to acting as court-appointed expert in hundreds of cases in the Netherlands, he has testified in Mauritius and for the International Criminal Tribunal for the Former Yugoslavia in The Hague.

John Burrows is a partner in Morgan Harris Burrows, a consultancy group specializing in crime risk management and crime reduction. He has published widely on a range of issues relating to policing, youth crime, drugs and the criminal justice process. His research into the criminal investigation process dates back to the early 1980s when he co-authored, with Roger Tarling, *Clearing Up Crime* (*Home Office Research Study* 73). He has also managed a series of research studies into the use of forensic science in crime investigations. He has held honorary posts at four British universities.

David Carson is a reader in law and behavioural sciences at the University of Portsmouth. His output – written, editorial and conference organization – has focused on promoting interdisciplinary co-operation and understanding between the behavioural sciences and law (see http://www.port.ac.uk/departments/academic/icjs/staff/title,14064,en.html).

Denis Clark is Principal Lecturer in Criminal Justice Studies at the University of Lincoln. He instigated and led the University of Teesside's MSc in Criminal Investigation and was course leader of a programme to teach police officers how to handle and manage covert human intelligence sources (informants). Prior to becoming a university lecturer, Denis served in the Metropolitan Police, leaving in 2000 as a detective chief inspector. He is the author of Bevan and Lidstone's *Law of Criminal Investigation* (2004) and legal editor of the journal *Police Professional*.

Max Craglia is the Research Co-ordinator of the unit of the European Commission–DG Joint Research Centre that has responsibility for the technical co-ordination of the Infrastructure for Spatial Information in Europe. Prior to joining the centre in 2005, Max was a senior lecturer at the University of Sheffield, teaching GIS for urban planners and applications of GIS to crime analysis.

Jonathan Crego, BSc (hons), PhD, has, with Bill Griffiths and John Grieve, designed and delivered critical incident training for the last 16 years. his design of the Minerva, Hydra and 10,000 volt debriefing methodologies took learning from the Taylor Report into Football Community Safety and, following the Stephen Lawrence Inqiury, he generated (with Bill Griffiths and John Grieve) the Strategic Management of Critical Incidents environment. Jonathan has carried out over 70 debriefing sessions dealing with 9/11, the Asian tsunami, the London bombings, multi-agency perspectives to child protection and murder reviews, both pre- and post-charge. He holds a research chair and is Co-director of the International Centre for the Study of Critical Incident Decision Making at the Department of Psychology, Liverpool University. His Hydra and Minerva methodologies are now operating at 31 locations internationally.

Emma Disley is a DPhil student at the University of Oxford. Her thesis explores contemporary criminal justice policy through a particular initiative to reduce persistent offending. Emma worked as a research officer at the University of Oxford Centre for Criminology during the first two years of her DPhil and now works part time as a research assistant at the National Policing Improvement Agency.

Jim Fraser is Professor of Forensic Science and Director of the Centre for Forensic Science at the University of Strathclyde. He is a past president of the Forensic Science Society and currently Associate Director of the Scottish Institute for Policing Research. He has extensive experience as an expert witness in criminal courts in the UK and has been involved in many high-profile cases. He also has significant experience in strategic and policy matters in relation to forensic science and has advised Scottish and UK parliamentary committees on these matters. He has lectured and published widely on forensic science and related issues. His current research interests include the interaction of science and law, particularly in relation to expert witness evidence and the effective use of forensic science in support of criminal justice.

Nicholas Fyfe is Professor of Human Geography in the School of Social Science at the University of Dundee and Director of the Scottish Institute for Policing Research. He is the author of *Protecting Intimidated Witnesses* (2001), the first in-depth study of a witness protection programme and, with James Sheptycki, of a Home Office-funded report on facilitating witness co-operation in organized crime investigations. He is currently carrying out a comparative study of community activism and crime prevention in Manchester and Auckland.

Robert Green has over 20 years' experience working in the field of forensic science and scientific support. During this time he has been responsible for the management of many serious and notable crime scenes. In addition he has undertaken consultancy work in both the UK and abroad to advance the application of forensic science. He has a double Masters from Canterbury where he is currently reading for his PhD in applied forensic science. He worked for the Forensic Science Service in the Research and Service Department before heading up the Forensic Science Section in the Police Standards Unit (PSU), where he leads a team of forensic scientists, fingerprint experts and other specialists who manage the forensic portfolio within the PSU. Foremost among the remit of the PSU's Forensic Science Team is the work Robert has led on cold-case review – Operation Advance. He was also the initiator of the current performance management regime on forensic science. He is Senior Lecturer in the School of Physical Sciences at the University of Kent and King's College London, where he provided input to the MSc in Forensic Science.

John Grieve, CBE, QPM, BA (hons), MPhil, has served in every rank in the Metropolitan Police, where he was the first Director of Intelligence and where he managed the service's intelligence project. He led the anti-terrorist squad and was the National Co-ordinator for Counter-terrorism during the 1996–8 bombing campaigns. He created and was the first Director of the Racial and Violent Crime Task Force in response to the Stephen Lawrence Inquiry. Retiring in 2002, he is now Chair of the Centre for Policing and Community Safety, an emeritus professor at London Metropolitan University, a senior research fellow at Portsmouth University and a commissioner for the peace process following the Good Friday Agreement. With Jonathan Crego and Bill Griffiths, he helped create critical incident immersive learning and pioneered the use of independent advisers and family liaison officers as fully engaged members of an investigation.

Bill Griffiths, BEM, QPM, joined the Metropolitan Police as a 20-year-old in 1967 and retired as Deputy Assistant Commissioner in 2005, having served mainly as a detective. As Director of Operations and Tasking, he was responsible for all serious and specialist crime investigations, including homicide, armed robbery, kidnap and fraud. He was the Metropolitan Police's lead on learning from the Victoria Climbié and Damilola Taylor public inquiries. He now leads the Commissioner's Development Initiative as Director of the Metropolitan Police's Leadership Academy. With John Grieve and Jonathan Crego, he helped design the Critical Incident Leadership Training programme, and he has been the Director of this programme for the last eight years. He has driven learning from these critical events into organizational learning and change.

Gisli H. Gudjonsson is a professor of forensic psychology at the Institute of Psychiatry, King's College London, and Head of Forensic Psychology Services at the Maudsley and South London NHS Trust. He has published extensively in the areas of psychological vulnerability, false confession, police interviewing and recovered memories. He pioneered the empirical measurement of suggestibility and provided expert evaluation in a number of high-profile cases, including those of the Guildford Four and the Birmingham Six (England), Henry Lee Lucas and John Wille (the USA) and Birgitte Tengs and Orderud (Norway).

Martin Innes is Professor and Director of the Universities' Police Science Institute at Cardiff University. He is author of the books *Investigating Murder* (2003) and *Understanding Social Control* (2003) and of a number of scholarly articles on various aspects of policing. He is the serving editor of the journal *Policing and Society*. Between April 2003 and July 2005 he led the research for the National Reassurance Policing Programme. His current research focuses on applications of the signal crimes perspective to understanding public reactions to crime and the use of intelligence by the police in relation to issues of national and neighbourhood security.

Tim John is Senior Lecturer in Criminology and Criminal Justice at the Centre for Criminology, University of Glamorgan. He has written extensively on proactive and intelligence-led policing. This has included, with Mike Maguire, two major reviews of intelligence-led policing on behalf of the Home Office. The most recent was the national evaluation of the roll-out of the National Intelligence Model (2003). He is currently undertaking research into the extension of intelligence principles and practice into partnership approaches to tackling crime and disorder issues. This included, in 2006 (with Colin Morgan and Colin Rogers), an evaluation of the Greater Manchester Against Crime Partnership Business Model.

Paul Johnson is Lecturer in Sociology at the University of Surrey. He has researched and published on the increasing use of genetic identity archives in both national and international criminal investigations. He is interested in the significance of DNA and other biometrics in relation to the securitization agenda of the European Union, the possibilities for transnational and supranational DNA databases, and the privacy issues raised by the police use of biometric data. Having recently completed a study of the NDNAD of England and Wales, he is currently researching the police uses of DNA in the 25 states of the European Union.

Les Johnston is a professor of criminology at the Institute of Criminal Justice Studies, University of Portsmouth. He has research interests in security governance and in public, commercial and citizen-based policing. He has published articles in many journals, including *Urban Studies*, *Policing and Society*, *Modern Law Review*, *British Journal of Criminology* and *Political Quarterly*. His books include *The Rebirth of Private Policing* (1992), *Policing Britain: Risk, Security and Governance* (2000) and (with Clifford Shearing) *Governing Security: Explorations in Policing* (2003).

Chris Lewis is a senior research fellow at the Institute of Criminal Justice Studies at the University of Portsmouth, where he researches into organized crime, particularly gun crime, covert operations, crime measurement (especially statistics of diversity) and comparative justice systems (particularly those in Europe, Africa and Japan). He was Assistant Director of Research at the Home Office from 1976 to 2003, where he covered statistics and research on all areas of criminal justice, immigration and community diversity.

Mike Maguire is a professor of criminology at Cardiff and Glamorgan Universities. He has published widely on policing topics, including crime investigation and its regulation, intelligence-led policing and complaints against the police. He conducted one of the first studies of the Police and Criminal Evidence Act 1984; a commissioned study for the Royal Commission on Criminal Procedure 1991; and three evaluations of major targeted policing initiatives under the recent Home Office Crime Reduction Programme. He has also written on burglary, violence, victim issues, prisons, probation, parole and resettlement. He is a co-editor of *The Oxford Handbook of Criminology* (4th edn 2007). He is a member of the Correctional Services Accreditation Panel and of the South Wales Probation Board, and is Senior Academic Adviser to the Home Office research team based in the Welsh Assembly.

Mario Matassa is a research fellow at the Mannheim Centre for Criminology at the London School of Economics. He worked previously at the Public Policy Research Unit, Goldsmiths College, the Home Office Policing and Reducing Crime Unit and Leeds University, where he completed his PhD on policing in a divided society. He is a consultant to the Metropolitan Police Service and has been involved in major studies of the policing of hate crimes. His publications include *Community Safety Structures: An International Literature Review* (with Adam Crawford) and the book chapter 'Policing and terrorism' (2003, with Tim Newburn).

Rob C. Mawby is Reader in Criminal Justice at the Centre for Criminal Justice Policy and Research, UCE, Birmingham. He is the author of *Policing Images: Policing, Communication and Legitimacy* (2002) and co-author of *Practical Police Management* (1998). He has undertaken consultancy and applied research projects for, among others, the European Commission, the Home Office and the Police Standards Unit. These have focused on diverse aspects of policing, including police accountability and police corruption, police–media relations, the effectiveness of intensive supervision projects for prolific offenders and the joint agency management of priority offenders.

Clare McLean is a research assistant at the Centre for Critical Incident Research, the School of Psychology, University of Liverpool. Clare has examined multi-agency collaboration in complex inquiries, decision errors and decision inertia. She has worked on a variety of operational debriefs in major inquiries and has provided internal reports for several police forces in the UK.

Becky Milne, BSc (Hons), PhD, is a principal lecturer at the Institute of Criminal Justice Studies, University of Portsmouth. She is the course leader of the FdA in Investigation and Evidence – a distance-learning degree programme specifically for investigators. She is a chartered forensic psychologist, an associate fellow of the British Psychological Society and an associate editor of the *International Journal of Police Science and Management*. Becky is the academic lead of the Association of Chief Police Officers' Investigative Interviewing Strategic Steering Group, and has worked closely with the police and other criminal justice organizations through the delivery of training in the enhanced cognitive interview, witness interview advising and the interviewing of vulnerable groups, and by providing case advice.

Bob Morris read history at Cambridge and is an honorary research fellow at both the History Department of the Open University and the Constitution Unit, Department of Political Science, UCL. During 1961–7 he worked at the Home Office. Among other things, he served as the Principal Private Secretary, the Home Office liaison officer with the Metropolitan Police and as Head of the Bill Team for the original police and criminal evidence legislation.

Tim Newburn is Professor of Criminology and Social Policy and Director of the Mannheim Centre for Criminology at the London School of Economics. He has written and researched widely on issues of crime and justice and, in particular, on policing and security. He has acted as adviser to the Home Office on various aspects of policing and to the Metropolitan Police on integrity and corruption. His recent books include *Policing, Surveillance and Social Control* (2001, with Stephanie Hayman), *Crime and Criminal Justice Policy* (2nd edn 2003), *Handbook of Policing* (2003), *Youth Offending and Restorative Justice* (2003, with Adam Crawford), *Criminal Justice and Political Cultures* (2004, with Richard Sparks), *Policing: Key Readings* (2005) and *Dealing with Disaffection* (2005, with Michael Shiner and Tara Young).

Peter Neyroud is a chief constable and the Chief Executive of the National Policing Improvement Agency. From 2002 to 2006 he was the Chief Constable of Thames Valley and has served in Hampshire and West Mercia. From 2004 to 2006 he was a vice-president of the Association of Chief Police Officers. From 2006 to 2007 he was a Home Office director with national responsibility, while building the NPIA, for police ICT and forensic science. He has written and published on police ethics and police management, is the editor of the new *Oxford Journal of Policing* and is a jury member for the Stockholm International Prize in Criminology. He is a member of the Sentencing Guidelines Council and an independent member of the Parole Board Review Committee.

Paul Roberts is Professor of Criminal Jurisprudence at the University of Nottingham School of Law, where he researches and teaches in the fields of criminal evidence, criminal justice and criminal law theory, with particular emphasis on philosophical, international and comparative perspectives. He has published over 60 articles, book chapters, research reports, notes and reviews on these topics, and is co-author (with Adrian Zuckerman) of *Criminal Evidence* (2004). He is also editor of the *International Journal of Evidence and Proof*, has acted as consultant to the Law Commission and the Crown Prosecution Service, and regularly lectures to the legal profession on topics of criminal evidence and procedure.

Amanda L. Robinson received her PhD in interdisciplinary social science from Michigan State University, with concentrations in criminology, sociology and industrial/organizational psychology. She is currently a senior lecturer in criminology and criminal justice at Cardiff University. She has conducted empirical research into American and British criminal justice systems. Specifically, her research interests include police discretion and decision-making, police performance measurement, community policing, violence against women, and sentencing policy and practice. She has published in *Policing and Society*, *Journal of Criminal Justice*, *Criminal Justice and Behavior*, *Violence against Women*, *Contemporary Justice Review* and *Policing: An International Journal of Police Strategies and Management*.

Stephen P. Savage is Director of the Institute of Criminal Justice Studies at the University of Portsmouth. He has researched and published in the areas of policy analysis, policing, miscarriages of justice and the politics of law and order. His publications include *Policing and the Power of Persuasion* (2000, with Sarah Charman and Stephen Cope), *Policy Networks in Criminal Justice* (2001, co-edited with Mick Ryan and David Wall) and *Police Reform: Forces for Change* (forthcoming 2007).

Kevin Smith has been investigating offences involving vulnerable witnesses since 1989. He is seconded to the Crime Investigation Doctrine Development Team of the National Centre for Policing Excellence but continues to be operationally involved in interviewing witnesses and suspected offenders, and in the provision of strategic interview advice. He is a member of the ACPO National Strategic Steering Group on Investigative Interviewing and sits on the Home Office Steering Group for Vulnerable and Intimidated Witnesses and the Intermediary Project Steering Committee. He is the author of *The Child Protection Investigator's Companion* (1994) and is currently writing another book about vulnerable and child witnesses. He holds a first-class honours degree in psychology, an MA in education and a PhD in social psychology.

Peter Stelfox is the Head of Investigative Practice at the National Centre for Policing Excellence (NCPE). He works with police practitioners, policy-makers and academics to develop and publish evidence-based practice for the investigation of crime. Before joining the NCPE he was Head of Crime Operations in the Greater Manchester Police with responsibility for the investigation of organized crime and homicide. He has an MA in police management and a doctorate in the investigation of homicide.

Nick Tilley is Professor of Sociology at Nottingham Trent University and Visiting Professor at the UCL Jill Dando Institute of Crime Science. He is also Senior Adviser to the Home Office Regional Research Team based in the Government Office for the East Midlands. He is author or editor of nine books and has published over 100 journal articles, book chapters and research reports for government offices.

Robin Williams is Reader in Sociology at the University of Durham. In the last five years he has been involved in researching police uses of forensic science in the UK and elsewhere. His work has been funded by the Home Office and by the Wellcome Trust. He is a member of the Policy, Ethics and Life Sciences Institute and convenes an interdisciplinary research group on 'Identities, technologies and society' at Durham University. His book (co-authored with Paul Johnson), *Genetic Policing: Using DNA in Crime Investigation*, will be published in 2007.

Tom Williamson was, until his death in 2007, a visiting professor at the Institute of Criminal Justice Studies, University of Portsmouth. He was a chartered forensic psychologist and had a doctorate from the University of Kent for his research into investigative interviewing. He was one of the founders of the PEACE method of interviewing. A former police officer, he retired from the post of Deputy Chief Constable of the Nottinghamshire Police in 2001, having previously served in all ranks to commander in the Metropolitan Police.

Alan Wright is a visiting professor at the Centre for Criminal Justice Policy and Research, UCE, Birmingham, with research interests in the fields of policing and crime investigation. Before entering academic work in 1985, he served in the Metropolitan Police for 25 years, mostly in the CID, where he worked on the Kray case and on other gang crime and homicide cases. He is the author of *Organized Crime* (2006) and *Policing: An Introduction to Concepts and Practice* (2002) and co-author of *Practical Police Management* (1998). He has lectured at several universities and is also currently an honorary research fellow at Keele University.

For Tom and Rita

Preface and acknowledgements

Criminal investigation is a subject that figures extensively in government policy, in the media and in the public imagination. In addition to fictional accounts in books, film and television, it has been the focus of many official reports and enquiries. Despite this evident interest, and in contrast to the sub-discipline of police studies which is now well established within British criminology, there has been relatively little systematic research by sociologists, criminologists and social psychologists into how criminal investigations are conducted. This is surprising given the fact that the subject has received the attention of two Royal Commissions since 1980 and high levels of publicity in a number of miscarriage of justice cases and government enquiries.

This handbook has been produced to remedy the lack of a readily accessible overview of the subject and to enable practitioners, academics and general readers to explore the salient issues of criminal investigation and some of its complexities. The primary aim of the handbook is to provide a comprehensive and authoritative text; setting out a rigorous and critical approach to a wide range of contextual knowledge and understanding about criminal investigation, including underpinning theory. To achieve this, it brings together experts in their particular fields to address key themes in the history, structures, processes, practice and governance of criminal investigation.

Our sincere thanks are especially due to those subject experts who contributed chapters of a very high quality to the handbook. Without their contribution, this volume could simply not have been produced. Our thanks are also due to a number of people who helped us to complete the work. Dr Rob Mawby (University of Central England), commented extensively on draft chapters of the manuscript and made many constructive comments. Peter Stelfox (National Centre for Policing Excellence) did likewise, and also made a number of very helpful suggestions for the Glossary. Michelle Antrobus and David Kershaw organised and successfully completed a mammoth task in editing and proof reading the manuscripts. Particular thanks are due to our publisher, Brian Willan, who brought patience, encouragement and a considerable amount of practical and intellectual support in seeing this project through to completion. As always we gratefully acknowledge the support provided by our families during the gestation and birth of this rather large volume.

Finally, and perhaps most poignantly, we would like to pay tribute to our co-editor Tom Williamson, whose contribution to this handbook cannot be over-emphasised. Sadly, Tom died before the handbook was published, although he was able to engage with the final proof stage and every area of the work bears his handprint. We dedicate this work to Tom and to his wife Rita, in the hope that it will prove a fitting memorial to Tom's life and work in this field.

Tim Newburn, London School of Economics
Alan Wright, University of Central England
April 2007

Chapter 1

Understanding Investigation

Tim Newburn

Understanding investigation

The police have many functions and responsibilities. Indeed, understanding the balance between these has led to considerable academic debate. For many commentators the core function of the police is the maintenance of order. Others point to the role of police forces as 'secret social services'. In the public mind, however, in addition to the provision of reassurance, it is undoubtedly the case that it is the prevention, investigation and detection of crime that is seen as the central part of the police mandate. Interestingly, crime investigation has not generally been a subject of significant academic scrutiny. That is beginning to change, however, and in this volume we examine the history, theory, policy and practice of investigation. As with all areas of policing, however, it is important to understand these activities in their broader institutional and social context.

It is now commonplace to observe that policing is changing markedly just as the world being policed is itself being transformed. The fact that such an observation is fast taking on the character of a cliché doesn't make it any less true. A number of important and fairly rapid changes have been affecting the structure and nature of British policing in recent decades. First, quite clearly for the bulk of the postwar period crime has been on the rise. That crime has fallen in the last decade doesn't mask the fact that over a longer time period the overall direction of change has been towards much higher levels of crime, affecting all communities. Secondly, ease of transportation and communication has changed the character of at least some criminal activity. Although much crime is still committed by local people within their own or neighbouring communities, there is an important strand of criminal activity that involves significant mobility – of people and goods – with important implications for how such activity is policed. For example, the creation by the Serious Organized Crime and Police Act 2005 of the Serious Organized Crime Agency (SOCA), which became operational in 2006, is a significant departure from the traditional policing structure in England and Wales. SOCA is charged by s. 2 of the Act with 'preventing and detecting serious crime', but also to 'contributing to the reduction of such crime in other ways and to the mitigation of its consequences'. Thus, from its inception it has been working to a different paradigm of investigation from either its predecessor organizations or police forces, and this new paradigm is expected to be better able to meet the crime challenge emanating from the changes in transportation and communication.

Like the whole of the crime control arena, the last 30 years have seen a remarkable politicization of policing. The emergence of a 'law and order' ideology has been particularly marked in neoliberal political economies such as the UK (Cavadino and Dignan 2006), as political parties compete to demonstrate their policies are the toughest on crime. By pushing law and order further up the political agenda, politicians have become more involved in the management of policing structures and resources. These political changes also forced a change in the function of policy-makers from their traditional distantiated role as Platonic guardians (Loader 2006) to a much more hands-on service delivery function. This meant that police organization, police pay and police performance are all matters on which politicians regularly offer views and around which they frequently seek to make political capital, with officials being tasked to drive through the subsequent political reforms. Finally, this process increased the gradual centralization of policing, which has been underway ever since formal police forces first covered the whole of England and Wales, and that has gathered considerable pace in the last 30 years or so.

Within policing, there has been a gradual shift in which increasing emphasis has been placed on crime control. All the classic studies in the sociology of policing observed, in their different ways, that the core functions of policing included the maintenance of order, the investigation, detection and prevention of crime, and a host of other 'service' tasks. This interest in policing coincided with the gradual emergence of the managerialist agenda of the 1980s and 1990s that took hold as government politicians sought to increase their oversight of all public services, including the police. This ostensibly enabled them to ask questions of how public money was being spent and, crucially, whether value for money was being achieved. Over time, there developed an increasing sense that politicians were less and less impressed with the efficiency and effectiveness of the British police service. This, combined with the general politicization of 'law and order', led the government increasingly to identify crime reduction as the number-one priority for the police. Crime control has become progressively defined as the key task in policing. Over the last decade and a half significant effort has been devoted to exploring organizational and technological means for improving police performance in this area. All aspects of policing, including investigatory capacities and techniques, have been affected by this shift with significant government investment in forensics, such as DNA testing and in improving the connectivity of information and communication technology, between forces and agencies.

The introduction of the New Police in the early nineteenth century was accompanied by considerable public scepticism and resistance. In persuading a reluctant Parliament and public, Peel and the other architects of the British police sought to design an institution that was obviously dissimilar in important respects from the military, or the gendarmerie model that Wellington had previously created in the Royal Irish Constabulary which was designed to pacify a largely indigent Catholic population and which became the model for colonial policing throughout the British Empire. Significantly, Peel also saw the need to differentiate the New Police from the continental model of policing that involved agents provocateurs and informers. As a consequence, the development of an investigative capability was eschewed in favour of patrol and it was some time before a formal criminal investigation function and department were created with grudging approval from the Home Secretary. From the 1870s, when criminal investigation was first fully established, this element of policing spread rapidly. Moreover, the development of this function was accompanied by stringent efforts by police managers to portray such work as requiring particular forms of expertise and to secure criminal investigation departments a degree of autonomy from their uniformed peers. In many respects such endeavours were highly successful for, by the mid-twentieth century, a certain cachet or glamour attached to plain-clothes work within the police service, however misleading the notion of detective 'expertise' may really have been.

Over time, a stereotypical picture of police detective work has built up. Maguire (2003: 367) suggests that the typical popular portrayal of such work contains the following six assumptions:

1 That it is 'reactive' (i.e. that the police respond to a crime complaint from the public rather than generate the investigation themselves).
2 That it is focused on an offence which has already taken place.
3 That the offence which is being investigated is clear from the outset.
4 That the inquiries are geared to uncovering the 'truth' about what happened.
5 That it is carried out by detective (CID) officers.
6 That the main investigative skills lie in discovering and interpreting 'clues' to find out 'who did it'.

He then goes on to note that, while it is perfectly possible to find cases that adhere to this general pattern, in practice day-to-day investigative work is very different. It is different for some of the following reasons. First, the vast majority of investigative work is 'suspect centred'. That is to say, it involves the surveillance of, and collection of intelligence on, what are sometimes euphemistically referred to as the 'usual suspects' and then working to link them to existing criminal activity. Secondly, there is a critical standpoint which views with great scepticism the claim that investigative work is focused on the search for the 'truth' and, by contrast, argues that it is more about constructing successful cases against known offenders leading to convictions (Sanders and Young 2003). Thirdly, and increasingly, there is a strand of investigative activity that is better thought of as *proactive* than *reactive*. There is growing emphasis upon the use of covert surveillance, informants and the like in contemporary investigative practice. Indeed, the overt aim of the National Intelligence Model – which aims to promote such activities – is precisely to alter the nature of police activity and to make it less reactive and less influenced by the latest event or 'crisis'.

Historically, criminal investigation has been organized in three main ways: primarily, into specific criminal investigation departments; into specialist squads such as robbery teams or squads focusing on particular problems such as organized crime; and, finally, into major inquiry teams set up in response to particularly significant events. Though there have been many notable successes, the history of criminal investigation in British policing has also come in for some extremely serious criticism. Indeed, and particularly since the 1970s, it has been regularly beset by scandal. The scandals have come in a number of forms, but have focused primarily upon allegations of corruption (not least in some serious crime squad in the Metropolitan Police in the 1960s and 1970s); some significant abuses of power leading to miscarriages of justice (particularly around the wrongful convictions of people accused of terrorism in the 1970s and 1980s); and more general incompetence (in the investigation of the Yorkshire Ripper case in the 1980s and the Soham murders leading to the Bichard Inquiry in 2005) and institutional racism (for example, in connection with the investigation of the murder of Stephen Lawrence in the 1990s).

Such scandals, together with a more pervasive sense that policing generally, and criminal investigation more particularly, was not especially efficient, have led to growing calls for reform. Initially – from the early 1980s – attempts at increasing police effectiveness focused on tighter managerial controls, greater external (government) scrutiny and tighter legislative control (via the Police and Criminal Evidence Act (PACE) 1984). Progressively, attention turned to what became known as 'crime management' and to the idea that such work could be managed more proactively, that crimes could be allocated to different categories according to their seriousness and the likelihood of clear-up (a form of policing 'triage') and that new methods could be found to increase effectiveness. As in so many areas of policing at the time, the Audit Commission were particularly influential. Their (1993) report, *Helping with Enquiries: Tackling Crime Effectively*, was highly critical of traditional case-based methods of inquiry and prompted the police to think more proactively, across cases, and to use forensic evidence and other intelligence in a more strategic manner.

The long-term outcome of this general pressure to increase efficiency and work more strategically has been the emergence, via the idea of intelligence-led policing (Tilley 2003), of the National Intelligence Model (NIM). Launched by the Association of Chief Police Officers (ACPO) in 2000, NIM was endorsed by government and, according to the National Policing Plan, was to be 'adopted by ALL forces to commonly accepted standards'. NIM is expected to work at three levels: basic command unit, force/regional and national/international in relation to serious and organized crime. It is described by at least some of its proponents as a 'business model', designed to enable police managers to allocate resources and, at its heart, is the aim of gathering and using 'intelligence' in a structured manner in relation to strategies, tactics, problems and targets. As such it shares certain characteristics with 'problem-oriented policing' though, arguably, should, if put into practice effectively, be more wide ranging in its impact. As with so many initiatives in policing, the key word here is *implementation*. It remains early days for NIM and, while there appears to be considerable commitment to the model, there is still a very long way to go before it can be claimed that it has been embedded successfully within the police service (Maguire and John 2004). The Human Rights Act 1998 meant that the intrusive surveillance the police had traditionally conducted as part of their intelligence gathering would in future be unlawful, and this led to the enactment of the Regulation of Investigatory Powers Act (RIPA) 2000 (as amended) which provided a framework for the interception of communications, surveillance and the use of covert human intelligence sources with regulation being provided by RIPA commissioners. Codes of practice are issued under the Act which has brought about the codification of aspects of best intelligence practice. One result of the legislation is to extend the remit of surveillance beyond the police and, currently, besides the 43 police forces in England and Wales, there are over 900 agencies that are now the beneficiaries of RIPA powers.

Studying investigation

In contrast to the subdiscipline of police studies which is now well established within British criminology, there has been relatively little systematic research by sociologists, criminologists and social psychologists into how criminal investigations are conducted. This is surprising for a number of reasons. First, criminal investigation is a staple of literary fiction and other media. From Sherlock Holmes through to modern-day bestsellers like Ian Rankin, Patricia Cornwell and P.D. James, criminal investigation fills bookshelves across the country. Relatedly, criminal investigation has been central to television portrayals of the police. Although a beat cop, and later a sergeant, George Dixon remains the apogee of television representations of British policing. Since the days of Dixon, however, some of the most famous TV cop programmes have focused on criminal investigation. *Softly, Softly, The Sweeney* (portraying a fictionalized flying squad) and even a significant element of *The Bill* all focus on the activities of the CID. In the USA the focus is even clearer, with *Hill Street Blues* and *NYPD Blue,* among many others, built around the lives of US detectives. The role of forensics has become a more recent genre, with television programmes like *CSI* proving to be immensely popular. Beyond popular portrayals, criminal investigation has also been the subject of considerable public and political attention, not least because of two Royal Commissions since 1980 as well as the very high levels of publicity attracted by a number of miscarriage of justice cases. In addition, there have been a number of more recent high-profile government inquiries such as those carried out by Lord Macpherson of Cluny into the death of Stephen Lawrence and by Lord Laming into the death of Victoria Climbie. Each of these reports has identified shortcomings in the way criminal investigations have been conducted and has made recommendations for improvement.

Despite the relative absence of academic scrutiny in this area, the study of criminal investigation is increasing in higher education institutions. Within the last decade, a number of centres have been established in universities to provide higher educational qualifications in investigation-related subjects. A Foundation Degree in Investigation and Evidence is now available. In mainstream criminology courses, students are beginning to take modules on criminal investigation as part of their studies. This will frequently take the form of one module and will cover the history of investigation, the structure of investigations, legal and technological changes in investigation, corruption, regulation and growth in professionalism.

Moreover, as we implied in the discussion of NIM earlier, there is a process of 'professionalization' going on in relation to investigation within the police service itself. ACPO launched a new training and development programme in late 2005 with the aim of enhancing the skills of investigatory officers and indeed all staff involved in such work. Such professionalization has developed only recently within the police service, partly because it is only relatively recently that criminal investigation has been viewed as in any way separate from other policing skills (even though CIDs have existed for over a century). A combination of legal and technical changes affecting the context and practice of investigation, together with a broader set of concerns about police effectiveness, including in criminal investigation, have brought this latest change about. The desire to stimulate greater professionalism has been supported by the creation of job descriptions and occupational standards covering all investigative roles. The end product has been the Professionalizing Investigation Programme (PIP), established by the Home Office and ACPO. According to its organizers, it has the key objective of:

> achieving professionalism in investigation across the complete spectrum of the investigative process. PIP includes an end to end National Learning and Development Programme designed to provide a career pathway for investigators and develop skills in investigation within the Police Service.
>
> PIP incorporates training, workplace assessment and ultimately registration for all existing and new to role investigators. The programme draws on the Practice Advice contained within Core Investigative Doctrine and is underpinned by the investigation and interviewing units contained within the National Occupational Standards developed by Skills for Justice.
>
> National training programmes with investigative elements have been designed to support PIP and to accurately reflect the levels of complexity at which investigators are expected to operate. (http://www.deliveringchange.org/faq.asp).

The consequence has been the development of an accreditation programme and the introduction of continuous professional development aimed at officers at all levels and police service staff involved in criminal investigation.

Indeed, the need to consolidate knowledge and understanding about criminal investigation has been further recognized by central government. In 2006 the Home Office announced the establishment of a National Policing Improvement Agency (NPIA). The agency, which will be formally established in 2007, is designed to support police forces to improve the ways in which they work. In due course, the NPIA will supersede the National Centre for Policing Excellence, which was established to provide evidence-based policies and practice in the field, and Centrex with its responsibilities in police training. The national investigative occupational standards developed by the Police Sector Skills Organization (PSSO) (now subsumed in the Skills for Justice organization) will provide the criteria for a competency-based model for investigators which is intended to lead at some point in the future to a form of 'licence to practice'. The PSSO conducted research for its Foresight Report and identified that the shortage of investigative skills was one of the most important challenges that the police service will face over the next five years.

A joint Home Office/ACPO conference in 2004 served to focus attention on the importance of investigation as a means of improving police performance. Volume crime has been receiving the attention of the Police Standards Unit, the Audit Commission and Her Majesty's Inspectors of Constabulary (e.g. HMIC 2003; Audit Commission 2006). In addition to the challenges facing the public police, there is now a growing plurality of provision. Investigators are employed by a number of public sector bodies, such as the Inland Revenue and the Department of Work and Pensions. In conjunction with the universities, these bodies have developed accreditation programmes for the training of their investigators. Civilian oversight bodies have also developed similar investigator-training programmes. Clearly, there is a very substantial set of changes underway both within and outside the police service. The gradual professionalizaton of investigation is leading to education and training demands that the higher education sector is now organizing itself to meet. In addition, the general changes to police training that are underway will only serve to increase this process. As a consequence, there would now appear to be a sizeable and growing practitioner audience consisting of investigators at all levels, both public and private, for whom there is as yet no comprehensive textbook that covers all the key areas of criminal investigation. It was with this in mind that we embarked on the *Handbook of Criminal Investigation*.

The volume

This text is not intended as a training manual or simply as a compendium of extant knowledge about particular crime types and their investigation. We have attempted to be significantly more ambitious. What we have sought to do in this volume is to provide a rigorous and critical approach to a wide range of contextual and practical issues, including underpinning theory. Chapters review existing knowledge and consider future directions. Rather than a dry summary of existing ideas, all the authors were given the freedom to write an essay that might capture the excitement of current developments as well as consider future prospects. Putting together such a book – even one as large as this one is – meant making some difficult decisions about what to include and what to leave out. Readers will have their own views, and we would be genuinely interested to hear about ideas that might arguably be included in a future edition.

The current volume is divided into five parts. The first part considers criminal investigation in comparative context from the perspective of various disciplines, including history, sociology, psychology and law. It addresses the question of how criminal investigation is best theorized and understood through each of these perspectives. How is criminal investigation moulded and shaped by the political, social and cultural forces, such as the mass media, that have seen modernity replaced by late modernity and the development of those more general forces summarized as globalization? In this regard when talking of 'modernity' we are referring to the social and technological changes that brought about the Industrial Revolution, including the recognition of the need for a police force. In contrast, late modernity is taken to describe an advanced stage of industrial capitalism in which massive social and technological changes, particularly in the area of communications – often summarized as 'globalization' – have begun to change the way in which nation-states are organized and operate. How has our growing understanding of the psychological affected the nature and processes of criminal investigation and how central is such knowledge to that set of practices we call investigation? And, crucially, how is criminal investigation shaped by the criminal law? What is the relationship between the two and in what ways is an understanding of jurisprudence central to the process of making sense of criminal investigation? These questions and others set the parameters for the initial part of the book and provide the basis for the more specific and detailed elements that follow.

The second part considers the organization of criminal investigation. It addresses a number of crucial questions. What are the international, national and local structures within which criminal investigation takes place? What is the rationale and impact of the National Intelligence Model? How is NIM working in practice and to what extent will it reorient police work in this area? How is the investigation of local crime and that of serious and serial crime organized? What provision is made for investigation by private bodies and public bodies which have hitherto been regarded as being outside the 'mainstream' of policing? How does this plurality of regulative and investigative activity affect the investigation of a range of offences, including such things as white-collar crime and fraud?

The third part examines the important subject of forensic science and the techniques that have been developed to support the investigative process. This part includes four chapters, the first of which examines the principles of forensic examination science. At its heart this looks at material traces of various sorts, from matter such as blood, saliva, semen, urine and hair, and physical and chemical traces like glass, fibres and paint, together with impression evidence such as handwriting, shoeprints and fingerprints. This is followed by a more particular examination of the *practice* of forensic investigation as it is carried out in the UK, and the part concludes with two chapters that examine, among other things, the practice of crime scene investigation, the growing use of biometric databases and how such work might be evaluated and assessed.

Part four examines investigative sources and process. This covers such issues as models of investigation, the use of covert surveillance and informant handling – a growing element in policing generally as we have described – practices and processes for dealing with victims and witnesses, and an examination of the practice of investigative interviewing. Finally, the section concludes with two chapters that examine different forms of crime profiling. The first focuses on that area of activity that has been made famous by television in recent years, however inaccurately – namely, offender profiling. The final chapter looks at the profiling of places using geo-demographic analysis and geographic information systems.

The final part examines some of the problem areas associated with the governance of criminal investigation, including its management, supervision and oversight. This part also examines such topics as critical incident management, investigative ethics and corruption, miscarriages of justice, and the growing importance of professionalization of the investigative process. We conclude with a brief future look. In drawing together some of the more important themes and developments covered in the previous twenty-seven chapters, and extrapolating forwards, we offer some views on the pressures likely to be brought to bear on criminal investigation during the next decade or more, and what these are likely to mean for these practices within and beyond policing. What seems undeniable is that we are now at the point where the study of criminal investigation becomes a much more coherent and important field. We hope that this first edition of the *Handbook of Criminal Investigation* will prove a useful guide to this developing area.

References

Audit Commission (1993) *Helping with Enquiries: Tackling Crime Effectively.* London: Audit Commission.

Audit Commission (2006) *Neighbourhood Crime and Antisocial Behaviour.* London: Audit Commission.

Cavadino, M. and Dignan, J. (2006) *Penal Systems: A Comparative Analysis.* London: Sage.

HMIC (2003) *Partners in Crime.* London: HMIC.

Loader, I. (2006) 'Fall of the "Platonic guardians": liberalism, criminology and the political responses to crime in England and Wales', *British Journal of Criminology*, 46: 561–86.

Maguire, M. (2003) 'Criminal investigation and crime control', in T. Newburn (ed.) *Handbook of Policing.* Cullompton: Willan Publishing.

Maguire, M. and John, T. (2004) *The National Intelligence Model: Key Lessons from Early Research.* London: Home Office.

Sanders, A. and Young, R. (2003) 'Police powers', in T. Newburn (ed.) *Handbook of Policing.* Cullompton: Willan Publishing.

Tilley, N. (2003) 'Community policing, problem-oriented policing, and intelligence-led policing', in T. Newburn (ed.) *Handbook of Policing*. Cullompton: Willan Publishing.

Part I

Criminal investigation in context

Understanding criminal investigation – as would be the case for any part of criminal justice – cannot properly be realized without having some sense of its historical and social context. It is providing this context that is the focus of the chapters in this first part of the volume. The part opens with Bob Morris's overview of the history of criminal investigation. In outlining the changing nature and organization of criminal investigation he identifies four main periods: what he refers to as the 'heroic period' covering the first 50 years after the introduction of the New Police; a further period lasting until the interwar years in which a process of organizational specialization got underway; and a third half-century-long period in which there developed central leadership and oversight of criminal investigation within the police service. Finally, there is the current era, starting in the early 1980s, in which further centralization, particularly by government, took hold and moulded crime investigation practices. What is clear from Morris's analysis of the history of investigation is that the forces that have shaped and changed policing generally are also those that have affected investigation more particularly. Though there are particular incidents – scandals, inquiries and serious crimes – that obviously bear on investigation much more significantly than other aspects of police work, in general terms it has been the gradual centralization, politicization and increasing managerial control of policing that can also be seen in investigation as elsewhere.

This point also comes across clearly in Matassa and Newburn's exploration of the social context of investigation. Here they identify, from among a broader range of social pressures, four linked processes that have had the greatest impact on contemporary criminal investigation. One of these is the aforementioned *centralization*. The impact of this can be seen in a number of different ways: the growing influence of central government over this aspect of policing; and the rise of national policing bodies responsible for aspects of investigation – notably the Serious and Organized Crime Agency – and of national training bodies such as the National Policing Improvement Agency.

Second is the broader set of changes associated with globalization which, in revolutionizing communications, have had an important impact on the nature of serious and organized crime and have stimulated the growth of transnational policing bodies with an increasingly global reach. The third trend is what they refer to as neoliberalization. In using this term, they are pointing to a number of linked changes in investigation, notably the increasingly managerialist nature of command and control in policing and, relatedly, the growth of marketization and competition and the consequent spread of private actors within the sphere of criminal investigation. Finally, they suggest that contemporary investigative practices are dominated by risk-oriented concerns. While it is important not to overstate the impact of such thinking on policing, there are numerous examples of its impact, including the growing influence of cost-benefit calculations in decisions about investigation; the redeployment of expertise from reactive to intelligence-led policing; the growth of surveillance technologies and of information technologies such as computer data storage and collation; and, linked with this, the gradual reorientation of policing as 'information brokerage'.

Below this general social context of policing there is a further way in which investigative practice and procedure can be understood. Anyone at all familiar with television portrayals of crime investigation, or with other fictionalized accounts, will be only too aware of such psychological issues as memory, intelligence and recall and their relationship to confessions and other testimony. Tom Williamson explores such issues and a range of other questions that form the psychological context of criminal investigation. Psychology has had a very significant impact on shaping policy and legislation regarding such issues as the questioning of suspects in custody, the interpretation of witness evidence and the problem of false confessions. Despite the difficulties – and they can be extensive – Williamson quotes research that suggests that adults demonstrate accurate recall of events up to 98 per cent of the time and that the mistakes that they do make are more likely to concern peripheral details rather than crucial information. The impact of psychology can possibly be seen in its most concrete form in the establishment of behavioural science units in many police forces. Established initially within the Federal Bureau of Investigation, such units have spread rapidly and tend to involve a combination of practitioners and professional psychologists, providing support, advice and expertise in situations as varied as hostage negotiations, major inquiries and the profiling of serial killers. The rise of more 'scientific' approaches to criminal investigation is yet another illustration of the trend towards professionalization that is described and analysed in a number of the chapters in this volume.

Having considered the social context, the legal and jurisprudential context of contemporary criminal investigation is considered in detail by Paul Roberts. The law structures criminal investigations in two important ways. First, the law specifies the objectives of criminal investigations. It defines the elements of a crime, sets out what must occur for a criminal conviction to be secured and details the nature of specific offences. Secondly, the law also seeks to regulate investigations. It does so by establishing the basis of police powers – via legislation such as the Police and Criminal Evidence Act

(PACE) 1984 and the Regulation of Investigatory Powers Act 2000. Roberts outlines the nature of each of the major police powers: stop and search, arrest, search, seizure, detention, interrogation, together with the rules relating to identification. Crucially, as he goes on to point out, it is vital not to lose sight of the limitations of the law, and of the necessity, therefore, of remedies when there is some abuse of powers. Perhaps most importantly, though also controversially, recent years have seen the passage of the Human Rights Act 1998, and Roberts suggests that there are grounds for 'cautious optimism' in regard to its potential 'to supplement the common law's traditional laissez-faire attitude towards the ill-defined powers of "citizens" in uniform' with a demand for an explicit legal basis for any investigative measure potentially infringing individuals' fundamental rights. However, set against this, as he notes in conclusion, there is the fact that the law has never presented an insurmountable obstacle to those who wish to exploit new technologies and processes of investigation. It is a difficult future to predict.

It is now all but impossible to separate our understanding of criminal investigation from mediatized images of such work. Public impressions of crime investigation are heavily mediated by television in particular. In the final chapter in this section, Rob C. Mawby explores such representations. In particular, he explores three themes: the variety of ways in which crime investigation has been portrayed through the media; the extent to which the British police have developed the practice of what he refers to as overt 'image work'; and, finally, the nature of police–media relations. The media have played a hugely important role in the construction of both positive and negative images of the police, and Mawby concludes with the interesting observation that the nature of contemporary communications offers the possibility in future of demystifying police work generally, and police investigative practice in particular.

Chapter 2

History of criminal investigation

Bob Morris

How has the recognizably 'modern' society of the last 200 years in England and Wales responded to investigative needs? Although there has been much recent attention paid to *policing*, relatively little systematic attention has been paid to criminal *investigation*. What follows will attempt, therefore, to trace investigation in England and Wales, from the creation of the Metropolitan Police to the present day.

Looking at developments over approximately 200 years, it is possible to discern four main timeframes:

1 The heroic period: 1829–78.
2 Organizational specialization: 1878–1932.
3 Central leadership: 1933–80.
4 Central initiative and control: 1981–the present.

Over the whole period there were, of course, many social and other changes that affected behaviour, perceptions of crime and investigative capacity. A number of developments were also event driven. As a full-time detective specialism grew, issues emerged about its control. Such contemporary influences will be identified in the course of this survey.

First, it is necessary to bear in mind one of the governing peculiarities of the English criminal justice system – the absence of a universal, independent system of public prosecution until 1986. While there were partial expedients, for example in the role of the Treasury Solicitor and that of the reformed Director of Public Prosecutions (DPP) from 1908, their focus was almost exclusively on the most serious offences – a handful of the total number prosecuted before the courts.

Unlike the situation in Scotland, Ireland, British India and British colonial territories, every prosecution in England and Wales was in law a private prosecution. Unsought by them, the role became one shouldered by the new forces. It gave a special authority to the police investigative function, the exercise of which was, until the entry into force in 1985 of the Police and Criminal Evidence Act 1984, carried out largely on the basis of uncodified powers. The lack of specific funding or of a continuous, adequately resourced central function meant that the prosecution function in England and Wales was, compared with the situation in other European states of comparable size, relatively immature. Well into the twentieth century it also lacked access to centrally organized and quality-controlled scientific advice and capacity.

The heroic period: 1829–78

While the establishment of the 'new' police from 1829 was clearly a deliberate break from previous arrangements, it did not overnight introduce fresh or standard levels of investigative expertise. The change was motivated by the executive's wish to control public order policing uniformly throughout the metropolis: 'Professional policing was the norm in London by the 1820s, but *centralization* remained controversial' (Reynolds 1998: 4).

In so far as there was a policing capacity available for investigative action in London, it was in the police offices set up by the Middlesex and Surrey Justices Act 1792, and not absorbed into the Metropolitan Police until 1839 (Beattie 2006). Outside London, the 'new' forces established under the Municipal Corporations Act 1835 and the County Police Act 1839 were modest affairs. In, for example, the Black Country of Staffordshire – a series of populous, contiguous industrial small towns and villages – build up was slow. One of the principal towns (Walsall) during 1835–40 possessed only one superintendent and three constables for a population that grew from 14,420 in 1831 to 19,587 in 1841.

Nor did the condition of society necessarily pose the sort of impediments to investigative success to which we have learnt nowadays to be accustomed. Travelling any distance was greatly facilitated by the railways in the nineteenth century and it was more difficult to invigilate. But rail travel did not provide the freedom made available by the arrival of cheap motor cars in the following century. In the late 1850s, for example, although trains allowed the Manchester pickpocket to travel to seaside Southport to work the crowds at one of Barnum's shows, they also allowed a Southport police officer to use the company telegraph to trace the offender (whose identity was unknown) through the ticketing system and have him detained on return to Manchester (Jervis 1995: 29–30). In 1894, a quick-thinking Hertfordshire divisional commander, guessing that an unidentified burglar might aim to return to London by the morning train, hurried to intercept it and divined successfully which of the passengers might be the culprit, arresting him with the stolen items on his person (Osborn 1969: 117–18).

The density, or anomic quality, of modern populations should not be anticipated. Speaking of the Black Country 1835–60, it was said that no great efforts of detection were necessary because 'the community seems to have been a tight one in which everyone knew everyone else' (Philips 1977: 60). As the population of England and Wales grew and became more intensely urban, it became commensurately more difficult to rely on the intimacy of smaller communities. But these processes worked only gradually, were not universal or simultaneous, and their onset should not be anachronistically assumed. Even in London, the persistence of nodal, village-like qualities cannot be overlooked.

Furthermore, it would be incorrect to assume that, until the explicit establishment of detective departments from the 1840s, there were no public officials undertaking investigative work after 1829. On the contrary, the establishment of such departments represented merely the bureaucratization and professionalization of the function rather than its invention. While it is generally understood that the small number of constables attached to Bow Street from the mid-eighteenth century and subsequently to all the other 1792 Act police offices undertook inquiries (including outside London) until disbandment in 1839, they had their less celebrated counterparts elsewhere. As observed of Staffordshire local constables, they were not illiterate incompetents and 'they tended to be long-serving' (Philips 1977: 62). Old Runners like Henry Goddard (1800–83) acquired a good deal of detective skill over a long career. Although the hero of his own anecdotes, his methods would be recognized today as exhibiting developed features of investigative professionalism which would have been learnt from former colleagues and by experience (Goddard 1956). Fulfilling similar functions in the City of London where they were attached to the Mansion House rather than the new force established in 1839, John and Daniel Forrester, who had operated since 1816 and 1820 respectively, were not stood down until 1857 (Rumbelow 1971: 197). Similarly, even in the Metropolitan force, where it has often been assumed there was no detective capacity between 1829 and 1842, there is evidence of some informal investigative specialization in a situation where the commissioners deployed officers to look into particular cases.

What was new about the Metropolitan Detective Department sanctioned by the Home Secretary in 1842 was not its investigative function but the *recognition* it gave to that function in an event-precipitated change. The immediate origins lay in the Russell and Good murders of 1840 and 1842. In the first, a peer, an uncle of a Cabinet minister who had also recently been Home Secretary (Lord John Russell), was murdered by his valet, Courvoisier, and the investigation conducted by the police patently left much to be desired. In the Good case, the suspect had partially dismembered his female victim and it took time for the suspect to be run to earth. These events received unfavourable newspaper comment and, although the original deployment of the Metropolitan Police had been predicated on a preventative rather than a detective design, the commissioners were brought in 1842 to recommend that the Home Secretary should sanction the establishment of a detective department.

The commissioners made their recommendations to the Home Secretary (Mayne 1842) with some hesitation. Spurred most immediately by criticism following the Good case, Mayne defended the Metropolitan force's record. He also went out of his way to denigrate the Bow Street Runners with whom the Metropolitan Police had co-existed until 1839, and to whose demise was attributed by some observers a loss of investigative capacity in London. True, he allowed, the Runners 'had advantage in tracing out some sorts of cases' but their methods included the fact that 'by at least some of them, a communication was kept up with the thieves or their associates, from whom occasionally they received information that led to detections, that might not otherwise have taken place'.

Pointing out that the commissioners already identified in each division 'individuals more peculiarly qualified from experience and superior intelligence' to undertake special inquiries, Mayne also indicated the problems that might arise in relations between a specialist detective body and the uniformed force, and was alive to the potential problems of supervision and control. Finally, recommending ostensibly an experiment, Mayne concluded that it should be possible to compensate for such disadvantages, envisaging that the new detectives would be under the 'immediate directions' of the commissioners.

There seems to have been no substantive discussion in the Home Office, which approved the proposals within the week. All but one of the eight officers (i.e. two inspectors and six sergeants) appointed were later identified from contemporary newspapers as having already acted in a detective capacity (Cobb 1957). If there had been discussion with the Home Office, it must have occurred before the paper was written rather than as a result of it. A consensus, rarely challenged, became established: there could be difficulties but careful supervision would overcome them.

Indeed, rather than its being challenged by the 1868 Departmental Committee (Metropolitan Police 1868a) set up in the wake of the Fenian Clerkenwell explosion, the committee recommended its considerable extension in the shape of attaching a corps of detectives to every Metropolitan Police division. Even where investigative arrangements have been shown to be fallible as in the Turf Fraud cases of 1877 (Dilnot 1928) or *The Times* corruption cases a century later (Cox *et al.* 1977), the response has been to reinforce the system rather than reform it. 'Rotten apples' have been discarded but otherwise the orchard has remained undisturbed.

Looking back, it is easy to characterize the 1842 change as paltry and inadequate, and to see as pusillanimous any future reluctance to challenge presumed policy-making inadequacies of 1842. But there would be a real danger of anachronism in adopting such a line. As Mayne pointed out in 1842, the nature of crime in London at the time did not justify any complicated architecture for the response. It is also the case that, although Mayne has been given the credit for detective innovation, that has been the result of what the investigative task *became* rather than what at the time it amounted to. In many ways, all that Mayne actually sought in 1842 was political endorsement of what had in any case been going on – unacknowledged – for some time.

Indeed, detective departments did not break out elsewhere in a pandemic rash. Just as it seems no great publicity was given to, or sought, for the new specialism in London in 1842 (Browne 1956: 122), so were other forces relatively slow to respond. While detectives were introduced in Birmingham later in the summer of 1842, the force was then under a Home Office commissioner and it may well have been influenced directly by the Metropolitan force's action (Reilly 1989: 16). By 1878 there were 16 detectives out of a total of 520 men. In the other London force, the City, there even seems to be some doubt about when exactly a detective department came formally into life. The best guess apparently is that it coincided with the departure of the Forrester brothers in 1857 (Rumbelow 1971: 194).

From 1856 one of the first Inspectors of Constabulary (General Cartwright) encouraged the appointment of plain-clothes officers in provincial forces, and stressed of Birmingham: 'the detective force is of the greatest importance and might be increased with advantage in co-operation with other forces' (HM Inspector of Constabulary 1857). In fact, there were never more than a small handful of detectives in the early days, and they were rarely consolidated into recognizable detective functions. In Worcestershire merely because officers were in plain clothes did not necessarily mean that they were investigators: 'Most plain clothes officers were used to serve summonses and court documents and were not actively involved in the investigation of crime' (Pooler 2002: 123). Sometimes resort to plain clothes could be purely temporary, as when the Chief Constable of Dorset ordered their wearing to apprehend vagrants in 1850 (Hann 1989: 33–4).

Not surprisingly, the larger urban forces like Birmingham developed a detective capacity ahead of county forces. Leeds, for example, had three plain-clothes officers in 1843 (Clay 1974: 24), and eleven detectives headed by a superintendent in 1878. Even small boroughs like Newport and Leicester had officers acting in a detective capacity in 1842 and 1843, respectively (Bale 1960: 56; Beazley 2001: 30). Rather later, Coventry recruited its first detective (from Liverpool) in 1858 (Sheppard 2000: 11) and Middlesbrough appointed its first in 1859 (Taylor 2002: 116).

As in so many aspects, the Metropolitan numbers greatly exceeded those anywhere else. Following the recommendations of the 1868 committee (Metropolitan Police 1868a), the central Detective Department's numbers were increased from 15 to 25. More significantly, nearly 200 detectives were appointed in the Metropolitan Police divisions. It is not clear how they were selected, but it is likely that they were in fact – rather like the men first appointed in 1842 – already operating in plain clothes on the divisions. The divisional detectives remained under the control of the divisional superintendents.

So far as investigative methodologies were concerned, in the beginning – and for a long time afterwards – pragmatism ruled. There was no formal training: informal apprenticeship was the rule, and one that outlasted the 'heroic' period. In retrospect this may seem an inadequate response by the managers of forces. From their point of view, however, circumstances did not justify any special training. Many of these issues were discussed during the proceedings of the Detective Departmental Committee set up following the Turf Fraud trials of 1877. In these trials a number of the central Detective Department's most experienced and senior officers were convicted of corruption (Dilnot 1928). Giving evidence to the committee, the commissioner's legal adviser, J.E. Davis (formerly a stipendiary magistrate in Stoke and Sheffield), who had been put in charge of the Detective Branch following the Turf Fraud scandals, opined: 'the majority of offences…are cases as to which you cannot help seeing in thirty minutes how incapable of further action they are' (Metropolitan Police 1878a: Q 5033). In his own evidence, the Metropolitan Commissioner, Henderson, put his judgement rather testily: 'The real practical fact is that in ninety-nine cases out of a hundred cases of crime, the detection is most humdrum work, and it only requires just ordinary care and intelligence. You do not want a high class mind to do it at all' (Metropolitan Police 1878a: Q 5251).

But, even if higher intellectual standards had been necessary or even desirable, they were not apparently to be found among the generality of early detectives. Davis dismissed the divisional as opposed to central Detective Department officers as 'the least informed and the least educated' officers (Metropolitan Police 1878a: Q 5009). The Head Constable of Leeds, William Henderson, was, if anything, more damning when giving evidence to the same committee: 'nineteen out of twenty of the detectives throughout the kingdom are very illiterate men' (1878a: Q 3806). Looking back 25 years from 1910, a Liverpool commentator recalled: 'the majority of the Force was very illiterate, many even of the higher officers being quite unable to write, much less spell, a short report so as to be reasonably intelligible' (Jones 1910: 39).

Controlling the investigators

The problem of effectively supervising the operations and probity of detectives was not solved by the form of their establishment in London in 1842. Corruption has a long history, has at times been allegedly extensive and, some would argue, is unavoidably endemic (Morton 1994; McLagan 2003). In a much quoted observation, one historian of the Metropolitan Police judged that, by 1922, 'the CID had become a thoroughly venal private army' (Ascoli 1979: 210).

The problem of institutional control was strongly implied in Mayne's 1842 memorandum: if there had been problems with the probity of the runners, then the same fallings from grace might afflict the Metropolitan detectives. The reassurance he offered to the Home Secretary was that the detectives would be 'under the immediate directions of the Commissioners'. In fact, it is inherently unlikely that Mayne was able to exercise an effective supervision even over the relatively small central Detective Department of his day, which never numbered more than 15 officers. Effective central control was even less likely in respect of the divisional detective system initiated in 1869 after Mayne's death. In their case, the divisional superintendents had neither the time nor the means to supervise the officers who were not subject to control from the centre either.

There was some fairly anxious, if inconclusive, discussion about these difficulties at headquarters from 1870 when the defects of the 1869 arrangement began to become apparent. A.C. Howard, one of the new-style district superintendents appointed following the 1868 committee, made some of the most thoughtful comments. With an Indian Police Service background, he was a persistent advocate of detective diaries, both to control and to direct detectives' work. The Indian Criminal Procedure Act actually required detectives to keep diaries.

Problems of control were addressed in a number of ways. The Turf Fraud scandal of 1877 had demonstrated a complete failure of supervision, in one case involving corrupt behaviour from 1872, but the ensuing departmental committee's recommendations concentrated on structural change rather than specifically on forms of control. The establishment in 1878 of what became known as the Criminal Investigation Department (CID) unified the divisional and central detective forces, though with continuing ambiguity in respect of the authority of local divisional superintendents. This was the model eventually adopted throughout the service in England and Wales but, while it responded to operational investigative imperatives, it did not address investigator control. In some ways, it made those problems worse by establishing the CID as an independent, self-referential satrapy within forces, the 'firm within the firm'.

The appliance of science

Tom Critchley, formerly Secretary to the Willink Royal Commission, maintained in his history that 'Detective work, during much of the nineteenth century, was the Cinderella of the police service' (Critchley 1967: 160). It is certainly true that in this early period there was little evidence of scientific sophistication. During the nineteenth century, 'science' for forensic purposes meant for most people the natural or physical sciences as largely, but not exclusively, deployed by the medical profession. It was only rather later that the contributions of the social and mathematical sciences became recognized and exploited. Moreover, for a good deal of the first hundred years, the forensic applications of the natural and physical sciences remained in their exploratory stages. The great toxicologist, Alfred Swaine Taylor, giving evidence in 1856 in the trial of the Rugeley poisoner, Palmer, had to persuade the jury that the victim had died of strychnine poisoning even though Taylor had no test available for finding its presence in the corpse (Ward 1998: 47–58). In the Smethurst case (a doctor accused of poisoning his pregnant mistress) in 1859, Taylor caused a crisis of confidence in the guilty verdict by having admitted that he had found the presence of arsenic but only because of contamination from his own testing apparatus. The Home Secretary sought further medical opinion and granted a free pardon, not because of any defect in the trial process as such but because of 'the imperfection of medical science' (Parry 1931: 21–2). Such 'imperfection' could lead, it has been claimed, to very rough justice in poison cases where it was as likely that an innocent party would be convicted and executed as that a guilty party would go free (Watson 2004: 3).

On the other hand, just as it would be wrong to assume that science was infallible, so would it be a mistake to think that whenever deployed it offered immutable standards of proof. Stephen's own change of tack about the evidence in a Warwick poisoning trial of 1781 showed how what was expected of standards of scientific proof could change over time. It was alleged that the victim, a bachelor baronet, had been poisoned with laurel water (a form of cyanide) by his brother-in-law who hoped, through his wife, to benefit from the victim's death. The evidence was almost entirely circumstantial and the medical evidence equivocal – the exhumation and post mortem on a much decayed corpse did not occur until some time after death. But the accused's demeanour had been thoroughly suspicious: he did all he could to conceal his involvement in the procurement of the poison and to impede the investigation. In his first account of the case, Stephen concluded that there was enough evidence to satisfy the jury and that 'It would have entirely satisfied me' (Stephen 1863: 335–6). In the second edition of the same work 27 years later, the latter comment was replaced by the observation that 'In the present day, I doubt whether the prisoner would have been convicted, because the medical evidence is far less strong than it might have been' (Stephen 1890: 229–30).

This anecdote illustrates that what science – medical or other – can offer varies over time, and so do the standards of proof expected of its deployment. In addition, vital as the scientific evidence is in itself, at least as important is *how* it is communicated to the court. It was said, for example, of the pathologist Bernard Spilsbury (1877–1947) that 'He could persuade a jury to accept a bad scientific proposition more readily than others could achieve acceptance of a right view' (Ward 1993: 111).

On the other hand, it has to be borne in mind that the best detectives, although rarely highly educated men, could and clearly did develop effective investigative practices, often showing considerable psychological insight. Whicher's report on his investigation into the Road murder of 1860 is an exemplary account of an intelligent assessment of motive and means. His inquiries built up a full and convincing picture of a determined and wilful adolescent, Constance Kent, credibly capable of murdering her half-brother. Summoned late to the scene, he was unable to identify and collect the physical evidence that could have persuaded the magistrates to commit for trial, but the suspect's later confession fully vindicated his conclusions.[1]

Organizational specialization: 1878–1932

Only 29 years of age, Howard Vincent, the first head of the newly established Metropolitan CID, was an adventurer in the burgeoning Victorian administrative state. He brought new energy and more system to the investigative function, moving on to enter Parliament in 1884. Among his innovations, Vincent did not wait for a complaint – hitherto the rule – before launching an investigation, for example into potential swindles (Littlechild 1893: 14). Vincent also wrested control of the *Police Gazette* from the clerk to the Bow Street court, making it a more useful organ for circulating police criminal intelligence.

As in 1842, the Metropolitan model was not after 1878 adopted with alacrity everywhere else, especially in the county forces. Summarizing the position in his district, HMI Lt Col Cobbe explained that the detective officers in the boroughs consisted of 50 officers of different ranks but that, in the counties, 'the officers in charge of divisions, assisted by their immediate subordinates, aid the constable on the "beat" in the detection of offences' (HM Inspector of Constabulary 1880). The long detective career of James Bent in the Lancashire force was typical: he never served in a separate detective department (Bent 1891).

The same 1880 HMI reports record that there were by then detectives in Hampshire but without recording how many. There were, in fact, at least two from 1874 when it is recorded that two were sent for a training attachment to the Metropolitan Police (Watt 2006: 19). The West Riding force – totalling 920 men – then seemed to have no recorded detectives at all. In Hertfordshire the first full-time plain-clothes officer did not appear at Watford until 1892 (Osborn 1969: 51); and, in 1893, Norwich had only two detective officers (Morson 2000: 79). One of the larger county forces, Kent, did not establish a detective department until 1896 and then with a strength of only four officers (Thomas 1957: 63). Essex seems to have had a few plain-clothes officers from the late 1850s, but did not set up a detective department until 1919, or give it a detective inspector until 1921, and only in 1932 was it named the CID (Scollan 1993: 127–8). Bedfordshire, whose small population gave rise to only 33 reported indictable offences in 1903, continued without headquarter detectives as such until 1931 (Richer 1990: 83, 121), and Monmouthshire until 1937 (Thomas 1969: 37). Herefordshire established a CID at HMI prompting in 1939 with two officers who had attended the Wakefield course (Hadley 1999: 40). Caernarvonshire first established a CID even later – in 1940 – with three officers in its force of 129. In the same year in Caernarvonshire, a total of only 402 crimes were recorded (Jones 1963: 76, 87). On the other hand, where a county force had also to operate in a significant town, detectives appeared much earlier, as for example in Warwickshire. There detectives were introduced into Aston in 1858, though the Birmingham force later swallowed the area in the 1911 expansion of the city's boundaries (Powell *et al.* 1997: 103).

The apparent slowness to precipitate an investigative specialty is not remarkable: most forces remained very small. In 1901, for example, the strength of only 21 of the 56 county forces in England and Wales exceeded 200. In the 125 boroughs (excluding the Metropolitan and City of London forces), the comparable number was 14. In addition, only a further 12 exceeded 100 men (Savill 1901: 258–63). The largest of all the provincial forces was Lancashire at 1,600.

It followed from this that the largest force, the Metropolitan Police totalling 15,800 in 1900, was far and away in the best position to develop further specialties within its CID. It did so, however, only slowly. Its main initial effort was put into criminal record-keeping from 1871. During the late nineteenth and throughout the twentieth centuries, it developed specialties in subjects where the size of London's population, and the concentration of various services of all kinds, threw up problems more often than elsewhere and in which the force developed expertise as a result. The most obvious example was the emergence of the Special Branch from 1881–3. Rather later examples included currency fraud, obscene publications and art and antique thefts.

Forensic resources

Granted the growth of organizational specialization in forces, it did not follow that there was an accompanying or commensurate growth in professional development. For identification purposes, following a relatively brief adoption of the Bertillon anthropometric system, Henry's fingerprint classification was adopted in 1902. In 1913 Llewellyn Atcherley, Chief Constable of the West Riding Constabulary, the third largest force outside London, issued the first edition of a painstakingly compiled work which commended a records classification system based on criminal methods of operation. A later edition (Atcherley 1932) claimed a wide circulation throughout the British colonial empire, as well as Denmark, China, Greece and Siam. It was no doubt influential in its day – recommended by HM Inspectors (HM Inspector of Constabulary 1913: 57-8) and much relied upon by forces outside London, if one provincial detective's views were typical (Totterdell 1956: 63–6).

The status of the investigative function was slow to rise. The apparent ineffectiveness of the police during the Ripper murders in 1888 did nothing for the service's reputation. Indeed, expectations of the expertise required were not high. For example, the 1919 report of the Desborough Committee – the first major review of policing in England and Wales since the 1850s – recommended against specialist training for detectives, opining that the requirement might 'adequately be met by experience and practical work' (Desborough 1919–20: Part II, para. 115). Investigation, in other words, remained an artisan craft devoid of any higher intellectual content.

It was the perceived gap between the investigative expertise required and actual detective practice that was exploited by Conan Doyle with Sherlock Holmes as a scientific paragon for ever upstaging the hapless Inspector Lestrade. And, in the memoirs that the officers themselves published signifying their growing self-consciousness as a special group, the artisan practitioners themselves naturally emphasized the craft basis of their expertise (see Hughes 1864 for an early example). A recent study of the social history of the Metropolitan Police over the period up to 1914 singled out detective job satisfaction as notably different from the instrumental attitude of most other policemen to their work (Shpayer-Makov 2002: 266). This group identity was fostered, among other things, by the closed character of the CID, its superior pay and the extent to which it determined its own work standards. This would have contributed to the robust self-belief of the retired Metropolitan detective in 1912: 'I believe it is pretty generally admitted that the Criminal Investigation Department, of which Scotland Yard is the centre, is to-day about the most efficient detective force in the world' (Fuller 1912: 27).

Such attitudes suggested a certain insularity. It was, after all, an officer – Edward Henry – originating in the *Indian* police service who devised a workable fingerprint technology. The point was further brought home by an American observer, Raymond Fosdick, in his 1915 comparative study of European police systems. Impressed by 'the typical Scotland Yard detective, cool, keen, patient, resourceful', he was not impressed by backward methodologies. Moreover, he judged that for the previous ten years there seemed to have been a deep-rooted opposition at Scotland Yard to change and innovation (Fosdick 1915: 313).

The fact is that investigators were not offered much help to bring themselves up to date. Not only was there no national guidance offered by the government (where the criminal justice responsibilities were fragmented) or the courts, but little was produced from within the system itself. In those circumstances, it is not surprising that the first comprehensive – 600 illustrated pages – handbook for investigators in English was a translation made on his own initiative and published in 1906 by the Madras prosecutor (an Englishman) from the German of an Austrian professor of criminology in Prague published originally in 1893, and only in 1924 published in England (Gross 1924). Three subsequent editions were published in 1934, 1950 and 1962 under the superintendence of the Metropolitan Police's Assistant Commissioner (Crime).

On the other hand, Fosdick's strictures stemmed to an extent perhaps from somewhat formulaic expectations. Where there was no central provision, there was none the less a good deal of unsung self-help, and forces made their own way, turning to such local expertise as was available. Public analysts started to become appointed from 1860. During the Fenian bombing campaign of the 1880s, it was the Professor of Chemistry at Liverpool, J.C. Brown, who was instrumental in providing the evidence to convict a bomb maker (Ward 1993: 185–6). In 1894, for example, Metropolitan Detective Inspector C.F. Baker (later Chief Constable of Hastings, 1895–1907) engaged the ammunition manufacturers, Eley, to depose about the bullet found in the brain of a murder victim.[2] The gunsmith family of the Churchills, especially the founder's nephew, Robert Churchill, were used to give expert evidence until the late 1940s in a period where Robert privately developed the use of the comparison microscope for forensic purposes (Hastings 1963).

Routinely, too, much practical assistance no doubt came from the police surgeons. Originally employed to look after the health of the officers, they developed advisory and investigative functions. For example, one Metropolitan surgeon, Graham Grant (whose guide, *Practical Forensic Medicine*, went into three editions from 1907), referred to his 'murder bag', a ready-packed collection of items for use at murder scenes which included equipment for producing contemporaneous sketches for evidential use as well as magnifying lenses and microscope slides. Grant provided scientific evidence leading to convictions (Grant 1920: 79–85, 113–15), and Wensley records help from the same quarter in a murder case (1931: 227). While police surgeons could be charged with amateurism and their knowledge was said to be often meagre (Ambage 1987: 50), such a view perhaps undervalues their utility, especially in everyday practical terms (Merseyside Police 1981: 27/1). That said, their employment directly by the police must have made it difficult for them always to maintain an adequate professional distance and independence. In at least one case, the over-identification with the police is palpable (Matthews 1959).

Effective investigative strategies included borrowing more expert capacity or reinforcing investigating teams. There was at first a casual and later a more deliberate sharing of investigative resource. Whicher's journey to Somerset in 1860 was just one example of the practice of despatching Scotland Yard detectives to the provinces to assist with the investigation of unusual or difficult local cases, especially murders. The practice of making Metropolitan detectives available, originating in the former use of Bow Street officers, was formalized in 1906 and subsequently offered at no cost.

It is difficult to assess the impact of these secondments, though their surviving records can be eloquent about the situations revealed in the forces they visited. For example, that there could still in 1908 be a lack of even elementary forensic scene of crime procedures outside London is illustrated by a Salisbury case.[3] Chief Inspector Walter Dew of the Yard was sent down to investigate the stabbing murder of a one-legged 12-year-old boy. When Dew arrived, no effort had been made to preserve the scene. On the contrary, the body had been washed and a determined attempt – not quite thorough enough – had been made to clear up all the bloodstains in the house. At the time, the Salisbury force consisted of fewer than 20 men for a population of 15,500. This did not represent a particularly low proportion of police to population at the time, but it meant that it was unlikely that there was much investigative sophistication. Indeed, the result of Dew's meticulous and careful report (against the weight of the evidence the mother was acquitted at her second trial) was a further Home Office circular advising promptitude in seeking Scotland Yard assistance and preserving the scenes of crime. According to Wensley, instancing two 1919 cases where the Yard was summoned two and six weeks respectively after the murders, delays remained common (1931: 212).

Reinforcement was almost as important as, if not more important than, investigative skill in the case of intractable inquiries. An 1934 murder saw the Brighton Chief Constable swiftly call for Metropolitan help over the case of a limbless and headless female torso found deposited in a trunk at the railway station's left-luggage office.[4] The legs turned up in a suitcase at St Pancras. The head and the rest of the body were never found. At one time, the Metropolitan investigating officer had 15 plain-clothes officers making house-to-house inquiries in Brighton, others tracing the trunk and suitcase manufacturers, and still more tracking down the 800 women (of whom 730 had been eliminated from inquiries within 16 weeks) reported missing at the time. The victim was never identified and, although a suspect was charged with an unrelated separate murder, the man was acquitted. In the end, an enormous inquiry ended with no 'result'.

Despite the fact that the local forces did not have to pay for Scotland Yard help, secondments do not appear to have been all that frequent. Basil Thomson, then the Yard's Assistant Commissioner (Crime), commented to the Desborough Committee in respect of requests from provincial forces: 'to ask for help they think is a confession of incompetence. The consequence is the number of cases I am asked about you can count on the fingers of one hand in a year' (Desborough 1919–20: Part II, Q 549). It was later reported that aid had been sought in only three cases in 1931, none in 1932, two in 1933, seven in 1934, one in 1935 and five in 1936 – a total of 18 cases in six years (Dixon 1938: 50).

Controlling the investigators

Detective diaries – an important instrument of supervision – were introduced gradually in the Metropolitan force, first for the central detectives from at least 1878 and by 1893 for divisional officers too. The first CID head, Howard Vincent, also took another tack. He issued in 1881 the first edition of a hortatory conduct manual directed at all police officers but with special advice for detectives (Vincent 1881) which, updated by the Yard itself, continued to be issued in successive editions until 1931, long after Vincent's death in 1908. Revisions to the first edition and to others after Vincent's death reflected, among other things, continuing senior officer concern about detective control (Morris 2006).

The courts provided relatively little influence or advice on the direction of investigation practices. True, the trial judge in the 1880 Titley case (a chemist selling abortifacients) objected to the way evidence had been obtained, but gave no directions other than negatively. The judges as a whole remained silent about how interrogations should be conducted, and until 1912 the sole published semi-authoritative advice on the subject was a Foreword contributed by the High Court judge, Henry Hawkins, in 1882 to Vincent's *Code*. When the *Judges' Rules* were issued in 1912, they were a pretty terse set of narrowly conceived injunctions, and arose from the fact that the Home Office had had to intervene after two judges had given conflicting directions in separate similar cases. Uncertainty and ambiguity about investigative powers remained. Although much discussed in the 1920s (Savidge Report 1928; Royal Commission on Police Powers and Procedures 1929), no significant changes were made to the law.

Central leadership: 1933–80

Although arguing that the non-county borough forces should be absorbed into the county forces, H.B. Simpson, the principal Home Office witness to the Desborough Committee in 1919, had accepted without question that the police should remain locally organized and controlled. Listening to this evidence had been the Secretary to the Committee, A.L. Dixon. He was later extremely dismissive of the attitude behind Simpson's testimony and based his own subsequent career on successfully espousing the opposite view. However, although it is true that the experience of the First World War had required the Home Office to take a more proactive line with policing than hitherto, Simpson's view was not simply idiosyncratic passivity. Rather, it voiced what had always generally been the position before 1914. That is, law and order were matters of local responsibility: the centre might assist and its police Inspectorate might advise forces, but the Home Office (with the arguable exception of London) had no direct operational responsibility.

Again, it is necessary to recall that most law and order services, including the criminal courts and prosecutions, were locally organized. This disaggregated universe was not only still largely funded locally but its very disaggregation was regarded as a virtue. What induced the centre to become more interventionist was its realization that the fragmented form of police organization was incapable unaided of measuring up to contemporary expectations drawing upon all the technological aids becoming available.

Dixon became the senior Home Office official heading police affairs between the two world wars. At first, intervening in investigative practices was not highest on Dixon's agenda after Desborough. Indeed, as the Committee's Secretary, he had no doubt been responsible for penning the report's dismissive sentence about detective training noted above.

However, 13 years after Desborough, Dixon took a significant initiative in leading a full examination of detective work and training in a departmental committee he chaired, and the importance of which he later compared with that of Desborough itself (Dixon 1966: 133). One of Dixon's aims was undoubtedly to use the committee, as he had sought to use the regular conferences of chief constables, as a means of redressing the inefficiencies he thought arose from the continued proliferation of so many small forces incapable of lifting their game in the way he thought changed social circumstances made imperative.

The committee finally reported in five volumes in 1938. It estimated that there were about 2,600 detectives in England and Wales in 1933, of whom 1,000 were Metropolitan officers, 1,100 in city and borough forces, and 450 in county forces. By 1938 the overall numbers had risen by about 450 overall, but in a service where there were still 181 separate forces.

The report made particularly important recommendations about detective training. Although Metropolitan detectives had had some formal training since at least about 1916, and the Home Office recommended the holding of district conferences of detectives in 1925, none of these initiatives constituted developed, formal training. As Dixon put it, the fact was that, in the counties, the men were spread too thinly and the detective's instruction 'would be gained by working with a more experienced officer – or by the light of nature'. While some instruction was given in the larger forces, 'nothing in the way of an accepted system of instruction, or doctrine, had been developed in respect of detective work generally' (Dixon 1966: 138).

The report was damning about existing courses where they existed and recommended a detailed syllabus for an eight-week full-time course. In addition to stressing the need for systematic behaviour at scenes of crime and the use of forensic aids, the core concentrated on offences, how to investigate them and against what evidential requirements. At the same time, there was a proper stress on observational and human skills, the latter, for example, in interrogation. While overall the emphasis may have been to lie heavily on the procedural, that fact itself reflected one of the abiding truths about bringing detective work home. After trials at Hendon and the West Riding, a national system of regional courses was instituted. Though stood down during World War Two, detective training continued to be developed thereafter, later within the Centrex arrangements – the Central Police Training and Development Authority, a non-departmental body – due under the Police and Justice Act 2006 to be absorbed by the National Police Improvement Agency.

Forensic resources

Although there was undoubtedly a considerable body of forensic science technique available in England and Wales in the early 1930s (Ambage 1987: 46), it was not organized specifically to meet police needs. There was a nascent facility at Nottingham under the auspices of the hyperactive Chief Constable, Athelstan Popkess, a similar enterprise at Bristol and a resource in Cardiff run by a local grammar-school chemistry master who happened to be the son of the Deputy Chief Constable. Two Derbyshire officers published in 1934 a fairly comprehensive handbook on what was available to assist investigation (Else and Garrow 1934).

What all this needed was system and Dixon was again the man of the hour. As part of the ideas he had been developing to promote efficiency in a fragmented service, and himself possessing a scientific bent, he pursued the issues. While the Detective Committee did not directly take on the subject, how to respond to the organizational question was very much part of the agenda taken up by Trenchard as a reforming Metropolitan commissioner.

The immediate outcome was the establishment in the spring of 1935 of a Metropolitan Police laboratory with a staff of six at the Metropolitan Police College, Hendon. Contrary to Dixon's thinking, a medical pathologist was appointed as head. This proved to be the wrong specialism and, for reasons of personality, the wrong man. With the departure of its sponsor, Trenchard, the laboratory withered in the hostility of the Metropolitan CID, which simply starved it of cases, partly by means of a typically Metropolitan device where permission to refer a case required four signatures. One of the scientists subsequently said of detective officer resistance: 'He reckoned he was a failure if he needed to use science' (Ambage 1987: 72). The fact, too, that the laboratory was located at the college so much hated by Metropolitan officers no doubt affected attitudes (Cuthbert 1958: 26–7). The situation improved with a new head, Henry Holden (a botanist), and a new Commissioner, Scott (a former Home Office official), who extended the positive patronage that had been withheld by Trenchard's successor, Game. The episode was a further illustration of how the Metropolitan force had escaped real accountability to its police authority, the Home Office (Morris 2004). Although it remained outside the 'Home Office' laboratories in what became known as the Forensic Science Service until 1996, the Metropolitan laboratory came into the mainstream of forensic science from the appointment of Holden, and became noted for innovative work. Outside London laboratories were established at Birmingham, Bristol, Cardiff, Nottingham and Preston in the years up to World War Two. The requirements placed upon them stretched the expertise of the staff and pushed them beyond their normal ranges of knowledge, so that external experts continued to be used.

Controlling the investigators

In theory, it could be expected that a prosecution system would have an important role in combating inadequate or corrupt investigative practices. In practice, the special features of the prosecution arrangements in England and

Wales up to 1986 were almost perfectly designed to minimize prosecutorial influence and discipline. The police were themselves in charge of most prosecutions by default, even after the DPP's office was reformed in 1908. From 1908 most DPPs were recruited from criminal barristers (Rozenberg 1987), especially those Treasury Counsel practising at the Central Criminal Court (Old Bailey). Accustomed to working closely with the police and living off police briefs, prosecutors were unlikely to develop habits inclined to bite the hands that fed them. The biographers of one of the most celebrated Old Bailey prosecuting counsel, Richard Muir, made brave attempts to insist to the contrary, as if such a defence were thought necessary (Felstead and Muir 1927: 306–7). The fact was that prosecutors – whether permanent officials employed by police authorities or lawyers in private practice – had to work closely with police officers, were not always brought in at the early stages of investigation and may not have had great influence on either investigative method or conduct. Some memoirs suggest a relationship with detectives that was close to symbiotic (Ensor 1958; Andrews 1968). Muir – to modern eyes – gave the game away in an alleged anecdote. On hearing that the celebrated Metropolitan detective, Wensley, was the officer in a case, Muir remarked: 'Oh, that's not likely to give me much trouble. There is sure to be a confession' (Felstead and Muir 1927: 307). Maintaining a proper professional distance could never have been easy and, as events proved, a high degree of reliance on confession evidence could not be sustained in the longer run.

Even the DPP, because of his use of local agents, did not rule directly over all the already highly unrepresentative cases that came to him. While it was convenient under the Police Act 1964 to require all complaints alleging criminal offences by police officers to the DPP to decide whether to prosecute, the system (which had generalized a prior Metropolitan Police practice) did not by itself bear directly on investigative practice, particularly when so many complaints turned on unresolvable conflicts of contradictory assertion in situations devoid of any independent witnesses.

As late as 1981, the Royal Commission on Criminal Procedure failed to find satisfactory prosecution arrangements *within* forces. The Metropolitan Police had established its own legal and prosecuting department only in 1932. Where there were independent prosecuting solicitors' departments outside London, it is possible that there was more prosecutorial control. Some of them were well established and relatively powerful bodies. Leeds, for example, had 11 prosecuting solicitors by 1974 (Clay 1974: 123). Setting them up universally had been one of the recommendations of the 1962 Willink Royal Commission, but by the time of the establishment nearly 25 years later of the Crown Prosecution Service (CPS) there were still six county forces that had not complied.

Speaking to the Departmental Committee in 1878 in the wake of the Turf Fraud scandal, Metropolitan Commissioner Henderson was frank: 'You authorise your officers to bribe people, and you are very much surprised that they fall themselves occasionally under temptation' (Metropolitan Police 1878a: Q 5194). Robert Mark made one of his reputations by the determination with which he faced problems within the Metropolitan Police (Mark 1978). The investigative function continued to be reviewed from time to time, the focus dependent on the circumstances that led to the review in the first place. The Royal Commission on the Police of 1962 was concerned primarily with constitutional questions of governance, the Criminal Law Revision Committee Report of 1972 with the law of evidence and the Royal Commission on Criminal Procedure of 1981 with issues of police powers following, among other things, the use made of them in a miscarriage of justice case which had been reviewed by a High Court judge.

Central initiative and control: 1981–the present

Increasingly in the last quarter of the twentieth century central government took the initiative in a controlling fashion. This was the consequence both of social changes, which saw crime rise up the political agenda, and government responses to specific stimuli. The police service itself was substantially reinforced: less than 85,000 strong in 1962 when the Willink Royal Commission reported, it rose to over 140,000 officers with substantial civilian support elements by 2007. A concomitant of this growth was the emergence of a new collective professionalism among chief officers. Their trade association – the Association of Chief Police Officers (ACPO) – developed a greater substance and public voice. By 1974 the service in England and Wales, which still had 125 forces in 1960, consisted of 43 forces and, while this consolidation – together with the overlay of regional crime squads established in the 1960s – had removed some of the inadequacies of the very small predecessor forces, it did not establish a consistently high level of confidence in the investigative process whose general characteristics have been very fully and insightfully described by Mike Maguire (2003).

Indeed, the degree of reliance on confession evidence in a notorious miscarriage of justice led not only to an inquiry undertaken by a High Court judge (Fisher 1977) but directly also to the appointment of the Royal Commission on Criminal Procedure tasked to review police powers and the prosecution system. The 1981 Report of the Royal Commission dealt comprehensively with police powers on the basis of careful and illuminating research about the investigative process and the real role of the detective within it. This brought out the fact that 'the majority of offenders were detected in circumstances that did not involve the exercise of detective skills', and 'about a quarter of detections were made following the questioning of someone arrested for another offence' (Philips 1981a: 17, 18).

The outcome was the Police and Criminal Evidence Act 1984, which was fundamentally a codification of investigative powers and procedures which set the professional standards for investigators. How far the Act actually changed investigative behaviour, especially in the case of interrogation, continues to be uncertain (Sanders and Young 2003), and the Macpherson Inquiry (1999) identified incompetence as well as racism as the cause of the failed investigation into the murder of Stephen Lawrence. However, there can be no doubt that the Act did much to bring hitherto unfettered detective discretion under scrutiny and control. Among other things, tape-recording of interviews – long resisted by the police – became adopted without the heavens falling. In the longer perspective, the extent to which the police service has moved from a reactive to a more proactive investigative model remains unclear. On the other hand, from the Police National Computer in the 1970s through to fingerprint matching and large inquiries management systems, information technologies have made vital contributions. In addition, the Crime Faculty at Centrex, offers a capacity for the modern training of detectives and a forum for the circulation of ideas and experience to a standard hitherto wholly unavailable.

Less reactive and more purposive was a series of organizational initiatives taken by the centre. In the past, expertise in the more specialized crimes had been in effect serviced nationally from within the Metropolitan Police which had developed units to deal with them, of which the Special Branch created in 1881–3 was the best known (Porter 1987: 35–49). At first informally and then deliberately, the benefit of these specialties was made available to other forces. The Police Act 1909 had recognized such special 'imperial' services with an annual Treasury subvention to compensate the London ratepayers.

In the end it made sense in 1992 to pull this work into a new central unit, the National Criminal Intelligence Service (NCIS). It was not a British FBI but it was a new species of police organization. As a statutory entity it brought to an end the grace-and-favour functions of the Yard and opened up participation not only to all the 43 forces in England and Wales but also on a multi-agency basis which incorporated the right skills (for example, from Customs and Excise and local authorities), whether they came from within the police service or not. Similar parallel developments had formed and eventually amalgamated regional crime squads, the cross-police authority functioning operational detective units, into the National Crime Squad in 1998 (Mawby and Wright 2003). The Serious Organized Crime and Police Act 2005 represented a further development by fusing NCIS and the National Crime Squad into a single national intelligence and operational entity. The appointment of a former head of the Security Service as its head has no doubt been intended as an important signal. The difference in orientation, operation and style from the glory days of the unreformed Flying Squad described by a former Metropolitan commissioner (Stevens 2005: 66–79) could hardly be more marked.

Also significant has been the funding basis of the new statutory bodies. Whereas earlier forms of centrally organized services – training establishments, laboratories – were funded by force contributions as common police services, the statutory bodies are centrally funded and, although with representative committees, centrally driven.

At the time of writing, it is not clear how far current central initiatives will successfully challenge the notion of locally based policing ostensibly preserved in the 1974 configuration of 43 forces and what, if any, will be the implications for investigative capacity. An Inspectorate of Constabulary review of force performance in respect of 'protective services' (O'Connor 2005) favoured reduction by amalgamation over various forms of improved co-operation between existing forces while preserving the local dimensions of policing in basic command units. These would function within new, larger structures which needed to have a minimum of 4,000 officers to be able to deliver services to an acceptable modern standard. The consultation launched in November 2005 hazarded that 12 was the right number of forces for these purposes.

In the immediate political context, it is clear that the spur for this initiative was the London suicide bombings of July 2005. Although unable to prevent all such events, the government can at least take the opportunity to offer organizational change as part of its response, thus in a way revisiting an agenda that has recognizably ancient roots in inspectorate assessments of 150 years ago. However, in the Commons debate on 19 December 2005, the government experienced some difficulty in gaining acceptance of its case. While the utility of the Serious and Organized Crime Agency (SOCA) for dealing with crimes of national significance was accepted, critics had not been convinced that larger forces would do anything to improve the investigation of purely local crimes. None the less, the then Home Secretary (Clarke), speaking in the debate, made some of his best points when placing a good deal of weight on the goal of improved investigative capacity, pointing out that only 13 of the 43 forces had fully resourced specialist murder units.

A subsequent change of Home Secretary allowed the new one (Reid) to review the whole question. He announced that only one amalgamation – the voluntary Cumbria/Lancashire merger – would go ahead. At the same time he stressed that the status quo was not an option but indicated that the government would be flexible about the *means* by which goals outlined by the inspectorate should be achieved. The Police and Justice Act is the vehicle for a number of initiatives, including the establishment of a National Police Improvement Agency (NPIA) which will, among other things, incorporate Centrex and the Police Information Technology Organization. The Home Secretary has also set up and chairs a National Policing Board which unites ACPO, the Metropolitan Police, the Association of Police Authorities, the inspectorate, the proposed NPIA and the Home Office. Driving what looks like a strong, proactive agenda, the board clearly has given a more ambitious, driving edge to former initiatives like the National Policing Plans made under the Police Reform Act 2002. Among other things, the board reviews investigation outcomes against the targets that have been set. The fact that contemporary governments struggle to maintain the legitimacy of the justice system generally means that investigation performance will remain a primary focus of political attention and support.

Forensic resources

Technically there were successes and failures. Successes included the successive uses of X-ray diffraction and paper chromatography, gas chromatography-mass spectrometry and related techniques, exploitation of electron microscopy and – most well-known – DNA analysis. Failures included professional lapses and worse – including by detectives – leading to the overturning of convictions in a number of cases, including some high-profile alleged IRA murders (Ward 1998: 208–14).

The latter experiences raised fundamental questions of accountability. In the 1930s Dixon's preferred model had been one where the scientists were not employed by the prosecutors, and that was achieved in the Home Office laboratories. However, if there were not equal access to defence as well as to prosecution, the distinction could not deliver a perceived difference. Such concerns have been addressed in two ways. Legislation (the Criminal Appeals Act 1995 and the Criminal Procedure and Investigations Act 1996) removed the post-appeal reviewing function from the Home Office to the independent Criminal Cases Review Authority and required greater prosecution disclosure to the defence to include matter that might favour the defence. The 1996 Act also included provisions for a code of practice for crime investigations. Secondly, there have been successive changes to the governance of the Forensic Science Service (FSS), some of which have been designed to increase its independence and to foster competition in what at one time was its captive market. In December 2005 it ceased to have trading-fund status and became a government-owned company. The object of the change is to allow the service the commercial independence to develop its business flexibly and efficiently in order to be able to compete in an increasingly challenging forensic environment. Although the FSS will continue to supply operational services to the National DNA Database (NDNAD), it will do so only contractually and the management of the NDNAD will be under the control of a separate body.

At the same time, discussing developments in 'traditional' forensic science should not overlook the considerable and growing contribution of the social sciences and statistical techniques. It was the research use of such resources that gave authority in many ways to the recommendations of the 1981 Royal Commission. The product of work undertaken within or under the auspices of what is now the Home Office Research, Development and Statistics (RDS) Directorate has helped to inform investigative techniques. Whereas formerly Home Office advice was sparing and communicated through rare and austere circulars, a whole series of occasional publications are issued to the police service, in the form, for example, of RDS *Findings*, online reports and *Briefing notes* and papers from the Policing and Crime Reduction Unit. There is now outside the laboratory an intellectual community analysing and debating issues formerly the preserve of the limited number of professional investigators compelled with little outside support to make the best of things by relying on their native wit and experience – which remain, of course, with energy and zeal, vital contributions to successful investigation.

Controlling the investigators

As again adumbrated by Mayne in 1842, the institutional problem within forces was what should be the proper relationship between detectives and the uniformed part of the service. The organizational pendulum swung over time between CID exclusivity and attempts to give an appropriate supervisory authority to local uniformed territorial commanders. Because he believed that the CID had become in many ways out of control, Robert Mark took strong steps to align CID management more closely with the main operational structure of the Metropolitan Police (Mark 1978: 120–5). However, resort to transferring 'failed' detectives to the uniform branch as a disciplinary measure was not calculated to improve the morale of the latter whatever it achieved in increasing control over the former. One of his successors, Paul Condon, volunteered a remarkable and frank admission to the Home Affairs Select Committee in 1997 about the extent of the problem in his force (HASC 1998: 1). Condon also firmly associated himself with a series of initiatives that have brought all chief officers and HM Inspectorate of Constabulary together in fresh attempts to confront corruption ideologically as well as managerially (HM Inspectorate of Constabulary 1999), a process informed by a literature review which should have finally laid the 'rotten apple' theory to rest (Newburn 1999), and discussed elsewhere in a context wider than one concentrating solely on investigative activity (Neyroud 2003).

The service has continued to grapple with this organizational problem to which there is no pat answer. Henderson, speaking to the 1878 Departmental Committee in the wake of the Turf Fraud, spoke one of the eternal truths: 'You authorize your officers to bribe people, and you are very much surprised that they fall themselves occasionally under temptation' (Metropolitan Police 1878a: Q 5194). Broadly, the old detective exclusivity has been modified in ways that attempt not to detract from detective skills but, rather, to see them deployed in more collaborative, multi-agency operational structures. Also relevant here is that the establishment of the Independent Police Complaints Commission by the Police Reform Act 2002 has removed the ability of the police to investigate their own alleged misdemeanours, the commission drawing on the investigative skills found in a great variety of non-police as well as police organizations.

Despite continuing concern about investigator control, there has been no real challenge to the organizational regime instituted in 1842. No one was surprised when the Royal Commission whose recommendations were instrumental in the establishment of the Crown Prosecution Service (CPS) for England and Wales in 1986 considered it best to build on what existed rather than consider starting afresh (Philips 1981a: 144). A later attempt (Roach 2002) to argue that the wrong turning was taken in 1842 and, more, that the investigative function should be put entirely under the wing of the prosecution function is unlikely to make headway in exactly that form. On the other hand, the greater prosecutor control over charging and the establishment of the new central bodies selectively to investigate the most serious offences could be seen as responses to such approaches.

Clarification and codification arrived only following the Philips Commission (1981) and the resulting Police and Criminal Evidence Act (PACE) 1984, with its attendant codes of practice. The later Royal Commission on Criminal Justice (Runciman 1993) recommended further changes dealt with in the Acts of 1995 and 1996 mentioned above. Since then successive Acts have made further adjustments to police powers (Regulation of Investigatory Powers Act 2000, Criminal Justice Act 2001, Police Reform Act 2002, Criminal Justice Act 2003, and the Serious and Organized Crime Act 2005). New codes of practice under PACE (as amended) and subsequent powers came into force from 1 January 2006. As already noted, the 2002 Act paved the way for a new complaints system in the Independent Police Complaints Authority, which became operational on 1 April 2004 and can conduct investigations entirely from its own resources rather than always remaining dependent on police investigation.

Conclusions

The investigative requirement does not stand still. Every age produces new targets, offers fresh techniques and demands different evidential standards. Modern preoccupations and state resources have greatly increased national investment not only in policing personnel but also in the intellectual effort devoted to investigative processes. Systems continue to develop – for example, increasing the responsibility of the CPS for charging can be expected to influence investigative methods and behaviour. The craft/artisan days of the detective may be over but the goal of professionalization is not to be regarded as attainable and finite. Rather, it is in each lifetime a journey of constant improvement.

Selected further reading

Emsley, C. and Shpayer-Makov, H. (eds) (2006) *Police Detectives in History, 1750–1950*. Aldershot: Ashgate. A series of essays which reach both further back into the past and beyond the UK into France, Germany, Australasia, the last days of colonial empire and the USA. They usefully expand the frame of reference and explain the influence of the political and legal environment on investigative practices.

Ward, J. (1998) *Crimebusting: Breakthroughs in Forensic Science*. London: Blandford. An accessible, popular account of mostly British leading cases written by a criminologist.

Wensley, F.P. (1931) *Detective Days*. London: Cassell. The best of the older detective memoirs. A convincing picture of London at the turn of the nineteenth century.

Stevens, J. (2005) *Not for the Faint-hearted: My Life Fighting Crime*. London: Weidenfeld & Nicholson. A detective who made it to the top of the tree operating towards the end and the turn of the twentieth century.

www.homeoffice.gov.uk. The Home Office website with portals to other criminal justice organizations. An indispensable source for tracing contemporary developments.

Notes

1 *Francis Saville Kent* MEPO 3/61.
2 *Florrie Dennis* MEPO 3/153.
3 *Teddy Haskell* MEPO 2/7823.
4 *Brighton Trunk Murder 1934* MEPO 3/1692.

References

Ambage, N.V. (1987) 'The origins and development of the Home Office Forensic Science Service, 1931–1967.' PhD thesis, Lancaster University.

Andrews, A. (1968) *The Prosecutor: The Life of M.P. Pugh, Prosecuting Solicitor and Agent for the Director of Public Prosecutions*. London: Harrap.

Ascoli, D. (1979) *The Queen's Peace: The Origins and Development of the Metropolitan Police, 1829–1979*. London: Hamish Hamilton.

Atcherley, L.W. (1932) *Criminal Investigation and Detection*. Wakefield: Chief Constable of West Riding.

Bale, I. (1960) *Through Seven Reigns: A History of the Newport Police Force*. Pontypool: Griffin Press.

Beattie, J. (2006) 'Early detection: the Bow Street Runners in late eighteenth-century London', in C. Emsley and H. Shpayer-Makov (eds) *Police Detectives in History, 1750–1950*. Aldershot: Ashgate.

Beazley, B. (2001) *Peelers to Pandas: An Illustrated History of Leicester City Police*. Derby: Breedon.

Begg, P. and Skinner, K. (1992) *The Scotland Yard Files: 150 Years of the CID*. London: Headline.

Bent, J. (1891) *Criminal Life: Reminiscences of Forty-two Years as a Police Officer*. Manchester: Heywood.

Browne, D.G. (1956) *The Rise of Scotland Yard*. London: Harrap.

Clay, E.W. (1974) *The Leeds Police, 1836–1974*. Leeds: Leeds City Police.

Cobb, B. (1957) *The First Detectives*. London: Faber.

Cope, N. (2004) '"Intelligence led policing or policing led intelligence" – integrating volume crime analysis into policing', *British Journal of Criminology*, 44: 188–203.

Cox, B., Shirley, J. and Short, M. (1977) *The Fall of Scotland Yard*. London: Penguin Books.

Criminal Law Revision Committee (1972) *Evidence (General): Eleventh Report (1972) of the Criminal Law Revision Committee* (Cmnd 4991). London: HMSO.

Critchley, T.A. (1967) *A History of the Police in England and Wales, 900–1966*. London: Constable.

Cuthbert, C.R.M. (1958) *Science and the Detection of Crime*. London: Hutchinson.

Desborough, Lord (1919–20) *Report of the Committee on the Police Service in England, Wales and Scotland* (Part I, PP 1919, Vol. XXVII, Cmd 253; Part II, PP 1920, Vol. XXII, Cmd 574 and 874). London: HMSO.

Dilnot, G. (ed.) (1928) *The Trial of the Detectives*. London: Bles.

Dixon, A.L. (1938) *Report of the Departmental Committee on Detective Work and Procedure* (5 vols). London: Home Office.

Dixon, A.L. (1966) 'The Home Office and the police between the two world wars.' Typescript, Home Office Library.

Else, W.M. and Garrow, J.M. (1934) *The Detection of Crime*. London: *Police Journal*.

Ensor, D. (1958) *I Was a Public Prosecutor*. London: Hale.

Felstead, S.T. and Muir, Lady (1927) *Sir Richard Muir: A Memoir of a Public Prosecutor*. London: John Lane.

Fisher, Sir H. (1977) *The Confait Case: Report by the Hon. Sir Henry Fisher* (HC 90). London: HMSO.

Fosdick, R.B. (1915) *European Police Systems* (reprinted 1972). New Jersey: Patterson Smith.

Fuller, R.A. (1912) *Recollections of a Detective*. London: Long.

Goddard, H. (1956) *Memoirs of a Bow Street Runner* (ed. P. Pringle). London: Museum Press.

Grant, C.G. (1907) *Police Surgeon's Emergency Guide*. London: H.K. Lewis.

Grant, G. (1920) *Diary of a Police Surgeon*. London: Pearson.

Gross, H. (1924) *Criminal Investigation: A Practical Textbook for Magistrates, Police Officers and Lawyers* (trans. J.C. Adam). London: Sweet & Maxwell.

Hadley, V. (1999) *Herefordshire Constabulary, 1857–1967.* Hereford: Hadley.

Hann, M. (1989) *Policing Victorian Dorset.* Wincanton: Dorset Publications.

HASC (1998) *Police Disciplinary and Complaints Procedures, First Report, Select Committee on Home Affairs, Session 1997–8, 15 January* (HC 258–1).

Hastings, M. (1963) *The Other Mr Churchill: A Lifetime of Shooting and Murder.* London: Four Square.

HM Inspector of Constabulary (England and Wales) (1857) *Report* (PP 1857–8). Vol. XLVII. London: HMSO.

HM Inspector of Constabulary (England and Wales) (1880) *Report* (PP 1881). Vol LI. London: HMSO.

HM Inspector of Constabulary (England and Wales) (1913) *Report* (PP 1914). Vol LXVII. London: HMSO.

HM Inspectorate of Constabulary (1999) *Police Integrity.* London: Home Office.

Hughes, A. (1864) *Leaves from the Notebook of a Chief of Police.* London: Virtue Brothers.

Innes, M., Fielding, N. and Cope, N. (2005) '"The appliance of science?" The theory and practice of crime intelligence analysis', *British Journal of Criminology,* 45: 39–57.

Jervis, R. (1995) *Chronicles of a Victorian Detective.* Runcorn: P. & D. Riley.

Jones, J.O. (1963) *The History of the Caernarvonshire Constabulary, 1856–1950.* Caernarvon: Caernarvonshire Historical Society.

Jones, W. (1910) *Police!!: An Illustrated and Descriptive History of the Liverpool and Bootle Police Past and Present in aid of the Liverpool and Bootle Police Orphanage, Liverpool.* Liverpool: Smith & Jones.

Littlechild, J.G. (1893) *Reminiscences of Chief-Inspector Littlechild.* London: Leadenhall Press.

Macpherson, W. (1999) *Report of the Stephen Lawrence Inquiry* (Cm 4262-1). London: HMSO.

Maguire, M. (2003) 'Criminal investigation and crime control', in T. Newburn (ed.) *Handbook of Policing.* Cullompton: Willan Publishing.

Mark, R. (1978) *In the Office of Constable.* London: Collins.

Matthews, A.D. (1959) *Crime Doctor.* London: John Long.

Mawby, R.C. and Wright, A. (2003) 'The police organisation' in T. Newburn (ed.) *Handbook of Policing.* Cullompton: Willan Publishing.

Mayne, R. (1842) *Memorandum to Home Secretary, 15 June 1842* (HO 45/252).

McLagan, G. (2003) *Bent Coppers: The Inside Story of Scotland Yard's Battle against Police Corruption.* London: Weidenfeld.

Merseyside Police (1981) *Police Detective Training Course Notes.* Loose-leaf folder.

Metropolitan Police (1868a) *Report of the Departmental Committee.* London: Home Office.

Metropolitan Police (1868b) *Evidence of the Departmental Committee.* London: Home Office.

Metropolitan Police (1878a) *Report of the Departmental Commission on Detective Police.* London: Home Office.

Metropolitan Police (1878b) *Evidence of the Departmental Commission on Detective Police.* London: Home Office.

Metropolitan Police (1879a) *Evidence of the [Departmental] Commission to Inquire into the State, Discipline and Organization of the Metropolitan Police Force (other than the CID).* London: Home Office.

Metropolitan Police (1879b) *Report of the [Departmental] Commission to Inquire into the State, Discipline and Organization of the Metropolitan Police Force (other than the CID).* London: Home Office.

Morris, R.M. (2004) 'The Metropolitan Police and government 1860–1920.' PhD thesis, Open University.

Morris, R.M. (2006) '"Crime does not pay": thinking again about detectives in the first century of the Metropolitan Police', in C. Emsley and H. Shpayer-Makov (eds) *Police Detectives in History, 1750–1950*. Aldershot: Ashgate.

Morson, M. (2000) *A Force Remembered: The Illustrated History of the Norwich City Police, 1836–1967*. Derby: Breedon.

Morton, J. (1994) *Bent Coppers*. London: Warner.

Newburn, T. (1999) *Understanding and Preventing Police Corruption: Lessons from the Literature. Police Research Series Paper* 1110. London: Home Office.

Neyroud, P. (2003) 'Policing and ethics', in T. Newburn (ed.) *Handbook of Policing*. Cullompton: Willan Publishing.

O'Connor Report (2005) *Closing the Gap: A Review of the 'Fitness for Purpose' of the Current Structure of Policing in England and Wales*. HM Inspectorate of Constabulary. London: Home Office.

Osborn, N. (1969) *The Story of the Hertfordshire Police*. Letchworth: Hertfordshire Countryside.

Parry, L.A. (1931) *Trial of Doctor Smethurst*. Edinburgh: Hodge.

Philips, Sir C. (1981) *Report of the Royal Commission on Criminal Procedure* (RCCP 1981a and 1981b, Cmnd 8092 and 8092–1). London: HMSO.

Philips, D. (1977) *Crime and Authority in Victorian England: The Black Country, 1835–60*. London: Croom Helm.

Pooler, B. (2002) *From Fruit Trees to Furnaces: A History of the Worcestershire Constabulary*. Pershore: Blacksmith.

Porter, B. (1987) *The Origins of the Vigilant State: The London Metropolitan Police Special Branch before the First World War*. London: Weidenfeld & Nicholson.

Powell, J.A., Sutherland, G. and Gardner, T. (1997) *Policing Warwickshire: A Pictorial History of the Warwickshire Constabulary*. Studley: Brewin.

Reilly, J.W. (1989) *Policing Birmingham*. Birmingham: West Midlands Police.

Reynolds, E.A. (1998) *Before the Bobbies: The Night Watch and Police Reform in Metropolitan London, 1720–1830*. Stanford, CA: Stanford University Press.

Richer, A.F. (1990) *Bedfordshire Police, 1840–1990*. Bedford: Hooley.

Roach, L.T. (2002) 'Detecting crime', *Criminal Law Review*, 379–90, 566–77.

Royal Commission on Police Powers and Procedures (1929) *Report* (Cmd 2497). London: HMSO.

Royal Commission on the Police (the Willink Report) (1962) *Final Report* (Cmnd 1728). London: HMSO.

Rozenberg, J. (1987) *The Case for the Crown*. Wellingborough: Equation.

Rumbelow, D. (1971) *I Spy Blue*. Bath: Cedric Chivers.

Runciman, Viscount (1993) *Report of the Royal Commission on Criminal Justice* (Cm 2263). London: HMSO.

Sanders, A. and Young, R. (2003) 'Police powers', in T. Newburn (ed.) *Handbook of Policing*. Cullompton: Willan Publishing.

Savidge Report (1928) *Report of the Tribunal in Regard to the Interrogation of Miss Savidge* (Cmd 3147). London: HMSO.

Savill, S. (1901) *The Police Service of England and Wales*. London: Police Review.

Scollan, M. (1993) *Sworn to Serve: Police in Essex, 1840–1990*. Chichester: Phillimore.

Sheppard, K. (2000) *True as Coventry Blue: The History of Coventry Police, 1836–1914*. Coventry: Coventry Newspapers.

Shpayer-Makov, H. (2002) *The Making of a Policeman: A Social History of a Police Labour Force in Metropolitan London, 1829–1914*. Ashgate: Aldershot.

Stephen, J.F. (1863) *A General View of the Criminal Law of England* (2nd edn 1890). London: Macmillan.

Stevens, J. (2005) *Not for the Faint-hearted: My Life Fighting Crime.* London: Weidenfeld.

Taylor, D. (2002) *Policing the Victorian Town: The Development of the Police in Middlesbrough, 1840–1914.* London: Palgrave Macmillan.

Thomas, D. (1969) *Seek Out the Guilty.* London: Long.

Thomas, R.L. (ed.) (1957) *The Kent Police Centenary.* Canterbury: Centenary Booklet Committee.

Totterdell, G.H. (1956) *Country Copper.* London: Harrap.

Vincent, C.E.H. (1881) *A Police Code and Manual of Criminal Law.* London: Cassell.

Ward, J. (1993) 'The origins and development of forensic medicine and forensic science in England, 1823–1946.' PhD thesis, Open University.

Ward, J. (1998) *Crimebusting: Breakthroughs in Forensic Science.* London: Blandford.

Watson, K. (2004) *Poisoned Lives.* London: Hambledon.

Watt, I.A. (2006) *A History of the Hampshire and Isle of Wight Constabulary, 1839–1966.* Chichester: Phillimore.

Wensley, F.P. (1931) *Detective Days.* London: Cassell.

Chapter 3

Social context of criminal investigation

Mario Matassa and Tim Newburn

Introduction

Robert Reiner has remarked that the 'police are like social litmus-paper, reflecting sensitively the unfolding exigencies of a society' (1992 cited in Newburn 2005: 676). When Robert Peel first established the modern British police in 1829,[1] widespread fear of continental-style policing inhibited the formation of a plain-clothes investigative branch. It was not until some years later, after such fears had partly abated and were superseded by fresh concern over rising crime, that the path was paved for the formation of the first team of detectives in the Metropolitan Police. Ironically, the wheel appears to have turned full circle. Whereas the British police was established under a condition of 'difference' (Emsley 2003) – and for some considerable time was different from many of its counterparts in the Western world – recent decades have witnessed something of a 'convergence in organization and style' (Reiner 2000: 202). Much of the reason for this convergence can be traced to broader socioeconomic changes, and it is these – which form the social context of criminal investigation – and their relationship to crime and mechanisms of social control which lie at the heart of this chapter.

Any attempt to encapsulate the current social context of criminal investigation is going to be a partial one at best. The last five decades have seen three Royal Commissions consider aspects of policing – though only one directly on the police. Between 2002 and 2005 the government produced one green and two white papers, and no less than eight parliamentary bills focusing on policing. There has been a plethora of inquiries exploring a range of issues with consequent reforms, and legislation affecting policing has been so extensive as to be almost impossible to summarize (Newburn 2003: 13). In addition to internal change, external factors continue to play a role in shaping the policing establishment. In the last quarter of the twentieth century the pace of societal change increased markedly. Captured under the banner of globalization, the changes that occurred, and that are increasingly coming to shape late modern society, are 'analogous' in scope to the 'rise of industrial capitalism' (Reiner 2000: 199). These changes are extraordinarily far-reaching with some arguing that even the state itself is undergoing a process of 'reinvention' (Osborne and Gaebler 1992), challenging its position as the primary guarantor of security.

For policing, one does not have to look too far to see the implications of these social transformations. Perhaps most obviously, the vocabulary of 'policing', with its traditional emphasis on the 'police', appears increasingly anachronistic. A reconceptualization of 'policing' is occurring (Crawford 2003) with a growing emphasis on 'security networks' (Shearing 1996) and policing 'beyond the police'. The transformations that have taken place have been variously hailed as post-Keynesian policing (O'Malley and Palmer 1996), risk-based policing (Ericson and Haggerty 1997; Feeley and Simon 1992) and 'pick 'n mix' policing (Reiner 1997). The changes coincide with an increasing emphasis on knowledge, and in particular knowledge of risk (Beck 1992). The demand for knowledge about risk has never been greater, elevating the police to the status of primary producers and disseminators of crime-based risk knowledge (Feeley and Simon 1992; Ericson and Haggerty 1997; Johnston 2000). Indeed, Ericson and Haggerty (1997) go so far as to define the police as 'knowledge workers'. Underpinning such developments is a move from disciplinary to actuarially based practices of crime control (Simon 1988; Feeley and Simon 1992, 1994). Attention is being redirected from the individual offender to the control and regulation of suspect populations through anticipatory strategies of risk assessment and prevention. Intelligence-led policing, problem-oriented policing and zero-tolerance policing have in common a shift from the reactive case-focused mentality of criminal investigation to proactive mechanisms for controlling risky populations.

The scope of inquiry has broadened to encapsulate the proliferation of agencies and actors, both public and private, who play a role in the function of policing (cf. Shearing and Stenning 1987; Johnston 1992; Jones and Newburn 1998). As policing becomes increasingly 'commodified' (Loader 1997), its exposure to global market forces adds greater complexity to the policing division of labour. An understanding of the current context of criminal investigation can no longer be gleaned adequately from within the confines of the sovereign state. Territorial borders are simultaneously being eroded and redrawn – physically, symbolically and virtually (cf. Zureik and Salter 2005). Crime and the mechanisms applied to its control are not bounded by geographical space. Recent terrorist atrocities on every continent bring added impetus to the emergence and development of 'transnational' policing arrangements (McLaughlin 1992; Anderson et al. 1995; Hebenton and Thomas 1995; Sheptycki 1997, 2000) and blur the distinctions between 'high' and 'low' policing. Emerging forms of collaboration between the security services and the police in the fight against terrorism are increasingly encroaching on efforts to tackle 'ordinary decent crime'[2] (Brodeur 1999; Bowling and Newburn 2007 forthcoming). Crimes such as drug and human trafficking, money-laundering, illegal immigration, football hooliganism and extreme-right movements are global concerns that mandate a concerted response across jurisdictions. Modern technology provides new opportunities for criminals – such as use of the Internet – and challenges for crime control practitioners (such as data management, protection and control across global policing networks). While the advent of DNA or biometric surveillance technology adds to the investigator's arsenal, the dangers of 'surveillance creep' (Nelkin and Andrews 1999) become all too real (Marx 1988).

At the core of this chapter we briefly review what we take to be the major contours of the social context of criminal investigation in recent decades. We organize this under three main headings: globalization (including the growing transnationalization of criminal investigation), risk and neoliberalization (itself covering three major sets of changes in pluralization, managerialism and centralization). Before this we begin with a few observations about the longer-term history of police investigation.

A brief history of police investigation

Police criminal investigative practice has changed markedly since the first unit of plain-clothes detectives was formed in 1842. The factors responsible for driving change are complex, rooted both in broader social transformations and internal pressures to reform. The latter have been instigated largely in response to shortcomings in practice – varying from corruption scandals and miscarriages of justice to high-profile investigative failures. The primary aims of reform have been to increase accountability, prevent corrupt practice and improve efficiency and effectiveness. There is, of course, considerable overlap between external and internal drivers of change. The nature and extent of crime, for instance, a variable beyond the capacity of the police to determine (and arguably influence overmuch), is one that continuously drives organizational change. Indeed, the factors driving change are varied and complex. However, a brief review of the history of criminal investigation will provide some insight into the ways in which current structures and practices have emerged.

When the 'New Police' came into being in 1829, resistance resulting in part from prejudice and partly from fear and suspicion (Emsley 2003; see also Ascoli 1979) inhibited the formation of a detective unit or plain-clothes branch. The principal aims of the police at the time were the prevention of crime and the maintenance of order, as opposed to investigation and detection. The emphasis placed at the time on prevention was crucial, both in allaying extant fears of 'continental policing' and in the subsequent form of social control that has developed in the UK and is dominant to this day (Hobbs 1988: 26–34). Indeed, it was not until 1842 that approval was finally secured for the formation of a small team of six plain-clothes officers. Although Rowan and Mayne, the force's first commissioners, acknowledged the potential benefits of establishing a plain-clothes wing, they were not overly keen to do so. Setting aside prevailing fears surrounding the continental system, their reluctance was in part fuelled by uncertainty over how to control and keep track of plain-clothes officers (Emsley 2003: 69). However, by 1877 concern over rising street crime enabled the formal establishment of a substantial and autonomous Criminal Investigation Department (CID) in the Metropolitan Police force, initially consisting of 250 officers. But even these early beginnings were blighted by scandal. At the time, three out of the four chief inspectors of the detective branch had been found guilty of corruption (Ascoli 1979: 143–6; Hobbs 1988).

Despite the rocky start, 'crime control' quickly came to be viewed as a major plank of the police agenda and senior officers in the investigative branch took every opportunity to distinguish themselves from their uniformed colleagues and to assert their autonomy and expertise in the field (Maguire 2003: 365). The Metropolitan Police effectively became a 'divided force, partitioned into two separate branches, each with rigidly defined functions' (Hobbs 1988: 41). This division has periodically been reinforced by external events. For example, when the uniformed branch's strategy of guarding likely targets was seen to fail, the establishment of the first specialist unit, the 'Special Irish Squad' – which later formed the nucleus of Special Branch – brought added kudos and consolidated CID's monopoly over investigative techniques.

Technological advances at the beginning of the twentieth century proved something of a milestone for investigative work. The introduction in 1901 of an effective fingerprinting system and, later that same year, the establishment of the Criminal Records Office brought some improvement to working practices, and facilitated the trend towards specialization and professionalism (Hobbs 1988: 43). Such technological advances enabled the CID further to consolidate its independent position and to expand its numbers.

Thereafter, the function of the CID remained relatively unchanged for the first half of the twentieth century. In 1938, the Departmental Committee on Detective Work, after five years of research, presented its findings in a highly critical report. It concluded that Britain was lagging seriously behind its counterparts in continental Europe and North America, leading to a 'general rationalization of detective work, involving systematic training, improved laboratory and forensic facilities, and a revamping of systems of communication' (Hobbs 1988: 45; Elmsley 2003). The impact of these measures was to increase the general efficiency of the CID and to distance further its function from that of uniformed police officers, a trend that has persisted throughout the history of police investigation.

Corruption, scandal and reform

Allegations of corruption, abuses of power and miscarriages of justice have been a persistent feature in the history of police criminal investigation. Added to this, criticism has recurrently been levelled at the perceived lack of transparency and accountability of investigative practice, coupled with more general criticism of its ineffectiveness. Such problems – and public criticism in particular – have often acted as an important stimulus for legislative and organizational reform.

The most damning series of scandals began in 1969. In November of that year journalists from *The Times* published transcripts of tape-recorded conversations between detectives and criminals in which they were discussing a deal to cover up serious crimes. The damage done was exacerbated by the pattern of obstruction, leaks and disappearing evidence experienced initially by officers from New Scotland Yard, and later by staff from Her Majesty's Inspectorate of

Constabulary (HMIC) charged with investigating the allegations. Throughout the 1970s further scandals erupted involving officers from the Drug Squad and the Obscene Publications Squad (Cox *et al.* 1977). A broad strategy of reform introduced by the then Commissioner, Robert Mark, included the establishment of A10, a specialist elite department charged with investigating complaints against the police, as well as the resignation of approximately 500 officers in anticipation of being investigated. Nevertheless, the pattern of scandal and corruption persisted. In 1978 there were even allegations that detectives had been involved in major armed robberies (Ball *et al.* 1979). This scandal was a by-product of the supergrass strategy – a tactic used for the most part to secure convictions against Irish terrorism on the mainland (and was eventually transported to Northern Ireland in 1981; cf. Greer 1988, 2001; Matassa and Newburn 2003). The scandal prompted the Commissioner, Sir David McNee, to set up Operation Countryman under the direction of the Dorset Chief Constable, Arthur Hambleton. The ensuing investigation quickly undermined any assumption that the previous commissioner's reforms had eradicated corruption in the force. Resistance to change was also only too visible. Officers were obstructed in their investigation by Yard pressure and the operation ultimately resulted in only two convictions (Reiner 2000: 63–4).

Nor did the matter end with the completion of Operation Countryman. The scandal had highlighted the issue of what is misleadingly described 'noble cause corruption'. It was, in part, instrumental in prompting the Prime Minister, James Callaghan, to announce the Royal Commission on Criminal Procedure (RCCP). Of particular concern was the behaviour of officers during the detention and interrogation of suspects – and particularly those suspected of being involved in Irish Republican terrorism – and the probity of the convictions that were secured as a result. There were widespread allegations of intimidation and violence during interrogation and the fabrication of evidence. Claims of malpractice were vindicated when, in October 1989, the Court of Appeal released the Guildford Four after new evidence revealed that the Surrey officers investigating the bombing lied at the trial (Reiner 2000). Shortly thereafter, further miscarriages of justice came to light, including the 'Birmingham Six', the 'Maguire Seven', the cases of Judith Ward and that of the four men convicted of the murder of Carl Bridgewater (see Chapter 25).[3]

The RCCP reported in 1981. Its most significant contribution was in forming the basis of what later became the Police and Criminal Evidence Act 1984 (PACE) (revised in 1991). The RCCP focused on the rights of suspects, a long-standing issue brought to a head by the 'Confait case' in which, it was eventually discovered, three teenage boys had been convicted of murder on the basis of false confessions. An official inquiry into the case, headed by Sir Henry Fisher, a High Court judge, found that the *Judges' Rules* – which at the time formed the basis for suspects' rights – had been abused. PACE introduced far-reaching procedural safeguards to guard against abuses of these powers. In brief, these included the appointment of a 'custody officer' who decides if detention is justified and maintains a custody record; limits on the duration of detention; and the tape-recording of interviews (cf. Zander 1985; Home Office 1995).

The extent to which the new rules and procedures have eradicated malpractice has been vigorously debated (cf. McConville *et al.* 1991; Morgan 1995; Maguire 2002). Many of the cases that came to light in the late 1980s, the police argued, had occurred prior to the introduction of the new reforms. However, in 1992 the Court of Appeal upheld the appeal of the 'Tottenham Three', who had been convicted of the murder of PC Blakelock during the 1986 Broadwater Farm riot, on the grounds that the accused's statements had not been recorded contemporaneously, as required under PACE. The case raised serious questions about the extent to which legislative reform had eradicated malpractice. Two further cases, the Yorkshire Ripper case and the Stephen Lawrence case, were to shine a critical spotlight back on to police criminal investigative practice. On this occasion the issues were incompetence and institutional racism. As Maguire (2003: 386) notes, the 'Ripper' case:

> was notable not just for the public fear it caused while the murders continued but also for the highly publicised misjudgements made by the enquiry team, in particular putting 'all their eggs in one basket' and failing to spot several strong indications of the identity of the murderer within the huge volume of material generated by the inquiry.

A number of reforms resulted, including the introduction of the HOLMES computer system, together with a number of strategic changes to reduce the burdens on senior investigating officers (Maguire and Norris 1992). The Stephen Lawrence case indicated that all remained far from perfect in the aftermath of such reforms.

On 22 April 1993, 18-year-old Stephen Lawrence was stabbed to death outside a bus shelter in Eltham, south London, by a gang of 'five white youths'. An extraordinary chain of events followed, culminating in the publication of the report of an official inquiry chaired by Lord Macpherson (1999). With regard to the investigation, the inquiry concluded: 'There is no doubt that there were fundamental errors. The investigation was marred by a combination of professional incompetence, institutional racism, and a failure of leadership by senior officers' (1999: para. 46.1).

Part one of the inquiry explored issues in relation to the investigation. Areas of criticism included the lack of direction and organization of the initial response, the provision of first aid, command and control at the scene of the murder, family liaison and victim support, the actions/inactions of senior investigating officers, the surveillance operation, the handling of suspects, the management of informants and issues relating to record-keeping. The inquiry was also highly critical of two internal reviews into the investigation that failed to expose the inadequacies. As a consequence of the inquiry report, a series of changes were introduced, including new standards and procedures for the management of murder scenes, new processes for logging decision-making, dedicated officers responsible for family liaison and, in London at least, the creation of dedicated murder investigation teams. The intention of some of the inquiry's recommendations was also that much greater emphasis be placed on community consultation and endeavouring to ensure community confidence as well as, more generally, seeking to prompt forces to think about the potential within their investigative policies and practices to discriminate, however unwittingly, against particular groups. Initial research suggests that forces still have some way to go, particularly with regard to institutional racism (Foster *et al.* 2005).

The social context of contemporary criminal investigation

In what follows we want to draw attention to what we take to be some of the key developments that have framed the changing nature of criminal investigation. Now, clearly, the 'social context' within which investigation takes places is more complex and variable than is possible to capture within a relatively short space. Consequently, we are only able to focus on elements of what appear to be the crucial sociological and political developments in recent times. In doing so, we organize the discussion under three broad headings: globalization, risk and neoliberalism. In short, we will argue that globalizing trends have led to the emergence of transnationalized police investigation; that risk orientation is transforming the ways in which investigation is perceived and undertaken; and, finally, that the forces of neoliberalism have resulted in growing trends towards privatization and managerialism in the investigative sphere.

Globalization

Policing does not take place in a vacuum but is responsive to the social, political, cultural and economic environment. Accordingly, the terrain of criminal investigation cannot be understood outside its context. The world is changing ever more rapidly and, with it, so too is the topography of policing and criminal investigation. The establishment of the modern police (whether one adheres to the orthodox or the revisionist perspective) coincided broadly with the development of modern society and specifically modern nation-states. The function of the police was to maintain the *internal* order of the *sovereign state* and to protect its citizens from the threat posed by crime and disorder. At least in the UK, policing – or more precisely, the police – came to symbolize nationhood. We are now, however, or so it is claimed, living in a 'post' or 'late' modern society (Harvey 1989; Giddens 1990; Kumar 1995) in which the modern state-system has been (is being) reconfigured and in which the traditional nexus between crime control and the state has been loosened. That is, the state's monopoly over crime control has been increasingly exposed (Garland 1996) as new modes of governance emerge. The idea of the 'police' as 'the monopolistic guardians of public order' (Crawford 2003: 136), if even only on a symbolic level (in practice, such a monopoly never really existed; cf. Jones and Newburn 2002), no longer holds true and in its stead a more diffuse patchwork of organizations and actors is emerging.

The forces driving these changes are complex and are most crudely subsumed under the label *globalization*. In a relatively short span of time, globalization has assumed a position of considerable prominence in contemporary social debate. In an even briefer period (10–15 years) it has become a staple of media and political discourse as well as public conversation. Zygmunt Bauman, one of the foremost observers of the phenomenon, regards it as 'by far the most prominent and seminal feature of our times' (2001 11). Yet despite its undisputed salience, it is a term commonly misunderstood and abused. The claim of globalization is that: 'Spatial barriers have collapsed so that the world is now a single field within which capitalism can operate, and capital flows become more and more sensitive to the relative advantages of particular spatial locations' (Waters 1995: 57–8). New information technologies have helped emancipate time from space (Bauman 2000) setting in motion 'a process (or set of processes) which embodies a transformation in the spatial organization of social relations and transactions – assessed in terms of their extensity, intensity, velocity and impact – generating transcontinental or interregional flows and networks of activity, interaction, and the exercise of power' (Held *et al.* 1999: 16).

Globalization is in many respects paradoxical. It is illusory in as much as it is a transitory state (Findlay 1999), a process that by definition is incomplete. Much of the debate on globalization is surrounded in hyperbole. There are three points that need to be made here. First, there is a tendency to overstate the ramifications of globalization, as though they were a given. Yet globalization in and of itself does not constitute a constant state. Whether one sees the process of globalization as linear or non-linear, or as a recent phenomenon or one with a long history, few dispute the fact that it signifies a process. It is a process of societal restructuring.

Secondly, there is an assumption in much of the literature that the net effect of globalization will be uniformity and homogeneity – epitomized in the phrase: 'There will be no there anymore; we will all be here' (Waters 1995: 124). On the contrary, the restructuring that is taking place is complex, simultaneously lending diversity and contradiction to societal structures (Johnston 2000). Globalization, as a paradoxical process, stimulates competing and contradictory tendencies. The permutations that emerge include globalization/localization, centralization/decentralization, cultural homogeneity/heterogeneity, security/insecurity, fragmentation/consolidation. In reviewing the contextual contours of the late-modern landscape it is not uncommon, indeed it is typical, to see competing processes at work. So, for example, while Coca Cola or McDonald's are frequently hailed as symbols of global cultural consumerism, simultaneously we see a rise in the importance of regional and local cultural variations. Thus, homogeneity and heterogeneity exist hand in hand. This is what is referred to as the Janus face of globalization (cf. Findlay 1999).

Thirdly, and following from the above, there is a tendency, both in contemporary sociological theorizing and in current policing discourse, to view the recent changes in society as epochal, suggesting a fundamental break from one kind of order to another. The transformations that have taken place in the field of policing have been hailed by one pair of authors as the 'end of public policing' (McLaughlin and Murji 1995) and by another as an 'era ... when one system of policing ended and another took its place' (Bayley and Shearing 1996: 585). There is no question that the changes that have taken place in the past few decades have been profound. Yet, hopefully, as the following will make clear, as easy as it is to highlight the novelty in current transformations, so too there is significant continuity. So, for example, the establishment of the Serious Organised Crime Agency (SOCA) has its antecedents in the regional crime squads in the mid-1960s. So, too, the origins of Special Branch can be traced as far back as the 1883–5 Fenian bombing campaign. As Jones and Newburn (2002: 142–3) recently argued, in considering the current field of policing, and more specifically in this case criminal investigation, it is important neither to 'exaggerate the degree of change' nor to lose sight of the 'consistencies and continuities'.

Transnationalization

Transnational policing structures have a history that dates back to the latter half of the nineteenth century.[4] Early measures in the mid-eighteenth century were instituted in response to social upheaval and revolution in an attempt to protect the established order (cf. Deflem 2002). The first permanent international agency – the International Criminal Police Commission (ICPC) – was established in the wake of World War One. It was later to become known as the International Criminal Police Organization (ICPO) – or more popularly, Interpol.[5] Interpol was never intended as an operational police force. It was designed to act as a clearing-house for information and intelligence between participating police forces and as a network forum for senior officers or a 'policeman's club' (Anderson 1989: 43). Over the years membership, initially 19, has increased tenfold. Technological developments also facilitated its development during that time. In February 1987 a computerized Criminal Information System replaced the manual system and an Electronic Archive System was introduced in 1990. These developments, among others, enhanced the flow and quality of information exchange between the national central bureaus. More recently Interpol further rationalized its organizational structure with the creation of a separate European Unit. At the 54th General Assembly in 1985, Interpol's involvement in anti-terrorist activity was established with the creation of a specialized group within the then Police Division to 'co-ordinate and enhance co-operation in combating international terrorism'. It was not, however, until 1987 that the group became operational. The then Secretary General is quoted as saying: 'it took 15 years from [Interpol's] lowest point at the Munich Olympic Games in 1972 to do something that could have been done in two years' (cited in Bresler 1992: 257).

A number of problems have been identified with Interpol. First, there have been persistent doubts about the security of Interpol's communications network (House of Commons 1990: 43; George and Watson 1992). Secondly, the ineffectiveness or inadequacy of Interpol's structures for tackling terrorism in the 1970s in part prompted European states to make other arrangements, notably the establishment of the Trevi Group (see below) and the European Police Working Group. Despite improvements in organizational structure, Walker maintains that Interpol remains the 'paradigm case of a *inter*national police organisation' that has 'never challenged the statist prerogative in police operations and lacks the legal, symbolic and material resources to be anything other than parasitic on national police authorities' (2003: 117).

Because of these restrictions, and in light of broader developments, Interpol's predominance in the international policing field has been largely superseded. Two related developments are particularly noteworthy: Schengen and Trevi.

The Schengen Convention has been described by Hebenton and Thomas (1995: 59–60) as the 'most complete model ... of international police co-operation within Europe'. Its origins lie in the Schengen Agreement (1985). Five EC member states (France, Germany, Belgium, the Netherlands and Luxembourg) originally signed up to the agreement. An Implementation Agreement enabled the signing of the convention in 1990 and, over the following two years, Spain, Portugal, Italy and Greece also signed up. The Schengen *acquis* now covers all EU member states with the exception of Britain and Ireland (cf. Maas 2005).[6]

The rationale behind Schengen was the promotion of economic liberalization through enhanced mobilization of capital, labour and goods within the territorial confines of participating states. This was to be achieved through the elimination of border controls. Simultaneously, external borders were to be strengthened through a series of compensatory measures, which included the harmonization of entry controls; the co-ordination of intelligence (through the establishment of the Schengen Information System (SIS)); the right of 'hot pursuit'; and other measures aimed at enhancing police co-operation. Although Schengen was a milestone in an unfolding pan-European policing edifice and, unlike Trevi, was sanctioned with a formal legal basis, it remained like its counterpart distinct from the legal organization of the supranational structure. Schengen was to a great extent overshadowed by developments that resulted in the establishment of the EU's own policing body, Europol. The Schengen arrangements were eventually incorporated by the Amsterdam Treaty (see below) into the new Area of Freedom, Security and Justice.

The platform for the launch of Europol was the Trevi Group, formed in 1976. Originally established as a European intergovernmental forum to tackle terrorism, its remit was eventually expanded 'to look ... at the mechanics of police co-operation in the European Community across the whole range of crime, the use of liaison officers and the creation of a common information system' (House of Commons 1990 cited in Hebenton and Thomas 1995: 71). By the early 1990s the Trevi Group was already far advanced in the development of a rapid and protected communications system for collecting and disseminating information on terrorism and other forms of cross-border criminality. At the European Council meeting in Luxembourg in 1991, the group presented plans for a common information system that was able to compensate for the erosion of borders and with the capacity to tackle international organized crime (Hebenton and Thomas 1995: 85). In a meeting later that year references were incorporated into the Treaty on Political Union under Article K.1.(9) for the creation of a European Police Office – or Europol as it is more commonly known.

Police co-operation was formally integrated into the EU with the passing of the Maastricht Treaty of 1992. With the evolution of the so-called 'third pillar' of the EC – to become the EU in November 1993 – to deal with justice and home affairs, Europol was to be established replacing both Trevi and the Co-ordinators Groups. A complex array of steering groups and working parties was established, responsible to a committee of senior officials known as the K4 Committee which in turn answers to the Council of Justice and Home Affairs Ministers. Although a permanent Project Team with a 50-strong multinational staff was soon after established in Strasbourg, progress in the early days was impeded by disagreement among member states over, among other things, the range of crimes covered in its mandate, the adequacy of the data protection system and the extent of jurisdiction of the European Court of Justice. These disagreements cast some considerable early doubt as to the adequacy of political and legal accountability as well as the very viability of the new organization (Walker 2003). As a consequence, Europol did not become fully operational until 1999, albeit with a revised constitutional basis set out in the Amsterdam Treaty (1997).

A number of important changes were made to the EU's new policing institution. On a constitutional level issues relating to the free movement of people – visa, asylum and immigration policy – were transferred from the Third to the First Pillar. Moreover, the powers of the European Court of Justice are more clearly recognized – although these fall short of ruling on issues surrounding the operations of domestic police forces and on matters concerning the preservation of law and order and internal security.

Regardless of the revisions made by Amsterdam, the powers invested in competent authorities within member states are substantial. Operational co-operation between the competent authorities is embraced and Europol is provided with the formal legal basis to:

> establish joint operational teams to support national investigations, the power to ask the competent authorities of the member states to conduct and co-ordinate investigations in specific cases ... the facility to promote liaison arrangements between prosecuting or investigating officials specialising in the fight against organised crime [and] the capacity to develop common measures for harmonisation of both substantive and procedural criminal law and to facilitate co-operation between criminal justice agencies (Walker 2003: 120–1).

Europol started limited operations in early 1994, specifically in relation to drugs (with the creation of the Europol Drugs Unit in 1993). Its mandate was extended in 1998 to include counter-terrorism (Rauchs and Koenig 2001) and in 2002 to deal with all serious forms of international crime. Europol supports members states by:

- facilitating the exchange of information, in accordance with national law, between Europol liaison officers (ELOs). ELOs are seconded to Europol by the member states as representatives of their national law enforcement agencies;

- providing operational analysis in support of member states' operations;

- generating strategic reports (e.g. threat assessments) and crime analysis on the basis of information and intelligence supplied by member states, generated by Europol or gathered from other sources; and

- providing expertise and technical support for investigations and operations carried out within the EU, under the supervision and legal responsibility of the member states concerned.

Europol is also active in promoting crime analysis and harmonization of investigative techniques within the member states. Activities specifically of interest to Europol include 'drugs-trafficking, human-trafficking, child pornography, money-laundering, Euro-counterfeiting, cyber crime, environmental crime, terrorism and racism' (Europol 2006).

At the European Council meeting at Tampere in October 1999 which focused on a single theme (an unprecedented move signalling the perceived importance of the issue) – the development of the Area of Freedom, Security and Justice – a number of further initiatives concerning police co-operation were announced, including a European Police Chiefs Operational Task Force, a European Police College and the establishment of Eurojust (which achieved formal legal status following the Treaty of Nice in 2001 and is intended to complement at judicial level the operational activities of Europol).

As we have noted, international contacts between police officers and institutions are not a new phenomenon. Until recently, however, it is reasonable to argue that the basis of these networks has been predominantly around 'knowledge work' (Ericson 1994: 149–76) – mostly IT based. That is to say, it has primarily been concerned with the 'collection, collation and dissemination' within 'informed space' of knowledge (Sheptycki 1998: 54–74, 71 fn. 2). Interpol, the Trevi Group and Europol in its early days all focused on developing more efficient mechanisms for the sharing of information and intelligence between law enforcement agencies. More recent developments within the EU signal the likelihood of an increased active operational role (Loader 2004). This has been given added impetus following the events of 11 September 2001 in America and, subsequently, the terrorist attacks in Madrid and London and elsewhere (Bunyan 2003; Gilmore 2003). The intensification of activity in this area seems likely to continue. Recent developments include proposals for a common European Border Guard and a European Public Prosecutor (Den Boer 2003).

Risk

One commentator has described risk as the 'world's largest industry' (Adams 1995: 31). In a relatively short period of time the 'logic of risk' (Ericson and Haggerty 1997) has assumed a dominant position in sociological and criminological theorizing. Writers such as Beck (1992) and Giddens (1990) locate the current preoccupation with risk in conditions of late modernity. Crudely, pre-globalized or modern society was characterized by known and calculable risks, rooted in scientific knowledge, a world which could be 'measured, calculated and therefore predicted' (Lupton 1999: 6). Under conditions of late modernity risks are distinguishable by their profusion, extensity and finality. For both Giddens (1999) and Beck, the 'risk society begins where tradition ends' (1998: 12). Moreover, for Beck (1992), the very processes of industrialization, modernization and globalization produce and exacerbate risk to the point where they are no longer constrained by the modern tools used to assess them or the technology used to contain them: 'Late modernity has transformed risk from a probabilistic, calculable artefact to risk as uncertainty, plagued by indeterminate knowledge and subject to a number of "it depends"' (Kemshall 2003: 8).

Risk has become a pervasive feature of contemporary living. Previously the preserve of specialists, risk has 'seep[ed] out ... to become part of the very idiom of our contemporary moral and political conversations' (Loader and Sparks 2002: 93). In other words, risk has been democratized and mainstreamed. Today every individual is confronted with myriad risks and must (indeed, is encouraged through 'responsibilization strategies'; Garland 2001) assume personal responsibility for monitoring and managing his or her own risk. For Giddens (1990), risk, security, danger and trust are determining characteristics of 'high modern' society. Douglas's (1992) 'cultural theory of risk' draws attention to the way that risk has become a 'way of thinking'. The identification of particular sources of threat reflects contemporary dispositions to crime, security and danger. In this sense, risk acts as a tool for making sense of, and negotiating, the contemporary landscape.

For some time now it has been evident that commercial risk management techniques are being applied in modern forms of crime control. Over 20 years ago, Cohen (1985) highlighted the increasing shift away from causal theories of crime to spatial and temporal explanations. Kemshall (2003), among others, argues that the identification, assessment, prevention and management of risk have become central to crime control policy and practice. The extent of the shift is such that some commentators claim we are witnessing a new era of justice, 'actuarial justice', in which the focus has shifted from the management of individual offenders and behaviour to the management of crime opportunities and aggregate risks (Feeley and Simon 1992, 1994): 'The new penology is ... less concerned with responsibility, fault ... diagnosis, or intervention and treatment of the individual offender. Rather, it is concerned with techniques to identify, classify, and manage groupings sorted by dangerousness. The task is managerial, not transformative' (Feeley and Simon 1992: 452).

There is little doubt that the new preoccupation with risk has impacted on police investigative policy and practice. The growing emphasis placed upon categorization and classification in policing is inscribed in strategies such as intelligence-led, problem-oriented and zero-tolerance policing (Tilley 2003). Underpinning all these strategies is a shift from the reactive investigation of individual offences to strategies aimed at controlling and managing suspect populations (Maguire 2000). Even traditional policing strategies are not immune. Johnston, for instance, argues that the orientation towards risk management has evoked the realization of a hybrid form of community policing, no longer based on traditional notions of sentiment and communitarian values, but on the identification and policing of 'communities of risk' (1997, 2000). In a seminal text Ericson and Haggerty (1997) argue that the preoccupation with risk, coupled with the availability of sophisticated information technology, has transformed the very function of policing and that they should now be viewed as, first and foremost, 'information brokers'.

Although there is significant dispute as to the extent to which policing has become infused by risk-based thinking (cf. the 'transformation debate' – Bayley and Shearing 1996: Jones and Newburn 2002), there can be no doubt that policing broadly, and criminal investigative practice specifically, is adapting to these new modes of thinking. Kemshall (2003: 120) usefully summarizes some of the key features of how risk is affecting the nature of contemporary policing:

- Cost-benefit calculations, for example of detectability and whether the case is worth pursuing.[7]

- The redeployment of expertise from the security services to intelligence-led policing.[8]

- The growth of surveillance technologies and the use of surveillance to gather key information (cf. Marx 2002).

- The growth of information technologies, such as computer data storage and collation (cf. Ericson and Haggerty 1997).

- The construction of police as 'information brokers', particularly in multi-agency arrangements for crime management, and the role of police officers in collecting, collating and disseminating risk information (adapted from Kemshall 2003: 120).

Neoliberalization

'Neoliberal' is a term much used and misused (Harvey 2005). In this context we use 'neoliberalization' simply as shorthand for those political and economic transformations associated with the deregulation of markets as part of a broader belief in the efficacy of markets as a method of organizing and regulating human conduct. These changes have seeped through most parts of the social fabric leaving few institutions and practices untouched. Policing is no exception. Again, all we can do in the space available is outline elements of what we take to be three of the more obvious consequences of neoliberalism for policing and criminal investigation. Two linked sets of changes concern the increasing managerialization of policing and, relatedly, the growing centralization of control over all public services, including the police. First, though, we explore what has variously been referred to as the marketization, commodification or privatization of investigation.

Pluralization

For a brief period in the mid-twentieth century the impression was created that the public police enjoyed something of a monopoly in the legitimate use of violence on behalf of the state. In other words, they and they alone were responsible for formal policing. Of course, this was always a fiction. But the fact that the myth developed at all is an indication of the position occupied by the police at that time. Much has changed since. For complex, and contested, reasons policing has become more complex. There is now an array of actors and providers: private security, local authority patrols and wardens, new auxiliaries and the like. Their proliferation has led to policing now generally being described as 'pluralized' (Jones and Newburn 2006). Criminal investigation is no exception, and there is now a range of private and civilian bodies working in prominent roles in this area of work.

Private investigation in Britain has a history that dates back to well beyond the introduction of the New Police in the nineteenth century. In the early eighteenth century, for example, inducements and rewards encouraged a mix of professional constables, watchmen and bounty hunters to engage in 'thief taking' (cf. Rawlings 2003). The Matrimonial Causes Act 1857 enabled the first detectives to take a more formal role in divorce cases and, in 1901, the range of investigative services offered was expanded with the establishment of Garnier's Detective Agency (see Chapter 11, this volume).

Today an array of 'home-based' firms, 'high-street' agencies, 'regional' agencies and 'prestige' companies (Gill and Hart 1997) offers a hugely expanded and diverse range of services. Johnston's review of the industry (Chapter 11, this volume) suggests approximately 90 areas in which investigators work. These range from more traditional practices, such as matrimonial investigations, missing persons and insurance claims investigation, to more contemporary forms of investigation, such as nanny investigations, Internet profiling, pre-home purchase investigations, risk management and hostage investigation and negotiation. Johnston, drawing on evidence from a 1992 report by the Institute of Professional Investigators (Button and George 2000, cited in Johnston, Chapter 11, this volume) estimates the total number of investigative agents in Britain to be around 15,000 and the overall value of the sector to be approximately £110 million (the bulk of which comes from corporate business).

Trying to make sense of the industry is far from simplistic. Prenzler (2001) offers a useful four-fold classification:

1 *Anti-fraud work*: undertaken for the most part for large insurance firms (but also for some self-insured private companies and some government insurance work).

2 *Legal work*: carrying out background work for lawyers in civil and less often criminal cases, as well as process serving.

3 *Commercial work*: includes electronic counter-measures, liability investigations, pre-employment screening, investigations into workplace theft, personal protection, repossessions and debt collection, and risk and security assessment.

4 *Domestic investigations*: missing persons, matrimonial, checking teenage drug use.

Until recently, and unlike the USA, Canada, Australia and many European countries, the private investigation sector in Britain remained largely unregulated. Some limited regulation has existed, such as the Interception of Communications Act 1985 and the Regulation of Investigatory Powers Act 2000. In addition, the Association of British Investigators and the Institute of

Professional Investigators provided a limited measure of self-regulation. Yet the industry has, to all intents and purpose, lacked a statutory framework for regulating operators. There are, however, signs that the situation is changing. The introduction of the Private Security Industry Act 2001 established the Security Industry Authority (SIA), an independent non-departmental body whose function is to license individuals operating in the private security industry – including private investigators (see Chapter 11, this volume). The aim ostensibly is to shift the industry closer in the direction of mainstream policing – a key element in the project to create a 'police extended family' – by encouraging a greater degree of professionalism (Crawford 2003). Yet, as Johnston points out, the legislation falls short of establishing compulsory licensing of firms, relying instead on working with existing self-regulatory measures.

Finally, it is important to consider some of the likely implications of recent developments both for public policing and for the private investigative industry. The first point to make, axiomatic though it may seem, is that under the current climate – the preoccupation with risk (coupled with contemporary threats posed by among other things, terrorism, serious organized crime and emerging forms of crime such as cybercrime), an increasingly fluid global marketplace and the dispersion of ever greater responsibility from public to private policing – it is perhaps inevitable that the scale of the private investigation industry, and the demand for its services, is only likely to increase. Secondly, and relatedly, this will undoubtedly raise some important and potentially awkward questions concerning the function of public policing in this regard. Are there elements of investigative work that are most appropriately carried out by public bodies? What are they and how might they be identified? Third, is the question of governance. As in all areas of policing, the increasingly complex patchwork of organizations and agencies, sometimes stretching across national boundaries, raises difficult questions of accountability. How, crucially, are these structures and networks to be held responsible for their actions?

Managerialism

A second set of changes associated with neoliberalism concerns the rise of what is generally referred to as 'managerialism' and the increasing centrality of a performance measurement culture together with the changing role of the state in relation to the management or governance of major institutions. With regard to the latter, the past two decades have seen a reconceptualization of the twin notions of government and governance. The previously held assumption that governance was the responsibility and prerogative of government no longer holds true. Commentators have described the modern state as 'stretched' (Bottoms and Wiles 1996), 'unravelling' (Crook *et al.* 1993) or 'hollowing out' (Jessop 1993). In such a view, the state is seen as disengaging, applying a form of 'rule at a distance' (Shearing 1996) or what Rhodes describes as 'governing without government' (1995). The notion of distanciated government is best captured by Osborne and Gaebler's (1992) analogy in which government increasingly assumes the function of 'steering' while responsibility for 'rowing' is devolved to public and private agencies and actors. Though much of this work hugely overstates the impact of such changes on the modern nation-state, it does capture an important shift in the way in which organizations are governed and managed.

The managerial philosophy underpinning the emerging relationship between public policing and the state comes in the form of new public management (NPM). The process began tentatively in the early 1980s under the government's Financial Management Initiative designed to promote economy, efficiency and effectiveness across the public sector. During the early 1990s the process accelerated with the publication of the 1993 Sheehy Inquiry into police responsibilities and rewards, and the white paper on police reform (subsequently to become the Police and Magistrates' Courts Bill). The former proposed radical changes to the internal organization and structure of the police. Although the force of police objection managed to neutralize many of the proposals made at the time, the production of the government's white paper during the same year clearly signalled the direction in which the wind was blowing. The subsequent Police and Magistrates' Courts Act 1994 introduced, among other things, national policing objectives and key performance indicators, costed 'business plans' for policing and the devolution of budgetary controls. New Labour did not flinch in progressing the reforms. The Police Reform Act 2002 established the Police Standards Unit (PSU), introduced an Annual Policing Plan and introduced powers to require police forces to take remedial action where they are judged to be inefficient or ineffective by Her Majesty's Inspectorate of Constabulary (HMIC).

As other chapters in this volume have outlined, there is now a very considerable initiative underway to 'professionalize' police investigative practice. Part of the impetus for this initiative came from the analysis of policing undertaken for and presented in the Policing White Paper published in 2001 (Home Office 2001). A brief outline of some of what the white paper had to say will illustrate the managerialist thrust of contemporary reform. The white paper raised concerns about falls in both detection and conviction rates and, in response, outlined what it took to be the key requirements for the police. These included:

- The police need a clear and *common* understanding of the theory and practice of investigation;
- There need to be clear strategies to tackle criminal gangs and persistent offenders;
- There need to be more effective means of *spreading good practice* in handling investigations (Home Office 2001: para. 3.16, emphasis added).

To achieve these aims the government proposed the introduction of a National Centre for Policing Excellence. Its role was to spread best practice and to validate such work. As such it would augment the work of the Police Standards Unit in monitoring and overseeing policing practice across the country. Linked with this, the white paper also looked forward to 'HMIC continuing to develop a more radical and challenging approach to inspecting the police service' (para. 7.12). It is at this point that the extent of the managerialist thrust of recent times becomes clear. The white paper went on to outline a range of systems for inspecting, auditing, influencing, managing and controlling what the police service does, including a broadened remit for HMIC; basic command unit inspections; the use of performance indicators to 'give the public a much clearer idea both of what we want the police service to achieve and how well they are achieving it' (para. 7.17); the construction of new performance management systems; the introduction of a National Policing Plan; and the introduction of a three-tiered approach to police governance, consisting of regulations, codes of practice and guidance. In relation to investigation the primary vehicle through which reform will be managed is the National Intelligence Model (see Chapter 8, this volume).

As should be clear, the twin thrust of recent developments is both managerialist and, in the main, centralizing.

Centralization

In theory, the model of policing in England and Wales presupposes 43 local police forces operating autonomously with accountability shared within each between the chief constable, the local police authority and the Home Office. The reality is very different. Over the years, the locus of power has shifted incrementally to the Home Office and to the chief constables, represented through the Association of Chief Police Officers (ACPO), at the expense of the local authorities (cf. Lustgarten 1986; Reiner 1991; Jones and Newburn 1997). The trend towards greater centralization of policing has a history that dates back to the formative years of the 'New Police' (Wall 1998). Newburn (2003) highlights four ways in which this process of centralization may be seen in the postwar years:

1   The progressive reduction in the number of police forces in England and Wales (and increased government powers of amalgamation).

2   The increased ability of police forces to co-ordinate their activities across force boundaries together with the formation of new, powerful national police organisations such as the National Criminal Intelligence Service (NCIS) and the National Crime Squad (NCS).

3   The formalisation of the activities of police representative bodies such as the Police Federation and, in particular, ACPO. And perhaps most significantly

4   The increase in government oversight of, and influence over, policing via legislative change and new managerial reforms.

There is little doubt that the trend is set to continue, frequently giving rise to claims of 'creeping nationalization'. Since 1945 the number of forces in England and Wales has been reduced from 200 to 43. Recently, the government announced proposals to reduce their number further in the wake of a report by HMIC that concluded that larger forces could better pool their resources in large investigations (reported in The *Observer*, 4 December 2005).

A second aspect of centralization that is of particular relevance here is the increased ability of forces to work across boundaries, together with the creation of national policing bodies. The trend is especially evident with regard to arrangements for tackling serious and organized crime. Regional crime squads (RCSs) were established in England and Wales in 1965 under the auspices of the Police Act 1964. They expanded significantly throughout the 1970s and 1980s, although the number of squads was reduced from nine to six in the early 1990s. Other contemporaneous developments included the Home Office appointment of a National Co-ordinator for Drugs Intelligence to oversee the creation of the National Drugs Intelligence Unit (NDIU) and the establishment of the National Football Intelligence Unit (NFIU) in 1989.

Within this *de facto* national policing establishment, there was increasing vocal support for further amalgamation. In May 1989 Sir Peter Imbert, then Commissioner of the Metropolitan Police, speaking in Oslo at the annual conference of the Heads of Police Forces in Capital Cities, spoke in favour of a national representative with executive authority, arguing that local authority and autonomy, although admirable, can impede international decision-making. The call was taken up in the autumn of 1989 when the then Home Secretary, Douglas Hurd, requested the RCS Executive Co-ordinator to prepare a report on a national criminal intelligence service in light of 'the increasing sophistication of criminal behaviour and the likelihood that this would increase further following the relaxation of controls on movement in 1992' (*Statewatch*, 2: 9 and cited in Hebenton and Thomas 1995: 116). By 1992 the NFIU, the NDIU, the regional criminal intelligence offices, as well as a variety of other bodies, were incorporated into the newly established NCIS. Shortly after, plans were revealed to create an operational unit to tackle serious and organized crime on a national level. These were realized with the creation of the National Crime Squad in 1998 under the auspices of the Police Act 1997 (which also placed NCIS on a statutory footing). Less than six years later, in February 2004, the government announced plans for the establishment of the Serious Organized Crime Agency (SOCA), which will amalgamate NCIS and NCS, and their partner agencies, into a single agency with national and transnational jurisdiction.

The government's strategy for tackling serious organized crime was set out in its white paper, *One Step Ahead: A 21st Century Strategy to Defeat Organised Crime*, published in March 2004. The central plank of the strategy involves the establishment of SOCA. On 7 April 2005, the Serious Organized Crime and Police Act received Royal Assent, formally establishing the new agency. SOCA has assumed principal responsibility for tackling serious and organized crime within, or affecting, England and Wales. Both the NCS and NCIS have been incorporated into the new dedicated agency, as well as the serious drug trafficking and recovery of related assets functions of HM Revenue and Customs and the UK Immigration Service's responsibilities for combating organized immigration crime. SOCA which initially comprised approximately 4,500 staff, will 'be intelligence-led, and have as its core objective the reduction of harm caused to the UK by organised crime' (NCIS

2005). The new agency represents the most recent phase in the broader trend towards the centralization of policing.

The potential benefits of establishing a 'one-stop shop' for tackling organized crime, set out in the government's Regulatory Impact Assessment (RIA), include, among other things:

> increasing the consistency and clarity of strategic approach both to intelligence and enforcement; developing and delivering an integrated harm reduction strategy; streamlining organisational efficiency, increasing accountability and limiting bureaucracy; developing proactive and long-term intelligence effort; delivering a clear system for proportionate, sharper and more flexible operational prioritisation and effort; delivering operations designed to detect, detain and successfully prosecute the most serious organised criminals through operations driven by intelligence and an appreciation of maximising impact; and, serving as a single point of contact for international partners enhancing relationships and better managing expectations at all levels (Home Office November 2004).

Conclusion

Our aim in this chapter has been to consider some of the key social developments that currently constitute the context of criminal investigation. The review has been necessarily partial, the choice of subjects limited and their coverage indicative. Yet, barring the deliberate omission, there are two dangers in a thumbnail review of this kind. First is the tendency to focus on the novel; on change at the expense of continuity. Second, and relatedly, is the temptation to view the transformations that are taking place as somehow unprecedented, even *epochal*. Throughout, we have been at pains to avoid these pitfalls. There is little doubt that, under the general banner of globalization, some potentially far-reaching transformations are taking place. The landscape of policing, and more specifically of criminal investigation, is changing in important ways and in a direction that is by no means certain. Let us recap. New forms of transnational crime are emerging and, with it, new sites of control are being established. New actors have entered the investigative arena and risk-based thinking has infused practice to the extent that control and management of risky populations become a core driving principle. Proactive investigation is argued to be taking precedence over the traditional reactive mentality. New threats dominate the field compelling new relationships between hitherto disparate agencies and a new performance regime is reconfiguring the traditional relationship between the public institutions of social control, the state and the citizen.

There can be no doubt that policing has changed, just as the society being policed has changed. And, arguably, over the past 20 or 30 years, the pace of change has accelerated. Under these circumstances it would be all too easy to lose sight of the consistencies and continuity in the historical trajectory of criminal investigative practice. In this regard it is worth bearing in mind that the recent creation of the SOCA has its antecedents in the regional crime squads of the 1960s. So, too, transnational policing structures are evolving, but they are by no means an entirely new phenomenon. And likewise, the rudiments of the private investigation industry predate the formation of the first plain-clothes investigation unit. Private investigative practices of varying size have operated in Britain since before the 'New Police' were created.

Finally, we wish to make a small number of observations about the potential implications of the current social context for criminal investigation. Since the very inception of formal, separate criminal investigatory capacity in policing in 1842 there has been a tendency within policing to draw a crude distinction between the uniformed and plain-clothes functions of policing. Recent events appear to have bolstered this trend. The creation of national and transnational policing institutions with a clear emphasis on serious organized crime and terrorism serves to compartmentalize the division of policing labour by function. The dangers are all too real. Speaking at the Richard Dimbleby Lecture in November 2005, Sir Ian Blair, Commissioner of the Metropolitan Police, recognized this danger, noting that policing must stop the drift towards the 'complex and the glamorous end' (cited in the *Guardian* 16 November 2005). He argued strongly against the further fragmentation of policing, a trend that is arguably evidenced by the increasing preoccupation with serious organized crime and terrorism. In this connection it is worth repeating some of the Commissioner's observations at greater length. He argued:

> What we should seek to avoid, at all costs, is a separation of local, neighbourhood policing from either serious criminal investigation or counter terrorist investigation. Every lesson of every police inquiry is that, not only the issues that give rise to anti-social behaviour, but also those that give rise to criminal activity and to terrorism begin at the most local level. I will give you two direct examples. The first is the dreadful death of the cockle pickers in Morecambe Bay. The inquiry into that stretched from overcrowded housing in Liverpool to the role of triad gangs in China: a single investigation. The second follows the failed bombings of 21st of July. A local authority worker identified the flat which three men shown on the CCTV images had frequented: this was the bomb factory. However, he also mentioned that he had found dozens of empty peroxide bottles in the wastebin. Had he had one of our neighbourhood policing teams in place then he probably would have told us about what he had found. Peroxide is the basis of the bombs. Thus national security depends on neighbourhood security. It will not be a Special Branch officer at Scotland Yard who first confronts a terrorist but a local cop or a local community support officer. It is not the police and the intelligence agencies who will defeat crime and terror and anti-social behaviour; it is communities (from the full text of the speech in the *Guardian* 16 November 2005).

Sir Ian's comments clearly point to the danger inherent in further widening the existing division between the uniformed and investigative functions of policing. The attendant dangers are all the more clear when one considers just some of the other developments discussed in this review. Clearly, over the past 20 years, the policing infrastructure has undergone some significant change. The field of policing, no longer confined to the borders of the sovereign state, has broadened. This brings us to our second observation. Some time ago Brodeur (1983) made the distinction between 'high' and 'low' policing. Increasingly, 'high' policing agencies, including the CIA in America and MI5 in Britain, are being drafted in to tackle serious forms of criminality. This adds a complex new dimension to the field of criminal investigation. Questions of national security, internal security and intelligence gathering have somehow become fused as a range of disparate agencies are enrolled in common cause. How (or the extent to which) such agencies will communicate in a world of vested and competing interests remains to be seen. But certainly the boundaries between 'high' and 'low' policing have all too suddenly become more much blurred.

Moreover, the state no longer holds even a symbolic monopoly over the mechanisms of social control. Criminal investigation is a lucrative and expanding market. The state itself encourages commercial investigative agencies to assume a role in the peripheries of criminal investigation (by joining the extended police family), while multinational corporations, for very different reasons (see Chapter 11, this volume), create a market for such services in their own right. A small number of transnational companies dominate the market providing a complex array of services that transcend the state. This raises a number of questions that are beyond our capacity to explore here. As security networks become increasingly complex, and as private forms of investigation increasingly encroach upon, and coalesce with, public policing, the difficulties of ensuring democratic accountability become all too real. It is here that some of the most important debates about the future of criminal investigation lie.

Selected further reading

There is no single comprehensive text covering all the issues discussed in this chapter. The *Handbook of Policing* (Newburn, T. (ed.) (2003) Cullompton: Willan Publishing) provides the most complete single source of reference to many of the issues touched upon with regard to the contemporary landscape of policing. The chapters by Newburn, Walker, Crawford and Maguire, respectively, provide good introductions to context and history, transnational developments, pluralization and criminal investigative practice. Robert Reiner's *The Politics of the Police* (2000 (3rd edn) Oxford: Clarendon Press) remains the best single text on British policing in the postwar era. Useful discussions of contemporary issues can also be found in *Policing Britain* (2000) by L. Johnston (London: Longman), R. Ericson and K. Haggerty's (1997) *Policing the Risk Society* (Oxford: Clarendon Press) and *Governing Security* (2002) by L. Johnston and C. Shearing (London: Routledge). Conveniently, many of the key papers on substantive policing issues have been housed under one cover in *Policing: Key Readings* (Newburn, T. (ed.) (2005) Cullompton: Willan Publishing).

Again, no single text can claim universal coverage of the broader sociological issues touched upon in this chapter. I. Loader and R. Spark's (2002) chapter, 'Contemporary landscapes of crime' (in M. Maguire et al. (eds) *The Oxford Handbook of Criminology* (3rd edn). Oxford: Clarendon Press), provides an excellent starting point and source of references. Other chapters in this collection are equally helpful. U. Beck's (1992) *Risk Society* (London: Sage), A. Giddens' (1990) *The Consequences of Modernity* (Cambridge: Polity Press) and Z. Bauman's (2000) *Liquid Modernity* (Cambridge: Polity Press) are all seminal texts by the key proponents of the late modern society debate. H. Kemshall's (2003) *Understanding Risk in Criminal Justice* (Maidenhead: Open University Press) is an accessible introduction to many of the issues. Generally, however, anyone seeking to keep abreast of current thinking would do well to scan the journals regularly, particularly the *British Journal of Criminology*, *Criminal Justice: The International Journal of Policy and Practice*, *Policing and Society* and the *British Journal of Sociology*.

Notes

1 In referring to the British police, we are focusing here on England and Wales. We acknowledge that these systems are quite distinct from their counterparts in Northern Ireland and the Channel Islands, and – to a lesser extent – Scotland (Newburn 2003: 16).
2 The euphemism stems from a term employed in Northern Ireland to distinguish between crimes perpetrated by political and non-political criminals.
3 Concern was also raised at the time over the cases of Chris Craig and Derek Bentley for the murder of a policeman and Timothy Evans for the murder of his wife and child in the 1950s.
4 Transnational policing bodies are taken here to mean those that draw their legitimacy from sources beyond individual states.
5 The commission's statutes formally changed its name in 1956.
6 Denmark has signed the Agreement but can choose within the EU framework whether or not to apply any new decisions. Although the UK and Ireland remain outside Schengen, the UK requested in March 1999 to participate in police and legal cooperation in criminal matters, the fight against drugs and the Schengen Information System (SIS). The request was approved in May 2000. Ireland made a similar request in June 2000, which was granted in February 2002.
7 The Head of the National Crime Faculty at Bramshill recently stated that criminal investigation is undergoing a fundamental shift 'from emphasis on resource allocation to [one on] detectability' (cited in Johnston 2000: 57).
8 This trend is particularly evident in response to recent developments over the policing of terrorism (cf. Matassa and Newburn 2003) and serious organized crime (Edwards and Gill 2003).

References

Adams, J. (1995) *Risk*. London: UCL Press.
Anderson, M. (1989) *Policing the World: Interpol and the Politics of International Police Co-operation*. Oxford: Clarendon Press.
Anderson, M., den Boer, M., Cullen, P., Gilmore, W., Raab, C. and Walker, N. (1995) *Policing the European Union: Theory, Law and Practice*. Oxford: Clarendon Press.
Ascoli, D. (1979) *The Queen's Peace: The Origins and Development of the Metropolitan Police, 1829–1979*. London: Hamish Hamilton.
Ball, J., Chester, L. and Perrott, R. (1979) *Cops and Robbers*. Harmondsworth: Penguin Books.

Bauman, Z (2000) *Liquid Modernity*. Cambridge: Polity Press.

Bauman, Z. (2001) *The Individualized Society*. Cambridge: Polity Press.

Bayley, D. and Shearing, C. (1996) 'The future of policing', *Law and Society Review*, 30: 585–606.

Beck, U. (1992) *Risk Society: Towards a New Modernity*. London: Sage.

Beck, U. (1998) 'The politics of risk society', in J. Franklin (ed.) *The Politics of Risk Society*. Cambridge: Polity Press.

Bottoms, A. and Wiles, P. (1996) 'Understanding crime prevention in late modern societies', in T. Bennett (ed.) *Preventing Crime and Disorder: Targeting Strategies and Responsibilities*. University of Cambridge, Institute of Criminology, Cropwood Series: Cambridge.

Bowling, B. and Newburn, T. (2007 forthcoming) 'Policing and national security', in B. Bowling and J. Fagan (eds) *Police, Community and the Rule of Law*. Oxford: Hart Publishing.

Bresler, F. (1992) *Interpol*. London: Sinclair Stevenson.

Brodeur, J.P. (1983) 'High policing and low policing: remarks about the policing of political activities', *Social Problems*, 30: 507–20.

Brodeur, J.P. (1999) 'Cops and spooks', *Police Practice and Research*, 1: 1–24.

Bunyan, T. (2003) 'The birth of the EU's Interior Ministry?', *Statewatch*, 13: 21–3.

Cohen, S. (1985) *Visions of Social Control*. Cambridge: Polity Press.

Cox, B., Shirley, J. and Short, M. (1977) *The Fall of Scotland Yard*. Harmondsworth: Penguin Books.

Crawford, A. (2003) 'The pattern of policing in the UK: policing beyond the police', in T. Newburn (ed.) *Handbook of Policing*. Cullompton: Willan Publishing.

Crook, S., Pakulski, J. and Waters, M. (1993) *Postmodernization: Change in Advanced Society*. London: Sage.

Deflem, M. (2002) *Policing World Society: Historical Foundations of International Police Co-operation*. Oxford: Clarendon Press.

Den Boer, M. (2003) 'Police and judicial cooperation in criminal matters: a dynamic policy area', in P. Van Der Hoek (ed.) *Public Administration and Public Policy in the European Union*. New York, NY: Dekker.

Douglas, M. (1992) *Risk and Blame*. London: Routledge.

Edwards, A. and Gill, P. (eds) (2003) *Transnational Organised Crime*. London: Routledge.

Emsley, C. (2003) 'The birth and development of the police', in T. Newburn (ed.) *Handbook of Policing*. Cullompton: Willan Publishing.

Ericson, R. (1994) 'The division of expert knowledge in policing and security', *British Journal of Sociology*, 45: 149–75.

Ericson, R. and Haggerty, K. (1997) *Policing the Risk Society*. Oxford: Clarendon Press.

Europol (2006) *Fact Sheet on Europol* (January) (available online at www.europol. eu.int).

Feeley, M. and Simon, J. (1992) 'The new penology: notes on the emerging strategy of corrections and its implications', *Criminology*, 30: 452–74.

Feeley, M. and Simon, J. (1994) 'Actuarial justice: the emerging new criminal law', in D. Nelken (ed.) *The Futures of Criminology*. London: Sage.

Findlay, M. (1999) *The Globalisation of Crime*. Cambridge: Cambridge University Press.

Foster, J., Newburn, T. and Souhami, A. (2005) *Assessing the Impact of the Stephen Lawrence Inquiry*. London: Home Office.

Garland, D. (1996) 'The limits of the sovereign state: strategies of crime control in contemporary society', *British Journal of Criminology*, 36: 445–71.

Garland, D. (2001) *The Culture of Crime Control: Crime and Social Order in Contemporary Society*. Oxford: Oxford University Press.

George, B. and Watson, T. (1992) 'Combatting international terrorism after 1992', in Y. Alexander and D.A. Pluchinsky (eds) *European Terrorism Today and Tomorrow*. Washington, DC: Brassey's Terrorism Library.

Giddens, A. (1990) *The Consequences of Modernity*. Cambridge: Polity Press.

Gill, M. and Hart, G. (1997) 'Policing as business: the organisation and structure of private investigation', *Policing and Society*, 7: 117–41.

Gilmore, W. (2003) *The Twin Towers and the Three Pillars*. Florence: European University Institute, Law Department.

Greer, S. (1988) 'The supergrass system', in A. Jennings (ed.) *Justice Under Fire*. London: Pluto Press.

Greer, S. (2001) 'Where the grass is greener: supergrasses in comparative perspective', in R. Billingsley *et al.* (eds) *Informers: Policing, Policy and Practice*. Cullompton: Willan Publishing.

Harvey, D (1989) *The Conditions of Postmodernity*. Oxford: Blackwell.

Harvey, D. (2005) *A Brief History of Neoliberalism*. New York, NY: Oxford University Press.

Hebenton, B. and Thomas, T. (1995) *Policing Europe: Co-operation, Conflict and Control*. London: Macmillan.

Held, D., McGrew, A., Goldblatt, D. and Perraton, J. (1999) *Global Transformations*. Cambridge: Polity Press.

HMIC (2004) *Baseline Assessment of the National Crime Squad, July 2004*. London: HMIC.

Hobbs, D. (1988) *Doing the Business: Entrepreneurship, the Working Class, and Detectives in the East End of London*. Oxford: Oxford University Press.

Home Office (1995) *Revised Code of Practice for the Detention, Treatment and Questioning of Persons by Police Officers*. London: Home Office.

Home Office (2001) *Policing a New Century: A Blueprint for Reform*. London: HMSO.

Home Office (2004) *Serious Organised Crime and Police Bill: Final Regulatory Impact Assessment*. London: Home Office.

House of Commons (1990) *Practical Police Co-operation in the European Community. Home Affairs Committee Report (7th Report) Session 1989–90*. London: HMSO.

Jessop, B. (1993) 'Towards a Schumpeterian workfare state? Preliminary remarks on post-Fordist political economy', *Studies in Political Economy*, 40: 7–39.

Johnston, L. (1992) 'British policing in the nineties: free market and strong state?', *International Criminal Justice Review*, 2: 1–18.

Johnston, L. (1997) 'Policing communities of risk', in P. Francis *et al.* (eds) *Policing Futures: The Police, Law Enforcement and the Twenty-first Century*. London: Macmillan.

Johnston, L. (2000) *Policing Britain: Risk, Security and Governance*. London: Longman.

Jones, T. and Newburn, T. (1997) *Policing after the Act*. London: Policy Studies Institute.

Jones, T. and Newburn, T. (1998) *Private Security and Public Policing*. Oxford: Clarendon Press.

Jones, T. and Newburn, T. (2002) 'The transformation of policing? Understanding current trends in policing systems', *British Journal of Criminology*, 42: 129–46.

Jones, T. and Newburn, T. (2006) *Plural Policing: A Comparative Perspective*. London: Routledge.

Kemshall, H. (2003) *Understanding Risk in the Criminal Justice System*. Maidenhead: Open University Press.

Kumar, K. (1995) *From Post-industrial to Post-modern Society*. Oxford: Blackwell.

Lee, M. and South, N. (2003), 'Drugs policing', in T. Newburn (ed.) *Handbook of Policing*. Cullompton: Willan Publishing.

Levi, M. (2003) 'Organised and financial crime', in T. Newburn (ed.) *Handbook of Policing*. Cullompton: Willan Publishing.

Loader, I. (1997) 'Private security and the demand for protection in contemporary Britain', *Policing and Society*, 7: 143-62.

Loader, I. (2004) 'Policing, securisation and democratisation in Europe', in T. Newburn and R. Sparks (eds) *Criminal Justice and Political Cultures: National and International Dimensions of Crime Control*. Cullompton: Willan Publishing.

Loader, I. and Sparks, R. (2002) 'Contemporary landscapes of crime, order and control: governance, risk and globalization', in M. Maguire *et al.* (eds) *The Oxford Handbook of Criminology* (3rd edn). Oxford: Clarendon Press.

Lupton, D. (1999) *Risk*. London: Routledge.

Lustgarten, L. (1986) *The Governance of Police*. London: Sweet & Maxwell.

Maas, W. (2005) 'Freedom of movement inside "Fortress Europe"', in E. Zureik and M.B. Salter (eds) *Global Surveillance and Policing: Borders, security, identity*. Cullompton: Willan Publishing.

Macpherson, Sir W. (1999) *The Stephen Lawrence Inquiry: Report* (Cm 4262-I). London: HMSO.

Maguire, M. (2002) 'Regulating the police station: the case of the Police and Criminal Evidence Act 1984', in M. McConville and G. Wilson (eds) *The Handbook of the Criminal Justice Process*. Oxford: Oxford University Press.

Maguire, M. (2003) 'Criminal investigation and crime control', in T. Newburn (ed.) *Handbook of Policing*. Cullompton: Willan Publishing.

Maguire, M. (2000) 'Policing by risks and targets: some dimensions and implications of intelligence-led crime control', *Policing and Society*, 9: 315–36.

Maguire, M. and Norris, C. (1992) *The Conduct and Supervision of Criminal Investigations. Royal Commission on Criminal Justice Research Report 5*. London: HMSO.

Marx, G.T. (1988) *Undercover: Police Surveillance in America*. Berkeley, CA: University of California Press.

Marx, G.T. (2002) 'What's new about the new surveillance? Classifying the change and continuity', *Surveillance and Society*, 1: 9–29.

Matassa, M. and Newburn, T. (2003) 'Policing and terrorism', in T. Newburn (ed.) *Handbook of Policing*. Cullompton: Willan Publishing.

McConville, M., Sanders, A. and Leng, R. (1991) *The Case for the Prosecution*. London: Routledge.

McLaughlin, E. (1992) 'The democratic deficit: European Union and the accountability of the British police', *British Journal of Criminology*, 32: 473–87.

McLaughlin, E. and Murji, K. (1995) 'The end of public policing? Police reform and the "New Managerialism"', in L. Noaks *et al.* (eds) *Contemporary Issues in Criminology*. Cardiff: University of Wales Press.

Morgan, R. (1995) 'Authors meet critics: the case for the prosecution', in L. Noaks *et al.* (eds) *Contemporary Issues in Criminology*. Cardiff: University of Wales Press.

NCIS (2005) *The National Criminal Intelligence Service Annual Report 2004/05*. London: HMSO.

NCS (2002) *National Crime Squad: Information Booklet*. London: NCS.

NCS (2004) *National Crime Squad: Corporate Plan, 2004 to 2007* (online report). London: NCS.

NCS (2005) *The National Crime Squad Annual Report, 2004/05*. London: HMSO.

Nelkin, D. and Andrews, L. (1999) 'DNA identification and surveillance creep', *Sociology of Health and Illness*, 21: 689–706.

Newburn, T. (2003) *Handbook of Policing*. Cullompton: Willan Publishing.

Newburn, T. (ed.) (2005) *Policing: Key Readings*. Cullompton: Willan Publishing.

O'Malley, P. and Palmer, D. (1996) 'Post-Keynesian policing', *Economy and Society*, 25 137–55.

Osborne, D. and Gaebler, T. (1992) *Reinventing Government*. Reading, MA: Addison-Wesley.

Prenzler, T. (2001) *Private Investigators in Australia: Work, Law, Ethics and Regulation. Report to the Criminology Research Council*. Brisbane: Griffith University.

Rauchs, G. and Koenig, D.J. (2001) 'Europol', in D.J. Koenig and D. K. Das (eds.) *International Police Cooperation: A World Perspective*. Lanham, MA: Lexington Books.

Rawlings, P. (2003) 'Policing before the police', in T. Newburn (ed.) *Handbook of Policing*. Cullompton: Willan Publishing.

Reiner, R. (1991) *Chief Constables*. Oxford: Oxford University Press.

Reiner, R. (1992) 'Policing a postmodern society', *Modern Law Review*, 55: 761–81.

Reiner, R. (1997) 'Policing and the police', in M. Maguire *et al.* (eds) *The Oxford Handbook of Criminology*. Oxford: Clarendon Press.

Reiner, R. (2000) *The Politics of the Police* (3rd edn). Oxford: Clarendon Press.

Rhodes, R. (1995) *The New Governance: Governing without Government*. Swindon: ESRC.

Shearing, C. (1996) 'Reinventing policing: policing as governance', in O. Marenin (ed.) *Policing Change: Changing Police*. New York, NY: Garland.

Shearing, C. and Stenning, P.C. (eds) (1987) *Private Policing*. Newbury Park, CA: Sage.

Sheptycki, J. (1997) 'Transnationalism, crime control and the European state system: a review of the literature', *International Criminal Justice Review*, 7: 130–40.

Sheptycki, J. (1998) 'The global cops cometh: reflections on transnationalization, knowledge work and policing subculture', *British Journal of Sociology*, 49: 57–74.

Sheptycki, J. (2000) *Issues in Transnational Policing*. London: Routledge.

Simon, J. (1988) 'The ideological effects of actuarial practices', *Law and Society Review*, 22: 772.

Tilley, N. (2003) 'Community policing, problem oriented policing and intelligence-led policing', in T. Newburn (ed.) *Handbook of Policing*, Cullompton: Willan Publishing.

Walker, N. (2003) 'The pattern of transnational policing', in T. Newburn (ed.) *Handbook of Policing*. Cullompton: Willan Publishing.

Wall, D. (1998) *The Chief Constables of England and Wales: The Socio-legal History of a Criminal Justice Elite*. Aldershot: Dartmouth.

Waters, M (1995) *Globalization*. London: Routledge.

Zander, M. (1985) *The Police and Criminal Evidence Act 1984.* London: Sweet & Maxwell.

Zureik, E. and Salter, M.B. (eds.) (2005) *Global Surveillance and Policing: Borders, Security, Identity*. Cullompton: Willan Publishing.

Chapter 4

Psychology and criminal investigation

Tom Williamson

Introduction

Information is frequently averred to be the lifeblood of an investigation. Psychological science can inform our understanding of the effectiveness of various methods for the elicitation of information from victims, witnesses and suspects that will have a bearing on the quality of the investigation and subsequent criminal justice processes. But a major problem exists in that, as investigators, lawyers and judges often receive no instruction in psychological theory as part of their training, they can remain in ignorance of basic psychological processes involved in the construction of testimony which are often at odds with lay or 'commonsense' knowledge (Yarmey 2003: 547). This knowledge gap may have disastrous consequences for their decision-making, and it can on occasions contribute to miscarriages of justice (see Chapter 25, this volume). The policy response to miscarriages of justice has been to tighten the legal and regulatory framework governing investigative interviewing and, in particular, the custodial questioning of suspects. More progress needs to be made in promoting a better understanding of psychological processes which would lead to more effective investigations and safer criminal justice. A trend can also be observed of the application of behavioural science to investigations.

This brief introduction to psychology and criminal investigations will examine three areas which illustrate where psychological research has, and is, affecting the regulation and practice of investigations. It begins by describing psychological research that shaped the legal and regulatory framework for criminal investigations in England and Wales in response to, *inter alia*, concerns about interviewee suggestibility, low intelligence, false confessions and an investigative culture characterized by an over-reliance on confession evidence. It considers the psychological research that contributed to the change in the law relating to the 'right of silence'. The second substantive section provides an overview of some of the psychological processes involved in the construction of testimony. Psychological research regarding the cognitive and social influences shaping memory for events demonstrates that it is a very malleable process, which has important implications for the reliability of witness testimony upon which most investigations are heavily dependent. This is particularly true of eyewitness testimony. Finally, the third section outlines the contribution of behavioural science units (BSUs) to more effective investigations as disseminators of psychological knowledge illustrated by reference to the concepts of offender profiling and investigative psychology to suggest that, in future, inductive knowledge-based systems of investigation may mean less reliance will be placed on deductive inferences, which is the traditional means of conducting investigations. (A more detailed discussion of offender profiling can be found in Chapter 20, this volume, and for a critical analysis of investigative interviewing see Chapter 19, this volume).

Psychology is often defined as *the scientific study of behaviour and mental processes*. The science of psychology has a very long history reaching back to Greek philosophers but from the time of its modern development in the nineteenth century, psychologists have found that their scientific studies have enabled them to make a contribution to investigations, as well as to civil and criminal trials (cf. Gudjonsson and Haward 1998: 6–22). It is worrying how difficult it has been for investigators and lawyers to comprehend the implications which psychological research has for the way they work (Fisher 1977; Williamson 1990; Heaton-Armstrong *et al.* 1999: ch. 19; Carson and Bull 2003: chs 5.1 and 5.3), with the result that there is frequently a tension between psychology and law, generally exacerbated by the lack of any mutual understanding.

The legal and regulatory framework for custodial questioning

Suggestibility, intelligence and false confessions

Wilhelm Wundt, one of the fathers of modern psychology, opened the world's first psychological laboratory in Leipzig, Germany, in the late nineteenth century where he conducted surprisingly sophisticated experiments into sensory and behavioural phenomena. One student, Schrenk-Notzing, presented evidence to a Bavarian court of laboratory experiments into suggestibility and errors of recall. In particular, he testified that witnesses in a murder trial had not distinguished between what they had seen and what had been reported in the press (Gudjonsson and Haward 1998: 10; cf. Hale 1980). Testimony was also studied by yet another Leipzig student, Cattel, of whom Gudjonsson and Haward (1998: 10) wrote: 'Cattel … examined experimentally the nature of testimony and revealed the effects of situational and individual differences, which are still being confirmed by more sophisticated methods a century later.'

Cattel's research into testimony was replicated by a French psychologist, Alfred Binet, and his colleagues, who went on to study differences between individuals in their intelligence (individual differences in suggestibility and intelligence are examined in more detail in Chapter 19, this volume).

Intelligence

One psychological factor that can affect testimony is the intellectual capacity of the witness, and psychometric tests have been developed which can assess the extent to which this particular ability is possessed. The first intelligence tests were developed at the beginning of the twentieth century (Binet and Simon 1905). These began to be used to test for aptitude in scholastic performance and for recruitment in employment. By distributing intelligence tests to thousands of children it was possible to develop age-level norms where each test item was age graded at the level at which a substantial majority of the children pass it. A child's mental age could be obtained by summing the number of items passed at each level and from this it is possible to establish whether the child's intelligence was above or below the average for his or her age.

The more familiar intelligence quotient (IQ) is an index that expresses intelligence as a ratio of mental age to chronological age multiplied by 100. Where IQ is given a value of 100, the mental age is equal to the chronological age. When represented on a graph, IQ scores tend to fall in the form of a bell-shaped curve, with most people's scores hovering around 100, but some people score much higher or lower than 100. Some 68 per cent of the population are likely to have average scores ranging from 85 to 115; some 16 per cent are likely to have scores from 115 to 145 and above, and these people are described as superior, very superior and gifted, depending on their score. Another 16 per cent are likely to have scores from 55 to 85 and, of these, 13.6 per cent will be in the 70–85 range and can be described as borderline mentally retarded; a further 2.2 per cent in the 55–70 range can be described as mildly mentally retarded; and 0.1 per cent with scores below 55 are described as severely to profoundly mentally retarded (Anastasia and Urbina 1997).[1] These tests have proved to be quite reliable and have a high test–retest correlation score (.90) and are fairly valid predictors of achievement in school with validity coefficients of about .50, where a perfect correlation would be 1.00 and nil correlation would be 0.

A person with below-average intelligence may have more difficulty in coping with the justice system, such as in being able to provide an account to investigators in the first instance, or later when dealing with challenges to the account in police interviews or in cross-examination at court. The issues of suggestibility and intelligence had a bearing on a miscarriage of justice in the case of Maxwell Confait, which involved three youths convicted of murder who were later found to be suggestible, to have below-average intelligence and to have made false confessions to the police (Fisher 1977).

False confessions

The issue over which lawyers, a judge and psychologists clashed was why the youths made false confessions. Maxwell Confait was a 26-year-old transvestite homosexual prostitute. During the night of 21/22 April 1972 a fire took place at 27 Doggett Road, London SE6. The fire brigade was called to extinguish the fire, and in a room on the first floor they found the body of Confait. On 24 April three youths were arrested and questioned and, as a result, confessions were said to have been made to the police by two youths, Ronald Leighton, then aged 15 years, and Colin Lattimore, then aged 18 years. The youths were charged with the murder of Maxwell Confait, and along with a third youth, Ahmet Salih, then aged 14 years, they were also charged with setting fire to 27 Doggett Road. At the trial in November 1972, Leighton was convicted of murder, Lattimore was convicted of manslaughter on the ground of diminished responsibility and all three were convicted of arson. In October 1975 the convictions were quashed by the Court of Appeal.

Exceptionally for Court of Appeal acquittals at the time, a government inquiry was conducted by a retired judge, the Hon. Sir Henry Fisher, who published his report in December 1977. In his findings Fisher was at pains to point out that the youths had not been physically assaulted by the police and that no police officer had deliberately falsified the record of oral answers given by the three youths to questions. All three youths gave evidence to the inquiry, and Fisher was concerned that they had personal characteristics which rendered them vulnerable during police questioning. Fisher described the youths in the following terms. Leighton was a difficult disturbed adolescent of limited intelligence whose reading age had been established by psychologists to be 9 years 6 months, and who had been attending a school for maladjusted boys. Intelligence tests showed that he had an IQ of 81. Salih was found to be intelligent, collected and articulate and made a favourable impression on the inquiry. Lattimore was classified as educationally subnormal (ESN[2]) and, from the age of 6, had successively attended three ESN schools. He behaved like a child of 8 and his IQ was estimated at approximately 60. He appeared to the inquiry to be 'suggestible'. He could neither tell the time nor add up the value of coins placed in front of him.

Attending the inquiry throughout was Barrie Irving, a psychologist who gave evidence to the inquiry where he addressed the question of why the boys acquiesced in a confession which they knew to be false. Drawing on psychological theories from cognitive and social psychology, he pointed to difficulties in processing information and to the influence of social factors such as custody. Irving proposed explanations for the confessions but these were firmly rejected by Fisher. Fisher said:

> Notoriously, a confession may be extracted by physical violence, or fear of physical violence; by a hectoring bullying approach and a kind understanding approach. It may also be extracted by a promise of favours if a confession is made. It is conduct of that kind which renders a confession inadmissible (1977: para. 12.127, 135).

The things which rendered a confession 'unreliable' were self-evident to Fisher, a lawyer. To Irving, a psychologist, they were far from self-evident. Fisher was concerned about the external factors and how they could be regulated through the Judges Rules; Irving was more concerned, as a psychologist, with the mental and social processes involved in custodial questioning which had led to the false confessions. One outcome of the Fisher Inquiry was that the government appointed a Royal Commission on Criminal Procedure. The growing pressure for a Royal Commission was given further impetus by the report from an inquiry arising out of the manner in which suspects in terrorist cases in Northern Ireland had been interrogated by the military and which had led to the only case where one European country has taken another to the European Court of Human Rights[3] (Bennett 1979). An indication that this may have also been on Fisher's mind can be seen from his reference to the effects of techniques designed to create disorientation. Fisher said: 'It is of course now a commonplace that disorientation can occur as a result of stress (lack of food, drink, sleep, sensory deprivation, fear)' (1977: para. 12.127, 135).

Concern about what happened to people during custodial questioning in ordinary investigations opened the door to psychological research studies for two Royal Commissions that examined the investigative process.The Royal Commission on Criminal Procedure (Philips 1982), under the chairmanship of a distinguished historian, commissioned a series of research studies to inform its findings. In the event a series of 12 excellent studies were produced, of which seven were produced by psychologists, the remainder by lawyers. The commission made recommendations for the investigation of offences which led directly to the Police and Criminal Evidence Act (PACE) 1984 and to the Code of Practice issued under s. 66 of the Act, which provided the first regulatory framework for the investigation of offences in England and Wales.

Once this regime was in place, public confidence in criminal justice was again undermined through a series of high-profile cases, some involving suspected terrorists, pre-dating PACE, that were overturned by the Court of Appeal on the basis that the confession evidence was unreliable (Gudjonsson 2003: 439, Table 16.1). This led to the Royal Commission on Criminal Justice (Runciman 1993) that was informed by 22 research studies, of which 15 could be said to be psychological in nature. Some of these studies continued to address the issue of protection for interviewees and suspects who were vulnerable (Gudjonsson *et al.* 1993; Chapter 19, this volume). An early finding of the research studies was the over-reliance on confession evidence.

Over-reliance on confession evidence

In a study of the work of detectives for the Royal Commission on Criminal Procedure, Steer (1982) showed that most offenders were found in circumstances that did not involve detective skills. Only about 40 per cent of offenders were detected following some kind of investigatory effort. Steer stressed the importance of interrogation in the detection and investigation of crime: one in four offences was detected when the police interviewed a suspect after his or her arrest for other offences, a pattern corroborated by other contemporary research (Bottomley and Coleman 1980; Steer 1982). Because these studies indicated the importance of questioning in the detection of offences, further studies were commissioned into police interrogation practices. Softley (1982) found in a study in four police stations that the great majority of suspects were interviewed even when the existing evidence against them was strong, and in 70 per cent of these cases the police believed that the information given by the suspect would help to secure a conviction. About 60 per cent of suspects made either a full confession or a damaging admission (Softley 1982). In a study at Brighton police station, Irving (1982) found a similar confession rate and that the main purpose of an interview was to obtain a confession. When cases being heard in the Crown Court were examined by two academic lawyers, it was found that 13 per cent would have failed to reach a *prima facie* standard without confession evidence, and a further 4 per cent would probably have been acquitted. Half the statements made by the accused amounted to a full confession (Baldwin and McConville 1982).

Prior to PACE the procedures for police questioning were set out in a Home Office circular entitled *The Judges Rules and Administrative Directions to the Police*, which are based on principles first developed in the nineteenth century. When the Judges Rules were first formulated in 1912 it was rare for the police to question suspects, reflecting a judgment by Lord Brampton that a constable should keep his eyes and ears open and his mouth shut. The Royal Commission on Police Powers and Procedure (1929: paras. 162 and 165) concluded that it was advisable for the police to avoid any questioning at all of persons in custody. It is therefore remarkable that over the next 50 years police interrogation became so central to the investigation of offences, leading the report of the Royal Commission on Criminal Procedure (Steer 1982: para. 2.7) to remark: 'Only comparatively recently does police questioning in custody seem to have become accepted practice.'

The Royal Commission on Criminal Procedure examined the Judges Rules and found them to be ineffective in controlling police practices during custodial questioning. The presumption behind the Judges Rules is that the circumstances of police questioning are of their very nature psychologically coercive. A similar point had been made in 1966 by the US Supreme Court in their landmark judgment in *Miranda*,[4] where the court held that custodial questioning was inherently coercive. The commission rejected the wording in the Judges Rules that the statement made by the person being questioned in custody should be voluntary, 'in the sense that it has not been obtained from him by fear of prejudice or hope of advantage, exercised or held out by a person in authority, or by oppression'. They considered that since custodial questioning was inherently coercive the notion of voluntariness should be replaced by the concept of whether the statement was reliable. Since the commission took the view that the present rules were unworkable, they stipulated that any rules applied to investigative arrangements should reach three principal standards if they were to command public confidence:

- Are they fair?
- Are they open?
- Are they workable?

This concept of the reliability of statements made to the police during custodial questioning was subsequently addressed through ss. 76 and 78 of PACE. Section 76 reverses the burden of proof and it is on the prosecution to demonstrate that nothing happened during custodial questioning that would render any statement to be unreliable and by virtue of s. 78, a statement can be excluded if it has been obtained unfairly. The commission recommended the introduction of tape-recording of all custodial questioning in order to ensure that the record of what was said was accurate and that it was said freely. The commission drew attention to the need for a greater appreciation of the effects of custody on suspects and the psychological vulnerabilities of all who had to face custodial questioning. This was described by the Royal Commission on Criminal Procedure in this way: 'it is equally important to convey to the detective in training a sharper awareness of the psychology of custody and interrogation and some basic analysis of and skills in methods of interviewing' (Steer 1982: para. 10.14).

The arrival of tape-recording and video-taping meant that police interrogations became available for scientific analysis, and this clearly revealed that there was a need for the police to be trained in investigative interviewing and to have an awareness of the psychological pressures inherent in custodial questioning (for a more detailed analysis of the psychological processes involved in custodial questioning and the psychology of confessions, Gudjonsson 1992, 2003; Kassin and Gudjonsson 2004; Williamson 2006; Chapter 19, this volume).

Tape-recording can be seen as a response to the requirement that the rules regulating custodial questioning should encourage openness, and the provision for legal advice to be freely available meant that interviewers encountered more lawyers and their clerks when questioning suspects in custody. Anecdotal evidence at the time from officers suggested that this was leading to a rise in interviews where suspects would exercise their right not to say anything in reply to police questions. This was supported by a research study involving 1,627 interviews conducted on ten police divisions of the Metropolitan Police (Williamson 1990: 294). It was found that 6 per cent of suspects did not answer any questions from the start of the interview, 6 per cent did not answer any questions relevant to the offence and a further 11 per cent did not answer some questions relevant to the offence. The number of full admissions was 13 per cent. In 23 per cent of cases the suspects were legally represented and, in this sample, 39 per cent exercised their right to silence, 54 per cent answered all questions put to them and 6.7 per cent admitted the alleged offence. There was a concern that the minority who exercised their right to silence included a disproportionate number of experienced criminals who exploited the system in order to obtain an acquittal. The extent to which suspects were exercising their right to silence was further examined in a study for the Royal Commission on Criminal Justice. It was found in a study of Crown Court cases that: 'defendants exercised their right to silence in relation to all questions in 11%–13% of cases and to some significant questions in a further 10% of cases' (Zander and Henderson 1993: 16. 53).

The majority on the commission did not believe that adverse inferences should be drawn from silence but went on to recommend pre-trial disclosure – namely, that when the prosecution case has been fully disclosed defendants should be required to offer an answer to the charges made against them at the risk of adverse comment at trial on any new defence they then disclose or any departure from the defence which they previously disclosed. The government's response was the Criminal Justice and Public Order Act 1994 and the revised Code of Practice which introduced a new caution: 'You do not have to say anything. *But it may harm your defence if you do not mention when questioned something which you later rely on in court.* Anything you do say may be given in evidence.'

Sections 34–39 set out the circumstances in which a court or jury may draw proper inferences from the fact that a person does not give evidence at trial or answer questions put to him or her by the police. Together with what had come about as a result of PACE, these changes marked the new legal framework for regulating custodial interviewing, and they have had a significant effect on the investigative culture.

In summarizing the effect of the legal and technological changes described in this section, it can be argued that they brought about a change in the investigative culture from one where there was an over-reliance on confession evidence in order to secure a conviction, and where interrogation was often seen as a shortcut in lieu of a more thorough investigation. The post-PACE investigative culture has become accustomed to being more accountable and complying with a due process model of investigation. It should be noted that progress towards a new investigative paradigm was partly enabled by psychologists, lawyers and investigators who collaborated to develop the investigative interviewing training model used in England and Wales to meet the higher standards required by the new legal and regulatory framework (Williamson 2006; Chapter 19, this volume). It also meant that, although interviews could make a greater contribution to the information flowing into the investigation, this potential had been hampered by investigators' lack of understanding of the basic psychological processes whereby testimony is constructed and therefore the degree to which it is safe to rely on, which will be examined in the next section of this chapter.

The psychology of the construction of testimony

From sensing something to conscious experience and recall

If psychologists contributed towards an established and settled legal and regulatory framework for investigative interviewing, the challenge facing psychologists who wish to promote a better understanding of the psychological processes involved in the construction of testimony should be seen as a work in progress. The English adversarial system of justice continues to rely heavily on oral testimony regarding past events. It is important for investigators, lawyers and judges to understand that what is perceived by a witness is a mental image constructed at the time of the event which is then reconstructed from memory to provide any subsequent account of the experience. Cognitive processes are active rather than passive, and people construct their perception of what happened and actively reconstruct the account they provide of it. The eye does not function in a way that is analogous to a video-recorder, nor the ear as an audio-recorder. There is a danger that investigators and lawyers are simply consumers of the account provided without having a greater awareness of how the account may have been distorted. The early psychologists experimented with the concept of the 'absolute threshold', which is the minimum magnitude of a stimulus that can be reliably detected from no stimulus at all. These values were then used to measure the relationship between the magnitude of some stimulus, such as the physical intensity of light or sound, and the resulting psychological experience, such as how bright the light is or how loud the sound is perceived to be. We should therefore note that the physical conditions prevailing at the time will affect what a witness experiences. It transpires that these cognitive processes are, in general, remarkably efficient and accurate.

Psychologists began to experiment to determine how stimuli are transmitted from the senses (sight, hearing, touch, smell and taste) to the sensory receptors in the brain. Each sensory stimulus must translate physical energy, such as sound waves and light waves, into electrical signals that can make their way to the brain. Each sensory organ has receptors that are specialized nerve cells which, when activated, pass the electrical signal to connecting neurons until the signal reaches its receiving area in the cortex of the brain. In the brain the electrical signals resulting from the physical stimuli are reconstructed to form the conscious sensory experience. The importance of this research is that it demonstrates that the perceptions of what we think we saw and heard derive from an active process of cognitive construction which constantly involves us in making hypotheses about what it is we think we have experienced – for example, was it a gun being discharged or a car backfiring that we heard? The ear registers the physical soundwaves reaching the hair cells in the inner ear as noise, but it is the brain that processes the information that allows us to decide whether it was a gun or a car. Sometimes our hypotheses or decisions are right and sometimes they are wrong. This can reflect the amount of 'attention' (see below) received.

Experiencing what we pay attention to

What a witness is able to tell investigators and a court will depend on what he or she perceived and how much attention he or she paid to it at the time. The study of perception deals with how organisms process and organize incoming raw sensory information in order to form a coherent representation. They then use that representation to solve problems, such as determining which part of the sensory environment to attend to. This enables them to determine where objects are, to recognize them, abstract information about them and keep the appearance of objects constant. An immediate problem is that, at any one time, our sensory organs are being bombarded with a vast amount of information from the environment. As we are normally not aware of all this sensory information, the implication is that the sensory systems and the brain have some mechanism to screen the incoming information. How the brain filters out some and selects other information is known as 'attention'. For example, it is possible to identify and trace a person's eye movements when he or she is looking at an object. A practical application of this kind of research has been to weapon focus, which is where a person pays rapt attention to a weapon in a scene. Victims of armed crime are often able to provide a detailed description of the weapon but seem to know relatively little about other aspects of the scene, such as the appearance of the person holding the weapon. Laboratory experiments show that eye fixations are on the critical object, the gun, not the rest of the scene (Loftus *et al.* 1987).

Another example relating to how auditory attention acts as a filter is the 'cocktail party' effect, first described by Cherry in 1953, where the sounds of many voices bombard our ears, but yet we are able to pick out one voice or conversations that have some significance for us and that we attend to. We may hear a number of conversations around us but remember little of what we do not actively attend to.

Different parts of the brain appear to be involved in processing sensory information using two different systems. The first represents the perceptual features of an object, and the second system appears to be designed to control when and how these features will be selected and then stored in memory (Matlin 2005: 68). If there has been no conscious attention, this makes it less likely that a witness will be able to provide accurate testimony. To press a witness beyond what he or she is capable of providing runs the serious risk of obtaining testimony based on confabulation or dissembling.

Remembering what we have experienced

Although witnesses at a scene may provide an account to the investigator, the adversarial system of trial, with its high dependence on oral testimony from the witness, imposes an enormous burden on witnesses to remember (under cross-examination) details of an event that may have occurred a long time ago. Well intentioned witnesses can easily feel trapped, can become flustered and can become confused in the account they are providing. To understand why this happens, we need to consider the processes in the brain that are the basis for creating and retaining the memories the witness is relying upon and how psychological understanding of these processes developed during the latter part of the twentieth century.

Psychologists consider that memory can be broken down into three discrete stages: encoding, storage and retrieval (Melon 1963). Encoding is when environmental information is translated into, and stored as, a meaningful entity. The storage stage is where this information is maintained over time. The third stage, retrieval, is where an attempt is made to pull from memory information that was previously encoded and stored.

Information arriving from the environment is first placed in a sensory store. The sensory store is transient, in that information decays over a time period ranging from a few tenths of a second (for visual information) to a few seconds (for the auditory sensory store). The proportion of information in the sensory store that is attended to is transferred into a short-term memory store, which is the store for information of which we are conscious. Usually, information in the short-term memory store will decay over a period of 20 seconds. Decay can be prevented through a process of rehearsal, such as occurs when we repeat a telephone number or a name we have heard. Information processed in short-term memory is passed to a long-term memory, which is the repository of all the information we store to be available to us. The size of this long-term store appears to be unlimited, and it represents our total acquired knowledge of the world.

These three memory stores were described in a theory put forward by Atkinson and Shiffrin in 1971. These different memories appear to correspond to different time intervals, and it seems we commit information to one of these memories subconciously. The short-term store (in which information is attended to) has recently been renamed the working memory to reflect the activities involved in managing sensory information, and this memory appears to have two distinct stores: a phonological buffer storing acoustic information, and a visual-spatial sketch-pad storing visual or spatial information (Baddeley 1986, 1990). Perhaps the most striking aspect of working memory is that it is very limited in capacity: most normal adults have a capacity of seven items, plus or minus two (Miller 1956; Baddeley 2000). Forgetting occurs because items decay over time or are replaced with new items. A problem for the investigator is that it is often difficult to know whether forgetting from long-term memory is due to a loss from storage (it is no longer there) or a failure in retrieval (it still exists but we cannot retrieve it). Retrieval can be affected by interference, which occurs when we try to use a cue to retrieve one item but other items become active and interfere with our recovery of the target item. Forgetting is a function of time – a great deal is forgotten within the first few hours but, after that, the rate of forgetting slows down (Ebbinghaus 1885; Bahrick and Phelphs 1987).

The more we organize the material we encode, the easier it is to retrieve. It is easier to retrieve a fact or episode if you are in the same context you encoded it. We tend to rehearse emotionally charged events, and this can improve retrieval from long-term memory. But a caveat needs to be added as repeating the story over and over can give rise to elaboration of the account to the extent that the final account bears little relation to the original story (Bartlett 1932). Retrieval can also be affected by anxiety. When people experience a frightening situation giving rise to stress or signs of panic, it is very difficult to retrieve even very familiar information. Another contextual effect is that recall is better when the dominant emotion during recall matches that during encoding.

It will be seen that the very accurate representation of the sensory experience evaporates quickly. What the investigator, lawyer and judge is left with is a partial description that cannot ever be as accurate. We can conclude, therefore, that what a well motivated witness is able to recall will be influenced by many factors, including, for example the following:

- Was the event actually perceived?
- What level of attention did the witness pay to it?
- What effort was made to memorize what happened?
- How long after the event did the witness provide an account?
- How many times has the witness provided an account?
- Has the account changed over time?

In particular, we should note that memory is both a constructive and reconstructive process. The brain does not work like a video-recorder. The memory for an event can, and does, depart from the objective reality that gave rise to it, both at the time it is formed (via constructive processes) and then later over time (via reconstructive memory).

Memories are also shaped by social influences

We may add new information that is suggested to us by others, as found by Schrenk-Notzing over a hundred years ago. We may generate schemas or hypotheses to provide a mental representation of a class of people, objects, events or situations and this would include social stereotyping (such as the personality traits or physical attributes of a whole class of people). These social processes also shape our perception of what we think we have experienced. One example of how memory can be affected by externally provided suggestions is found in the classic experiment of Loftus and Palmer (1974). Subjects were shown a film of a car accident and divided into two groups that were treated identically, except for a single word in one of the questions. One group was asked: 'How fast was the car going when it hit the other car?' The other group was asked: 'How fast was the car going when it smashed into the other car?' The 'smashed' group provided a higher speed estimate than the 'hit' group, which could indicate the social effect of leading questions. All the subjects returned a week afterwards when they were asked a series of additional questions. One of the questions was: 'Did you see any broken glass?' (There had been no broken glass.) Those who were in the 'smashed' group were more likely to include incorrectly the presence of broken glass. This phenomenon has been replicated many times, sometimes with varying degrees of success, but it illustrates how easily a real event can be remembered incorrectly with respect to incidental details, particularly when misleading or inaccurate cues are introduced. There are disagreements as to the mechanisms that cause the misinformation effect, but it appears that subtle changes in words can encourage subjects to report non-existent details of events they have not experienced.

This does not mean that witness testimony is generally badly flawed. One study found that middle-aged adults showed accurate recall for public events 98 per cent of the time (Howes and Katz 1992). The mistakes that people do make relate mainly to peripheral details rather than the central information about important events (Sutherland and Hayne 2001), and it has been found that it is unhelpful to try to remember too many small details (Schacter 2001). As a result, some witnesses may be particularly vulnerable during cross-examination, where their account may generally be accurate although wrong on some point of detail. If they are pressed they may respond by unwittingly making up the information that is being sought. Even well intentioned witnesses can make things up.

For example, when subjects are asked to remember a list of words such as mad, fear, hate, rage, temper, fury, ire, wrath, happy, fight, hatred, mean, calm, emotion and enrage, then later they are asked to recall whether the word 'anger' was contained in the original list, many subjects will report remembering the critical non-presented word, 'anger', as having been present in the original list. Roediger and McDermott (1995) claim that these results demonstrate that people remember events that never happened. It is also possible to create a memory of an entire fictional event. Several psychological experiments have been conducted where subjects have been asked to recall events that had never actually happened, such as a ferry sinking, yet they provided very detailed accounts. Some 52 per cent of participants claimed to have seen a non-existent film of the sinking of a ferry, and participants also either increased or decreased their levels of false reporting depending on whether a confederate claimed to have seen, or not to have seen, the film (Granhag et al. 2003). In a similar experiment using a different event (the death in a car crash of Diana, Princess of Wales) Ost (2001) found that 44 per cent of participants claimed to have seen a non-existent video of the moment of the crash on television. Not all subjects in these types of experiments remember false events but, in general, about 25 per cent do.

Not only do subjects remember events that they have imagined but they can be very confident about the account they provide. This has important implications for the way in which the adversarial system of justice works and how proof is established (see Chapter 16, this volume, for a discussion of alternative models and of the assessment of probability). The factors that may well influence the accuracy of the account include poor initial encoding (due to short duration), poor lighting and lack of attention; some post-event interference or information suggested by others; and motivation and opportunity to rehearse the reconstructed memory (Penrod and Cutler 1995). In a study of 45 experiments that examined the relationship between confidence and accuracy, it was found that, in half those studies, there was a positive relationship between confidence and accuracy; in the other half there was no relationship or a negative relationship. The encoding circumstances that may contribute to poor memory can lead people to fill gaps in their memory with salient information they could draw from their knowledge of the world. Given that there may be no correlation between accuracy and confidence (Deffenbacher 1980; Stephenson 1984), we need to pay attention to the circumstances leading up to a confident memory. The memory reconstruction process can form the basis for memories that are incorrect but seem real and that are recounted with considerable confidence. This latter effect is particularly likely to be the case when people collaborate in remembering an account (Clarke and Stephenson 1999).

Leaving aside the possibility of fabricated accounts, a particular problem has been recovered memories. Thousands of people who have sought counselling have, during certain types of therapy, developed memories of sexual abuse and brutalization (Loftus and Pickrell 1995; Gudjonsson 1997; Brown et al. 2000; Ost 2006). Sometimes this is facilitated by participating in support groups consisting of other people who have recovered or are trying to recover repressed memories for abuse. In some instances the memories developed are psychologically impossible, such as remembering being abused when they were three months old. Participation in the group may have encouraged the person to report his or her experience, but it may also have encouraged confabulation and embellishment of events. Suggestive information can alter the details of a recent event but can also plant entirely false beliefs in the minds of people (Porter et al. 1999; Ost 2006). The problem for the investigator and the court is that there is little that can be done to differentiate true memories from those that have been suggestively planted. According to Loftus (2003):

> Apart from bearing on the controversy about repressed memories that has plagued our society for more than a decade, the modern research does reveal important ways in which our memories are malleable, and it reveals much about the rather flimsy curtain that sometimes separates memory and imagination.

These difficulties arising from memory being malleable highlight the importance of good interviewing techniques and models of interviewing, such as the PEACE model in the UK and the cognitive interview (Fisher and Geiselman 1992), which can help minimize the problems inherent in eliciting accurate testimony from witnesses. There are a number of common features in good investigative interviewing models, including the following:

- Careful preparation prior to the interview, including being aware of the conditions that would have affected what the witness was able to perceive.

- Establishing a rapport with the interviewee, treating him or her with respect and demonstrating cultural sensitivity.

- Being careful when dealing with those who are vulnerable, suggestible or suffering from learning difficulties, although it should be noted that the identification of vulnerabilities remains a problem (Gudjonsson *et al.* 1993).

- Allowing the witness to provide an account without interruption from the interviewer – sometimes known as 'free recall'.

- Checking and clarifying the account provided against what is known or can be ascertained.

- Concluding the interview on a positive note and leaving the interviewee with an invitation to provide additional information in the event he or she remembers something new (Williamson 2006).

There is no doubt that interviewing practice would be improved if practitioners had a better understanding of the basic psychological processes involved in the construction of testimony.

Eyewitness identification is particularly malleable

In a study of miscarriages of justice in the USA where the convicted person had subsequently been completely exonerated as a result of DNA testing, it was found that the most common contributory factor was mistaken identity, which occurred in 52 per cent of cases. Caucasians misidentified African-American defendants in 35 per cent of cases, but African-Americans also misidentified other African-Americans in 24 per cent of the cases

(Scheck *et al.* 2000). Research in the State of Massachusetts has revealed that mistaken eyewitness testimony has been a factor in over half the known wrongful convictions in the state (Fisher and McKenzie 2004: 19). Cutler and Penrod (1995) estimate that there are 4,500 erroneous convictions each year in the USA arising from faulty eyewitness identification.

It is possible to trace guidance on identification procedures in England and Wales from Home Office Circulars in 1905, 1925 and 1926, but the examination of these procedural documents usually commences from the Home Office circular on ID parades (9/1969) and, since 1984, the relevant guidance is contained under the aegis of PACE and the codes of practice (Fisher and McKenzie 2004: 7). As a result of a series of miscarriages of justice based on erroneous identification, a judicial inquiry was held in 1977 under Lord Devlin, who was the first judge to call for psychological research to be conducted on identification parades. The key stated case in England and Wales on identification is *Regina* v. *Turnbull*.[5]

There have been several recent reviews of the literature on eyewitness testimony (see Thompson *et al.* 1998; Memon *et al.* 2003: 108–25). In field experiments conducted in realistic settings, such as where customers were engaged in non-stressful transactions with clerks in shops for one or more minutes and were tested after short delays, the average accuracy when presented with photographs where the target person (the clerk) was present was 42 per cent, and false identification when the targets were not present was 36 per cent (Yarmey 2003: 544). According to Memon *et al.* (2003), by 1995 there were over 2,000 publications addressing eyewitness (un)reliability. These studies have consistently confirmed that eyewitnesses can be mistaken and that they often perform at a level not better than chance or by tossing a coin.

Intelligence, gender and race are not particularly useful predictors of identification accuracy. Children over five years do not differ significantly from adults with respect to correct identification, although they are more inclined to make a choice when the target is absent, and in this respect they are the same as seniors (60–80 years) (Memon *et al.* 2003). Subjects with high blood-alcohol are more likely to make a false identification from a target absent display (Dysart *et al.* 2002). Wells *et al.* have observed that 'the confidence that an eyewitness expresses in his or her identification during testimony is the most powerful single determinant of whether or not observers of that testimony will believe that the eyewitness made an accurate identification' (1998: 620).[6] Sporer *et al.* (1995) found that the confidence–accuracy relationship was stronger for witnesses who make an identification than for those who say the target is not present.

Turning now to psychological research relating to the targets (the suspect), it appears that gender has no effects on facial recognition, but attractiveness does, with greater recall for either attractive or ugly faces. Malleable target characteristics include recognition being impaired by disguises and changes in facial appearance. When people are asked to describe faces they mostly refer to hairstyle (27 per cent), eyes (14 per cent), nose (14 per cent) and face shape (13 per cent). Therefore simple changes in hairstyle or facial hair may be detrimental to recognition performance (Shepherd and Ellis 1996).

There is an extensive literature on cross-race bias (Yarmey 2003: 548). According to one study, people are 1.38 times more likely to recognize correctly someone of their own race and 1.50 times less likely to identify falsely someone of their own race (Meissner and Brigham 2001). If witnesses are shown photographs of suspects and then attend a line-up, they are more likely to identify a person whose photograph they had seen regardless of whether that person is the perpetrator. Collaboration between witnesses can lead to introducing new erroneous information into their account. In one study participants separately saw a video which they believed to be the same but was of the same event seen from different perspectives. Some 71 per cent of witnesses reported erroneous details acquired during the discussion that they could not have seen on the video, including 60 per cent who reported seeing a theft they could not have seen – it was their co-witness who had seen the theft. Four studies of line-ups indicate that 90 per cent of mock witnesses expected the target to be present despite clear instructions that the target might not be present. Some 95 per cent did not recall the instruction; 17 per cent felt under pressure to choose from the line-up; 78 per cent said that they would expect the target to be there in real life; and only 48 per cent made the correct identification decision (Memon *et al* 2003: 117–22).

Regulation of eyewitness identification

Given the frailty and malleability of human memory, it has been suggested that investigators should adopt a similar approach to the identification evidence as they do to how they preserve physical or forensic trace evidence. Wells (1995) has argued that there should be an analogous chain of preservation of psychological eyewitness evidence, along the lines of treating memory as if it were trace evidence. The latest PACE code of practice in relation to identification evidence commenced on 31 March 2003. This code is probably the most advanced of its kind in the world. An evaluation of the accuracy of eyewitness information has been made in the UK on behalf of the Home Office (Kebbel and Wagstaff 1999). The guidance goes a long way to minimize the risk of extreme misuse of identification evidence. As a result of the recommendations from an expert group of specialists, the Department of Justice in the USA has also published a guide on obtaining best identification evidence, in which Wells played a significant role (Yarmey 2003: 551–2). However, no regulation can get over the problem identified by Loftus (2003) that our memories are malleable and, without the proper safeguards and in the absence of other probative evidence, investigators and prosecutors may well be building their cases on something no more reliable than chance. Caveat emptor.

The challenge facing psychologists is how to convince investigators, lawyers and judges of the benefits to the quality of investigations and justice that would flow from a better understanding of psychological processes. One way in which psychological knowledge is being disseminated in law enforcement is through the growing influence of behavioural science units, which are briefly discussed below.

Behavioural science: applying psychological knowledge to investigations

The science of psychology impinges on investigations in many more areas than just custodial questioning and witness testimony. There is perhaps no better example of the growing importance that investigators attach to these other areas of psychology than in the way in which psychological knowledge and understanding are being spread in police and law enforcement agencies through the creation of specialist behavioural science units (BSUs), which are both contributors to, and consumers of, research in the evolving discipline of investigative psychology. The first unit was probably that formed by the FBI in the 1980s, which conducted a series of studies of people convicted of murder and serial killings. The methodology employed in these studies has been criticized, but it did lead to systematic attempts to develop offender profiles (for a critical analysis and description of how offender profiling is done and what the main components are, see Chapter 20, this volume).

In the UK the first BSU was established at the National Police College, Bramshill, Hampshire in the late 1990s, and it is now part of the National Crime and Operations Faculty. The intention was to bring operational officers, researchers and crime trainers together in a virtuous cycle, where experience in the field would inform the research agenda and the results of research would inform the teaching curricula for investigators. The unit is structured in such a way that inquiries are channelled through a help-desk and directed to behavioural advisers, geographic profilers and advisers on physical evidence.[7] There are two important databases: one of experts who have registered with the unit whom investigators can be referred to; and a large database of serious violent crimes, which is the responsibility of the Serious Crime Analysis Section (SCAS). The SCAS database is being used in over 20 research projects. There are currently five full-time and around 30 part-time behavioural investigative advisers (BIAs). The work of these BIAs is subject to peer review, audit and inspection as a result of measures introduced by the Association of Chief Police Officers in April 2001 following judicial criticism in a high-profile case. The process is the responsibility of a chief constable assisted by senior academic advisers. During 2005, 120 requests had been received for BIA support, and over 500 reports had been prepared since the scheme commenced. The range of advice that can be provided is extensive and includes the following:

- Crime scene assessment.
- Predictive profiling.
- Prioritizing suspects.
- Suggestions to assist with main lines of inquiry.
- Investigative interviewing strategies.
- Media strategies.
- Familial DNA prioritization.

A contemporary issue is the training and continuous professional development of the BIAs. A competency framework has been produced, and there are well established links with academia.

The BIAs are part of a network of people employed in BSUs in Europe, North America and other countries. A typical example is the BSU of the Sûreté du Québec (Quebec Provincial Police) in Montreal, Canada. The unit consists of six police officers, four of whom are trained polygraph operators and interviewers, and two of whom are offender profilers. Psychological advice is provided by an investigative forensic psychologist, who is employed on a full-time basis within the unit. During 2004, the Sûreté BSU dealt with 250 polygraph interviews, of which nearly half related to alleged sexual offences on children. It is of interest to note that almost 90 per cent of the suspects taking the test are considered to have produced a truthful denial. The BSU also undertakes around 300 written statement analyses, researches into false allegations, conducts threat assessments of anonymous letters and undertakes risk assessments for certain police operations. The members of the unit and the psychologist are available on a call-out rota to attend serious incidents, including hostage negotiations and other crisis situations (such as dealing with snipers).

A dilemma facing BSUs is how far to make their operational responses and tactics available in the public domain. While it is understandable that members of BSUs would worry about the use that criminals could make of this information, it is surprising how much information is readily available in written or visual media.[8] The BSU in Quebec gave careful consideration to publication of a psychological approach it had developed to hostage and crisis negotiation, and decided that the benefit of sharing their approach with other police agencies was worth the risk that it might inform potential hostage takers (St-Yves *et al.* 2001).

The FBI unit consisted of practitioners and psychologists who had close connections with academic researchers. This early research identified a number of further potentially useful research questions. Taking just one example, there is currently growing interest in the perceived link between animal cruelty and violence against people, including serial homicides (Merez-Perez and Heide 2004). The research literature indicates that there may be a link between juvenile bedwetting, fire setting and torturing small animals. In a study of 45 violent offenders and 45 non-violent offenders in a maximum security prison in Florida, Merez-Perez and Heide found that there was indeed a correlation between violent offenders and their experiences of abuse of farm animals, animals in the wild, companion animals and stray animals. This included setting fire to an animal, dismembering an animal and tying animals together to watch them fight. The violent offenders in the survey showed little remorse for their past acts. These findings may contribute to a better understanding of the developmental pathways involved in the aetiology of serious and serial violence against people and to the identification of risk factors that could assist in earlier, preventative intervention (Merez-Perez and Heide 2004).

Investigative psychology

As personified in the approach of Sherlock Holmes, the fictional detective, the traditional approach taken by investigators (and offender profilers) has been to make inferences on a *deductive* basis. This method is unreliable for making robust inferences, and this fact lies at the heart of many of the criticisms of offender profiling (see Chapter 20, this volume). One of the most interesting recent developments is the application of *inductive* reasoning, which lies at the heart of empirical science. This methodology requires that data are collected across a range of cases to test hypotheses about the co-occurrence of various features and this has led to the development of the discipline of investigative psychology. Investigative psychology proposes an inductive model of an investigative cycle where information leads to inference and then to action. These three strands are included in the definition of investigative pyschology as:

> the systematic, scientific study of:
>
> (a) investigative information, its retrieval, evaluation and utilisation;
> (b) police actions and decisions, their improvement and support; and
> (c) the inferences that can be made about criminal activity, its
>   development, differentiation and prediction,
>
> [whose] objective is to improve criminal and civil investigations (Canter and Youngs 2003: 177).

This is a much more scientific approach to investigations, going beyond deductive reasoning and traditional attempts at profiling. It may lack the appeal of some fictional accounts of deductive investigations, but it is much more likely to be a basis for a science of investigation that will emerge in the twenty-first century. The systematic collection of data will enable investigators to interrogate the databases for answers to questions that they should find helpful, such as the offender's salient features, the geography of where searches for the offender should be carried out, which crimes have been committed so far by this offender and where the offender will commit the next offence. Canter and Youngs (2003: 201–2) conclude that 'Investigative Psychology provides a holistic perspective on the investigation of crime, showing that all aspects of the detective's work are open to scientific psychological examination'.

Inductive investigative models will require the establishment of databases of relevant crimes (such as the Serious Crime Analysis Section) supported by information technology networks and commercially available analytical tools that will permit hypothesis testing. For example, such models would enable analysts to explore the geodemographic and distance relationships between stranger rapists and their offences (Rossmo *et al.* 2004). This information would have many practical applications, including, for example, establishing the parameters of house-to-house inquiries. This vision of science-based investigative psychology is an excellent example of the progression that is possible from traditional deductive investigations to new methodologies, where the collection and analysis of data will lead to intelligence-led and knowledge-based investigations (Williamson in press). The paradigm shift from deductive to inductive investigative methodologies has yet to be achieved, but it appears that a process of change is underway.

Conclusion

This chapter has illustrated how psychology has already had an influence on shaping the legal and regulatory framework in England and Wales regarding custodial questioning. A current challenge for psychologists is to convince investigators, lawyers and judges that they need a better understanding of the psychological factors that affect the reliability of witness testimony and the weight it should be given. An appropriate level of understanding of psychological processes should become a core competence for investigators, lawyers and judges, as this would improve their decision-making and reduce the risk of some of the biases inherent in current systems that have led to miscarriages of justice. The practical benefits to investigators from the science of psychology are being demonstrated through behavioural science units that employ practitioners and psychologists who are extending the influence of psychology in investigations through activities such as offender profiling. But we need to go beyond offender profiling, and if a science of investigative psychology is to develop during the twenty-first century, it will require the data, databases, networks and analytical tools that will enable a progression from traditional deductive investigations to inductive, knowledge-based investigations. This begins with the collection of accurate and reliable information, which will make such a paradigm shift possible.

Selected further reading

Smith, E.E., Nolen-Hoeksema, S., Fredrickson, B. and Loftus, G.R. (2003) *Atkinson and Hilgard's Introduction to Psychology* (14th edn). Belmont, CA: Thomson Wadsworth. An excellent introductory textbook to psychology that is written in a very accessible style. The book is organized in such a way that it provides a comprehensive reference to the science that would be of value to investigators.

Gudjonsson, G.H. and Haward, L.R.C. (1998) *Forensic Psychology: A Guide to Practice.* London: Routledge. Forensic psychology went through a long gestation period in the UK. This is an excellent historical account that includes descriptions of the techniques used.

Adler, J.R. (ed.) (2004) *Forensic Psychology: Concepts, Debates and Practice.* Cullompton: Willan Publishing. Forensic psychology sometimes seems to be trying to fight its way out of the narrow definition it has been given in the UK by the British Psychological Society. This is a very readable textbook that takes a broad perspective and that is popular with students.

Gudjonsson, G.H. (2003) *The Psychology of Interrogations and Confessions: A Handbook.* Chichester: Wiley. Mullin, C. (1990) *Error of Judgement: The Truth about the Birmingham Bombings.* Dublin: Poolbeg. Victory, P. (2002) *Justice and Truth: The Guildford Four and Maguire Seven.* London: Sinclair-Stevenson. These three books discuss miscarriages of justice. Gudjonsson (2003) is a comprehensive analysis of miscarriages of justice and expert psychological testimony that led to acquittals. Victory (2002) is especially helpful for its chronology of events.

Memon, A., Vrij, A. and Bull, R. (2003) *Psychology and Law: Truthfulness, Accuracy and Credibility* (2nd edn). Chichester: Wiley. Carson, D. and Bull, R. (eds) (2003) *Handbook of Psychology in Legal Contexts.* Chichester: Wiley. Memon *et al.* (2003) discuss areas where the law and psychology have come together. Carson and Bull (2003) is a recent comprehensive handbook of the legal contexts of psychology.

Acknowledgements

The author would like to thank three anonymous reviewers and Professor Gisli Gudjonsson for their helpful comments on an early draft of this chapter.

Notes

1 Expressions describing intellectual deficits vary across different countries and disciplines. In England and Wales the expression 'learning difficulties' is generally used (see Chapter 18, this volume, for special measures for interviewing witnesses who are vulnerable, including those with learning difficulties). In England and Wales, IQ assessments falling in the range 70–79 are considered to be borderline.
2 The term in use at the time.
3 Ireland *v.* United Kingdom (1978) 2 EHRR 25.
4 Miranda *v.* Arizona (383) US 1966.
5 (1977) QB 224.
6 For a fuller discussion of confidence and accuracy, see Clark and Stephenson (1999).
7 Information provided by Adam Gregory, Senior Behavioural Investigative Adviser.
8 In one serial homicide being investigated in London, the killer actually telephoned the murder squad and said that he had read the FBI book on serial killing and that he knew he had to kill at least four people to be classified as a serial killer (personal knowledge).

References

Anastasia, A. and Urbina, S. (1997) *Psychological Testing* (7th edn). New York, NY: Prentice Hall.
Atkinson, R.C. and Shiffrin, R.M. (1971) 'Human memory: a proposed system and its control processes', in K.W. Spence (ed.) *The Psychology of Learning and Motivation: Advances in Research and Theory.* New York, NY: Academic Press.
Baddeley, A.D. (1986) *Working Memory.* Oxford: Clarendon Press.
Baddeley, A.D. (1990) *Human Memory: Theory and Practice.* Boston, MA: Allyn & Bacon.
Baddeley, A.D. (2000) 'The magic number and the episodic buffer', *Behavioral and Brain Sciences*, 24: 117–18.
Bahrick, H.P. and Phelps, E. (1987) 'Retention of Spanish vocabulary over eight years', *Journal of Experimental Psychology: Learning, Memory and Cognition*, 13: 344–9.
Baldwin, J. and McConville, M. (1982) *Confessions in Crown Court Trials. Royal Commission on Criminal Procedure Research Study 5.* (Cmnd 8092). London: HMSO.
Bartlett, F.C. (1932) *Remembering: A Study in Experimental and Social Psychology.* Cambridge: Cambridge University Press.
Bennett, H.G. (1979) *Report of the Committee of Inquiry into Police Interrogation Procedures In Northern Ireland* (Cmnd 7497). London: HMSO.
Binet, A. and Simon, T. (1905) 'Méthodes nouvelles pour le diagnostic du nouveau intellectuel des abnormaux', *Année Psychologie*, 11, 191–244.
Bottomley, A.K. and Coleman C.A. (1980) 'Police effectiveness and the public: the limitations of official crime rates', in R.V.G. Clarke and J.M. Hough (eds) *The Effectiveness of Policing.* Farnborough: Gower.

Brown, R., Goldstein, E. and Bjorklund, D.F. (2000) 'The history and zeitgeist of the repressed-false-memory debate: scientific and sociological perspectives on suggestibility', in D.F. Bjorklund (ed.) *False Memory Creation in Children and Adults.* Mahwah, NJ: Lawrence Erlbaum Associates.

Canter, D. and Youngs, D. (2003) 'Beyond "offender profiling": the need for an investigative psychology', in D. Carson and R. Bull (eds) *Handbook of Psychology in Legal Contexts.* Chichester: Wiley.

Carson, D. and Bull, R. (eds) (2003) *Handbook of Psychology in Legal Contexts.* Chichester: Wiley.

Cherry, E.C. (1953) 'Some experiments on the recognition of speech with one and two ears', *Journal of the Acoustical Society,* 23: 975–9.

Clarke, N.K. and Stephenson, G.M. (1999) 'Getting heads together: police collaborative testimony', in A. Heaton-Armstrong *et al.* (eds) *Analysing Witness Testimony: A Guide for Legal Practitioners and Other Professionals.* London: Blackstone.

Cutler, B.L. and Penrod, S.D. (1995) *Mistaken Identification: The Eyewitness, Psychology, and the Law.* Cambridge: Cambridge University Press.

Deffenbacher, K. (1980) 'Eyewitness accuracy and confidence: can we infer anything about their relationship?', *Law and Human Behaviour,* 4: 243–60.

Deffenbacher, K., Cross, J., Handkins, R. Chance, J., Goldstein, A., Hammersley, R. and Read, J.D.D. (1989) 'Relevance of voice identification research to criteria for evaluating reliability of an identification', *Journal of Psychology,* 123: 109–19.

Devlin, Lord (1979) *Report to the Secretary of State for the Home Department of the Departmental Committee on Evidence of Identification in Criminal Cases.* London: Home Office.

Dysart, J.E., Lindsay, R.C.L., MacDonald, T.K. and Wicke, C. (2002) 'The intoxicated witness: Effects of alcohol on identification accuracy', *Journal of Applied Psychology,* 87: 107–75.

Ebbinghaus, H. (1885) *Uber das gedachthis.* Leipzig: Dunckes & Humbolt.

Fisher, Sir H. (1977) *Report of an Inquiry by the Hon. Sir Henry Fisher into the Circumstances Leading to the Trial of Three Persons on Charges Arising out of the Death of Maxwell Confait and the Fire at 27, Doggett Road, London, SE6.* London: HMSO.

Fisher, R.P. and Geiselman, R.E. (1992) *Memory Enhancing Techniques for Investigative Interviewing: The Cognitive Interview.* Springfield, IL: Charles C. Thomas.

Fisher, S.Z. and MacKenzie, I. (2003) 'A miscarriage of justice in Massachusetts: eyewitness identification procedures, unrecorded admissions and a comparison with English law', *Public Interest Law Journal,* 13.

Granhag, P.-A., Strowall, L. and Billings, F.J. (2003) '"I'll never forget the sinking ferry"': how social influence makes false memories surface', in M. Vanderhallen *et al.* (eds) *Much Ado About Crime: Chapters on Psychology and Law.* Belgium: Uitgeverij Politeia.

Gudjonsson, G. (1992) *The Psychology of Interrogations, Confessions and Testimony.* Chichester: Wiley.

Gudjonsson, G.H. (1997) 'False memory syndrome and the retractors: methodological and theoretical issues', *Psychological Inquiry,* 8, 296–9.

Gudjonsson, G.H. (2003) *The Psychology of Interrogations and Confessions: A Handbook.* Chichester: Wiley.

Gudjonsson, G.H., Clare, I., Rutter, S. and Pearse, J. (1993) *Persons at Risk During Interviews in Police Custody: The Identification of Vulnerabilities. Royal Commission on Criminal Justice Research Study* 12. London: HMSO.

Gudjonsson, G.H. and Haward, L.R.C. (1998) *Forensic Psychology: A Guide to Practice.* London: Routledge.

Hale, M. (1980) *Human Science and Social Order: Hugo Munsterberg and Origins of Applied Psychology.* Philadelphia, PA: Temple University Press.

Heaton-Armstrong, A., Shepherd, E. and Wolchover, D. (eds) (1999) *Analysing Witness Testimony: A Guide for Legal Practitioners and Other Professionals*. London: Blackstone.

Howes, J.L. and Katz, A.N. (1992) 'Remote memory: recalling autobiographical and public events from across the lifespan', *Canadian Journal of Psychology*, 46, 92–116.

Irving, B. (1982) *Police Interrogation: A Case Study of Current Practice. Royal Commission on Criminal Procedure Research Study* 2 (Cmnd 8092). London: HMSO.

Kassin, S.M. and Gudjonsson, G.H. (2004) 'The psychology of confessions. A review of the literature and issues', *Psychological Science in the Public Interest*, 5: 35–69.

Kebbel, M.R. and Wagstaff, G.F. (1999) *Face Value? Evaluating the accuracy of eyewitness information. Police Research Series Paper* 102, London: Home Office.

Loftus, E.F. (2003) 'Repressed memories are a dangerous belief', in E.E. Smith *et al. Atkinson and Hilgard's Introduction to Psychology*, 14th edn. Belmont, CA: Wadsworth.

Loftus, E.F., Loftus, G.R. and Messo, J. (1987) 'Some facts about "weapon focus"', *Law and Human Behaviour*, 11: 55–62.

Loftus, E.F. and Palmer, J.C. (1974) 'Reconstruction of automobile destruction', *Journal of Verbal Learning and Verbal Behaviour*, 13: 585–89.

Loftus, E.F. and Pickrell, J.E. (1995) 'The formation of false memories', *Psychiatric Annals*, 25: 720–5.

Maas, A. and Kohnken, G. (1989) 'Eyewitness identification: simulating the "weapon effect"', *Law and Human Behaviour*, 13, 397–408.

MacLeod, A.D. (1995) 'Undercover policing: a psychiatrist's perspective', *International Journal of Law and Psychiatry*, 18: 239–47.

Matlin, M. (2005) *Cognition* (6th edn). Chichester: Wiley.

Meissner, C.A. and Brigham, J.C. (2001) 'Thirty years of investigating the own-race bias in memory for faces: a meta-analytic review', *Psychology, Public Policy, and Law*, 7: 3–35.

Melon, A.W. (1963) 'Implications of short-term memory for a general theory of memory', *Journal of Verbal Learning and Verbal Behaviour*, 2: 1–21.

Memon, A. Cronin, O., Eaves, R. and Bull, R. (1996) 'An empirical test of the mnemonic components of the cognitive interview', in G.M. Davies *et al.* (eds) *Psychology and Law: Advances in Research*. Berlin: De Gruyter.

Memon, A., Vrij, A. and Bull, R. (2003) *Psychology and Law: Truthfulness, Accuracy and Credibility* (2nd edn). Chichester: Wiley.

Merez-Perez, L. and Heide, K.M. (2004) *Animal Cruelty: Pathway to Violence Against People*. Walnut Creek, CA: Alta Mira Press.

Miller, G.A. (1956) 'The magical number seven plus or minus two: Some limits on our capacity for processing information', *Psychological Review*, 63: 81–97.

Milne, R. (1997) 'Application and analysis of the cognitive interview.' Doctoral dissertation, University of Portsmouth.

Ost, J. (2006) 'Recovered memories', in T.M. Williamson (ed.) *Investigative Interviewing: Developments in Rights, Research and Regulation*. Cullompton: Willan Publishing.

Penrod, S. and Cutler, B. (1995) 'Witness confidence and witness accuracy: assessing their forensic relation' (special issue: 'Witness, memory and law') *Psychology, Public Policy and Law*, 1: 817–45.

Philips, Sir C. (1982) *Royal Commission on Criminal Procedure* (Cmnd 8092). London: HMSO.

Porter, S., Yuille, J.C. and Lehman, D.R. (1999) 'The nature of real, implanted, and fabricated memories for emotional childhood events: implications for the recovered memory debate', *Law and Human Behaviour*, 23: 517–37.

Roediger, H.L. and McDermott, K.B. (1995) 'Creating false memories: remembering words not presented in lists', *Journal of Experimental Psychology: Learning, Memory, and Cognition*, 21: 803–14.

Rossmo, K., Davies, A., and Patrick, M. (2004) *Exploring the Geo-demographic and Distance Relationships between Stranger Rapists and their Offences. Special Interest Series Paper* 16. London: Home Office. Research, Development and Statistics Directorate.

Royal Commission on Police Powers and Procedure (1929) *Report* (Cmd 3297). London: HMSO.

Runciman, Viscount (1993) *Report of The Royal Commission on Criminal Justice* (Cm 2263). London: HMSO.

Schacter, D.L. (2001) *The Seven Sins of Memory.* Boston, MA: Houghton Mifflin.

Scheck, B., Neufeld, P. and Dwyer, J. (2000) *Actual Innocence: Five Days to Execution, and other Dispatches from the Wrongly Convicted.* New York, NY: Doubleday.

Shepherd, J.W. and Ellis, H.D. (1996) 'Face recall: methods and problems', in S.L. Sporer *et al.* (eds) *Psychological Issues in Eyewitness Identification.* Mahwah, NJ: Erlbaum.

Softley, P. (1982) *Police Interrogation: An Observational Study in Four Police Stations. Royal Commission on Criminal Procedure Research Study* 4. (Cmnd 8092) London: HMSO.

Sporer, S.L., Penrod, S.D., Read, D. and Cutler, B.L. (1995) 'Choosing, confidence, and accuracy. A meta-analysis of the confidence-accuracy relation in eyewitness identification studies', *Psychological Bulletin*, 118: 315–27.

Steer, D. (1982) *Uncovering Crime: The Police Role. Royal Commission on Criminal Procedure Research Study* 7 (Cmnd 8092). London: HMSO.

Stephenson, G.M. (1984) 'Accuracy and confidence in testimony: a critical review and some fresh evidence', in D.J. Muller *et al.* (eds) *Psychology and Law.* Chichester: Wiley.

St-Yves, M., Tanguay, M. and St-Pierre, J. (2001) 'Following the rhythm of a crisis: the SINCRO model', *International Criminal Police Review*, 491: 4–9.

Sutherland, R. and Hayne, H. (2001) 'The effect of postevent information on adults' eyewitness reports', *Applied Cognitive Psychology*, 15: 249–63.

Thompson, C.P., Herrmann, D.J., Read, J.D., Bruce, D., Payne, D.G. and Toglia, M.P. (eds) (1998) *Eyewitness Memory: Theoretical and Applied Perspectives.* Mahwah, NJ: Erlbaum.

Wells, G.L. (1995) 'Scientific study of witness memory: Implications for public and legal policy', *Psychology, Public Policy, and Law*, 1: 726–31.

Wells, G.L., Small, L., Penrod, S., Malpass, R.S., Fulero, S.M. and Brimacombe, C.A.E. (1998) 'Eyewitness identification procedures: Recommendations for lineups and photospreads', *Law and Human Behaviour*, 22: 603–47.

Williamson, T.M. (1990) 'Strategic changes in police interrogation: an examination of police and suspect behaviour in the Metropolitan Police in order to determine the effects of new legislation, technology and organisational policies.' Unpublished PhD thesis, University of Kent.

Williamson, T.M. (ed). (2006) *Investigative Interviewing: Developments in Rights, Research and Regulation.* Cullompton: Willan Publishing.

Williamson, T. (ed.) (in press) *Knowledge Based Policing: Current Conceptions and Future Directions.* Chichester: Wiley.

Yarmey, A.D. (2003) 'Eyewitnesses', in D. Carson and R. Bull (eds) *Handbook of Psychology in Legal Contexts.* Chichester: Wiley.

Yarmey, A.D. and Jones, H.P.T. (1983) 'Is the psychology of eyewitness identification a matter of common sense?', in S. Lloyd Bostock and B.R. Clifford (eds) *Evaluating Witness Evidence: Recent Psychological Research and New Perspectives.* New York, NY: Wiley.

Zander, M. and Henderson, P. (1993) *The Crown Court Study. The Royal Commission on Criminal Justice Research Study* 19. London: HMSO.

Chapter 5

Law and criminal investigation

Paul Roberts

Understanding law

Criminal investigations are obviously 'something to do with' the law. But there are many significantly varied ways and different senses in which 'the law' (whatever that is taken to mean) can relate to criminal investigations. Before launching into detailed discussion of particular laws and legal doctrines and assessing their practical significance, some of the nuances of this relation should be made explicit. The first part of this chapter therefore clarifies the concept of 'law' in its relationships with criminal investigations and supplies some jurisprudential background. The second part presents a critical survey of the police powers most central to criminal investigations and clarifies their basis in law. The third part explores the distinction between 'police powers' in legal theory and the realities of investigative practice. It also outlines the legal remedies potentially available to those whose rights have been breached during the course of a criminal investigation. Finally, in conclusion, the last part briefly considers the influence of science and technology on the legal regulation of criminal investigations and the scope for reform.

Jurisdiction and authority of positive law

Modern law is state-centric, in the sense that the national state is taken to be the primary and paradigm source of legal authority (Hart 1994: ch. 10; Brownlie 2003: ch. 6). In the simplest model, each national state is coterminous with one, single and unified legal jurisdiction. In reality, the simple model of legal sovereignty is complicated by the complexities of British constitutional arrangements, and increasingly anachronistic in a globalizing legal environment.

The UK contains multiple legal jurisdictions. Specifically regarding criminal law, the principal legal jurisdiction is England and Wales, and its law is properly referred to as English law. Scotland, Northern Ireland and smaller territories such as Jersey, Guernsey and the Isle of Man each have their own separate criminal justice systems, which bear many similarities to English law and legal institutions, but also striking differences. The law applicable in England and Wales is the exclusive focus of this chapter.

In the grip of 'globalization' (Beck 2000; Twining 2000), national legal sovereignty has lately become immensely more complex, and unstable. State-centric law is currently undergoing a process of transformation into something resembling 'cosmopolitan law' (cf. Eleftheriadis 2001; Hirsh 2003), a law which to an unprecedented extent is open to international influences and which derives part of its authority from beyond the nation-state. Legal authority is now partly vested in international organizations such as the United Nations (UN) and the World Trade Organization (WTO), in regional institutions such as the European Union (EU) and the Council of Europe (CoE), and in more amorphous notions of the 'international community' and international civil society. Rather than a simple transfer of sovereign legal authority from national to international entities, we should instead think in terms of the permeability, pooling, blending and reconstitution of national sovereignty and legal authority (MacCormick 1999).

Though the state-centricity of modern Western law has been in slow decline since the early twentieth century, national law remains staunchly secular and positivistic (in sharp contrast to traditions in which law is essentially an extension of religious teaching, like the Jewish *Torah* or Islamic *Sharia*; see Glenn 2004). 'Positive' law is the law *posited* by constitutionally-validated processes of law creation, such as parliamentary legislation. Legal positivism insists on a conceptual distinction between valid law – the law of the land – and its moral evaluation. Law is law if it has the right constitutional pedigree, regardless of its content (Raz 1985). Legal positivism in this sense has nothing to do with the 'positivistic' (empiricist) epistemologies sometimes encountered, and lampooned by their critics (e.g. Taylor *et al.* 1973: chs 1–2), in the physical and social sciences.

The meaning and sources of law

When lawyers talk about 'the law' they are usually referring to legal norms – the rules, principles, doctrines and other recognized legal standards of positive law. In the pronouncements of politicians and policy-makers, and in the idiom of journalists and taxi-drivers, however, 'the law' is frequently invoked in a more promiscuous, expansive fashion, to embrace various aspects of legal process, procedure and institutional practice, as well as referring to legal norms in the strict, narrow sense.

Sometimes the processes, procedures and institutional practices of law are prescribed by legal norms. As later sections of this chapter expound in detail, police investigations are structured by a raft of legal rules and codes, and criminal trial procedure is governed by complex rules of evidence. On other occasions, however, the processes, procedures and practices of law have little if anything to do with legal norms. They are instead dictated by occupational culture, professional ethics and expertise, organizational (including resource) constraints and the judgements of individual or group decision-makers, be they police, prosecutors, defence lawyers, judges or juries. It is consequently rather uninformative to say, with a flourish, that 'the law' is responsible for this or that, or that 'the law' should be reformed, etc. Does this mean that new laws must be created, or that institutional practices must be changed? If practices must be changed, does this necessitate legislation, or only an operational programme of better training and supervision? Would legislation even have any capacity, or authority, to alter the behaviour in question? And so on. In this chapter, 'law' is understood in the narrower, analytically more precise and useful sense designating legal norms – rules, principles, doctrines and other recognized legal standards of positive law.

A discussion of the relationship between law and criminal investigations in England and Wales will naturally focus on the norms of English criminal law and criminal procedure. According to traditional legal theory, these norms have two, and only two, authentic sources: legislation and case law. The UK Parliament legislates, *inter alia*, for the criminal law jurisdiction of England and Wales. Parliamentary activity in the field of penal law expanded throughout the course of the twentieth century, to the point where criminal justice professionals can barely keep pace with the unceasing torrent of new statutes. Second to Parliament in the orthodox hierarchy of lawmakers come the higher-tier courts, whose principal business is to determine appeals arising from first instance trials. In criminal matters, the main source of legal precedents is the Court of Appeal (Criminal Division), from which a further appeal lies to the House of Lords – i.e. the Law Lords sitting in their judicial capacity.

Legislation and case-law precedents are indubitably the most prolific and influential sources of criminal law, but they do not tell the whole creation story. Today, the sources of cosmopolitan law are increasingly numerous and diversified. Below the level of primary legislation enacted by Parliament is a plethora of delegated legislative powers, codes of practice, administrative regulations and informal or 'soft' legal norms, some of which have a major bearing on criminal investigations. Parliament frequently delegates the power to make laws of this type to ministers of state and their governmental departments, or to senior officials such as chief constables or the Director of Public Prosecutions (DPP). We can also look for sources of modern law above the level of ordinary legislation. It is characteristic of the cosmopolitan turn in modern legality that English criminal law has lately opened up to an unprecedented extent to supra-national norms.

The most notable recent development, for our purposes, is the Human Rights Act 1998, the main provisions of which came into force on 2 October 2000. The Human Rights Act (HRA) 1998 gives legal effect in England and Wales to the substantive rights guaranteed by the European Convention on Human Rights (ECHR), and requires English courts to take account of the interpretative jurisprudence of the Strasbourg-based European Court of Human Rights (ECtHR).[1] The ECHR guarantees the right to life (Article 2); freedom from torture or degrading treatment or punishment (Article 3); freedom from slavery (Article 4); the right to liberty and security of the person (Article 5); the right to a fair trial (Article 6); the right not to be convicted under a retroactive penal statute (Article 7); the right to respect for one's private and family life, home and correspondence (Article 8); and rights to freedom of thought, conscience and religion (Article 9); freedom of expression (Article 10); and freedom of assembly and association (Article 11). All these rights are either directly related to criminal proceedings (Articles 5–7), or plainly bear upon various aspects of penal law. Most of the enumerated rights are subject to exceptions explicitly stated in the ECHR itself, or else developed through the ECtHR's now massive and rapidly expanding case law.[2]

By arming courts for the first time with something approaching a modern Bill of Rights (cf. Straw and Boateng 1997), the HRA 1998 has already spurred judicial activism and creativity in law-making (see, e.g., Roberts 2002; Choo and Nash 2003), and its impact might conceivably continue to deepen and expand. Parliament has consciously encouraged judges to be bold defenders of citizens' human rights by imposing on the courts a strong interpretative obligation to construe parliamentary legislation, whether past or future, to be in conformity with the enumerated convention rights,[3] unless the words of a UK statute cannot plausibly bear any such meaning – signalling Parliament's deliberate intention to contravene the ECHR. In accordance with traditional constitutional theory, the UK Parliament remains sovereign and supreme and can, in principle, enact any law it chooses for loyal judges to apply. Beyond the limits of interpretational latitude, therefore, English courts are restricted to issuing a 'declaration of incompatibility' between English law and the ECHR in cases of irresolvable conflict.[4] Whether or not such breaches of the UK's international legal obligations[5] are subsequently rectified, having been solemnly pronounced by the judges, remains Parliament's business.

The legal structure of criminal investigations

There are two different senses in which the law can be said to 'structure' criminal investigations. Law specifies the *objectives* of criminal investigations, and also seeks to *regulate* their conduct.

Criminal investigations, in the standard case,[6] are orientated towards cracking unsolved crime, identifying perpetrators, launching prosecutions, proving guilt at trial and bringing offenders to justice. When engaged in this kind of prosecution-orientated activity, as opposed to collecting general intelligence, maintaining order or undertaking other routine policing tasks, an investigator's objectives are dictated by criminal law. Criminal law defines the elements of a crime and the criteria of criminal responsibility, which taken together specify the facts that must be proved at trial in order to secure a criminal conviction. Legal definitions of criminal offences are also highly salient to the early stages of criminal investigations, long before courtroom litigation is in prospect. By working back from what must be demonstrated at trial, the investigative task assumes concrete form and structure. Each element of the offence(s) alleged must be proved, and each potential plausible defence must be *dis*proved, by evidence admissible in court. It is the job of the investigator to unearth, recover, procure, amass, sort, compile, test, evaluate and arrange this evidence as compelling proof of the offender's guilt. In the ways and means of discovering and generating evidence of various types, and from an array of different sources, lie the investigator's science, arts and craft.

Though families of offences typically share elements in common, each separate criminal charge can be regarded as presenting the investigator with its own distinctive investigative goals and probative challenges. According to the best estimates, there are upwards of 8,000 different offences in English criminal law (Ashworth 2000: 226), every one specifying a unique set of objectives for investigation. The offences most commonly encountered in practice are described in the practitioner manuals *Archbold* (Richardson 2005) and *Blackstone's Criminal Practice* (Murphy and Stockdale 2005). This chapter will not stray any further on to the terrain of substantive criminal law *qua* source of investigative objectives, but will instead concentrate on the second sense in which law structures criminal investigations, through their legal regulation. This is the (procedural) law *of* criminal investigations, as opposed to the (substantive) criminal law routinely enforced by police and prosecutors.

A topography of investigative police powers

Law facilitates criminal investigations by conferring instrumentally useful powers on the police, yet also constrains criminal investigations by subjecting police conduct to legal prohibitions, restrictions and procedural requirements. English statutes, case-law and delegated legislation contribute extensively both to the permissive and to the restrictive facets of legal regulation, as we shall see. At the same time, many significant police powers lack any explicit foundation either in statute or at common law.

It is well known that much of the business of contemporary 'policing' is carried out by agencies other than the traditional public police, including an 'extended (public) policing family' and a burgeoning private security sector. For all this acknowledged 'postmodern' diversity (cf. Reiner 1992; de Lint 1999) in the policing function, however, the public police remain central to most people's conception of 'policing' and still undertake the bulk of investigations relating to 'crime' as popularly conceived. While the explicit focus of the following discussion is 'the police' in this orthodox sense, many of the rules and principles discussed in this section and the next can be extrapolated, with appropriate modifications, to the work of specialist agencies conducting criminal investigations (Serious Fraud Office, HM Revenue and Customs, Health and Safety Executive, etc.).

Implicit common law powers

In continental European jurisdictions police powers are typically specified in the national police law or code of criminal procedure. The existence of an explicit textual basis for the exercise of potentially coercive police powers is regarded in continental legal theory as an essential requirement of the rule of law facilitating democratic control and accountability of policing.

A remarkable feature of common law jurisdictions like England and Wales is that they start from the opposite premiss. The guiding assumption in England and Wales is that conduct, whether official or private, is permitted under the general law unless expressly forbidden.[7] When applied to ordinary citizens, this assumption favours individual liberty, personal autonomy and private freedom from governmental interference, and is consequently generally applauded by liberals and democrats. The argument for extending the same presumption to state officials, who in various spheres of activity wield considerable coercive power and influence over others, is less obviously consistent with liberal principles of limited government, individual freedom and democratic accountability. The explanation for this doubtful approach to the legality of police powers is bound up with the historical evolution of British policing.

In most jurisdictions modern police forces were originally imposed by more or less autocratic governments as the domestic counterpart of state armies used in wars of national defence and foreign conquest. Modern British policing, by contrast, began life as a limited, gradualist experiment in 'policing by consent' (see generally Reiner 2000: ch. 1). At least in official rhetoric, nineteenth-century police officers were nothing more than 'citizens in uniform' patrolling the streets for the benefit, and with the approbation, of ordinary law-abiding citizens. Whether foundation myth or empirical reality (or a bit of both), the ideology of citizens in uniform fostered a common law tradition of implicit police powers which endures, albeit increasingly attenuated, to this day (Dixon 1997: ch. 3).

The upshot of this historical legacy is that much of what police investigators do on a day-to-day basis requires no explicit legal authorization in England and Wales. Just as you or I can stop a stranger in the street to request directions, to ask the time, to solicit a donation to charity or for any other lawful purpose, the police are similarly entitled to stop a stranger in the street and ask him or her what he or she is doing, whether he or she has seen anything suspicious, where he or she lives, etc. Just as a journalist can 'door-step' you for a story, so the police can go round to the house of a potential witness and ask him or her to give a statement. Any conduct that takes place in plain view is liable to be observed, photographed, recorded and reported, by amateur or professional sleuths; any property or other matter (say, blood spatters or a fingerprint) abandoned in the street or other public venue can be recovered by the police as evidence, just as it might be appropriated by a tinker or made into modern art by a passing conceptualist. Since any citizen is entitled at common law to arrest a person who has committed a criminal offence and take him or her before a magistrate, citizens who happen to be wearing uniforms can hardly be prevented from doing the same.[8] And, most strikingly of all, anybody, including a police officer, may employ reasonable and proportionate force – including lethal force if circumstances so dictate – in self-defence, defence of another person or in the prevention of crime.[9]

That a great deal of investigative policing neither has nor requires explicit legal authorization is a point worth underlining. Rather than reaching for their statute books at every turn, the police can often achieve their investigative objectives simply by asking nicely or paying attention to their environment. Still, this dish should not be overcooked, in the first place because police power is often exercised coercively; and, secondly, because the modern trend is towards providing explicit statutory bases both for new and long-established police powers, thereby bringing English law into closer conformity with continental European ideals of legality.

If a stranger stops you in the street to ask a question, or a journalist knocks on your door for a story, you are perfectly entitled to ignore or rebuff his or her approaches, and you are not even obliged to be civil about it. If the stranger tried to press the point, by forcibly detaining you on the spot, he or she would be acting unlawfully, both committing a crime (common assault) and inflicting a civil law wrong which might be actionable in damages. Likewise if the journalist forced his or her way into your house and refused to leave without a story. But matters are rather different when one's interlocutor is a police officer. The police might initiate interactions with citizens on a consensual footing requiring no explicit legal authorization, but if the 'softly, softly approach' fails to elicit the desired response police officers can fall back on a raft of explicit statutory powers authorizing them to behave in ways which would constitute assault, threatening behaviour, blackmail, kidnapping, theft, burglary, trespass or criminal damage if resorted to by an ordinary member of the public.

Explicit police powers can be conceptualized, generically, as norms conferring legal immunities from criminal and civil liability on police officers acting in the course of their duty. The modern tendency has been to equip the police with an ever-expanding range of new and newly extended legal powers of surveillance, stop-and-search of individuals and motor vehicles, entry and search of private premises and seizure of potential evidence or contraband, arrest, detention prior to charge, custodial interrogation, and formal identification. Each of these groups of police powers is examined in greater detail below.

An incidental by-product of the proliferation of statutes conferring coercive police powers is that a greater proportion of police activities now boasts an explicit legal basis than was previously the case. Basic precepts of criminal investigation have also been spelt out for the first time, notably including the elementary proposition that '[i]n conducting an investigation, the investigator should pursue all reasonable lines of inquiry, whether these point towards or away from the suspect'.[10] A platitude, perhaps, but one which investigators have not always sufficiently taken to heart, as notorious miscarriages of justice – such as the tragic case of Timothy Evans (see Kennedy 1961) – ruefully attest. The juridification of police investigations has been reinforced by the ECHR, which holds that intrusive law enforcement activity will normally breach individuals' Convention rights unless explicitly authorized by domestic legislation.[11] To this extent, the regulation of criminal investigations in England and Wales has moved closer to embracing fully the rule-of-law ideal. That this achievement has been won through a massive expansion of potentially authoritarian police powers might, however, be regarded as a Pyrrhic victory for liberal legality.

Surveillance, deception and proactive policing

Most investigative policing is reactive, in the sense that the police are responding to a complaint from a member of the public, who will usually be the direct victim of criminality or an eyewitness to an alleged crime. This is a notably efficient way of initiating and progressing criminal investigations, especially in comparison with routine beat-policing which may (or may not) reassure the public, but contributes only marginally to criminal detection. For certain crimes, however, reactive policing is patently inadequate. So-called consensual crimes, such as smuggling, money-laundering, selling restricted items to under-age consumers, drug-taking and trafficking, pimping, prize-fighting, pornography, consensual incest or voluntary euthanasia (that is, murder, in English law), generally occur in private and their participants are not inclined to complain to the police, or even to regard themselves as genuine victims. Reactive policing is also notoriously powerless to assist victims who are physically unable or too afraid to speak out, including abused children, battered spouses and those in thrall to international people traffickers, labour gang-masters and forced prostitution rings. In order to combat these vicious and, as it would appear, increasingly prevalent offences against the most vulnerable people in our society, the police have turned to 'proactive' methods of criminal investigation. In this, they have been greatly assisted by modern technological innovations facilitating telephone-tapping, secreted listening and recording devices, and other forms of covert surveillance.

English law has traditionally taken a rather relaxed, some might say unacceptably complacent, attitude towards proactive policing methods. In fact, until quite recently the courts were not really interested in how evidence was procured and did not regard even police illegality as having any bearing on the fairness of a criminal trial.[12] So long as the evidence was reliable and court proceedings were themselves conducted with procedural propriety, the dictates of legality were satisfied and the police were free to employ informers, undertake covert surveillance of suspected individuals or premises and use deception and chicanery to trap a suspect into confessing guilt or revealing the whereabouts of incriminating evidence without judicial interference. The concept of a 'fair trial' essentially ended at the courtroom door. Only if the police resorted to threats, violence or inducements which could be regarded as rendering a suspect's subsequent confession 'involuntary'[13] might a court step in to exclude the confession at trial.

Today, the law's traditional indifference to proactive policing techniques has been significantly modified, if not entirely abandoned (Ormerod and Birch 2004; Roberts and Zuckerman 2004: ch. 4). There is still no substantive defence of police 'entrapment' in English criminal law.[14] Just as journalists are at liberty to 'go undercover' to investigate institutional corruption or to infiltrate a criminal gang in order to pen an insider-exposé, it is in principle lawful for police officers to employ informants, 'plants', stings, honey-traps/rat-traps and other creative methods of deception in order either to catch the criminally inclined red-handed or to procure proof of previously consummated crimes. Observing that offenders themselves lie, cheat and do a lot worse to their innocent victims,[15] the courts are prepared to tolerate a certain amount of deception in law enforcement as a necessary evil in the service of the greater good. In keeping with the common law's implicitly permissive approach, the police require no explicit legal authorization to undertake covert or deceptive operations in public places. Yet there are now well recognized, if imprecise, limits to how far the police can go in weaving their webs of deception (see generally Birch 1994; Ashworth 1998).

Legal regulation of proactive policing methods operates chiefly through three, overlapping and convergent, doctrinal strands. First, s. 78 of the Police and Criminal Evidence Act (PACE) 1984 provides that 'unfair' prosecution evidence will be excluded if 'having regard to all the circumstances, including the circumstances in which the evidence was obtained, the admission of the evidence would have such an adverse effect on the fairness of the proceedings that the court ought not to admit it'. Secondly, at common law English trial judges have the power to 'stay' a prosecution as an 'abuse of process' if there has been 'a serious abuse of power' amounting to 'acts which offend the court's conscience as being contrary to the rule of law'.[16] A stay is not technically an acquittal, but it amounts to much the same thing for all practical purposes. A third doctrinal strand is supplied by Article 6 of the ECHR guaranteeing the right to a fair trial. Significantly, the ECtHR has ruled that improper conduct during police investigations can render a subsequent trial 'unfair',[17] which parallels English courts' creative application of PACE s. 78 to pre-trial conduct. The combined effect of these mutually reinforcing procedural rules is that evidence is liable to be excluded at trial if the judge decides that the investigative means employed to procure it were unfair. Instances of flagrant or egregious police misconduct, moreover, run the risk of permanently derailing a prosecution by impelling the trial judge to stay the proceedings as an abuse of process.

The crucial question thus becomes: what, precisely, is 'unfair' in criminal investigations? The concept of fairness is notoriously indeterminate, and the test of 'serious abuse of power... offend[ing] the court's conscience' is barely less expansive or open to competing interpretations. It is necessary to consult precedent cases for further guidance on distinguishing between fair and unfair investigative means. For while (as some would have it) all is fair in love and war, the Court of Appeal and the House of Lords have not accepted that all is fair in criminal investigations.

Police deception is inherently neither fair nor unfair; everything depends on the circumstances, which consequently require careful and detailed examination. It is not unfair in English law for police undercover agents to behave as an 'ordinary' smuggler,[18] drug-dealer[19] or hit-man[20] would behave in order to attract 'business' from willing punters voluntarily engaging in criminality. If the officer is relatively passive and the suspect 'makes all the running' in the criminal transaction, the suspect will not usually have any valid grounds for complaint when his or her statements to the officer, or any incriminating articles or information procured in consequence of his or her statements, are later used against him or her at trial. In these circumstances, the courts will say that the suspect 'applied the trick to himself'[21] and that criminal conviction is no more than the suspect deserves. This rubric covers simple deceptions at the police station – e.g. placing a detainee together with his or her suspected accomplice in a bugged cell to see if they will strike up an incriminating conversation[22] – as well as elaborate sting operations, such as setting up a fake jewellers' shop and waiting for thieves and fences to try to sell stolen goods to undercover officers posing as 'dodgy' salespeople.[23] The same principle applies to 'test purchases' of alcohol, cigarettes or 18-rated videos to clearly under-age purchasers working for the police,[24] and to undercover trading standards officers hailing mini-cabs which are not licensed to make random street pickups in that vicinity.[25]

The line of fairness is crossed, however, if undercover officers take the initiative and appear to entice or cajole a suspect into committing an offence that he or she might not otherwise have had the inclination or nerve to go through with. The borderline is somewhat blurred, because police officers are not precluded from conduct which can be regarded as a necessary part of maintaining their 'cover', including active participation in criminality[26] and even making requests of the suspect,[27] if this is what the average 'ordinary punter' might reasonably be expected to do in soliciting drugs, procuring a hitman or taking part in organized gang violence, etc. But if undercover officers press too long and hard they will be regarded by trial judges not as investigating crime but as creating it, and any ensuing criminal prosecution is likely to be stayed as an abuse of process.[28]

Various aspects of covert and proactive policing methods have lately been subjected to formal statutory regulation, partly in response to the UK government's serial reverses before the ECtHR.[29] The principal statute is now the Regulation of Investigatory Powers Act (RIPA) 2000, an elaborate piece of legislation regulating the interception of telecommunications, intrusive surveillance and the use of 'human intelligence sources' (i.e. informants – a.k.a. police 'snitches', 'grasses' and 'snouts'). Unless the relevant parties consent,[30] the police may not intercept messages passing along a public or private postal or telecommunications system without first obtaining a warrant from the Home Secretary,[31] which can only be granted in relation to a named individual or premises[32] for the purpose of preventing or detecting serious crime, complying with the UK's international legal obligations or safeguarding national security.[33] Further detailed constraints and safeguards are expounded in a dedicated Code of Practice, issued pursuant to RIPA 2000, s. 71.[34] The workings of the system are overseen by an Interception of Communications Commissioner appointed by the Prime Minister (Thomas 2005), and there is an Investigatory Powers Tribunal to adjudicate complaints of investigative abuses.[35]

Interestingly, lawful interception of telecommunications is a purely investigative measure in England and Wales. The fruits of telephone tapping cannot generally be given in evidence in criminal proceedings.[36] This restriction does not reflect governmental tenderness for citizens' privacy, however. It is a concession to the security services, who fear that adducing telephone intercepts in criminal trials will inevitably lead to revelations of sensitive operational details concerning their personnel and methods, anticipating that defence lawyers would be certain to demand further information about when, where, how, why and by whom interceptions had been made. The status of telephone intercepts remains a matter of ongoing controversy. Relinquishing cogent evidence of guilt in the prosecution's possession and possibly allowing dangerous criminals to remain at large sits uneasily with the official policy of being 'tough on crime', and from time to time the government lets it be known that it is thinking of making intercept evidence admissible, always instantly provoking howls of very public protest from the intelligence and security communities (Leigh and Norton-Taylor 2003; Norton-Taylor 2005). Whether a British government will ever be prepared to incur the wrath of its security services in order to further its crime control agenda remains to be seen, although it is perhaps significant that this Rubicon has not yet been traversed, despite ample legislative opportunity.[37]

Covert surveillance and the use of human intelligence sources are governed by Part II of RIPA 2000,[38] and further elaborated in additional Codes of Practice.[39] As a general rule, these methods may only be authorized if they are necessary and proportionate for pursuing legitimate crime control or security objectives. 'Directed' covert surveillance aimed at procuring private information about a person,[40] and 'intrusive' covert surveillance targeting domestic premises or private vehicles where an individual is present or employing an electronic surveillance device,[41] are subject to progressively more stringent authorization procedures[42] and approval by specially appointed 'surveillance commissioners' (Leggatt 2005). Failure to follow designated protocols in requesting or conducting covert surveillance runs a serious risk of any subsequently-discovered evidence being excluded under PACE, s. 78. It would also almost certainly constitute a breach of Article 8 of the ECHR[43] and potentially expose investigators to civil liability.[44]

Stop, search and seizure

The power to stop and search individuals and vehicles has obvious investigatory potential. Purely random stop-and-search is unlikely to be an especially efficient form of criminal investigation, but even random 'fishing trips' sometimes discover illegal drugs, stolen goods, concealed weapons and the like. Of course, police stops need not be entirely random. The exercise of stop-and-search powers is more typically targeted on individuals, places or activities arousing investigators' suspicions.

General powers of stop-and-search are contained in Part I of PACE and its associated Code of Practice A,[45] the latest edition of which entered into force on 1 January 2006.[46] Section 1 of PACE empowers all constables, whether or not in uniform, to search any person or vehicle in a public place (which includes commercial premises, private yards or gardens, or other spaces to which the public generally has free access, at least until directed to leave by the owner) for stolen goods, offensive weapons or articles made or adapted for use in crime. The officer must have reasonable grounds for suspecting that items of the anticipated class will be found. As a matter of general principle:

> [p]owers to stop and search must be used fairly, responsibly, with respect for people being searched and without unlawful discrimination

... The intrusion on the liberty of the person stopped or searched must be brief and detention for the purposes of a search must take place at or near the location of the stop.[47]

In addition, lawful searches must satisfy certain procedural requirements, such as informing the person to be searched of the officer's name and police station and of the reason for the search.[48] If the proper procedures are not followed, or if the officer lacked reasonable grounds for conducting any search in the first place, the search will not be lawful, and if it was conducted without consent it will constitute an assault, potentially exposing the officer to civil liability in damages and possible criminal prosecution. Constables only enjoy immunity from an ordinary citizen's exposure to potential criminal liability while exercising their powers in accordance with the letter of the law. Moreover, 'using the powers fairly makes them more effective'.[49] Section 1 of PACE was invoked to stop and search 851,200 persons and vehicles in the financial year to April 2005 (Home Office 2005a).

Flanking PACE's omnibus power of stop-and-search on reasonable suspicion, a raft of subject-matter-specific statutes confers additional stop-and-search powers in relation, *inter alia*, to drugs,[50] protected wildlife,[51] terrorist offences[52] and the security of civil aviation.[53] There are also supplementary powers of a more general nature. Section 60 of the Criminal Justice and Public Order Act (CJPOA) 1994 empowers a senior police officer to designate a particular area in which 'serious violence' or the carrying of dangerous weapons is anticipated for a period of 24 hours. During this period a constable may stop and search any person or vehicle within the designated area for offensive weapons or dangerous instruments notwithstanding the absence of particularized suspicion. Designation pursuant to s. 60 thus effectively supplies a categorical presumption of suspicion in relation to anybody who happens to be present within the designated area. A measure of accountability is provided by the requirement that a person stopped and searched under s. 60 is entitled to obtain within a period of 12 months a written statement recording that the stop took place.[54]

The rationale for this provision is chiefly preventative: the idea is to identify potential troublemakers and disarm them before trouble flares up. However, since carrying an offensive weapon in a public place is in itself a criminal offence,[55] s. 60 can properly be classified as an investigative power. What is more, a police officer of the rank of superintendent or above may extend the period of designation for a further 24 hours, but only where relevant offences are known or reasonably suspected to have occurred.[56] The power to extend the period of s. 60 designation is therefore clearly investigative, to facilitate the detection of offenders and confiscation of their weapons. Some 41,300 s. 60 searches were conducted in 2004–5, resulting in almost 1,200 arrests (Home Office 2005a: 11).

Each of the stop-and-search powers just mentioned comes equipped with a complementary power for the police to seize any contraband or dangerous item for which they were searching.[57] Seizure powers are clearly (among other things) investigative measures, authorizing the police to collect material evidence that might later be presented in court.

Prior to the major rationalization and consolidation of police powers effected by PACE, local police forces had accumulated a bewildering diversity of stop-and-search powers conferred by piecemeal legislation and local bye-laws (Philips 1981: 25–6). As we have just seen, however, PACE is by no means the exclusive source of current police powers of stop-and-search, and the modern trend is towards further extensions and ad hoc additions. Back to the future, the historic consolidation appears to be progressively deconsolidating. A notable recent extension is contained in ss. 44–46 of the Terrorism Act (TA) 2000. Adapting the model pioneered by s. 60 of the CJPO Act 1994, s. 44 of the TA 2000 authorizes a senior police officer to designate an area in which the police may then stop and search any person on foot or in a vehicle for any items of a kind which could be used in connection with terrorism. The twist is that the designation may last for up to 28 days,[58] and is subject to unlimited renewal.[59] Authorizations under s. 44 will presumably continue to be utilized until the 'war on terror' is won, and that by all accounts will not be any time soon.

Continual extension of police powers of stop-and-search naturally raises concerns that civil liberties of free movement, privacy, assembly and expression are progressively being eroded. Stop-and-search on the public highway is relatively unintrusive compared with the more extensive police powers considered below, but being stopped and searched can still be an inconvenient, vexatious, embarrassing, intimidating and even possibly degrading experience. Most people would resent the intrusion if they thought they were being stopped without good cause. Some citizens may experience the additional resentment that they are, or feel themselves to be, singled out for 'police harassment' on discriminatory grounds of colour, race or religion. Discriminatory policing, in any form, is corrosive of standards of legality and propriety in the administration of criminal justice and threatens to undermine the ideals of pluralistic democracy.

Even where partly or wholly unfounded, perceptions of discriminatory, heavy-handed or unfair treatment are counter-productive for police investigations. Rumours of police misconduct may precipitate a loss of confidence in the trustworthiness of law enforcement, especially within communities which come to perceive themselves as victims of the very officials who, invested with the state's monopoly on legitimate violence, are supposed to be the guarantors of citizens' liberty and security. One consequence of this tragic estrangement between police and policed is to choke off the flow of information regarding particular unsolved crimes and general criminal intelligence which are the life-blood of efficient and effective investigative policing. Alas, the frequently troubled history of police–community relations in the UK provides ample empirical foundation for this hypothesis (Scarman 1981; Bowling and Phillips 2002: chs 5–6; CJS 2004).

Arrest

Arrest was not originally conceived as an investigative power. In historical perspective (Stephen 1883: 190–4), the main purposes of arrest were, first, to restrain a person from committing, or continuing to commit, breaches of the peace and, secondly, to bring suspected offenders before a magistrate in order to commence criminal proceedings against them or, in relation to more minor matters, to extract a formal promise not to repeat their disorderly behaviour (a 'bind over'). There are also well established powers to arrest persons who present a physical danger to themselves or to others in order that they be removed temporarily to a place of safety.[60]

Arrest with a view to detention and questioning is obviously an investigative step. However, the legality of arrest for the explicit purpose of custodial interrogation remained doubtful until a landmark ruling of the House of Lords in 1984,[61] thereafter promptly endorsed by Parliament. Section 37(2) of PACE 1984 authorizes the continued detention of a person at a police station where 'his detention without being charged is necessary to secure or preserve evidence relating to an offence for which he is under arrest *or to obtain such evidence by questioning him*' (emphasis added). Prior to this clarification, or development, of the law of arrest, suspects interrogated at police stations were often said – in what became the standard euphemism, parroted by the media without apparent irony – to be 'helping the police with their inquiries'. Suspects questioned in these circumstances were, in legal parlance, 'volunteers' who were legally at liberty to withdraw their co-operation and leave the police station at any time. In reality, many suspects, fearful of the greater trouble they might get into if they refused to co-operate, doubtless regarded their freedom of choice as significantly more constrained, and some probably inferred that they were under arrest even though, technically speaking, they were not (Philips 1981: 53). Although s. 37(2) arguably extended the scope of police powers subsequent to arrest, it none the less clarified the legal status of police station detainees and dispensed with dubious euphemisms. The law regulating custodial detention and interrogation is surveyed in the section on 'Detention and custodial interrogation', below. Arrest can further be regarded as a significant investigative step because it triggers various evidence-gathering powers of search and seizure, including those discussed in the next section of this chapter.

Criminal courts are authorized to issue warrants for the arrest of suspects who breach their conditions of bail, fail to answer to a court summons or breach a penal order.[62] Like the powers of courts to issue warrants for the arrest of witnesses under subpoena,[63] however, the warrant procedure is clearly an adjunct to criminal adjudication. Investigative arrests are generally effected under statutory powers without a warrant.

From 1 January 2006, the English law of arrest underwent major change pursuant to the Serious Organized Crime and Police Act (SOC&PA) 2005. Under the original scheme enacted in ss. 24 and 25 of PACE 1984, a fundamental distinction was drawn between 'arrestable offences' – essentially, those offences carrying a maximum penalty of at least five years' imprisonment, plus miscellaneous crimes so designated by Parliament – and all other offences. Section 24 authorized any person to arrest without warrant anyone who was committing, or had committed, an arrestable offence, or was suspected on reasonable grounds of having done so. This was a statutory recapitulation, in relation to serious offences, of the ancient common law right to effect a citizen's arrest (Stephen 1883: 192–3). Police constables were invested with additional powers under s. 24 to arrest on reasonable suspicion that an arrestable offence was about to be committed, and under s. 25 to effect an arrest in relation to less serious offences not designated 'arrestable' where the 'general arrest conditions' applied. By way of counterpart to the policy of commencing criminal trial proceedings for less serious offences by summons directing the accused's voluntary attendance at court rather than invoking the coercive power of arrest (Philips 1981: 48–9), the general arrest conditions encompassed circumstances in which proceeding by way of summons would be impractical: where the suspect gave no name, or the officer reasonably suspected that a false name had been given; where the suspect refused to provide a satisfactory address for the service of a summons; and where an arrest was necessary to prevent personal injury (including self-harm) by the suspect, damage to property, obstruction of the highway, offences against public decency or to protect the welfare of a child or other vulnerable person. (It was therefore misleading to think of the offences excluded from the ambit of s. 24 as 'non-arrestable' offences; they were, rather, 'only-arrestable-when-the-general-arrest-conditions-apply' offences.) Part of this jurisdiction was clearly designed to enable police officers to take appropriate action when confronted by exigent threats to person or property. Arrest to ascertain a suspect's true identity or place of residence, however, is also directed towards furthering criminal investigations and prosecutions.

SOC&P Act 2005 dispenses entirely with the concept of 'arrestable offence'. PACE, s. 25 is repealed, and new ss. 24 and 24A inserted.[64] Section 24 now authorizes *constables* to arrest without warrant any person who is about to commit, is in the process of committing or has committed *any* offence, or is suspected on reasonable grounds of committing offences in the past, present or future. Constables also retain the power to arrest any person reasonably suspected of having committed an offence which the constable has reasonable grounds for suspecting has occurred.[65] In other words, an arrest can still be lawful even if no crime has actually taken place, a power never afforded to ordinary members of the public and now extended from arrestable offences to all offences. Summary arrest by a constable under s. 24 must, however, be regarded by the constable on reasonable grounds as 'necessary'[66] for one of the purposes specified by subs. 24(5). The specified purposes mostly recapitulate the old, now defunct, 'general arrest conditions', but add two explicitly investigative objectives: 'to allow the prompt and effective investigation of the offence or of the conduct of the [suspect]'; and 'to prevent any prosecution of the offence from being hindered by the disappearance of the person in question'. Section 24 of PACE 1984, as amended by the 2005 Act, thus both conceives arrest as a quintessentially investigative step, and confers generously formulated powers on constables to take this step in relation to *any* offence. Parliament's inhibition against encouraging over-hasty resort to coercive powers of arrest appears to have been overcome.

This development is somewhat mitigated by the simultaneous promulgation of a new Code of Practice bringing arrest within the framework of the PACE codes for the first time.[67] Code G emphasizes that:

The right to liberty is a key principle of the Human Rights Act 1998. The exercise of the power of arrest represents an obvious and significant interference with that right. The use of the power must be fully justified and officers exercising the power should consider if the necessary objectives can be met by other, less intrusive means ... When the power of arrest is exercised it is essential that it is exercised in a non-discriminatory and proportionate manner.[68]

These are valuable statements of principle which police officers should certainly take to heart. However, the concept of 'reasonable grounds for believing' is so indeterminate and s. 24(5)'s list of justified objectives so all-encompassing that it is difficult to believe that Code G will exert much practical restraint on decisions to make an arrest. Civilians, on the other hand, have no business conducting criminal investigations. Section 24A of PACE consequently preserves the power to make a citizen's arrest in relation to ongoing or completed indictable (as opposed to 'arrestable') offences, but now limited to situations in which 1) it is not reasonably practicable for a constable to make the arrest instead;[69] and 2) the person making the arrest has reasonable grounds for believing that an arrest is necessary to prevent physical injury, damage to property or the suspect's 'making off before a constable can assume responsibility for him'.[70] Citizens may arrest criminal suspects in the circumstances envisaged but must hand over detainees to professional investigators at the first reasonable opportunity.

The utility of arrest as an investigative tool has greatly been enhanced by judicial rulings confirming the legality of pretextual, or 'holding', charges. To effect a lawful arrest, the arresting officer must inform the suspect that he is being placed under arrest, making it clear that the suspect is no longer at liberty to leave the officer's custody and explaining the grounds on which the arrest is being made ('I am arresting you on suspicion of burglary...', etc).[71] But what if the stated reason for making the arrest is really just a pretext for exposing the suspect to custodial interrogation on another, more serious matter? The courts might have denounced any such attempt to expand the permissible scope of detention for questioning, declaring that a pretextual arrest could not be a lawful arrest. Instead, it has been decided that pretextual arrests are perfectly lawful, whether the real intention is to question the suspect in relation to other matters[72] or to get him out of his house so that concealed listening devices can be planted there in the suspect's absence[73] or to trick the suspect into making incriminating admissions while confined with his criminal associates in a bugged police cell.[74] The only proviso is that the arresting officer must genuinely apprehend reasonable grounds for suspicion in relation to the pretextual or 'holding' charge which are communicated to the suspect as the reason for his arrest. Ulterior motives, in other words, do not invalidate an otherwise lawful arrest.

The use of holding charges to investigate serious crimes might be regarded as sensible, if not ingenious, police work. Pretextual arrest might equally be said, recalling that the legality of detaining suspects for questioning *in any circumstances* was disputed until the 1980s, to press an inherently controversial investigative technique too far. The analogous tactic of pretextual stop-and-search has been bitterly contested in the USA, where it has been shown that highway patrol officers frequently stop motorists on the pretext of minor traffic violations in order to search their cars for drugs and other contraband (Alschuler 2002; Gross and Livingston 2002). The flames of this debate have been fanned by the allegation, which in some states is underpinned by empirical data (cf. Pager 2004), that black and Hispanic motorists are statistically much more likely to be stopped for minor traffic violations than whites. The clear implication is that minority ethnic citizens are being singled out disproportionately for pretextual traffic stops on the basis of racist generalizations predicting their involvement in drug-dealing and dishonesty offences. By adopting these discriminatory investigative strategies, critics have provocatively charged, the police have created the de facto 'crime' of 'driving while black' (Harris 1997).[75] Despite the clear risks of unfair prejudice, conflict and alienation presented by this duplicitous investigative strategy, the US Supreme Court has upheld the constitutionality of pretextual traffic stops.[76]

Entry, search and seizure, incidental to arrest or pursuant to a warrant

PACE provides for search and seizure incidental to an arrest. Persons arrested outside the confines of a police station may be subjected to a relatively unintrusive 'pat-down' search, partly to deprive them of any weapons or other dangerous objects concealed about their person, but also to recover contraband or anything else that might be evidence in relation to an offence.[77] Searches are restricted, first, by object, to evidence which the investigating officer has reasonable cause to believe may be in the arrested person's possession; and, secondly, in scope, to the extent reasonably required for discovery of such evidence. In public, a person may be required to remove only an outer coat, jacket and gloves – not a hat, or any other more intimate item of clothing. But searches of suspects' mouths – e.g. to recover hastily concealed drugs or incriminating pieces of paper, which suspects sometimes try to swallow when they anticipate imminent apprehension – are explicitly authorized.[78]

A constable may enter and search any premises or vehicle where the arrested person was apprehended, or any place frequented by a suspect immediately prior to his or her arrest in relation to an indictable offence.[79] Parliament intended to confer an appropriately circumscribed investigative power: the constable must have reasonable grounds for believing that the premises or vehicle contains material of evidentiary value in relation to an offence for which the suspect has been arrested or a related offence, and that the type of search to be conducted – in terms of its focus, thoroughness and duration – is necessary to recover material of that kind.[80] The police are entitled to seize and retain any item discovered in that location, possibly against the wishes of the person from whom it was seized, which is believed in good faith to be required as evidence for a later trial,[81] or in order to return suspected stolen goods to their rightful owner.[82]

More extensive powers of search and seizure apply to arrested persons detained at a police station. On arrival, the designated custody officer[83] must ascertain whether the suspect is in possession of unlawful or dangerous items, or material which may be evidence in connection with an offence, and may direct that the suspect is subjected to a strip search or an intimate search for these purposes, provided that no less intrusive measure would suffice.[84] A strip search involves the removal of more than outer garments or shoes and socks.[85] It may be conducted only by a constable of the same sex as the person being searched.[86] 'Strip searches shall not be routinely carried out if there is no reason to consider that articles are concealed.'[87] Intimate searches are examinations of bodily orifices other than the mouth (which, as we have seen, can be inspected by a constable on the street). Emergencies aside, intimate searches should normally be conducted by a suitably qualified medical practitioner, at a police station or medical facility.[88] 'The intrusive nature of such searches means the actual and potential risks associated with intimate searches must never be underestimated.'[89] Whereas strip searches may be undertaken to recover evidence which the custody officer reasonably believes to be in the suspect's possession,[90] intimate searches cannot generally be conducted for evidential purposes – only to deprive the suspect of dangerous items. However, intimate searches are specifically authorized for the purposes of recovering drugs that may have been possessed with intent to supply or export,[91] which is at least partly an investigative exercise in securing evidence of drug-dealing. Dangerous articles and material of evidential value may be seized and retained, on the same terms as items recovered from non-intimate searching. Thus, intimate searches may incidentally produce admissible evidence of offending[92] even though they may not be authorized for explicitly investigative purposes.

Police station detainees can be subjected to various procedures in order to confirm and record their identity. Verification of a suspect's identity is crucial for the purposes of any ongoing investigation, but also may contribute to future investigations, if not by identifying the perpetrator directly then at least by eliminating known offenders with a similar pattern of criminality or characteristic 'MO'[93] from a particular inquiry. 'Rounding up the usual suspects' through dragnet arrests and interrogations is time-consuming and often unproductive; checking the usual suspects' vital statistics on a database is the modern, efficient way of investigative policing.

The physical person of a suspect is an important source of information and potential evidence in modern criminal proceedings. Suspects who are arrested and detained at a police station in relation to a 'recordable offence'[94] may have their fingerprints taken without their consent.[95] The same applies to those who have been charged with, convicted of, or cautioned regarding a recordable offence.[96] Bodily samples are categorized as 'intimate' or 'non-intimate' within the PACE regime.[97] Intimate samples include blood, semen, tissue fluid, urine, pubic hair, dental impressions and swabs taken from any bodily orifice other than the mouth. Intimate samples can be taken only on the authority of a senior police officer, and with the consent of the suspect[98] (and, in the case of juveniles, with their guardian's consent[99]). However, refusal to consent to such a request carries an evidentiary price if the case goes to trial: juries are directed that they may draw 'such inferences as appear proper' from the accused's refusal, without good cause, to accede to a well founded police request for an intimate bodily sample to be taken by a properly qualified health professional.[100] Non-intimate samples, which include saliva, skin impressions, hair (other than pubic hair) and mouth swabs, can generally be taken with or without a police station detainee's consent, provided that the investigating officer has reasonable grounds for believing that the sample will have evidential value in proving, or disproving, the suspect's involvement in a recordable offence.[101] The definition of 'non-intimate sample' was expanded by CJPOA 1994 to allow the police, without consent, to pluck head-hair with its roots intact, in order to facilitate DNA testing.[102] PACE also authorizes non-intimate searches in order to ascertain whether the suspect has any distinguishing marks, such as a recent injury, tattoo or body piercing, which might confirm his or her involvement in a crime. Any such mark may be photographed for evidential purposes, and retained for use in subsequent investigations.[103]

The Criminal Justice and Police Act (CJ&PA) 2001 introduced important new amendments to the PACE scheme for taking and retaining fingerprints and bodily samples. Fingerprint records, bodily samples and any data derived from them no longer have to be destroyed if the suspect is later acquitted or released without charge.[104] Instead, this material may be retained and stored in databases for the purposes of 'speculative searching'[105] – that is, comparing genetic material[106] recovered from unsolved crime scenes against the fingerprint records or DNA profiles of previously identified suspects, in the hope of finding a 'match' revealing the perpetrator of an unsolved crime. DNA evidence is enormously powerful, but it is neither infallible in theory nor foolproof in practice (Lempert 1991; Redmayne 1997; Donnelly and Friedman 1999). Speculative searching is particularly controversial, because it purports to generate very strong, possibly overwhelming, evidence against a person whose only evidential connection to a crime is a matching fingerprint or DNA profile generated from a scientific database. Should this acontextual identification be enough, in isolation, to convict the accused of any criminal offence importing blame and censure, let alone a very serious offence like rape, robbery or murder? Is society's faith in science and scientific experts sufficient to sustain the legitimacy of a criminal conviction founded almost exclusively on the appliance of science? While these profound questions are being pondered, the House of Lords has already rejected the collateral complaint that DNA databases unreasonably infringe the right to respect for private life guaranteed by Article 8 of the ECHR, especially in relation to people who have never been convicted of, or even charged with, any criminal offence.[107] PACE has been amended so that suspects must now be informed that their footwear impressions, fingerprint records or saliva and hair samples may be retained and used in speculative searching.[108] It must be doubtful, however, whether many suspects will appreciate the full implications of this formal notification. Moreover, even those *CSI* aficionados among the suspect population who do grasp the implications of speculative searching remain powerless to prevent the police from lawfully taking fingerprints and non-intimate hair and saliva samples, with or without their consent.

An alternative source of evidence derives from searches of premises and seizure of relevant items conducted under the authority of a warrant issued by a magistrate or judge. Legislative powers of search and seizure under judicial warrant are explicitly investigative. PACE Code of Practice B[109] regulates the execution of search warrants under the general provisions of the 1984 Act and a host of miscellaneous statutes.[110] On application by a constable under s. 8 of PACE, a magistrate may issue a warrant authorizing the search of premises (including vehicles, vessels and temporary structures[111]), provided that there are reasonable grounds for believing 1) that an indictable offence has been committed; and 2) that the specified location contains material with substantial evidentiary value for the investigation. Application for a search warrant is intended as a remedy of last resort, since '[p]owers of entry, search and seizure... may significantly interfere with the occupier's privacy' and '[t]he right to privacy and respect for personal property are key principles of the Human Rights Act 1998'.[112] An officer should apply for a warrant only if it is not practicable to obtain the material sought in any other way.[113] To avoid speculative 'fishing expeditions', the application must particularize both the premises to be searched and the material the constable expects to find there.[114] Each warrant permits a single entry, not repeated visits,[115] unless multiple entry is specifically authorized.[116] Only material within the scope of the warrant may be searched for, and, if discovered, seized and retained. 'Searches must be conducted with due consideration for the property and privacy of the occupier and with no more disturbance than necessary.'[117] Prior to conducting the search the warrant must be shown to the occupier of the premises, who must also be supplied with his or her own copy accompanied by an official 'Notice of Powers and Rights'.[118] If the premises are unoccupied at the time of the search, a copy of the warrant and notice must be displayed prominently for the occupier to find on his or her return.[119] An executed warrant must be endorsed with information detailing the conduct of the search and also recording which, if any, items were seized as potential evidence. An executed and properly endorsed warrant is then deposited with the court for a period of 12 months, during which time the occupier of the premises is entitled to inspect it.[120] These safeguards are designed to ensure that search warrants are granted and executed only in accordance with the strict letter of the law, underlining the significance of this notably intrusive investigative step. After all, 'an Englishman's home is his castle',[121] and its ramparts are not lightly to be breached. Nor, more prosaically, should the police be tearing up a householder's floorboards or dismantling his or her hi-fi if they are supposed to be looking for stolen desktop computers or similar large items.[122] The procedural safeguards regulating the execution of search warrants granted under s. 8 of PACE apply *mutatis mutandis* to the raft of additional statutory provisions under which magistrates may grant search warrants in relation to specified offences (drugs, firearms, obscene publications, terrorism, etc.).[123]

Certain types of material attract special legal immunities from police search and seizure. Items subject to legal professional privilege (lawyer–client communications, plus communications with third parties in connection with ongoing or contemplated litigation; see Roberts and Zuckerman 2004: 235–8) cannot be the subject of a search warrant[124] or warrantless entry and search incidental to an arrest.[125] Other types of confidential material, such as personal employment or medical records, confidential business information and journalistic sources, are categorized either as 'excluded material'[126] or 'special procedure material'[127] within the PACE scheme. Access to such information is limited (but not, in fact, 'excluded': 'highly restricted material' would have been a more accurate designation). Application must be made to a circuit judge who may grant an order for access or, exceptionally, a warrant for search and seizure.[128] If relevant material is in the hands of, say, a solicitor or bank manger, an order for production, usually demanding compliance within seven days, would normally suffice. In other circumstances, however, prior notification might lead to the concealment or destruction of evidence, and only a search warrant authorizing the police to turn up to the premises and demand entry unannounced can safeguard the interests of the investigation. In any event, the judge will not grant a production order or search warrant in relation to excluded or special procedure material unless the officer making the application has demonstrated, on the balance of probabilities, that 1) there are reasonable grounds to believe that the premises contains material of substantial evidentiary value to the investigation of an indictable offence; 2) there is no other, less intrusive, means for securing access to the material; and 3) it would be in the public interest, all things considered, to grant the order. The judge retains a broad discretion to ensure a proper balancing of interests, weighing personal privacy and confidentiality on one side of the scales against facilitating criminal investigations and the effective administration of justice on the other. A production order or search warrant should never be granted except on the basis of full information and with appropriate circumspection.[129]

Finally, various statutes authorize the police and other investigators, such as customs officials and tax inspectors, to demand the production of documents and other information for particular specified purposes, particularly in commercial contexts.[130] Such investigative powers are typically given sharper teeth by the provision of penal sanctions for non-compliance. There is a no general legal objection to forcing citizens to provide information under threat of penalty; indeed, this happens all the time in relation to tax returns, entries on the electoral register, applying for a driving licence, claiming social security benefits, completing the periodic population census and so forth. If such information is then used in a subsequent criminal trial to prosecute the person who provided it, however, this would seem to trench on the privilege against self-incrimination. The accused has been forced, under threat of penalty, to provide the prosecution with self-incriminating evidence. English courts have none the less upheld convictions based in part on information compelled in this way, pointing out that the privilege against self-incrimination is an important, but not an absolute, right at common law and in the jurisprudence of the ECtHR.[131] The true scope of the privilege against self-incrimination, and investigators' inversely corresponding mandate to coerce self-incriminating evidence from suspects, are matters of ongoing legal controversy (see Roberts and Zuckerman 2004: ch. 9).

Detention and custodial interrogation

We saw above that, under ss. 24, 24A and 37 of PACE, suspects may be arrested and detained in a police station for the explicit investigative purpose of custodial interrogation. The police station is a pivotal site of information gathering and 'case construction' (Sanders 1987; McConville *et al.* 1991; Baldwin 1993a; Roberts 1994). Custodial interrogation is an opportunity for investigators to turn perhaps vague suspicions of the detainee's involvement in criminality into hard evidence of particular offences, by inducing the suspect to confess directly or to disclose valuable intelligence revealing other perpetrators or crimes. From the suspect's perspective, any damaging admissions made in the police station may effectively seal his or her fate, even if the suspect's words were ill-judged or misinterpreted. False or coerced confessions have been a major source of miscarriages of justice in recent history (Dennis 1993; JUSTICE 1994; Walker 1999). The duration of pre-charge detention and the conditions and conduct of police interrogation consequently exert a decisive influence on the progress and outcome of many criminal investigations (Sanders and Young 2007: chs 4–5; Ashworth and Redmayne 2005: ch. 4).

Section 37 of PACE 1984 requires that investigative questioning in relation to any particular offence must cease as soon as there is sufficient evidence to support a formal criminal charge. Questioning may continue in relation to other alleged or suspected offences, but the police are prohibited from using custodial interrogation to build up a case beyond the charging threshold. Police interviews and the duration and conditions of detention are further regulated in minute detail by PACE Code of Practice C governing 'detention, treatment and questioning' – the 'DTQ Code'.[132] In brief, suspects may be detained without charge on the authorization of police officers for up to 36 hours,[133] but this period can be extended on application to a magistrate for a maximum of 96 hours[134] – that is, four days in the police cells without charge. The duration and conditions of detention are subject to periodic reviews by the appointed custody officer,[135] who is tasked with monitoring the treatment of detainees and ensuring their welfare.[136] For those detained on suspicion of terrorist offences, however, the maximum period of detention without charge has recently been extended to 28 days[137]. With the backing of senior police officers, the government had attempted to persuade Parliament to authorize a maximum period of 90 days' detention for uncharged terrorist suspects, with the implication that a person who had done nothing more blameworthy than being suspected – however erroneously – of terrorist activity could have been locked up for longer than many convicted thieves and burglars.[138] But Parliament was unpersuaded by an argument predicated on investigative necessity yet bereft of concrete evidence or examples, and the government suffered an embarrassing defeat in the House of Commons.[139] Still, the maximum duration of detention without charge for terrorist suspects was doubled to 28 days. Vulnerable, confused or intimidated suspects have been known to make false confessions after very much shorter periods of custodial detention.

Prior to the enactment of PACE, police cells and interview rooms were secretive, dark corners of criminal process that were in practice almost impervious to external scrutiny. Detainees could be held incommunicado and deliberately isolated and pressurized, and were sometimes subjected to physical abuse.[140] Complaints of police brutality emerged from time to time, but the courts evinced little inclination to intervene on any systematic basis. The Royal Commission on Criminal Procedure, which reported in 1981, acknowledged that police detention was an inherently coercive experience, such that suspects might feel compelled to speak and risk making ill-conceived admissions, even if they had been informed of their 'right to silence' (which many, apparently, were not) (Philips 1981: ch. 4).

PACE implemented most of the Royal Commission's key recommendations. Suspects could no longer be held incommunicado,[141] and they would henceforth have a statutory right to consult privately with a solicitor at any time.[142] Custodial legal advice has since been provided free of charge to suspects who request it under the publicly funded duty solicitor scheme (Bridges 2002; Cape 2002). Police sergeants with no direct involvement in ongoing investigations, newly designated as 'custody officers', would take primary responsibility for ensuring that suspects were properly treated within the confines of the police station.[143] The common law test of 'voluntariness' for admissible confessions was superseded by more carefully crafted legal standards of oppression and reliability contained in s. 76 of PACE (Wolchover and Heaton-Armstrong 1996; Roberts and Zuckerman 2004: 449–64). In light of their pronounced susceptibility to making unreliable confessions (see, e.g., Confait Inquiry 1977), special provision was made for juveniles and mentally disturbed adults to be accompanied by an independent person, such as a relative, social worker or mental health professional, to protect vulnerable detainees' interests and provide reassurance and support during police interviews.[144] Most significant of all, s. 60 and PACE Code E provided for the tape-recording of all police interviews with suspects.[145] This effectively put an end to allegations of 'verballing' in the police station – that is, falsely attributing to suspects incriminating oral statements allegedly made during conversations with police officers. In the days before tape-recording, suspects would not infrequently claim that investigating officers had concocted incriminating 'confessions', or even lied about conducting whole interviews that never occurred, while police officers denied any impropriety and accused suspects of making malicious allegations. It was almost impossible for courts to get to the bottom of such disputes months after the event, when neither party could be shaken from its story. Tape-recording – in some instances now upgraded to video-recording[146] – today supplies an unassailable account of *what* was said during police interview, liberating the courts to concentrate on the evidential significance of suspects' admissions. This ostensibly prosaic technical innovation made a profound impact on the conduct of criminal investigations and prosecutions. Thornton (2004: 691) remarks: 'The days when a good case could be ruined by a bit of police nonsense were mostly over; police evidence became respectable again. And PACE became a solid framework, firmly in place for the introduction of the Human Rights Act 1998.'

Yet, it would be naïve to suppose that this, or any other, package of legislative reforms could at a stroke guarantee the reliability of every confession tendered at trial. Policing exemplifies the seemingly infinite human capacity for neutralizing institutional constraints. Although the police station is now a highly regulated and scrutinized environment for conducting interviews with suspects, arrestees can still be driven to the police station 'by the scenic route' creating ample time for them to make unrecorded admissions in transit, if not when first apprehended at the scene (Moston and Stephenson 1993). It has been proposed, in turn, that police officers should carry portable tape-recorders in order to authenticate such spontaneous statements (e.g. Wolchover and Heaton-Armstrong 1991), but cost and inconvenience have thus far proved insurmountable objections to making hand-held recording devices standard issue for patrol officers. (The rapid development of communications technologies suggests that this judgement should be revisited: these days, cell phones with the capacity to make video-recordings are smaller than ordinary police radios.) Even within the legally sanitized and closely scrutinized environment of the police station, moreover, one finds a significant gap between the higher aspirations and strict letter of PACE and the realities of confinement and interrogation experienced by suspects. Responsibility for this gap must be laid primarily at the door of the police, but their derelictions have been aided and abetted by defence solicitors (and legal advisers who are not solicitors) and by the courts.

Section 58(1) of PACE provides in unequivocal language that 'A person arrested and held in custody in a police station or other premises shall be entitled, if he so requests, to consult a solicitor privately at any time'. In *Samuel*[147] the accused's request to see a solicitor was denied because the police thought that legal advice might jeopardize the progress of the investigation, perhaps by encouraging Mr Samuel to exercise his right to remain silent. The Court of Appeal held that the trial judge should probably have excluded Samuel's confession under s. 78 of PACE, because he had been 'denied improperly one of the most important and fundamental rights of a citizen'.[148] In *Alladice*,[149] however, the appeal court indicated that delay or dubious refusals of a suspect's request to see a solicitor would not lead to the automatic exclusion of any subsequent admissions. In the absence of deliberate bad faith, it was 'not possible to say in advance what would or would not be fair'.[150] Mr Alladice was regarded as a professional criminal who 'knew the score' and was perfectly capable of exercising his rights without the benefit of professional legal advice. The Court of Appeal was consequently able to conclude that the presence of a solicitor would have made no difference either way to Alladice's conduct or prospects. Yet, even on the dubious supposition that certain suspects are their own best legal advisers, is it really safe to assume, counterfactually, that a lawyer would not have provided material assistance to a suspect who was obliged to manage as best he or she could without professional legal advice?

As well as providing the suspect with expert legal assistance, as s. 58 contemplates, the presence of a defence legal representative in the police station brings reassurance and emotional support to suspects who may be fearful or disorientated by their unfamiliar surroundings and daunting predicament. Police station detainees are often in more desperate need of a friendly (non-police) face and a cigarette than expert legal counsel. The presence of somebody independent of the police during interrogation also supplies an additional layer of scrutiny and accountability. Incidents can occur before or after the tape-recorder is switched on or off (Fenwick 1993). Audio-only tape-recording is restricted to capturing the verbal part of communication, whereas the true meaning of speech is sometimes embedded within the bodily and facial gestures accompanying the spoken word (cf. McConville 1992; Barnes 1993).

Initial police opposition to the introduction of legal advisers into the police station was fuelled by the expectation that lawyers would encourage their clients to remain silent and thus frustrate police attempts to secure confessions. In fact, even before Parliament exposed suspects to the risk of adverse inferences being drawn at trial from 'significant silences' during police interview,[151] silence was rejected as an unintelligent blanket strategy by experienced advisers (Philips 1981: paras. 4.43–4.46; McConville and Hodgson 1993: 193; Dixon 1997: 236–58). Detainees are usually advised to co-operate fully with police inquiries, unless – exceptionally – their interests would be better served by temporary unresponsiveness, for example because the police are themselves withholding information pertinent to the inquiry. A combination of police persistence, ineffectual legal representation and suspects' natural inclination to extricate themselves from trouble as quickly as possible entails that few detainees consistently exercise their right to silence throughout a series of interviews (Leng 1993: 20; McConville and Hodgson 1993: 195; cf. Zander and Henderson 1993: para. 1.2). As for those few who do remain silent throughout, the police treat non-cooperation as suspicious and have been more likely to charge such suspects than those who fully co-operate by answering questions.

Despite these empirical findings, and in the teeth of the Runciman Royal Commission's contrary recommendation (Zander 1994), the last Conservative administration was determined to enact legislation limiting suspects' right to silence. Sections 34–38 of the CJPO Act 1994 now permit juries to draw adverse inferences from a suspect's failure to explain him or herself at the earliest reasonable opportunity, from a suspect's failure to account for his or her presence at the scene of a crime or for a suspect's possession of incriminating articles or marks on his or her clothing, and from a suspect's election not to testify in his or her own defence at trial. The CJPO Act 1994 may have loosened a few tongues in the police station (Bucke et al. 2000; Jackson 2001), but its overall impact on the progress and outcomes of criminal investigations is bound to be marginal, given the evident unpopularity among suspects and their legal advisers of electing to remain silent during police interrogation. Moreover, suspects pressured to speak by the threat of forensic penalties do not necessarily tell the truth or reveal anything useful to the investigation. It has been argued, to the contrary, that penalizing silence during police interrogation encourages guilty suspects to lie, which in turn undermines the credibility of innocent explanations and increases the risk of miscarriages of justice (Seidmann and Stein 2000).

Most legal commentators are critical of the 1994 Act's silence provisions (e.g. Birch 1999; Jackson 2001; Leng 2001; Dennis 2002). Legislative intervention greatly complicated the law on pre-trial silence. Judges are now obliged to give, and jurors to attempt to comprehend and apply, tortuously complex directions explaining which, if any, inferences can be drawn, in which circumstances, and for what purposes.[152] These linguistic farragos appreciably lengthen trials and generate avoidable appeals. Perhaps the most disappointing interpretational development has been the Court of Appeal's insistence that a suspect remains vulnerable to adverse inferences even where he or she has remained silent on the good faith advice of his or her lawyer.[153] Apparently, suspects are expected to distinguish between sound and ill-considered legal advice to remain silent and to reject the latter, calling into question the practical value of providing supposedly expert legal counsel in the first place (Cape 1997; Choo and Jennings 2003). Taken together with the decision in *Alladice*, it is barely any exaggeration to say that the courts have conspired with Parliament to eviscerate the suspect's right to custodial legal advice conferred by s. 58 of PACE.

Formal identification procedures

Like confessions, identification evidence – more precisely, *mis*identification evidence – is recognized as a potent source of miscarriages of justice, stretching back more than a century (Devlin 1976; Pattenden 1999: ch. 1). Mirroring the law's approach to confession evidence, evidence of identification is subject to a complex, PACE-based scheme of legal regulation.

Extensive behavioural science research, conducted over the last three decades, has amply demonstrated the shortcomings of purported identifications of the accused by eyewitnesses (Wells and Loftus 1984; Kapardis 1997: chs 2–3). The fact that a scrupulously honest and very confident eyewitness could none the less still be mistaken poses an acute challenge to a trial system predicated on evaluating oral testimony through cross-examination and close scrutiny of the witness's demeanour (Wellborn 1991; McKenzie and Dunk 1999; Roberts and Zuckerman 2004: 212–21, 490–6). If – as modern science insists (Cohen 1999) – remembering is a creative, actively willed but partly subconscious process, then the image of a suspect first seen in police custody or in a gallery of 'mugshot' photographs could easily become interpolated into the witness's, now half-forgotten – and possibly always faulty – recollection of the original incident. Yet vigorous cross-examination will not shake an honest eyewitness in the courtroom. A more promising forensic strategy is to ensure that appropriate formal identification procedures are conducted with scrupulous procedural rectitude, in an attempt to insulate identification evidence from well documented corrupting influences. This is the approach adopted by PACE.

Identification procedures are governed by PACE Code of Practice D,[154] which specifies a hierarchy of identification procedures to be considered whenever the suspect's identity is unknown or disputed. The process is overseen by designated 'identification officers', police officers of at least inspector rank who are not directly involved in the current investigation (and who are thus less likely, through unconscious body language or otherwise, to give witnesses inappropriate 'hints' as to the identity of the suspect).[155] When PACE was first enacted, the live identification parade where the suspect lines up with eight or more 'foils', supposedly resembling him or her in physique and appearance, was regarded as the optimal procedure. In practice, however, parades can be problematic, especially if the suspect has unusual distinguishing features or hails from a minority community from which an adequate number of foils cannot be recruited in time (highly dubious practices such as foils 'blacking up' and wearing wigs are not unknown; see Tinsley 2001). Revised versions of Code D consequently prioritize video parades, whereby 'the witness is shown moving images of a known suspect, together with similar images of others who resemble the suspect'. None the less, the identification officer, in consultation with colleagues, may still elect to hold a live parade, or even invite the witness to pick out the suspect from an informal 'group identification', if the identification officer judges this appropriate in the circumstances.[156] But a witness must never be shown photographs, artist's composites or e-fit images unless the identity of the suspect is currently unknown (thus precluding his or her participation in formal identification procedures).[157]

Live parades and, albeit to a lesser extent, video identifications,[158] require the suspect's consent and practical co-operation. If such is not forthcoming, the identification officer may resort to less satisfactory identification procedures, including covert 'street' identifications[159] and direct confrontation of a suspect by the witness.[160] Despite their admitted deficiencies, even these substitute procedures provide some opportunity for testing the strength of a witness's recall close to the time of the events in question and outside the highly charged atmosphere of a courtroom with its stylized, rigidly choreographed interactions.[161] Code D ensures that identification procedures of whatever description are planned, monitored and properly recorded, minimizing risks of contamination and supplying an invaluable evidentiary celluloid or paper trail to inform the jury's deliberations at trial. Code D also contains significant due-process rights for the accused to be informed of pending investigative steps and to make representations,[162] although the value of such procedural guarantees is arguably undercut by the fact that non-cooperation may expose a suspect to covert or otherwise unconsented identification procedures in any event (Roberts and Clover 2002).[163]

Pre-trial identification procedures are complemented by special rules of court, laid down in *Turnbull*.[164] Most dramatically, if the prosecution's case rests exclusively or substantially on poor-quality identifications – e.g. a 'fleeting glimpse' of a stranger in the dark – the judge should direct an outright acquittal. Where eyewitness testimony is better quality or flanked by supporting evidence, the trial judge's summing-up should include a '*Turnbull* warning' explaining how mistaken identifications have caused miscarriages of justice in the past, and specifically drawing jurors' attention to factors potentially affecting the quality of the identification in the instant case (the offender was not previously known to the witness; the light was fading; sightlines were blocked by obstacles; the offender was only observed for a few fleeting moments; etc.). In this way, the jury is instructed to assess eyewitness identification with particular circumspection, and the contextual features emphasized by the judge might well, in an evidentially close case, tilt the balance towards acquittal.

While PACE Code D requires police investigators to follow optimized standard procedures for generating new evidence of identification, the

Turnbull rules provide an incentive for investigators and prosecutors to build criminal cases that do not rely exclusively on eyewitness accounts. If at all possible, an eyewitness's positive identification should be supported by confirmatory evidence such as fingerprints, fibre transfers or CCTV video footage. Relying on the testimony of a single eyewitness is now a high-risk prosecutorial strategy, because the case is likely to be thrown out of court if the judge, for whatever reason, is less impressed by the quality of the witness's identification than the prosecutor had hoped or expected.

English law has none the less resisted arguments for introducing a formal corroboration requirement (e.g. Dennis 1984; Jackson 1999: 195; cf. Devlin 1976: paras. 4.27–4.42), mandating that a conviction could never be based solely on contested identification evidence. The extent of the law's commitment to safeguarding the accused from mistaken (mis)identification is also called into question by a recent House of Lords' decision, holding that evidence generated through alternative identification procedures would not automatically be excluded under s. 78 of PACE just because the accused had been denied a parade in contravention of Code D.[165] Their Lordships acknowledged that the accused has a legitimate interest in being able to take part in a parade, inasmuch as a witness's failure to identify the accused when presented with a fair opportunity to do so can be regarded as (somewhat) probative of innocence. But the only remedy for this breach of investigative procedure was held to be a curative direction in the trial judge's summing-up, informing jurors that 'the suspect has lost the benefit of that safeguard and that the jury should take account of that fact in its assessment of the whole case, giving it such weight as it thinks fair'.[166]

Realities and remedies

The preceding section has indicated the type, range and extent of formal legal measures available to police officers (and *mutatis mutandis* to other official investigators) in the conduct of criminal investigations in England and Wales. But the 'law in the books' is, at best, an uncertain guide to the 'law in action'. Formal legal authority may be invoked to immunize investigators from criticism or legal liability, but otherwise serve only as a pretext for what the police were going to do anyway, law or no law. Sanders and Young (2007: 61–2) thus characterize certain police powers, or their exercise on certain occasions, as 'presentational' rather than truly 'inhibitory'. There is something to be said for encouraging fidelity to legal rules even as a matter of convenience or habituation, but this should not be equated with wholehearted allegiance to the rule of law in a constitutional democracy.

For much of the practical business of policing, law is strictly superfluous to investigators' requirements, since citizens' 'consent' pre-empts the need to invoke formal police powers of stop, search,[167] arrest, detention and interrogation (see, further, Dixon 1997: ch. 3; Sanders and Young 2000: chs 2–4). Most people co-operate willingly with police requests for information, because they genuinely want or feel obliged to help, or because they wrongly assume they have no real choice in the matter, or because they correctly perceive that being obstructive will get them nowhere. Though one is legally entitled to be unco-operative,[168] being standoffish or obstreperous with police officers is liable to provoke a coercive reaction[169] – not least because a citizen who refuses to help the police more or less *ipso facto* generates 'reasonable suspicion' – and even risks non-cooperation later being interpreted by a jury as evidence of guilt in the event of subsequent prosecution and trial. Rather than functioning as a series of limitations on state power buttressing liberty and individuals' rights, the laws of policing might instead be regarded as a set of additional resources, augmenting the ubiquitous 'Ways and Means Act' of immemorial policing lore, which serve primarily to facilitate criminal investigations in the interests of order, security and penal justice. We do not disparage these indisputably legitimate interests by encouraging candid recognition that law is always a limited tool for regulating criminal investigations.

The limitations of law in policing

The corpus of empirical research evaluating the impact of PACE and related reforms conclusively refutes two propositions: it is wrong to say, with the hard-bitten cynics and prophets of doom, that PACE has failed to exert any discernible impact on the practical realities of policing; and it is equally false to claim, now donning rose-tinted spectacles, that PACE has always functioned as legislators intended and its supporters dared to hope. The truth lies somewhere in between these polar extremities.

Law's inherent limitations as a technology of regulation can in part be ascribed to the practical realities of routine interactions between police and citizens. Parliament has been alive to the risk that carefully crafted legal limits on police investigations may be eroded by citizens' ill-informed or coerced 'consent' to officers' demands. PACE is shot through with requirements that suspects must be informed of their rights not to co-operate (and of any associated risks of withholding co-operation), and given explanations of what is going to happen to them and why, and what their options are, if any.[170] Information is often supplied in writing to be digested and signed as accurate and understood, with ample opportunity to comment or set the record straight.[171] Above all, as we have seen, suspects have a statutory right to custodial legal advice, provided free of charge to all police station detainees regardless of means, at a cost of over £150 million p.a. to British taxpayers (Legal Services Commission 2005: 43). PACE Code of Practice C even requires multilingual posters advertising the duty solicitor scheme to be placed prominently in every police station charging area,[172] no effort being too great or detail too trivial in the drive to ensure that the availability of free legal advice is communicated effectively to suspects. Yet none of these safeguards, nor any others that might be devised, is foolproof against suspects who are too suspicious or fatalistic, too inarticulate, or slow-witted, or suggestible to invoke them. Experience teaches that there is no procedural right so robust or attractive that it cannot be disdained or bargained away for some real or perceived advantage. And there are always police officers willing to provide inducements to elicit suspects' co-operation, not infrequently abetted by defence lawyers whose principal strategy, more often than not, is to encourage their clients to do a deal and plead guilty.

Despite the concerted efforts of recent years, it remains the case that fewer than half, and possibly only around a third, of police station detainees actually receives legal assistance (Hodgson 1992; Brown 1997; cf. Zander and Henderson 1993: para. 1.3.3). Why do a majority of suspects decline the offer of gratis legal advice? Empirical research points to a variety of personal and contextual influences, but one recurring factor is the various 'ploys' devised by police officers to persuade suspects to be interviewed before the duty solicitor arrives, or to forgo legal advice altogether (Sanders and Bridges 1999; Sanders and Young 2007: ch. 5). By inducing suspects into 'voluntary' waivers of their right to see a solicitor the police have in practice been able to neutralize s. 58 of PACE while notionally still 'going by the book'.

The qualifications and performance of advisers who do attend police stations and sit through interviews have also attracted criticism. Many advisers are not legally qualified solicitors, but rather 'law clerks' or solicitors' assistants. This poses the question whether such individuals are capable of advising suspects regarding, for example, the technical criteria of legal liability or detailed rules of evidence and procedure. There are documented cases of 'advisers' being manifestly incompetent and woefully inept (e.g. McConville et al. 1994: 60–2, 146, 266–7). Notwithstanding the adversarial structure of English criminal process, defence legal advisers have been exposed as passive, compliant and reliant upon the police for information about the suspect's situation (Baldwin 1992; Hodgson 1994; McConville et al. 1994: ch. 5). Although a confrontational approach will not always be in a client's best interests (Roberts 1993), researchers have branded defence legal advisers 'pusillanimous' (Baldwin 1993b) and found them 'prepared to sit passively through interrogations conducted in a hostile atmosphere and where there were open attempts to intimidate or belittle the suspect' (McConville et al. 1994: 113). Empirical researchers' criticisms are borne out by the case of the 'Cardiff Three',[173] in which the Court of Appeal remarked that 'the solicitor appears to have been gravely at fault for sitting through this travesty of an interview' without attempting to protect his client from being 'bullied and hectored' by 'hostile and intimidating' questioning.[174]

Since the early 1990s successive governments have demanded higher standards of service from defence legal advisers by implementing more rigorous schemes of training and accreditation (Bridges and Hodgson 1995), latterly within the framework of franchises awarded by the Legal Services Commission and the introduction of salaried public defenders (Cape 2002). The symbiotic relationship between practice and regulation is constantly evolving, and real improvements doubtless continue to be made (though Cape 2004's prognosis is more pessimistic). But there are limits to what can be achieved merely by changing the rules, because working practices and process outcomes are significantly influenced by the institutional and procedural contexts, occupational cultures and professional ideologies of police officers and defence legal advisers. Law reform must be carried forward on multiple fronts and levels if real progress is to be made. Working to improve the ethical standards of police interviewing is, for example (Zuckerman 1992;

Shepherd and Milne 1999), at least as important as putting up informational posters in custody suites. It is not sufficient that police officers and lawyers merely *know* the rules they are meant to be following – albeit that even imparting basic knowledge is a major organizational challenge when criminal procedure law is beset by almost perpetual reform. More ambitiously, criminal justice professionals must be brought to embrace the underlying rationales for legal regulation, motivating their conscientious compliance with legal rules, not through threats of sanctions for misconduct, but as an extension of their professional pride and personal ethical responsibility for doing justice according to law (see generally Kleinig 1996; Banks 2004: chs 1–2; Ashworth and Redmayne 2005: ch. 3).

While suspects cannot necessarily be trusted to further their own best interests in the course of criminal investigations, most police officers are beyond the scope of effective supervision and de facto legal accountability for most of the time they devote to investigative tasks. This is a second major, and cumulative, practical limitation on law as a regulatory mechanism. If suspects, intermittently in cahoots with prosecutors and defence lawyers, collude in police impropriety, who else will ever know, when nobody is motivated to complain? A well documented discovery of the sociology of policing is that police work inverts the standard organizational pyramid of top-down bureaucratic hierarchy and functional differentiation (Reiner 1997: 1009). The most junior beat police officers enjoy the greatest levels of occupational discretion in the police organization, while chief constables and other senior officers are subjected to rigorous institutional audit and the intense glare of the media spotlight (cf. Katz 2006). Out on the street, police officers are often at liberty, practically speaking, to be a law unto themselves. Formal procedures in the police station are more closely regulated by the law of criminal procedure, as we have seen. Still, even here, illegalities can be condoned, records can be doctored, deals can be struck before the tape-recorder is switched on, etc.

The role of custody officer, tasked with compiling a formal custody record for each detainee, was devised to provide independent oversight of the treatment of suspects at the police station (Philips 1981: paras. 3.111–3.113). Yet there is a natural tendency for members of any organization to support their colleagues in conflicts with 'outsiders', a tendency most pronounced in organizations, such as the military and the police, whose members develop close bonds of mutual reliance and support in the face of shared perils. While deliberate collusion in serious lawbreaking is probably rare,[175] slight adjustments in working routines to minimize the real impact of imposed change, exploiting institutional adaptation and inertia, are commonplace in any complex occupational bureaucracy. The chequered history of PACE's partial successes and unanticipated side-effects confirms the status of the police organization as a prototypical adaptive bureaucracy. If suspects can be detained only on the word of the custody officer,[176] but refusing authority to detain means turning down the request of a trusted colleague to the visible amusement and vindication of criminal suspects ('toe-rags', 'scrotes', 'obnoxious shits' in police argot; Choongh 1998: 623), reasonable suspicion for holding the suspect will invariably be found to exist (McKenzie *et al.*

1990: 24–6). If the legality of detention must be reviewed periodically,[177] very few suspects will be released before the first six-hourly review, even though greater numbers would have been released more promptly before a formal system of timed reviews was put in place, ostensibly for the benefit of suspects (Bottomley *et al.* 1991). And so on.

Again, the claim is not that legal regulation of policing is wholly impotent and pointless. Law reform has exerted real, empirically demonstrated effects on the conduct of policing, albeit not always in the manner or to the extent which legislators contemplated. The lesson lies precisely in the limitations of law reform, and the importance of augmenting regulation through law with other modalities of professional socialization, including on-the-job training and supervision by more experienced officers. Police officers are more likely to understand, remember and be motivated to follow a legal rule if its underlying rationale is appreciated, in both senses of being perspicuous to its addressees and endorsed by their personal conviction. Police training should aspire to inculcate in officers an appreciation of the laws which govern their professional conduct and to inspire their allegiance to the ideal of democratic policing under the rule of law. Such training should challenge the demoralizing misconception circulating among serving officers that the greater part of policing law is merely bureaucratic 'red tape' involving pointless form-filling and other 'paperwork', which is to be completed with mechanical uninterest whenever it cannot be evaded altogether. The ethos of rule-of-law policing imparted to new recruits during their initial period of training thereafter requires positive reinforcement through the example, instruction and advice of superior officers in the routine conduct of criminal investigations. Alas, leadership, direction and effective supervision of less experienced officers have been alarmingly scarce commodities in criminal investigations of the recent past (Baldwin and Moloney 1992; Maguire and Norris 1994). Best practice has not been disseminated throughout the police organisation, and elementary mistakes have been repeated without learning from experience (Maguire and Norris 1992; Irving and Dunnighan 1993; Bridges 1999). The police have latterly adopted a discernibly more professional, 'scientific' and 'intelligence-led' approach towards the planning, execution, and critical self-appraisal of criminal investigations (e.g. Brown and Cannings 2004; HMIC 2004; Nicol *et al.* 2004; National Crime Squad 2005; NCIS 2005). These changes in organizational culture and practice stand to be every bit as significant in improving the conduct and outcomes of criminal investigations as the law reform activities of legislators and judges.

At a more generic level, law must reconcile the conceptual limits of prophylactic regulation with the demands of practical efficacy in subjecting human conduct to the governance of rules. We have seen that the law of police powers characteristically employs open-ended phrases such as 'reasonable grounds for suspecting', 'reasonably required' or 'the fairness of the proceedings', investing police officers with considerable operational latitude to apply (extend, mould, bend, disapply, etc.) the abstract legal standard to each more or less unique factual scenario calling for the exercise of their discretion. At the limit, this must necessarily be so, because it is literally impossible for legislators to anticipate and make provision for every potential configuration of facts and circumstances in advance. That being said, the conceptual hinterlands of prophylactic legislation are really beside the point for present purposes, because excessively elaborate legal constraints on policing would cease to be practically effective long before the inherent, epistemological and linguistic limitations of legislation were reached.

In theory, the legislature ought to be able to reduce the scope for operational discretion by enacting increasingly comprehensive legal rules dictating how police investigators must behave, in an expanding range of scenarios, in ever finer detail. In reality, the notion that Parliament could ever micro-manage policing through legislation is a mirage. For the price of more detail is correspondingly greater complexity, and complexity breeds uncertainty, confusion, error, normative conflict and scope for reinterpretation of applicable legal rules. The extent of lawful operational discretion can certainly be reduced by enacting detailed legislation. But there comes a point at which greater detail and complexity paradoxically produce *more* operational discretion, not less. A police officer obliged to follow five short and clear directives might be more constrained by law than his or her counterpart who is subject to twenty-five multi-part directives containing somewhat obscure and potentially conflicting passages, which permit – indeed, practically invite – the officer to pick and choose between them. It is not possible to generalize about the precise location of this tipping-point, where greater legislative detail would only be counterproductive in terms of limiting policing discretion; it is no easy matter even to say where the tipping-point bites in particular cases. But appreciating that this fulcrum is conceptually ubiquitous should curb enthusiasm for ever more fine-grained regulation of policing. Practically minded investigators would, in any event, simply ignore legislation perceived as too complex to accommodate the operational imperatives of their daily working lives, and instead utilize simplified summaries or digests (officially approved or otherwise). Open-ended legal standards like 'reasonable suspicion', for all their admitted short-comings, consequently have more to recommend them than first meets the eye.

In summary, the inherent limitations of prophylactic legislation, the counterproductive tendencies of excessive complexity and the operational imperatives of criminal investigations (mediated by the variable cognitive capacities and motivation of individual police officers) combine to place tangible constraints on the scope for effective legal regulation of policing. A further, possibly decisive, missing ingredient in recent efforts to subject criminal investigations to the rule of law is the political will to enact robust legal standards; and to weather the storm of the inevitable backlash against them, even at the cost of electoral disadvantage and, conceivably, some reduction in police effectiveness and citizens' security. This history can be seen in microcosm in the fluctuating fortunes of PACE Code A, which at one time has included provisions expressly framed to constrain discriminatory exercises of stop-and-search powers,[178] only for anxieties around gang violence[179] and, most recently, terrorism[180] to generate spoiling provisions which effectively cede the ground that had been gained and even flirt with full-scale retreat.

Remedies for police illegality

Remedies are the alter-egos of rights. A right without a remedy for its breach exists in name only. A 'bare' right of this kind may exert moral force and be capable of guiding the conduct of the willing, but in the absence of legal redress for its violation is powerless to restrain either deliberate defiance or careless disregard. Indeed, English law has traditionally focused on providing remedies rather than specifying rights, in striking contrast to the rights-based jurisprudential traditions of continental Europe. The Human Rights Act 1998 may in retrospect prove to have shifted rights from the margins to the centre of English legal thinking, but for the time being the orthodox primacy of remedies – *ubi remedium, ibi jus* – retains its hold over the English common lawyer's legal imagination and continues to influence the conduct and outcomes of criminal litigation.

Inevitably, given their centrality to English criminal jurisprudence, remedies have already featured in the foregoing exposition. We have seen that if the police exceed their explicit legal authority, they risk incurring criminal liability (e.g. for assault in effecting an unlawful arrest) or civil liability to pay damages (e.g. for trespassing on private property after an unlawful entry), and possibly both together (excessive force in making an otherwise lawful arrest may constitute both a criminal assault and a tortious – civil wrong – trespass to the person). Conversely, police officers *qua* 'citizens in uniform' are generally speaking at liberty to do whatever it is lawful for ordinary citizens to do without incurring any legal liability.

So far as criminal prosecutions are concerned, it might be objected that police officers cannot truly be equated with ordinary citizens in the eyes of the law. Criminal justice professionals may be reluctant to co-operate in the conviction and punishment of 'one of their own', while juries and magistrates are generally impressed by police testimony and routinely convict on officers' evidence. There is an immediate and systematic credibility deficit when allegations of misconduct are levelled against police officers, often by people who are themselves repeat offenders with long and unflattering criminal records. Against this, England and Wales has benefited from an independent Crown Prosecution Service (CPS) since 1986,[181] and there are plenty of examples of police officers being prosecuted and convicted for illegality or corruption[182] (as well as contentious examples of criminal charges against police officers not being proceeded with (Webb and Harris 1993; Crickmer 2001; Cowan 2006), and equally controversial acquittals (Mullin 1993; Travis 1995)). Perhaps police defendants tend to get the benefit of the doubt more often than they should, always bearing in mind that police officers facing criminal trial are no less entitled to the presumption of innocence than any other person standing accused. But the CPS is keenly aware of its responsibilities, and the potential for public embarrassment, when criminal charges are brought against serving police officers (e.g. CPS 2005), and English juries and magistrates are perfectly well aware that police officers sometimes themselves break the law, or even become corrupted into a life of crime. It is possible to trust the police in general, while simultaneously seeking to expose, isolate and punish those who, as experience has demonstrated, abuse the trust reposed in their office.

Victims of tortious civil wrongs inflicted by serving police officers may sue for damages in the civil courts, whether or not a parallel criminal prosecution is launched. The chief constable, representing the local police authority, is constructively liable for civil wrongs perpetrated by any lower-ranking police officer acting in the course of his or her duty,[183] which means that claimants can attempt to recover damages from public funds and it is no bar to recovery that the individual officer at fault lacks any financial assets worth pursuing. Juries have sometimes made exorbitant awards of exemplary 'punitive' damages against chief constables running to hundreds of thousands of pounds, though such sums tend to be drastically reduced on appeal.[184] Only a very small minority of fortunate claimants achieves this level of success in civil actions against the police, however. Success in civil litigation generally requires disposable income, knowledge of one's legal rights and how to enforce them, a strong sense of injustice, confidence that 'the system' will deliver redress to the righteous, patience, tenacity and spare time; those most often the victims of civil wrongs inflicted by the police, however, are typically blessed with few if any of these advantages.

An alternative avenue for seeking redress for police wrongdoing is the official police complaints system. Originally placed on a statutory footing by the Police Act 1964, its latest incarnation is the Independent Police Complaints Commission (IPCC).[185] The key challenge for the IPCC is to generate public confidence and maintain credibility in the eyes of potential complainants. These objectives, most commentators agree (Reiner 2000: 184–7; Sanders and Young 2007: 612 ff.), eluded the IPCC's various predecessors, partly owing to a generalized suspicion that the police cannot be trusted to investigate allegations of wrongdoing brought against fellow officers with vigour and impartiality, and partly because only a very small percentage of complaints were ever upheld. In the last year of operation of the old system, for example, fewer than 4 per cent of the 25,376 complaints finalized to March 2004 were substantiated (Home Office 2004). Renewed efforts have consequently been made to emphasize the independence of the IPCC and the impartiality of its procedures (IPCC 2005). Whether recent reforms will make any tangible impact on complainants' limited chances of success, however, remains to be seen. It is entirely possible that the majority of complaints brought to the IPCC are ill-founded, and some are doubtless malicious (the police deal daily with individuals from whom most of us would wish to steer clear). Without claiming that past efforts have always been adequate or dismissing the capacity of well targeted reforms to improve outcomes, we should squarely face the fact that devising and operating a complaints system that is simultaneously efficient, effective, fair to all parties, consistent with the operational demands of policing and enjoys public confidence presents a formidable challenge.

We have seen that many police 'illegalities' involve breaches of the detailed Codes of Practice which place flesh on the bones of primary legislation. While some of these breaches may also constitute crimes and/or civil wrongs, most do not. PACE specifically provides that breaches of the PACE Codes of Practice shall not *ipso facto* give rise either to criminal or to civil liability, but that evidence of any such infringement is always admissible in a subsequent criminal trial if relevant to any issue in the proceedings.[186] In this way, breaches of the codes, if 'significant and substantial',[187] can be invoked by the defence in support of an application to the trial judge to exclude evidence obtained in consequence of the breach, or even, in particularly egregious cases, for having the whole proceedings stayed as an abuse of judicial process.

The evidential fruits of proactive policing are particularly vulnerable to exclusion whenever undercover operations have involved official illegality, or suspects' rights appear to have been undermined. Section 78 will bite on conduct not strictly necessary for maintaining an undercover identity if the officer's interaction with a suspect effectively amounts to a covert interrogation, for suspects are entitled to various procedural protections during a formal police interview, as we have seen, and undercover operations cannot be allowed to outflank this protective legal framework.[188] Likewise, repeated attempts to trick a suspect into making admissions by insinuating a police informant as his prison cellmate while detained on remand, and after the suspect has already indicated that he has nothing more to say, may undermine the substance of the suspect's 'right to silence'/privilege against self-incrimination, contravening Article 6 of the ECHR[189] and leaving any subsequently procured admissions vulnerable to being excluded under s. 78.[190] Undermining a suspect's right to custodial legal advice under PACE s. 58, for example, by lying to his solicitor about the existence of incriminating evidence, is also likely to incur judicial censure.[191] It is arguable that any breach of a suspect's most basic 'constitutional' rights (including Article 6 fair trial guarantees) should point decisively towards an exclusionary remedy (cf. Ashworth 2003; Mahoney 2003; Ormerod 2003), but English courts have yet to embrace this categorical approach as a matter of general principle.[192]

Any features of a police investigation bearing adversely on the reliability of prosecution evidence will contribute towards the argument for exclusion. Thus, failure to adhere to the numerous recording requirements imposed on investigating officers by the PACE Codes of Practice might not of itself constitute sufficiently serious impropriety to trigger s. 78, but will often do so if by extension the breach calls into question the authenticity or reliability of police evidence. This might occur where the suspect's alleged admissions were not recorded on tape, or where there is no permanent record of an undercover officer's interactions with a suspect to dispel any suspicions of official 'crime creation' by an agent provocateur. The same principle governs simple one-off deceptions as much as elaborate, extended undercover operations, such as the ill-fated attempt to ensnare Colin Stagg for the Wimbledon Common murder of Rachel Nickell through the charms of a female undercover officer, to whom Stagg was supposed to confess his darkest secrets in accordance with a 'psychological profile' of the murderer. The plan went sour, and the trial judge threw the case out of court (Roberts and Zuckerman 2004: 171–3).

Exclusion of evidence and, all the more so, judicial stays are controversial remedies for police illegality. The implication of excluding unlawfully obtained evidence is often that (in the celebrated phrase of Judge Cardozo) 'The criminal is to go free because the constable has blundered',[193] and this is not a consequence that can be accepted lightly by a system of justice whose over-riding objective is conviction of the guilty (see, further, Roberts 2006). Evidence may be deemed inadmissible for different reasons: where police illegality has potentially undermined the reliability of a confession, for example, its exclusion at trial can be said to promote truth-finding and guard against miscarriages of justice by shielding jurors from misleading evidence. But in other situations police illegality does not affect the reliability of incriminating material (as where an unlawful search unearths stolen goods, for example), and here, at least, guilty defendants are effectively awarded an unmerited forensic windfall by the exclusion of evidence tainted by police illegality. On one view, it is misguided to free criminals and, in effect, penalize victims of crime in response to police misconduct during the course of a criminal investigation. If the accused has been wronged at the hands of the police he or she should pursue an appropriate remedy in a separate legal action, without affecting the admissibility of relevant and reliable evidence of the accused's own guilt in the current proceedings (Wilkey 1992; Pizzi 1999: ch. 2). The contrary view is that police illegality, at least of the more serious sort, threatens the integrity of criminal proceedings and could only anticipate a morally flawed verdict if adduced and relied upon in spite of its tainted provenance. So sometimes the criminal must indeed go free, not primarily in order to censure the constable's 'blunder' (or deliberate law-breaking) or to reward the accused with a remedy he or she scarcely deserves, but to preserve the moral authority of criminal adjudication and the possibility of dispensing justice according to law (Mirfield 1997: ch. 2; Roberts and Zuckerman 2004: 150–60).

The traditional legal remedies of criminal prosecution, civil suit, official complaint and evidentiary exclusion have lately been augmented by novel human rights actions. Police misconduct in the course of a criminal investigation may constitute a violation of the European Convention on Human Rights if it involves unlawful killing (Article 2), torture or inhuman or degrading treatment (Article 3), unlawful deprivation of liberty (Article 5), lack of respect for private life (Article 8), or unjustified infringement of freedom of expression (Article 10) or public assembly (Article 11). In addition, as previously observed, evidence obtained through police impropriety may contravene the right to a fair trial guaranteed by Article 6. Since the UK conceded the right of petition to individual applicants in 1966, it has been possible to lodge a complaint directly with the European Court of Human Rights (ECtHR) in Strasbourg, once all domestic remedies have been exhausted without success. However, the limited jurisdiction of the ECtHR must be appreciated. The Strasbourg court has no power to allow an appeal against a criminal conviction or to alter a sentence imposed in an English criminal trial. The job of the ECtHR is to determine whether states parties to the convention, specifically for our purposes the UK, have discharged their obligations under international law to 'secure to everyone within their jurisdiction the rights and freedoms' guaranteed by the ECHR.[194] If an applicant succeeds in showing that representatives of the state, such as police officers conducting a criminal investigation, have breached one of his or her ECHR rights, the applicant may be awarded 'just satisfaction',[195] which can include monetary compensation but more often than not, in relation to the routine breaches of Articles 5 and 6 which occupy most of the court's time, constitutes merely a declaration that the applicant's right has been wrongfully infringed. The formality of this redress, coupled with the fact that it can take several years to secure a judgment from the ECtHR, considerably diminishes the practical utility of direct applications to Strasbourg as a frontline remedy for police illegality.

Since the Human Rights Act 1998 came fully into force on 2 October 2000, litigants in English legal proceedings can rely directly on those convention rights enumerated in Schedule 1 to the Act, which includes all the substantive and procedural guarantees liable to be breached in the course of criminal investigations. For example, the accused in a criminal trial in England and Wales can now argue that evidence procured through police impropriety should be excluded because it breaches his or her Article 6 right to a fair trial, instead or in addition to making a parallel argument for exclusion under s. 78 of PACE.[196] In addition, s. 8 of the HRA 1998 authorizes civil courts to award damages for breaches of convention rights, where this is deemed 'necessary to afford just satisfaction'[197] in accordance with the principles developed by the ECtHR.[198] It is unlikely that English courts will be any more generous towards complainants alleging police impropriety, or indeed any more accessible to them, than the ECtHR itself has been in this regard. English courts interpreting convention rights are required to 'take into account' pertinent Strasbourg jurisprudence.[199] None the less, it remains open to an applicant, once all domestic remedies have been exhausted, to argue before the ECtHR that the English courts have misinterpreted the convention and consequently failed to give full effect to the applicant's rights, in granting an appropriate remedy or in any other respect. By this circuitous route, a person convicted of a criminal offence in England and Wales partly in consequence of investigative impropriety might ultimately succeed in having his or her conviction quashed, by winning on a point of interpretation before the Strasbourg court and then launching a fresh appeal to the Court of Appeal (Criminal Division) in order to persuade the English judges to adopt the ECtHR's interpretational ruling. Only an English court has the jurisdiction to quash a guilty verdict pronounced by an English jury, but it may conceivably be prompted to do so by the jurisprudence of the ECtHR. The Strasbourg court thus continues to serve as the ultimate guardian of convention rights, even in the era of the Human Rights Act.

Finally, it is worth mentioning that redress for police impropriety can also be pursued in a more indirect fashion by seeking to influence policy formation and operational priorities. Some measure of citizen involvement in shaping local policing policy promotes responsive law enforcement and democratic accountability, which in turn boost public confidence and encourage a successful partnership approach to policing. If citizens of a democracy, who fund policing through taxation and 'pay' for its presence – and absences – in their daily lives, do not approve of the way in which the policing power is being exercised, mechanisms should be in place to enable them to express their dissatisfaction and precipitate official reflection and change. Participation in a general election every four or five years patently affords insufficient opportunity to engage meaningfully with detailed issues of policing. Continuous involvement in the micro-politics of local policing is the ideal, and there are various institutional models and procedural devices for putting the ideal into practice. 'Civilian review boards' (Goldsmith and Lewis 2000) and rotating 'citizen advocates' (Bibas 2006) have been proposed by commentators to undertake a range of functions, from the supervision of police patrols to combat racial bias in stop-and-search (Hecker 1997), to reviewing indictments and charging decisions to ensure that the interests of justice are not being subordinated to organizational preferences for efficient case management, to involvement in allocating policing resources and agenda setting to promote responsiveness to local concerns. Variations on these models have been implemented in many legal jurisdictions, especially in North America. Citizen involvement in policing policy-making is more modest and indirect in England and Wales, principally effected through local councillor membership of police authorities, the governing bodies of county forces. The constitution and function of police authorities are also mandated by law,[200] but a description of the complex legislative framework of police governance is beyond the scope of this chapter (see Reiner 2002; Jones 2003).

Concluding remarks: the scientific horizon

Like politics in general (with which it shares an etymological root; Reiner 2000: 7), policing is the art of the possible in the service of an ideal – specifically in relation to criminal investigations, an ideal of justice. The parameters of investigative powers and strategies are ultimately fixed by the scientific horizon of criminal detection – 'forensic science' in its original, broad sense, indicating science applied to the administration of justice. One day it might be technologically possible to dispense with anything resembling our current practices of 'criminal investigation', and with them most of the law governing stop-and-search, arrest, pre-charge detention, interrogation, identification procedures and the rest. But for as long as infallible truth machines, omniscient surveillance, precognition of future events and similar marvels remain the stuff of science fiction (and political dystopias), criminal investigations and prosecutions incorporate and adapt what they can from the best available repertoire of contemporary scientific fact.

The development of fingerprinting in the early years of the twentieth century revolutionized the science of criminal detention (Moenssens et al. 1995: ch. 8). Roughly a century later, DNA technology has inaugurated a second, still more consequential scientific revolution in criminal investigations in our own time. Further technological innovations, such as the use of iris-recognition software to confirm identity, are said to be close at hand, although one must sometimes be wary of excessive hype and dubious predictions. Genuine revolutions in the science of criminal detection are infrequent, but DNA profiling – already now extended beyond its original application to homicides, rapes and serious assaults to become routine in the investigation of 'volume' crimes like burglaries and thefts from vehicles (Forensic Science

Service 2004: 23) – fully merits that accolade. Meanwhile, personal computers, video-recordings (including CCTV images), mobile telephones, email and the Internet have cumulatively wrought profound effects, both on patterns of criminal offending and on the work of investigating and prosecuting crime and bringing offenders to justice.

The law is an inherently conservative normative system, and consequently tends to lag behind the cutting edge of science. Sometimes this means that the law can be outflanked. The system of authorizing searches of private property by judicial warrant, for example, was conceived long before anybody had ever imagined – let alone developed – technologies to 'see' through solid objects by ultrasound, detect the presence of life-forms by infrared imaging or conduct intrusive surveillance from high-resolution spy-satellites in the sky. Equipped with these and other similar surveillance devices, investigators are no longer beholden to judges through the warrant process every time an intrusive search of private residential premises is contemplated; and new legal controls must be devised and implemented, as to some extent they have been in England and Wales,[201] if unbridled technology is felt to pose unacceptable threats to personal privacy and the democratic accountability of investigative policing. At other times new legislation is required to facilitate technological advances in criminal investigations, for example in establishing – and then expanding – the National DNA Database (NDNAD) (Williams et al. 2004; House of Commons Science and Technology Committee 2005: Part 4) by authorizing police officers to extract genetic material (usually a mouth swab or hair root) from suspects and to retain their DNA profiles, which could not have been achieved in reliance on existing statutory or residual common law powers of search and seizure.[202] Speculative searching of the NDNAD to identify unknown perpetrators from crime-stain samples presents one of the greatest investigative opportunities, and also one of the most serious challenges to established legal doctrine and practice, of the immediate future.

Whether running to catch up with technology or paving the way for its forensic reception, the essential questions for law and its reform are always the same: do investigative powers strike an appropriate balance between liberty, privacy and security, for individuals and their families and society at large? Is this balance achieved without unfair discrimination on prohibited grounds of race, religion, sex, age, etc.? Does the framework of law ensure democratic accountability of policing and criminal investigations, in answer to Juvenal's timeless conundrum, *Quis custodiet ipsos custodes*? And is the domestic legal framework in compliance with applicable standards of international human rights law, a question of increasing salience in a globalizing legal environment? Practical responses to these questions are encapsulated in the law of stop-and-search, covert surveillance, arrest, search and seizure, detention, custodial interrogation and formal identification procedures surveyed in this chapter, within the broader framework of jurisprudential reasoning and principle and mediated by the processes of the 'law in action' which have also been considered.

Looking to the immediate future, there are grounds for cautious optimism in the potential of the Human Rights Act 1998 to supplement the common law's traditionally laissez-faire attitude towards the ill-defined powers of 'citizens in uniform' with a demand for an explicit legal basis for any investigative measure potentially infringing individuals' fundamental rights. Certain measures – such as relying on evidence probably procured by torture abroad[203] – may even be entirely off-limits. But against this hope must be set the observable fact that the law has never presented a serious obstacle to expanding police powers in order to capitalize on the investigative potential of new technologies; indeed, judges have sometimes seemed to go out of their way to accommodate policy-makers' reflex expansionism.[204] In a time of phoney wars, on crime, on drugs, and – above all – on terror, the prospect looms large that the insatiable pursuit of security through criminal investigations (as one facet of law-and-order policing in general) will exact an exorbitant price on liberty, privacy, human rights and democratic accountability, and that the cost will be borne disproportionately by those in society least able, and in justice least fairly expected, to bear it.

Selected further reading

Reiner, R. (2000) *The Politics of the Police* (3rd edn). Oxford: Oxford University Press. This is the best general introduction to policing. It is both authoritative and eminently readable, and includes chapters on 'cop culture', the sociological investigation of policing practice and the relationship between police powers and accountability.

Reiner, R. (1997) 'Policing and the police', in M. Maguire *et al.* (eds) *The Oxford Handbook of Criminology* (2nd edn). Oxford: Oxford University Press. Reiner's contribution to the second edition of the *Oxford Handbook of Criminology* remains an excellent introductory overview of policing.

Bowling, B. and Foster, J. (2002) 'Policing and the police', in M. Maguire *et al.* (eds) *The Oxford Handbook of Criminology* (3rd edn). Oxford: Oxford University Press; Sanders, A. and Young, R. (2002) 'From suspect to trial', in M. Maguire *et al.* (eds) *The Oxford Handbook of Criminology* (3rd edn). Oxford: Oxford University Press. Both these chapters, in the third edition of *The Oxford Handbook of Criminology*, are also valuable starting points for further study.

Dixon, D. (1997) *Law in Policing: Legal Regulation and Police Practices*. Oxford: Oxford University Press. This book is the most illuminating systematic treatment of the relationship between law and policing.

Zander, M. (2006) *The Police and Criminal Evidence Act 1984* (5th edn). London: Sweet & Maxwell. The standard reference work on PACE law.

Ashworth, A. and Redmayne, M. (2005) *The Criminal Process* (3rd edn). Oxford: Oxford University Press; Sanders, A. and Young, R. (2007) *Criminal Justice* (Oxford: 3rd edn). Oxford University Press. These texts are the market leaders for more general treatments, placing policing within the broader context of criminal process. Ashworth and Redmayne is the more theoretically astute work, with a strong human rights dimension. Two chapters are specifically devoted to questioning suspects and gathering evidence. On several topics, however, richer sociological detail and more extended legal analysis can be found in Sanders and Young, which contains over 200 pages on stop-and-search, arrest, pre-charge detention and police questioning.

Notes

1   HRA 1998, s. 2.
2   Free to access online via the court's website (www.echr.coe.int/echr).
3   HRA 1998, s. 3.
4   HRA 1998, s. 4.
5   ECHR, Art. 1.
6   Investigations may sometimes be undertaken for ulterior motives or even in bad faith. Ulterior motives are not necessarily to be deprecated (e.g. investigators may intend to disrupt and deter further criminal activity by organized crime groups without any realistic prospect of ever launching a criminal prosecution against named individuals). But I take these to be marginal cases for present purposes.
7   *Malone* v. *Metropolitan Police Commissioner* [1979] Ch 344, Ch D, 366–7.
8   See the 'Arrest', below.
9   *Beckford* v. *R* (1987) 85 Cr App R 378, PC; *R* v. *Pagett* (1983) 76 Cr App R 279, CA; Criminal Law Act 1967, s. 3.
10   Code of Practice issued pursuant to Part II of the Criminal Procedure and Investigations Act 1996, para. 3.4.
11   For example, *Khan* v. *UK* (2001) 31 EHRR 45.
12   *Fox* v. *Chief Constable of Gwent* [1986] 1 AC 281, HL; *R* v. *Leatham* (1861) 8 Cox CC 498: but cf *Kuruma* v. *R* [1955] AC 197, PC.
13   *DPP* v. *Ping Lin* [1976] AC 574, HL; *Ibrahim* v. *R* [1914] AC 599, PC.
14   *R* v. *Sang* [1980] AC 402, HL.
15   For example, *R* v. *Mason* [2002] 2 Cr App R 628, CA, *per* Lord Woolf CJ.
16   *R* v. *Horseferry Road Magistrates' Court, ex p. Bennett* [1994] 1 AC 42, HL.
17   *Teixeira de Castro* v. *Portugal* (1998) 28 EHRR 101.
18   *R* v. *Latif; R* v. *Shahzad* [1996] 1 WLR 104, HL.
19   *R* v. *Looseley; Attorney-General's Reference (No 3 of 2000)* [2001] 1 WLR 2060, [2001] UKHL 53.
20   *R* v. *Smurthwaite; R* v. *Gill* (1994) 98 Cr App R 437, CA.
21   *R* v. *Christou and Wright* (1992) 95 Cr App R 264, CA, 269.
22   *R* v. *Bailey and Smith* (1993) 97 Cr App R 365, CA.
23   *R* v. *Christou and Wright* (1992) 95 Cr App R 264, CA.
24   *DPP* v. *Marshall* [1988] 3 All ER 683, DC; *Ealing LBC* v. *Woolworths plc* [1995] Crim LR 58.
25   *Nottingham City Council* v. *Amin* [2000] 1 Cr App R 426, DC.
26   *R* v. *Latif; R* v. *Shahzad* [1996] 1 WLR 104, HL.
27   *R* v. *Looseley; Attorney-General's Reference (No 3 of 2000)* [2001] 1 WLR 2060.
28   The House of Lords endorsed the trial judge's decision to stay the prosecution in *Attorney-General's Reference (No 3 of 2000)*, where undercover officers who had previously supplied contraband to the accused had subsequently induced him to procure heroin for them on the basis of 'a favour for a favour'.
29   *Khan* v. *UK* (2001) 31 EHRR 45; *Chalkley* v. *UK* (2003) 37 EHRR 30; *Halford* v. *UK* (1997) 24 EHRR 523; *Malone* v. *UK* (1985) 7 EHRR 14.
30   RIPA 2000, s. 3.
31   Section 7.
32   Section 8.
33   Section 5.
34   *Interception of Communications Code of Practice*, brought into force by SI 1693/2002 (available online at www.security.homeoffice.gov.uk/surveillance/ripa-updates/).

35   RIPA 2000, ss. 65–70.
36   Section 17. There are limited exceptions facilitating proof of crimes constituted by illegal interference with telecommunications and associated offences against the administration of justice or breaches of official secrets (s. 18).
37   Most recently in the form of a Private Member's Bill on Interception of Communications (Admissibility of Evidence), introduced into the House of Lords by Lord Lloyd of Berwick in the autumn of 2005, and still before Parliament at the time of writing; see HL Debs, 18 November 2005, cols 1301–1336.
38   If covert surveillance involves trespass or interference with property or wireless telegraphy ('bugging and burgling' operations), further statutory restrictions are triggered under the Police Act 1997 or the Intelligence Services Act 1994 (depending on the officials concerned).
39   *Covert Surveillance Code of Practice*, brought into force by SI 1933/2002; *Covert Human Intelligence Sources Code of Practice*, brought into force by SI 1932/2002 (both available online at www.security.homeoffice.gov.uk/surveillance/ripa-updates/).
40   RIPA 2000, s. 26(2).
41   Section 26(3).
42   Sections 28 and 32, and *Covert Surveillance Code of Practice*, Parts 4 and 5.
43   See n. 29 above.
44   See 'Remedies for police illegality below'.
45   PACE Code A, *Code of Practice for the Exercise by Police Officers of Statutory Powers of Stop and Search* (2005 edn); see http://police.homeoffice.gov.uk/operational-policing/powers-pace-codes/.
46   Home Office Circular 56/2005.
47   PACE Code A, paras. 1.1–1.2.
48   PACE 1984, ss. 2–3 and Code A, Parts 3 and 4.
49   PACE Code A, para. 1.3.
50   Misuse of Drugs Act 1971, s. 23(2).
51   Wildlife and Countryside Act 1981, s. 19; Badgers Act 1992, s. 11; Deer Act 1991, s.12; Poaching Prevention Act 1862.
52   Terrorism Act 2000, ss. 42–45.
53   Aviation Security Act 1982, s. 27(1); Aviation and Maritime Security Act 1990, ss. 2 and 22.
54   CJPOA 1994, subss. 60(10) and (10A).
55   Contrary to s. 139 of the Criminal Justice Act 1988.
56   CJPOA 1994, s. 60(3).
57   PACE 1984, s. 1(6); CJPOA 1994, s. 60(6); PACE Code of Practice B, Part 7.
58   TA 2000, s. 46(2).
59   TA 2000, s. 46(7).
60   Mental Health Act 1983, ss. 135 and 136; Children and Young Persons Act 1969, s. 32.
61   *Holgate-Mohammed* v. *Duke* [1984] AC 437, HL.
62   Magistrates Court Act 1980, s. 13; Supreme Court Act 1981, s. 80(2).
63   Criminal Procedure (Attendance of Witnesses) Act 1965, s. 4; Magistrates Court Act 1980, s. 97.
64   SOC&PA 2005, s. 110.
65   Section 110(1), inserting PACE 1984, s. 24(3).
66   PACE 1984, s. 24(4).
67   PACE Code G, *Code of Practice for the Statutory Power of Arrest by Police Officers* (2005 edn).

68 PACE Code G, paras. 1.2–1.3.
69 PACE 1984, s. 24A(3)(b).
70 Subsection 24A(3)(a) and (4).
71 PACE 1984, s. 28; PACE Code G, para. 3.3 and n. 3; *Edwards* v. *DPP* (1993) 97 Cr App R 301, DC.
72 *R* v. *Mason* [2002] 2 Cr App R 628, CA; *Allan* v. *United Kingdom* (2003) 36 EHRR 12.
73 *R* v. *Chalkley and Jeffries* [1998] QB 848, CA.
74 *R* v. *Mason* [2002] 2 Cr App R 628, CA.
75 The debate has more recently been extended to random passenger searching at airports and other transit points thought to be vulnerable to terrorist attack, which critics say is disproportionately and unfairly targeted on Muslims and Asians. Airport security staff and others are accused of creating the 'crime' of 'flying while brown' (Shora, 2002).
76 *Whren* v. *US* 517 U.S. 806, 116 S Ct 1769 (1996).
77 PACE 1984, s. 32(2).
78 Section 32(4).
79 Sections 18 and 32(2)(b).
80 Subsections 18(3) and 32(3).
81 Subsections 18(2) and 19(3)–(4); *Malone* v. *Metropolitan Police Commissioner* [1980] QB 49, CA.
82 Powers of Criminal Courts (Sentencing) Act 2000, s. 148.
83 PACE 1984, ss. 36–39; see 'Detention and custodial interrogation', below.
84 Subsections 54(6) and 55(2).
85 PACE Code C, *Code of Practice for the Detention, Treatment and Questioning of Persons by Police Officers* (2005 edn), Annex A, B.9.
86 PACE 1984, s. 54(9) and PACE Code C, Annex A, B.11(a).
87 Code C, Annex A, 10.
88 PACE 1984, subss. 55(4), (5) and (8).
89 Code C, Annex A, 1.
90 PACE 1984, subss. 54(3)–(4) and PACE Code C, para. 4.2.
91 Section 55(1)(b).
92 Section 55(12)(b).
93 Modus operandi – a particular mode of offending or 'criminal signature', such as a distinctive way of gaining entry to a property, an innovative method of fraud or an unusual means of luring victims.
94 National Police Records (Recordable Offences) Regulations 2000, SI 2000/1139, covering virtually all 'traditional' criminal offences, excluding minor road traffic infractions.
95 PACE 1984, s. 61(3) and Code D, para. 4.3. Any person may consent to having his or her fingerprints taken by the police under the PACE regime. Further investigative powers to take fingerprints without consent pertain to immigration matters under the Immigration Act 1971 and the Immigration and Asylum Act 1999; see PACE Code D, paras. 4.10–4.15.
96 PACE 1984, subss. 61(4) and (6).
97 Sections 62–63 and PACE Code D, Part 6.
98 Subsections 62(1) and (1A), and PACE Code D, paras. 6.2–6.4.
99 Section 65(1).
100 Section 62(10).
101 Section 63 and PACE Code D, paras. 6.5–6.9.
102 Section 63A(2), as inserted by CJPOA 1994, s. 56.
103 PACE 1984, s. 54A and Code D, paras. 5.1–5.11.

104   Section 64, as amended by CJ&PA 2001, s. 82.

105   PACE 1984, s. 63A(1).

106   Or other systematically collected information, such as footwear impressions; see PACE 1984, s. 61A and Code D, paras. 4.16–4.21.

107   *R (S)* v. *Chief Constable of South Yorkshire Police* [2004] 1 WLR 2196, [2004] UKHL 39, HL.

108   PACE 1984, ss. 61(7A), 61A(5), 62(7A) and 63(8B), and Code of Practice D, Note for Guidance 6E and Annex F.

109   *Code of Practice for Searches of Premises by Police Officers and the Seizure of Property Found by Police Officers on Persons or Premises* (2005 edn).

110   For example, TA 2000, sch. 5; Misuse of Drugs Act 1971, s. 23; Theft Act 1968, s. 26. Code B also governs searches without a warrant pursuant to various statutory authorizations – e.g. Transport and Works Act 1992, s. 30(4); Road Traffic Act 1988, s. 6E(1); Criminal Justice Act 1988, s. 139B; Explosives Act 1875, s. 73(b).

111   PACE 1984, s. 23.

112   Code B, para. 1.3.

113   PACE 1984, s. 8(3).

114   Section 15(6).

115   Section 15(5).

116   PACE 1984, subss. 8(1C) and (1D) inserted by SOC&PA 2005, and Code B, paras. 3.6(db) and 6.3A.

117   Code B, para.6.10, adding that '[r]easonable force may be used only when necessary and proportionate because the co-operation of the occupier cannot be obtained or is insufficient for the purpose'.

118   Code B, para. 6.7.

119   PACE 1984, subss. 16(5)–(7).

120   Subsection 16(9)–(12).

121   Cf. *R (Bright)* v. *Central Criminal Court* [2001] 1 WLR 662, DC, at [90].

122   Cf. Code B, Note for Guidance 6A: 'Whether compensation is appropriate depends on the circumstances in each case. Compensation for damage caused when effecting entry is unlikely to be appropriate if the search was lawful, and the force used can be shown to be reasonable, proportionate and necessary to effect entry.'

123   Code B, paras. 2.3, 6.7–6.8 and Part 8.

124   PACE 1984, ss. 8(1)(d) and 10.

125   Sections 18(1) and 19(6).

126   Subsections 11–13.

127   Sections 14(1)–(2).

128   PACE 1984, s. 9 and sch. 1.

129   *R (Bright)* v. *Central Criminal Court* [2001] 1 WLR 662, DC.

130   For example, Insurance Companies Act 1982, ss. 43A and 44 (investigations into insurance companies); Companies Act 1985, ss. 434 and 447 (production of company documents to inspectors and Secretary of State); Insolvency Act 1986, s. 433; Company Directors Disqualification Act 1986, s. 20; Building Societies Act 1986, s. 57; Financial Services Act 1986, ss. 105 and 177; Banking Act 1987, ss. 39, 41, and 42; Criminal Justice Act 1987, s. 2.

131   *Brown (Margaret)* v. *Stott* [2003] 1 AC 681, PC: cf. *Saunders* v. *UK* (1996) 23 EHRR 313.

132   *Code of Practice for the Detention, Treatment and Questioning of Persons by Police Officers* (2005 edn).

133   PACE 1984, ss. 41(1) and 42(1)

134 Sections 43–44. The overall time limit is set by s. 44(3).

135 Section 40 and Code C, Part 15.

136 Section 39(1) and Code C, para. 1.1A and Part 2.

137 TA 2000, sch. 8, para. 36, as amended by the Terrorism Act 2000, sch. 8, para 36, as amended by the Terrorism Act 2006, s. 23(2), with effect from 25 July 2006. The maximum period of detention was originally set as seven days.

138 Taking account of automatic remission, 90 days' detention equates to a sentence on conviction of six months' imprisonment. In 2004, 44.8 per cent of convicted burglars were sentenced to immediate custody. The average length of sentence imposed on burglars convicted in magistrates' courts was 4.5 months (Home Office 2005b: Tables 2.13 and 2.16).

139 The government's 90-day proposal was defeated by 322 votes to 291; HC Debs vol. 439, cols 378–386 (9 November 2005).

140 For example, R v. McIlkenny et al. (1991) 93 Cr App R 287, CA; Abid Hussain v. R [2005] EWCA Crim 31.

141 PACE 1984, s. 56 and Code C, Part 5.

142 Section 58.

143 See n. 136, above.

144 PACE 1984, ss. 57 and 77, and Code C, paras. 3.12–3.20, 6.5A, 11.15–11.20, and Annex E.

145 PACE Code E, Code of Practice on Audio Recording Interviews with Suspects (2005 edn). With limited exceptions, it is mandatory to record interviews with suspects in relation to indictable offences triable in the Crown Court, while interviews relating to summary offences may be recorded at investigators' discretion; paras. 3.1 and 3.3 and Note for Guidance 3A. Interviews with terrorist suspects detained pursuant to s. 41 or sch. 7 of the TA 2000 are governed by a separate Code of Practice.

146 See PACE Code F, Code of Practice on Visual Recording with Sound of Interviews with Suspects (2005 edn), extending Code E mutatis mutandis to video-recording.

147 R v. Samuel [1988] QB 615, CA.

148 Ibid. 630. Cf. PACE Code C, Annex B.

149 R v. Alladice (1988) 87 Cr App R 380, CA.

150 Ibid. 386.

151 CJPOA 1994, s. 34.

152 See, e.g., R v. Webber [2004] 1 Cr App R 40, HL; R v. Petkar and Farquhar [2004] 1 Cr App R 22, CA; and the Judicial Studies Board's Specimen Directions, Part IV 'Defendant's failures' (available online at http://www.jsboard.co.uk/criminal_law/cbb/).

153 R v. Beckles [2005] 1 Cr App R 23, CA; R v. Howell [2005] 1 Cr App R 1, CA.

154 Code of Practice for the Identification of Persons by Police Officers (2005 edn).

155 Code D, para. 3.11.

156 Code D, paras. 3.14, 3.16.

157 Code D, para. 3.3 and Annex E.

158 Once a video image of the suspect has been obtained, his or her co-operation is no longer required to conduct a video parade including his or her image. Video images may be retained for use in future criminal investigations, pursuant to PACE 1984, s. 64A, if taken at the police station or while the suspect was under arrest; see Code D, paras. 3.30–3.32, 5.12–5.15.

159 Code D, Annex C.2.

160 Code D, para. 3.23 and Annex D.

161 So-called 'dock identifications', where the witness identifies the accused in court, have long been disfavoured at common law; *R v. Cartwright* (1914) 10 Cr App R 219, CCA.

162 Code D, paras. 3.15, 3.17–3.18. As further disincentives to non-cooperation, suspects are informed that their refusal to participate in a contemplated identification procedure, and any attempt to frustrate it (e.g. by deliberately altering their appearance), may be given in evidence at trial; para. 3.17(v) and (ix).

163 If the suspect makes him or herself 'unavailable', a video parade may employ '[a]ny suitable moving or still images... and these may be obtained covertly if necessary' (Code D, para. 3.21). Furthermore, 'a photograph [i.e. any still or moving visual image; para. 2.16] may be obtained without the person's consent by making a copy of an image of them taken at any time on a camera system installed anywhere in the police station' (para. 5.15). This is all subject to para. 3.22's over-riding proviso that 'Any covert activity should be strictly limited to that necessary to test the ability of the witness to identify the suspect'.

164 *R v. Turnbull* [1977] QB 224, CA.

165 *R v. Forbes* [2001] 1 Cr App R 430, HL.

166 *Ibid.* [33].

167 PACE Code A, para. 1.5, states firmly that: 'An officer must not search a person, even with his or her consent, where no power to search is applicable. Even where a person is prepared to submit to a search voluntarily, the person must not be searched unless the necessary legal power exists.' But if the suspect is compliant, and lawful search powers are relatively open-ended, who will ever be in a position to complain?

168 *Rice v. Connolly* [1966] 2 QB 414, DC; *R v. Director of Serious Fraud Office, ex p. Smith* [1993] AC 1, HL, 30–1.

169 For example, failure to provide one's name and address may precipitate arrest and detention: cf. PACE Code G, paras. 2.9 and 3.7.

170 For example, PACE Code B, paras. 5.2 and 6.12A; Code C, paras. 3.21, 6.1, 10.1–10.4, 10.10, 11.2, 12.5, 16.2; Code D, paras. 4.7, 4.19, 5.16 and 6.8; Code G, paras. 3.1–3.5.

171 For example, PACE Code A, paras. 4.2 and 4.12; Code B, paras. 5.1, 6.7–6.8 and 7.12–7.13; Code C, paras. 3.4, 11.11–11.14, 16.3 and Annex D.

172 PACE Code C, para. 6.3 and Guidance Note 6H.

173 *R v. Paris, Miller and Abdullahi* (1993) 97 Cr App R 99, CA.

174 *Ibid.* 103.

175 By a rough estimate, less than 1 per cent of serving police officers in England and Wales is potentially corrupt (Miller 2003). This is reassuringly low by international standards; see, e.g., Beck and Lee (2002).

176 Within six hours of detention in the first instance, and subsequently at nine-hour intervals; PACE 1984, s. 37(1)–(3).

177 Section 40(3) and Code C, Part 15.

178 For example, Code A (1991 edn), para. 1.7.

179 Code A (1997 edn), para. 1.7AA and Note for Guidance 1H.

180 TA 2000, s. 44; cf. Code A (2005 edn), para. 2.2.

181 Pursuant to the Prosecution of Offences Act 1985.

182 For example, *R v. Kassim* [2006] 1 Cr App R (S) 4, CA; *R v. Hesse* [2004] 2 Cr App R (S) 42, CA; *R v. Roberts* [1999] 1 Cr App R (S) 381, CA; *R v. Witchelo* (1992) 13 Cr App R (S) 371, CA.

183 Police Act 1996, s. 88.

184 *Thomson* v. *Metropolitan Police Commissioner; Hsu* v. *Metropolitan Police Commissioner* [1998] QB 498, CA (limiting exemplary damages to a maximum award of £50,000).
185 Police Reform Act 2002. See www.ipcc.gov.uk/.
186 PACE 1984, subss. 67(10) and (11).
187 *R* v. *Keenan* [1990] 2 QB 54, CA, 69–70.
188 *R* v. *Christou and Wright* (1992) 95 Cr App R 264, CA; cf. *R* v. *Bryce* (1992) 95 Cr App R 320, CA.
189 *Condron* v. *UK* (2001) 31 EHRR 1; *Saunders* v. *UK* (1996) 23 EHRR 313, ECtHR.
190 *Allan* v. *United Kingdom* (2003) 36 EHRR 143, ECtHR.
191 *R* v. *Mason* [1988] 1 WLR 139, CA.
192 Cf. *Mohammed* v. *State* [1999] 2 AC 111, PC.
193 *People* v. *Defore* 242 NY 13 (1926) at 21, 24–5.
194 ECHR, Article 1.
195 ECHR, Article 41.
196 *R.* v. *Looseley; Attorney General's Reference (No 3 of 2000)* [2001] UKHL 53; [2001] 1 WLR 2060.
197 Section 8(3).
198 Section 8(4).
199 Section 2(1).
200 Police Act 1996; Police Reform Act 2002.
201 Regulation of Investigatory Powers Act 2000.
202 PACE 1984, ss. 63 and 64, as successively amended by the Criminal Justice and Public Order Act 1994, the Criminal Justice and Police Act 2001 and the Criminal Justice Act 2003.
203 *A* v. *Secretary of State for the Home Department* [2005] UKHL 71.
204 Cf. *Attorney General's Reference (No 3 of 1999)* [2001] 2 AC 91, HL.

References

Alschuler, A.W. (2002) 'Racial profiling and the constitution', *University of Chicago Legal Forum*, 163.
Ashworth, A. (1998) 'Should the police be allowed to use deceptive practices?', *Law Quarterly Review*, 114: 108.
Ashworth, A. (2000) 'Is the criminal law a lost cause?', *Law Quarterly Review*, 116: 225.
Ashworth, A. (2003) 'Exploring the integrity principle in evidence and procedure,' in P. Mirfield and R. Smith (eds) *Essays for Colin Tapper*. Oxford: Oxford University Press.
Ashworth, A. and Redmayne, M. (2005) *The Criminal Process* (3rd edn). Oxford: Oxford University Press.
Baldwin, J. (1992) 'Legal advice in the police station', *New Law Journal*, 18 December: 1762.
Baldwin, J. (1993a) 'Police interview techniques: establishing truth or proof?', *British Journal of Criminology*, 33: 325.
Baldwin, J. (1993b) 'Legal advice at the police station', *Criminal Law Review*, 371.
Baldwin, J. and Moloney, T. (1992) *Supervision of Police Investigations in Serious Cases. RCCJ Research Study* 4. London: HMSO.
Banks, C. (2004) *Criminal Justice Ethics: Theory and Practice*. Thousand Oaks, CA: Sage.

Barnes, M.S. (1993) 'One experience of video recorded interviews', *Criminal Law Review*, 444.

Beck, A. and Lee, R. (2002) 'Attitudes to corruption amongst Russian police officers and trainees', *Crime, Law and Social Change*, 38: 357.

Beck, U. (2000) *What Is Globalization?* Oxford: Polity Press.

Bibas, S. (2006) 'Transparency and participation in criminal procedure', *New York University Law Review*, 81: 911.

Birch, D. (1994) 'Excluding evidence from entrapment: what is a fair cop?', *Current Legal Problems*, 73.

Birch, D. (1999) 'Suffering in silence: a cost-benefit analysis of Section 34 of the Criminal Justice and Public Order Act 1994', *Criminal Law Review*, 769.

Bottomley, K., Coleman, C., Dixon, D., Gill, M. and Wall, D. (1991) 'The detention of suspects in police custody: the impact of the Police and Criminal Evidence Act 1984', *British Journal of Criminology*, 31: 347.

Bowling, B. and Phillips, C. (2002) *Racism, Crime and Justice.* Harlow: Longman.

Bridges, L. (1999) 'The Lawrence Inquiry – incompetence, corruption, and institutional racism', *Journal of Law and Society*, 26: 298.

Bridges, L. (2002) 'The right to representation and legal aid', in M. McConville and G. Wilson (eds) *The Handbook of the Criminal Justice Process.* Oxford: Oxford University Press.

Bridges, L. and Hodgson, J. (1995) 'Improving custodial legal advice', *Criminal Law Review*, 101.

Brown, D. (1997) *PACE Ten Years On: A Review of the Research. Home Office Research Study* 155. London: HMSO.

Brown, R. and Cannings, A. (2004) *Approaches to Intelligence-led Vehicle Crime Reduction. Home Office Development and Practice Report* 25 (available online at www.homeoffice. gov.uk/rds).

Brownlie, I. (2003) *Principles of Public International Law* (7th edn). Oxford: Oxford University Press.

Bucke, T., Street, R. and Brown, D. (2000) *The Right of Silence: The Impact of the Criminal Justice and Public Order Act 1994. Home Office Research Study* 199. London: Home Office.

Cape, E. (1997) 'Sidelining defence lawyers: police station advice after *Condron*', *International Journal of Evidence and Proof*, 1: 386.

Cape, E. (2002) 'Assisting and advising defendants before trial,' in M. McConville and G. Wilson (eds) *The Handbook of the Criminal Justice Process.* Oxford: Oxford University Press.

Cape, E. (2004) 'The rise (and fall?) of a criminal defence profession', *Criminal Law Review*, 401.

Choo, A.L-T. and Jennings, A. (2003) 'Silence on legal advice revisited: R v. *Howell*', *International Journal of Evidence and Proof*, 7: 185.

Choo, A.L-T. and Nash, S. (2003) 'Evidence law in England and Wales: the impact of the Human Rights Act 1998', *International Journal of Evidence and Proof*, 7: 31.

Choongh, S. (1998) 'Policing the dross: a social disciplinary model of policing', *British Journal of Criminology*, 38: 623.

Cohen, G. (1999) 'Human memory in the real world', in A. Heaton-Armstrong *et al.* (eds) *Analysing Witness Testimony.* London: Blackstone.

Confait Inquiry (1977) *Report of an Inquiry by the Hon Sir Henry Fisher into the Circumstances Leading to the Trial of Three Persons on Charges Arising out of the Death of Maxwell Confait and the Fire at 27 Doggett Road, London SE6.* London: HMSO.

Cowan, R. (2006) 'Met officers in "Table Leg" shooting will not face action', *Guardian*, 10 February.

Crickmer, G. (2001) 'As 999 chase deaths continue to soar, why has no police driver faced prosecution?', *Sunday Express*, 11 November.

Criminal Justice System (CJS) (2004) *Race and the Criminal Justice System: An Overview to the Complete Statistics, 2002–2003* (available online at www.homeoffice.gov.uk/rds/).

Crown Prosecution Service (2005) *Deaths in Custody – the Role of the Crown Prosecution Service* (available online at: www.cps.gov.uk/publications).

de Lint, W. (1999) 'A post-modern turn in policing: policing as pastiche?', *International Journal of the Sociology of Law*, 27: 127.

Dennis, I. (1984) 'Corroboration requirements reconsidered', *Criminal Law Review*, 316.

Dennis, I. (1993), 'Miscarriages of justice and the law of confessions: evidentiary issues and solutions', *Public Law*, 291.

Dennis, I. (2002) 'Silence in the police station: the marginalisation of Section 34', *Criminal Law Review*, 25.

Devlin, Lord (1976) *Report to the Secretary of State for the Home Department of the Departmental Committee on Evidence of Identification in Criminal Cases* (HC 338). London: HMSO.

Dixon, D. (1997) *Law in Policing: Legal Regulation and Police Practices*. Oxford: Oxford University Press.

Donnelly, P. and Friedman, R.D. (1999) 'DNA database searches and the legal consumption of scientific evidence', *Michigan Law Review*, 97: 931.

Eleftheriadis, P. (2001) 'The European Constitution and cosmopolitan ideals', *Columbia Journal of European Law*, 7: 21.

Fenwick, H. (1993) 'Confessions, recording rules and miscarriages of justice', *Criminal Law Review*, 174.

Forensic Science Service (2004) *The National DNA Database Annual Report 03/04* (available online at www.forensic.gov.uk/).

Glenn, H.P. (2004) *Legal Traditions of the World* (2nd edn). Oxford: Oxford University Press.

Goldsmith, A. and Lewis, C. (eds) (2000) *Civilian Oversight of Policing: Governance, Democracy and Human Rights*. Oxford: Hart.

Gross, S.R. and Livingston, D. (2002) 'Racial profiling under attack', *Columbia Law Review*, 102: 1413.

Harris, D.A. (1997) '"Driving while black" and all other traffic offenses: the Supreme Court and pre-textual traffic stops', *Journal of Criminal Law and Criminology*, 87: 544.

Hart, H.L.A. (1994) *The Concept of Law* (2nd edn). Oxford: Oxford University Press.

Hecker, S. (1997) 'Race and pre-textual traffic stops: an expanded role for civilian review boards', *Columbia Human Rights Law Review*, 28: 551.

Her Majesty's Inspectorate of Constabulary (HMIC) (2004) *A Report on the Investigation by Cambridgeshire Constabulary into the Murders of Jessica Chapman and Holly Wells at Soham on 4 August 2002* (available online at www.inspectorates.homeoffice.gov.uk/hmic/).

Hirsh, D. (2003) *Law against Genocide: Cosmopolitan Trials*. London: Cavendish.

Hodgson, J. (1992) 'Tipping the scales of justice: the suspect's right to legal advice', *Criminal Law Review*, 854.

Hodgson, J. (1994) 'Adding injury to injustice: the suspect at the police station', *Journal of Law and Society*, 21: 85.

Home Office (2004) *Police Complaints and Discipline*. Home Office Statistical Bulletin 17/04 (available online at www.homeoffice.gov.uk/rds).

Home Office (2005a) *Arrests for Recorded (Notifiable Offences) and the Operation of Certain Police Powers under PACE. Home Office Statistical Bulletin* 21/05 (available online at www.homeoffice.gov.uk/rds).

Home Office (2005b) *Sentencing Statistics 2004. Home Office Statistical Bulletin* 15/05 (available online at www.homeoffice.gov.uk/rds).

House of Commons Science and Technology Committee (2005) *Forensic Science on Trial. Seventh Report of Session 2004–05* (HC 96-I). London: HMSO.

Independent Police Complaints Commission (2005) *Annual Report* (HC 608). London: HMSO.

Irving, B. and Dunnighan, C. (1993) *Human Factors in the Quality Control of CID Investigations. RCCJ Research Study* 21. London: HMSO.

Jackson, J.D. (1999) 'Trial procedures,' in C. Walker and K. Starmer (eds) *Miscarriages of Justice: A Review of Justice in Error*. London: Blackstone.

Jackson, J.D. (2001) 'Silence and proof: extending the boundaries of criminal proceedings in the United Kingdom', *International Journal of Evidence and Proof*, 5: 145.

Jones, T. (2003) 'The governance and accountability of policing,' in T. Newburn (ed.) *Handbook of Policing*. Cullompton: Willan Publishing.

JUSTICE (1994) *Unreliable Evidence? Confessions and the Safety of Convictions*. London: JUSTICE.

Kapardis, A. (1997) *Psychology and Law: A Critical Introduction*. Cambridge: Cambridge University Press.

Katz, I. (2006) 'The year of living dangerously – a year in the life of Britain's most controversial policeman', *Guardian* (G2), 30 January.

Kennedy, L. (1961) *10 Rillington Place*. London: Grafton.

Kleinig, J, (1996) *The Ethics of Policing*. Cambridge: Cambridge University Press.

Legal Services Commission (2005) *Annual Report 2004/05*. London: HMSO (available online at www.legalservices.gov.uk/).

Leggatt, Sir A. (2005) *Annual Report of the Chief Surveillance Commissioner to the Prime Minister and to Scottish Ministers for 2004–2005* (HC 444). London: HMSO (available online at www.surveillancecommissioners.gov.uk/).

Leigh, D. and Norton-Taylor, R. (2003) 'MI6 fights to block phone tap evidence: secret service fears lifting ban on court use would aid terrorists', *Guardian*, 14 October.

Lempert, R. (1991) 'Some caveats concerning DNA evidence as criminal identification evidence: with thanks to the Reverend Bayes', *Cardozo Law Review*, 13: 303.

Leng, R. (1993) *The Right to Silence in Police Interrogation: A Study of Some of the Issues Underlying the Debate. RCCJ Research Study* 10. London: HMSO.

Leng, R. (2001) 'Silence pre-trial, reasonable expectations and the normative distortion of fact-finding', *International Journal of Evidence and Proof*, 5: 240.

MacCormick, N. (1999) *Questioning Sovereignty*. Oxford: Oxford University Press.

Maguire, M. and Norris, C. (1992) *The Conduct and Supervision of Criminal Investigations. RCCJ Research Study* 5. London: HMSO.

Maguire, M. and Norris, C. (1994) 'Police investigations: practice and malpractice', *Journal of Law and Society*, 21: 72.

Mahoney, R. (2003) 'Abolition of New Zealand's *prima facie* exclusionary rule', *Criminal Law Review*, 607.

McConville, M. (1992) 'Videotaping interrogations: police behaviour on and off camera', *Criminal Law Review*, 532.

McConville, M. and Hodgson, J. (1993) *Custodial Legal Advice and the Right to Silence. RCCJ Research Study* 16. London: HMSO.

McConville, M., Hodgson, J., Bridges, L. and Pavlovic, A. (1994) *Standing Accused*. Oxford: Oxford University Press.

McConville, M., Sanders, A. and Leng, R. (1991) *The Case for the Prosecution: Police Suspects and the Construction of Criminality*. London: Routledge.

McKenzie, I. and Dunk, P. (1999) 'Identification parades: psychological and practical realities', in A. Heaton-Armstrong *et al.* (eds) *Analysing Witness Testimony*. London: Blackstone.

McKenzie, I., Morgan, R. and Reiner, R. (1990) 'Helping the police with their inquiries: the necessity principle and voluntary attendance at the police station', *Criminal Law Review*, 22.

Miller, J. (2003) *Police Corruption in England and Wales: An Assessment of Current Evidence*. Home Office Online Report 11/03 (available online at www.homeoffice.gov.uk/rds/).

Mirfield, P. (1997) *Silence, Confessions and Improperly Obtained Evidence*. Oxford: Oxford University Press.

Moenssens, A.A., Starrs, J.E., Henderson, C.E. and Inbau, F.E. (1995) *Scientific Evidence in Civil and Criminal Cases* (4th edn). Westbury, NY: Foundation Press.

Moston, S. and Stephenson, G.M. (1993) *The Questioning and Interviewing of Suspects Outside the Police Station*. RCCJ Research Study 22. London: HMSO.

Mullin, J. (1993) 'Guildford Four case detectives cleared', *Guardian*, 20 May.

Murphy, P. and Stockdale, E. (eds) (2005) *Blackstone's Criminal Practice 2006*. Oxford: Oxford University Press.

National Crime Squad (2005) *Annual Report 2004/05* (HC 211). London: HMSO.

National Criminal Intelligence Service (2005) *Annual Report* (HC 212). London: HMSO.

Nicol, C., Innes, M., Gee, D. and Feist, A. (2004) *Reviewing Murder Investigations: An Analysis of Progress Reviews from Six Police Forces*. Home Office Online Report 25/04 (available online at www.homeoffice.gov.uk/rds/).

Norton-Taylor, R. (2005) 'Intelligence agencies and police at odds over wiretap evidence', *Guardian*, 8 February.

Ormerod, D. (2003) 'ECHR and the exclusion of evidence: trial remedies for Article 8 breaches?', *Criminal Law Review*, 61.

Ormerod, D. and Birch, D. (2004) 'The evolution of the discretionary exclusion of evidence', *Criminal Law Review*, 767.

Pager, C.K.W. (2004) 'Lies, damned lies, statistics and racial profiling', *Kansas Journal of Law and Public Policy*, 13: 515.

Pattenden, R. (1999) *English Criminal Appeals, 1844–1994*. Oxford: Oxford University Press.

Philips, Sir C. (1981) *Report of the Royal Commission on Criminal Procedure*. London: HMSO.

Pizzi, W.T. (1999) *Trials Without Truth*. New York, NY: NYU Press.

Raz, J. (1985) 'Authority, law and morality', *The Monist*, 68: 295.

Redmayne, M, (1997) 'Presenting probabilities in court: the DNA experience', *International Journal of Evidence and Proof*, 1: 187.

Reiner, R. (1992) 'Policing a postmodern society', *Modern Law Review*, 55: 761.

Reiner, R. (1997) 'Policing and the police', in M. Maguire *et al.* (eds) *The Oxford Handbook of Criminology* (2nd edn). Oxford: Oxford University Press.

Reiner, R. (2000) *The Politics of the Police* (3rd edn). Oxford: Oxford University Press.

Reiner, R. (2002) 'The organization and accountability of the police', in M. McConville and G. Wilson (eds) *The Handbook of the Criminal Justice Process*. Oxford: Oxford University Press.

Richardson, J. (ed.) (2005) *Archbold: Criminal Pleading, Evidence and Practice 2006*. London: Sweet & Maxwell.

Roberts, A. and Clover, S. (2002) 'Managerialism and myopia: the government's consultation draft on PACE – Code D', *Criminal Law Review*, 837.

Roberts, D. (1993) 'Questioning the Suspect: The Solicitor's Role', *Criminal Law Review*, 368.

Roberts, P. (1994) 'Science in the criminal process', *Oxford Journal of Legal Studies*, 14: 469.

Roberts, P. (2002) 'Drug-dealing and the presumption of innocence: the Human Rights Act (almost) bites', *International Journal of Evidence and Proof*, 6: 17.

Roberts, P. (2006) 'Theorising procedural tradition: subjects, objects and values in criminal adjudication', in A. Duff *et al.* (eds) *The Trial on Trial, Volume 2. Judgment and Calling to Account*. Oxford: Hart.

Roberts, P. and Zuckerman, A. (2004) *Criminal Evidence*. Oxford: Oxford University Press.

Sanders, A. (1987) 'Constructing the case for the prosecution', *Journal of Law and Society*, 14: 229.

Sanders, A. and Bridges, L. (1999) 'The right to legal advice', in C. Walker and K. Starmer (eds) *Miscarriages of Justice: A Review of Justice in Error*. London: Blackstone.

Sanders, A. and Young, R. (2007) *Criminal Justice* (3rd edn). Oxford: Oxford University Press.

Scarman, Lord (1981) *The Scarman Report: The Brixton Disorders, 10–12 April 1981*. Harmondsworth: Penguin Books.

Seidmann, D.J. and Stein, A. (2000) 'The right to silence helps the innocent: a game-theoretic analysis of the Fifth Amendment Privilege', *Harvard Law Review*, 114: 431.

Shepherd, E. and Milne, R. (1999) 'Full and faithful: ensuring quality practice and integrity of outcome in witness interviews', in A. Heaton-Armstrong *et al.* (eds) *Analysing Witness Testimony*. London: Blackstone.

Shora, K. (2002) 'Guilty of flying while brown', *Air and Space Law*, 17: 4.

Stephen, J.F. (1883) *A History of the Criminal Law of England. Volume I*. London: Routledge/Thoemmes.

Straw, J. and Boateng, P. (1997) 'Bringing rights home: Labour's plans to incorporate the European Convention on Human Rights into UK law', *European Human Rights Law Review*, 71.

Taylor, I., Walton, P. and Young, J. (1973) *The New Criminology*. London: Routledge & Kegan Paul.

Thomas, Sir S. (2005) *Report of the Interception of Communications Commissioner for 2004* (HC 549). London: HMSO.

Thornton, P. (2004) 'Trial by jury: 50 years of change', *Criminal Law Review*, 683.

Tinsley, Y. (2001) 'Even better than the real thing? the case for reform of identification procedures', *International Journal of Evidence and Proof*, 5: 99.

Travis, A. (1995) 'Joy Gardner trio escape police action', *Guardian*, 13 July.

Twining, W. (2000) *Globalisation and Legal Theory*. London: Butterworths.

Walker, C. (1999) 'Miscarriages of justice in principle and practice', in C. Walker and K. Starmer (eds) *Miscarriages of Justice: A Review of Justice in Error*. London: Blackstone.

Webb, G. and Harris, D. (1993) 'Birmingham Six police are cleared of perjury', *London Evening Standard*, 7 October.

Wellborn, O.G. (1991) 'Demeanor', *Cornell Law Review*, 76: 1075.

Wells, G.L. and Loftus, E.F. (eds) (1984) *Eyewitness Testimony: Psychological Perspectives*. Cambridge: Cambridge University Press.

Wilkey, M.R. (1992) 'Why suppress valid evidence?', in M.J. Gorr and S. Harwood (eds) *Controversies in Criminal Law*. Boulder, CO: Westview Press.

Williams, R., Johnson, P. and Martin, P. (2004) *Genetic Information and Crime Investigation*. London: Wellcome Trust.

Wolchover, D. and Heaton-Armstrong, A. (1991) 'Cracking the Codes', *Police Review*, 12 April: 751.

Wolchover, D. and Heaton-Armstrong, A. (1996) *Confession Evidence*. London: Sweet & Maxwell.

Zander, M. (1994) 'Abolition of the right to silence, 1972–1994', in D. Morgan and G. Stephenson (eds) *Suspicion and Silence*. London: Blackstone.

Zander, M. and Henderson, P. (1993) *Crown Court Study. RCCJ Research Study* 19. London: HMSO.

Zuckerman, A.A.S. (1992) 'Miscarriage of justice – a root treatment', *Criminal Law Review*, 323.

Chapter 6

Criminal investigation and the media

Rob C. Mawby

Introduction

The relationship between crime and the media is a much debated subject and a diverse area of study that encompasses a variety of research approaches. These have considered, *inter alia*, media representations, contents and effects and have focused on offenders, victims and institutions (Leishman and Mason 2003; Reiner 2002, 2003; Jewkes 2004). Drawing on the rich body of literature and research, this chapter examines three distinct, but related, aspects of criminal investigation and the media. The first part of the chapter charts the longstanding media fascination with criminal investigation and explores historical and contemporary representations of investigators and the investigation function. In doing so, it considers the place of criminal investigation in the construction of the police image and the symbolic importance that is attached to the police crime-fighting role. Secondly, acknowledging that the police have always engaged to varying degrees with the news and entertainment media, the chapter examines the extent to which the British police have developed the practice of overt 'image work'.[1] It considers how this intersects with the processes of crime investigation through a discussion of the 'newsworthiness' of crime and its investigation. Thirdly, because media developments make the investigation of serious crime a particularly visible, sometimes exposed, policing function, the chapter focuses on police–media relations during such investigations. The chapter concludes that, in our media-dominated society, the processes of criminal investigation have become increasingly public and this has the potential both to idealize and to demystify the police as effective crime fighters.

The public police have consistently promoted their image as crime fighters and investigators despite crime fighting being neither their primary activity nor their most impressive quality. As Martin Innes (2002: 67–8) has summarized, sociological studies examining how police officers construct their social world converge with the literature on the mediated representations of policing to suggest that the dominant image is one of the crime fighter: a 'myth' that has served to legitimate the police role to both sections of the public and to police officers themselves. This myth is regularly debunked through studies of what the police actually do (Bayley 1996; PA Consulting Group 2001). Nevertheless, Innes (2002: 68) identifies that the police detective function and the investigation of serious crime retain a central role in terms of 'how policing is symbolically constructed'.

The symbolic role of the police as crime fighters was described by Peter Manning (1971, 1997, 2003) as an 'impossible mandate', a consequence, he argued, of the police's claim to control crime 'although crime, in many respects, was not in their command' (2003: 63). The encouragement of the public to think of the police in such idealized terms led Manning to warn that the police mandate was 'fraught with difficulties ... They have defined their task in such a way that they cannot ... hope to honor it to the satisfaction of the public' (1971: 155). In identifying the impossible mandate and the investment in it by both police and public, Manning drove to the heart of what is at stake in the contested terrain of police–media relations. This mystification of the police as crime fighters also forms part of what Robert Reiner (2003: 250–260) has called 'police fetishism' which embodies 'the assumption that the police are a functional prerequisite of social order, so that without a police force there would be chaos and uncontrolled war of all against all'. He observes (2003: 276) that media stories generally continue to reproduce police fetishism. Nevertheless, in recent years, the media have provided a context in which the police service's ability to conduct criminal investigations effectively has been questioned as well as praised. While criminal investigation has been at the core of images of policing for the best of reasons, it has also brought scandal, evidenced through miscarriages of justice (e.g. the Guildford Four, the Birmingham Six, released in 1989 and 1991, respectively); accusations of racism and incompetence (e.g. the investigation into the murder of Stephen Lawrence in 1993); administrative failure (e.g. the investigation into the murders of Holly Wells and Jessica Chapman in Soham, Cambridgeshire, in 2002); and allegations of the 'execution' of innocent people (e.g. the shooting of Brazilian Jean Charles de Menezes during the investigation into the London bombings of July 2005).

Images of criminal investigation

Emerging images

Images of policing as crime fighting and the drama of criminal investigation are staple ingredients of modern media content; this holds across the entertainment and news media in diverse formats and is not a recent phenomenon. The crime-fighting image has been propagated through all forms of media since at least the eighteenth century. In this respect, there has been consistent media interest in the investigation of crime and, equally, police interest, on the part of both public and private policing agencies, in courting the media. For example, prior to the establishment in London of the 'new' Metropolitan Police in 1829, earlier upholders of law and order indulged in marketing their services and promoting their reputation. The Bow Street magistrates Henry and John Fielding in the 1750s spread news of their crime-fighting successes through pamphlets and their newspaper, *The Covent Garden Journal* (Rawlings 1995: 140). The Fieldings were early exponents of 'managing' the media: John advertised in newspapers, requesting victims and witnesses to take information to Bow Street, from where it was distributed to 'thief-takers' and magistrates, thereby increasing the chances of detection (Rawlings 2003: 59). The brothers combined their skills in pamphleteering and in using newspapers for publicity to exploit crime panics with the purpose of securing financial support from the government for their crime-fighting ambitions. With their establishment of a small force of relatively reliable thief-takers, who later became known as the Bow Street Runners, policing was moving towards greater professionalism; crime detection was coming to the fore, increasingly with the image of professional investigators 'at the heart of the detection process' (Rawlings 2003: 60).

Coinciding with the establishment of the Metropolitan Police in 1829, mid-nineteenth-century Britain experienced increasing literacy and saw the growth of different forms of media. Raymond Williams charted in the 1840s alone: 'the effective establishment of a popular Sunday press ... the growth of new kinds of periodical ... the coming of cheap fiction ... the development of minor theatres ... the rise of the music halls' (1961: 72–3). Underpinning these changes were technical progressions (e.g. the introduction of steam-printed newspapers) that were exploited and commercialized by entrepreneurs, but at the same time the first public libraries (1850) were being established. This mixture of 'commercial exploitation ... and enlightened public provision' (Williams 1961: 74) provided channels to develop and spread images of policing. Collectively, they comprised a stage where tensions about the acceptability of the new police were played out (Mawby 2002a: 10; Reiner 2003: 264). It was also during this period that a body of popular literature emerged providing mainly positive representations of policing to the growing numbers of the reading public. This included the reminiscences of detectives, detailing their successful cases, but also bogus memoirs, often written by journalists (Cox 1992: xiv). These proved extremely popular (Lawrence 2003: 127) and are an early example of the blurring of fact and fiction which is a central feature of contemporary policing representations (Leishman and Mason 2003, 2005).

In contrast to the bogus memoirs, but also combining fact with fiction, Charles Dickens and Wilkie Collins based fictional characters on real police officers. Two of the original detectives appointed to work from Scotland Yard in 1842 were used as models for Dickens' Inspector Buckett in *Bleak House* and Collins' Sergeant Cuff in *The Moonstone* (Ascoli 1979: 119). Dickens was especially active in promoting the work of detectives (e.g. in his *Detective Anecdotes* in 1850). Through such works, Symons (1985: 46) argues that Dickens 'played a considerable part in forming the public view of detectives and changing the hostile or critical working-class attitude to the police'.

It was not only police-focused detective fiction that became popular in the nineteenth century: a number of fictional private detectives emerged,

Table 6.1 Overview of the mediation of criminal investigation

Protagonist	Type	Source/description
1. Police professional	*Police detective fiction*	1. Imagination: pure fiction (e.g. the novels of Ian Rankin featuring Inspector John Rebus or the novels of Ruth Rendell featuring Chief Inspector Wexford, both adapted for TV) 2. Real detectives: Fictional detectives based on real people (e.g Charles Dickens based *Bleak House*'s Inspector Bucket on Sgt Field, one of the first members of the 'Detective' at Scotland Yard) 3. Real crimes: Fictional detectives investigating real unsolved crimes (e.g. Detectives Barlow and Watt, from television's *Z Cars*, *Softly Softly*, revisiting the Jack the Ripper case in *Second Verdict*; BBC 1973) 4. Real crimes: fictional detectives based on real people investigate fictional crimes that resemble true crimes (e.g. Wilkie Collins basing Sgt Cuff on Scotland Yard's Inspector Whicher to investigate a murder resembling the Constance Kent case of 1865 in *The Moonstone*; Haste 1997: 162–3)
	Police memoirs and biographies	Factual career-based: narratives of improvement/career success stories (Lawrence 2003), and/or celebrated cases (e.g. books by retired senior officers; Sillitoe 1955; Mark 1978; Hellawell 2002)
	Police false memoirs	Imagination: pure fiction but purports to be real (e.g. George Dixon's 'autobiography' in which he thanks Ted Willis (the actual writer) in the acknowledgements; Dixon 1960)
	Police factionalized memoirs	Real detectives embellishing or reinventing their careers (e.g. Fabian of the Yard (Fabian 1955) and Vidocq of the Paris Sûreté, who published his *Memoires* in 1828; Morton 2005)
2. Amateur investigator	*The police 'outsider'*	Police outsiders undertake parallel inquiries that may embarrass or outshine the police or hold them to account. Typically the amateur dilettante in novels/TV drama (e.g. Agatha Christie's Miss Marple and Hercule Poirot)
	The police 'insider'	An amateur 'civilian' investigator, but with other specialist skills, joins the police investigation. Medical doctors, psychologists, forensic scientists provide the silver bullet that solves the crime. Used extensively in entertainment media, but reflecting actual practice (e.g. television's *Silent Witness*, *Dangerfield* and *Cracker*)

Table 6.1 *continued*

Protagonist	Type	Source/description
3. Other (non-police) statutory investigator	*Specialist investigators*	Dramatized accounts of the criminal investigation work of other public, government and military agencies including Customs and Excise, the military police and MI5 (TV examples include *The Professionals, Spooks, The Knock, Redcap, Rose and Maloney*)
4. Professional private security industry investigator	*Private investigators*	Most often based on the cases of fictional professional private investigators (e.g. Jim Rockford, Phillip Marlow, Sam Spade). In Livingstone and Hart's (2003) typology, these would come under their 'Hired Gun' (other types are the 'Watchman' – e.g. *Inspector Gadget* and the 'Gangster')

pioneering the genre in which a gifted amateur detective investigates crimes that the police are apparently too stupid to solve. Indeed, in his typology of popular images of the police detective, Brearley notes that the 'Bumbler' detective is often upstaged by such characters (Brearley 2005).[2] The first literary amateur detective is accredited to the imagination of Edgar Allan Poe, who introduced Auguste Dupin in 1841 in *The Murders in the Rue Morgue*. The following year, Dupin appeared in Poe's *The Mystery of Marie Roget*, which was based on the real unsolved murder of Mary Rogers in Chicago; with this blurring of fact and fiction, Poe had developed the 'crime faction detective short story' (Haste 1997: 13). In Britain, Conan Doyle introduced the celebrated Sherlock Holmes in 1887 in *A Study in Scarlet*. The genre is still popular today in a number of forms. These 'police outsiders' tend to undertake parallel inquiries to the police, often antagonizing their professional counterparts. However, the gifted amateur also appears as a 'police insider'. As amateur detectives but professional psychologists or surgeons, these 'insiders' align with the policing professionals, e.g., in the television series *Silent Witness*, (BBC 1996 to the present) and *Dangerfield*, (BBC 1995 to the present). In between these two types are the gifted amateurs who float between insider and outsider, called in by the desperate professional detectives, but also mistrusted and routinely challenged, e.g. academic psychologist, Dr Tony Hill, in *Wire in the Blood*, (ITV 2002 to the present). Table 6.1 summarizes the different ways in which crime investigation has been represented, though it does not take account of the types that emerge through factual programmes and the news media.

Television crime fighters

Television has been the dominant medium in terms of mass entertainment since the mid-1950s and several scholarly analyses of media representations of law enforcement have included television (Reiner 1994, 2000; Reiner *et al.*

2001; Lichter *et al.* 1999, 2002; Leishman and Mason 2003). In his analysis of the crime genre of fiction, Reiner (2000: 149–60) distinguishes between *criminal tales* and *law enforcement* stories and classifies the latter into 12 ideal types of representation, providing a framework in which contrasting policing images can be placed. These types range from 'classic sleuth' (e.g. *Inspector Morse*, ITV 1987–2000), to 'police procedural' (*Z-Cars*, BBC 1962–78) to 'police community' (*The Bill*, ITV 1984 to the present) to 'community police' (*Dixon of Dock Green*, BBC 1955–76). While these types can be distinguished in terms of 'hero', 'crime', 'villain', 'victim' and other organizing characteristics, closer examination highlights the importance for each type of criminal investigation in their construction. This is obvious for programmes such as *Inspector Morse* in which the protagonists' *raison d'être* is clearly crime investigation; it may not be so obvious for programmes such as *Dixon of Dock Green* which has come to be regarded as an exemplar of the 'police officer in society', benign guardian and crime preventor, rather than crime sleuth. Yet the radio revival of *Dixon* in 2005 confirmed the crime-fighter role. BBC Radio 4 broadcast six half-hour episodes adapted from original screenplays written by Ted Willis. In these, George Dixon was not the stereotypical 'plodding' beat officer; he knew his patch and investigated crimes using all his experience and the networks of goodwill that he had established within the community. For example, in episode two, *Needle in a Haystack* (broadcast 22 June 2005), Dixon investigates a stall-holder whom he suspects of dealing illicit drugs. He cultivates an informer, makes his inquiries and subsequently recovers stolen barbiturates which are traced back to the suspected stall-holder/dealer.

Similarly, although *The Bill* is not predicated upon crime fighting, being described by Leishman and Mason (2003: 63) as a 'police soap opera', it nevertheless relies on the police crime-fighting role to structure its storylines. Since the late 1990s, *The Bill* has tracked the moral ambiguity of policing (Leishman and Mason 2003: 103–4, 2005). However, like other police dramas, it also reinforces the impossible mandate by over-emphasizing the ability of the police to solve crime. Paul Mason undertook a contents analysis of 24 episodes of *The Bill* screened between June and December 1990 and found that the Sun Hill police had a detection rate of 78 per cent that compared very favourably with the then national detection rate of 34 per cent (Mason 1992: 18). Even in series therefore that ostensibly are about the wider role of public policing, the crime-fighting role of the police remains of symbolic importance and tends to be exaggerated.

In addition to his typology of law enforcement stories, Reiner (1994) has plotted dialectically the development of the police drama and the representation of the police as a caring or controlling organization (reflecting the police *force*/police *service* debate). He argued that *Dixon of Dock Green* was the thesis, presenting the police as carers, *The Sweeney* (ITV 1975–78) was the antithesis in which the police were portrayed as controllers and *The Bill* was the synthesis in which care and control (force and service) were interdependent. Leishman and Mason continued this dialectical analysis, taking *The* (old) *Bill* as the new thesis, *Between the Lines* (BBC 1992–94) as the antithesis and *The* (new) *Bill* as the new synthesis, by way of the transitional texts of *Prime Suspect* (ITV 1991–2006) and *Cracker* (ITV 1993–2006), in which the role of the crime fighter is primary. *Prime Suspect* with Helen Mirren as the senior detective officer, Jane Tennyson, was a significant development in the portrayal of women police officers (Brunsdon 2000: 204–8, Creeber 2001; Leishman and Mason 2003: 95–6). It illustrated the difficulties that women face in the masculine world of the criminal investigation department (CID). *Cracker* represents the emergence of a plethora of representations emphasizing the appliance of science. These include 'medico-detective' dramas (Leishman and Mason 2003: 102) and programmes that foreground the role of scientific certainty in police work, notably the extremely successful *CSI: Crime Scene Investigation* (Channel 5 2001 to the present).

These developments, of course, are not entirely novel. For example, in the late 1960s, *The Strange Report* (ITV 1968-9) featured Anthony Quayle as former Home Office criminologist Adam Strange, who was deployed on particularly difficult unsolved cases. He routinely solved these, drawing on his specialist expertise and the tools and techniques of his home's forensic laboratory. However, with regard to criminal profilers at least, while they are a successful formula for television entertainment programmes, their actual use is more controversial. McGrath and Turvey's (2003) analysis of the US 'Beltway Snipers' case suggests a relationship between profilers' public announcements and the subsequent behaviour of the sniper team (which killed ten and wounded three people between 2 and 22 October 2002 by shooting covertly from a hidden platform in a modified car). Their analysis exposes both the fallibility of criminal profilers and the news media's thirst for their views whether they were officially advising the inquiry or had been brought in as specialist commentators by media organizations. In Britain, the efficacy of profilers was questioned by the investigation into the 1992 murder of Rachel Nickell. Detectives brought in forensic psychologist and profiler Paul Britton, who helped to build a case against Colin Stagg using a 'honey trap' ploy. The police subsequently charged Stagg with murder, but when the case reached the Old Bailey, Britton's evidence was dismissed and the prosecution withdrew its case.

Since Leishman and Mason's update of Reiner's initial dialectical analysis, there have been further developments which may yet spawn the transitional texts that lead to the new thesis. One such development has been the emergence of police dramas that have abandoned the classic formula of 1) crime unfolds; 2) investigation ensues; and 3) crime is solved and the balance of law and order is usually restored. These series have developed in both time directions. We have series such as *New Tricks* (BBC 2003 to the present) which features the work of the Unsolved Crime and Open Case Squad and *Waking the Dead* (BBC 2000 to the present) which features a Cold Case Squad investigating unsolved crimes using new technology. In one respect, such series focusing largely on frustratingly unsolved crimes infer police fallibility in the same way that *Crimewatch UK* and its siblings do, though this is turned around into reassurance, suggesting that new technology and scientific methods can reach the parts earlier detectives could not.

While some programmes have focused on unsolved crimes of the past, others have looked to uncommitted crimes of the future. Examples have emerged on television (*Murder Prevention*, Channel 5 2004) and also in the cinema (*Minority Report* in 2002) of pre-emptive police strikes to prevent crimes – what might be termed 'pre-crime investigation'. In the case of *Minority Report*, set in 2054, this involves the nightmare visions of 'Pre-Cogs', who foresee criminal events in the future, prompting the 'pre-crime' squad to arrest and incarcerate people before they offend. Similarly, on television, *Murder Prevention* is premised on the basis of closely surveilling 'imminent killers', whom the police suspect are preparing to murder, and apprehending them at the point before they commit the offence, once there is sufficient evidence of intent to kill. Reviewing the series, Andrew Billen congratulated the makers on writing an allegory of the invasion of Iraq in 2003. He wrote: 'the series can legitimately be read as a symbol of the perils of pre-emptive action on the world stage: motives may be good, but outcomes are uncertain and the means are highly dubious' (Billen 2004). In reading *Murder Prevention* this way, Billen illustrates only the most recent example of police drama series acting as a vehicle for wider messages. For example, Hunt (1999: 146) analysed the two *Sweeney* films set in the 1970s and concluded, 'these were not happy times and these are not happy films' and, more recently, Brunsdon (2000: 196) has argued convincingly that the police series is 'a privileged site for the staging of the trauma of the break-up of the post-war settlement'.

While, according to its creator, Declan Croghan, *Murder Prevention* is 'the first pre-crime drama ever, anywhere' (Channel Five press release 11 October 2004), its inspiration is the actually existing Homicide Command of the Metropolitan Police Service (MPS). The MPS introduced three murder suppression teams in October 2001 'to deal with those who are deemed to have the propensity to kill, will carry it out imminently and are beyond the operational capability of boroughs to monitor' (Metropolitan Police Authority 2002). In criminal investigation it would appear that truth can be as strange as fiction.

Criminal investigation and factual programming

It is not only fiction-based programming that focuses on criminal investigation; it also features prominently in factual programmes. Historically, factual television programmes about policing have been either 1) investigative critical programmes that question police practices, competence and integrity, or 2) broadly supportive information-based documentaries made with police co-operation. Investigative critical programmes have provided regular opportunities to take to task the shortcomings and failings of an accountable public sector organization. Programmes such as *World in Action* (ITV 1963–98), *Panorama* (BBC 1953 to the present) and *Rough Justice* (BBC 1980 to the present) have exposed flaws in criminal investigations that have had the most serious of consequences. Subsequent to these, drama-documentaries that blur fact and fiction have provided very public examinations of how the police conduct the investigation of crime. A number of programmes have been made on the investigation into Stephen Lawrence's murder – e.g. *The Murder of Stephen Lawrence* (ITV 1999) and *The Colour of Justice* (BBC 1999) which was also a theatre production. Others have showcased earlier examples of police fallibility e.g. the 'Yorkshire Ripper' investigation. Peter

Sutcliffe killed 13 women before he was finally arrested in January 1981, after having been interviewed and released on nine occasions. The investigation was reconstructed in ITV's *This is Personal: The Hunt for the Yorkshire Ripper* (2000), and was also the subject of *Real Crime: The Hunt for Wearside Jack* (ITV 2001), which investigated why West Yorkshire Police detectives were taken in by a hoaxer who diverted resources from the investigation (see Hellawell 2002: ch. 11 and, in contrast, Wright 2002: 82–3).

With regard to information-based documentaries, following Roger Graef's groundbreaking *Police* (BBC 1982), there is now a plethora of 'fly on the wall' programmes. These follow both routine police work and elite squads. For example, series such as *Mersey Blues* (BBC 1999) and *Murder Blues* (BBC 2005) have been devoted to crime investigation. *Murder Blues* followed the difficult work of unarmed detectives from the MPS 'Operation Trident' squad as they investigated fatal and non-fatal gun crime within London's black communities. It emphasized a holistic approach showing officers investigating crimes, but also working at community events, youth conferences and with advertising campaigns to discourage young people from aspiring to gang membership. In *Mersey Blues*, the charismatic Detective Chief Inspector Elmore Davies featured prominently, respected by his team and boosting flagging morale. However, in an episode called *A Fair Cop*, Davies was exposed as a corrupt officer and subsequently sentenced to five years' imprisonment for passing confidential information to a known criminal in exchange for £10,000. Such outcomes are the exception and in recent years these police 'ride-along' documentaries have been criticized for their blurring of information provision and entertainment, and for producing programmes which resemble public relations productions (Hill 2000a, 2000b; Kilborn *et al* 2001).

A third form of factual programming which has assumed great significance for the mediation of crime investigation is that of the 'crimescarer', the most celebrated exponent being *Crimewatch UK* (BBC 1984 to the present). This strand differs from the other two in that it involves public participation, a dialogue between the police and viewers; it is predicated upon crime investigation being a joint venture. Crimescarers emerged in numbers in the 1980s, characterized by a focus on real, unsolved crimes which are dramatically reconstructed and viewers are asked to provide information that may assist with detection. Examples, similarly structured, emerged in Europe, the USA and Australia (Breslin 1990: 352–7). While *Crimewatch UK* was based on the German programme, *Aktenzeichen XY ... Ungelost*, in the UK the origins of crimescarers lie in *Police Five* (ITV 1962–90) and its 1970s spin-off, *Junior Police Five*, fronted by Shaw Taylor, who ended each five-minute programme of requests to the viewers for information on featured crimes by exhorting viewers to 'Keep 'em peeled'. *Police Five* attracted little controversy, but other crimescarer programmes that sprang up in the 1980s, including *Crimestoppers, Crime Stalker, Michael Winner's True Crimes* and *Crime Monthly*, were criticized for their style, content and their role in generating anxiety (Home Office 1989; Hill 2000a). The Grade Report commented on the genre thus: 'We are very concerned by this rapid escalation in coverage with its over-emphasis on violent crime. It will inevitably reinforce erroneous impressions of a major increase in violent crime, fuel fears about copycat crimes and push up the level of anxiety and fear about individual safety' (Home Office 1989: 32 para. 4.39).

Crimewatch UK has assertively countered such accusations. It began inauspiciously and somewhat hesitantly with three pilot programmes, having secured the support of just three police forces following negotiations with the Association of Chief Police Officers (ACPO) and the BBC (Schlesinger and Tumber 1994). In 2004 *Crimewatch UK* celebrated its twentieth anniversary, claiming that the 2,923 cases it had featured had resulted in 450 convictions and 879 arrests. During this period the format of reconstructions, rogues galleries and feedback on previously featured cases has remained consistent. According to Yvonne Jewkes (2004: 166), this is a 'tried and tested formula of representing a limited range of very serious crimes perpetrated against a restricted category of victims'. It has been criticized for other reasons, including: 1) it promotes unrealistic expectations of crime detection – this was one of ACPO's initial fears regarding co-operation with the programme makers; 2) it promotes crime as entertainment – Schlesinger and Tumber (1994: 262–63) found that the police recognized and accepted the programme's entertainment value while the BBC emphasized the 'public good of helping solve crimes'; 3) it uses reconstructions that are sensationalist – despite some convincing arguments that this is the case (e.g. see Jewkes 2004: 154–61), this is rejected by Nick Ross (Miller 2001: 14–15) and others who point to the *BBC Producers' Guidelines* that the programme must abide by; 4) it creates or increases fear of crime – this is much debated and, despite the programme makers' reassurances, cannot be cursorily refuted (Schlesinger and Tumber 1994: 266–7; Leishman and Mason 2003: 24, 115; Jewkes 2004: 160–1); 5) it reinforces conservative family and gender roles and relations (Jewkes 2004); and 6) it encourages 'copy-cat' crimes. Again this is denied by Ross (Miller 2001: 14) but is supported by Gill's survey of armed robbers (2000: 34). Despite these criticisms, *Crimewatch UK* is less obviously exploitative than its rivals, is successful in terms of capturing an audience and, on the face of it, in terms of crime investigation. It has achieved a level of respectability and is regarded as a BBC flagship (Jewkes 2004:157). This has been helped by using established and respected BBC journalists. The original presenter Nick Ross has become a media authority on crime and is currently chair of the Advisory Board of the Jill Dando Institute of Crime Science at University College, London. This institute was named in honour of Ross's erstwhile co-presenter, whose tragic murder in 1999 was reconstructed on the programme.

The police service, after its initial suspicion, has supported *Crimewatch UK*. From a policing perspective, it is effective image work in that it engages the public as partners in fighting crime. During times of concern about crime and the ability of the police to control it, *Crimewatch UK* presents the police investigating and solving real crimes. On the programme the police are not present just to be interviewed, they have moved centre-stage and have become mediators themselves. In this televised version of policing, they are clearly constructed as crime investigation experts, legitimating their power and the crime-fighting role. Although the programme is based on as-yet unsolved crime and, according to Nick Ross, is often the last resort of detectives (Miller 2001:10), this is balanced by updates on featured cases that have been solved, by the spin-off programme *Crimewatch Solved*, and by books celebrating solved cases (Ross and Cook 1987; Miller 2001).

Police image work and the news media

Crimescarers and information-based documentaries have been criticized for the level of complicity between the police and programme makers. This reflects the ongoing theoretical debate concerning 'crime and the media' which has always included sub-debates about 'policing and the media'; these have incorporated discussions about where the balance of power lies. Reiner has summarized these debates thus: analyses of media representations of law and order and policing have tended to be either 'hegemonic' or 'subversive' (2000: 139–47, 2002: 376–77, 406–8, 2003: 261–2). Proponents of the former perspective point to the police as being in a position to provide access to information, to select and filter information, thus placing them in a position of dominance in relation to media agencies, which become 'propagators of a dominant ideology' (Reiner 2000: 139). In contrast, proponents of the latter perspective perceive the media as a threat to morality and authority, and fear that media representations undermine respect for the police service. Within this debate, influential commentators (Hall *et al* 1978; Ericson *et al* 1989) have argued the police drive the relationship. Being gatekeepers to information enables them to use 'proactive publicity' for damage control and to 'promote and protect the image of their organization as accountable' (Ericson 1995: 147–9).

Since these arguments were put forward, however, the context in which both the police and media organizations operate has changed: it is now infinitely more complex and accordingly more difficult for an agency such as the police to control (Mawby 1999). Organizational and technological changes have led to an explosion of media outlets, particularly news based. News distribution formats have changed. Most notably there is now 24-hours rolling news, cable and satellite television stations, commercial radio stations and Internet news providers. Technological advances in the media have also had an impact. The use of lightweight cameras, camcorders and even cameras on mobile telephones has eased the access of all to the media and has increased the speed at which events are mediated locally and nationally.[3] These developments have increased the level of scrutiny to which the police are subjected. In this context, viewing the police as gatekeepers to information, who can dominate the media agenda, is one-dimensional and simplistic. Rather the police-media relationship is a series of co-existing relationships that ebb and flow in terms of dominance and control and the balance of power differs over time and location and at national and local levels (Mawby 2002a; see also Leishman and Mason 2003: 44). Nevertheless, it is equally simplistic to suggest that the police will not attempt to manage and control their relationship with the media. In this media-dominated society, public organizations must attend to the 'management of visibility'

(Thompson 1995) and the police service now has many 'image workers' engaged in promoting and protecting the police image. These police employees include press officers, marketing professionals, public relations officers and corporate identity specialists (Mawby 2002a: ch. 4; Mawby and Worthington 2002).

While policing agencies have always practised image work (Mawby 2002a: ch. 1), since the late 1980s the police service has taken significant steps towards professionalizing activities to promote and project the police image. At the national level, ACPO established a Media Advisory Group (MAG) in 1993. This fulfils a co-ordinating role and disseminates advice to forces on policy and practice. A further step towards professionalization was made in 1998 through the establishment of the Association of Police Public Relations Officers (APPRO). At the local level, forces have developed media strategies and their press offices are now routinely managed and staffed by civilian communications specialists, far removed from earlier incumbents, who were generally police officers or civilian administrators (Mawby 2002b). Although press offices were originally established for the purpose of conducting reactive and proactive press relations, the trend is now towards a broader role. The traditional 'press bureau' has given way to 'media services' departments which co-ordinate communications activities force-wide. Press officers work at strategic and tactical levels, communicating with external agencies and also providing support to operational colleagues – backstage by enabling them to communicate more effectively, and frontstage by acting as a buffer between the media and operational officers. In short, police–media relations is now professional – it is guided by strategy and policy, it has its own processes, and it is managed by specialist communicators or conducted by police officers who have been trained and advised by specialists.

Image work intersects with the business of criminal investigation in different ways. At one level forces will work with media production companies who wish to develop dramas and fact-based programmes around crime and policing. Programme makers may wish to negotiate access to specialist crime investigation squads and the police will consider the legal issues, together with the implications for transparency, positive images and operational integrity. For example, the *Murder Prevention* production team had an initial meeting with the MPS, but further co-operation was declined. Through actively engaging with media organizations, police forces seek to influence the images of crime investigation that appear through the entertainment media. The history of such co-operation and collaborations, however, confirms that the police cannot control the outcome. For example, following the screening of the first episode of *The Cops* on BBC2 on 19 October 1998, Greater Manchester Police (GMP) and Lancashire Constabulary, who had co-operated with the film-makers, registered dismay at the results. They worried that the series, a drama filmed in documentary style, would have a negative impact on their reputation. *The Cops* painted a powerful and disturbing picture of policing contemporary Britain, and both GMP and Lancashire Police refused to co-operate with the making of the second series (Mawby 2003). A similar reaction had followed the first screening of *Z Cars* in 1962, a series that went on to become an influential representation of policing during its 18-year run.

At another level, image work is central to the police–news media relationship. It is part of the 'bread and butter' work of police press officers to appeal for information about reported crimes, to publicize and explain crime levels and occurrences, and to service media requests for information. Crime is perennially a core media interest and before considering how the police deploy image work to assist criminal investigation, it is first necessary to consider from a media perspective the place of crime in the construction of news.

Crime and newsworthiness

In his classic account of crime reporting in the British press, Steve Chibnall identified eight 'professional imperatives which act as implicit guides to the construction of new stories' (1977: 23). These were *immediacy, dramatisation, personalisation, simplification, titillation, conventionalism, structured access* and *novelty*. These are the criteria for newsworthiness – a term that 'encapsulates the perceived "public appeal" or "public interest" of any potential news story' (Jewkes 2004: 227). As Jewkes (2004: 38, 227) explains, newsworthiness is determined by news values, which are 'the professional, yet informal, codes used in the selection, construction and presentation of news stories'. Despite Chibnall's study being of the press alone and from a different media age, his work remains influential; Leishman and Mason (2003: 32–5) recently revisited the eight imperatives, arguing that they have become even more significant. In contrast, Jewkes has argued that the media world and audience sophistication have changed beyond recognition from the mid-1970s when Chibnall was writing. Accordingly, she reappraises Chibnall's imperatives and reformulates the values that shape crime news in the first decade of the twenty-first century. First she argues that three news values underpin all the others – namely, *crime* itself; *negativity* (the majority of crime stories are essentially negative); and *novelty* (the news must tell us something new). These three values run through the 12 other values that now shape crime news – namely *threshold, predictability, simplification, individualism, risk, sex, celebrity, proximity, violence, spectacle, children* and *conservatism* (see Table 6.2).

It is informative to consider these news values in relation to the considerable body of research on the extent of crime in the news and the pattern of crime news. Reiner (2002: 379–93; see also Reiner 2003: 268) has undertaken a comprehensive review of these studies and the reader is referred to his nuanced analysis. However, to summarize somewhat crudely, Reiner concludes, albeit noting variances over time, across the media, and also between markets, that: 1) crime stories are prominent in all media and always have been; 2) the news media concentrate on violent crimes against individuals and do not accurately reflect official statistics. The risks of becoming a victim of violent crime are overplayed and the risks of becoming a victim of property crime are underplayed; 3) the demographic profiles of media victims and offenders are not representative of actual victims and offenders recorded in the criminal justice system; and 4) the news media

Table 6.2 Jewkes' 12 news values for a new millennium

News value	Description
Threshold	Events have to meet a level of perceived importance or drama to be considered newsworthy. The threshold will differ depending on whether the news professionals work at local, regional, national, global level
Predictability	Predictable news stories (e.g. the release of crime figures) allow news organizations to plan ahead
Simplification	Reducing the news to a minimum number of themes or parts (e.g. 'drugs and crime'). Whenever possible social situations must be reduced to binary oppositions
Individualism	Individual definitions of crime and responses to crime are preferred to complex explanations. Political, social and conceptual issues are reduced to conflict between individuals (e.g. the Prime Minister's views on law and order compared with those of the Leader of the Opposition)
Risk	Misrepresentation of the risk of crime. Media present serious crime as random, meaningless and unpredictable; we are all potential victims
Sex	Over-reporting of crimes of a sexual nature. Misrepresentation of women victims
Celebrity or high-status persons	The level of deviance required to attract media attention is significantly lower for celebrities than for 'ordinary' citizens. Applies to celebrities as offenders and victims
Proximity	Proximity is both spatial – the geographical nearness of an event – and cultural – the relevance of an event to an audience. Proximity varies between local and national news. Cultural proximity can pertain to perpetrators and victims; more coverage will be afforded to missing 'respectable' girls than 'tearaway' council-estate lads
Violence	Violence fulfils the media's desire to present dramatic events in the most graphic possible fashion
Spectacle and graphic imagery	Quality pictures help to demonstrate the 'truth' of a story. Violent acts with a strong visual impact will receive media attention. Increased use of CCTV footage and video footage shot by amateur witnesses
Children	Any crime involving children can be lifted into news visibility; both children as victims and children as offenders
Conservative ideology and political division	A version of 'populist punitiveness' dominates. This agenda emphasizes deterrence and repression and voices support for more police, more prisons and a tougher criminal justice system

Source: Summarized from Jewkes (2004: 40–60)

sharply criticize police deviancy and ineffectiveness, but on the whole they present positive images of police effectiveness and integrity.

Reiner's conclusions, in conjunction with the identified news values, elucidate the high media profile of crime and its investigation, and explain why serious crimes, such as murder and rape, attract greater interest than 'everyday' crimes such as burglary and car theft. Crime and its investigation tick many of the news value boxes and serious crimes, particularly, have a high quota of newsworthiness. It is in these cases that the processes of police image work, the business of criminal investigation and the professional imperatives of the news media intersect most sharply. In the final section of the chapter, we will focus on this aspect of criminal investigation and the media.

Serious crime investigation and the media

In cases of serious crime the performance of the police as investigators is played out most publicly: the symbolic role of the police as crime fighters is held up for scrutiny and appraised by the media, by celebrated former police investigators enrolled by media organizations to provide the 'inside track' and ultimately by the viewing, reading and listening audiences. Consequently, media handling in serious crime investigations has become a major issue, acknowledged by Home Office research as a critical skill required by senior investigating officers (SIOs) (Feist 1999). The Home Office report, *The Effective Detective*, identified 22 skill categories for effective SIOs, one of which was 'managing the communications process' which includes managing the media and developing appropriate media strategies (Smith and Flanagan 2000: 53). These Home Office studies belatedly recognized that the management of media relations during serious crime investigations is complex. In such circumstances, from the police perspective media relations is two edged: it is important for both negative and positive reasons. In terms of the former, the media can be an extra problematic issue for the investigation; in terms of the latter, the media can be deployed as an investigative resource (Innes 1999). Let us consider each of these in turn.

On the one hand, the media can be used to assist generally in generating information; they can act as a conduit to a wide public audience through reporting on the crime, providing coverage of press conferences, and issuing descriptions of people wanted to 'assist with inquiries'. They can also be used to reinvigorate investigations that have not been solved and where the police have pursued all available lines of inquiry. In his study of the media as an investigative resource in murder investigations, Innes (1999: 276–7) reported, based on fieldwork observations and analysis of case files, that the police attempted to use the media tactically to achieve a number of purposes, including: 1) to flush out the killer as a result of publicizing the crime; 2) to put pressure on the killer who may then behave strangely and prompt someone close to contact the police; 3) to shame someone shielding a killer to turn him or her in; 4) to publicize photographs and descriptions of suspects to encourage a public response; 5) to seek further witnesses and information; and, controversially, 6) to use the media as a means of developing suspicions they have about individuals close to the victim (e.g. involving such individuals in press conferences).[4] Innes' study is an insightful contribution to our understanding of how the police interact with and use the media, though it presents the perspective of investigating officers and does not take account of the growing, mainly unseen role of the police's own media professionals, who have become increasingly involved in all aspects of police–media relations (Mawby 1999, 2002a, 2002b). Its perspective also foregrounds managing and using the media rather than coping with their intrusions.

On the other hand, and more problematic from the police point of view, the news media can present a number of challenges to the progress of high-profile serious crime investigations. Research conducted in 1994 on the management of serious crime investigations produced the somewhat surprising finding that SIOs considered the task of 'managing the media' to be among their most onerous responsibilities (Berry et al. 1995). To take one example, the case of Fred and Rose West,[5] Gloucestershire police found themselves besieged and overwhelmed by the national and international media during this investigation. The experience was not positive: the SIO and Deputy SIO described media intrusions at both personal and professional levels. At the personal level this included journalists covertly following off-duty members of the police investigation team and attempting to eavesdrop on their conversations. At the professional level it included: 1) the media conducting parallel inquiries independently of the police investigation and setting up their own telephone hot-lines to attract information; 2) media-directed inquiries – journalists suggesting new lines of inquiry which they thought should be pursued 'in the public interest'; 3) journalists gaining access to witnesses, victims and members of the West family and buying their stories, sometimes prior to the police conducting interviews with the same people; 4) interference with evidence (e.g. guards had to be mounted to protect potential search and excavation sites); and 5) the 'bugging' of press conference venues with electronic listening devices in order to pick up 'off the record' information.

For this investigation at least, the fourth estate were summed up by one detective not as an investigative resource but as 'uncontrollable, no morals or integrity, no financial limits, no loyalty to each other – scumbags'. The intrusion reached a level that threatened a media-driven investigation and a trial by media. Rose West's solicitors argued (unsuccessfully) that she should not be tried as a fair trial was not possible given the extent and tone of the press coverage. Interviews with detectives in other forces provided further examples of media intrusions; though less serious, none the less they had potentially debilitating effects on the investigation being undertaken (Berry et al. 1995).

Although the West case was exceptional, the patterns of media intrusion described are recognizable in other high-profile investigations, including the case of the Yorkshire Ripper, the investigation into the abduction and murder in 1993 of 2-year-old James Bulger from a Liverpool shopping mall by Robert Thompson and Jon Venables (both aged 10), and the abduction and murder of Sarah Payne by a convicted paedophile in 2000. However, most recently the resonations are with the investigation into the murder of two 10-year-olds, Holly Wells and Jessica Chapman, in Soham. The investigation resulted in the conviction of school-caretaker Ian Huntley, but also serious criticism of the police (Bichard 2004).[6] As Leishman and Mason (2003: 44) noted:

> the interaction between police and media – perhaps unparalleled in terms of immediacy and unprecedented in intensity – demonstrated by turns the fact that control of context in unfolding major incidents is a fluid rather than a fixed phenomenon. At first praised for the professional way that the media was handled in terms of keeping the story in the public eye, Cambridgeshire Police soon came to experience the three 'E's of police-media relations – expectation, exhortation and excoriation.

The media pressures brought to bear on actual crime investigations are alluded to regularly in fictional investigations. Television detectives commonly come under pressure to achieve results not only from their superiors, but also from the media. A pertinent example arises in the *Inspector Morse* episode 'Happy families', in which an aggressive media pack becomes antagonistic towards Morse. At a press conference, Morse is disdainful of the media, prompting his superior, worried about the public perception of the investigation, to berate him afterwards with the words 'we need them on our side – you were bloody superior – there are more than just *Guardian* readers out there you know!' Consequently, Morse is stood down from the next press conference, in favour of his assistant, Sergeant Lewis, who gives a virtuoso performance. Unlike Morse, he is at ease with the media, handling their questions with assurance and good humour. This is noted by Morse, who becomes increasingly bewildered and disturbed by the media's intrusions as the investigation flounders. While a drama, this episode highlights the tensions that can exist in police–media relations and the pressure that the media can exert on the investigators. It also signals a clash between the old and new context of crime investigation and the skills required by SIOs – Morse's contempt for, and inability to engage with, the media contrasts sharply with Lewis's relaxed manner.

Given the benefits that the media can bring to an investigation, and also the need to manage the potentially negative aspects of media interest, what can a SIO and his or her investigation team do to 'manage' the media? To answer this question the Home Office commissioned research that examined 16 case studies and included interviews with the SIO and media liaison officer in each case (Feist 1999). Feist recognized the complexity of media relations during serious crime investigations and the need to systemize this aspect of the investigation. He concluded (1999: 35) that an effective media strategy is 'an integral part of an investigative strategy, rather than a presentational luxury' and suggested that strategies should include the following eight objectives. To:

Table 6.3 Towards a media strategy

Planning imperatives	The considerations: what needs to be done?
1. *The management of media interest*	Anticipate and plan for: • the level of media interest (local, regional, national, international?) • the types of media that will be attracted (print, radio, television?) • the longevity/sustainability of media interest (local media interest may sustain longer than national; local press interest may sustain longer than radio and television interest) • the time commitment required of the SIO from the media and the likely questions to be asked at different stages • the post-charge issues – e.g. is pre-emptive legal action required about possible media interference in the case?
2. *The disclosure and and generation of information*	Ongoing information management: • determine at the initial stage the information that should be released and that which should be retained for the most effective progression of the investigation • review the disclosing and retaining of information as the investigation progresses • consider the timing of the release of information in order for it to have its greatest impact • determine the target audiences in disclosing information and appealing for further information. Who are the audiences and what is the most effective medium for reaching them? • plan the main messages that need to be communicated and subsequently reinforced • following the disclosure of information, monitor how it is interpreted and communicated through the media.
3. *Managing potential media consequences*	Assessment of the implications of media interest and the actions of journalists in terms of: • preserving and protecting the crime scene • witnesses and the potential for their evidence being compromised by media 'interference' (e.g. payments by the media for witness accounts) • the victim and and his/her relatives, friends, associates. The media presentation of the victim can influence the willingness of family and friends to co-operate with the police. SIOs, with their press officers, need to anticipate potential media interpretations of aspects of the investigation

Table 6.3 *Continued*

Planning imperatives	The considerations: what needs to be done?
	• execution of legal process. Once criminal proceedings become active following the charging of offenders, the media are bound by the subjudice ruling and by the Contempt of Court Act 1981. SIOs need to consider the appropriateness of pre-trial and during-trial media briefings
4. *Human resource management*	The SIO and his and her management team will need to consider: • the integration of force media liaison personnel into the investigation team at management level • the human and time resources required to manage the interface with the media • the processes for including the media liaison officer in the running of the investigation, so that he or she works as part of the investigation team and not as a semi-detached 'bolt-on' to it • the media training implications for members of the investigation team • planning for resourcing the response to media-focused activities (e.g. resourcing phone lines following a televised crime reconstruction)

Source: Derived from Feist (1999).

1 use the media to acquire information required by the investigation;
2 manage media interest to minimize potential misinformation;
3 manage media interest to minimize interference with scenes, witnesses, victims and their relatives, and suspects;
4 inform the public accurately about the crime and the police approach to its investigation;
5 give due concern to the portrayal of victims, the sensibilities of their relatives, and the response of the community;
6. minimize concern over the fear of crime;
7 disseminate relevant crime prevention and security advice; and
8 demonstrate the professionalism of the police service
    (summarized from Feist 1999: 3).

To operationalize these objectives, although Feist's research does not set out a fixed template for an effective media strategy, he suggests that SIOs consider similar factors when constructing a strategy. These include: 1) the management of media interest; 2) the disclosure and generation of information; 3) managing potential media consequences; and 4) human resource management. The appropriate considerations under each of these headings are listed in Table 6.3. It is in these areas that police image workers can support and advise the investigation team. As media professionals they can provide guidance on the level and types of media interest that the investigation will generate. They can work 'backstage' assisting the SIO and his or her team with advice on information disclosure and on managing the consequences of media involvement. They can also work 'frontstage' liaising directly with media representatives, thereby acting as a 'buffer' between detectives and the media and allowing the investigation team to concentrate on substantive matters. Where the media demand to speak to the SIO, the press officer can broker and manage these appearances and can prepare the SIO for the questioning. Press officers can also act as a buffer between the media and members of the victim's family. Employing such measures allows the SIO to concentrate on the investigation and makes the maximum use of the skills of the police-employed media professionals, which in turn will help to meet the requirements of the media. This will help facilitate the 'natural symbiosis of interest for both the media and the police in respectively providing and obtaining media coverage' (Innes 1999: 285).

Conclusion: the publicness of crime investigation

To conclude, the police–media relationship is longstanding and complex, with recurring themes of conflict and reciprocity. The media have created police heroes and villains, have idealized the police, but have also exposed failing policing systems and practices. The police have been consistently interested in communicating through the media for instrumental and symbolic reasons. Amid great changes over time in types of media, in the speed and range of communication and in the techniques of media presentation and management, the crime investigation function has proved to be a central focus for the police–media relationship, being of particular interest to the police, the media and to consumers of both policing services and media outputs. However, in a context of mounting media saturation, criminal investigation has become an increasingly public spectacle and, at times, almost a participatory process. The police-watching public(s), through absorbing a stream of policing fiction and faction, through being let into the media world of exemplary and flawed detectives, and by being educated and entertained by the science of investigation, may think they know about criminal investigation. In the case of serious crime investigations, this most sacred and revered of operational functions has been laid bare. This is, of course, a partial and distorted picture: media consumers are completing their own 'half-formed pictures' (Mawby 2003). In this context, the 'impossible mandate' remains central to analyses of policing and retains its explanatory power. In contrast, the days of 'police fetishism' may be numbered; as the processes of criminal investigation become ever more visible, there exists the potential not only to idealize, but also to demystify the police as effective crime fighters.

Selected further reading

Reiner, R. (2002) 'Media made criminality: the representation of crime in the mass media', in M. Maguire *et al.* (eds) *The Oxford Handbook of Criminology* (3rd edn). Oxford: Clarendon Press. Reiner, R. (2003) 'Policing and the media', in T. Newburn (ed.) *Handbook of Policing.* Cullompton: Willan Publishing. Both these chapters provide excellent, accessible overviews of crime, policing and the media.

Jewkes, Y. (2004) *Media and Crime.* London: Sage. An extremely useful book that includes chapters on the construction of crime news and on 'crimewatching'.

Leishman, F. and Mason, P. (2003) *Policing and the Media: Facts, Fictions and Factions.* Cullompton: Willan Publishing. This book considers the blurring of factual and fictional accounts of criminal investigation.

Mawby, R.C. (2002) *Policing Images: Policing, Communication and Legitimacy.* Cullompton: Willan Publishing. Focuses on how the police have developed the practice of 'image work'.

Innes, M. (1999) 'The media as an investigative resource in murder enquiries', *British Journal of Criminology*, 39: 269–86. This article provides a detailed account of how detectives seek to use the media during murder inquiries.

Notes

1 By image work I mean the activities police forces engage in to project meanings of policing. It includes overt activities (e.g. media and public relations activities) but also the mundane practices of police work, which also communicate images of policing (e.g. routine patrol work) (Mawby 2002a).

2 Brearley's typology identifies 'four sequentially emerging and enduring sets of images' in the popular development of the police detective in England and Wales, namely: 1) 'Bullies'; 2) 'Bumblers'; 3) 'Boffins'; and 4) 'Bureaucrats' (Brearley 2005).

3 An example of the speed and global reach of communications appeared in the *Guardian* on 30 March 2005 under the heading 'Long distance "crime" alert'. The report tells of an Australian in Boorowa, New South Wales, who was browsing the Internet and watching webcams trained on the sea front at Exmouth in Devon, England (through www.exmouthcam.co.uk). While doing so, he witnessed what appeared to be a robbery and alerted Devon and Cornwall Police to this by telephoning to report what he had seen from 12,000 miles away.

4 Following several cases in which people appearing at press conferences were subsequently charged with the crime under investigation, concern was expressed about police motives and tactics (Innes 1999: 280). ACPO guidance provides that victims' relatives should not be used at press conferences until they have been eliminated from the inquiry (Feist 1999: 27).

5 Fred West was accused of committing 12 murders between 1971 and 1994. The remains of nine victims were found buried at the family home, 25 Cromwell Street, which was besieged by the media. West committed suicide while on remand in prison; in 1995 his wife Rose was convicted of ten murders and jailed for life (see Bennett 2005).

6 The Bichard Inquiry reported in June 2004, finding 'errors, omissions, failures and shortcomings' across all organizations that had contact with Ian Huntley.

References

Ascoli, D. (1979) *The Queen's Peace*. London: Hamish Hamilton.

Bayley, D.H. (1996) 'What do the police do?', in W. Saulsbury *et al.* (eds) *Themes in Contemporary Policing*. London: PSI Publishing.

Bennett, J. with Gardner, G. (2005) *The Cromwell Street Murders: The Detective's Story*. Stroud: Sutton Publishing.

Berry, G., Izat, J., Mawby, R.C. and Walley, L. (1995) *The Management and Organisation of Serious Crime Investigations*. Stafford: Staffordshire University. Unpublished report to the Home Office Police Operations Against Crime (POAC) programme.

Bichard, M. (2004) *The Bichard Inquiry Final Report*. London: HMSO.

Billen, A. (2004) 'Iraq as thriller: a six part series offers a surprising allegory of the war', *New Statesman*, 8 November.

Brearley, N. (2005) 'The rise and fall of the modern detective: the media construction of criminal investigation and the golden age of policing.' Paper presented at the British Society of Criminology conference, Portsmouth, July 2004, and at the University of Central England, Criminal Justice Policy and Research seminar series, February 2005.

Breslin, J. (1990) *America's Most Wanted*. London: Harper & Row.

Brunsdon, C. (2000) 'The structure of anxiety: recent British television crime fiction', in E. Buscombe (ed.) *British Television: A Reader*. Oxford: Clarendon Press.

Chibnall, S. (1977) *Law-and-order News: An Analysis of Crime Reporting in the British Press*. London: Tavistock.

Cox, M. (ed.) (1992) *Victorian Tales of Mystery and Detection*. Oxford: Oxford University Press.

Creeber, G. (2001) 'Cigarettes and alcohol: investigating gender, genre and gratification in *Prime Suspect*', *Television and New Media*, 2: 149–66.

Dixon, G. (1960) *Dixon of Dock Green: My Life*. London: William Kimber & Co.

Ericson, R.V. (1995) 'The news media and account ability in criminal justice', in P.C. Stenning (ed.) *Accountability for Criminal Justice*. Toronto: University of Toronto Press.

Ericson, R.V., Baranek, P.M. and Chan, J.B.L. (1989) *Negotiating Control – a Study of News Sources*. Toronto: University of Toronto Press.

Fabian, R. (1955) *Fabian of the Yard*. London: Heirloom Modern World Library.

Feist, A. (1999) *The Effective Use of the Media in Serious Crime Investigations*. Policing and Reducing Crime Unit Paper 120. London: Home Office.

Gill, M. (2000) *Commercial Robbery*. London: Blackstone Press.

Hall, S., Critcher, C., Jefferson, T., Clarke, J. and Roberts, B. (1978) *Policing the Crisis: Mugging, the State, and Law and Order*. London: Macmillan.

Haste, S. (1997) *Criminal Sentences: True Crime in Fiction and Drama*. London: Cygnus Arts.

Hellawell, K. (2002) *The Outsider*. London: HarperCollins.

Hill, A. (2000a) 'Crime and crisis: British reality TV in action', in E. Buscombe (ed.) *British Television: A Reader*. Oxford: Clarendon Press.

Hill, A. (2000b) 'Fearful and safe: audience response to British reality programming', *Television and New Media*, 1: 193–213.

Home Office (1989) *Standing Conference on Crime Prevention Report of the Working Group on the Fear of Crime*. London: Home Office.

Hunt, L. (1999) 'Dog eat dog: the *Squeeze* and the *Sweeney* films', in S. Chibnall and R. Murphy (eds) *British Crime Cinema*. London: Routledge.

Innes, M. (1999) 'The media as an investigative resource in murder enquiries', *British Journal of Criminology*, 39: 269–86.

Innes, M. (2002) 'Organizational communication and the symbolic construction of police murder investigations', *British Journal of Sociology* 53: 67–87.

Jewkes, Y. (2004) *Media and Crime.* London: Sage.

Kilborn, R., Hibberd, M. and Boyle, R. (2001) 'The rise of the docusoap: the case of *Vets in Practice*', *Screen*, 42: 382–95.

Lawrence, P. (2003) '"Scoundrels and scallywags and some honest men ..." Memoirs and the self-image of French and English policemen *c*.1870–1939', in B. Godfrey *et al.* (eds) *Comparative Histories of Crime.* Cullompton: Willan Publishing.

Leishman, F. and Mason, P. (2003) *Policing and the Media: Facts, Fictions and Factions.* Cullompton: Willan Publishing.

Leishman, F. and Mason, P. (2005) 'From *Dock Green* to docusoap: decline and fall in TV copland', *Criminal Justice Matters*, 59: 22–3.

Lichter, S.R., Lichter, L.S. and Amundson, D. (1999) *Images of Government in TV Entertainment.* Washington, DC: Partnership for Trust in Government (available online at http://www.trustingov.org/research/govtv/TVStudy.pdf).

Lichter, S.R., Lichter, L.S. and Amundson, D. (2002) *Images of Government in TV Entertainment, 1998–2001.* Washington, DC: Partnership for Trust in Government (available online at http://www.trustingov.org/research/govtv/mediarpt.pdf).

Livingstone, K. and Hart, J. (2003) 'The wrong arm of the law? Public images of private security', *Policing and Society*, 13: 159–70.

Manning, P.K. (1971) 'The police: mandate, strategies and appearances', in J.D. Douglas (ed.) *Crime and Justice in American Society.* Indianapolis, IN: Bobbs-Merrill.

Manning, P.K. (1997) *Police Work: The Social Organization of Policing* (2nd edn). Prospect Heights, IL: Waveland Press.

Manning, P.K. (2003) *Policing Contingencies.* Chicago, IL: University of Chicago Press.

Mark, R. (1978) *In the Office of Constable.* London: Collins & Son.

Mason, P. (1992) *Reading* The Bill*: An Analysis of the Thames Television Police Drama.* Bristol: Bristol and Bath Centre for Criminal Justice.

Mawby, R.C. (1999) 'Visibility, transparency and police media relations', *Policing and Society*, 9: 263–86.

Mawby, R.C. (2002a) *Policing Images: Policing, Communication and Legitimacy.* Cullompton: Willan Publishing.

Mawby, R.C. (2002b) 'Continuity and change, convergence and divergence: the policy and practice of police–media relations', *Criminal Justice*, 2: 303–25.

Mawby, R.C. (2003) 'Completing the "half-formed picture"? Media images of policing', in P. Mason (ed.) *Criminal Visions: Media Representations of Crime and Justice.* Cullompton: Willan Publishing.

Mawby, R.C. and Worthington, J.S. (2002) 'Marketing the police: from a force to a service', *Journal of Marketing Management*, 18: 857–76.

McGrath, M. and Turvey, B.E. (2003) 'Criminal profilers and the media: profiling the Beltway Snipers', *Journal of Behavioral Profiling*, 4: 1–20.

Metropolitan Police Authority (2002) *Performance Report: Homicide.* Report 06, 13 June (available online at http://www.mpa.gov.uk/committees/x-pspm/2002/020613/06.htm).

Miller, H. (2001) *Crimewatch Solved.* London: Pan Macmillan.

Morton, J. (2005) *The First Detective.* London: Ebury Press.

P.A. Consulting Group (2001) *Diary of a Police Officer.* Police Research Series Paper 149. London: Home Office (available online at http://www.policereform.gov.uk/docs/prs149.pdf).

Rawlings, P. (1995) 'The idea of policing: a history', *Policing and Society*, 5: 129–49.

Rawlings, P. (2003) 'Policing before the police', in T. Newburn (ed.) *Handbook of Policing.* Cullompton: Willan Publishing.

Reiner, R. (1994) 'The dialectics of Dixon: the changing image of the TV cop', in M. Stephens and S. Becker (eds) *Police Force Police Service*. London: Macmillan.

Reiner, R. (2000) *The Politics of the Police* (3rd edn). Oxford: Oxford University Press.

Reiner, R. (2002) 'Media made criminality: the representation of crime in the mass media', in M. Maguire *et al.* (eds) *The Oxford Handbook of Criminology* (3rd edn). Oxford: Clarendon Press.

Reiner, R. (2003) 'Policing and the media', in T. Newburn (ed.) *Handbook of Policing*. Cullompton: Willan Publishing.

Reiner, R., Livingstone, S. and Allen, J. (2001) 'Casino culture: media and crime in a winner-loser society', in K. Stenson and R.R. Sullivan (eds) *Crime, Risk and Justice: The Politics of Crime Control in Liberal Democracies*. Cullompton: Willan Publishing.

Ross, N. and Cook, S. (1987) *Crimewatch UK*. London: Hodder & Stoughton.

Schlesinger, P. and Tumber, H. (1994) *Reporting Crime*. Oxford: Clarendon Press.

Sillitoe, P. (1955) *Cloak without Dagger*. London: Pan Books.

Smith, N. and Flanagan, C. (2000) *The Effective Detective: Identifying the Skills of an Effective SIO. Policing and Reducing Crime Unit Police Research Series Paper* 122. London: Home Office RDS.

Symons, J. (1985) *Bloody Murder: From the Detective Story to the Crime Novel* (2nd edn). Harmondsworth: Penguin Books.

Thompson, J.B. (1995) *The Media and Modernity: A Social Theory of the Media*. Cambridge: Polity Press.

Williams, R. (1961) *The Long Revolution*. Harmondsworth: Penguin Books.

Wright, A. (2002) *Policing: An Introduction to Concepts and Practice*. Cullompton: Willan Publishing.

Organization of criminal investigation

How is criminal investigation organized? What are the main structures and systems? Which organizations are involved in such activity, and how is such work undertaken in areas such as high-volume crime and major crime inquiries? These are some of the core questions explored in Part 2 of the Handbook. The part opens with a look at international structures and transnational crime. As we noted in the Introduction to this book, the changing nature of communications and transport associated with the overall social transformation we have come to know as 'globalization' has had an impact on criminal opportunities as in all other areas of activity. Serious and organized crime involving the trafficking of goods (from drugs to weapons), the trade in people (from organizing immigration to trafficking for prostitution and slavery) to the enormous possibilities opened up by the electronic trade in money, are all evidence of the dramatic impact of globalization on crime. Criminal investigation has progressively reorganized itself in response, and Chris Lewis examines a number of the key structures such as the United Nations, Interpol and Europol, as well as some of the newer, more specific powers such as the European Arrest Warrant. He illustrates some of the continuing variation that exists in the investigation of organized crime across the EU, and argues that both national jurisdictions and transnational bodies have generally been slow to change their structures and to move their resources in response to the changing nature of the problems they have to confront.

Back at the domestic level, Tim John and Mike Maguire examine the history, nature, development and effectiveness of the National Intelligence Model (NIM). Modern intelligence systems, they argue, really began to develop in the 1970s and 1980s during which a series of proactive investigative techniques were developed. The term 'intelligence-led policing' is a more recent development and refers to the development of intelligence beyond specialist squads into mainstream policing. This approach to policing has emerged for a number of reasons, they argue, including concerns about the perceived effectiveness of reactive policing, advances in technology, limitations of investigative interviewing and confession evidence, and increasing emphasis on serious and organized crime, together with the pressures of new public management. Perhaps not surprisingly it has taken some time for the new structures and processes associated with the NIM to bed down within the police service, and John and Maguire suggest that, in most forces, NIM priorities are still very much police, and crime control, driven. 'It is only in the last year or two', they suggest, 'that some police forces have begun to engage non-police partners in anything more than a token manner in their own NIM decision-making procedures and – perhaps more importantly – that intelligence products have begun to influence to any significant degree the activities of agencies other than the police.' It is in this area that some of the more important developments are likely to emerge in coming years.

The NIM is eventually intended to restructure and reform all aspects of policing. One area where there are significant challenges, but also huge potential, is in the investigation of high-volume crime. Nick Tilley, Amanda Robinson and John Burrows, drawing heavily on a large research study they have conducted, look at the investigation systems and processes used by forces in tackling volume crimes such as burglary and vehicle crime. Resources and their allocation form a very significant element in decision-making. As Tilley and colleagues outline, there are a number of crucial questions that need to be asked by police managers, including which cases warrant police attention at the scene, which need an urgent response, which should be followed up by scenes of crime officers and possibly by CID, and so on. From the outset, they say, a process of triage is in operation. In terms of investigative processes, they identify two 'ideal types'. The first – the *procedural* processes – are characterized by clear protocols governed by specific predetermined questions and practices in an 'assembly-line' version of the investigative process. By contrast, the *discretionary* process, as it sounds, is more flexible and tailored to the perceived needs of the individual case. The pressure, as the earlier chapter by John and Maguire illustrated, is pushing policing further in the direction of more flexible and proactive approaches.

At the other end of the spectrum from volume crime are major crime inquiries. Volume crime, by definition, occurs in large numbers. Major crime inquiries, for example in response to murder and other very serious offences, are less frequent. Research on volume crime investigation has tended to suggest that it is routinized and ordered, that much of the activity involved is information work and that accounts of the crime itself are in part a reflection of police methods. Though major crime inquiries are arguably slightly less routinized than volume crime, the general findings from previous research apply remarkably well to this area of activity. In his overview of the area, Martin Innes argues that criminal investigation is about the endeavour of bringing a degree of order to the disorderly and an attempt to manufacture certainty out of uncertainty. In doing so, he suggests, investigators become involved in three inter-related sets of activities. First, they 'identify and acquire'. This concerns the acquisition of those things – information, materials, intelligence and suspects – that provide the basis for understanding 'who did what to whom'. Secondly, they 'interpret and understand'. This is a sense-making process in which they classify information and utilize existing narratives to order and understand the phenomena acquired in the first stage. Finally, they 'order and represent'. That is to say, they use the particular narrative or narratives as a template for the generation of an account of the particular incident – including its pre-history and post-event activities. Investigatory decision-making and case construction are, in Innes' terms, ongoing accomplishments; they are phenomena that evolve, and understanding this can aid our understanding of how investigations work, as well as what can go wrong.

Our discussion so far, as is the case with so much work on policing, has focused on the *public* police – that is, local constabularies and related national and international bodies. However, there is of course a vast array of other bodies involved in criminal investigation. Les Johnston's chapter explores 'private investigation' as it has developed and currently operates. Crucially, as he reminds us, little if any of this is new. Pinkerton's operated during the American Civil War in the nineteenth century. However, what we have now is a larger, and more technically competent and highly structured, private investigatory sector. Estimates of the numbers employed in such activity in the UK vary, but the number probably exceeds the 15,000 estimated by Button and George in the early 1990s. The work undertaken in this sector is divided by Johnston into four main categories: anti-fraud work undertaken primarily for large insurance firms; background legal work, forensic-evidence gathering and process serving; commercial inquiry including debugging, pre-employment checks, personal protection and risk assessment; and, finally, domestic investigations including checking fidelity, children's drug use, missing persons and abducted child recovery. Two of the general trends outlined by Matassa and Newburn in Part 1 – transnationalization and risk orientation – are also having a profound structuring impact on the private investigatory sector and are further blurring the boundaries between the private and public sectors or, as Johnston argues, rendering such a distinction generally inappropriate.

Chapter 7

International structures and transnational crime

Chris Lewis

Conceptual framework

The years since 1950 have seen an unprecedented development of a large number of international institutions and instruments in all political, social and economic areas. This development aims to reduce conflict and inequality, ease international co-operation and speed economic development. It also responds to the increased movement of goods, services and people, itself a reaction to improved communications as reflected in cheaper transportation and the growth of IT.

Criminal justice has been no exception to this development. Bilateral arrangements between countries that sufficed before the 1950s have gradually been replaced by frameworks that cover groupings of countries. Such frameworks aim to avoid criminals exploiting 'safe havens' and differences between criminal justice systems.

The need for international co-operation in criminal justice investigation parallels the need for co-operation within a single jurisdiction. It is taken for granted that Hampshire Police Force in England should obtain full co-operation from all other criminal justice agencies in England and Wales when they pursue a case. But modern criminals are as likely to pursue their activities from outside England and Wales or to flee abroad once their crime has been committed. The need for co-operation between jurisdictions therefore falls into the following broad categories:

- The need for authorities to pursue their investigations outside their area of jurisdiction:

  - by having easier access to pursuing and interviewing suspects and witnesses; and
  - by better access to documentary evidence, including records on computer, video-tapes or phones.

- Improved extradition proceedings.
- Mutual legal assistance between respective agencies.
- The transfer of proceedings to another jurisdiction, if appropriate.
- The recognition of judgements from other jurisdictions.
- If appropriate, the implementation of such judgements in other jurisdictions.
- The setting up of supranational agencies for investigation and judgement where appropriate and acceptable.
- Ensuring evidence from another jurisdiction can be produced in an acceptable way.
- Transferring prisoners where this is appropriate.

This chapter considers the response to these needs, what international instruments and structures have been set up and their broad success. More details can be found in the selected further reading section and the references at the end of the chapter (the websites given in the chapter and in the references, however, will supply more up-to-date information).

The broad conclusion of the chapter is that much has been achieved in international co-operation but developments have been piecemeal. EU developments, in particular, have been late in coming and much more remains to be done.

Need for international co-operation in investigation and policy development

Crimes that have in some way been 'organized'[1] or 'transnational' are not new. Some crimes have always been organized abroad or have been committed in more than one state, and the criminal has often escaped abroad after committing a crime. However, recent developments in illegal markets, technology, transport and commercial structures have increased the likelihood of such cross-border crimes.

The increase in international travel has meant that criminals can go abroad to see the environment where they plan the crime. If their home state has good crime prevention strategies, they can move where their particular type of crime is more likely to succeed. After the crime, they can move to where extradition is difficult. The coming of multinational companies with common practices in different countries means that they can be targeted more easily, and the growing wealth of many states leads to more money for the average person. This leads to increased spending in illegal markets, such as sex and drugs.

The demand for drugs has led to a vastly increased market, usually supplied by illegal imports along well established trade routes. Estimates of the turnover in this market are enormous, amounting to $160 billion at the end of the twentieth century (Reuter 1998). The demand for personal services and the growth of the sex industry have led to a large increase in both legal and illegal migration from poorer to richer countries to provide low-cost services. Some estimates put the turnover of illegal immigration and human trafficking at the same order of magnitude as the drugs industry (see e.g., FATF 2005).

New technologies, such as the Internet, mean that new types of crime have evolved, associated with hacking, identity theft, denial of service attacks, or other computer fraud. Such crimes are committed in a virtual world. Money resulting from criminal activity can be easily moved between states, despite money-laundering measures that financial institutions now need to obey.

Although there are very few measures of crime that cross borders (Savona et al. 2005), it is generally accepted by commentators that such crimes have increased greatly over the last 20 years. In particular, the police at the start of the twenty-first century are much more likely to need to contact their colleagues abroad, judges are much more likely to be asked to extradite a criminal or sign an arrest warrant, and prison authorities are more likely to need to transfer inmates back to the country of the origin to complete their sentences.

A greater need for international co-operation in justice has grown in the last 20 years. However, it is clear that, despite the various developments listed in this chapter, the response has been inadequate, particularly in Europe. Despite growing co-operation between investigating authorities, there remain frequent examples where investigations and prosecutions have been held up because the criminal or defendant has moved from one country to another, making use of the slowness of existing procedures, the concern that member states of the EU have with giving up their sovereignty and the recentness of all these developments that still makes co-operation across states an unfamiliar operation to the average police detective.

Some commentators (e.g. Joutsen 2005) have commented that the everyday practices of extradition and mutual assistance are based on instruments developed many years ago. The more recent developments (international terrorism, new technologies that facilitate crime, cheap transport, freedom of movement) call for a much faster change to investigative procedures across boundaries than so far achieved. Whether either the governments or the populations of the EU are willing to accept such faster changes remains to be seen. We start by examining current international organizations that exist in the general area of countering crime and terrorism.

United Nations

Despite colossal efforts by the present Secretary General, the UN remains influential but largely impotent in the fight against international terrorism and organized crime.

Many conventions have been published,[2] and a 2001 resolution obliged member states to take action against the financing of terrorism; to suppress the provision of safe havens; to share information with other states; to criminalize active and passive assistance for terrorists; and to ratify the existing international conventions and protocols. However, such a resolution is a long way from actually achieving action and most states have not yet obeyed previous similar resolutions.

The main reason behind this slow progress is that the UN does not possess the authority or resources to ensure member states follow the conventions and protocols agreed within its assemblies and committees. There are also some member states that are unwilling to sign up to certain anti-terrorism measures because a significant part of their populations are at least tacitly supportive of some terrorist activity.

In an attempt to speed up progress, in preparation for the sixtieth anniversary meeting of the UN in September 2005, the Secretary General pressed hard for agreement at that meeting on 'The Five Ds'[3] of action against terrorism: to dissuade disaffected groups from choosing terrorism as a tactic; to deny terrorists the means to carry out attacks; to deter states from supporting terrorist groups; to develop the capacity of states to prevent terrorism; and to defend human rights and the rule of law. He also pressed states to agree on a definition of 'terrorism'.

However, discussions prior to that meeting were largely unsuccessful in getting UN member states to come to an agreement even on the definition of 'terrorism' or to sign up to anything very specific on measures against terrorism. There were signs that some member states were beginning to lose patience with this slow progress. The final 2005 report was disappointingly vague, reflecting deep disagreement. Previous exhortations were simply repeated and further discussions urged.[4]

Interpol

Interpol has 182 members. It supports organizations seeking to prevent or combat international crime. Its main roles are public safety, the prevention of terrorism, the disestablishment of criminal organizations and fugitive investigation support. It is also concerned with trafficking in drugs or persons, and financial and high-tech crime. It aims to provide a unique global police communications system, with a range of criminal databases and analytical services, as well as giving proactive support for police operations throughout the world (see www.interpol.int).

Any law enforcement agency could at any time need to trace a key offender at large within the international community. Interpol circulates internationally identification details and judicial information about wanted criminals. Its 'red notices' of wanted criminals have been recognized in many countries as having a legal basis for provisional arrest. Its fugitive investigative support subdirectorate provides investigative support to ongoing international fugitive investigations to locate and arrest fugitives; to co-ordinate and enhance international co-operation in the field of fugitive investigations; to collect and disseminate best practice and expert knowledge; and to conduct and co-ordinate relevant research.

Interpol has been involved with international terrorism since 1985. It works to develop a programme to build national and international capacity to counter bio-terrorism. It has a Fusion Task Force to identify terrorist groups and their membership, and its weapons projects include 'orange' notices to warn of threats from small arms, parcel bombs and radiological, chemical and biological threats. Its Weapons Electronic Tracing System (IWeTS) makes it easier to trace firearms that have moved internationally, and its Terrorism Watch List permits instant access to information on fugitive terrorists and suspected terrorists, as well as to a list of over 5,000 stolen passports.

Interpol produces crime statistics as well as criminal strategic analyses. Operational analyses aim to achieve a specific law enforcement outcome, such as an arrest, seizure or forfeiture of assets or disruption of a criminal group. Strategic analyses are used to inform higher-level decision-making and to provide early warnings of emerging issues.

Interpol is also actively involved in providing help to investigating authorities in member states about a large number of specific types of crime:

- *Crimes against children, trafficking in women and people smuggling*: these are top priorities. There is a forum to exchange information on current trends and investigations, to raise awareness, build competences and identify best practice.

- *Thefts of cultural property or works of art*: the main work is in raising awareness.

- *Vehicle crime*: training is given to improve investigations of cross-border crime. Codes of conduct are issued to minimize the chance of being a victim of carjacking, and codes are issued for recovering stolen vehicles from other countries.

- *Drugs*: Interpol makes links between drug cases being conducted by national administrations that would otherwise seem unrelated. It produces strategic and tactical intelligence reports and shares new investigative techniques. Fact sheets are produced for each drug, dealing with supply routes, traffickers and users.

- *Financial crime*: Interpol publishes details of risks of fraud, together with preventive and investigative methods (e.g. counterfeit money orders, lottery fraud, fraudulent reconstruction tenders after natural disasters, disaster charity fraud and 'Nigerian' 4-1-9 letters). It works on crime prevention with commercial organizations.

- *Identity cards*: Interpol works with the private sector to minimize identity theft.

- *Environmental crime*: it takes a lead on poaching, in trafficking in ozone-depleting substances, in the use of illegal pesticides, the illegal diversion of rivers, trafficking in endangered species and the illegal dumping of hazardous waste.

- *Information technology*: Interpol co-ordinates expertise from around the world.

- *Forensic developments*: it co-ordinates information on technologies available in fingerprinting, DNA profiling and disaster victim identification.

European Union

At the beginning of the 1990s, justice and home affairs were outside the competence of the EU, with each member state making its own co-operative arrangements within the terms of the various European conventions agreed under the aegis of the Council of Europe.[5] Since then, developments within the EU on co-operation within the justice and home affairs area have been relatively speedy. The Treaty on European Union in 1993 incorporated justice and home affairs into its institutional framework, and the Amsterdam Treaty of 1999 incorporated the Schengen Rules on freedom of movement.[6] The treaties of Maastricht and Tampere strengthened the ideas of judicial co-operation. Various terrorist incidents, starting with the 11 September 2001 attacks in the USA, followed by the Madrid bombings of March 2004, added impetus to these developments.[7] It is too early to say whether the London bombings of July 2005 will have a similar effect.

The agreed aim of the political leaders of the EU was to create an 'Area of Freedom, Security and Justice' within the EU. The strategy to achieve this was to create structures and protocols within the criminal justice agencies of different countries and at international level. Little interest was placed on consulting with the populations within the EU, or of educating those who would benefit from such arrangements. As a result, the organizations and protocols set up between 1993 and 2003 developed rather in a somewhat haphazard way (see Norman 2005 for a critical view of historical developments).

Little attention was paid to this lack of a strategic approach because the EU Commission plan was always to incorporate the strategic approach to justice and home affairs into the proposed EU Constitution, and it was taken for granted that such a constitution would eventually be agreed.

Legally speaking, as all member states agreed to justice and home affairs becoming part of the EU competences in the 1993 treaty and then signed up to Maastricht and Tampere, then, despite the rejection of the EU Constitution, there is no barrier to the continued development of co-operation on justice and home affairs. It should be recognized, as stated by Walker (2003: 117), that 'the EU may today be hosting the most audacious and potentially far-reaching experiment in transnational policing', but we should also note that, in several areas, member states have been slow at implementing ideas put forward by the EU Commission, and this lack of complete enthusiasm may well become more exaggerated following the rejection of the treaty on the Constitution.

It may be that EU energies will be concentrated on achieving an agreed revision of their budget system for some years at the expense of developments in criminal justice. At the time of writing it is difficult to say what will happen to EU justice and home affairs developments. The rejection of the treaty on the EU Constitution by France and the Netherlands in the spring of 2005 has left more detailed discussion in limbo. The terrorist incidents in London in July 2005 have reinforced the need for a more strategic approach to crime and justice. Initial attempts to negotiate the return of a terrorist suspect from Italy to the UK to assist in the investigation process were quite slow as both countries showed their unfamiliarity with the details of how to work with European arrest warrants (EAWs) (see below).

High-profile events such as this do tend to spur on developments such as the EAW. However, the reader interested in detailed developments on such European issues will need to keep up to date by frequent reference to the EU and the Europol websites (e.g. http://www.europol.eu.int). These are in great detail although they tend to concentrate on the ambitions of the central authorities rather than the agreed position of member states. In particular, the websites pertaining to the Directorate of Justice and Home Affairs lay out very detailed developments since 1993 (http://europa.eu.int/comm/ justice_home/glossary/wai/glossary_e_en.htm). They give a definition of all the terms used in the justice area, and the systems and agreements that have been set up over the last ten years.

At the apex of this work is the Justice and Home Affairs Council, which brings together justice and interior ministers from all member states to progress a key aim of the EU to create an Area of Freedom, Security and Justice. This involves developing and implementing co-operation and common policies in the justice and home affairs sectors. The main developments so far are the setting up of the European Police Office (1995), the European Ombudsman (1995), Eurojust (2002) and the European Judicial Network (1998) (see http://europa.eu.int/pol/justice/index_en.htm).

Europol

The European Police Office, Europol, is the most well known of the EU agencies concerned with crime and justice. It was founded in 1995 and is based in The Hague, with nearly 500 police officers, analysts and officials, many seconded from the police forces of the 25 EU member states. It also has bilateral or strategic arrangements with other states such as Switzerland, Norway, Bulgaria, Columbia and Russia. Its 2005 budget was over €63 million (see also http://www.europol.eu.int/index.asp?page=facts).

Europol aims at improving the effectiveness and co-operation of the competent authorities in preventing and combating terrorism, unlawful drug trafficking and other serious forms of international organized crime. Its mission is to make a significant contribution to the EU's law enforcement action with an emphasis on targeting criminal organizations.

Counter-terrorism activity is one of Europol's priority crime areas. However, despite this it was not able to help the Spanish police before the Madrid bombings in March 2004 or the British police before the July 2005 bombings. In fact, the Madrid bombings gave a spur to Europol's anti-terrorist activities, which had been rather limited. For example, the first response was to reactivate the Counter-terrorism Task Force, the second was to recruit some more staff for specific anti-terrorist activities. The main immediate successes were the effective intelligence gathering before and during the 2004 Athens Olympic Games and European Football Championships.

Despite all this, Europol tends to work in the background on essential, but non-headline-grabbing, initiatives such as terrorism infrastructure (the financing of terrorism, the role of alternative remit systems, the role of non-governmental organizations, the problems of forged or stolen documents, the role of incendiary devices, and the use of chemical, biological, radiological and nuclear substances or other weapons of mass destruction). It also supports law enforcement against drug trafficking, immigration networks, terrorism, the forgery of euros, trafficking in humans, child pornography, illicit vehicle trafficking and money laundering. It facilitates the exchange of information between liaison officers seconded from member states by providing operational support, by generating threat assessments, providing expertise and technical support for investigations and operations, promoting crime analysis and harmonization of investigative techniques, and by establishing a computerized system to allow the input, access and analysis of data.

Europol publishes an annual *EU Organized Crime Report* (Europol 2004). This puts together reports from each member state about the situation on organized crime. Europol also publishes overviews on trafficking and money laundering (full details can be found at http://www.europol.eu.int/index. asp?page=publications&language).

This listing of Europol structures and policies gives some idea of the day-to-day activity of the liaison and policy officers and analysts. For example, each country has between two and eight officers seconded to Europol, but they remain in contact with their colleagues back home – not only with their police HQ staff but also more and more with local field officers. It is likely that this close working together of practitioners from all countries of the EU will result in more changes within individual countries, as seconded officers return to their home states with a greater recognition of the common problems they all face and the need for common solutions.

Three examples of specific actions that show the day-to-day influence of Europol are as follows:

- As a result of co-ordination of intelligence between local officers engaged in anti-maritime crime, Europol, together with police from member states, was able to take action to investigate and solve the theft from the French port of St Tropez of expensive pleasure boats which had been transported to Lithuania.

- A frequent action of Europol is to co-ordinate 'controlled deliveries' of drugs. As a result of intelligence obtained by Europol on the port of entry of drugs and the route to be taken, Europol enables state police forces to monitor closely the drugs as they go through several member states so that the state of the final 'drug drop' can intercept and arrest those involved. Broad details of drug routes are published in *Drugs Information Bulletins*.

- In 2004, in close co-operation with eight member states, Europol shared intelligence about a Pakistani illegal immigration facilitation network that resulted in a simultaneous operation in Belgium, the UK and Greece and in the arrest of the main target criminal.

European Ombudsman

The European Ombudsman has a limited, but important, role in safeguarding human rights against poor or corrupt administration in EU affairs. Since its origins in 1995, the European Ombudsman has dealt with over 10,000 grievances from EU citizens, companies, organizations and public bodies against community institutions and bodies. Its remit is much wider than justice and home affairs and it concentrates on the right of each EU citizen to good administration. Some of the most common problems are unnecessary delay, refusal of information, discrimination and abuse of power. It has issued a European code of good administrative behaviour. Complaints against national, regional or local authorities are dealt with by national authorities.

Eurojust

Eurojust was set up in 2002 to enhance the effectiveness of the competent authorities of member states when dealing with the investigation and prosecution of serious cross-border and organized crime. Its college comprises 25 senior judges or prosecutors from each EU state, supported by a small administrative team. It is expected to grow in the future. It stimulates and improves co-ordination of investigations and prosecutions between competent authorities; it improves the co-operation by easing the execution of international mutual legal assistance and the implementation of extradition requests; and it supports states in investigations into cross-border crime.

Eurojust is based in The Hague. It has privileged partnerships with liaison magistrates, the European Judicial Network and organizations such as Europol and the European Anti-fraud Office. It is also regarded as a legal melting pot from which subsequent developments to strengthen the European judicial area will be defined (more information can be found at its website – www.eurojust.eu.int).

European Judicial Network

The European Judicial Network (EJN) was set up in 1998 to improve judicial co-operation between EU member states to combat organized crime, corruption, drug trafficking and terrorism (www.crimjust.eu.int/about-ejn. aspx). It is a practical structured mechanism of EU judicial co-operation and operates to identify and promote those in member states who play a practical role in the area of judicial co-operation in criminal matters. It thus creates a network of experts who execute mutual legal assistance requests. The EJN has some 250 contact points in the 25 member states of the EU. These are 'active intermediaries' who make judicial co-operation between member states more straightforward (e.g. in combating serious and organized crime).

The website (www.ejn-crimjust.eu.int/ejn_tools.aspx) gives access to many mutual assistance tools, the most useful of which is the EAW (see below). Other useful tools on the site are Atlas, which allows the immediate identification of the competent authority to receive and execute a mutual assistance request; Fiches Belges which gives concise legal and practical information on 43 investigation measures, in every member state (e.g. tracing and intercepting of (tele)communications, sequestration of assets, cross-border operations, examination, body search and expert evaluation); assistance in drafting rogatory letters to go to authorities abroad; SOLON, which assists in the avoidance of problems of translation between different legal terminologies; and the texts of the relevant EU instruments on judicial co-operation in criminal matters.

European arrest warrant

The European arrest warrant (EAW) aims to replace lengthy extradition procedures within the EU by an improved and simplified judicial procedure of the surrender of people for the purposes of conducting a criminal prosecution or executing a custodial sentence or detention. It was introduced in 1993. A warrant can be issued if the person whose return is sought is accused of an offence for which the maximum penalty is a year or more in custody or if that person has been sentenced to more than four months in prison.

An EAW should be executed as soon as possible. Their use means faster investigative procedures and no more political involvement. If the EAW procedures are followed correctly, then member states can no longer refuse to surrender a national to another state. The EAW guarantees that the person involved has his or her human rights respected, including access to legal representation and an interpreter. There are agreed grounds for refusal, such as not being re-tried for the same crime, being under age or if a time-limitation or statute amnesty is in force.

The EU Commission reported in 2005 that, despite some initial delays, the EAW was operational in most cases and its impact was positive. It also reported that over 2,600 EAWs had been issued, 653 people had been arrested, 104 people had been surrendered and that the average time to execute a warrant had fallen from 9 months to 43 days. However, these numbers are really very small in comparison with the potential need, and the EU itself has complained that several member states are still delaying responding to EAWs or attempting to set new reasons for refusal. Moreover, few practitioners in each member state had experience of working through an EAW request successfully. It seems clear, therefore, that there is still a long way to go before all states accept the EAW in the detail the EU Commission would support (for more information on the EAW, see http:/europa.eu.int/comm/justice_home/fsj/criminal/extradiction/fsj_criminal_extradition_en.htm).

European Judicial Network on Civil and Commercial Cases

This is a network of (mainly) information sources to help individuals and firms in Europe to improve access to justice by pursuing their cases in other civil jurisdictions within the EU. It is not concerned with investigation as such but is included here for completeness, as another arm of the institutions set up after the important conference in Tampere in the autumn of 1999. A good idea of the considerable extent to which this network has already developed can be obtained from their website (http//europa.eu.int/comm/justice_home/ejn/index.en.htm). This also gives a good idea of how far the EU Commission feels co-ordination and harmonization should go across Europe.

Extradition and mutual judicial assistance

The EAW aims to replace the long-agreed system of extradition between countries. The internationally agreed legal instruments on extradition and judicial assistance predate the involvement of the EU in justice affairs and can be used for countries outside the EU or where EU procedures are not easily followed. Most extradition provisions follow the following six basic principles:

1 *Nationality*: many states do not extradite their own nationals.

2 *Nature of offences*: it is an accepted principle that political offences may not give rise to extradition.

3 *Double criminality*: Extraditable offences are those that are punishable in the requesting state and punishable in the requested state if committed there.

4 *Non bis in idem*: extradition must be refused if the person has already been tried for the same offence.

5 *Specificity*: an individual may only be tried for offences cited in the request.

6 *Capital punishment*: extradition can be refused if the individual is likely to suffer the death penalty.

The major instruments relevant to the European area are as follows:

• The *European Convention on Extradition* (1957) provides for the extradition of persons wanted for trial or to carry out a sentence; it does not apply to political or military offences, and any country may refuse to extradite its own citizens if the person claimed risks the death penalty. It need not apply to fiscal offences. A request for provisional arrest must be sent via Interpol or directly to the competent authorities, and a reply must be sent without undue delay.

• The *European Convention on Mutual Legal Assistance in Criminal Matters* (1959) sets out rules for the enforcement of rogatory letters of a party that aim to procure evidence or to communicate the evidence in criminal proceedings undertaken by the judicial authorities of another party.

• The *UN Model Treaty on Extradition* (1990) sets out a framework to assist member states interested in negotiating and concluding bilateral arrangements for co-operation in crime prevention and criminal justice.

• The *Rules of Procedure and Evidence of the International Criminal Tribunal for the Former Yugoslavia* (1994) go into detail about The Hague tribunal.

• The *EU Convention on Extradition* (1995) supplements the 1959 convention by giving more detail about, for example, the person sought and the time in which certain actions need to be taken.

• The *Rome Statute on the International Criminal Court* (1998) establishes the court as complementary to national criminal jurisdictions, sets down in detail how it will be governed and the crimes it can judge (genocide, crimes against humanity, war crimes and the crime of aggression).

- The *EU Convention on Mutual Legal Assistance* (2000) is a proposal for mutual assistance between member states but has not yet been ratified by sufficient member states for it to come into force. The types of assistance which could be requested under this convention are broadly those that one would expect between parties within the same jurisdiction: restoring stolen objects discovered abroad to their original member state; transferring, for a short period, a person to another member state to assist in an investigation; allowing hearings by video or telephone conferencing; setting up joint investigation teams by two or more member states; officers of another member state carrying out covert investigations; and requesting the competent authorities of another member state to intercept/transmit telecommunications.

(More details and hyperlinks can be found at www.interpol.int.)

Because of the lack of ratification of the EU convention, the European Commission has proposed a European Evidence Warrant to obtain evidence. Such a warrant would be the first step towards a single mutual recognition instrument that could activate the mutual legal assistance convention. This would replace mutual legal assistance in the same way that the EAW has replaced extradition. However, this has not yet come into force and, given current concerns about the EU's future, is likely to remain in abeyance for the next few years at least.

Many commentators (e.g. Joutsen 2005) have commented that the everyday practice of extradition and mutual assistance is based on instruments that were developed many years ago, before the coming of international terrorism, cheap transport, freedom of movement and modern technologies that facilitate crime across borders. Joutsen (2005) comments that the available tools 'have regrettably not evolved to keep pace with developments in crime'. This implies the need for international co-operation to move faster than international criminals. However, as we have seen from the EU experience, national governments tend to put a brake on developments in international co-operation because of their fears that they are giving up some powers once they sign up to such cross-border instruments as the EAW.

The EU has come late to the idea that justice is something that would benefit from being developed in a central fashion, and this has unfortunately come at a time when the populations of the EU are feeling more isolated from European developments. The subterfuge of trying to formalize justice arrangements within the now defunct European Constitution has not gone down well with the citizens of EU states. It would have been better to take steps to educate them about the need for wider central powers to cope with cross-border crime and investigation.

The coming of city terrorism to Spain in 2003 and London in 2005 highlighted the need for better arrangements for pursuing intelligence and criminals across borders. The anomalies that have so far followed the investigative process into the 21 July suspected London bombers have meant that, because one of the suspects moved to another country before arrest, there has been little consistency of process, either in investigation or in the remand, bail or charging. This is in itself acting against the efficient progress of the cases and, unless a speedy procedural solution is discovered, it could lead to miscarriages of justice.

EU Anti-fraud Office

The EU has been more effective in setting up structures to deal with criminal actions against its own structures, perhaps recognizing more clearly the potential for such actions and the need for an early solution to reassure the public. The EU Anti-fraud Office (OLAF) is an independent investigation service within the European Commission, set up in 1999 to fight fraud, corruption and any other irregular activity (including misconduct) within EU institutions. It conducts full internal and external investigations and organizes close and regular co-operation with fraud and other authorities in EU states. It supplies EU states with support and technical know-how to help in their anti-fraud activities. It contributes to the anti-fraud strategy of the EU by attempting to strengthen the relevant legislation. OLAF runs an Anti-fraud Communicators Network, which includes the spokespersons for the national fraud investigation systems of EU states. This network aims to prevent fraud through the free flow of information; to create a permanent dialogue between OLAF and EU states; and to inform the public about anti-fraud activities.

OLAF has 300 agents, most of whom have worked with national agencies and who come from police, judiciary, financial, customs and agricultural, etc. fields. They have access to specialized external databases (e.g. to identify the movements of ships and containers, imports and exports, etc.). They also have data on over 50 million businesses worldwide with contact details, financial information, names of principal directors, etc. (OLAF 2002, 2003).

OLAF proposed in a green paper in 2001 that there should be a European Prosecutor to initiate action on fraud against the EU. Any prosecution would be carried out in the national courts of EU states and there would be a deputy European prosecutor in each member state to conduct the prosecutions. However, this proposal has not found much support and remains on the drawing board. The success of OLAF relative to the failure of the proposal for a European Prosecutor highlights the difficulties of getting member states to change their structures.

Financial Action Task Force

The Financial Action Task Force (FATF) is an intergovernmental body that aims to develop national and international policies against money-laundering and terrorist funding. Created in 1989, it attempts to generate the political will to bring about legislative and regulatory reform (see www.fatf-gafi.org). Its mission is to spread the anti-money-laundering message across the globe; to monitor the FATF recommendations; and to review and publish money-laundering trends and countermeasures. Probably the most important of these for the average investigator in any particular country is the extent to which the FATF analysis of current trends in money laundering can assist in developing policies in his or her country. The annual FATF *Typologies Reports* (FATF 2005) contain a large amount of detail, including case studies and regulatory frameworks of use to investigators. For example:

- *Alternative remittance systems* (ARS): these are systems for transferring money outside the banking sector. Most of these transfers are legitimate, but FATF concludes that there is a significant illegal aspect to the ARS.

- *Vulnerabilities in the insurance sector*: FATF research has indicated that there is a low detection of money laundering within the insurance sector in comparison with other parts of the financial services industry.

- *Proceeds from trafficking in humans and illegal migration*: FATF claims that this is the most lucrative of all organized crime activities and represents a global challenge of the same proportions as the illegal trafficking in drugs and firearms.

Other commentators have tried to draw together the international response to money laundering (Joyce 2005). Their broad conclusion is similar to other aspects of the international response – that the criminal is developing faster than the internationally agreed methods to counter his or her activities.

Country differences in dealing with organized crime

This section deals with the differences in the ways the countries of the EU cope with the investigation and recording of organized crime. It includes some results from a 15-nation study carried out for the EU Commission by Transcrime and the universities of Trento, Paris and Huddersfield.[8] The main purpose of the study was to look at measurement systems and to make recommendations to the EU about how such systems might be better harmonized. The study came about from an acknowledgement that measurement systems for organized crime throughout the world were deficient (see Lewis 2005).[9]

Traditional differences in police and legal systems that are normally associated with different types of jurisdiction (e.g. the 'Anglo-Saxon model' versus the 'European model') seem to be less important than the more modern structures set up, or not set up, to deal especially with organized or transnational crime. For example, all EU states contribute to Interpol and Europol, whether or not they have a particular type of police system (or systems), a strong or weak prosecution service, an examining magistrate structure or an adversarial or non-adversarial court system.

In broad terms, some EU states tend to be proactive in dealing with organized crime and in co-operating with others, looking at organized crime structures and developing proactive policies to deal with developments before they occur. Such countries have set up national structures to deal with organized crime (e.g. the BundesKriminalamt (BKA) in Germany or the Serious and Organized Crime Agency in the UK, due to be set up in 2006). Other countries, however, tend to treat each crime on its merits and to react to it as organized crime as and when it occurs. These differences often parallel the differences in the definitions and measurement systems used for organized crime.

Definitions used for organized crime

The definition of organized crime used by the EU is contained in the document 6204/2/97Enfopol 35 Revision 2. According to this definition, there are 11 characteristics of organized crime, as set out below. At least six of these criteria should be present before a crime or criminal group is classified as organized, and among these should be items 1, 2, 5 and 11:

1 Collaboration between more than two people.
2 Each person has his or her own appointed tasks.
3 The group is stable and of long or unlimited duration.
4 Some form of discipline or control is used.
5 Serious criminal offences have been committed or are suspected.
6 Operations on an international level.
7 Use of violence or other means of intimidation.
8 Use of commercial or businesslike structures.
9 Engaged in money laundering.
10 Exerting undue influence as regards the political sphere, the media, public agencies, judicial authorities or the business sector.
11 Determined by the pursuit of profit or power.

In 2004, only ten out of 15 member states used this definition. National definitions prevail elsewhere. Even in countries that use the EU definition, it is not used uniformly: in eight of these countries it coexists with other national definitions used alternatively or cumulatively to collate information on criminal groups. The way in which the two types of definition interact is sometimes unclear and, in some cases, the EU definition is applied differently because of a conscious choice or because of different interpretations of the 11 criteria contained in the definition itself.

The uniform collection of data on and, hence, the investigation of organized crime is thus hampered by the lack of a common use of the EU definition and by its varied application. This lack of harmonization will impact badly on the comparability of the picture among countries and in the extent to which countries can co-operate in their work against organized crime.

Offence and offender-based systems for recording and investigating organized crime

The 15 EU states use offence-based, offender-based and mixed systems to record and analyse organized crime data. Seven states have an offence-based system. This means that the unit of analysis of the data collection systems for these countries is the offence. Data are collected on all offences, and various techniques or presumptions are then used to identify, among all reported crimes, those offences committed by organized criminal groups.

In four countries the organized crime data-collection system is offender based. The unit of analysis is the person suspected or discovered to be a member of an organized crime group, and data on organized-crime-related offences flow from information on the crimes carried out by the group's members. Four states have a dual approach where, in addition to organized crime data collected as part of the general crime data-collection system, specific information on organized criminals is also collected.

An offence-based recording system is reactive – it reacts to an offence already committed. An offender-based system, on the other hand, is proactive, and makes possible the collection of intelligence information that could enable the prevention of organized criminal events. Also, offender-based systems do normally provide a reliable picture of organized crime because the information they collect is based on the monitoring of organized crime members, rather than the somewhat artificial techniques used to identify organized crimes in offence-based systems.

The different types of recording also reflect the organizational structure of each country. Countries with offence-based systems tend to be less proactive in crime prevention measures against organized criminals and, hence, less able to assist countries that have more proactive policies.

The types of data collected on organized crime by different countries

Most EU states collect a good deal of data on organized crime, but there is a great deal of variation. Most countries collect data on the following:

- *Suspects*: name, age, gender, nationality, function in the organization, previous criminal history, crimes suspected of, known associates.

- *Organized crime groups*: name, core activity, number of members, nationalities in the group (or ethnic predominance, if any), structure, role of the members in the group, geographical areas where active, crimes committed, modus operandi, relationship to other groups, use of violence (within the group, against members of other organized crime groups, or against others or those outside the criminal world), use of corruption.

Having a number of common variables does not imply full harmonization or comparability of information. This is because of the different methods used for the same variables, different data collection techniques, dissimilar legal and police systems, and the timing of recording, as well as the different amount of detail recorded. Some countries collect information on the basis of standardized forms that often lead to less detailed but more nationally comparable information, while others opt for more flexible templates, which pay more attention to the complexities of reality, but lead to less comparability.

It is also necessary to establish whether their respective data systems enable states to understand the level of organized crime's penetration and corruption of their legal economies. Few countries can claim success in this. In a limited number of countries only are the following crucial variables collected:

- Connections to companies used for criminal activities or the abuse of legal entities.
- Political/judicial manipulation or the penetration of enforcement agencies.

- The employment of skilled workers (such as lawyers, chemists, experts, technicians).
- The financial aspects of the groups (such as profits earned).

A predetermined set of variables on organized crime is not common to all states. There is, however, a tendency to collect information on the crimes typically related to organized crime, namely:

- *Drugs manufacturing*: precursor chemicals (or product), location, method.

- *Drug trafficking*: routes, groups involved, methods, links to other groups, information on the drug involved (type of drug, amount), modus operandi, means of transport, smuggling routes, contacts, violence used, weapons used, links to firm/organization (or the use of legitimate businesses).

- *Trafficking in human beings*: routes, countries of origin, transit and destination, identity of facilitators, modus operandi.

- *Money laundering*: source of money, links to firm/organization, buildings, places or addresses, means employed (money transfers, loan-back constructions, underground banking, etc.), use of legitimate business.

Organizations co-operating in data gathering and investigation in different countries

In all EU states the main organizations collecting data and investigating organized crime are local or regional police forces, while the co-ordinating body is a specific office set up within the national police. This simple organizational structure is enriched in most states by specific authorities, such as customs, financial intelligence units, immigration services, etc. However, information from such groups rarely exists in standard formats and it is difficult to share this with other groups.

Almost completely lacking is a coherent approach among the national agencies to collecting information on organized crime from the business or commercial sector. It is known, however, that banks, insurance companies and other financial institutions have a great deal of internal data on crimes perpetrated against them. The national authorities tend not to access this information. This mainly due to a belief, not necessarily correct, that private industry will not share such information with the authorities in case competitors are given inside knowledge of the extent to which they are threatened.

However, in many cases information is shared within an industry, as many businesses realize that a common approach against organized crime can be effective. The police, however, have been slow to forge links with the business sector in their national action against organized crime. The extent to which businesses have developed their own security arms to cope with organized crime is also very much under-researched, especially in the international context (for comments on this, see Walker 2003).

Wider availability of data on organized crime

A balance has to be struck between informing the public about the state of crime and organized crime in a country and not letting organized crime groups become aware of the extent to which the police have knowledge of their activities. Thus each country has to make an annual report to Europol on the extent of its organized crime. These reports are put together in a full report for all member states. This full report is kept for the use of the justice agencies in each member state, but an abridged version is placed on the Europol website each year, including country profiles for each state (www.europol. eu.int/EUOrganisedCrimeSitRep/2004/EUOrganisedCrimeSitRep2004.pdf).

More important, perhaps, is the extent to which data from local agencies of the police, customs, etc., having been collated by central authorities, are then fed back to the local agencies. The purpose of doing this would be to show the extent to which local information is part of a pattern, and whether crime prevention and detection policies being used in other parts of the country, or even in other countries, could be replicated in local areas.

Feedback from the co-ordinating bodies to the collecting organizations is now provided in nine EU states. This enhances co-operation between local and central levels because the collecting agencies receive something in return for their collaboration, something that may be extremely useful in solving ongoing investigations or in discovering new cases. The local agencies therefore become aware of the added value of a nationally organized crime data collection system and contribute to it more actively.

UK structures for organized crime

The current UK structures for investigating organized crime were due to be modified in 2006 with the setting up of the Serious and Organized Crime Agency (SOCA). Apart from SOCA, however, the following bodies and legislation are used in the UK in the investigation of organized crime.

The National Criminal Intelligence Service (NCIS) publishes a routine threat assessment that describes and assesses the threats to the UK from serious organized crime and that looks at how these threats are likely to develop. Criminals such as paedophiles often use encryption to protect their electronic information, and local forces frequently lack the facility to investigate such technical issues. The National Technical Assistance Centre (the NTAC) will provide a central capacity to produce text, audio or video from lawfully intercepted communications and lawfully seized encrypted computer material. NTAC supports the needs of law enforcement for a continuing flow of intelligence and evidence.

The Proceeds of Crime Act 2002 includes tough powers for police and customs officials to investigate and seize the money criminals make from, and intend to use in, their activities. Structures include the Assets Recovery Agency to investigate and recover criminal assets, a civil recovery scheme in cases where criminal prosecution cannot be brought and the power to tax an individual or business where income profit or gain is suspected of being derived from crime.

The Regulation of Investigatory Powers Act 2000 provides for a range of investigative powers, by a variety of public authorities. It takes account of technical changes (such as the growth of the Internet) and includes such powers as the interception of communications, the use of covert surveillance and the investigation of electronic data protected by encryption, while also providing for independent judicial oversight of its powers.

The UK also participates in the EU AGIS initiative to improve understanding of how agencies could work well together against serious and organized crime. AGIS is a five-year EU-funded programme (2003–7) for police and judicial co-operation in criminal matters. It focuses on organized crime and on encouraging co-operation between law enforcement agencies and judicial bodies. AGIS also aims to encourage co-operation with new member states and covers the areas of training, exchange schemes for personnel, studies, research and establishing networks, conferences and seminars. Bids must have European added value.

However, the British keenness for structural change continues, and proposals have recently been made for a radical restructuring of local police forces to make them more able to cope with modern-day crime and terrorism (HMCIC 2005). These proposals are based on an analysis that has identified a future policing environment characterized by widespread enterprising organized criminality; proliferating international terrorism and domestic extremism; a premium on intelligence, expertise and the smart use of capacity; and an increasing risk concerning public and intrusive media.

The analysis implies a major development in capacity. To achieve this, changes would be needed to the whole configuration of policing above basic command unit level so that forces would be on a scale large enough to respond dynamically but local enough to understand the diverse contexts within which they operate. The conclusion is that strategic force realignment is the most appropriate option, with forces being regrouped against a framework of design considerations – forces must exceed a critical mass and must have regard to the criminality of their populations and to their local geographical conditions. At the time of writing it is not clear whether this initiative will result in a small reduction in the current number of 43 forces (e.g. to 30) or whether a much more radical restructuring to, perhaps, a dozen or so forces will result.

UK threats from terrorism

Much of this information, as one would expect, is classified and not available to the general public. However, a certain amount of information is available to the public on the threat to the UK of terrorism. The main points are listed below, but more detail can be found on the MI5 website (www.mi5.gov.uk/output/Page4.html).

This advice and, in particular, the co-ordination of authorities in London, has improved considerably over the last few years, especially since 11 September 2001. The response to the 7 July 2005 bomb attacks was generally regarded as very positive and was the result of extensive planning and full co-ordination in the four years since 11 September 2001. The main success of this improved planning was the importance placed on getting all London-based organizations to take terrorism seriously and to recognize that, although an attack or attacks were regarded as inevitable, the consequences that followed from such an attack could be minimized with proper planning. In the event this proved to be the case, with minimum consequential disruption. The remainder of this section describes specific aspects of terrorist threats to the UK.

The UK *Threat Assessment, 2004–5* describes and assesses the activities of serious organized criminals as they affect the UK. It informs law enforcement priorities for tackling serious organized crime and proposed changes to legislation, operations and policy.[10] The current threat to the UK from organized crime is high, and it comes from Class A drug trafficking, organized immigration crime, fraud, money laundering, criminal possession and the use of firearms, hi-tech crime, sex offences against children (including online pornography) and child abuse. Other significant areas are armed robbery, kidnap, vehicle crime (including freight), crimes against cultural property and the environment, counterfeit currency, wildlife and intellectual property crime.

Threats from international terrorism include a unique combination of factors associated with al Qaeda – the global reach, capacity, resilience, sophistication, ambition and lack of restraint of those involved. Advice is given by the National Security Advice Centre (NSAC), which contributes to the protection of key government assets, and by the UK's Critical National Infrastructure (CNI), such as communications, emergency services, energy, finance, food, government and public service, public safety, health, transport and water. This advice is relevant to a broad range of organizations both private and public, and shows the high value placed on maintaining essential services and on supplying protection against national emergencies of all kinds, including terrorism. Emphasis is placed on security planning for all organizations, the protection assets and bomb protection. The ten top guidelines (www.mi5.gov.uk/output/Page167.html) involve:

- risk assessment;
- planning security;
- improving security awareness;
- ensuring basic housekeeping for businesses, schools, etc.;
- looking at access points to premises;
- improving physical measures;
- improving mail-handling procedures;
- making employer recruitment fully robust;
- protecting information and data; and
- business continuity.

One of the reasons for the relative success in coping with international terrorism is the experience the security services have had with Northern Ireland-related terrorism over the last 30 years. The current estimation (August 2005) is that dissident Irish Republican terrorist groups still present a serious threat to British interests, although this could change if current IRA plans to discontinue violence and to destroy weapons gain general credibility.

Despite the Iraq experience, or perhaps because of it, the UK security services continue to warn of the need to be worried about the spread of weapons of mass destruction, which encompass nuclear, biological and chemical weapons. The UK also has obligations under such agreements as the Nuclear Non-proliferation Treaty, the Chemical and Biological Weapons Conventions and the Missile Technology Control Regime.

Future scenarios

The development of effective transnational co-operation in the detection and elimination of crime is likely to remain behind the criminal or terrorist's ability, either organized or working alone, to disrupt modern societies. National jurisdictions and transnational bodies have proved very slow at changing their structures and moving their resources to where they could best be deployed, whether this be disrupting supply routes for the illegal traffic in drugs, money, stolen goods or human beings, coping with terrorist activity or dealing with the international criminal when caught. All international bodies, from the UN to the EU, have proved inadequate to the task, and the recent report on the World Summit (UN 2005) – agreed in September 2005 – only serves to show up the difficulties in getting disparate countries to agree on anything in the international criminal field.

However, the pressure from international criminals and terrorists is unlikely to go away. The countries with the largest resources are usually those with democratic populations, and these countries have the most to lose, both in the destruction of resources and in popular support. They will have to react to this quickly and, if current international bodies are inadequate to the task, then it is likely that others will be set up.

The UN has shown itself to be inadequate to the task and one possible, if pessimistic, scenario is of a new body being set up, or of an existing one being modified to cope with terrorism and transnational crime as an effective counterweight to the UN. Such a body would perhaps be based mainly on the rich countries and fronted by the G8 group or some slightly wider body. Given the way that Europe has been subjected to terrorist attacks, Europol might well become more involved than it has been.

Such a structure could work through a mixture of better intelligence and research, better investigation within the jurisdictions involved, greater control at the borders and tighter discipline within the jurisdictions, especially when terrorism is a product of a disaffected minority within a country. This is likely to have benefits in reducing terrorism but it will also involve some restrictions on human rights. Big business will also need to be brought in and market factors brought to bear, through taxation and regulation. This could even lead to relaxations in the illegality of drugs and other currently illegal industries, although this would mean that UN treaties would effectively be ignored. This would likely be accompanied by the effective nationalization of such markets within countries to incorporate the taxation and regulatory aspects necessary if national governments wished to control the level of crime they would permit their countries. Such a scenario is one possible result of the lack of progress by international agencies in coping with terrorism and transnational crime.

Selected further reading

Joutsen, M. (2005) 'International instruments on cooperation', in P. Reichel (ed.) *Handbook of Transnational Crime and Justice*. London: Sage. The concept of international co-operation is well covered in this chapter by the Finnish scholar, Matti Joutsen.

Sheptycki, J. and Wardak, A. (2005) *Transnational and Comparative Criminology*. London: Glasshouse Press. This is a recent collection of papers on comparative criminology. It contains chapters on area studies, transnational crime and transnational control responses.

Fijnaut, C. and Paoli, L. (2004) *Organised Crime in Europe: Concepts, Patterns and Policies in the European Union and Beyond*. Springer Dordrecht. This book is divided into the areas of the history of organized crime, contemporary patterns of organized crime and organized-crime control policies.

Reichel, P. (2005) *Handbook of Transnational Crime and Justice*. London: Sage. This handbook follows a similar pattern to Fijnaut and Paoli (2004), but it covers a wider span of countries. It has four sections: a historical overview; transnational crime in the twenty-first century (terrorism, antique theft, computer and environmental crime, drug and human trafficking, war crimes and genocide, money laundering and measurement); cross-national and international efforts to combat transnational crime; and regional and special issues.

Notes

1 For a comprehensive and up-to-date review of the history of organized crime, see Part I of Fijnaut and Paoli (2004: 21–235).

2 For a summary of the legal instruments applying to the international action against terrorism see the short paper by the Counter Terrorism Executive Directorate of the UN (www.un.org/News/dh/infocus/terrorism/CTED_legal_instruments.pdf).

3 See, for example, Kofi Annan's article in the *Toronto Globe and Mail* on 11 March 2005 (www.un.org/News/ossg/sg/stories/articleFull.asp?TID=3&Type=Article).

4 See the final report on the 2005 World Summit (e.g. http://daccessdds.un.org/doc/UNDOC/GEN/N05/511/30/PDF/N0551130.pdf?OpenElement).

5 Both the EU and the Council of Europe (CoE) have varied in membership over the period since the 1950s. The CoE has always been an organization of states that meet together to discuss common problems, without much in the way of common authority. Because of this informal structure there have been few constraints on the subjects the CoE has been prepared to discuss. The EU is a collection of states that have agreed to centralize some of their powers in a growing collection of treaties, agreements, central structures and publicly accepted phenomena, such as a common currency and freedom of movement. The EU limits the topics it is prepared to discuss and, until the 1990s, justice and home affairs were outside its remit. The EU grew from a group of 15 states

in 1973 (Austria, Belgium, Denmark, Finland, France, Germany, Greece, Ireland, Italy, Luxembourg, the Netherlands, Portugal, Spain, Sweden and the UK) to become a group of 25 states in 2004 with the addition of Cyprus, Czech Republic, Estonia, Hungary, Latvia, Lithuania, Malta, Poland, Slovakia, and Slovenia. There are plans for Bulgaria and Romania to join the EU in 2007, with Croatia also likely to be admitted soon. Discussions with Turkey have also started. The CoE has always had a much wider membership than the EU and, in October 2004, included Albania, Andorra, Armenia, Austria, Azerbaijan, Belgium, Bosnia & Herzegovina, Bulgaria, Croatia, Cyprus, Czech Republic, Denmark, Estonia, Finland, France, Georgia, Germany, Greece, Hungary, Iceland, Ireland, Italy, Latvia, Liechtenstein, Lithuania, Luxembourg, 'The former Yugoslav Republic of Macedonia', Malta, Moldova, Monaco, the Netherlands, Norway, Poland, Romania, the Russian Federation, San Marino, Serbia & Montenegro, Slovakia, Slovenia, Spain, Sweden, Switzerland, Turkey, the UK and Ukraine, with Belarus as a candidate country.

6 The Schengen Pact in 1995 led to all 15 member states (apart from the UK and Ireland) abandoning border controls except on the EU's external borders.

7 It needs to be recalled that, with the exception of the opt-out from Schengen, nearly all the developments covered in this chapter apply to the UK as well as to all other member states of the EU, a fact not always recognized by commentators.

8 The 15 nations included in this study were the member states of the EU before May 2004. These were Austria, Belgium, Denmark, Finland, France, Germany, Greece, Ireland, Italy, Luxembourg, the Netherlands, Portugal, Spain, Sweden and the UK. Full details of the methodology of the study are given in Savona *et al.* (2005).

9 Lewis (2005) considers the available literature on the measurement of organized crime.

10 An unclassified version is at www.homeoffice.gov.uk/docs4/threat_assess_2005.pdf and a fuller, classified version is available to those who need to know about it in more detail.

References

Europol (2004) *EU Organised Crime Report, Open Version, December 2004* (available online at http://www.europol.eu.int/publications/EUOrganisedCrimeSitRep/2004/ EUOrganisedCrimeSitRep2004.pdf).

Fijnaut, C. and Paoli, L. (2004) *Organised Crime in Europe: Concepts, Patterns and Policies in the European Union and beyond*. Springer: Dordrecht.

Financial Action Task Force (2005) *FATF Annual Typologies Report, 2004–5* (available online at www.fatf-gafi.org/dataoecd/16/8/35003256.pdf).

Haberfeld, M. and McDonald, W.H. (2005) 'International co-operation in policing', in P. Reichel (ed.) *Handbook of Transnational Crime and Justice*. London: Sage.

HMCIC (2005) *A Review of the 'Fitness for Purpose' of the Current Structure of Policing in England and Wales* (available online at www.homeoffice.gov.uk/hmic/closing gap.pdf)

Joutsen, M. (2005) 'International instruments on cooperation', in P. Reichel (ed.) *Handbook of Transnational Crime and Justice*. London: Sage.

Joyce, E. (2005) 'Expanding the international regime on money laundering in response to transnational organized crime, terrorism and corruption', in P. Reichel (ed.) *Handbook of Transnational Crime and Justice*. London: Sage.

Levi, M. (2002) 'The organisation of serious crimes', M. Maguire *et al.* (eds) *The Oxford Handbook of Criminology* (3rd edn). Oxford: Oxford University Press.

Lewis, C. (2005) 'Data sources on organized crime', in E. Savona *et al.* (eds) *Developing am EU Statistical Apparatus for Measuring Organized Crime: Assessing its Risk and Evaluating Organised Crime Policies*. Trento and Milan: Transcrime.

Norman, P. (2005) 'European policing strategies and transnational crime: from governance to institutional development and operational strategies', in J. Sheptycki and A. Wardak (eds) *Transnational and Comparative Criminology*. London: Glasshouse Press.

OLAF (European Anti-Fraud Office) (2002) *Europe Confronts Cross-border Fraud.* European Commission.

OLAF (European Anti Fraud Office) (2003) *The fight against fraud and transnational crime: OLAF and international co-operation.* European Commission.

Reichel, P. (ed.) (2005) *Handbook of Transnational Crime and Justice*. London: Sage.

Reuter, P. (1998) 'UN International Drug Control Program: World Drug Report', *Journal of Policy Analysis and Management*, 18: 730–3.

Savona, E., Lewis, C. and Vettori, B. (2005) *Developing an EU Statistical Apparatus for measuring Organised Crime: Assessing its Risk and Evaluating Organised Crime Policies.* Trento and Milan: Transcrime.

Sheptycki, J. (2005) 'Relativism, transnationalism and comparative criminology', in J. Sheptycki and A. Wardak (eds) *Transnational and Comparative Criminology*. London: Glasshouse Press.

Sheptycki, J. and Wardak, A. (eds) (2005) *Transnational and Comparative Criminology,* London: Glasshouse Press.

UN (2005) *Report of World Summit 2005* (available online at http://daccessdds.un.org/doc/UNDOC/GEN/N05/511/30/PDF/N0551130.pdf?OpenElement).

Walker, N. (2003) 'The pattern of transnational policing', in T. Newburn (ed.) *Handbook of Policing*. Cullompton: Willan Publishing.

Chapter 8

Criminal intelligence and the National Intelligence Model

Tim John and Mike Maguire

The history of the police use of criminal intelligence in the UK has been characterized by a long period of evolution followed by rapid recent change. Initial reluctance in the nineteenth century to allow the police to perform investigative, and particularly covert investigative, functions gradually thinned, allowing the use of criminal intelligence to develop, at first within specialist units and the CID, and more recently into mainstream uniform work. The tactical, operational use of intelligence has grown considerably since the early 1990s, but – arguably more important – *strategic* intelligence has increasingly been used as the basis for managerial decision-making and prioritization of the use of resources. Intelligence-led decision-making frameworks, as exemplified by the National Intelligence Model, are also beginning to broaden out from the police into the multi-agency partnership activities (especially the work of local Crime and Disorder Partnerships) that are evolving as a major component of current responses to crime problems.

This chapter explores a number of the above issues. It begins with a very brief historical account of the use of intelligence within the police, examining reasons for its rapid expansion towards the end of the twentieth century. It then considers both tactical and strategic uses of criminal intelligence in modern policing, looking in turn at the development of 'intelligence-led policing', the National Intelligence Model and initiatives involving partnership with other agencies.

The development of intelligence

The use of intelligence is certainly not unique to modern times. Commentators on its history (e.g. Grieve 2004) quite often refer to the Chinese strategist Sun Tzu and his military treatise *The Art of War*, written 2,000 years ago, with its references to spies and intelligence. Spying and intelligence-gathering have also been used by many rulers over the centuries to maintain control over their internal political enemies (notoriously, for example, by Machiavelli).

The establishment of policing systems was critical to the emergence of modern centralized states in the nineteenth century, and in many cases this led to the development of more sophisticated and bureaucratic forms of intelligence collection and analysis. For example, in the 1820s, Eugene-Francois Vidocq, the first head of the Paris Sûreté, operated on behalf of the French government a sophisticated system of surveillance, using an innovative card index system of intelligence files on hundreds of people designated as criminals or enemies of the state (Morton 2005). In England, middle-class dislike of 'continental' policing methods of this kind delayed the development of the use of intelligence by the 'new police', but such concerns were largely forgotten in the 1880s, when the 'Special Irish Squad' was set up in response to Fenian bombing campaigns in London – a detective unit which later developed into the modern Special Branch (Critchley 1978; Ascoli 1979). Further encouragement was given to the development of intelligence methods by the establishment of spy networks during both world wars (Emsley 2002; Maguire 2003).

The development of modern intelligence systems and practices began in earnest in England and Wales in the 1970s and 1980s, as the potential uses of advances in computer-based storage and analysis of information came to be recognized. A report for the Association of Chief Police Officers, the Baumber Report (ACPO 1975), set out a vision for the much more systematic use of intelligence by the police. In doing so, the report made it clear that, for this to be effective, 'intelligence' had to be understood as something more than simply information. While it had become common to refer to, for example, 'intelligence from a police informant', Baumber argued that criminal intelligence as a modern policing concept requires that such a piece of information is put together with others and some form of analysis is performed in order to produce a fuller picture (see also Willmer 1970; Sheptycki 2004). The report put forward the following definition of intelligence, which has subsequently become broadly accepted: 'Criminal intelligence can be said to be the end product of a process often complex, sometimes physical, and always intellectual, derived from information that has been collated, analysed and evaluated in order to prevent crime or secure the apprehension of offenders' (ACPO 1975: para. 32).

Baumber and a series of other reports over the next 20 years (ACPO 1978, 1986, 1996) also consistently highlighted the benefits of developing criminal intelligence processes and procedures more systematically across *all* policing functions. However, such processes still tended to be restricted to specialist units rather than affecting 'mainstream' policing. Intelligence developments mainly took place in tandem with other covert policing activities. In particular, they were closely associated with a growth in the recruitment and cultivation of informants and the use of physical and electronic surveillance. Taken together, these were described as 'proactive' policing techniques (Maguire and John 1995) and tended to be deployed by specialist detective teams. This association retained intelligence work as a covert policing function. However, with a strong lead from Kent in the mid-1990s (Maguire and John 1995; Amey *et al.* 1996), the systematic production of intelligence increasingly came to be used to inform and direct a range of police activities at both operational (tactical) and strategic levels, and a number of forces underwent major restructuring and resource reallocation to implement 'intelligence-led' models (HMIC 1997).

The term 'intelligence-led policing', then, is most accurately used to refer to this relatively recent development of intelligence beyond specialist ('proactive') squads into mainstream policing. In the UK, the culmination of this process is represented by the embedding of the National Intelligence Model (NIM) into every basic command unit (BCU) in the country. Introduced in 1999 by the National Criminal Intelligence Service, the NIM subsequently became the responsibility of ACPO, thereby signalling its wider relevance. All police services in England and Wales were required by ACPO to be 'NIM compliant' by April 2004 while ACPOs set a target date of December 2006 for Scottish forces.

Reasons for the growth of intelligence-led policing

A number of factors that account for the growth of interest in, and adoption of, intelligence-led policing in the UK context have been identified elsewhere, by the present authors and others.[1] In essence, they may be summarized as follows:

Perceived ineffectiveness of reactive policing

From the mid-1980s onwards, there was increasing frustration in central government and among police senior ranks with failures to achieve reductions in crime rates or increases in detection rates, despite increased investment in personnel and technology. Arguments for the wider adoption of proactive methods and intelligence-led models often included reference to these failures, focusing particularly on the shortcomings of reactive approaches to investigation. The Audit Commission (1993: 40), for example, claimed that: 'The police and the rest of the criminal justice system are caught in a vicious circle of reactive policing in which crime threatens to overwhelm them'.

In many cases, it was argued, reactive techniques may not be capable of producing the required evidence. Common offences such as burglary often present officers with a crime scene that yields no fingerprints, no eyewitnesses and no forensic evidence. By contrast, intelligence-based methods could potentially yield powerful alternative forms of evidence such as:

- surveillance records of targeted suspects' movements;
- records of financial dealings and associations with others;
- indications from informants about the location of stolen property or the sites of planned offences;
- direct police observation (and sometimes photographic or video-recorded evidence) of criminal acts;
- (though relatively unusual) statements from undercover officers (Maguire and John 1995: 5).

The Audit Commission, like others, saw a particular role for such methods in relation to what have since become known as 'prolific' offenders – i.e. frequent offenders responsible for disproportionate amounts of crime (Home Office 2004). Intelligence-led strategies, it argued, should target these individuals, the rationale being that if they were 'taken out of circulation', there would be a significant reduction in crime rates.

Limitations on interviewing and 'confession evidence'

Another factor leading to the search for new investigative strategies has been a reduction in the number of cases in which police are able to rely on uncorroborated 'confession evidence' to secure a conviction. Traditionally, the confession was something of a cornerstone for reactive policing. Until the mid-1980s, it was relatively easy for the police to arrest suspected offenders (or to ask them to attend the police station 'voluntarily') without any strong evidence, and to submit them to lengthy and robust questioning in the hope of eliciting an admission. Concerns about abuses of such powers led to the setting up of the Royal Commission on Criminal Procedure in 1979 and eventually to the passing of the Police and Criminal Evidence Act (PACE) 1984. The safeguards introduced under the Act, such as an impartial custody officer, a right to free legal advice, strict time limits on the length of detention and the tape-recording of interviews, have subsequently made it more difficult for the police to engage in 'fishing expeditions', to detain suspects without firm grounds for doing so, to make informal deals with them or to apply physical or psychological pressures to induce them to confess. The introduction of the independent Crown Prosecution Service, also in the mid-1980s, together with reduced trust in confession evidence on the part of judges following a series of high-profile miscarriages of justice (Walker and Starmer 1999), also meant that prosecutions were less likely to proceed or succeed without stronger corroborative evidence.

There were disputes about the extent to which these changes improved the protection of suspects in practice,[2] but they had an effect in spurring police officers to seek other forms of evidence before making an arrest.

Advances in technology

The impact of advances in technology on extending the potential of proactive policing techniques has been, and will continue to be, considerable. This is particularly the case in the rapid development of intelligence databases. Until relatively recently an intelligence system consisted of card files maintained by a collator and (hopefully) cross-indexed. Accessing information from the system involved manual trawls through the cards. As a result the searches were relatively crude and frequently reliant on the local knowledge of the collator. The development of computerized intelligence systems has vastly extended the potential of the information held within them to be both retrieved and analysed. Although who has access to the system varies from force to force, many allow all officers access to search for information and to develop intelligence packages; the potential for performing effective searches has also increased exponentially with the ability to use keywords as the basis of the search. Importantly, too, the scope for analysis of the information retrieved has been extended greatly through the development of dedicated intelligence analysis tools such as 'I2' and 'Watson', which allow flexible manipulation of the data along with pictorial representation of the results, as well as various mapping tools which assist in spatial analysis. Police forces now employ many (mainly civilian) intelligence and crime analysts, whose principal job is to create intelligence products for both strategic and tactical use (see below).

Increased focus on serious and organized crime

Concern about increasingly sophisticated methods used by criminals involved in serious and organised crime has led to the need to develop equally sophisticated tactics to target them. Consequently there has been a considerable investment in improving and linking intelligence on a national and international level. This process has seen the introduction of national agencies, most recently the Serious Organised Crime Agency (SOCA) in 2006. This agency and its predecessors, notably the National Criminal Intelligence Service and the National Crime Squad, have worked closely with the security services, hence enhancing police expertise and experience in the use of intelligence. Recent responses to terrorist threats have strengthened these links.

Pressures for more efficient and effective use of resources

The increasing emphasis by government since the early 1980s on more efficient and effective use of resources, reflected now in the ubiquity of target-setting, performance monitoring, auditing and inspection, has also had an impact on the development of intelligence. It has been broadly accepted that intelligence-based decision-making – especially through the NIM tasking and co-ordinating processes (see below) – potentially allows resources to be allocated and used in a more 'rational' and cost-effective manner. Such a rationale creates a need for accurate and timely intelligence products to help decision-makers assess the nature and scale of current crime problems and prioritize responses.

Intelligence processes in practice

The production of intelligence has four main stages: collection, evaluation, analysis and dissemination/actioning. At its most effective, these form part of a circular process (the 'intelligence cycle') with a regular 'flow', whereby disseminated intelligence triggers operational responses which in turn produce new information to be fed back to the intelligence unit for new analysis and so on. In this section we look briefly at the intelligence cycle, then at each of the above stages, considering in particular issues that can constrict the flow.

The intelligence cycle

Good intelligence is rarely produced solely from one-off 'tips' from informants. Rather, it emerges from a longer-term process of incrementally increasing knowledge. This process may be set in motion by a vague report about a specific individual suspected of committing crime, or by rumours about a criminal enterprise about which little is currently known. The latter is frequently a starting point in the investigation of fraud (Levi 1981).

A process is therefore necessary to ensure that intelligence is collected and analysed in a logical and structured manner. A commonly adopted strategy for ensuring this is for the intelligence resources at a particular level of the organization to be sited at one location and directed and operated by specialists – usually called an 'intelligence unit'. This forms a key part of what should be an ongoing cycle, rather than a process with a beginning and an end. A typical example of an intelligence cycle is outlined by Ratcliffe (see Figure 8.1).[3]

In short, information is collected and its veracity and importance evaluated before it is analysed in further depth. A 'package' (i.e. an intelligence file on a group of offenders or a set of criminal activities) may then be developed by the intelligence unit and disseminated back into the field. At this point it may be actioned by, for example, a surveillance team following the offenders in the hope of 'catching them in the act' or at least gathering evidence of criminal activities. Much more often, the intelligence will require further development by field intelligence officers or others. In either case, these actions should produce further information to feed back into the system – hence the cycle continues. However, as will be illustrated below, there are points at which the flow of intelligence may be constricted, with a knock-on effect on the whole cycle.

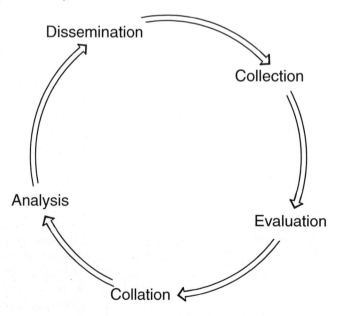

Figure 8.1 The intelligence cycle
Source: Ratcliffe (2002: 57)

Collection

Apart from standard records of reported crimes, arrests and convictions, the most common form of raw material used by intelligence analysts consists of 'intelligence logs' produced by other police officers. In many cases, these are simply sightings of known offenders by patrol officers – pieces of information which are on their own of little use, but when put together with other information (for example, a spate of burglaries in a specific area at a specific time) may become valuable. Other logs may be based on information from members of the public, passed on, for example, in conversations with patrol officers or through telephone calls to the police or schemes such as 'Crimestoppers'.

In addition, information may be obtained from registered informants. In this case, particular sensitivities arise concerning the protection of the sources and of the information that they provide. The Regulation of Investigatory Powers Act 2000 provided a statutory footing for the activities of informants and undercover police officers (referred to as 'covert human intelligence sources', or CHISs) to bring the authorized use of such sources within the requirements of the Human Rights Act 1998 (see Chapter 17, this volume). A number of commentators, however, have criticized the Act for providing only minimal guidance (see, for example, Whitaker 2001; Sharpe 2002) as to the limits of the activities of such sources, provided that they act 'in accordance with the law'. These minimal safeguards have, however, become supplemented with specific guidelines that provide for measures such as the specialist handling of CHISs by dedicated source units (DSUs), requirements for prior authorization before contact is made with a source, and the creation of 'sterile corridors' within which only authorized personnel may gain access, in order to preserve the integrity of operations and the confidentiality of sensitive material (for a summary of such measures and their practical application, see ACPO Centrex 2005).

While these are the 'traditional' sources of police intelligence, recent years have seen an expansion in the range of sources available, including regular supplies of information from other agencies (including prisons and probation services, as well as non-criminal justice public and private sector organizations such as local councils, banks and building societies), in many cases facilitated by data-sharing protocols (John *et al.* 2006).

Problems with the collection and transmission of information to intelligence units – which result in insufficient good information entering the system – have been identified as one of the main threats to the effectiveness of intelligence cycles (see Maguire and John 1995; Barton and Evans 1999). There are a number of reasons for failures in this respect, but one of the most important remains cultural resistance to the sharing of information. This has been recognized as a facet of detective culture, which has traditionally rewarded individual initiative in following up 'leads' and being identified as a 'good thief-taker' (Maguire and Norris 1992). While detective practice has changed considerably in recent years (Maguire 2000), there are undoubtedly still leftovers of individualistic thinking and attitudes. Where uniform officers are concerned, there is a risk that they may see themselves as so remote from the world of intelligence and crime investigation that they feel no motivation to enter data into a system in which they have no clear involvement and no recognition for the eventual result. Without commitment from the majority of staff, even those without direct involvement in intelligence or investigation, insufficient information will be fed into the system to make it effective.

Evaluation

Part of the Baumber definition of intelligence included a stipulation that information is *evaluated* as part of the process of converting it into intelligence. Operationally this is crucial, in order to be as certain as possible that the information is accurate and that the source (particularly covert sources such as informants) can be relied upon. Moreover, in the light of previous findings against the UK by the European Court of Human Rights (see Maguire and John 1996), and the incorporation of the European Convention on Human Rights into UK law under the Human Rights Act 1998, a formal system of evaluation is important in creating a paper trail to demonstrate that any operations resulting from intelligence have been proportionate and necessary. Police evaluation mechanisms traditionally involved an assessment, on a scale of 1–4, of the source of the information and of the quality of the information itself: a process known as the '4 × 4' system. More recently, the police and other agencies who deal with intelligence have adopted the '5 × 5 × 5' system (see Table 8.1). This adds an additional dimension, a 'handling code', which regulates the dissemination of the information to other parties. This has been described by Sheptycki (2004: 12) as 'essentially a risk assessment for dissemination'.

The advantage of the 5 × 5 × 5 system is that it allows for the prioritization of investigative resources according to the quality of intelligence received. It is therefore an important feature underlying the decision-making process of a more intelligence-driven police service. Nevertheless, there are some important management issues associated with the use of this system. If intelligence is to be shared with colleagues or managers (as it should be) there is a temptation for those who have received the information to give it as high a rating as possible to make themselves look effective; hence objectivity can potentially be lost. To counter this it is common practice for the information to be evaluated by an independent intelligence officer, usually responsible for the intelligence process as a whole. However, there is some suggestion that these officers might err in the other direction and be overcautious in their evaluations of intelligence and its dissemination (particularly following the passing of the Human Rights Act 1998).

Following the conviction of Ian Huntley for the murders of Jessica Chapman and Holly Wells, the Bichard Inquiry was set up by the Home Secretary to review the intelligence sharing between Humberside and Cambridgeshire Police. Huntley was the school caretaker in Soham and it became apparent that he had come to the attention of Humberside Constabulary nine times between 1995 and 1999 concerning alleged sexual offences. The Bichard Report (2004) found serious shortcomings in the handling and dissemination of intelligence by the two police forces concerned, and by extension expressed

Table 8.1 The 5 × 5 × 5 system of evaluation

Source evaluation	
A	Always reliable
B	Mostly reliable
C	Sometimes reliable
D	Unreliable
E	Untested

Intelligence evaluation	
1	Known to be true without reservation
2	Information known personally to the source but not to the reporting officer
3	Information is not known personally to the source but there is corroboration by information already recorded
4	Information that is not known to the source and cannot be corroborated
5	Information that is suspected to be false

Handling code	
Code 1	Permits dissemination to other law enforcement and prosecuting agencies (such as the Benefits Agency) including agencies abroad where there are sufficient safeguards to protect the rights of individuals
Code 2	Permits dissemination to non-prosecuting agencies (such as credit card companies)
Code 3	Permits dissemination to foreign agencies where no, or inadequate, legal safeguards to protect the rights of individuals exist; however, this is only on the grounds of substantial public interest
Code 4.	Permits dissemination only within originating agency/force with internal recipients
Code 5	Permits dissemination to other agencies but only in accord with specified conditions such as 'no further dissemination' or 'to be discussed with originator and documented below'

Source: Adapted from Sheptycki (2004: 11–12).

concerns about the national position. Although progress in developing an intelligence culture had been made with the introduction of the NIM, it concluded, variations in local interpretation of the NIM detracted from uniformity and therefore the ability for information and intelligence to be shared. One of the report's key recommendations was that an infrastructure should be developed which allows national intelligence sharing. In response, a *Code of Practice on the Management of Police Information*, with instructions aimed at increased uniformity in procedure, was published in 2005 and supplemented by more detailed guidance in 2006 (ACPO Centrex 2006).

Analysis

Cope (2003: 340, emphasis added), drawing upon Gill (2000), sees crime analysis as involving 'the synthesis of police *and other relevant data* to identify and interpret patterns and trends in crime, to inform the police and judicial practice'. As will be discussed in more detail below when we consider the GMAC initiative, crime analysis is increasingly being used to inform the crime-related activities of a number of other agencies, particularly the statutory partners identified in the Crime and Disorder Act 1998. In so doing, the 'other relevant data' referred to by Cope are growing in scale, variety and importance, allowing more medium to long-term multi-agency initiatives to be considered and implemented.

Cope (2003: 340) goes on to describe the potential benefits that can accrue through crime analysis:

> Engaging in the process of analysis suggests patterns of crime can be identified among offenders, offences, victims, spaces and places. Crime analysis supports the prevention, reduction and investigation of crime by providing the police with information that enables them to prioritise interventions. Local crime analysis identifies the location of crime problems, criminal targets and vulnerable victims to prevent and reduce crime, while investigative analysis assists with solving crimes and the prosecution of offenders by providing information for presentation at court.

Innes *et al.* (2005: 44, emphasis in original) classify these various strands into four modes of intelligence that are routinely manufactured:

> *Criminal Intelligence*: detailing the activities of a 'known' suspect or suspects.
>
> *Crime Intelligence*: enhancing the police's understanding about a specific crime or series of crimes.
>
> *Community Intelligence*: based upon data provided to the police by 'ordinary' members of the public.
>
> *Contextual Intelligence*: relating to wider social, economic and cultural factors that may impact upon levels of crime and patterns of offending.

In practice, the majority of this work is conducted by crime (tactical) and intelligence (strategic) analysts, based within intelligence units. Analysis is a fairly new career but one that has received significant impetus since the introduction of the NIM. The role is also developing away from simply a focus on the visual representation of data and intelligence using crime pattern analysis and mapping technology, to using these tools to provide advice on resourcing and prioritization to senior police managers (John and Maguire 2004). These developments are, however, patchy. A review of the roll-out of the NIM found considerable variance in the support provided to analysts, partly arising through some managers' misinterpretation of what the role entailed (John and Maguire 2004). Without good understanding and support from senior managers, the study found, analysts were frequently used simply to provide management information and to create graphical representations of areas, with opportunities for creative interpretation of problems and potential responses being minimized. Cope (2004: 201), in reviewing the integration of borough crime analysis within two police forces, also identified cultural and understanding gaps between police and analysts:

> The level of mutual misunderstanding between the police and analysts in the research created a potentially dangerous and depressing self-fulfilling prophecy. The analysis had become a descriptive formality, partly because the analysts lacked the quality of information to improve their products. Officers were unable to ask the right questions of analysis and their mistrust of it, because it was descriptive and did not tell them anything, also contributed to their reluctance to share information with analysts. Without a detailed understanding of their mutual roles, processes, epistemologies and expertise, the hope of developing a productive relationship seems unachievable.

Dissemination/actioning

As underlined by Mackay and Ratcliffe (2004: 155):

> The function of dissemination is to ensure that the finished intelligence product is circulated to those that need to see it. An intelligence product which remains locked up in the intelligence unit and is only read by intelligence personnel, fails to achieve the primary objective of intelligence, and that is to influence decision making.

Perhaps the greatest pragmatic problem associated with the intelligence cycle, particularly in terms of tactical and operational policing, concerns difficulties in ensuring that the criminal intelligence that is produced is actually followed up and used operationally. Several early studies of intelligence-led policing found instances in which appropriate response units were not available to act in a timely way on the products of intelligence (Maguire and John 1995; Barton and Evans 1999). It is often only those officers (or civilians) with direct investigative experience of criminal intelligence who are fully committed to taking up the intelligence emerging from these units and developing it and actioning it further. To those outside this 'clique', the potential or relevance of intelligence to their daily function may be unclear (Maguire and John 1995). As intimated above, partly to ameliorate such problems, the past few years have seen a determined move towards elevating the use of intelligence right across the police service. This has included not only enhancements to organizational systems for producing and using tactical intelligence, but major advances in terms of *strategic* intelligence. In both areas, the NIM has been at the heart of the changes. The model makes considerable inroads in institutionalizing in a central way the value of intelligence to determining and rationalizing police business, and providing appropriate responses for resultant actions to be taken.

Intelligence-led policing and the NIM

The NIM was first piloted in England and Wales in 2000 by the National Criminal Intelligence Service. Subsequently, the government's first National Policing Plan, covering the period 2003–6, required all 43 police forces in England and Wales to adopt the NIM and be compliant with its procedures by April 2004 (Home Office 2002). The model therefore represents what is in Britain an unusually determined attempt from 'the centre' to standardize policing practice and, indeed, to do so around a particular policing paradigm – intelligence-led policing.

The NIM owes some of its heritage to experiments in two police divisions in Kent, under the leadership of Chief Constable David Phillips. This represented the first attempt to introduce intelligence-led policing in a systematic manner into the day-to-day work of ordinary police stations (Maguire and John 1995; Amey *et al.* 1996). Although weaknesses were identified in the way it was operationalized, the basic idea of placing intelligence at the heart of local decision-making – which extended to the intelligence unit directing aspects of both uniform and CID daily activities (for example, tasking patrol officers to gather specific information to be used in planning target operations) – was viewed as a considerable improvement over more ad hoc initiatives undertaken by other forces in response to the Audit Commission's (1993) call to move towards proactive strategies.

While much of the early discussion generated by the Audit Commission report and the Kent experiments focused purely on new approaches to crime investigation – i.e. tactical intelligence – as time went on a number of academics and police policy-makers began to take a wider view of intelligence-led policing (see Hale *et al.* 2005). A developing association with evidence-based prioritization of resources, supported by increasingly sophisticated analytical capacity, opened up the prospect of intelligence-led policing becoming a management tool that could potentially direct resources across policing organizations – encompassing, for example, traffic, patrol and partnership activities. Crucially, it was recognized, the required policing response to a problem identified through intelligence analysis might not be a proactive policing tactic, but might equally encompass community or partnership solutions.

The most important product of this new thinking, the NIM, was always intended by its creators to embrace a wide range of police business. The NIM identifies the core business of policing as 'managing crime', 'managing criminals', 'managing localized disorder', 'managing enforcement and community issues' and 'reducing opportunities for crime'. This implicitly emphasizes its distinction, as discussed above, from proactive policing strategies and their main focus on prolific and serious offenders. The NIM draws upon a range of intelligence sources, including 'community' and 'contextual' intelligence, as well as intelligence on crime or criminals, and is therefore much broader than a focus on criminal intelligence.

The following section will identify the central tenets of the NIM. It will be followed by a discussion of recent initiatives that form the basis for the next phase of development – evolving the model to encompass the work not only of the police but of other key partner agencies. The Greater Manchester Against Crime (GMAC) initiative will form the basis for this aspect of the discussion.

Core elements of the model

The model recognizes the management of policing as taking place at three levels or tiers. Level 1 is concerned with local area policing (basic command unit); Level 2 with force/regional issues; and Level 3 with national and international threats. The NIM's management processes are essentially replicated at each level, allowing, in principle, for information from each BCU to be collated at force level, and therefore to inform decision-making at that level, and in turn for products from each force to be collated at Level 3 to inform national strategy and decision-making. For example, the problem of drugs can be tackled holistically and contemporaneously through appropriate responses at each level – Level 1 focusing on users, street dealers and the impact of drugs on communities, Level 2 on significant dealing networks and Level 3 on importation (John and Maguire 2003).

The NIM seeks to reinforce key areas of policing activity – or policing 'business', as it is usually referred to in the model – at each of these levels. As noted above, the core business areas it identifies are wide ranging, encompassing disorder and community problems as well as crime. The outcomes sought through the NIM process are defined in similarly broad terms: 'community safety', 'reduced crime', 'arrested/disrupted criminals', 'managed hotspots' and the control of 'potentially dangerous offenders' (see Figure 8.2, which shows the Level 1 example from the NCIS CD-ROM 1999). It is further specified that these outcomes may be achieved through a variety of policing methods and resources: 'intelligence, reactive investigation, proactive operations, and patrol resources' (NCIS 1999).

The above definitions make it clear, then, that it is a misconception to regard the model solely as a more sophisticated form of the kind of 'proactive policing' advocated by the Audit Commission (1993) in its exhortation to 'target the criminal, not the crime', or simply as an advance from the use of individual 'proactive' tactics (intelligence, surveillance and informants) to a more integrated 'intelligence led' system for targeting prolific offenders. Certainly, many elements of the latter are present in the NIM, but this is only part of the story. The model specifies its 'business', its 'outcomes' and available resources as encompassing a considerably broader remit than that previously understood as being the preserve of intelligence-led policing. It specifically includes tasks such as managing 'disorder' and 'community

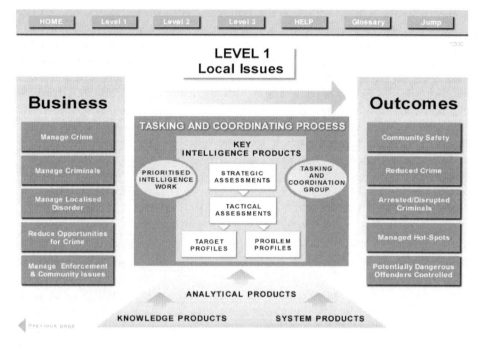

Figure 8.2 The NIM process at Level 1
Source: NCIS (1999)

issues' within its 'business', and places 'community safety' among its desired outcomes. It also recognizes ownership of reactive and patrol resources, and not just of resources such as surveillance teams and informant handling.

With the business and outcomes identified, the remainder of the model describes the process by which these desired outcomes may be achieved – using analysis to identify and prioritize problems and to determine the appropriate strategy for addressing them.

The driver of business at each level is the Tasking and Co-ordinating Group (TCG), comprising managers who can agree and allocate appropriate resources. At basic command unit level, for example, the chair will typically be the superintendent, with a membership of inspectors and other resource owners (not necessarily limited to police personnel – drawing, for example, on local partners such as local authorities). The TCG is the owner of 'business' at its particular level, and is responsible for achieving the relevant outcomes. The decision-making of the group is informed by a variety of *'intelligence products'* produced by analysts.

There are four key intelligence products: strategic assessments, tactical assessments, target profiles and problem profiles. Longer-term (typically annual or six-monthly) goals at each level are set on the basis of the *strategic assessment*. Strategic assessments are informed by analysis of problems challenging the level in question, and by priorities 'imposed' on the level by other internal or external bodies. A Level 1 strategic assessment will therefore encompass the priorities established within the local Crime and

Disorder Audit, but will also take account of the force strategic assessment, the UK Threat Assessment (effectively the Level 3 strategic assessment) and Home Office-imposed performance indicators and targets. At each level, an appropriate 'control strategy' is set on the basis of the strategic assessment, allowing the priorities for the forthcoming period to be set. Due to the nature of the transference of information upwards through the levels, once the model 'matures', commonly identified local priorities identified through strategic assessments should begin to inform priority setting by, for example, the Home Office, and therefore become significant precursors for future actions – thus aligning the priorities set between the levels. Of course, centrally created strategies are often influenced by the exigencies of national politics, which do not necessarily reflect local needs, so whether this actually occurs remains to be seen.

The more frequent *tactical assessments* (typically created on a fortnightly basis – John and Maguire 2004) manage the control strategy and propose and review actions taken against it. They normally combine a review of previously set priorities and activities with an assessment of newly arising problems needing decisions on prioritization. Finally, the *target profiles* and *problem profiles* are more specifically geared towards operational managers, providing intelligence on specific criminals or crime and disorder issues.

The intelligence products are, in turn, based on nine analytical products, which are simply analytical techniques specified by the NIM. Below is a very brief summary of the nine analytical products based on both NCIS (1999) and force-produced guidance, and on a review of the content of a range of such products (for a more detailed discussion of these products, see Cope 2003):

1 *Crime pattern analysis*: identifies crime series, crime trends, hotspots and general profiles of those responsible for committing crime. It therefore allows detailed pictures of crime to be developed, in order to facilitate more accurate prioritization and more effective response decisions.

2 *Market profile*: an ongoing assessment of the details of criminal markets – key factors, networks, criminal assets and associated criminal trends. Owing to its breadth, it will frequently encompass other analytical products (such as network or crime pattern analysis) dependent on the nature of the market. It allows prioritization of which elements of the market can be addressed and resourced by applying the tactical menu.

3 *Demographic/social trend analysis*: allows longer-term predictions of future demands on police activities, partly by more in-depth analysis of social factors underlying aspects of crime or disorder. It will also be used to identify (predict and therefore resource) seasonal trends in crime and other relevant activity.

4 *Criminal business profile*: builds up a detailed modus operandi of criminal enterprises. It 'examines all aspects of the way criminals operate, including how victims are selected, how the crime is committed, methods of disposing and removing of the proceeds and the weaknesses in systems

and procedures which the criminal exploits' (Crime Reduction Toolkit 2005). It is used to inform decisions on tactical responses and to identify legislative or policy needs.

5 *Network analysis*: a detailed breakdown of the individuals and activities that comprise an identifiable criminal network. It is used to inform strategic planning and tactical operational decisions.

6 *Risk analysis*: identifies the risks posed by criminal individuals or organizations to the public, to individual victims or categories of victims and to law enforcement agencies. The risk analysis will also form the basis for decisions on prioritization at both strategic and tactical levels.

7 *Target profile analysis*: provides a detailed picture of the activities, associations and lifestyles of individuals identified as meriting special attention in relation to a particular crime or disorder problem (for example, as serious or prolific offenders). This analysis will also include a breakdown of techniques that have worked or failed against the target in the past. It will also be an important determinant of target selection (prioritization) and appropriate tactical responses.

8 *Operational intelligence assessment*: based around specific operations, this is an ongoing assessment of, for example, new intelligence about associates or activities. One stated purpose is to maintain the focus of the operation and prevent 'mission creep' (i.e. to ensure that the investigation retains its original focus without getting diverted into other avenues of inquiry that might come to light).

9 *Results analysis*: assesses the impact of the responses adopted and is used subsequently to identify 'what works' and to disseminate good practice.

The identification and definition of these nine products within the model offer, in theory at least, the potential both for greater standardization of the products provided by analysts and (more importantly) for much wider understanding among managers in the police and other organizations of the techniques available to analysts and what it is possible for them to provide. Moreover, as can be seen from the breadth of the analytical products and the variety of information sources upon which they are potentially drawn, the move away from criminal, covertly gained, information or intelligence is significant.

In summary, then, the model splits policing into the two overarching fields of core policing 'business', and its required 'outcomes'. The link between them is the tasking and co-ordinating process. Tasking and co-ordinating operates in two mutually dependent modes, strategic and tactical, and is informed by four key 'intelligence products'. These, in turn, are based upon nine 'analytical products' (or techniques). The key resulting driver is the control strategy, which is addressed through the tactical menu (or set of operational responses). This general structure is replicated at the three distinct levels of policing: mutual dependence is again apparent, with priorities set at each level ultimately influencing those at the others.

The emergence of partnership-based intelligence

As noted earlier, in recent years there has been a development beyond 'intelligence-led policing', towards partnership-based intelligence systems and models. One of the most advanced of these at the time of writing is the GMAC (Greater Manchester Against Crime) Partnership Business Model. This is worth describing in some detail. At the time of writing, the Home Office is conducting a national consultation exercise which seems likely to result in a framework to facilitate similar developments being introduced nationally (Home Office 2006).

The GMAC Partnership Business Model

The GMAC Partnership Business Model (GMAC PBM) is designed to provide a framework for partnership working in the fields of crime and disorder management and community safety. It was developed by a multi-agency team on behalf of Crime and Disorder Reduction Partnerships (CDRPs) in Greater Manchester. With the NIM as its foundation, the team sought to build a structure whereby a multi-agency approach across ten local authorities could contribute to a pooled resource for the conurbation, which constitutes the county of Greater Manchester. At the heart of the enterprise is a dedicated 'data-hub' containing datasets from a range of different organizational sources, including police, fire service, probation, health and social services (John *et al.* 2006). The analysts are employed not by the police, but by each individual CDRP with additional analytical resources provided at county level. In addition to the NIM itself, the development of the GMAC model needs to be understood in the context of two parallel developments: the CDRP agenda, and problem-oriented policing.

The initiative grew out of discussions in early 2002 involving a number of individuals both within and without Greater Manchester, emerging from a recognition that problem-oriented policing would only work effectively if delivered within a CDRP setting. In the absence of a national equivalent, the GMAC PBM seeks to create a framework and process by which this can be achieved using a structured, business-focused approach. Given the centrality of partnership approaches to current government crime and disorder policy, these latter points have been perceived as a substantial area for improvement in the operation of the NIM nationally. A baseline assessment of GMP's progress in implementing NIM, conducted by the NCIS NIM implementation team in December 2002, identified specific improvements that could be made in the force's analytical and partnership data-sharing capacities. Reflection on this baseline assessment was a contributory factor to the development of the GMAC PBM.

The original feasibility report for the development of the model (then referred to by the cumbersome title of the 'Crime and Disorder Strategic Analysis and Business Process Model') produced an outline vision to use NIM principles to address CDRP business through the development of appropriate structures and working practices (Rigby 2003). The report drew upon the Audit Commission's (2002) report *Community Safety Partnerships* and its findings that:

> community safety partnerships need to focus on three areas for improvement:
> - Ownership and organisational behaviour, in particular leadership... and making community safety a part of core business
> - A sustained focus on a limited number of priorities, balancing local needs with national policy, setting action plans and targets...
> - Effectively using their capacity and systems to deliver community safety, improving performance management, prioritising resources... (2002: 1).

In short, it was concluded, the opportunity provided by the Crime and Disorder Act 1998 to move towards genuinely multi-agency crime reduction approaches was frustrated by the absence of a formal decision-making structure to support those initiatives. At the same time, the advantages that the NIM offered as such a structure, and in particular as a means of prioritizing resources, remained largely confined to the police, with little engagement from partners. It was therefore within this context that the relevant steering group sought to integrate the two streams of development by adopting NIM-based business processes explicitly within a partnership environment.

These two policy drives (intelligence-led policing and partnership approaches) are further viewed by GMAC as consistent with Goldstein's (1979) original concept of 'problem-oriented policing' (POP). Goldstein's principal concern was to reduce the extent of what he called 'means over ends' policing, whereby too much time was spent in responding to individual incidents as they arose, rather than adopting strategies to eliminate the underlying cause(s) of those incidents. From the 1990s onwards, POP has been adopted on quite a wide scale by police forces (and latterly CDRPs) in England and Wales. The GMAC PBM seeks to support POP delivery.

As with the NIM, the GMAC PBM is explicit about its business and the desired outcomes that it seeks to contribute to and achieve. The model aimed from the outset to increase the status and relevance of community needs – as business and outcome criteria, but more specifically as a key driver for the work of the partnerships. At the time of its development, this was of central importance to partners, while its relevance has subsequently been reinforced by the government's commitment to the 'neighbourhood policing' and 'new localism' agendas (Home Office 2005a, 2005b). In this context, one of its major contributions is to the aspiration for ownership of the whole crime-reduction process by the partnerships, with the police as just one member.

The structures and processes of the NIM itself have already been discussed in some detail above. What follows is a brief outline of the structure and form of the GMAC PBM, based largely on the GMAC Toolkit, to identify key areas of development.

As can be seen from Figure 8.3, the structures and priorities of the GMAC model are closely based upon those of the NIM, with some relabelling to

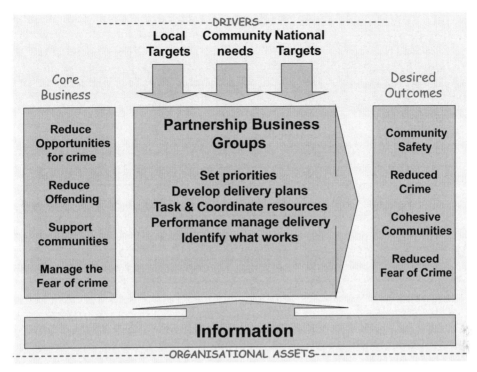

Figure 8.3 GMAC Partnership Business Model
Source: Crime Reduction Toolkit 2.1 (2005: 5)

reflect the partnership and community focus of this particular approach. As with the NIM's tasking and co-ordinating groups, the Partnership Business Groups operate in two modes: strategic and tactical. These are discussed briefly in turn.

Strategic Partnership Business Groups

At the core of the model, managing the process, are the Partnership Business Groups (PBGs). The strategic PBGs will typically meet every three months. The cycle for local and Greater Manchester strategic PBGs is offset so that one can inform the other. Locally the meetings are generally chaired by the Chief Executive and/or the Police Divisional Commander. Membership is defined locally. The Greater Manchester strategic PBG comprises chief officers from the police, fire service, strategic health authority and probation, and is chaired by the Chair of the Association of Greater Manchester Authorities' (AGMA) lead on community safety. The functions of the strategic PBG are to set the priorities of the partnership, make significant resource decisions and make policy decisions. The group 'have a high level strategic focus, meeting quarterly, giving guidance to the new Partnership Business Steering Group, dealing with the blockages and issues getting in the way of effective partnership working' (Greater Manchester Community Safety Team 2006: 6).

In essence, the strategic PBGs determine priorities and the resourcing of agreed actions. In doing so, they take into account local and national crime-reduction targets as well as assessments of community needs. The key resource available to them in making these decisions is the *Strategic Assessment* (see below). The group members are acutely aware that if their agreed aims are to be achieved, the organizational assets of partners need to be mobilized and information needs to be shared.

Tactical PBGs

The local tactical PBGs meet at least monthly, and often fortnightly. Locally, they are usually chaired by the Community Safety Manager and/or a senior police officer. Membership is defined locally. The function of the local tactical PBG is formally defined as to: manage performance against priorities; to develop and manage delivery plans, task and co-ordinate resources; to implement policy decisions; and to commission analysis and research. In performing these functions it is accountable to the strategic PBG.

The Greater Manchester Partnership Business Steering Group performs the county-level tactical function. It is chaired by the AGMA lead for community safety, and membership includes senior officers of Greater Manchester partnership organizations and community safety heads of service from the ten local authorities. It performs similar functions to the local PBGs although it adds to its remit issues such as encouraging closer partnership working. This group meets monthly and has responsibility for overseeing delivery against priorities set by the Executive Group in response to the annual *Greater Manchester Strategic Assessment*. It also has the role of ensuring that action is taken on the development of priorities and strategies for work at a county level (Greater Manchester Community Safety Team 2006: 6).

Informational resources

Overall, the GMAC PBM allows the organizational assets of the partnership members to be drawn together, considerably extending the breadth of information that can be used to inform the key document – the annual *Strategic Assessment*. The potential for a more holistic view to be reached is a considerable advance over similar documents derived from police-only data (even where supplemented with open-source information). Strategic analytical partnership co-ordinators (SAPCs) are the primary resource for analysing the data and, sometimes in partnership with others, including local authority liaison officers, authoring the *Strategic Assessments*. Nine analytical techniques are employed to interpret data and present findings. Much of the relevant data is stored in, and accessed from, a data warehouse – the data-hub. Moreover, under the GMAC PBM, the annual assessment is supported by a six-month review and two additional three-month updates.

The GMAC PBM therefore represents a significant national development in strategic planning for CDRPs. Its combination of NIM-based structures and processes with the broad range of data maintained in the data-hub and frequently analysed by trained staff is consistent with developments proposed by the Home Office in the current review of CDRPs (Home Office 2006).

Wider implications

The introduction of the GMAC PBM was achieved over a short period through strong leadership and commitment by key senior figures across a range of agencies, and through a strong and enthusiastic implementation team. These groups actively encouraged joint ownership of the model and successfully achieved broad buy-in and support for it. The significance of this approach is pertinent to proposals for a national reconstitution of CDRPs. Had the model been imposed rather than owned, the roll-out might have received resistance rather than being embraced. An independent evaluation of the GMAC PBM scheme (John et al. 2006) found strong support for the initiative throughout all the geographical areas that it encompasses. Particularly positive areas highlighted were: the availability of data; the quality and contribution of *Strategic Assessments*; improved co-ordination of resources; clearer accountability; and the benefits of co-ordinated partnership approaches in difficult areas. The scheme was seen to offer a sense of identity, drawing partnership agencies together and supporting one another in the process. Since the establishment of GMAC it is considered that joint working between partner organizations has improved particularly at the higher levels, but also throughout the CDRPs.

The evaluation also identified the *Greater Manchester Strategic Assessments*, in particular, as being exemplars in their field. The range of data from the range of agencies available to the analysts was seen to reinforce potentials for significant progress to be made in the prioritization of business that can be addressed through partnership approaches. The data availability, analytical tools and business process have also been positively received in reviews by Chainey and Smith (2006) and HMIC (2005). The latter saw the GMAC PBM as providing:

> a clear NIM-based performance management process that includes Opportunity Strategies underpinned by Delivery Plans. Strategic partnership business groups set priorities, make significant policy or resource decisions, and hold the 'doing group' to account. The 'doing group' is the Tactical Partnership Business Group, meeting either monthly or fortnightly. This group manages the delivery plans and the SARA problem-solving package delivery. The process operates at both local and county levels. (HMIC 2005: 61)

In sum, the GMAC PBM represents a significant development in extending the relevance of joint CDRP activities. It draws upon the NIM, but with a sharper focus on community issues and priorities. It supports partners in approaching their shared interests in a strategic manner, basing their decisions on a broad knowledge base – and provides process and structure for actions to be taken in a co-ordinated manner.

Summary and concluding comments

This chapter has charted the development of the use of intelligence by the police. It has demonstrated that, drawing upon experience of military intelligence, the police use of the method has evolved over a considerable period of time. Until quite recently, the development and use of intelligence were seen largely as the province of specialist proactive units, and associated with the gathering of particular kinds of information by covert means. Its use expanded considerably in the 1990s, underpinning a shift in crime control strategies, particularly in relation to organized crime, away from detection and prosecution, and towards the disruption of ongoing criminal activity (Maguire 2000; Innes and Sheptycki 2004). Such strategies, however, remained primarily enforcement focused, rarely looked beyond short-term operational results and paid little attention to community priorities (a narrowness of vision not helped by the growing emphasis placed by government on simplistic crime-related performance indicators). The advent of the NIM opened the way for a change in the general understanding of intelligence, showing how analysis of data from a wider range of sources could be used to direct police activities and make more effective use of resources. Intelligence has thereby gradually become integral not simply to tactical and operational concerns, but to strategic business planning. This shift has caused some commentators (eg Maguire and John 2006) to question the accuracy of the title of the NIM and to argue that it would be more accurately described as a business model – a 'National Policing Model'.

Nevertheless, until very recently NIM processes have remained in practice very much driven by police – and particularly crime control – targets and priorities (John and Maguire 2004). It is only in the last year or two that some police forces have begun to engage non-police partners in anything more than a token manner in their own NIM decision-making procedures and – perhaps more importantly – that intelligence products have begun to influence to any significant degree the activities of agencies other than the police (particularly the statutory partners under the Crime and Disorder Act 1998). The latter kinds of development, as evidenced in this chapter by the GMAC initiative, are beginning to show real signs of the potential for the NIM (or equivalent structures) to support a broader community safety agenda and genuinely to incorporate mid- to long-term considerations in strategic planning. The involvement of the other agencies encourages the use of a much wider range of data in both strategic and tactical analysis, allows serious consideration to be given to non-enforcement ways of conceptualizing and dealing with problems, and focuses police attention more closely on community priorities (including non-crime issues).

While this chapter has emphasized the positive potential of the NIM, it is still very much early days, and it has to be recognized that there is no guarantee that this potential will be fulfilled. Its implementation on a national scale undoubtedly carries some risks. These include the dangers that 1) the range and quality of the information reaching strategic TCGs are inadequate to allow well informed decision-making; and 2) the members of TCGs (and equivalent decision-making bodies such as the GMAC PBGs) are led too much by extraneous demands, such as performance targets, and ignore the messages that come through in the intelligence products such as Strategic Assessments. On the first point, it seems essential both to increase understanding of intelligence processes among police officers and to address the feelings of some that they are excluded from them or their results. It is also important to spread knowledge about intelligence-led approaches to crime control to a much wider audience, and to involve more local agencies in the sharing and analysis of relevant information as well as in decision-making processes arising from this, perhaps taking a lead from initiatives such as the GMAC PBM. On the second risk, it is critical that the NIM begins to work as it should at a national level, whereby national crime reduction strategies are influenced as much by 'bottom up' priorities and intelligence as by national interests and by short-term politically driven concerns, some of which may have little basis in evidence from local areas. Concerns that too much of the 'flow' has been too much from the top downwards have been expressed by many commentators, especially in relation to hastily devised centrally directed policy initiatives such as the 2002 Street Crime Initiative (see, for example, Skinns 2003; Grimshaw 2004; Maguire 2004; Curran et al. 2005).

Finally, during the same period as the NIM has been promoted and 'rolled out' across the country, a number of other major policing philosophies and initiatives have been promoted at national level and urged upon local forces. Some local forces, too, have adopted or adapted other policing models from elsewhere. In some cases, implementation of the NIM has dovetailed fairly comfortably with existing approaches, and the more far-sighted and strategically aware police managers have been able to 'add value' by blending them together. For example, Lancashire Constabulary, which for some time had been strongly promoting POP among its officers, linked POP principles and practice closely into the NIM processes, with considerable success (John and Maguire 2003; see also Tilley 2003). Clearly, the two approaches have much in common, including a focus on removing the underlying cause of problems rather than constantly responding to individual incidents, and an emphasis on planning actions on the basis of analysis (as in the SARA – Scanning, Analysis, Response, Assessment – approach used in POP; see Leigh et al. 1996, 1998), so the 'marriage' in this case was relatively straightforward. In other cases, however, there is a risk that, if not used in the open-minded way that its designers intended, NIM may act as a barrier to innovation.

Selected further reading

For broad-ranging discussions of the changing role of intelligence in the control of crime, see Gill, P. (2000) *Rounding up the Usual Suspects? Developments in Contemporary Law Enforcement Intelligence*, Aldershot: Ashgate; Innes, M. and Sheptycki, J. (2004) 'From detection to disruption: intelligence and the changing logic of police crime control in the United Kingdom', *International Criminal Justice Review*, 14, 1–14; and Maguire, M. and John, T. (2006) 'Intelligence Led Policing, Managerialism and Community Engagement: Competing Priorities and the Role of the National Intelligence Model in the UK'. *Policing and Society*, 16(1), 67–85.

For a succinct account of the thinking and principles underlying the analysis and use of criminal intelligence, see Innes, M., Fielding, N. and Cope, N. (2005) 'The appliance of science? The theory and practice of crime intelligence analysis', *British Journal of Criminology*, 45, 39–57.

The relationship of intelligence-led policing with other current models of policing is discussed usefully in Tilley, N. (2003) 'Community policing, problem-oriented policing and intelligence-led policing' in T. Newburn (ed.) *Handbook of Policing*, Cullompton: Willan.

For practitioners' perspectives on operational issues in the use of intelligence, see J. Ratcliffe (ed. 2005) *Strategic Thinking in Criminal Intelligence*, Annandale: New South Wales Federation Press, especially the chapters by Flood, Grieve, Mackay and Ratcliffe.

For more detail about the National Intelligence Model, see ACPO Centrex (2005) *Guidance on the National Intelligence Model* www.acpo.police.uk/asp/policies/Data/ nim2005.pdf.

Notes

1 More detailed discussions of these factors can be found in, for example, Maguire and John (1995), Gill (2000), Maguire (2000), Tilley (2003), Flood (2004) Grieve (2004), John and Maguire (2003, 2004), and Innes *et al.* (2005).
2 See, for example, Brown (1989), Irving and McKenzie (1989), McConville *et al.* (1991), Dixon (1992); for an overview of PACE, see Maguire (2002).
3 For slightly different versions of the intelligence cycle, see also Barton and Evans (1999: 10) or Friedman *et al.* (1997).

References

ACPO (1975) *Report of the Subcommittee on Criminal Intelligence* (the Baumber Report). London: Association of Chief Police Officers.
ACPO (1978) *Third Report of the Working Party on a Structure of Criminal Intelligence above Force Level* (the Pearce Report). London: Association of Chief Police Officers.
ACPO (1986) *Report of the Working Party on Operational Intelligence* (the Ratcliffe Report). London: ACPO.
ACPO (1996) *Report on International, National and Inter-force Crime*. London: Association of Chief Police Officers.
ACPO Centrex (2005) *Guidance on the National Intelligence Model*. Wyboston: Centrex/ NCPE (available online at www.acpo.police.uk/asp/policies/Data/nim2005.pdf).
ACPO Centrex (2006) *Guidance on the Management of Police Information*. Wyboston: Centrex/NCPE (available online at http://police.homeoffice.gov.uk/news-and-publications/publication/operational-policing/CodeofPracticeFinal12073. pdf?version=1).
Amey, P., Hale, C. and Uglow, S. (1996) *Development and Evaluation of a Crime Management Model. Police Research Series Paper* 18. London: Home Office.
Ascoli, D. (1979) *The Queen's Peace: The Origins and Development of the Metropolitan Police, 1829–1979*. London: Hamish Hamilton.
Audit Commission (1993) *Helping with Enquiries: Tackling Crime Effectively*. London: HMSO.

Audit Commission (2002) *Community Safety Partnerships*. London: Audit Commission.

Barton, A. and Evans, R. (1999). *Proactive Policing on Merseyside. Police Research Series Paper* 105. London: Home Office.

Bichard, M. (2004) *Bichard Inquiry Report*. London: Home Office.

Brown, D. (1989) *Detention at the Police Station under the Police and Criminal Evidence Act 1984*. London: HMSO.

Chainey, S. and Smith, C. (2006) *Review of GIS based Information Sharing Systems. Home Office Online Report* 02/06 (available online at http://www.homeoffice.gov.uk/rds/pdfs06/rdsolr0206.pdf).

Cope, N. (2003) 'Crime analysis: principles and practice', in T. Newburn (ed.) *Handbook of Policing*. Cullompton: Willan Publishing.

Cope, N. (2004) 'Intelligence led policing or policing led intelligence?', *British Journal of Criminology*, 44: 188–203.

Crime Reduction Toolkit (2005) *Criminal Business Profiles* (available online at http://www.crimereduction.gov.uk/toolkits/ui020504.htm).

Critchley, T. (1978) *A History of Police in England and Wales*. London: Constable.

Curran, C., Dale, M., Edmunds, M., Hough, M., Millie, A. and Wagstaffe, M. (2005) *Street Crime in London: Deterrence, Disruption and Displacement*. London: Government Office for London.

Dixon, D. (1992) 'Legal regulation and policing practice', *Social and Legal Studies*, 1: 541.

Emsley, C. (2002) 'The history of crime and crime control institutions' in M. Maguire *et al.* (eds) *The Oxford Handbook of Criminology*. Oxford: Oxford University Press.

Flood, B. (2004) 'Strategic elements of the National Intelligence Model', in J. Ratcliffe (ed.) *Strategic Thinking in Criminal Intelligence*. Annandale: New South Wales Federation Press.

Friedman, G., Friedman, M., Chapman, C. and Baker, J.S. (1997). *The Intelligence Edge*. London: Random House.

Gill, P. (2000) *Rounding up the Usual Suspects? Developments in Contemporary Law Enforcement Intelligence*. Aldershot: Ashgate.

GMAC (2003) *GMAC Toolkit* (GMAC internal document).

Goldstein, H. (1979) 'Improving policing: a problem oriented approach', *Crime and Delinquency*, April: 234–58.

Greater Manchester Community Safety Team (2006) *Business Plan* (GMAC internal document).

Grieve, J. (2004) 'Developments in UK criminal intelligence', in J. Ratcliffe (ed.) *Strategic Thinking in Criminal Intelligence*. Annandale: New South Wales Federation Press.

Grimshaw, R. (2004) 'Whose Justice? Principal drivers of criminal justice policy, their implications for stakeholders, and some foundations for critical policy departures.' Paper presented at the British Criminology Conference, July (available online at http://www.britsoccrim.org/volume7/005.pd).

Hale, C., Uglow, S. and Heaton, R. (2005) 'Uniform styles II: police families and policing styles', *Policing and Society*, 15: 1–18.

HMIC (1997) *Policing with Intelligence: Criminal Intelligence*. London: Home Office.

HMIC (2005) *Baseline Assessment Greater Manchester Police* (available online at http://inspectorates.homeoffice.gov.uk/hmic/inspect_reports1/baseline-assessments-ho-0506/gmp-baseline05.pdf).

Home Office (2002) *The National Policing Plan, 2003/2006*. London: Home Office.

Home Office (2004) *Prolific and Other Priority Offender Strategy: Initial Guidance: Catch and Convict Framework*. London: Home Office.

Home Office (2005a) *Neighbourhood Policing: Your Police, Your Community, Our Commitment*. London: Home Office (available online at http://police.homeoffice. gov.uk/news-and-publications/publication/community-policing/neighbourhood_ policing.pdf?version=1).

Home Office (2005b) *The National Reassurance Policing Project*. London: Home Office (available online at http://www.reassurancepolicing.co.uk).

Home Office (2006) *Review of the Partnership Provisions of the Crime and Disorder Act 1998 – Report of Findings*. London: Home Office.

Innes, M., Fielding, N. and Cope, N. (2005) 'The appliance of science? The theory and practice of crime intelligence analysis', *British Journal of Criminology*, 45: 39–57.

Innes, M. and Sheptycki, J. (2004) 'From detection to disruption: intelligence and the changing logic of police crime control in the United Kingdom', *International Criminal Justice Review*, 14: 1–14.

Irving, B. and McKenzie, I. (1989) *Police Interrogation: The Effects of the Police and Criminal Evidence Act 1984*. London: Police Foundation.

John, T. and Maguire, M. (2003) 'Rolling out the National Intelligence Model: key challenges', in K. Bullock and N. Tilley (eds) *Crime Reduction and Problem-Oriented Policing*. Cullompton: Willan Publishing.

John, T. and Maguire, M. (2004) *The National Intelligence Model: Early Implementation Experience in Three Police Force Areas. Cardiff University Working Paper Series 50*. Cardiff: Cardiff University (available onlilne at http://www.cardiff.ac.uk/ schoolsanddivisions/academicschools/socsi/publications/abstracts/wrkgpaper50-ab.html).

John, T., Morgan, C. and Rogers, C. (2006) *The Greater Manchester Against Crime Partnership Business Model: An Independent Evaluation* (Centre for Criminology, University of Glamorgan, internal document).

Leigh, A., Read, T. and Tilley, N. (1996) *Problem Oriented Policing: Brit Pop. Crime Detection and Prevention Series Paper 75*. London: Home Office.

Leigh, A., Read, T. and Tilley, N. (1998) *Brit Pop II: Problem Oriented Policing in Practice. Policing and Reducing Crime Unit, Police Research Series Paper 93*. London: Home Office.

Levi, M. (1981) *The Phantom Capitalists: The Organisation and Control of Long-firm Fraud*. London: Heinemann.

Mackay, D. and Ratcliffe, J. (2004) 'Intelligence products and their dissemination', in J. Ratcliffe (ed.) *Strategic Thinking in Criminal Intelligence*. Annandale: New South Wales Federation Press.

Maguire, M. (2000) 'Policing by risks and targets: some dimensions and implications of intelligence-led crime control', *Policing and Society*, 9: 315–36.

Maguire, M. (2002) 'Regulating the police station: the case of the Police and Criminal Evidence Act 1984', in M. McConville and G. Wilson (eds) *The Handbook of the Criminal Justice Process*. Oxford: Oxford University Press.

Maguire, M. (2003) 'Criminal investigation and crime control', in T. Newburn (ed.) *Handbook of Policing*. Cullompton: Willan Publishing.

Maguire, M. (2004) 'The crime reduction programme: reflections on the vision and the reality', *Criminal Justice*, 4: 213–38.

Maguire, M. and John, T. (1995) *Intelligence, Surveillance, and Informants: Integrated Approaches. Police Research Group Crime and Prevention Series Paper 64*. London: Home Office.

Maguire, M. and John, T. (1996) 'Covert and deceptive policing in England and Wales: issues in regulation and practice' *European Journal of Crime, Criminal Law and Criminal Justice*, 4: 316–34.

Maguire, M. and John, T. (2006) 'Intelligence led policing, managerialism and community engagement: competing priorities and the role of the National Intelligence Model in the UK', *Policing and Society*, 16: 67–85.

Maguire, M. and Norris, C. (1992) *The Conduct and Supervision of Criminal Investigations. Research Study 5, Royal Commission on Criminal Justice.* London: HMSO.

McConville, M., Sanders, A. and Leng, R. (1991) *The Case for the Prosecution: Police Suspects and the Construction of Criminality.* London: Routledge.

Morton, J. (2005) *The First Detective: The Life and Revolutionary Times of Eugene-Francois Vidocq, Criminal, Spy and Private Eye.* London: Trafalgar Square.

NCIS (1999) *NCIS and the National Intelligence Model.* London: National Criminal Intelligence Service.

Ratcliffe, J. (2002) 'Intelligence-led policing and the problems of turning rhetoric into practice', *Policing and Society*, 12: 53–66.

Rigby, B.V. (2003) *Feasibility Report* (Manchester GMCRSG internal document).

Sharpe, S. (2002) 'Covert surveillance and the use of informants', in M. McConville and G. Wilson (eds) *The Handbook of the Criminal Justice Process.* Oxford: Oxford University Press.

Sheptycki, J. (2004) *Review of the Influence of Strategic Intelligence on Organised Crime Policy Practice. Special Interest Paper* 14. London: Home Office Research, Development and Statistics Directorate.

Skinns, L. (2003) 'Responsibility, rhetoric and reality: practitioners' views on their responsibility for crime and disorder in the community safety partnerships.' Paper presented at the British Criminology Conference, July (available online at http://www.britsoccrim.org/volume6/007.pdf).

Tilley, N. (2003) Community policing, problem-oriented policing and intelligence led policing', in T. Newburn (ed.) *Handbook of Policing.* Cullompton: Willan Publishing.

Walker, C. and Starmer, K. (1999) *Miscarriages of Justice: A Review of Justice in Error.* London: Blackstone Press.

Willmer, M. (1970) *Crime and Information Theory.* Edinburgh: Edinburgh University Press.

Whitaker, Q. (2001) 'Surveillance and covert human intelligence sources under the regulation of Investigatory Powers Act 2000', in K. Starmer, M. Strange and Q. Whitaker (eds) *Criminal Justice, Police Powers and Human Rights.* London: Blackstone Press.

Chapter 9

The investigation of high-volume crime

Nick Tilley, Amanda Robinson and John Burrows

This chapter focuses on the detection of high-volume crimes. For the purpose of this discussion, these have been defined as domestic burglary, non-domestic burglary, theft of and theft from motor vehicles.[1] Collectively in the mid-1990s, these offences accounted for about half of all the recorded crime in England and Wales. In 2005 they accounted for just less than 30 per cent. This fall in share of the 'crime cake' is a function both of changed counting rules and steady falls in burglary and vehicle crime over the past decade.

The chapter begins with some introductory remarks on the terms used to categorize and count crime detections, the challenges faced in detecting volume crimes as against other types of crime, the significance of 'crime mix' in shaping overall detection rates by area, and how rates have been affected by crime-recording practices. It next points out how the sheer numbers of volume crimes – and the limited resources available to investigate them – strongly dictate what can be achieved. It goes on to examine processes of investigation and ways that cases are cleared, and then distinguishes two 'ideal types' of investigative activity. Finally, proactive approaches to investigation are discussed.

The discussion draws on a range of literature but relies heavily on a recent study in which the authors have been involved. This tracked some 3,000 volume crime cases, half detected and half undetected, from first police report to case outcome. These cases were from eight police basic command units (BCUs) comprising 'pairs' drawn from the four highest crime BCU 'families'[2] in England and Wales, where each pair had one BCU with a relatively high and the other with a relatively low detection rate (Burrows *et al.* 2005a). In addition to the case-tracking exercise, the investigative systems and processes within these BCUs were mapped in some detail. There are two reasons for focusing on this study. First, it describes the largest study conducted anywhere to date of volume crime investigation. Secondly, it provides an up-to-date perspective on investigative practices and outcomes. This study will be referred to as 'the eight BCU study'.

Table 9.1   Recorded crime: detection rates by selected individual offences, 2004–5

	Number of offences	Number of detections	Detection rate (%)
Burglary in a dwelling	318,921	49,949	16
Aggravated burglary in a dwelling	2,538	1,106	44
Total burglary in a dwelling	*321,459*	*51,055*	*16*
Burglary in a building other than a dwelling	358,061	37,885	11
Aggravated burglary in a building other than a dwelling	453	153	34
Total burglary in a building other than dwelling	*358,514*	*38,038*	*11*
TOTAL BURGLARY	*679,973*	*89,093*	*13*
Aggravated vehicle taking	11,121	5,263	47
Theft or unauthorized taking of motor vehicle	230,729	31,692	14
Theft from vehicle	496,681	37,935	8
Theft of and from vehicles	*738,531*	*74,890*	*10*
TOTAL VIOLENT CRIME	1,184,702	586,523	50

Source: Nicholas *et al.* (2005).

Introductory remarks

Counting detections

Overall, headline detection statistics, those 'cleared up' by the police, include both sanction and non-sanction detections. There are various ways of categorizing them. The detection statistics routinely published by the Home Office distinguish between sanction detections and non-sanction detections. Sanction detections comprise any that are associated with at least the potential for a sanction to be administered. They include crimes where a charge is put, where a caution is administered, and where the suspect asks that the offence be 'taken into consideration' (TIC) at sentence. Non-sanction detections, often described as 'other' or 'administrative' detections, include all those that do not lead to any further action. A substantial number were at one time obtained through 'prison interviews' with convicted suspects who could 'write off' past offences by admitting to them while completing their sentence. In 1995, interviews with convicted prisoners accounted for over 18 per cent of all detections nationally (Barclay and Tavares 1999). The practice was disallowed by the Home Office from April 1999, following a series of scandals about police fiddling crime figures (Davies 2003).

Another distinction often made is between 'direct detections', which refer to sanction detections excluding TICs, and 'indirect detections', which refer to

Table 9.2 Recorded crime: distribution of forms of detection for selected crime types, 2004–5

	Number	Charge/ summons %	Caution %	TIC %	Fixed penalty %	Other (administrative) %
Violence against the person	548,107	46	16	0	5	32
More serious violence	21,759	75	6	0	0	19
Other offences against the person	526,348	45	16	0	6	32
Common assault	93,003	24	11	0	0	65
Harassment	137,308	48	12	0	24	15
Other wounding	238,564	44	20	0	0	36
Sexual offences	20,761	71	11	1	0	17
Indecent assault	8,201	70	9	0	0	21
Rape of a female	3,975	83	2	0	0	15
Robbery	17,655	78	3	5	0	14
Burglary	89,093	51	6	35	0	9
Burglary in a dwelling	51,055	49	4	37	0	10
Burglary in other building	38,038	54	8	32	0	7
Theft and handling stolen goods	334,476	54	19	14	2	11
Theft from vehicle	37,935	32	8	53	0	7
Theft or unauthorized taking of a motor vehicle	36,955	57	9	24	0	10

Source: Nicholas *et al.* (2005).

TICs and non-sanction detections. Direct detections account, across all crime types, for between about three fifths and two thirds of all detections. Tables 9.1 and 9.2 show, respectively, the numbers of offences and detections and types of detections for various crime types. It is clear that TICs account for a substantial proportion of all detections of the volume crime types focused on in this chapter: for over a third of all burglary detections, a quarter of detections of theft of or unauthorized taking of a vehicle and more than half the detections of thefts from a vehicle.

Why the detection rate?

The headline detection rate (as shown in Table 9.1) has long been subject to criticism, and alternative measures of investigative outcome have been mooted (see Burrows 1986a): an issue that is returned to later. Essentially, it provides a measurement of *police effectiveness* – their ability to find out who committed a particular offence, regardless of the method or outcome of the case. The window the police mainly operate in is that between the report of an offence and the identification of the offender – what occurs prior to, or after, these stages the police have less influence over (e.g. public reporting practices, prosecutorial charging decisions, etc.).[3] Thus, counting detections represents a choice to focus on the performance of the police as opposed to other criminal justice actors.

Put another way, a detection – be it sanction or otherwise – does not mark the end of the road in criminal justice terms. The fact that a sanction detection is achieved so far as the police are concerned does not mean that the Crown Prosecution Service will proceed with a prosecution or that the prosecution will result in a case that is proved to the satisfaction of the court and results in the offender's conviction.[4]

How the detection rate is measured constitutes another important choice. The published overall headline detection figures can be said to give an optimistic picture of detection – the number *cleared up* in relation to *those recorded by the police*. The most pessimistic detection rate estimate would focus on *all crimes* (whether recorded or not) as the denominator and *crimes for which individuals were convicted* as the numerator. The picture each conveys is, of course, very different. For example, data from 1997 indicate that 1 in 4 recorded domestic burglaries were detected but only 1 in 50 led to a conviction in court. For theft of motor vehicles the corresponding figures are 1 in 5 and 1 in 17. For theft from motor vehicles they are 1 in 8 and 1 in 315 (Barclay and Tavares 1999).[5] Neither representation is 'correct' or 'incorrect'. They simply reflect different start and finish points in the attrition process.[6]

Arguably, for many members of the public, what really matters is the proportion of offences that lead to convictions in court. This reflects the number of offenders who are held to account for their offences, yet compared with detection rates these figures largely remain out of the public view. The choice and measurement of detection rates as a key performance indicator reflects political and pragmatic considerations rather than transparency.

Challenges to detecting crimes of different types

Different types of crime vary widely in their rates of detection. This in part relates to the nature of the offence and the nature of the challenges typically facing the investigator. For example, in violent offences there is direct contact between the victim and the offender, with the opportunity this brings for victims to observe the offender. In many cases they will already know the offender and be able to tell the investigator who it was. On the one hand this is an obvious benefit; however, this same feature can often also hinder police attempts at detection for some types of violent crime, such as cases of sexual assault where the perpetrator is known, or domestic violence. Victims may be reluctant to co-operate with police due to fear of retaliation from the suspect, or concern that their case will not be taken seriously. In these types of cases, the challenge facing police is not one of identifying a suspect, but rather of collecting evidence and encouraging victims to participate in the investigation and prosecution of their cases.[7]

Where an incident of shop theft is discovered the offender is also very often found at the same time. Even if the offender is not apprehended at the time, the discovery of the offence is associated with seeing it happen, albeit that it is not always possible later to obtain an accurate description of the offender. Similarly, for drug-trafficking crimes the offender's apprehension is often also what leads the incident to be recorded. The rates of detection for violent crimes, shop theft and drugs-trafficking offences are thus relatively high, reflecting these greater opportunities for detection. Hence, in 2004–5 the recorded rate of detection for trafficking in controlled drugs was 92 per cent, that for theft from a shop 61 per cent, and that for violent offences against the person 53 per cent (Nicholas *et al.* 2005).

Volume crimes – thefts of and from motor vehicles, domestic burglary and non-domestic burglary, but also offences like bicycle thefts – present more substantial challenges to the investigator. The offence is generally discovered some time after the crime was committed, the offender rarely has contact with the victim, and he or she may be seen by no one who would know that an offence was taking place. In 2004–5, the official detection rate for bicycle theft was 5 per cent, that for domestic burglary 16 per cent, that for non-domestic burglary 11 per cent, that for theft of a motor vehicle 14 per cent and that for theft from a vehicle 8 per cent. The detection rates for these sorts of offence increase very substantially where there is direct contact with the offender, as in 'aggravated' offences. For example, in 2004–5 the detection rate for aggravated domestic burglary was 44 per cent, for aggravated non-domestic burglary 34 per cent and for aggravated vehicle theft 47 per cent (Nicholas *et al.* 2005).

There are also differences in conditions for detection between different types of volume crimes. In thefts of motor vehicles, for example, the nature of the crime means the main crime scene is absent! Not surprisingly, until or unless the vehicle is recovered, the opportunity to collect evidence linking the suspect to the crime is low. In contrast, many commercial organizations have CCTV systems which may produce images of the offenders in cases of non-domestic burglary. Domestic burglaries may take longer to commit than thefts from motor vehicles, thus increasing the chances that the offender will be seen and/or identified by witnesses. However, once the property has been entered the offender is within private space and the prospects of being seen by witnesses are much reduced. These types of differences between crime types help explain the variations in the forms of, and obstacles to, their detection. We consider these issues further in due course.

The impact of crime mix on detection rates

The very marked differences in detection rate that are found between major crime types reflect variations in the difficulty of detection. Overall, detection rates by area reflect in large part variations in the mix of crimes with which forces have to deal. Burrows and Tarling (1982), who developed a model of influences on investigative performance with a view to determining the 'main drivers' of overall detection rates, found 'crime mix' consistently proved to be the main determinant. Where there is a relatively high proportion of the

Table 9.3 Crime variations in crime mix: hypothetical data

Crime type	Area A	Area B
Trafficking in controlled drugs	50	100
Violent crimes	100	200
Shop theft	100	150
Bicycle theft	150	100
Domestic burglary	150	50
Non-domestic burglary	50	150
Theft of motor vehicles	150	100
Theft from motor vehicles	250	150
Total	1,000	1,000

easier-to-detect crime types a high overall detection rate can be expected, and where there is a low proportion of easier-to-detect crimes a low detection rate can be expected. Let us assume a crime mix consisting only of the types described so far in each of two hypothetical police areas where there are 1,000 crimes (see Table 9.3). If the national detection rates for each crime type are applied, one area achieves a higher detection rate than the other: Area A ends up with 248 detections for the 1,000 crimes, a rate of about 25 per cent and Area B ends up with 365 detections, a rate of about 37 per cent.

Thus, in this scenario, the variations in crime mix and the differences in investigatory challenges posed by different types of crime would seem almost fully to explain the variations in overall detection rates. But, as the commentary that follows indicates, the picture is very rarely as straightforward as this.

The impact of recording practices on detection rates

There are two important qualifications to the picture of detection rates painted so far. The first relates to the crime number denominator: the count of offences in relation to which detection rates are calculated. So far the figures used have mostly referred to recorded offences. These are incidents that, in the main, have been reported to and classified as crimes by the police. It is obvious that not all offences are reported and the British Crime Survey (BCS) suggests that, of those that are reported, not all find their way into the records. Hence, in 2004 it was estimated that 61 per cent of domestic burglaries were reported and of these, 77 per cent were recorded – 47 per cent of the total. For thefts of vehicles, 95 per cent were reported of which 92 per cent were recorded – 87 per cent of the total. In the case of thefts from motor vehicles, just 45 per cent were reported, of which 75 per cent were recorded – 34 per cent of the total (Nicholas et al. 2005).[8]

These are the most recent national figures available at the time of writing. Historically, police recording practices have varied widely across place and time, meaning that the denominator for detection rates was unreliable. The police might know about offences in that they have been reported but not necessarily recorded: indeed, the UK research on criminal investigations in the 1970s and 1980s laid great emphasis on the practice of 'cuffing' reported offences – refusing to commit allegations to paper, often until they appeared to be 'solvable' – and the impact this could have on the detection rate (see McCabe and Sutcliffe 1978; Burrows and Tarling 1987 for a broader perspective). Therefore variations in detection rates across place and time could never be fully disentangled from differences in police recording practices. The National Crime Recording Standard has been introduced in an effort to standardize recording practices. It had become operational in all police services by 2004–5, so the figures for that year should be more reliable than those for earlier years, although this has not yet been verified empirically.

The significance of 'volume' for volume crime investigation and detection rates

It is easy to see how a vicious circle of increasing volume crime and decreasing detection can develop. Because offences are hard to detect, they are popular with offenders and committed in high numbers; because the crimes are committed in high numbers the time available to investigate each is limited, although – because of the nature of the offence – significant time is needed; because little time is spent investigating each offence the detection rate falls still lower; because the detection rate falls the offences become increasingly popular with the offending community and they are encouraged to commit even more of them. In the case of vehicle crime and burglary the advent of mass consumption in the postwar years provided a rich supply of targets and a ready market for stolen goods in which this spiral could operate. This pattern was evident in the 1980s. From 1981 to 1991 the number of recorded domestic burglaries increased by 78 per cent (from 349,001 to 622,969), the number of non-domestic burglaries by 61 per cent (from 368,579 to 594,210), the number of thefts of or unauthorized taking of motor vehicles by 75 per cent (from 332,590 to 581,901) and the number of thefts from motor vehicles by a whopping 141 per cent (from 379,640 to 913,276) (Home Office 2006). Over this same period, the number of police officers increased by only 6.3 per cent, to 127,100 officers (Barclay et al. 1993).[9]

The point has already been made that the high-volume property crimes focused on in this chapter tend to be harder to detect than specific types of non-volume crime where there is – say – contact between victim and offender, or where the discovery of the offence involves simultaneous identification of the offender. But differences in investigative opportunties also apply *within* the population of high-volume crimes focused on here: they will range from the very easy to detect to the very difficult to detect. We have already noted the much higher detection rates achieved for aggravated offences where there is perpetrator/victim contact compared with those where there are no aggravating circumstances. Amongst those where there are no aggravating conditions, difficulty of detection will also vary. In some cases the offender will be unlucky, lazy or slapdash and either be caught at the scene or leave large amounts of evidence enabling him or her easily to be caught. In other cases a careful and skilled offender will leave few clues, making the offence much more difficult to detect. The chapter turns later to the types of evidence most often found in practice in the investigation of volume crimes, and the supply of leads (as revealed in the work of police officers attending scenes of crime). For now, all that is assumed is that there is variation among high-volume crimes in the investigative challenges posed, and limited – as well as variable – resources to investigate them.

The impact of resources on detection rates

To what extent are detection rates a product of police resource levels? The detection of volume crime is not, of course, the only responsibility of the police: resources are needed to meet other policing imperatives or to devote to other locally or nationally determined priorities. The difficulty of establishing precisely what resources are channelled into crime investigation has long inhibited research into this question. Studies that have investigated the relationship have been obliged to adopt indices like police personnel per capita or expenditure on the police per capita.[10] For our present purposes, the numbers of police officers in relation to the number of volume crimes represent the best measure of the *potential* resources available for their detection.

Recent work by Tilley and Burrows (2005), which analysed attrition data across 266 BCUs in 41 forces, goes beyond establishing a simple, one-dimensional relationship and argues that finite police resources can lead to two likely consequences. On the one hand, as resources diminish it would be expected that only the easier-to-detect cases will be cleared up, reducing the overall detection rate because there will not be the resources to devote to the identification of offenders responsible for the harder to detect cases. On the other, as the number of volume crimes per police officer rises, other things being equal the number of easy-to-detect offences *per police officer* will also rise. In these circumstances the number of detections per police officer is also liable to increase, as less time will be needed per detection, given that laborious efforts to identify the offender will be not be required.

Tilley and Burrows (2005) found clear evidence in support of these suppositions when looking at national variations in the police-officer-to-crime ratios and their relationship to detection rates and numbers of detections per police officer. Their analysis indicated that *detection rates* tend to fall as the volume of crimes per officer increases. Specifically, for every 10 additional recorded volume crimes per officer, the force detection rate falls by 1.5 per cent. However, the more crimes there are for each officer to investigate, the more they detect, since they have more opportunities for detection, yielding an increase of 0.25 *detections per officer* for every 10 additional volume crimes. This seemingly incompatible situation is reconciled with the notion that, with a small number of officers in relation to the total amount of crime, it is possible to have a relatively large number of detections per officer, but a low overall detection rate (and vice versa).

'Doing' volume crime investigation

Limitations on the resources available mean that the police will be unable to investigate every volume crime to the extent they would a major crime. The police are therefore faced with having to decide which cases warrant significant attention. Building on the notion that detection difficulties vary, Eck (1983) suggested that three types of cases might be identified: 1) self-solvers; 2) cases that might be solved with some investigative effort; and 3) those which cannot be solved with a reasonable amount of effort or cannot be solved at all. He advocated a 'triage system' where an initial decision is made as to those cases where the conditions for detection look promising, and are therefore worthy of investigative resources, compared with those that are so unpropitious that allocating efforts would not be worth while. In practice, decisions about how and where to allocate resources constitute an inescapable feature of the whole investigative process for volume crime:

1 Which cases warrant police attendance at the scene?
2 Which cases warrant an urgent response?
3 Which cases warrant the expenditure of extended investigative effort at the scene of the crime?
4 Which cases warrant examination by a scenes of crime officer (SOCO)?
5 Which cases warrant follow-up work by the criminal investigation department or other specialist investigative unit?
6 Which cases warrant efforts to find, detain and question any suspect identified?
7 Which cases warrant file preparation efforts for the Crown Prosecution Service?
8 Which cases warrant prosecution?

'Triage' is happening throughout. Implicitly, if not always explicitly, decisions are taken about prioritization and allocation of investigative resources. As we go through the typical stages of the investigative process below (remembering that policies and practices can vary widely between police forces, and often within them), the patterns of investigative decision-making will become clear. It also will be clear that Eck's detectability criterion is not the only one being utilized by the police as they triage cases of volume crime.

The basic process in practice

Most volume crimes are reported by telephone. Investigation begins with the call handler, who takes some information on the basis of which a decision is taken about the initial response. The case may be closed and filed as undetected if there appear to be no prospects of detection. This rarely happens in cases of domestic burglary, in part because of its perceived seriousness and in part because attendance has the dual purpose of victim reassurance as well as crime investigation. For vehicle crimes, especially theft of vehicles, the decision will often be taken not to allocate an officer to attend the incident (Amey *et al.* 1996; Gill *et al.* 1996). The reasons have

Table 9.4 Police officer crime scene attendance patterns by crime type

Crime type	Family A BCUs		Family B BCUs		Family C BCUs		Family D BCUs	
	AH %	AL %	BH %	BL %	CH %	CL %	DH %	DL %
Domestic burglaries	99.0	92.6	98.5	89.4	95.7	98.1		
Non-domestic burglaries	97.8	97.7						
Thefts from motor vehicles			62.0	38.9			84.4	40.4
Thefts of motor vehicles					12.9	7.7	80.4	4.4

Note: The figures are taken from 3,000 tracked cases, using weighted data to deal with the over-representation of detected cases. The crime types are those that were sampled in each BCU.
Source: The eight BCU study.

both to do with the relatively lower seriousness of these offences and the likelihood that few leads will be obtained by attendance. Table 9.4 shows the patterns of officer attendance across BCUs, as found in the eight BCU study. The BCUs are in family pairs, the 'H' BCUs having relatively high detection rates and the 'L' BCUs relatively low ones. The overall pattern of attendance, by crime type, is broadly consistent with what had been found in earlier research.

Assuming, however, a police officer is allocated to attend, a decision will be taken about the urgency with which he or she should do so – the incident will be 'graded'. If the incident is happening at the time of the call or is known to have happened very recently, the police are likely to be asked – or could decide – to attend urgently. This is found across the board (Coopers and Lybrand 1994) and specifically for burglary and vehicle crimes (Gill *et al.* 1996). Attendance may be deemed urgent also for especially vulnerable and distressed victims (Coopers and Lybrand 1994; Gill *et al.* 1996). Just as Table 9.4 shows the wide variation between BCUs, research has shown that the actual rates of urgent attendance vary widely by police service. One study found a range from 2 per cent to 55 per cent across 33 forces (Coopers and Lybrand 1994).

Response times vary by crime types and the circumstances of the offence. For example, Coupe *et al.* (2002 cited in Jansson 2005) found that non-domestic burglaries graded as 'immediate' were attended in an average 4.5 minutes as against 9.6 minutes for those graded 'early'.

Once at the scene further details will be taken by the attending officer from the person reporting the incident, normally the victim or a witness: how the crime was committed, when it was committed, what was lost, attributes of the building or vehicle, attributes of the victim, suspicions as to who might have committed the offence and so on. The investigative activity most frequently conducted at a crime scene is a victim interview, undertaken in 9 out of 10 cases or more according to research in the USA (robberies and

Table 9.5 SOCO attendance rates by volume crime type

Crime type	Family A BCUs		Family B BCUs		Family C BCUs		Family D BCUs	
	AH %	AL %	BH %	BL %	CH %	CL %	DH %	DL %
Domestic burglaries	77.4	85.2	100.0	85.2	94.0	63.1	85.6	62.7
Non-domestic burglaries	67.9	73.7	41.5	73.7	41.4	27.2	55.7	34.4
Thefts from motor vehicles	2.5	4.1	21.7*	4.1	27.8	5.2	64.6	13.2
Thefts of motor vehicles	4.1	9.8		9.8	53.9	13.9	32.5	40.8
All volume offences	31.0	33.6	46.1	35.5	47.0	34.2	55.1	34.8

Notes: BCUs provided data covering all cases, regardless of the crime types for which cases were tracked.
*This is a combined figure from both types of motor vehicle crime.
Source: The eight BCU study.

burglaries; Eck 1983) and the UK (domestic burglary; Coupe and Griffiths 1996). Neighbour interviews are also common, occurring in just over half of domestic burglary incidents (Coupe and Griffiths 1996). Other investigative activities could include area searches, property checks, taking witness statements, scanning any available CCTV footage and so on, but these occur less routinely. The average time spent at scenes of detected burglaries was found by Coupe and Griffiths (1996) to be 53 minutes compared with 29 minutes for undetected burglaries.

On the basis of the record taken at the scene (assuming that the crime was not detected at the time), a decision is then taken about further investigation. In some instances it may be decided that there is nothing to be gained from further work and the case will be filed as 'undetected'. In others a SOCO (often now referred to as a 'crime scene examiner') will be asked to examine the scene for 'contact trace material' and/or the case may be referred on for further investigation either by CID or uniformed officers. While the officer first attending the crime scene will normally advise on the attendance of a SOCO, some research has indicated that they are often ill-equipped to make the decision (Tilley and Ford 1996). In the case of more serious volume crime offences, notably domestic burglary, the default position is often that a SOCO will be routinely dispatched to examine the scene, as shown in Table 9.5.

In relation to those scenes examined by SOCOs, decisions have to be taken as to the thoroughness of the search and about what types of physical evidence to collect. In volume crimes priority will normally be given to fingerprints and DNA traces, though shoe marks may also be taken. Of burglary dwelling crime scenes visited by SOCOs in 2002–3, fingerprints were taken in 31 per cent and shoe marks were taken in 12 per cent (Rix 2004). DNA was recovered from 6 per cent (MHB 2004), and this figure – increasing year by year – represents the impact of central government support for the collection of DNA evidence (Bradbury and Feist 2005). A wide range of other materials, such as glass, fluff, instrument marks and tyre tracks, may in principle be available but are rarely collected in volume crimes. A recent study of seven police forces in England and Wales found that the recovery rates of forensic material in volume crime cases are influenced by a number of factors, including force and BCU-level SOCO resources, individual SOCO workloads and the extent of integration of scientific support into the investigative process (Williams 2004).

Decisions about whether to conduct further investigation, subsequent to the initial scene attendance, may be made by a shift supervisor, a crime management unit, a specialist intelligence squad or CID. If there is no promising physical evidence, or if there are thought to be no worthwhile leads from the initial response to the incident, it may be filed as 'undetected'. If not so filed at this point, some further investigation may be conducted. For example, initial leads may be chased up, general community inquiries may be undertaken or the attributes of the incident may be looked at to see whether they form a likely part of a series, or are associated with the methods of a known criminal, or informants may be consulted. Further investigative efforts may then be directed at the case, informed by these sources of intelligence. What is done will very much depend on the nature of the leads that are available (Eck 1983). When these are checked and found to lead nowhere the case will then eventually be filed as 'undetected'.

The screening processes for what is often referred to as 'secondary investigation' are clearly difficult. In dealing with volume crime, selectivity is clearly needed in the allocation of scarce specialist investigative resources. If too many cases are screened in, the amount of investigative effort per case will be too thin to make progress, wasting resources. If too few are screened in, the number of detections is liable to be unduly small given the resources available, again wasting time and resources.

The issue is highlighted in research examining a screening algorithm that was developed in the USA to find out which case attributes and leads were most promising for detecting burglaries. The algorithm was developed by Greenberg et al. (1973) and then a post hoc test was conducted by Eck (1979) across some 13,000 cases. The factors identified by Greenberg et al. included witness reports, usable fingerprints, suspect information, vehicle descriptions, and range of time occurrence. The strength of the model was apparent, in that the vast majority of outcomes (detected versus not detected) were correctly predicted. On the other side of the coin, however, more than half the detections that actually occurred might have been lost had the model alone been used to allocate investigative effort.

Softer methods of screening for secondary investigation have been used in Britain (Coupe and Griffiths 1996; Gill et al. 1996; Jacobson et al. 2003). They have been found to be limited by poor-quality initial information and lack of systematic, standardized methods. In practice, vehicle crimes are rarely screened in for secondary investigation (Gill et al. 1996), while more than one third of domestic burglaries have been found to be followed up with CID visits after the initial attendance (Coupe and Griffiths 1996). In secondary investigation, much time appears to be spent simply duplicating what was originally done (Coupe and Griffiths 1996).

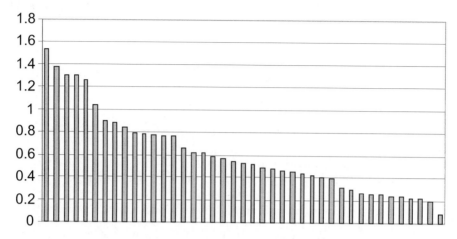

Figure 9.1 TICs per non-TIC sanction detection, all volume crimes by police service, 2003–3
Note: This omits two police force areas for which data were not available
Source: Tilley and Burrows (2005)

Obtaining an account of the offender's past offending

The investigative story does not end with the identification of a suspect, whether from primary or secondary investigation. When a suspect is arrested and charged, he or she may be asked about other offences he or she would like to have 'taken into consideration' (TICs) by the courts. These cases are detected indirectly. This is not to say that no investigative skills are needed. Interviewing clearly comprises one major tool of crime investigation. Indirectly detected cases will often include those that had previously been filed undetected. Rates vary enormously by area, perhaps reflecting both effort and skill at detecting cases through TICs. Figure 9.1 shows the number of TICs per direct detection by police service for all volume crimes in 2002–3. It is clear that TICs are pursued much more commonly in some police services than in others. Indeed, it is in the differing use of TICs that much variability in detection rate is explained. Once a person has been charged, case file preparation for the transmission to the Crown Prosecution Service (CPS), decisions on prosecution within the CPS and adjudication in court take place. These stages, though, lie beyond police investigation *per se*.

As indicated earlier, up to 1999 there was another means by which offenders could 'clean the slate' by admitting to their past offending – through the practice of obtaining prison write-offs. Leaving the issue of the appropriateness of this mechanism to one side, it remains crucially important to grasp – particularly in the light of our growing knowledge about persistent and prolific offenders – what a potentially dramatic impact the recording of past offending can have. In seeking to account for the differences in burglary detection rates between police areas, Burrows (1986a) concluded that clear-up rates 'give little or no indication of police effectiveness in arresting burglars … police areas achieving high burglary clear up rates often owe their success to local procedures designed to ensure that the burglars they arrest give a full account of their past offending'. The crux of the problem was expressed in an allied publication (Burrows 1986b: 82):

> If it is acknowledged, as most seem to do, that the majority of burglaries are committed by regular offenders, the failure to interview them successfully about past offences they may have committed will mean that the police cannot ever hope to achieve 'high' detection rates: even the theoretical arrest of all the burglars operating in an area – who, say, committed 10 offences each – would only produce a 10% clear up rate if all those caught refused to pass on any information about other burglaries they had carried out.

This issue rarely enters either the public debate about detection rates, or indeed – as the police service has been pushed to focus on arrests and sanction detection rates[11] – the debate in more informed circles, where even the value of TICs is questioned. But it remains a simple platitude that, to the extent that volume crime offences are committed by the same individual(s), detection rates will understate police investigative success *unless* the police give adequate attention and, perhaps, sufficient inducements are available to offenders, to document past offending.

Drivers of triage processes

The point has been made that triage processes occur throughout the investigative process, through various screening practices. What is screened in and what is screened out at each stage is, at one level, a matter of both apparent probability of detection and crime seriousness. This is not surprising. The public would expect greater efforts to be devoted to more serious crimes. Yet, in the interests of good resource management it is to be expected that attention will be paid to the potential pay-off from investigative processes. There is a balance to be struck between focusing on the opportunities for detection and focusing on the seriousness of offences.

It is again no surprise that, at another level, the balance varies across, and even within, police services. Several reasons for this are possible, including variations in resource levels because better resourced police areas will be able to be less discriminating about what and how they investigate. Furthermore, the proportion of resources devoted to investigation may be higher in some places than in others, depending on judgements made about policing priorities (e.g. crime prevention or crime detection?). Some forces may be more adept at spotting promising cases for further investigative efforts than others. Finally, there are differences of opinion about the benefits that are derived from obtaining admissions about past offending. It is clear that in some areas TICs are deemed a legitimate and useful form of detection, for both the police and the public to know that someone is being held to account for an offence. In contrast, TICs may be discouraged in other areas because there is no guarantee that they will be followed up in court and/or affect the sentence (Burrows *et al.* 2005a).

How volume crimes are detected

The discussion moves now from what is done to try to detect volume property crimes to what in practice leads to their detection. The detection of crime involves two conceptually separate stages: (1) the identification of a suspect, and (2) the collection of evidence that establishes that the suspect committed the crime, before an arrest can be made and a charge put. In many cases the same evidence does both jobs, but not always. Indeed, cases where a single source is sufficient to identify a suspect and then link him or her to the crime, with sufficient certainty to detect the case, are rare.

A wide range of clues, or types of evidence, may be involved in the detection of an offence. For example:

1 The suspect may be caught red-handed committing the offence.
2 The suspect may be stopped and found in possession of incriminating objects, say stolen goods, or the tools that may have been used in committing an offence.
3 A receiver of stolen property may implicate the suspect in the offence.
4 A known offender may be found close to the scene of a crime very soon after the offence.
5 A witness – the victim or another – may recognize the suspect as he or she commits the crime.
6 A witness may see the offender and be able to furnish a description.
7 A witness may recall suspicious behaviour or a suspicious vehicle and be able to provide some information relating to the offender or his or her activities.
8 Members of the community may routinely talk to police officers about suspicious persons and their suspicious movements.
9 A series of offences using a common method may be identified and a suspect identified for one, with the remainder imputed to him or her.
10 The offence may bear a strong resemblance to offences known previously to have been committed by the suspect.
11 An informant may suggest to the police who committed an offence or is committing offences of a particular kind or in a particular area.
12 A co-offender may be persuaded to inform on his or her collaborator.
13 The offender may leave physical evidence of some sort that may link him or her to the scene of the crime, and this may be collected and traced to him or her.
14 The offender may inadvertently take away physical evidence linking him or her to the scene of an offence.
15 The offender may be arrested for another offence and admit to the crime.
16 A suspect may be persuaded to admit to an offence while being interviewed.
17 The offender may ask that the offence be taken into consideration when being brought to book for an offence detected to him or her.

18 The victim may have a strong hunch as to who the offender is, perhaps a neighbour, past partner or other relative.
19 The offender may be caught on CCTV while committing the offence.
20 A known offender is caught on CCTV acting suspiciously in the area of the offence around the time the crime was committed.

The data to hand about detection do not permit a very fine-grained account of the role played by different types of evidence. Each case is unique and unravelling what led to its detection is complex. Tracking down leads obtained, their pursuit and then gauging their relative role in detecting cases is difficult. The paper trail from the investigative process involves many components[12] and can – even for volume crimes that are undetected – be substantial: but it remains only a partial record of investigative activity, a function of that which those involved choose to record. The analysis of data contained in case files from the eight BCU study does, however, allow us to describe the role of broad categories of evidence in the direct detection of volume crime.

Offender caught at or near the scene of the crime

The most obvious way in which a crime can be detected is through the offender being caught and arrested red-handed. This clearly depends on the offence being noticed as it happens and on the availability of someone to detain the offender. It is in the nature of most volume crime offences that this will not normally occur. Indeed, it is the potential to avoid this situation that presumably makes burglary and car crime attractive propositions for those disposed to commit property crimes.

Nevertheless, a small proportion of unlucky or inept offenders will be noticed as they offend, or they will behave in ways that make others sufficiently suspicious of their behaviour that they intervene in ways that lead the offender to be detained by either themselves or by third parties.

Table 9.6 shows the status of volume crime offences when reported. It is clear that offences are reported in progress in only a small minority of cases and the vast majority of those reported in progress are reported as the offender leaves the scene of the crime.

The benefits to detection opportunities provided by reports of offences in progress is obvious in Figure 9.2, which shows the percentages of cases directly detected in relation to the stage of the offence as it was reported. It is clear that the chances of a crime being directly detected are greatly enhanced when the incident is reported in progress and that the earlier it is reported in the course of the crime the greater the likelihood of detection. It shows that at least 30 per cent of those cases that were reported when the offender was entering the vehicle or property or was still in the vehicle or property were directly detected, for each of the four crime types. Furthermore, at least 10 per cent were directly detected when the offence was reported as the offender left the vehicle or premises. These figures compare with at most around 5 per cent when the offence was reported at a later stage.

Table 9.6 Status of volume crimes when reported to the police

	Domestic burglary	Non-domestic burglary	Theft from motor vehicles	Theft of motor vehicles	Total
Offender entering property/vehicle	1.0%	1.1%	.5%	.4%	.7%
Offender inside property/vehicle	2.0%	3.1%	1.2%	1.3%	1.7%
Offender leaving property/vehicle	10.6%	9.1%	7.6%	5.2%	8.8%
Not in progress	86.4%	86.7%	90.8%	93.1%	88.8%
Total	100.0%	100.0%	100.0%	100.0%	100.0%
Unweighted N	1093	357	723	744	2,917

Note: Weighted data.
Source: The eight BCU study.

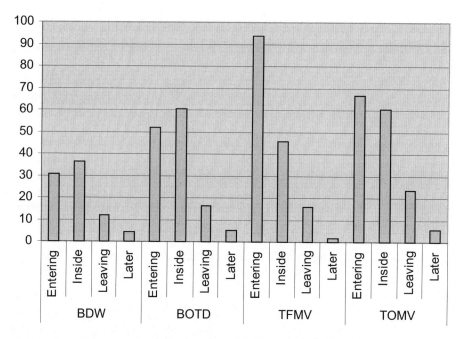

Figure 9.2 Direct detention rates by stage of offence when reported
Notes: 1. Weighted data from the eight BCU study, analysis supplementary to that in Burrows *et al*. (2005a) 2. BDW refers to burglaries in dwellings; BOTD refers to burglaries in buildings other than dwellings; TFMV refers to thefts from vehicles; and TOMV refers to thefts or unauthorised taking of motor vehicles.

The net effect of the low absolute numbers of crimes reported in progress, and their relatively higher direct detection rate, is that a high proportion of all detections relate to offences that were reported as they were happening. For domestic burglary, detections of crimes reported in progress constitute 37 per cent of all detections. The corresponding figures for non-domestic burglary, theft from and theft of motor vehicles are 51, 56 and 32 per cent. Overall, in a third (34 per cent) of all volume crimes that were directly detected, the main evidence for the detection was that the offender was caught at or near the scene of the crime.

In relation to offences reported in progress, various studies have shown that speedy police attendance is associated with an increased probability of detection (Spelman and Brown 1981; Blake and Coupe 2001). Coupe and Griffiths (1996) found that 43 per cent of detected domestic burglary cases involved offenders being caught in the act or near the scene. Although numbers of offences reported in progress might be small, they form a substantial proportion of detected volume property crimes, where police are able to catch the offender red-handed or where the trail is still very hot.

Victim or witness information

For those detected offences where the offender is not caught red-handed, information obtained by the investigator from victims and witnesses often appears to be critical. Coupe and Griffiths (1996) found that information from victims and witnesses about suspects played a large part in detecting domestic burglaries. Some 34 per cent of detected cases had suspects that were initially identified through interviews with victims and witnesses, almost all of whom (94 per cent) were questioned by the initial response officer. Burrows (1986b) found that the public provided the suspect's name for just over one half of detected cases. The eight BCU study found, across all volume property crime types, that in 55 per cent of directly detected cases the 'first suspect links' were made from the initial response to the incident, and that of these about 80 per cent came from information gleaned from the victim or another witness. Put another way, victim or witness information accounted for a little more than 40 per cent of all first links to offenders. The eight BCU study also found that, for 18 per cent of all volume crimes the main evidence that allowed the crime to be detected came from victims or other witnesses.

Physical evidence, including CCTV

Physical evidence forms a third major source for identifying a suspect or confirming his or her presence at the scene. While research into criminal investigations in the 1970s and 1980s provided little support for physical evidence playing any significant role in volume crime investigations, Coupe and Griffiths (1996) found – in relation to detected cases of domestic burglary – that forensic evidence had been used in 17 per cent of cases. More recently the eight BCU study, across all property volume crime types, found that physical evidence had provided the first links to a suspect in 24 per cent of cases, and was the main evidence allowing a case to be detected in 27 per cent of cases.

The apparent increase in the contribution of physical evidence in the decade between Coupe and Griffiths (1996) and the eight BCU study can be attributed, at least in part, to the development of the National DNA Database (NDNAD) and the National Automated Fingerprint Identification Service (NAFIS) and generally improved forensic techniques (Bradbury and Feist 2005). While both NDNAD and NAFIS have enabled DNA and fingerprints, respectively, found at the scene of a crime to be more easily linked to individuals with 'previous form', this has not been the only development. In recent years, the national DNA Expansion programme has injected very substantial funds into expanding the DNA database, and led to the training and funding of more SOCOs (see MHB 2004). Moreover, more advanced forensic techniques have been regularly developed and made more accessible (including, for example, super-sensitive means of retrieving DNA traces that are not visible to the human eye), and such developments have significantly changed the way in which the police service applies the different forensic techniques (the impact has been investigated by Burrows and Tarling 2004; Burrows *et al.* 2005b).

CCTV accounted for about 2 in 10 of the detections initiated through physical evidence in the eight BCU study. Of course the greater proportionate use of physical evidence generally may also have to do with reductions in the usability of other evidence types.

Other evidence

In the eight BCU study, almost 80 per cent of volume property crime direct detections were found to have been detected principally through catching the offender at or close to the scene (34 per cent), through information from the victim or witnesses (18 per cent) or through physical evidence (27 per cent). In Coupe and Griffiths' (1996) study of domestic burglary, detectives cited these same types of evidence as the most important in almost 80 per cent of detected cases.

The eight BCU study found that the principal evidence for the remainder of direct detections included the offender being found in possession of stolen goods (12 per cent), offender interviews (9 per cent) and – interestingly, in the context of the debate about proactive investigation (see below) – a tiny number where an informant played the key part (0.5 per cent). Similarly, Coupe and Griffiths (1996) found that informants were deemed to have played the most important part in 4 per cent of detections, interview admissions in 2 per cent, stolen property in 2 per cent and that vehicle description or registration numbers played the key part in 11 per cent.

Table 9.7 shows a model devised for the eight BCU study where different evidence types are brought together to estimate their respective contributions to detection rates. The data include the three types of property volume crimes for which sufficient cases were available: domestic burglary, theft from motor vehicles and theft of motor vehicles.

The final column on the right shows the proportion of cases providing the types of lead shown in the left-hand column. It is clear, unsurprisingly, that the odds of detection are increased massively if the offender is caught

Table 9.7 Multivariate (binary logistic regression) model of direct detection

Factor	Domestic burglary	Theft from motor vehicles	Theft of motor vehicles	Cases
	Exp(B): number of times the odds of detection increases for each occurrence of this factor			With this feature %
Was an offender *caught at the scene*? (Y/N)	184.4	207.4	75.4	2.4
Number of sources giving *a name* (caller, witness, IP or CCTV)	5.0	3.5	8.0	2.8
Number of *types of forensic material available* (finger-prints, shoe marks, DNA, glass or fibre from scene or property recovered)	2.5	5.2	8.0	17.4
Number of *other potential leads* (descriptions, offender vehicle details)	1.4	1.4	4.6	20.8
R^2 overall measure of *model performance* (range: from zero, no explanation, to one, fully explains outcome)	.353	.406	.526	

Note: This is the Nagelkerke 'pseudo' R^2 measure of the amount of variance explained by the model. Weighted data; unweighted (N = 2,111).
Source: The eight BCU study.

at the scene, though this is a rare eventuality. Specific names of suspects are also available quite infrequently, but nevertheless play a significant part in raising the odds of detection. Physical evidence is available for a much higher proportion of cases, and again the amount of it increases the odds of detection. Finally 'other' leads are available in still more cases but raise the odds of detection only modestly compared with the other types. The R^2 values shown in the bottom row show quite a good fit, most especially for theft of motor vehicles.

It should be remembered that not all direct detections will lead to convictions, as discussed earlier. Overall, the eight BCU study found that:

• in 18 per cent of volume property crimes a direct detection suspect was identified;

- in 8 per cent of cases an arrest was made (so for 10 per cent of cases there was a suspect, but no arrest);
- in 7 per cent of cases a charge was made (so in 1 per cent of cases an arrest was made, but no charge levelled);
- in 6 per cent prosecutions followed (so in 1 per cent of cases a charge was levelled but no prosecution followed); and
- in just over 4 per cent of cases the suspect was convicted (so in almost 2 per cent of cases there was a prosecution but no conviction).[13]

For the vast majority of volume crime cases, no suspect emerges, making them extremely difficult to detect. A named suspect is not necessarily, of course, an offender and it is no surprise that, either because of this or because there is insufficient corroborating evidence, many suspects will not be arrested. Only relatively few of those arrested are not charged and of those charged only a relatively small number are not prosecuted, although these 'attrition losses' take place only after significant investigative investment. Following prosecution, of course, some cases do not prove strong enough to secure a conviction. Here the failure to convict comes at the end of a great deal of effort, which was in the event wasted. The post arrest stages of case processing lie beyond the scope of this chapter. They are, though, important for the effectiveness and efficiency of the criminal justice system as it deals with volume crimes.

Ideal types of delivering the investigative process

Two ideal types of delivering the investigative process emerged from the eight BCU study: the procedural and the discretionary. In the *procedural* there are specified set rules mandating what will be done by way of investigating volume crimes. Call handlers ask predetermined questions. There are established criteria determining which cases will be attended by a police officer. The officer attending the scene will ask a set of specified questions and undertake closely defined investigative activities. Explicit rules will define cases where a crime scene examiner is called. Assuming the crime scene examiner attends, the nature of the scene examination is laid out in advance, specifying priorities, searches and materials to be recovered. And similarly, procedures apply in carrying out arrests, conducting interviews, TIC taking, case-file preparation and prosecution. Importantly, rules determine which cases are filed undetected or detected, and when these decisions are made. The procedural approach allows a good deal of division of labour, where cases can be passed from one stage of standard processing to the next. Specialists can undertake the required work at any stage. This is 'assembly line' volume crime investigation, analogous to volume car manufacturing. The procedural model is attractive in volume crime investigation, where the lesser importance of the offences and scarce resources available for investigation mean that detailed attention to the particulars and a commitment to identify and follow up all potential leads is not possible in all cases, or is not required as it would be for major crimes. Much research relating to the detection of volume property crime potentially feeds into a procedural model, which promises 'best bets' or specific best practices for allocating investigative efforts (Greenwood 1970; Greenberg *et al.* 1973; Eck 1979 1983; Audit Commission 1993; Jacobson *et al.* 2003).

In contrast, the *discretionary* method of delivering investigation leaves scope for judgement at each point in the investigative process, and is more characteristic of investigative efforts relating to major crimes. The call handler asks questions that are germane to the case. Whether an officer is asked to attend and who attends is a function of judgements made about the merits of the individual incident. The police officer attending the incident determines what lines to pursue, what evidence to collect and whether to call a crime scene examiner on the basis of the individual case. The officer makes these decisions on the basis of his or her professional judgement. The crime scene examiner looks at the case and decides what contact trace material to look for and collect on the basis of the individual case. Decisions about further lines of investigation, analyses of contact trace material, suspect interviews, charges to be laid, efforts to elicit TICs, file preparation and prosecution are likewise made on the basis of professional judgements concerning the merits of individual cases. While the discretionary approach allows some division of labour, it is minimized and where there is division of labour there is discussion about the case and its needs. This is 'craft' volume crime investigation, analogous to craft production.

Each of these is an 'ideal type' in the sense that it describes an idealized model that recognizably captures a way of operating that is consistent and internally coherent, and whose rationale can be sought. The procedural model is clearly attractive where there are large numbers of cases to process and limited resources to process them, and where the workforce may lack the time or skills sensibly to exercise discretion in relation to individual cases, one by one. The procedural model ought to maximize avoidance of ill-informed, maverick or ill-judged decisions about cases. No one would, we think, want to employ the procedural model for very serious crime. There is a strong interest in investigating each major crime as fully as possible – looking for and pursuing any leads that can be unearthed. Short of unethical practice, anything goes. Efforts at detection are as uninhibited as possible by specified set procedures proscribing and prescribing particular activities. The attraction of the discretionary model is that each case is given high-quality, committed individual attention. It turns on having a workforce with the skills and time properly to consider each case on its merits.

That said, there are always departures from ideal types. Discretion is seldom entirely eliminated, even in areas most exhibiting procedural characteristics (see Gill *et al.* 1996). Moreover, those operating in the most discretionary areas still conduct some work within specified procedures. Indeed were they not to do so, for example in relation to the collection, labelling and provision for continuity in relation to physical evidence, such evidence would likely become invalidated. What we find, however, are areas which begin with discretion and apply rules when needed as against those that begin with rules and allow discretion when unavoidable.

The highest detection BCU found in the eight BCU study was largely discretionary. It was populated by experienced police officers with close contacts with the local community. Another relatively high detection largely procedural BCU operated with inexperienced, but well supervised officers. A low detection discretionary BCU was staffed by inexperienced officers. A low detection procedural BCU was staffed by inexperienced but rarely supervised officers. Context is critical in determining which style will yield the higher detection rate. Neither can be advocated unequivocally. It is likely that, with very high-volume crimes and relatively inexperienced officers, the scope for a highly discretionary approach will be rather limited. The price for adopting the procedural approach, however, is that some leads will be lost and some effort wasted. The better the procedures, of course, the lower will be the cost in terms of wasted effort and forgone detections.

It appears widely to be assumed that some version of the procedural model will tend to prevail generally. A wide range of factors all tell in favour of maximizing the use of standard methods, including: large case numbers; accountability for doing what can reasonably be expected; net benefits where officers are inexperienced; the popularity of evidence-based best practice research and guidance; the imperative for the conduct of standard and well formulated procedures in the prosecution of cases; and the risks of wrongful conviction where maverick approaches are adopted. Yet, it is unlikely that discretion can entirely be eliminated. Police investigators face complex cases where rules are unlikely ever to be adequate for all eventualities.

Proactive volume crime investigation

The emphasis so far in this chapter has been on reactive investigation. The Audit Commission (1993: 32) advocated a proactive approach, saying:

> A consequence of steeply rising workload, some duplication of effort and the tendency for detectives to get bogged down in paperwork is that the pattern of CID activity is highly reactive. The focus of effort is on the crime incident rather than the criminal. There is a cyclical process at work – the focus on crimes pulls officers away from the proactive work that is needed to identify and apprehend prolific criminals, who therefore carry on committing the crimes which generate the reactive burden for the police.

This approach to crime investigation was strongly supported by – among others – the Home Office, ACPO and HMIC under the banner of the 'Tackling crime effectively' (TCE) initiative. But, notwithstanding the guidance issued,[14] what precisely is involved in proactive investigation is not self-evident (Maguire 2003). It certainly includes, for example: assembling and analysing intelligence of various kinds, including that gleaned from informants; covert surveillance; identifying crime series; focusing on prolific and persistent offenders; the use of specialist squads to target people, places and crime types; and efforts to disrupt crime business by homing in on key crime processes, such as the disposal of stolen goods or offender networks.[15]

Table 9.8 The relationship between volume-crime detection rates and proactive unit(s) specifically tasked to carry out proactive investigations of volume crimes

	High detection rate	Low detection rate
Comparison A (family 2)	AH	AL
	Yes: burglary unit and dedicated proactive squad (subsequently disbanded)	*Yes*: Burglary squad both reactive and pro-active units within it
Comparison B (family 4)	BH	BL
	50/50: no proactive units for burglary or vehicle crime but offender management team focusing on persistent offenders and use of forensic intelligence packages	*No*: focus is predominantly on local policing team (LPT) arrangement and, while a specific operation supplements this, they deal primarily with processing suspects detained from reactive activities
Comparison C (family 10)	CH	CL
	Yes: sector support team focused exclusively on volume crime	*Yes*: proactive burglary team (as well as robbery unit)
Comparison D (family 13)	DH	DL
	50/50: Three proactive units: proactive crime team (level 1 and 2 organized crime); general-purpose vehicles team and proactive crime team	*Yes*: tactical CID team focusing on burglary (dwelling), vehicle crime and drug offences

Source: The eight BCU study.
Note: 'Yes' indicates that units were operating that were specifically tasked to carry out proactive investigations of volume crime; '50/50' that while there were no such specific arrangements, some volume crime cases would be likely to be dealt with by other units (as detailed); and 'no' that there were no such arrangements.

The National Intelligence Model, and the tasking and co-ordination groups set up as part of it, are key vehicles for proactive work.

Subsequent work by the Audit Commission (1996) found that adopting proactive approaches led to falls in burglary and a rise in detections. There is also some evidence from an American study that a proactive Repeat Offender Project (ROP), which targeted active offenders, led to the arrest of individuals with longer crime records than a control group, though fewer arrests overall (see Sherman and Eck 2002).

Few of the individual volume-crime detections identified in the eight BCU study could, however, be traced directly to proactive investigative activities. Nevertheless, the work of that research project did find out what was being attempted by way of proactivity in the eight BCUs studied, as shown in Table 9.8. This study found no straightforward link between the level of undertaking proactive investigation in a BCU and its detection rate. However, even fierce exponents of the use of proactive work in this area are not likely to find this surprising, and would argue that proactive investigation is more likely to manifest itself in terms of *crime reduction and prevention*, rather than in detection.

The limited and relatively weak evidence on the results of proactive investigation may reflect the fact that proactive approaches are quite recent, have taken quite a long time to bed down (cf. Maguire and John 2003), and research into its impact is so far scarce. There is also continuing ambiguity over the nature and purpose of proactive investigation (Jansson 2005). It is possible that what is involved in proactivity, and the evidence of its effects on investigation, may become clearer in the future.

Conclusion

The distinctive challenge of volume property crime detection follows from the nature of the offences and their large numbers. The potentially covert nature of the crimes makes them attractive to offenders and at the same time hard to detect. Their large numbers mean that each cannot receive the investigative attention that would be devoted to a violent or more serious crime. The result is an – entirely unsurprising – very low detection rate. The high attrition rate, especially when the start and end points are numbers of crimes committed (rather than recorded) and numbers leading to convictions (rather than detections), means that the risk to offenders is very low and hence potential deterrence is very limited, a situation liable to encourage more offending.

The nature of the efforts made to detect volume property crimes follows from the nature of their unique challenge to the police. Police areas with more investigative resources can detect more offences, whereas those that are more pressed will be confined to detecting the most straightforward, 'self-solving' cases. Screening (or triage) is an inevitable corollary of high numbers of hard-to-detect cases in most policing areas. Decisions have to be made about where to spend scarce investigative resources, such as sending uniformed officers to attend cases and conduct the initial inquiries, referring cases to scenes of crime officers for the collection of forensic evidence, or having members of the CID conduct secondary investigations. In some places the decisions about what to do and where to allocate effort are largely made on the basis of set procedures, with specialist teams conducting specialist activities. In other places, decisions are largely made by individual officers on the basis of what they deem to be the merits of the case. Each approach has its advantages and disadvantages, although the former – 'procedural approach' – tends to prevail in British policing.

In practice, volume property crime detections follow mainly from catching offenders close to or at the scene in that small minority of cases that are promptly reported or reported in progress; from conducting thorough initial investigations that result in information being gleaned from victims or witnesses that yields a link to a suspect; or from collecting physical traces left inadvertently by the offender at the scene of the crime. The ability of police to maximize their performance in relation to these three areas is dependent upon a number of factors, including the crime mix, levels of resources, their relationship to the community and the style of investigation that is encouraged among officers.

So far the evidence available about the nature and consequences of proactive approaches to investigations, a further response to the large numbers of cases that have to be contended with by the police, is too limited to come to any firm conclusions about their prospects. However, at the time of writing, the philosophy of adopting a proactive approach to crime investigation continues to enjoy widespread support.

Selected further reading

Bradbury, S. and Feist, A. (2005) *The Use of Forensic Science in Volume Crime Investigations: A Review of the Research Literature*. RDS Online Report OLR 43/05. London: Home Office. This comprises a comprehensive and systematic review of research relating to the use of physical evidence in the investigation of volume crimes. It can be downloaded free from the Internet.

Burrows, J., Hopkins, M., Hubbard, R., Robinson, A., Speed, M. and Tilley, N. (2005) *Understanding the Attrition Process in Volume Crime Investigations. Home Office Research Study* 295. London: Home Office. This comprises a large-scale study of the investigation of domestic burglary, non-domestic burglary, and theft of and theft from motor vehicles. It is available in hard copy but can also be downloaded free from the Internet.

Eck, J.E. (1983) *Solving Crimes: The Investigation of Burglary and Robbery*. Washington, DC: Police Executive Research Forum. This is a classic and highly influential American study of processes of investigation in cases of robbery and burglary.

Jansson, K. (2005) *Review of Volume Crime Investigations. RDS Online Report* OLR 44/05. London: Home Office. This comprises a systematic review of studies of volume crime investigation. It can be downloaded free from the Internet.

Maguire, M. (2003) 'Crime investigation and crime control', in T. Newburn (ed.) *A Handbook of Policing*. Cullompton: Willan Publishing. This is very readable account of the development of crime investigation in Britain up to the present day.

Notes

1 This is a narrower definition than that used by ACPO (2001), which includes robbery, theft and acquisitive crimes linked to drugs.
2 'Families' are a Home Office classification that clusters the 318 BCUs in England and Wales into 14 families in terms of their similarity across 18 socio-

    demographic and geographic attributes (Harper *et al.* 2001; Sheldon *et al.* 2002; Hall *et al.* 2003a, 2003b).

3 However, police do have *some* influence over other areas of the criminal justice process, as evidenced by changes in reporting practices as public confidence increases, or higher charging and conviction rates due to improvements in police evidence collection.

4 Indeed, a crime that is cleared up by means of a charge will remain 'detected' even if the offender is found not guilty.

5 There are no figures here for non-domestic burglary. This is because this offence is not covered in the British Crime Survey which deals with crimes against individuals and households. The Home Office Commercial Victimization Survey has investigated crime only against a subset of non-domestic premises – retailers and a subset of manufacturers. It cannot be used to estimate total numbers of non-domestic burglaries.

6 The issue of reporting and recording volume crime is picked up again later in this chapter.

7 Variations in police ability to meet this challenge are reflected in the enormous differences across forces for detections of offences of violence against the person (a range of 27–81 per cent) (Nicholas *et al.* 2005).

8 As the BCS covers only crimes against individuals and their households, an indication of the percentage of non-domestic burglaries that are reported and recorded cannot be derived.

9 By 2005, the situation had changed again. The numbers of recorded crimes had fallen and the number of police officers had risen. From 1991 to 2004–5, recorded numbers of domestic burglaries decreased by 49 per cent, non-domestic burglary by 40 per cent, thefts of motor vehicles by 60 per cent and theft from motor vehicles by 19 per cent (to the figures shown in Table 9.1). At the same time, numbers of police officers went up by 12 per cent, to a little under 143,000 full-time equivalents (Bibi *et al.* 2005).

10 Many of these studies are quite dated, such as Carr-Hill and Stern (1979) and Burrows and Tarling (1982).

11 Prison write-offs, of course, involved no additional sanction; rather, a 'trade' between the police and the offender.

12 Obtaining the most comprehensive picture does require, for example, bringing together the records held by control rooms (often derived from computer aided dispatch (CAD) systems), custody records, SOCO records, full statements from witnesses, prosecution files, etc. – as well as the 'case file' (see Burrows *et al.* 2005a).

13 In addition to these figures, 6 per cent of cases were detected through TICs.

14 The 'campaign' included issuing the TCE management handbooks to every BCU commander in England and Wales.

15 The ways in which intelligence is mobilized vary also by area (Burrows *et al.* 2005a). In some there is much reliance on community contacts from which information on suspects is routinely derived. In others there is more reliance on specific known informants. In others still, intelligence is built up by looking systematically at cases, individual and crime business profiles. In some areas there is a fairly clear break from primary to secondary investigation, with cases passed over from uniformed officers to CID or specialist squads. In other areas, this distinction is not made at all clearly. In some there is a high degree of officer ownership from initial scene attendance onwards. In others the case is passed from one relatively specialized unit to another.

References

ACPO Crime Committee (2001) *Investigation of Volume Crime Manual*. London: Association of Chief Police Officers.

Amey, P., Hale, C. and Mieczkowski, T. (1996) *Development and Evaluation of a Crime Management Model. Police Research Series Paper 18*. London: Home Office.

Audit Commission (1993) *Helping with Enquiries: Tacking Crime Effectively*. London: HMSO.

Audit Commission (1996) *Detecting a Change: Progress in Tackling Crime: Bulletin*. London: HMSO.

Barclay, G. with Drew, C., Hatton, R. and Abbot, C. (1993) *Digest 2: Information on the Criminal Justice System in England and Wales*. London: Home Office.

Barclay, G. and Tavares, C. (1999) *Digest 4: Information on the Criminal Justice System in England and Wales*. London: Home Office.

Bibi, N., Clegg, M. and Pinto, R. (2005) *Police Service Strength. Home Office Statistical Bulletin 12/05*. London: Home Office.

Blake, L. and Coupe, R.T. (2001) 'The impact of single and two-officer patrols on catching burglars in the act', *British Journal of Criminology*, 41: 381–96.

Bradbury, S. and Feist, A. (2005) *The Use of Forensic Science in Volume Crime Investigations: A Review of the Research Literature. RDS Online Report 43/05*. London: Home Office.

Burrows, J. (1986a) *Investigating Burglary: The Measurement of Police Performance. Home Office Research Study 88*. London: HMSO.

Burrows, J. (1986b) *Burglary: Police Actions and Victims' Views. Home Office Research and Planning Unit Paper 37*. London: Home Office.

Burrows, J., Hopkins, M., Hubbard, R., Robinson, A., Speed, M. and Tilley, N. (2005a) *Understanding the Attrition Process in Volume Crime Investigations. Home Office Research Study 295*. London: Home Office.

Burrows, J. and Tarling, R. (1982) *Clearing up Crime. Home Office Research Study 73*. London: Home Office.

Burrows, J. and Tarling, R. (1987) 'The investigation of crime in England and Wales', *British Journal of Criminology*, 27: 229–51.

Burrows, J. and Tarling, R. (2004) 'Measuring the impact of forensic science in detecting burglary and autocrime offences', *Science and Justice*, 44: 217–22..

Burrows, J., Tarling, R., Mackie, A., Poole, H. and Hodgson, B. (2005b) *Forensic Science Pathfinder Project: Evaluating Increased Forensic Activity in Two English Police Forces. RDS Online Report 46/05*. London: Home Office.

Carr-Hill, R.A. and Stern, N.H. (1979) *Crime, the Police and Criminal Statistics*. London: Academic Press.

Coopers and Lybrand (1994) 'Evaluation of Call Grading' (unpublished).

Coupe, T. and Griffiths, M. (1996) *Solving Residential Burglary. Crime Detection and Prevention Paper 77*. London: Home Office.

Davies, N. (2003) 'Fiddling the figures', *Guardian*, 11 July (available online at http://www.guardian.co.uk/criminaljustice/story/0,13733,996547,00.html).

Eck, J.E. (1979) *Managing Case Assignments: The Burglary Investigation Decision Model Replication*. Washington, DC: Police Executive Research Forum.

Eck, J.E. (1983) *Solving Crimes: The Investigation of Burglary and Robbery*. Washington, DC: Police Executive Research Forum.

Gill, M., Hart, J., Livingstone, K. and Stevens, J. (1996) *The Crime Allocation System: Police Investigations into Burglary and Auto Crime. Police Research Series Paper 16*. London: Home Office.

Greenberg, B., Oliver, S.Y. and Lang, K. (1973) *Enhancement of the Investigative Function. Volume 1. Analysis and Conclusions.* Springfield, VA: National Technical Information Service.

Greenwood, P. (1970) *An Analysis of the Apprehension Activities of the New York City Police Department.* New York, NY: Rand Institute.

Hall, R., Vakalopolulou, V., Brunsdon, C., Charlton, M. and Alvanides, S. (2003a) *Maintaining Basic Command Unit and Crime and Disorder Partnership Families for Comparative Purposes: 1 April 2002 Results. RDS Online Report* 39/03. London: Home Office.

Hall, R., Vakalopolulou, V., Brunsdon, C., Charlton, M. and Alvanides, S. (2003b) *Maintaining Basic Command Unit and Crime and Disorder Partnership Families for Comparative Purposes: 1 April 2003 Results. RDS Online Report* 40/03. London: Home Office.

Harper, G., Williamson, I., See, L., Emmerson, K. and Clarke, G. (2001) *Family Ties: Developing Basic Command Unit Families for Comparative Purposes. Briefing Note* 4/01. London: Home Office.

Home Office (2006) *Recorded Crime Statistics, 1898–2004/5* (available online at http://www.homeoffice.gov.uk/rds/pdfs/100years.xls).

Jacobson, J., Maitland, L. and Hough, M. (2003) *Investigating Burglary. Home Office Research Study* 264. London: Home Office.

Jansson, K. (2005) *Review of Volume Crime Investigations. RDS Online Report* 44/05. London: Home Office.

Maguire, M. (2003) 'Crime investigation and crime control', in T. Newburn (ed.) *A Handbook of Policing.* Cullompton: Willan Publishing.

Maguire, M. and John, T. (2003) 'Rolling out the National Intelligence model', in K. Bullock and N. Tilley (eds) *Crime Reduction and Problem-oriented Policing.* Cullompton: Willan Publishing.

McCabe, S. and Sutcliffe, F. (1978) *Defining Crime.* Oxford: Blackwell.

MHB (2004). *Evaluation of the DNA Expansion Programme, 2002/3.* London: Home Office Research, Development and Statistics Directorate (available online via the ACPO intranet).

Nicholas, S., Povey, D., Walker, A. and Kershaw, C. (2005) *Crime in England and Wales 2004-5. Home Office Statistical Bulletin* 11/05. London: Home Office.

Rix, B. (2004). *The Contribution of Shoemark Data to Police Intelligence, Crime Detection and Prosecution. Home Office Findings* 236. London: Home Office.

Sheldon, G., Hall, R., Brunsdon, C., Charlton, M., Alvanides, S. and Mostratos, N. (2002) *Maintaining Basic Command Unit and Crime and Disorder Partnership Families for Comparative Purposes. RDS Online Report* 06/02. London: Home Office.

Sherman, L.W. and Eck, J.E. (2002) 'Policing for crime prevention', in L. Sherman *et al.* (eds) *Evidence-based Crime Prevention.* London: Routledge.

Spelman, W. and Brown, D.K. (1981) *Calling the Police: Citizen Reporting of Serious Crime.* Washington, DC: Police Research Executive Forum.

Tilley, N. and Burrows, J. (2005) *An Overview of Attrition Patterns in the Investigative Process. RDS Online Report* 45/05. London: Home Office.

Tilley, N. and Ford, A. (1996) *Forensic Science and Crime Investigation. Crime Detection and Prevention Series Paper* 73. London: Home Office.

Williams, R. (2004) *The Management of Crime Scene Examination in Relation to the Investigation of Burglary and Vehicle Crime. Home Office Findings* 235. London: Home Office.

Chapter 10

Investigation order and major crime inquiries

Martin Innes

Investigation is an act in three 'movements'. Whether we are concerned with a specific investigative activity, or a more complex investigative process comprising connected practices and lines of inquiry, these three inter-related movements are always present. The first movement involves 'identifying and acquiring' that which forms the basis of an investigation. The key task is to separate out what is relevant to the particular concerns of an individual investigation from that which is potentially available, but not relevant. This process of identifying and acquiring informs the second movement of the act, which is 'interpreting and understanding'. Interpreting and understanding is where information is translated into intelligence or knowledge. This phase involves inferences and hypotheses being constructed and the particular piece of information being fitted together with other things that are known. The third movement of investigation is 'ordering and representing' the information in a way that warrants the interpretations and understanding that have been constructed. This is about configuring new knowledge with extant knowledge held by the investigator(s) in a format that enables a solution to the question that is the focus of the investigation to be established and communicated. This may involve communication as evidence, or as a narrative suitable for wider cultural consumption.

These three movements collectively provide the act of investigation with its most basic sense of form, process and structure. As such, they constitute the foundations of what we might usefully term 'the investigation order' – that is, the sequence of information organizing, interpreting and communicating practices that enable an investigation to construct an account of how and why an event happened. The basic function of the investigation order is the reduction of uncertainty. An investigation is enacted because there is some doubt about an event or condition that it is predicted a process of investigation can help to determine. The investigation order articulates how the police do *not* undertake their investigative activities in a random or unstructured manner. Rather, they are guided by a complex array of formal and informal policies, systems, guidelines, procedures and conventions (Innes 2003a).

Applied to the field of police crime investigations, conceiving of police inquiries as seeking to reduce uncertainty through a structured process illuminates aspects of both their proactive and reactive work. As Maguire (2000) notes, proactive investigations are governed by a risk management logic where the uncertainty to be resolved is to establish whether a particular actor or actors are likely to engage in criminal activities that can be prevented in some manner, or for which they can be arrested. In contrast, reactive investigations are *ex post facto*, occurring after a criminal act has been performed, where the fundamental task is to establish 'who did what to whom, when, where, how and why?'

In this chapter I will use the conceptual apparatus outlined above to illuminate the conduct of major crime inquiries into homicides, as a particular type of large-scale reactive police investigation. My aim is to provide an overview of some of the key policies, processes and practices that collectively shape the ways in which major crime inquiries are performed. In so doing, I will also address issues of decision-making and the connections between policing major crime and other aspects of 'police business' in an effort to show the complex ways in which major crime procedures are structured. The chapter commences with a brief overview of the literature on crime investigation in order to identify some key research findings that are relevant to understanding the conduct of major crime inquiries. It then focuses upon the three phases of the investigation order identified above, before considering the role and nature of investigative decision-making. The final part of the chapter turns to consider how and why some investigations encounter problems.

The social organization of investigation

In direct contrast to the high profile that homicide investigations have in the mass media, empirical research on the conduct of major crime investigations remains comparatively rare. The reasons for this appear to be fourfold: (1) access has proven difficult to negotiate, with the police somewhat reluctant to provide assistance to researchers due to a number of security, legal and resource concerns; (2) until comparatively recently, data have not been available in a form especially conducive to the conduct of either qualitative or quantitative secondary analyses; (3) certainly in the UK, the historically low base numbers for criminal homicide compared with other types of volume crime have meant that political priority was consistently focused upon the latter rather than the former; and (4) connected to point 3, any potential concerns about system and process errors in the conduct of major crime investigations have been assuaged by the fact that the detection rate has consistently been in the region of 90 per cent for all criminal homicide cases.

Given that there is this dearth of research focused specifically upon major crime investigations, it is potentially instructive to look across studies of other types of police investigation in order to identify how they can inform our understandings of major crime inquiries. Three key relevant findings can be identified:

1 Investigative work is routinized and ordered.
2 Investigations are forms of information work.
3 Accounts of the crime are artefacts of police methods.

Routinization

Studies of the investigation of volume crime have tended to stress the mundane realities of detective work and the fact that much of what is performed is a form of bureaucratic crime management – doing paperwork and reviewing case files (Ericson 1993). Crime solutions are, for most types of volume offending, comparatively rare, and when they do occur tend to be a product of the quality and quantity of information provided to police by members of the public cast as victims or witnesses, rather than any actions taken by police investigators (Greenwood *et al.* 1977). The image that emerges from research is in direct contrast to the glamorous media fictions of the hard-bitten detective, possessed of some intuitive insight into the thought processes of the 'evil' criminal actor.

Ultimately, though, this portrayal should not be that surprising as the key function of formal organizations is the rationalization and routinization of action (Scott 1998). In my own ethnographic research on homicide investigation, I found that a majority of major inquiries tended to be highly routinized and standardized, albeit different in terms of scale and resources when compared with volume crimes (Innes 2003a). I differentiated between 'self-solving', 'whodunit' and 'hybrid' cases, analytic classifications that echo David Simon's (1991) journalistic work in Baltimore and what he labelled 'dunkers' and 'whodunits'. My observational work suggested that the process structures of many police homicide inquiries fitted a 'self-solver' model of the investigative process, where due to the circumstances in which they occurred, the identification of a suspect was a comparatively routine and uncomplicated matter (Innes 2002b). This was helped by the fact that, at an early stage of their inquiries, police received sufficient quality and quantity of information to enable them to identify a suspect. This was usually either because they had witnesses to a fatal altercation who were able to provide clear leads about the identity of a possible suspect, or, alternatively, in a significant number of homicides, due to the circumstances in which they occurred, potential suspects self-incriminated. Consequently, in responding to these incidents the police work gravitated to a significant degree around constructing a case for the prosecution (McConville *et al.* 1991). The more complex and difficult-to-solve 'whodunit' cases constituted only a minority of those that the police dealt with, despite the fact that it is these type of investigations that are publicly projected as the archetype of what police detectives do (Reiner 1997). Even in these cases, a distinct sense of order and structure to the conduct of the police work was discernible. The hybrid category was used to cover those that fell somewhere between the two ideal types of self-solver and whodunit.

Differentiating between self-solvers, hybrids and whodunits is important in that it reflects how cases are not easily comparable units (Manning 1988). The circumstances surrounding a death can make it more or less easy for police to establish what has happened and, ultimately, the police do not control all the factors that determine whether a successful outcome is likely to be achievable or not.

Information work

Studies of police responses to volume crime have repeatedly emphasized the degree to which detectives are engaged in doing things with information (Willmer 1970; Hobbs 1988; Manning 1988). Likewise, major crime inquiries are in essence forms of information work (Innes 2003a). Detectives are engaged in trying to identify information, interpret its meaning and assemble it into a form that will enable them to establish whether a crime has occurred, if so how, and who is responsible for its commission. In so doing they are actively involved in converting this information into several key modes: knowledge – information that has had its validity and reliability established and can thus be attributed a factual status; intelligence – information of varying provenance that can be used internally by the police organization to plot future actions and lines of inquiry; and evidence – information that has been assembled into a format suitable for use in the legal process with its particular dictates and conventions (Maguire 2003).

There are a number of key sources of the different types of information that investigators work with. These will be discussed in more detail presently, but can be summarized as follows:

- Physical materials from the scene of the crime and other locations which are subject to various forensic analyses.
- Verbal accounts from witnesses and possibly suspects concerning their perceptions as to what is alleged to have happened.
- Intelligence held in police databases or by other agencies on possible suspects for the crime.

These different types of information involve different problems and issues for officers in terms of identifying them, and assessing levels of validity and reliability. The availability of information also serves to structure the process of investigation. In most major crime inquiries the process is structured by a fairly rapid shift from a low information to a high information state (Feist and Newiss 2001; Innes 2002a). At the commencement of an inquiry, the police's problem is that they often need to acquire information in order that they can start to assemble a plausible account of what has occurred. However, as they start to implement their routine procedures and as lines of inquiry are established to enable some basic information to be collected, this initial problematic is replaced by a second one, which is more akin to an information management issue (Innes 2003a). Thus, as the police's investigative activity starts to gain momentum, attention becomes more concerned with sorting information and identifying those leads that need to be developed through further lines of inquiry.

This shift from a low to high information state is an important dynamic in terms of understanding the workings of the investigative system's approach, but also how the processual aspects of the investigation order unfold. In the early stages of an inquiry, standard operating procedures can be implemented to start to generate an information flow. As more information starts to be acquired then it must be processed in order to ascertain whether it increases the team's stock of knowledge and whether it justifies launching a further line of inquiry to follow it up. Consequently, as a police inquiry starts to alter from a low to high information state, so the focus of the investigative practices being performed by officers should shift to become more suspect focused.

Artefacts of investigative method

Reflecting these issues outlined above, investigations are best conceptualized as a constructive enterprise (McConville *et al.* 1991). The account that police produce of the crime is an artefact of the methods they employ to inquire into it. The police do not simply uncover the facts of the case; rather, they constitute them through the deployment of certain investigative methods and techniques. Thus the police account of an incident is not something that is discovered but something that is actively manufactured, as a result of the lines of inquiry that are established, and how information is interpreted and made sense of.

Understanding that the details of an incident are artefacts of police methods is especially pertinent to considering the issue of how and why investigations sometimes get it wrong. Significant attention has focused on a number of historic and more recent miscarriages of justice relating to major crime inquiries (see Chapter 25, this volume). The concern here has been with a problem of 'false positives' where, for a variety of reasons, police have identified and prosecuted someone as a prime suspect, securing a conviction, only for key aspects of their evidence to be undermined at a later date. Recent examples are the cases of Sally Clarke and Trupti Patel, who were convicted of killing their babies, only for key expert evidence that the police had relied upon to be discredited at a later date. Such instances have caused much public consternation about the conduct of investigations and in some cases have led to major reforms of investigative practice. There is, though, a second type of problem in major crime investigations that has received less attention, which is concerned with 'false negatives'. A false negative can be said to have occurred when the police fail to identify an incident as having a criminal cause, when it did in fact have this.

The false negative problem is relevant to the conduct of major crime inquiries due to the fact that the presence of criminal agency can be difficult to detect. For example, the serial murders committed by Dr Harold Shipman are an instance where people voiced their suspicions about aspects of his activities, but for a long time these concerns were dismissed. Over 40 years ago now, Havard (1960) noted particular difficulties in detecting homicides among the very young and very old, and voiced a concern that there was a possibility of a significant amount of 'secret homicide' remaining undetected among these segments of the population. What these recent cases demonstrate is that, despite advances in scientific techniques and knowledge, such issues remain, and that the capacity to establish accurately the cause of death in suspicious circumstances is constrained. It is also worth noting that cases such as these often present particular challenges for police investigators. Suspicions in these types of cases often only arise due to statistical irregularities being detected in the work of individual healthcare professionals or others, by which time the body of the deceased, an important source of evidential material for police, has been buried or cremated.

The methods that police use in the earliest stages of their investigation are then highly consequential. Research on homicide has long recognized the presence of 'victim-precipitation' (Wolfgang 1958) and that fatal exchanges often involve a complex set of actions and reactions, where who ends up as a victim and who a perpetrator is opaque (Luckenbill 1977; Brookman 2005). Under such conditions it is the responsibility of the police, informed by opinions provided to them by a variety of experts, to produce a degree of clarity and certainty in terms of identifying what happened, in what sequence and why. As this implies, in practice major investigations are often somewhat laborious undertakings, marked by painstaking attention to detail. We can now return to the conceptual framework outlined at the start of this chapter to understand how detectives perform this work.

Identifying and acquiring

As the first of the three key interconnected movements that collectively make up the investigation order, identifying and acquiring, is concerned with locating and securing access to those things that are likely to be relevant in establishing who did what to whom and why. In the course of an investigation police will seek to acquire and identify a number of different objects, including the following:

- Perceptual information from witnesses (and possibly victims) that describes what they saw or heard.
- Physical materials that, when subject to appropriate kinds of test, may reveal something about the incident and how it happened.
- Intelligence data from police or other agency databases that might in some way be of use to the investigation.
- Possible suspects who are individuals that can reasonably be connected to the crime.

It has long been an orthodoxy of police thinking and methodology in respect of homicide that a quick and effective response to the scene of a possible crime is imperative in terms of being able to identify and acquire correctly those materials necessary for conducting a successful investigation (ACPO 1998). In UK police parlance this has become known as 'the golden hour' principle. The logic of this is that a slow or lethargic police response increases the potential for large quantities of contact trace materials at the scene of a crime to be either deliberately or unwittingly damaged. Likewise, as time passes, so the probability that any witnesses will lose detail and clarity in terms of what they can remember increases, and the greater potential there is for any offender to 'cover his or her tracks'.

This need for speed in response has been tempered by an accompanying recognition of a need for control, in order that any materials at a scene can be preserved. For at the same time as forensic technologies have improved in their capacity to identify and recover contact trace materials, they have also been responsible for revealing just how fragile such material traces can be and how carefully they need to be handled (see Chapter 14, this volume). As a consequence, there are now standard operating guidelines applying for all officers who are first on the scene of a potentially suspicious fatality. They are supposed to administer first aid if required, secure any possible suspects if there are any, but most importantly secure the scene and preserve it intact (Geberth 1995). From this point on, there is also clearly formulated guidance for all other officers about who can and cannot access the scene (ACPO 1998). However, in the chaos and confusion that often surrounds responding to sudden deaths there is evidence to suggest that, to varying degrees, these guidelines are frequently breached (Macpherson 1999; Innes, 2003a).

Investigative systems

One crucial factor determining how quickly material that might be relevant to the police's inquiries is identified are the resources available to an investigation. The majority of volume crime investigations will be handled by either an individual officer or, at most, by a small team of specialist officers. In contrast, in the UK, major crime investigations frequently involve large teams of investigators. The large number of investigators means that lines of inquiry are not just sequenced in a series, but run in parallel also. Indeed it is not unusual, at the peak of activity on a major crime investigation, to have upwards of ten distinct lines of inquiry running simultaneously (Innes 2003a). A second area of difference relates to how it is increasingly the case that, for the vast majority of volume crime incidents, unless a solution is fairly apparent at an early stage, then it will receive only the most cursory form of response by the police. In contrast, major crime inquiries can still be actively under investigation months and sometimes years after the original offence was committed.

Given that significant resource investment is often made to try to solve many major crimes, it is helpful to understand the organization of the roles and personnel involved in responding to a suspicious death as a form of system. The work of a murder squad is based upon a division of labour between several key roles. This division of labour and the separating out of distinct roles within a team approach were formally established as part of the police service's response to the failings identified in the Yorkshire Ripper investigation (Byford 1981). The key roles are as follows:

- *Senior investigating officer (SIO)*: responsible for leading an investigation, for setting the strategic direction to be followed by the team and for taking key decisions. When first introduced the role of SIO was envisaged as being responsible on a day-to-day basis for the conduct of an inquiry under his or her command. But, increasingly, a distinction is being established in practice between the SIO, who remains in overall charge of an inquiry and engages in strategic decision-making, and the role of the investigating officer, who is less senior and responsible for day-to-day matters.

- *Major incident room:* the co-ordinating hub for the investigative activity. Its activities are divided between 'investigation management' and 'information management' (Innes 2003a). The former concerns co-ordinating the various coterminous lines of inquiry, and checking the progress of individual actions and all other key tactical management functions. The information management functions relate to processing and analysing the incoming data generated by the various lines of inquiry, establishing further lines of inquiry on the basis of the emerging analysis and defining the implications that this information has in terms of understanding the crime.

- *The outside inquiry team:* responsible for the conduct of the investigative actions and lines of inquiry. These are the officers 'on the ground' who will interview witnesses, inquire into the background of suspects and so forth.

- *Specialist investigators:* for a long time now, detectives have been used to involving specialists in their work, particularly in respect of dealing with physical contact trace materials. With the advances in the forensic sciences over recent years, most notably with respect to the capture, processing and interpretation of DNA, the roles of forensic investigators have become increasingly integral to the conduct of major investigations (Williams *et al.* 2004).

- *Media liaison:* as is the case with the specialist investigators, media liaison has come to play an increasingly central role in major crime inquiries. Such incidents frequently generate local media and, often, national media interest. Having a professional approach to this aspect is important so that it does not interfere with the conduct of the basic lines of inquiry, but also in order to try to reassure the public about what is being done to apprehend the perpetrator of a violent crime.

Depending upon the particular circumstances of the incident in question, it is standard practice to have anything from ten to 50 officers working on a single major crime inquiry and an explicit formula is provided in the ACPO murder manual (1998) for calculating the minimum number of officers to be assigned to different types of case. The number of officers supposed to be assigned is a function of the status of the victim, the circumstances of his or her assault and the degree of publicity it is thought the case will attract.

The co-dependencies that exist between these different roles mean that, in effect, the murder squad functions as a kind of 'soft' system. Different units of the investigative team are assigned specialist functions, which are connected to and interdependent with all the other functions. Thus actions in one part of the system shape and influence what happens in the other parts.

Identifying and acquiring suspects

In any police investigation, the moment where a suspect is identified can represent an important shift in the nature and focus of inquiries. Generally, at these points activities shift from trying to understand how the crime occurred to a more explicit focus upon the individual(s) under suspicion and testing what data are available to substantiate or refute any suspicions about their involvement. For reasons discussed previously, in a significant proportion of major crime inquiries the identity of a prime suspect is fairly apparent and comparatively easily established. Where suspects are not readily forthcoming, police follow a number of procedures to establish possible suspects for the crime. For these whodunit cases, a 'hierarchy of suspicion' is evident in how police consider potential candidates for being viewed as possible suspects. In the immediate aftermath of a fatal interaction, police attention often focuses upon the family and close friends of the deceased. Because the aetiology of homicide demonstrates that most victims will know the person who fatally assaults them (Polk 1994), in the early stages of an inquiry, particularly when it is in a low information state, investigators will be looking carefully at those close to the deceased in an effort to divine whether there are any indicators of suspicion (Brookman 2005). This will include trying to establish which individuals had the means, motive and opportunity to commit the crime. Equally important, though, in the police's eyes is whether any of those near to the victim have a previous criminal history.

It is a regular occurrence on major crime inquiries for a large number of individuals to be considered as potential suspects, only to be eliminated. As an inquiry gathers momentum and when no potential suspects are identified from the family and friends, the police instigate a 'bureaucratic mode of suspicion' (Matza 1969). Through this mode they will look at the characteristics of the crime and match them to known local active offenders in an area as a way of identifying another subsection of the general population who can be considered as suspects. For example, in a case reported in Innes (2003a) concerning the killing of an elderly couple where the assailant gained entry to their property through a downstairs window, the police instigated intelligence-led research into the whereabouts of known burglars in the area. Similarly, during the investigation into the murder of a young girl, the SIO on the case instructed his officers to look at the movements of known sex offenders across the local area.

If indicators of suspicion do not suggest any likely suspects or it is the case that all possible suspects have been eliminated from among the family and friends of the deceased person, and from among the known population of local offenders, then the police will more genuinely open up the scope of their inquiries to consider anyone as a possible suspect. In the first instance, though, their suspicions are directed towards particular individuals and groups of individuals who, it is considered, are more likely to be in possession of the means, motive and opportunity to commit a fatal assault.

Interpreting and understanding

As the police start to acquire information from a number of different sources on an investigation, then, as part of the investigation order, they also start to engage in a sense-making process. Crucial to this sense-making are a number of narratives about how and why different types of homicides tend to occur. However, in addition to their representational functions, in the context of major crime investigations, these case narratives facilitate a particular form of reasoning by detectives.

People kill and are killed in a variety of circumstances and ways, but what is remarkable about studying fatal violence is just how stable the motivational underpinnings remain. For, although there have been significant recent declines in homicide rates in some countries such as the USA, proportionately the motivational patterns appear relatively stable. In the majority of Western countries most people who kill will invoke their fatal violence upon their partner, some other family member or acquaintance. That such patterns exist tends to reflect that homicide is a 'hot' or 'expressive crime' taking place in emotionally charged circumstances, rather than being a product of 'cool' calculating logic (Katz 1988; Miethe and Regoeczi 2004) – although, of course, this is not to say that 'instrumental' homicides do not occur, because they do and must be investigated by the police.

Ultimately, then, the motivations and reasons why people perform homicidal acts are fairly limited. This is implicitly reflected in studies of this crime type, where it is commonplace to see a typology of different types constructed. For example, Ken Polk (1994), in his study of fatal violence committed by males, identifies four key master-types of homicide:

1 *Homicide in the context of sexual intimacy*: relates to those cases where the perpetrator kills his or her current or former partner for some reason. Most often this will be a form of jealousy or sense of proprietariness.

2 *Confrontational homicide*: takes place in public situations and is part of a fairly spontaneous argument, often, but not exclusively, between young men whose honour has been slighted in some fashion.

3 *Homicide in the course of other crime*: the death results from engaging in some other form of criminal activity. This might include robbery, burglary or sexual assault.

4 *Homicide as a form of conflict resolution*: relates to a scenario where a conflict has been escalating over an extended period of time, between people well known to each other. Violence is invoked by one or other of the parties as a method of social control.

During the course of my own research on police murder investigations, it was noted that police officers routinely talked in terms of seven key types of homicide (Innes 2003b). The precise contours of the different types were never explicitly articulated, but the fact that this was so is illustrative of the extent to which the types were assumed to be part of the working knowledge of competent investigators. Whereas the typologies constructed by researchers tend to be organized around some aspect of the structure or process of a fatal interaction, the classes utilized by police tend to be more pragmatically oriented, implicitly encoding what organizational experience has taught are likely to be key problems when responding to different scenarios of fatal violence. That they invoked such forms of classification was part of how detectives organized their understandings of what issues were likely to be involved when responding to such incidents. The officers studied were found to differentiate between:

- domestic homicides;
- confrontational homicides;
- child murders;
- criminal cause homicides;
- sexual murders;
- stranger murders; and
- serial murders.

Encoded to these distinct classes of homicide was an implicit understanding of what the core features of such crimes tended to be and the investigative problems that are routinely encountered in responding to them. For example, in domestic homicides, there was an understanding that the fatal violence would need to be set against a backdrop of the relationship between victim and perpetrator. As such, not only did detectives differentiate between types of homicide, but in so doing, they also maintained an awareness of ideal-type narratives for each of these types. That is, as far as detectives are concerned, most homicides follow fairly familiar sequences in terms of how they unfold. So domestic homicides will have a particular set of motives and will be enacted to an ordered series of moves and countermoves by the protagonists. Likewise, confrontational homicides tend to follow a fairly predictable sequence of events and so forth. There are, of course, permutations and situational inflections in these seven criminal homicide master-types, but the array of these, in terms of what the law and juridical interests are concerned with, is finite.

The definition of narrative as a socially organized and structured story is well established (Maines 2001). A narrative has discernible phases and themes, and often communicates a notion of morality in its telling. In the context of murder inquiries, case narratives have both a prospective and retrospective function. The retrospective function is concerned with assembling an *ex post facto* account of the case in order that others may be persuaded and convinced that the police now know whether a case should be defined as criminal homicide and, if so, who caused the death of another. This retrospective accounting quality will be addressed in the following section on ordering and representing. For now, though, this chapter focuses on the prospective functions of case narratives.

When conducting inquiries, police detectives draw upon these case narratives to assist them in organizing their present and future actions. Given a particular set of circumstances these narratives function as a stock of 'recipe knowledge' providing a sense of how to go on with an investigation and what are the issues that are most likely to be encountered when investigating a particular type of crime. In effect, they inform decisions about what lines of inquiry to pursue and when. By assigning an incident to one of several different master narratives at an early stage of an investigation, the narrative structure provides investigators with a sense of what are likely to be the key points at issue, where evidence might be located and the sorts of problems that might be encountered by investigators. In effect, then, these narratives provided the basis of a mode of reasoning that was predictive: informing decisions about what future directions the inquiry should take in terms of the lines of inquiry to be undertaken and leads pursued.

The significance of narrative reasoning is that it assists detectives to make sense of what is often conflicting, ambiguous and contingent information. It is commonplace in major inquiries to produce large volumes of information related to the incident, and what narrative reasoning endows is a capacity to establish how relevant a particular item is likely to be. Particularly because information that is forthcoming from lines of inquiry does not always point in the same direction, it has to be interpreted and validated in the light of what else is known.

Narrative reasoning and the assembling of a case narrative in the conduct of major crime inquiries are closely intertwined with the construction of abductive inferences. Many accounts of police investigative work have sought to explain how information is made sense of by reference to either inductive or deductive modes of inference (Kind 1987). In so doing, they are trying to unpack the cognitive processes involved in terms of how detectives make sense of the information that is generated by their lines of inquiry.

There is a tension, however, between these formal concepts of inference drawing and the more messy, contingent processes that are empirically described by detectives themselves. For example, my earlier work suggests that detective work is a combination of art and science and it is common to hear detectives make reference to intuition, hunch and 'getting lucky' when they try to describe how they do what they do. The problem with suggesting that detective reasoning is based upon either inductive or deductive inferences is that it neglects the ambiguous, uncertain and contingent nature of the data that detectives are working with. For much of the investigative process there may be a few key facts about the case that are known to have happened, and a lot more information that, from the point of view of detectives, may or may not be true, but cannot be verified as reliable or unreliable until such time as other forms of information become available.

Reflecting the importance of uncertainty, contingency and ambiguity in the conduct of major crime, based upon my observational work, I would suggest that much of the time murder squad detectives are engaged in drawing abductive inferences. Originally coined by the philosopher Charles Sanders

Peirce (1955), the concept of abduction has come to refer to a process of reasoning to the best explanation (Josephson and Josephson 1996). Particularly in the earlier phases of an investigation, where there is still much to be known and what is currently known is contingent upon facts still to be established, detectives use abductive inferences to synthesize the distribution of evidence and thereafter to project the most likely explanation for this distribution. In effect, they are saying 'what is the best, most plausible reason, given what is known at the current time, to explain how these circumstances came to be?' It is here that narrative reasoning and abductive inference connect, for it is the ordered nature of narrative that provides the 'abducer' with a sense of what is to be explained.

That detectives draw upon narrative structures in making sense of the information generated through their lines of inquiry also provides potential insight into how and why some inquiries go wrong. That is, officers become subject to a form of confirmation bias, whereby they interpret new information in a way that supports the narrative that they are in the process of constructing, even though this material could quite feasibly be placed under another description and thus interpreted differently.

Ordering and representing

Having considered how narratives assist detectives in interpreting and understanding the information generated by their lines of inquiry, I will now turn to the issue of how these same narrative structures contribute to the output of an investigation. As identified above, the power of the concept of narrative is in illuminating the organized ways in which certain stories are presented, and this captures how the narrative form is involved in the ordering and representing work that detectives engage in as part of their investigations.

In assembling their accounts of how and why particular crimes happened, detectives are effectively working to an implicit template. They are aware of the fact that the legal frame establishes certain points to prove when constructing a prosecution case, and that there are certain features and characteristics that tend to make a story about a crime plausible and believable. Case narratives assist officers in the task of assembling the knowledge and evidence that they have generated into a form coherent with the dictates and conventions of the criminal law and its systemic processes. Fitting the details of a particular incident to an extant narrative structure is a way of organizing a murder inquiry's knowledge in a way that is likely to work as the case moves into the adversarial world of the law courts. In this sense the narrative performs both a technical function, in that it assists in assembling knowledge into a format that will meet with the procedural and ultimately epistemological rules of law, and a social function, in that police are aware that, as modes of communication, these narratives are likely to be important in terms of persuading a jury of the strength of a case. If a jury is to believe allegations against a suspect 'beyond reasonable doubt', then it is important that they understand the story of the crime. A narrative structure employed by the police provides a sense of order and coherency to the account that is being proposed. Moreover, part of the narrative function is to try to anticipate how aspects of the police case may be contested by suspects and their legal representatives, and to pre-empt any such attempts to undermine the overall credibility of the account.

Thus, although individual case narratives will necessarily reflect the situational contingencies pertaining to a particular incident, in terms of how police investigators bring together the various pieces of information that they generate, they are all based upon three key components:

1 *The pre-history*: concerns relevant events and information that take place outside the immediate lead-up to the fatal interaction, but that nevertheless have some bearing upon the course of events that are the principal focus of police attention.

2 *The fatal interaction order*: the main and most obvious focus of any police investigation. Borrowing from Goffman (1983), it is possible to suggest that police are involved in plotting in 'high resolution' micro-level detail the sequence of actions and reactions involved in the conduct of the fatal interaction itself.

3 *The post-event actions*: this element of the narrative focuses upon what was done after the fatal event that is relevant to understanding the incident. Included here are the actions performed by actors connected to the incident itself (for example, did the suspect try to dispose of his or her clothes or talk to anyone?), but also the roles assumed by police and other emergency agencies in responding to the event. So included in this element of the narrative is a more reflexive concern with the conduct of the investigation.

These legally oriented narratives also inform a more internally directed form of organizational story-telling that takes place within the investigative team, and between the members of the murder squad and other facets of the police organization. Suffused with the moral values and norms of police culture, this dimension of ordering and representing not only captures the basic elements of the case, but also evaluates whether it was a good investigation or not, and how individuals performed. It is well established that police culture is heavily dependent upon the stories that cops tell themselves about themselves (Shearing and Ericson 1991; Innes 2002b) and this internally directed form of organizational communication feeds into the sorts of narrative reasoning identified in the previous section on interpreting and understanding. Additionally, though, the police are also involved in externally representing the findings of a major crime investigation via mass-media outlets.

Mediated narratives

An important facet of the narratives that detectives fashion in major crime inquiries is their external projection via mass-media channels. As Manning (2003), among others, notes, in an era of 'thin' public trust in social institutions, forms of police impression management have become increasingly widespread. On murder inquiries, relations with the media are now routinely managed by professional press officers, reflecting the high degree of public interest that such crimes can sometimes generate (Mawby 2002).

From time to time, journalists in the national and local media fixate upon a story of how one person caused the death of another. When such a situation transpires, the circumstances surrounding the fatal interaction and the progress of police inquiries into them are often the subject of intense scrutiny and comment. While the incident burns brightly on the media radar it often acquires the qualities of what elsewhere I have termed a 'signal crime', articulating public thinking about otherwise abstract issues of crime, deviance and security (Innes 2003b). And then at some point, the story ceases to be of such interest and it fades into the background, although some of these stories do become akin to a collective memory shared by the members of a community, framing their attitudes to crime and punishment more generally.

The mediated narratives that are constructed of such cases only exceptionally capture the detailed, complex and intricate work performed by police investigators. Neither are the impacts of media attention upon these cases or public understandings of police investigative work straightforward. By way of illustration, let us consider two of the most high-profile investigations in the UK of recent years: the Soham murders of Holly Wells and Jessica Chapman by Ian Huntley; and the murder of the schoolgirl Amanda Dowler in Surrey by a person as yet unknown. Both these cases received extensive and intense media interest. The interesting thing about comparing them is that in the former case, the assailant was identified and convicted, and yet the investigation was widely understood to have been poor and resulted in two major inquiries into its conduct (one of which was the Bichard Report 2004 that is having fairly significant impacts across many public services in relation to information management processes and structures). In contrast to this, the murder investigation by Surrey Police into the death of Amanda Dowler has, as yet, failed to produce a publicly identifiable suspect. Despite this, it is generally perceived by police and journalists as a well run and good investigation and, consequently, has for the most part avoided public criticism.

Concatenated decision-making

The conceptual framework outlined in the previous sections provides some understanding of how detectives engaged in an investigative process make sense of the information generated through their lines of inquiry to produce a narrative account of the crime setting out who did what to whom and why. Significantly, however, and as alluded to in the discussion of 'interpreting and understanding', this sense making is an ongoing accomplishment that is tied to the conduct of investigative actions. Thus the evolving account that police are building up over the course of an investigation informs the selection and performance of investigative actions. This connection between the knowledge available to an investigative team and the conduct of their investigative actions directs us towards a consideration of decision-making. For it is the concept of decision-making that keys us in to the ways that detectives select between possible alternative lines of action according to the information they have available to them at any given point. Thus, broadly speaking, in the early stages of an investigation, investigative decision-making is situated in a low information setting where consequential decisions for the subsequent trajectory of the investigation have to be taken informed by few reliable data. It is in part for this reason that, at the commencement of an inquiry, investigators are comparatively reliant upon standard operating practices and procedures. But then as an investigation develops the nature of the decision-making problem that must be addressed alters. Rather than a lack of incident-relevant information, in a more mature investigation difficulties are often the result of too much information, and the issue is identifying the valid, reliable and relevant material.

The systemic organization of major crime inquiries places the SIO in a position where he or she has responsibility for taking strategic decisions in respect of the overall direction of an investigation. When SIOs are operating in the full glare of the media spotlight, as they sometimes are on major crime responses, much attention often focuses upon the decisions taken by the SIO in terms of whether the trajectory of the investigation seems to be correct and warranted. Similarly, in a number of the key reviews into problematic major crime inquiries over the years, including the Byford Report (1981), the Macpherson Report (1999) and the Bichard Report (2004), SIO decision-making has featured as a key concern, albeit one that has not been subject to a systematic treatment.

In terms of understanding the dynamics and mechanics of a major crime inquiry, though it is important to be cognizant of the extent to which decisions taken by SIOs are intertwined with and dependent upon decisions taken by other actors within the investigative system. To understand how and why this is, a concept of 'concatenated decision-making' can be introduced to try to articulate the levels of complexity that are present.

As Stelfox and Pease (2004) note, the study of how detectives process and react to information when investigating crimes has not been a major feature of research. Relatedly, neither has the conduct of their decision-making. Making and taking decisions are a crucial part of investigative work and occur at all levels and phases of major crime inquiries. Decisions have to be made about whether an incident should be treated as a crime; what physical materials to collect at a scene; whether a witness account should be believed; if and when to arrest possible suspects; among many others. An important quality of these decisions in major crime investigations is that they are 'concatenated'. By this I mean that a decision taken at one point of an investigation effectively structures and frames the possibilities for other subsequent decisions.[1] For example, a decision taken at an early stage of an inquiry to treat an incident as being a likely domestic homicide rather than, say, an assault by a stranger, will shape subsequent decisions about where to look for possible validating evidence and how the deceased's partner is to be viewed.

One way to think about decision-making in major crime investigation is to focus on the content of the decisions that are made. On this basis, five key decision types are found in the conduct of major crime investigations:

1 *Policy decisions*: taken by the SIO and his or her management team, set the broad parameters for an investigation.

2 *Knowledge decisions*: are concerned with how particular units of information should be interpreted and treated by the inquiry team. That is, should they be understood as useful and contributing to the narrative of the case that is being developed, or should they be discarded as misinformation or disinformation?

3 *Action decisions*: relate to what should be done, when and by whom. Action decisions look at the performance of key tasks and their order and timing.

4 *Logistic decisions*: concern the support infrastructure for an investigation. How many staff members should be available to the different components of the investigative system and for how long?

5 *Legal decisions*: are essentially to do with how the investigation is related to the broader legal context in which it is located.

While focusing upon the substantive content of the decisions taken is undoubtedly helpful, I want to explore a rather different approach, related more directly to the notion of concatenation set out previously.

In thinking about the nature of concatenated decision-making, it is helpful to think along two key decision dimensions: the first hierarchical, the second sequential. Addressing the issue of the hierarchy, of decision-making first, a basic distinction can be made between 'strategic' and 'tactical' decisions. Strategic decisions are responsible for setting the broad contours and direction of an investigation and will usually be made by the SIO or his or her deputy. These may concern logistical issues (such as the phasing in and out of investigative resources) or they may be more directly concerned with the conduct of the investigative work by, for example, specifying the profile of individuals to be treated as potential suspects. Tactical decisions are more local in terms of their effects and concern how strategic directions are to be carried out.

A second, more sequentially based, distinction can also be used in terms of separating 'upstream decisions' and 'downstream decisions'. Upstream decisions can be thought of as the preceding decisions that have functioned to produce a particular decision-making context at a particular point in time. These are the things that have been done to place an individual in a particular set of circumstances and to provide him or her with a particular decision to make in the here and now. In contrast, downstream decisions are the consequent decisions that will be made available at some point in the future of an investigation by what is done at the present time. It is important to stress that notions of upstream and downstream decisions are always relative attributes in that they position a particular decision in relation to all the others that impact upon the conduct of an inquiry. Thus it helps us conceive of how any one decision in a homicide investigation is framed by a concatenated series of previous decisions and, in turn, how the particular decision will frame subsequent ones.

In analysing the conduct of any investigation, upstream decisions will frame the conduct of those that are downstream from them. And while the strategic decisions will set the parameters for any tactical decisions that have to be taken, it is also the case in a well run investigation that tactical upstream decisions should inform and influence those strategic decisions that are downstream. The contents of these various decision modes will focus upon policy, knowledge, action, logistical and legal issues, respectively. By bringing these contents and modes together, we can start to appreciate the complex nature of decision-making in the conduct of major crime inquiries.

Problematic major investigations

Throughout this chapter I have been seeking to illuminate some key facets of how murder inquiries are conducted. The focus has been upon how a plethora of data that are routinely generated by the lines of inquiry performed by detectives is made sense of and how this impacts upon the decisions they take. On the basis of a clear-up rate that is routinely around the 90 per cent level, we must presume that the policies, processes and practices that are employed in homicide investigations are reasonably effective – although, of course, it does not follow that they are efficiently run.[2] When major police inquiries do get it wrong, a considerable amount of public concern tends to result. In the course of the preceding discussion I have several times alluded to how and why major investigations do not function as they should. This is now an appropriate point at which to bring these points together in a coherent way.

In thinking about why investigations sometimes go wrong or struggle, the first thing to state is that some cases are simply much harder to solve than others. Although this is implied in the distinction between self-solvers and whodunits, it is nevertheless important that this be rendered explicit. Some investigations experience problems because the circumstances in which a death occurred mean that the incident is fairly intractable. In other cases, however, the police do make mistakes and errors, and the attribution of failure can be more directly levelled at them (Nicol *et al.* 2004).

In the section on 'identifying and acquiring', the system-based organization of major inquiries was noted, together with the importance of the 'golden hour' principle. Taken together, these are frequently sources of problems in major investigations in that, if the right amount of resources is not available at the right time in a major investigation, this can result in the inquiry overall running in a less than optimum fashion. The issue is that, in organizational systems, an error in one component can induce problems in other components. So, in effect, because of how the investigative system is designed, any problem can be compounded as its effects move through the system (Nicol *et al.* 2004). The issue here is that major crime inquiries are resource intensive and thus securing sufficient resources to conduct the requisite lines of inquiry in a timely manner can sometimes be difficult. If there is a cluster of cases or one long-running high-profile case, these can impact upon the organization's capacity to deliver other policing services. The problem of securing appropriate resources is potentially becoming more pronounced as elements of the investigative system become more technically advanced and specialist skills are increasingly required.

This is important in that it directs us to considering the nature of the connections between major investigations and other aspects of police 'business'. It is sometimes tempting to separate off the police's investigative work and to see it as being markedly different from other aspects of policing. But increasingly the interconnections between major crime and other policing activities and concerns are being recognized. Due to limitations on space, this section will remark on just two that are currently particularly important: the impact upon community intelligence provision and issues of reassurance.

Given that, as with volume crime, the success of major crime investigations is highly dependent upon the quantity and quality of publicly provided information, if police–community relations in an area are poor, then the flow of information and intelligence is likely to be constrained. In turn, there is a widespread perception within the police that the capacity to solve major crimes is a key influence in shaping levels of public reassurance, and community trust and confidence in the institution more broadly. Such issues were most obviously foregrounded in the aftermath of the Stephen Lawrence investigation.

One outcome resulting from the Lawrence case was increased attention being paid to what has become known as community impact assessment (CIA). Although as yet relatively unsophisticated and underdeveloped, the logic of a CIA is to try to calibrate the impact a major crime is having upon a local community and to understand if it is generative of any wider fears and tensions among particular communities. It seems likely that, in the coming years, a more coherent methodology will be required for the conduct of CIA, as will standardization of procedures and practices for the purposes of 'community impact management'.

If the assessment and management of community impacts are about dealing with what might be termed the 'tertiary victims' of major crimes (in the form of community members), and the direct victim is the 'primary victim', then important innovations have also occurred recently in police responses to 'secondary victims'. By 'secondary victims' is meant the family and friends of the deceased person who are harmed by the death that has occurred. As a result of a number of cases, including the Stephen Lawrence murder, there has been a growing recognition that the police's treatment of the families of homicide victims, in particular, was lacking in consistency and professionalism (cf. Rock 1998, 2004) and that, in the midst of a very difficult time, families needed more and better support. With this in mind, the role of the family liaison officer (FLO) has become a fairly standard part of managing major crime inquiries. Specialist officers who have undergone training are now placed with families to help them cope with the aftermath of the violent death of a loved one. While the primary function of these FLOs is to provide emotional and practical support, they can also make an important contribution to the progress of an investigation. Because they can become close to the victim's relatives, they are especially well placed to pick up any indicators of suspicion that may be helpful in progressing the main investigation. These are areas where the conduct of major investigations has been significantly reformed recently, and where reform is likely to continue in the near future.

Perhaps one of the most routinely encountered problems in major crime investigations has to do with information management and the attendant issue of information overload (Innes 2003a). In the process of setting up a major crime investigation, police rapidly start to acquire large amounts of information about a range of issues connected to the case in question. The issue then becomes how to process these data and to start to make sense of them – in effect moving from the 'identifying and acquiring' phase to the 'interpreting and understanding' phase. But often, if lines of inquiry are insufficiently precisely defined, then the volume of information being acquired overwhelms the capacity to sort and interpret it. For, as the model of concatenated decision-making suggests, lots of information coming in has a profound downstream effect on an investigation as it generates a large number of additional actions to check the validity and reliability of the information.

Conclusion

Investigating crime is fundamentally about the manufacture of certainty from uncertainty. Investigations are conducted where there either is or is likely to be contested or ambiguous knowledge about how a particular incident transpired. The police investigator is required to identify the causes of this act and to attribute responsibility for them. In this chapter the focus has been on how the conducting of major investigations can be understood as an ordered and structured sense-making process, and the ways this process connects with investigative decision-making. In addressing these issues the chapter has also touched on the organization of major inquiry teams and the functions of narrative as a mode of reasoning, and of representation.

The conduct of major investigations is notable for the level of detail and the 'high resolution' account that murder squad detectives seek to assemble into the pre-history and the actual performance of a deadly interaction. In addressing these issues, this chapter has sought to illuminate two under-remarked upon, yet central, facets of how investigations are conducted. How detectives make sense of the various streams of information they access when conducting an investigation, and the procedures they invoke to assemble a coherent explanatory narrative account of what they believe has taken place, are central to improving our understanding of the conduct of major investigations. Similarly, the ways that this sense-making work connects with the decisions that are taken, in deciding between possible paths of investigative activity is crucial to comprehending the dynamics of the investigative process as a whole. The concept of the investigation order attends to both these issues.

Selected further reading

Innes, M. (20030 *Investigating Murder: Detective Work and the Police Response to Criminal Homicide*. Oxford: Clarendon Press. This is the most in-depth and detailed study of major crime investigations yet conducted. It shows how the work of detectives responding to major crimes can be understood as concerned with the manufacture of knowledge.

Ericson, R. (1981) *Making Crime: A Study of Detective Work*. Toronto: University of Toronto Press. This book discusses the conduct of detective work in its more routine forms, attending particularly to its bureaucratic case-processing elements. It provides a useful counterpoint to the typically sensationalist treatments that police detectives are subject to in mass-media and true crime accounts.

Maguire, M. (2003) 'Criminal investigation and crime control', in T. Newburn (ed.) *Handbook of Policing:* Cullompton: Willan Publishing. This chapter provides a good overview of some of the key issues and themes relating to current research and practice in the area of crime control.

Notes

1 This approach is informed by the theoretical work of Beach (1997).
2 Indeed, the question of whether similar clear-up rates could be sustained under a different and possibly less intensive resourcing formula is one that is ripe for research.

References

Association of Chief Police Officers (1998) *Manual of Murder Investigation*. London: ACPO.

Beach, L. (1997) *The Psychology of Decision Making: People in Organizations*. Thousand Oaks, CA: Sage.

Bichard, M. (2004) *The Bichard Inquiry Report*. London: HMSO.

Brookman, F. (2005) *Understanding Homicide*. London: Sage.

Byford, L. (1981) 'The Yorkshire Ripper Case: Review of the Police Investigation of the Case' (unpublished).

Ericson, R. (1993) *Making Crime* (2nd edn). Toronto: University of Toronto Press.

Feist, A. and Newiss, G. (2001) *Watching the Detectives: Analysing Hard-to-solve Murder Investigations*. London: Home Office.

Geberth, V. (1995) *Practical Homicide Investigation*. New York, NY: CBC Press.

Goffman, E. (1983) 'The interaction order', *American Sociological Review*, 48: 1–17.

Greenwood, P., Chaiken, J. and Petersilia, J. (1977) *The Criminal Investigation Process*. Lexington, MA: D.C. Heath.

Havard, J. (1960) *The Detection of Secret Homicide*. Basingstoke: Macmillan.

Hobbs, D. (1988) *Doing the Business*. Oxford: Oxford University Press.

Innes, M. (2002a) 'Organizational communication and the symbolic construction of police murder investigations', *British Journal of Sociology*, 53: 67–87.

Innes, M. (2002b) 'The process structures of police homicide investigations', *British Journal of Criminology*, 42: 669–88.

Innes, M. (2003a) *Investigating Murder: Detective Work and the Police Response to Criminal Homicide*. Oxford: Clarendon Press.

Innes, M. (2003b) 'Signal crimes: media, murder investigations and constructing collective memories', in P. Mason (ed.) *Criminal Visions*. Cullompton: Willan Publishing.

Innes, M. (2004a) 'Signal crimes and signal disorders: notes on deviance as communicative action', *British Journal of Sociology*, 55: 335–55.

Innes, M. (2004b) 'Reinventing tradition? Reassurance, neighbourhood security and policing', *Criminal Justice*, 4: 151–71.

Josephson, J. and Josephson, S. (1996) *Abductive Inference: Computation, Philosophy, Technology*. Cambridge: Cambridge University Press.

Katz, J. (1988) *The Seductions of Crime: Moral and Sensual Attractions in Doing Evil*. New York, NY: Basic Books.

Kind, S. (1987) *The Scientific Investigation of Crime*. London: Forensic Science Service.

Luckenbill, D. (1977) 'Criminal homicide as a situated transaction', *Social Problems*, 25: 176–86.

Macpherson, W. (1999) *Report of an Inquiry into the Investigation of the Murder of Stephen Lawrence*. London: HMSO.

Maguire, M. (2000) 'Policing by risks and targets: some dimensions and implications of intelligence-led crime control', *Policing and Society*, 9: 315–36.

Maguire, M. (2003) 'Criminal investigation and crime control', in T. Newburn (ed.) *Handbook of Policing*. Cullompton: Willan Publishing.

Maines, D. (2001) *The Faultlines of Consciousness*. New York, NY: Aldine de Gruyter.

Manning, P. (1988) *The Narc's Game*. Cambridge, MA: MIT Press.

Manning, P. (2003) *Policing Contingencies*. Chicago, IL: University of Chicago Press.

Matza, D. (1969) *Becoming Deviant*. Englewood Cliffs, NJ: Prentice Hall.

Mawby, R. (2002) *Policing Images: Policing, Communication and Legitimacy*. Cullompton: Willan Publishing.

McConville, M., Sanders, A. and Leng, R. (1991) *The Case for the Prosecution: Police Suspects and the Construction of Criminality*. London: Routledge.

Miethe, T. and Regoeczi, W. (2004) *Rethinking Homicide: Exploring the Structure and Process Underlying Deadly Situations*. Cambridge: Cambridge University Press.

Nicol, C., Innes, M., Gee, D. and Feist, A. (2004) *Using Progress Reviews to Improve Investigative Performance*. London: Home Office.

Peirce, C.S. (1955) *Philosophical Writings of Peirce*. New York, NY: Dover Publications.

Polk, K. (1994) *When Men Kill*. Cambridge: Cambridge University Press.

Reiner, R. (1997) 'Media made criminality', in M. Maguire *et al.* (eds) *The Oxford Handbook of Criminology* (2nd edn). Oxford: Oxford University Press.

Rock, P. (1998) *After Homicide: Practical and Political Responses to Bereavement*. Oxford: Clarendon Press.

Rock, P. (2004) *Constructing Victims' Rights*. Oxford: Clarendon Press.

Scott, W. (1998) *Organizations: Rational, Natural and Open Systems*. London: Prentice Hall.

Shearing, C. and Ericson, R. (1991) 'Culture as figurative action', *British Journal of Sociology*, 42: 481–506.

Simon, D. (1991) *Homicide: A Year on the Killing Streets*. London: Coronet Books.

Stelfox, P. and Pease, K. (2004) 'Cognition and detection: reluctant bedfellows', in M. Smith and N. Tilley (eds) *Crime Science*. Cullompton: Willan Publishing.

Williams, R., Johnson, P. and Martin, P. (2004) *Genetic Information and Crime Investigation*. London: Wellcome Trust.

Willmer, M.A.P. (1970) *Crime and Information Theory*. Edinburgh: Edinburgh University Press.

Wolfgang, M. (1958) *Patterns in Criminal Homicide*. Philadelphia, PA: University of Pennsylvania Press.

Chapter 11

Private investigation

Les Johnston

Introduction

This chapter is in five parts. The first considers how the term 'private investigation' is to be defined. The second looks at the historical trajectory of private investigation in North America and Britain. Sections three and four, respectively, examine the structure and functions of the private investigative sector. Section five explores the issues of efficacy, ethics and regulation in respect of private investigation. The final section reflects back on issues raised previously in the chapter to consider the changing character of the public–private interface in security governance.

Matters of definition

The concepts of 'private investigation' and 'private investigator' are by no means easy to define. Gill and Hart (1997a) note that the Latin root of the term 'investigator' (*vestigium*) has both a literal meaning ('footprint') and a figurative one ('something lost or that has passed before'). An investigator is, therefore, 'someone who "tracks" or "traces out" something that is missing; something that has occurred, or something that was or is known by someone but remains hidden'; and a private investigator is someone who 'either runs or is employed by a business which provides investigative services for a fee' (Gill and Hart 1997a: 550, fn. 1).

However, as with many such definitions, qualification and refinement are immediately demanded. Prenzler (2001) notes that the term 'private investigator' has both a specific legal meaning (the character of which will vary between different jurisdictions) and a number of generic meanings (which may or may not correspond to the former). He notes that, in Australia, while licensing arrangements have drawn a distinction between 'private investigators', 'commercial agents' and 'process servers', the first term is used, generically, to incorporate the other two. A similar conflation of terms – 'professional investigator', 'private investigator', 'private detective' – is apparent in the UK (George and Button 2000). Here, definitional precision is undermined by the disparate occupational groups – forensic accountants, journalists, store detectives, solicitors and even psychics (reportedly used by both MI5 and the CIA) – engaging in investigative activity (Button 1998). George and Button's definition of 'professional investigators', their own preferred term, mirrors this complexity:

> Individuals (whether in house or contract) and firms (other than public enforcement bodies) who offer services related to the obtaining, selling or supplying of any information relating to the identity, conduct, movements, whereabouts, associations, transactions or character of any person, groups of persons or association, or of any other type of organization (2000: 88).

The definition of private investigation adopted in this chapter is broadly in accord with that provided by George and Button (2000), notwithstanding their recognition that any definition is relatively arbitrary. However, an important qualification should be added concerning the nature of the agents involved in the investigative process. In exploring the growth of 'insurance fraud policing', Ericson et al. (2000) note the expansion of formal bodies, such as special investigative units (SIUs), in the insurance industry (see also Johnston 1992). However, they also draw attention to the processes whereby 'the conduct of market conduct' is routinely regulated. Some of this regulation will be carried out by SIUs, but much of it is encapsulated in internal regimes of audit, inspection, surveillance, call monitoring, training and such like. Such practices, far from being the exclusive preserve of specialist investigative agents, are 'embedded' (Shearing and Stenning 1983) in the everyday work roles of organizational members.

The historical trajectory of private investigation

In Britain the rudiments of the private investigation industry lay in the thief-takers and bounty hunters that preceded and continued after the establishment of the new police in 1829. By far the biggest boost to commercial investigative activity came with the Matrimonial Causes Act 1857 which enabled detectives to develop a specialist role in the field of divorce. However, as Draper (1978) notes, these early detectives did not always confine themselves to the collection of evidential facts – some used paid co-respondents to fabricate 'hotel evidence' on behalf of their clients. During this period, the other main area of activity was hiring out detectives to infiltrate factories and workmen's clubs in order to collect evidence about potential strikes and labour disputes. In 1901, Garnier's Detective Agency was established, becoming one of the first to offer a wide range of investigative services.

The development of the private investigative sector in the USA was both more rapid and more pervasive. Allan Pinkerton, a Glaswegian, and previously the first detective in the Chicago Police, established a detective agency in 1850. The company offered the first systematic and comprehensive commercial detective service, combining files, special agents and criminological techniques (Bowden 1978). Among its first major clients were a number of railroad companies and the US Post Office. As well as being involved in infiltrating labour unions, Pinkerton's activities ranged from the detection and pursuit of outlaws (such as the James Gang and Butch Cassidy) to political espionage. Indeed, the American Civil War (1861–5) was a major factor in the company's development, Pinkerton operating behind Confederate lines during the hostilities.

That Pinkerton's company was called 'the Pinkerton National Detective Agency' (Churchill 2004) was no mere accident, one commentator suggesting that it 'provided America with something we have always boasted we didn't need and never had: a national police force' (O'Toole 1978: 28). Of particular significance here was the fact that, from its inception, the agency operated within the security framework of the state. Nowadays, evidence of this can be seen in the regular take-up by Pinkerton executives of senior public police positions, and in personnel and information exchange between the agency and other key public organizations, including the International Association of Chiefs of Police, the FBI and the US military (Churchill 2004). In recent years those links have become 'transnationalized', with major US companies like Pinkerton and Wackenhut having been absorbed by huge international corporations (Johnston 2000b, 2006).

How do these developments relate to our understanding of the historical trajectory of private policing, in general, and of private investigation, in particular? One influential account of the historical trajectory of private policing suggests that it has involved 'a glacial drift from a detection to a protection speciality' (Morn 1982: ix). Morn's point is that, during the course of the twentieth century, private security organizations abandoned their earlier criminal investigation/detection functions in order to specialize in the protection of property. Simultaneously, he suggests, state police forces concentrated more and more on the detection of crime, abandoning some of their patrol functions. Bayley and Shearing make a similar point, suggesting that a division of labour may now be observed 'where the public police increasingly specialise in investigations and counterforce operations while private police become decentralised, full-service providers of visible crime prevention' (2001: 19).

Undoubtedly, these accounts of the historical trajectory are accurate. However, certain caveats have to be made. One concerns my earlier point that the 'conduct of market conduct' is now embedded within the rules and practices of commercial organizations. This suggests that an important qualification needs to be made in respect of Morn's (1982) 'glacial drift' theory. For while it is true that the state police sector has usurped some of the investigative functions once carried out by the private police sector, that usurpation has been at the expense of *specialist* private investigators rather than of commercial agents *per se*. The embedding process confirms that many investigative functions remain located in the routine practices of the marketplace.

A second caveat relates to the mentality that shapes investigative practices. In meeting the needs of their clients, private investigators are invariably concerned with the pursuit of instrumental ends. Unlike police detectives, who collect evidence for constructing cases within a system of public justice, private investigators aim only to minimize the economic, social or personal losses of their clients. Instrumentalism is driven by a proactive, risk-based mentality, the object of which is to anticipate, recognize and appraise risks and, having done so, to initiate actions that will help to minimize their impact on clients. Previous analysis of the relationship between public and private police (e.g. Cunningham and Taylor 1985) has tended to make a clear demarcation between their respective mentalities. However, commentaries on the salience of the risk mentality within neoliberal governance (Beck 1992; O'Malley 1992; Johnston and Shearing 2003) note its diffusion across a wide range of organizations, including public sector ones. This begs two questions. First, is there potential for the private investigative sector to expand the scope of its work? Secondly, how far is the mentality of risk likely to penetrate police investigative practice? We consider these issues in the concluding section of the chapter.

A final caveat concerns the increasingly significant role played by the private investigative sector in the arena of transnational security governance, a development that may be linked to what Manning (2000) has termed 'the commodification of information'. Academic research in this area is minimal – such studies of private investigation as there are invariably having a national or local focus. Again, this issue is considered in the concluding section.

The structure of the private investigation industry

> The Investigative industry [in Britain] is made up of many small firms, lone operatives, partnerships, companies and some larger organisations, some of which incorporate other security and forensic related services throughout the country and internationally (www.psiact.org.uk/posi. htm (retrieved 23 August 2005).

This chapter focuses primarily on the work of businesses contracted to provide investigative services to clients.[1] Calculating the size and structure of the investigative sector is difficult for a number of reasons. For one thing, many investigative personnel work on a casual or *ad hoc* basis. For another, while it is relatively easy to enter the industry, those lacking access to appropriate networks (see below) are likely to find it difficult to obtain much work. As a result, the sector experiences a high turnover of personnel.

Having said that, evidence on the broad features of the investigative sector is relatively consistent across jurisdictions. In 1985 the first Hallcrest Report (Cunningham and Taylor 1985) found that more than 50 per cent of investigative firms in the USA reported gross annual revenues of less than $100,000 and that the median number of full-time employees was three. The US Department of Labor estimated that, in 2002, around 48,000 people were employed in private investigative work. Of these, about a third were self-employed, including many who held secondary investigative jobs; almost a fifth worked in investigation and security services, including private detective agencies; and another fifth worked on an 'in-house' basis for the retail industry. The remainder worked mainly in state and local government, legal services firms, employment services, insurance companies, and in credit intermediation and related activities (US Department of Labor, Bureau of Labor Statistics 2005).

Private investigators in Australia, like those in America, have long been licensed by the state. Despite this, Prenzler (2001) points out that variations in licensing categories make precise calculation of the size of the investigative sector difficult. At the time of his research, Prenzler estimated that in three states – South Australia (3,681 agents), New South Wales (around 15,800 agents) and Queensland (1,520 agents) – private investigators held about one third of all security licences.

Interviews with 40 investigators in New South Wales and Queensland, the majority of whom were owners or directors of investigation firms, revealed that just over half classified their companies as small or medium, the maximum number of employees in any one company being 50. Half the respondents had had previous military, police or corrective experience, those with law enforcement experience being the largest single group.

In Britain, a 1992 report by the Institute of Professional Investigators (cited in George and Button 2000) estimated the total number of investigative agents to be around 15,000. Of these, 6,000 were employed as sole operators or in small partnership; 8,000 were individual investigators; and 1,000 were employed as in-house investigators. The same report suggested that the overall value of the sector stood at around £110 million, £90 million of which came from corporate business, £10 million from private individual business and £10 million from overseas business. George and Button (2000: 91), while accepting that it is difficult to assess the reliability of these figures given the lack of supportive evidence, concur that a figure of 15,000 investigators provides a realistic estimate and suggest an approximate sector size of around £225 million. Further to that, they note that the sector is characterized by hundreds, if not thousands, of small operators, with no evidence of clear market domination. The one exception to this is in respect of the corporate investigations market where a few companies (Argen, Carratu International, Control Risks, Kroll, Network Security Management and Pinkerton) dominate.

The only significant empirical study of the investigative sector in Britain was undertaken by Gill and Hart (1997a, 1997b, 1997c, 1999).[2] The first and most striking fact uncovered by this study was the limited longevity of companies. Over one third of the sample agencies were under five years old, a further quarter having operated only for between five and ten years. In total, almost two thirds of firms in the sample had been operating for ten years or less.

As for turnover, the authors found that slightly more than half the companies (50.5 per cent) earned £40,000 or less. Of those companies earning more than that figure, two thirds claimed an annual turnover of less than £100,000 and, overall, only 12.2 per cent of the companies sampled generated turnovers in the range £201,000–£1 million. Nearly 60 per cent of all businesses were sole traders, 23 per cent being partnerships and 16 per cent limited companies. Relating turnover to company size showed almost three quarters of the lower income group, compared with less than half the high earners, to be sole traders. By contrast, nearly a quarter of those with high turnovers were limited companies, compared with less than 7 per cent of the low income group. However, while most private investigation agencies are small businesses, owned and run by one or two people, the relationship between structure and turnover was found to be relatively complex. Some successful small businesses had built up considerable turnovers but were reluctant to become limited companies. One reason given for this was that the resulting obligation to publish annual reports might make them vulnerable to aggressive or underhand tactics by rivals. Consequently, some small traders had larger turnovers than some limited companies.

Gill and Hart (1997b) found that the recruitment of investigative staff would normally occur through personal contacts rather than through advertising. Initial contact might be initiated through a professional association. More often, however, it would be the product of informal networks built upon prior professional and personal contact. As is the case in other jurisdictions, they found that the majority of individual investigators were former police officers, though a significant minority had experience in military, customs and excise and in the commercial and financial sectors. Lower income agencies were likely to employ or to be run by former police officers, while higher earning ones tended to employ more business specialists.

Just over two thirds of the sample companies employed between one and three investigators, the remainder (29 per cent) employing four or more.[3] Having said that, Gill and Hart (1997b) found no one-to-one relationship between numbers employed and scope of work. One company cited in the study employed 22 full-time staff operating almost exclusively within a 50-mile radius on small inquiries. By contrast, another company employed nine specialist staff to carry out inquiries for blue-chip international corporations. Gauging overall numbers employed in the sector was, however, difficult. Companies frequently drafted in casual help for tasks such as surveillance. Often, this would be done on an informal basis, family members sometimes being recruited to deliver legal papers or to help trace addresses. In addition to that, administrative staff would often play a role in investigation as, for example, when searching databases and other online services.

The other crucial factor in investigation is the subcontracting of work by one company to another. This practice is widespread for a number of reasons. The original firm might lack sufficient resources or specialist expertise to do the work; or it might have no operatives in the location where the work needs to be carried out. On some occasions, firms may also contract out work when they need illegal or unethical activities to be undertaken, such as accessing the Police National Computer or other confidential sources (George and Button 2000). All private investigation work – but particularly that involving subcontracting – depends on informal networks. As well as other investigative companies, membership of networks may include solicitors, finance houses, corporate clients, insurance companies and building societies

(Gill and Hart 1997b). The situation in Britain is similar in many respects to that in Australia. There Prenzler (2001: 31) found that the industry was 'based largely on sub-contracting of "operative" work, usually to single operators'. This extensive use of subcontracting – particularly in respect of work undertaken for the insurance industry – was attributed in part to alleged disincentives for taking on employees, such as unfair dismissal legislation and payment of entitlement; and in part on the feeling that subcontracting offered flexibility to companies and performance incentives to operators.

Gill and Hart (1997b) suggest that four ideal types of investigative businesses may be identified. 'Home-based' firms have low annual turnovers and sole-trader status. They are often run by former police officers who draw upon spouses and partners for administrative support and who gain the bulk of their business from the local legal profession. This type of investigator rarely invests in professional training and has no plans for business expansion. Like 'home-based' firms, 'high-street' agencies are also locally based, the main difference being that the latter invest in office premises. 'High-street' agencies are either sole-traders or partnerships usually staffed by former CID officers and/or non-police generalists often with experience of debt collection or bailiff work. Normally they will employ part-time administrative staff and may call upon other local investigators when required to do so. Such agencies serve the local legal profession and will also provide claims investigation services. They may attend occasional seminars but financial constraints limit their commitment to training. 'Regional' agencies tend to be limited companies with regional or even national branch offices. Being larger organizations they employ more people, have significantly higher turnovers and are likely to operate with standardized charges. They may invest in training and some will have structured programmes for new recruits. 'Prestige' companies are usually London based and offer high-level fraud investigation and due diligence services to blue-chip businesses. They will often employ fewer personnel than 'high-street' agencies but their investigators will have an elite civilian, police or military background. Often they will subcontract practical work out to 'high-street' companies, using their expertise to manage cases and to prepare specialist reports.

Private investigative functions

Outlining and categorizing the functions undertaken by private investigative agencies is no easy task. A recent 'overview of the private investigation industry' (retrieved on 19 December 2005 from www.psiact.org.uk/posi.htm) lists around 90 areas of work undertaken by investigators (see the Appendix to this chapter for an adapted version of this list). These range from the relatively predictable (fraud investigation, physical, technical and remote surveillance and due diligence inquiries) to the less predictable (pre-home purchase investigations, genealogical investigations and nanny investigations).

Haselden (1990) suggests that private investigative activities can be divided into four functional areas: commercial, legal, matrimonial and industrial. Prenzler (2001) offers a similar four-fold classification:

- *Anti-fraud work* is undertaken primarily for large insurance firms but also for some self-insured private companies and government insurance agencies. Such work will be either 'factual' (interviewing claimants, establishing an interview record, undertaking further inquiries where necessary) or 'surveillance' based. The latter is highly routinized, the client providing a list of suspect claims with supporting documentation, the investigator tracking that person for a specified period. Usually, these cases involve claims of physical disability, investigative agents trying to find evidence to disprove the veracity of claims. Insurance work also covers a wide range of other areas, including stolen vehicles, accidents, arson, welfare and benefit fraud.

- *Legal work* was the main source of employment before insurance companies began wholesale outsourcing of their work. It includes carrying out background or factual work for lawyers in civil and sometimes in criminal cases; locating and analysing forensic evidence; and process serving.

- *Commercial inquiry* is a growing area of work and includes electronic counter measures (debugging), liability investigations, pre-employment checks, investigations into workplace theft and harassment, copyright investigations, personal protection, repossessions and debt collection, and risk and security assessment.

- *Domestic investigations* include checking fidelity, checking teenage drug use, missing persons and abducted child recovery. Although this is the best known area of private investigative work, the matrimonial component of domestic investigation has reduced in the last 30 years.

Attempting to place disparate activities into discrete functional boxes is, in some respects, a limited exercise. Areas of activity may breach categorical boundaries and the work undertaken within categories may vary according to specific conditions, such as the nature of the client or the size of the company. Nevertheless, classification does enable us to impose some order on an otherwise disorderly field. Gill and Hart's (1997a) analysis of the investigative sector in the UK distinguishes seven areas of activity: process serving, claims investigation, road traffic accident inquiries, matrimonial inquiries, criminal investigations, fraud investigations and asset tracing/due diligence inquiries.

Process serving was by far the most common function identified, 90 per cent of companies in their sample undertaking this work. The next most common was insurance-related work (including both insurance claims and road traffic accident inquiries), one respondent providing evidence that work in this area for his company had doubled each year for the previous three years. As in Prenzler's (2001) Australian research, Gill and Hart's (1997a) respondents also noted that technological factors – such as video-recording – had increased the quality of surveillance and with it insurers' confidence in the investigative sector. Despite changes in British divorce law and the desire of many investigators to offload the 'snooper' image linked to carrying out such work, 68 per cent of Gill and Hart's (1997a) sample continued to undertake matrimonial inquiries, making it the third most commonly provided service.

As for the other categories, slightly more than half the companies sampled undertook criminal investigations. Usually, private investigators working in the criminal justice field do so on behalf of the defence, checking the accuracy of police evidence and looking for witnesses who might undermine the case for the prosecution. By contrast, criminal investigations for private companies usually aim to establish the causes of loss and of any guilt associated with such loss. Many companies, fearful of reputational damage, will avoid prosecuting alleged offenders, preferring to deal with matters on an informal basis. Gill and Hart (1997a) describe the case of a driver suspected of theft who was persuaded to resign from his job by an investigator using techniques that would have breached the Police and Criminal Evidence Act 1984 and that would have led to the case's dismissal had it ever gone to court. On the other hand, managers wishing to draw upon the public justice system in order to deal with theft against their companies are often forced to employ private investigators because of police disinterest in corporate loss.

Half the companies sampled by Gill and Hart (1997a) provided fraud investigation services though two thirds of these were from the higher income-earning agencies. Many of the 'prestige' companies specialized exclusively in this area of activity – one which, at the upper end, is highly lucrative and, because of concerns about corporate reputation, is least likely to result in engagement with the public justice system. A similar breakdown of service provision was found in respect of asset tracing and due diligence inquiries where higher-end companies were also the most active.

Several things may be said about these various investigative functions. First, they have undergone a changing trajectory during the last 30 years. On the one hand, the introduction of 'no-fault' divorce removed some of the demand for matrimonial investigation. Simultaneously, insurance-related work expanded. Whereas, in the past, the tendency of insurance companies had been to accept most claims so as to avoid negative publicity, the combination of increased competition with massive claim inflation forced the introduction of rigorous investigative regimes. Significantly, this change was facilitated by technological factors, one of which – the video-camera – both increased the quality of surveillance evidence and the confidence of the insurance industry in those using it (Prenzler and King 2002)[4].

Secondly, such functional change has coincided with a shift in clientele. Gill and Hart (1999) note that, while private investigators may, in the past, have received much of their business from private individuals, the bulk of it is now obtained from insurance firms and other private companies. While this is undoubtedly true, it is only part of the story. Later, I shall argue that corporate–client relationships pose issues that have not been addressed by existing studies of the investigative sector. Adequate analysis of these relationships demands consideration not only of investigative structures and functions within national jurisdictions (such as the UK, the USA or Australia) but also across such jurisdictions.

Thirdly, some aspects of commercial investigative work (e.g. claims investigation) are relatively uncontroversial, while other aspects (e.g. bugging and debugging) are less so. In respect of the latter, George and Button (2000) cite the example of a firm of builders which, having lost a succession of tenders, called in investigators to scan their offices for bugs. Having found one in the estimator's office, the company instructed the investigators to leave it there so that misinformation could be fed to the competitor responsible for planting it. Those deploying such reactive methods would presumably justify them on grounds of *quid pro quo*. However, the proactive use of bugging and other forms of covert surveillance raises more serious ethical issues. In some instances 'corporate deviance' may, effectively, be contracted out to commercial security companies, investigative agents being complicit in unethical and extra-legal activities.[5]

Efficacy, ethics and regulation

Clients employ private investigators primarily in order to ensure that their affairs remain private. On the one hand, individuals with personal problems want to have them resolved sensitively, discreetly and confidentially. On the other, corporate clients want to avoid publicity in order to protect their company's reputation and market share. Further to that, corporate goals are instrumental rather than social, companies wanting to prevent loss and minimize risk to their assets rather than to enforce the law and prosecute offenders.

Bearing these points in mind, what evidence is there regarding the efficacy of private investigation? Quantitative data on this subject are virtually non-existent. In a rare example, Benson (1998) cites data from Reynolds (1994) regarding the Railroad Police, a body established in the USA after the First World War. The Railroad Police, it is argued, were able to compile 'a remarkable record of effectiveness, particularly relative to public police' (Benson 1998: 347) due to their ability to specialize in a single area of detection and enforcement. Between the end of the First World War and 1929, freight claim payments for robberies fell by 92.7 per cent. This success, it is claimed, has continued to the present, the clearance rate for reported crimes in 1992 standing at 23.2 per cent compared with a rate of 8.1 per cent for the public police. Benson (1998) also claims that comparison of the US's private and public bail systems shows the former to be more efficient in terms of defendants failing to appear in court (14 per cent compared with 27 per cent for the public system) and in respect of fugitive rates after three years (less than 1 per cent compared with 8 per cent).

In a similar vein, Prenzler and King (2002) cite quantitative evidence from Australia on the decision to initiate an anti-welfare fraud drive in 1999. This scheme, which involved contracting out surveillance work on suspicious cases that were resistant to formal investigation, proved to be highly successful. In 1999–2000, 1,446 cases were referred to surveillance providers. In due course, 1,063 of these cases were finalized, of which 747 (70 per cent) resulted in debt or reduced payment. In all, over $4 million of 'savings to future outlays' were made and over $3.9 million dollars identified for recovery action (Prenzler and King 2002: 3, Table 2).

More often, however, evidence on the efficacy of private investigation takes a qualitative form. Prenzler and King's (2002) interviewees estimated that they were able to achieve positive results in between 70 per cent and 90 per cent of cases involving such things as loss recovery, the dropping of suspect insurance claims and locating missing persons. Perhaps not surprisingly, a large majority had positive views about the contribution they made to society. In respect of fraud, one said: 'There is a lack of appreciation by the public of the professionalism of the industry ... and the benefits to the taxpayer of stopping fraud against government' (Prenzler and King 2002: 4). Another commented: 'With every debtor that we can locate and induce to pay their debts ... [we're] assisting [the client] recover his debts and preventing him passing on his losses to the public' (Prenzler and King 2002: 4).

Of course, efficacy cuts both ways. Companies contract private investigators to deal with their problems in order that the solutions they come up with may be kept 'in-house'. Yet, during the course of that process, agents may be transformed from investigators into prosecutors; those who contract them may come to sit in judgement on the accused; and criminal acts which impact on the public interest may remain private matters by virtue of going unreported (Lipson 1975). As Cunningham *et al.* (1990: 301) put it, under such a system of private justice the offender's treatment may vary greatly and unpredictably, the 'guilty' employee facing 'suspension without pay, dismissal, job reassignment, job redesign (elimination of some job duties), civil restitution agreements, or criminal prosecution'.

Equally difficult problems may arise in respect of non-corporate clients. Prenzler (2001) quotes two disturbing examples. In the first, an investigator described how he had almost assisted in the attempted murder of a third party after he located a woman on behalf of a New Zealand investigator in a domestic violence case. In the second, an agent who specialized in domestic matters stated:

> In one case I was asked to trace four people. I found one of them and gave the client the details. A few weeks later the police were knocking on my door. The person I located was found dead – with a crossbow bolt through the head. Apparently he was a Crown Law witness. So were the other three on my list (Prenzler 2001: 41).

Examples such as these raise broader issues regarding the ethical position of private investigators. In the Australian research around one third of respondents believed legal non-compliance by investigators to be widespread. However, a large majority of interviewees claimed that unethical and illegal conduct occurred at the margins, and a similar majority thought that conduct had improved during the last 20 years (Prenzler 2001; Prenzler and King 2002). Misconduct may, of course, have a variety of sources and take a range of different forms (Button 1998): sometimes individuals of a dubious character penetrate the industry in order to engage in illegal acts; sometimes unethical or illegal acts may arise from the investigator's ignorance of proper legal or ethical procedures; and sometimes agents, working at the margins of the law, cross the boundary into extra-legal activities.

This last case is particularly significant as many commentators have suggested that investigators tend to push the law to its limits without necessarily breaking it. One reason for this is that the work undertaken – much of it involving accessing confidential information – inevitably operates at the ethical-legal margins. Another factor concerns the moral dilemmas private investigators claim to experience, an issue exemplified in Gill and Hart's (1999) analysis. Many of their respondents, while claiming to operate within ethical boundaries, cited examples where clients, including members of the legal profession, had asked them to perform illegal or unethical acts. Usually, these requests involved gaining unlawful access to confidential information, such as bank accounts – though some also cited instances of being asked to organize murders or serious assaults. Most investigators said they 'drew the line' at such illegal or unethical requests believing that, by breaking the law, they risked losing their professional reputations. However, many of the same investigators believed that a 'moral precedent' existed when they were working on behalf of innocent business victims subjected to malicious behaviour by professional criminals. As one interviewee put it: 'we've got to do something to help. The people we investigate are professionals and by that I mean they're bloody devious' (Gill and Hart 1999: 256). Here, agents felt it justifiable to 'cut corners' – such as by impersonating someone to gain his or her bank details – in order to achieve the 'right' moral outcome.

Ironically, in Britain, the existence of such practices has often been cited as a reason for *not* subjecting the investigative sector to statutory regulation. After all, it has been argued, statutory regulation would merely grant private investigators a 'licence to snoop', thereby legitimizing existing unethical practices. As Button (1998) points out, however, there have also been other reasons for Britain's long-standing resistance to the regulation of private investigation. One has been that the police have pushed for regulation only in those areas which most affect their core activities, such as alarm installation, guarding services and door supervision. Another has been that the expansion of the guarding sector – and, with it, of representative trade associations willing to demand regulation on that sector's behalf – has left the smaller investigative sector isolated from the lobbying process.

As a result Britain, unlike countries such as the USA, Canada, Australia, New Zealand, Belgium, the Netherlands, Germany, Finland or Spain, has lacked a statutory framework for regulating private investigators.[6] Such regulation as exists has been of two types: limited regulation of *investigations* through legislation such as the Interception of Communications Act 1985 and the Regulation of Investigatory Powers Act 2000; and *self-regulation* of investigators either through the Association of British Investigators (ABI) or the Institute of Professional Investigators (IPI).[7] While these bodies operate codes of practice and disciplinary systems, their regulatory efficacy is limited. George and Button (2000) estimated some years ago that the combined membership of ABI and IPI amounted to fewer than 1,000 members. Furthermore, expulsion from these organizations does not prevent former members from continuing as private investigators should they choose to do so.

In Britain, the situation is now changing with new regulatory systems being introduced under the Private Security Industry Act 2001. Button (1998) suggests that a regulatory regime needs to satisfy three conditions. First, it should provide a system of licensing for employees and firms that requires minimum standards of character and competence to be met. Secondly, there should be a code of practice regulating the activities of private investigators. Finally, the regulatory body should be entirely independent of the investigative sector and should have adequate funds and expertise to perform its functions effectively. How far does the 2001 Act meet these conditions?

The Act establishes an independent non-departmental body, the Security Industry Authority (SIA), the main function of which is to license individuals operating in those sectors of the private security industry – including private investigators – defined by the Act as subject to regulation. Licences are based upon the individual being defined as a 'fit and proper' person following a criminal records check, while other conditions – such as adherence to a code of conduct – may be imposed through secondary legislation (Button 2002). The main weakness of the legislation is that it does not propose the compulsory licensing of firms, limiting itself instead to working with existing self-regulatory schemes. For that reason Button (2002) concludes that, while the legislation is to be welcomed, there is a need for it to be extended to establish compulsory minimum standards for firms as well as for employees.[8]

Final comments: beyond the public–private interface

The final section of this chapter reflects further on two issues raised earlier regarding the changing character of the public-private interface: the first concerning the impact of the risk mentality on the scope and character of investigative practices within and across the sectors; the second concerning the increasingly significant role played by private investigative bodies in transnational security governance.

The risk mentality and investigative practice

Previously I suggested that writers on the salience of the risk mentality within neoliberal governance have commented on its diffusion across a wide range of public and private sector organizations. Given this situation, what potential is there for the risk-oriented private investigative sector to expand the scope of its work? For instance, if suitable regulatory systems were to be put into place, could private investigators play an enhanced role in the provision of services to victims of financial or, indeed, of other types of crimes? This possibility should not be dismissed out of hand. After all, private investigators do provide victims with services which the state is unable or unwilling to provide. Prenzler (2001: 48) makes the following observation:

> Interview respondents were virtually united in the view they could provide greater justice to victims of wrongs if governments would

allow greater controlled access to information. There was no support for a carte blanche approach. Respondents understood the inherent risks associated with access to databases but presented strong arguments in favour of restricted access to an application system – with reasons required for each application and regular audits of these transactions by regulatory authorities.

Arguably, then, there is a case for such matters to be debated provided that rigorous regulation is the *quid pro quo* of any extended involvement. Surprisingly, however, in a British criminal justice system which, for more than a decade, has been dominated by 'partnership' and 'multi-agency' models of provision, little, if any, consideration has been given to the enhanced role of private investigators. This rebuttal has nothing to do with the state's dismissal of the commercial security sector *per se*. On the contrary, the Police Reform Act 2001 makes the accreditation of commercial security companies a key element in the project to establish a 'police extended family', such companies being conceived as key partners in the future delivery of what Brodeur (1983) has called 'low policing'. Yet, far from being regarded as a potential partner of the public police in this domain, British private investigators have tended to be seen by the authorities as at best a nuisance and at worst a danger.[9] This attitude is by no means universal. Gill and Hart (1997c) contrast British attitudes with those found in the USA where investigators enjoy both a higher professional status and a closer working relationship with police than their British counterparts. As Gill and Hart (1997c) argue, the situation in the USA is the result of long-established cultural factors – not least American reverence for individualism and the free market. While in Britain long-held historical suspicions about the dangers of 'snooping' by the state or by commercial bodies may, for better or worse, be changing – witness the dramatic growth of CCTV surveillance over the last 20 years – it remains to be seen whether private investigators will enjoy an enhanced role in the future.[10]

One also has to consider the extent to which some of the practices undertaken by state and commercial security organizations have begun to coalesce as a result of the diffusion of the risk mentality. One consequence of this is that state police, in the manner of private police, are more and more inclined to adopt instrumental forms of action. A good example is the police's deployment of 'techniques of disorganization' against organized criminals (Johnston 2000a: 60), the rationale being that those who cannot be brought to justice through conventional means should be subjected to maximum disruption and disorganization. This raises a second question. How far is risk-based thinking likely to impact on state police investigation?

The 'test-bed' for this issue is the National Intelligence Model (NIM), a model firmly grounded in the risk mentality. As Maguire (2003) affirms, if applied correctly, the NIM allows for investigative solutions to be sought outside the criminal justice system. These might include 'gathering information about the nature of particular criminal markets in order to find ways of "disrupting" them and the criminal networks that control them' (Maguire 2003: 387). Of course, previous attempts to adopt similar risk-oriented strategies have met with only limited success. Radcliffe (2002) points to the difficulties of trying to export the British 'intelligence-led' model to the 'idiosyncratic local policing' environments of Australia, while Gill (2000) suggests that, for all its emphasis on proactivity, the model's application in Britain involved little more than 'rounding up the usual suspects'.

As yet, the progress of the NIM is difficult to gauge. John and Maguire (2004) note problems in respect of both ownership and understanding of the model, pointing to 'large "knowledge gaps" about the NIM among all ranks'; and to resistance derived either from ignorance or from dislike of the model's '"academic" structure and language'. Effective implementation, they suggest, will depend upon the provision of both training and 'creative efforts to win "hearts and minds"' (John and Maguire 2004: 5). Undoubtedly, resistance born out of the traditions of police culture will continue to influence the direction of the NIM. It is, however, undeniable that public sector organizations, such as the police, are increasingly structured, organized and oriented by the mentality of risk. In the longer term, while cultural factors will undoubtedly have a significant impact on how that mentality affects investigative practices, they are unlikely to resist its advances.

Private investigation in a transnational context

Existing evidence on the structure and functions of the private investigative sector is limited in two respects. First, there is a relatively small amount of academic research on private investigation. Secondly, the limited evidence that does exist invariably focuses on the investigative sector within single (regional or national) jurisdictions. This chapter has drawn extensively on valuable research undertaken by Gill and Hart in Britain and by Prenzler and King in Australia. Yet, neither body of work makes reference to developments at the transnational level, an area where our lack of knowledge about companies providing investigative and other services is often in inverse proportion to their global significance.

Manning noted some years ago that the US government, in co-operation with large corporations (many of them part of the defence industry), had broadened its definition of 'the national interest' to include industrial ideas with R&D potential (Manning 2000: 4). Transnational security consultancies such as The Control Risks Group, Kroll Inc., Carratu International, ArmorGroup, Wackenhut (now part of Group 4 Securicor) and Pinkerton (now part of Securitas)[11] are particularly active participants in this growing field of 'information policing': a field which sits firmly within George and Button's (2000) definition of 'professional investigation'. These companies offer a range of services to corporate clients and to governments including the provision of business/competitor intelligence, due diligence inquiries, forensic audits, background checks on individuals and businesses, advice on hostage negotiations, crisis management services and services to facilitate corporate restructuring.

Consider three examples. The Risk Advisory Group, like several other global security consultancies, provides specialist advice to clients contemplating investment in potentially profitable but unstable business markets, such as those in Eastern Europe.

ArmorGroup, which declares itself 'an international defensive protective security company', has, in the recent past, provided consultancy services to multinational companies undertaking oil pipeline and other projects in Russia, Kazakhstan, Ecuador and Colombia. In December 2005, Kroll Government Services Inc., a subsidiary of Kroll Inc. (which markets itself as 'the risk consulting company' and is sometimes labelled 'Wall Street's private eye'), was awarded a $17 million contract by the US Department of Homeland Security's (DHS) Transport Security Administration (TSA) to conduct background checks on TSA screeners and other employees. This is one of several major contracts held by Kroll with DHS departments, including one for US Customs and Border Protection. Kroll, which has offices in more than 60 cities on six continents, has also set up a partnership with another risk consultancy, World-Check, to protect corporate clients against money laundering.

How should these developments be considered in the wider context of democratic security governance? There is no reason in principle why transnational commercial security should be unable to contribute to the collective good, provided it is located within an appropriate governmental regime (Johnston 2000b). However, the difficulties of establishing transnational regulatory systems are considerable (Nossal 2001) and there is some justification for saying that the transparency of private security practices have reduced at the same time as the role and significance of companies have increased.[12]

There are four reasons for suggesting this, all of them related to the changing character of what has traditionally been regarded as the 'public–private' interface. First, conflicts such as those in Afghanistan and Iraq, coupled with counter-terrorist demands following 9/11, have fuelled an expanding market for security services and a parallel growth in defence and security budgets both in North America and Europe. At the same time states have contracted out many security and peace-keeping duties to commercial suppliers, such as 'private military companies'. This process has been most marked in the USA where critics have suggested that the opacity of contractual processes and the fudging of civil–military distinctions have enabled government to evade public scrutiny of its actions – effectively, by mobilizing 'rule at a distance' strategies. The result has been to make it difficult to know where the state 'begins' and 'ends'. Secondly, that process has been facilitated by the long-established 'revolving door' of personnel exchange between commercial, military and state security, a process dating back to the days of Alan Pinkerton. All transnational companies providing business risk and investigative services pride themselves on the fact that their key personnel have prior experience as senior police officers, military officers, state security operatives or financial executives.[13] Third, and related to the previous point, is the fact that the traditional divisions drawn between state security, military security, commercial security and the police become increasingly difficult to sustain as commercial security companies engage in military or peace keeping duties and the police and criminal justice system becomes more and more militarized (Kraska 1999). Fittingly, a fourth and final reason brings us back to what has become the staple diet of private investigative work: insurance. In 2004 a new dimension was added to the ever more complex public–private interface when Kroll Inc. was acquired by Marsh & McLennan Companies Inc., a global insurance company with annual revenues exceeding $12 billion (information retrieved on 26 January 2006 from http://www.krollworldwide.com/about/history/). The insurance industry it seems has, itself, become a significant player in global security governance.

The result of these four processes is that the traditional distinction between 'public' and 'private' spheres (however 'blurred' the boundaries or 'fuzzy' the edges are claimed to be) is unable to capture the 'nodal' character of security governance (Johnston and Shearing 2003). However, in a world where the collection, collation and deployment of 'information' for risk management purposes are central to the governance of security, one thing is certain: transnational companies offering investigative and other information-based services will play an increasingly significant role.

Selected further reading

Button, M. (1998) 'Beyond the public gaze', *International Journal of the Sociology of Law,* 26: 1–16. A useful review of the characteristics of private investigators and of the main issues concerning their accountability and regulation.

Gill, M. and Hart, G. (1997) 'Exploring investigative policing: a study of private detectives in Britain', *British Journal of Criminology,* 37: 549–67. An discussion of the role of private investigators in the context of four key issues: competence, legitimacy, relationship with the public police and future challenges in managing a diverse policing structure.

Gill, M. and Hart, G. (1997) 'Policing as business: the organisation and structure of private investigation', *Policing and Society,* 7: 117–41. An analysis of private investigation as a business enterprise culminating in the classification of investigative agencies into 'home based', 'high street', 'regional' or 'prestige' enterprises.

Prenzler, T. and King, M. (2002) *The Role of Private Investigators and Commercial Agents in Law Enforcement. Trends and Issues in Crime and Criminal Justice* 234, Canberra: Australian Institute of Criminology (6 pp.). An examination of the role of private investigators and commercial agents in Australia, drawing upon 40 in-depth interviews carried out in Queensland and New South Wales.

Acknowledgements

I am grateful to my colleague, Dr Mark Button, and Dr Rob C. Mawby for providing material used in the writing of this chapter. Any views expressed in the chapter are, however, solely those of the author.

Appendix: functions undertaken by the private investigation sector

Accident claims investigation
Adoption and post-adoption inquiries
Anti-corruption investigation
Asset investigation
Assisting bailiffs as creditors' representatives
Assisting counsel

Background and lifestyle investigation
Bankruptcy investigation
Blackmail investigation
Bodyguard services
Business interruption claims investigation

Civil proceedings investigation
Competitor intelligence
Computer crime investigation
Copyright infringement investigation
Corporate security investigation
Counterfeit investigation/anti-counterfeiting
Credit vetting
Crime prevention
Criminal defence investigation

Debt recovery
Director/staff loyalty investigation
Drug testing/screening
Due diligence inquiries (personal and corporate)

Electronic surveillance countermeasures
Employers' liability claims investigations
Executive and diplomatic protection
Expert witness services

Financial investigation
Forensic accounting
Forensic science services
Fraud investigation
Fraud prevention
Fraudulent claims investigation

Genealogy investigations
GPS/GSM vehicle, plant, freight tracking
Grey market and parallel trading investigation

Hostage investigation

Industrial espionage investigation
Information security investigation
Internet profiling
Internal loss (shrinkage) investigation
Investigations into applications for planning, liquor, gaming, betting office
    licences

Life insurance claims investigation
Locating missing persons, animals, property
Locus reports

Marine claims investigation
Matrimonial investigations
Missing persons inquiries
Mortgage protection claims investigation

Nanny investigation

Obtaining statements as to means

Patent infringement investigation
Peace-of-mind investigations
Pre- and post-employment investigation
Pre-home purchase investigation
Private medical claims investigation
Probate inquiries
Process serving
Product contamination/tampering investigation
Professional indemnity claims investigation
Property claims investigation
Public liability claims investigation

Recovery of abducted minors
Repossessions
Risk management
Road traffic accident injury claims investigation
Road traffic accident investigations (non-injury)

Sale and hire of video, polygraph equipment
Statement taking
Status (pre-sue) investigation
Surveillance (physical, technical, remote, electronic)

Tenancy investigation
Test purchasing
Theft claims investigation
Theft investigations (non-insurance)
Tracing beneficiaries

Travel claims investigation

Undercover operations

(Adapted from www.psiact.org.uk/posi.htm.)

Notes

1 It should not be forgotten, however, that many investigators are employed on an 'in-house' basis by organizations such as banks, insurance companies, local authorities, government departments and retailers. Such in-house investigators may be divided into three types: those employed in investigation departments (as often as not, part of wider security/loss-prevention departments); lone investigators employed to carry out inquiries; and security managers whose responsibilities include investigative functions (George and Button 2000).
2 The study was based upon a postal survey which elicited 206 responses from 1,700 distributed questionnaires (a response rate of 12.1 per cent) followed by observation of and interviews with respondents (number unspecified).
3 In Prenzler's (2001) Australian study (see also Prenzler and King 2002), just over half the sample companies employed between one and three investigators, the remaining 47.5 per cent employing four or more.
4 One qualification should be added. While insurer's direct use of investigators has certainly grown, they have always – though not always wittingly – used investigators indirectly. In the 1980s at least one company of loss adjusters is known to have retained the services of two freelance private investigators (both former police officers) to carry out background enquiries if claims appeared suspicious. Sometimes insurance companies would be notified of such private investigative involvement. Frequently, they would not be. In other words, by means of 'sub-sub-contracting' arrangements, insurers remained unaware of the extent to which loss adjusters deployed private investigators. (I am very grateful to Rob C. Mawby for providing this information).
5 Such practices are by no means the preserve of 'cowboy' companies. Allegations of impropriety have been directed at several major security corporations, including Wackenhut. (This example is described in the final section of the chapter.)
6 See Button (2002: 121–5) for a comparative analysis of private security regulatory systems.
7 See web links to ABI (http://www.theabi.org.uk/visitor/index.htm) and IPI (http://www.ipi.org.uk/).
8 The SIA website states that 'The development of licensing in [the private investigative] sector is in its early stages and we are still considering how we can ensure that the licensing scheme we establish is appropriate and reasonable … Subject to the outcome of an RIA [regulatory impact assessment] the SIA may launch the licensing of private investigators in 2006 (England and Wales)/2007 (Scotland)' (retrieved from http://www.the-sia.org.uk/home, 20 December 2005).
9 Thus, previous analysis of the relationship between public police and private investigators in Britain has tended to focus on problems such as ex-police officers, now employed in private investigation, gaining access to police data sources by invoking 'the old-pals act', and in-post police officers eliciting employment in the private investigative sector through 'moonlighting'.
10 In some areas of work, such as debt recovery, there is already evidence of an expanded role. Bailiffs have already been used to recover unpaid council tax from debtors and it has recently been proposed that private debt recovery agents should collect unpaid child maintenance (see Wintour 2006).

11 See the following links:
    The Control Risks Group (http://www.crg.com/);
    Kroll Inc. (http://www.krollworldwide.com/);
    Carratu International (http://www.carratu.com/);
    ArmorGroup (http://www.armorgroup.com/index.asp);
    Wackenhut (http://www.wackenhut.com/);
    Pinkerton (http://www.ci-pinkerton.com/);
12 Consider an example of alleged corporate deviance and 'cover-up'. Some years
    ago the Wackenhut Corporation was under contract to the Alyeska Pipeline
    Service Company, a consortium involved in Alaskan oil exploration and extraction.
    In 1991 the House Interior Committee met to hear allegations about covert
    surveillance alleged to have been conducted by Wackenhut against Charles Hamel,
    an environmental 'whistle-blower'. A number of former Wackenhut employees
    testified to having been involved in activities intended to discredit both Hamel
    and Alyeska employees who had accused the company of environmentally
    unsound practices. Wackenhut had also, apparently, used unlicensed investigators
    while carrying out this work (US House of Representatives 1991).
13 See Johnston (2000b: 31) for an example relating to Pinkerton.

References

Bayley, D. and Shearing, C. (2001) *The New Structure of Policing: Description,
    Conceptualization and Research Agenda.* Washington, DC: National Institute for
    Justice.

Beck, U (1992) *Risk Society: Toward a New Modernity.* London: Sage.

Benson, B.L. (1998) 'Crime control through private enterprise', *Independent Review*, 2
    (3) Winter: 341–71.

Bowden, T. (1978) *Beyond the Limits of the Law.* Harmondsworth: Penguin Books.

Brodeur, J.-P. (1983) 'High policing and low policing: some remarks about the policing
    of political activities', *Social Problems*, 30: 507–21.

Button, M. (1998) 'Beyond the public gaze', *International Journal of the Sociology of Law*,
    26: 1–16.

Button, M. (2002) *Private Policing.* Cullompton: Willan Publishing.

Churchill, W. (2004) 'From the Pinkerton's to the PATRIOT Act: the trajectory of
    political policing in the United States, 1870 to the present', *New Centennial Review*,
    4: 1–72 (available online at http://muse.jhu.edu/cgi-bin/access.cgi?uri=/journals/
    new_centennial_review/v004/4.1churchill.html&session=76730859).

Cunningham, W.C., Strauchs, J.J. and Van Meter, C.W. (1990) *Private Security Trends
    1970 to 2000: The Hallcrest Report II.* Boston, MA: Butterworth-Heinemann.

Cunningham, W.C. and Taylor, T. (1985) *Private Security and Police in America: The
    Hallcrest Report I.* Boston, MA: Butterworth-Heinemann.

Draper, H. (1978) *Private Police.* Brighton: Harvester.

Ericson, R., Barry, D. and Doyle, A. (2000) 'The moral hazards of neo-liberalism:
    lessons from the private insurance industry', *Economy and Society*, 29: 532–58.

George, B. and Button, M. (2000) *Private Security. Vol. 1.* Leicester: Perpetuity Press.

Gill, M. and Hart, G. (1997a) 'Exploring investigative policing: a study of private
    detectives in Britain', *British Journal of Criminology*, 37: 549–67.

Gill, M. and Hart, G. (1997b) 'Policing as business: the organisation and structure of
    private investigation', *Policing and Society*, 7: 117–41.

Gill, M. and Hart, G. (1997c) 'Private investigators in Britain and America: perspectives
    on the impact of popular culture', *Policing: An International Journal of Police Strategy
    and Management*, 20: 631–40.

Gill, M. and Hart, G. (1999) 'Enforcing corporate security policy using private investigators', *European Journal on Criminal Policy and Research*, 7: 245–61.

Gill, P. (2000) *Rounding up the Usual Suspects: Developments in Contemporary Law Enforcement Intelligence*. Aldershot: Ashgate.

Haselden, R. (1990) 'Licence to snoop', *Weekend Guardian*, 8–9 September.

John, T. and Maguire, M. (2004) *That National Intelligence Model: Key Lessons from Early Research*, Online Report 30/04. London: Home Office.

Johnston, L. (1992) *The Rebirth of Private Policing*. London: Routledge.

Johnston, L. (2000a) *Policing Britain: Risk, Security and Governance*. Harlow: Longman.

Johnston, L. (2000b) 'Transnational private policing: the impact of global commercial security', in J. Sheptycki (ed.) *Issues in Transnational Policing*. London: Routledge.

Johnston, L. (2006) 'Transnational security governance', in J. Wood, B. Dupont, (eds) *Democracy, Society and the Governance of Security*. Cambridge: Cambridge University Press (2006): 33–51.

Johnston, L and Shearing, C. (2003) *Governing Security: Explorations in Policing and Justice*. London: Routledge.

Kraska, P.B. (1999). 'Militarizing criminal justice', *Journal of Political and Military Sociology*, 27: 205–15.

Lipson, M. (1975) *On Guard: The Business of Private Security*. New York, NY: Quadrangle/New York Times Book Co.

Maguire, M. (2003) 'Criminal investigation and 'Crime control', in T. Newburn (ed.) *Handbook of Policing*. Cullompton: Willan Publishing.

Manning, P. (2000) 'Policing new social spaces', in J. Sheptycki (ed.) *Issues in Transnational Policing*. London: Routledge.

Morn, F. (1982) *The Eye that Never Sleeps*. Bloomington, IN: Indiana University Press.

Nossal, K.R. (2001) 'Global governance and national interests: regulating transnational security corporations in the post cold-war era', *Melbourne Journal of International Law*, 2: 459–76.

O'Malley, J. (1992) 'Risk, power and crime prevention', *Economy and Society*, 21: 252–75.

O'Toole, G. (1978) *The Private Sector: Private Spies, Rent-a-cops, and the Police-industrial Complex*. New York, NY: Norton & Co.

Prenzler, T. (2001) *Private Investigators in Australia: Work, Law, Ethics and Regulation. Report to the Criminology Research Council*. Brisbane: Griffith University.

Prenzler, T. and King, M. (2002) *The Role of Private Investigators and Commercial Agents in Law Enforcement. Trends and Issues in Crime and Criminal Justice* 239. Canberra: Australian Institute of Criminology.

Radcliffe, J.H. (2002) 'Intelligence-led policing and the problems of turning rhetoric into practice', *Policing and Society*, 12: 53–66.

Reynolds, M.O. (1994) *Using the Private Sector to Deter Crime*. Dallas, TX: National Center for Policy Analysis.

Shearing, C. and Stenning, P. (1983) 'Private security – implications for social control', *Social Problems*, 30: 493–506.

US Department of Labor, Bureau of Labor Statistics (2005) *Occupational Outlook Handbook* (available online at http://www.bls.gov/oco/ocos154.htm#empty).

US House of Representatives (1991) *Oversight Hearings on Alyeska Covert Operations*. 4 November.

Wintour, P. (2006) 'Debt collectors to collect unpaid child maintenance', *Guardian*, 19 January.

Part 3

Forensic techniques

As has been noted at various points in this volume, criminal investigation has long been a staple of popular culture. Indeed, it appears that modern television is all but obsessed with forensic science. From *Cracker* to *Crime Scene Investigation*, the schedules are now full of images of highly skilled experts and technicians 'cracking' crime through the appliance of science. Now, of course, the success of such dramas is in part that they play to our long-held desire for security and to our belief in the efficacy of scientific knowledge in making the world a better and safer place. One doesn't need to be a signed-up member of the society of postmodern relativists, however, to recognize that there is as much wishful thinking in this as there is truthful representation. Of course, forensic sciences don't lead straightforwardly to a massive hike in clear-up rates or necessarily to solutions to the most complex criminal investigations. And, yet, clearly they have huge potential and represent a significant advance. But how do we assess them? Separating the factual wheat from the fictional chaff is the primary purpose of the chapters in this part. What are forensic techniques, what do they involve and what are their promises and limitations?

In the opening chapter, A.P.A. Broeders examines the principles of forensic identification science. The examination of trace materials – such as glass, fibres, tool marks or biological matter – is generally focused on attempting to answer two questions. First, whether there is any relationship or connection between the trace and the incident being investigated. Secondly, what the origin of the trace is. Establishing the latter doesn't necessarily lead to being able to conclude that the former also exists. The establishment of an association between a trace and a single unique source is called *individualization*. Broeders goes on to examine the ways in which associations and relationships may be established and how criminalists then go about drawing and communicating their conclusions. This brings us back quickly to the issue of certainty – for essentially nothing is certain. As he puts it, 'all evidence is probabilistic'. Nothing is incontrovertible – even DNA evidence. That said, it is worth bearing in mind that fingerprint practitioners have long relied upon the assumption that each individual carries unique fingerprints; something which they may regard as setting it apart from other forms of probabilistic identification. In making this claim, fingerprint practice seems to regard the chance of misidentification (given that sufficient detail is available) as impossible, rather than simply as vanishingly small. Nevertheless, the probabilistic basis of most evidence is the point at which the skill and expertise of the forensic scientist are most required – not simply in collecting, analysing and understanding such evidence, but in assessing and presenting the conclusions in an appropriate and reliable manner.

Robert Green's chapter looks at the way in which forensic science support is used in the investigation of volume crime such as burglary and car crime. Until the mid-twentieth century the bulk of such forensic work was undertaken by police forces themselves. The creation of civilian scenes of crime officers in the early 1970s and the separation of the Forensic Science Service from the Home Office in the late 1980s were important developments. In relation to the investigation of volume crimes there is, not surprisingly, a considerable problem of capacity. At all stages of the investigation process there is what Green refers to as 'attrition': not all scenes are attended; of those that are, evidence isn't always collected for analysis; where it is, analysis isn't always undertaken; and so on. Not surprisingly, performance varies quite considerably among police forces, and Green suggests that differing patterns and procedures in relation to deployment, management and use of technology, as well as variations in investigative skills, account for the bulk of existing variation, and should therefore also be the focus for those seeking to improve performance.

Robin Williams and Paul Johnson evaluate the current evidence of forensic crime scene investigation. Echoing some of Martin Innes' earlier observations about the investigation of serious crime, Williams and Johnson argue that a significant element of the forensic process at the crime scene involves the attempt to 'reconstruct' the sequence of events being investigated. Although there are similarities with the work undertaken by detectives, there are also some important differences, not least the fact that attempts at forensic reconstruction involve an interaction between physical and other forms of evidence and, arguably, a more formalized process of verification/falsification. Using the examples of fingerprint and DNA collection, Williams and Johnson show how much of the work of forensic examiners, though bounded by clear organizational rules and procedures, is essentially improvised in character. Forensic science is, however, expanding and growing in influence, as Jim Fraser outlines in some detail in the final chapter in this part. Despite this, there remains considerable ignorance of forensic science within the police service. As a subject it is almost completely absent from probationer training, and several inquiries have suggested a lack of commitment or engagement among some senior officers. However, knowledge generally continues to increase, with 'published manuals and policies, implementation of new roles, investigative use in individuals cases, formal reviews of investigations and implementation of new scientific techniques and technologies' all having an effect. However, as Williams and Johnson argue, written manuals on such work 'give us access to such rules but they fail to tell us anything meaningful about the ways in which daily routines are the outcomes of spontaneous decision-making based on both formal mechanisms and situation[al understandings]'. What the following part attempts to do is to get behind the formal rules and some of the mythology to provide a detailed account of work in this increasingly important area of criminal investigation.

Chapter 12

Principles of forensic identification science

A.P.A. Broeders

Criminalistics is the science of individualization (Kirk 1963a).

Introduction

This chapter examines the determination of the origin of material traces. This process is traditionally called identification, as in fingerprint identification, but is more correctly termed *individualization* or *source attribution*. From a logical point of view, the process is most appropriately referred to as *inference of identity of source*.

Material traces may constitute either physical or biological evidence. Biological evidence includes organic matter like blood, saliva, semen, urine and hair, as well as botanical material such as plants, insects and pollen. Physical evidence not only includes a wide range of physical and chemical traces like glass, fibres and paint, but may also take the form of impression evidence, such as handwriting, tool marks, striation marks, shoeprints and fingerprints.

Among the various forensic identification disciplines, there is one that over the last century has earned itself a reputation for reliability that has so far remained unparalleled as well as largely unchallenged. This is *dactyloscopy*, the comparative examination of fingerprints (more properly called 'friction ridge patterns'). Traditionally, fingerprint examiners have always used categorical conclusions, with a positive identification carrying the implication that a crime-scene finger mark originates with absolute certainty from a particular finger. However, we shall see that unique source attribution – especially if this is claimed to have a categorical or deterministic rather than a probabilistic character – is not logically possible, barring forensically rather exceptional circumstances. Indeed, it appears that the less far-reaching – usually verbal – probabilistic conclusions that tend to be widely used in the other traditional forensic identification disciplines, as in handwriting, paint or firearms examination, are also somewhat problematical. The findings of a comparative examination undertaken with a view to establishing the source of a particular trace or set of traces do not strictly allow the type of probabilistic source attributions, be they of a quantitative or of a verbal nature, that have traditionally been used – and for the most part continue to be used – by the vast majority of forensic practitioners. A logically correct way to express the value of the findings of a source attribution examination of trace material, and thereby to express the weight of the trace evidence, is the one used in forensic DNA analysis. This takes the form of a so-called *likelihood ratio*. This concept is similar to that of the *diagnostic value*, a measure which has found wide acceptance in fields such as medicine and psychology as a way to express the value of any diagnostic test result (see, for example, www.rapid-diagnostics.org/accuracy.htm).

The limitations of the classical approach to source attribution are illustrated by means of an examination of the basic principles of the traditional identification disciplines and a discussion of the partly implicit and partly incorrect assumptions underlying this model. The chapter ends with a discussion of the so-called 'positivity doctrine', which – in spite of its demonstrably flawed logical basis – continues to be almost universally adhered to by practitioners of dactyloscopy throughout the forensic world.

Forensic science under attack

Although regular viewers of TV shows like *CSI* or Discovery Channel's *Forensic Detectives* might be forgiven for thinking otherwise, it would appear that all is not rosy in the forensic garden. Contrary to the powerful images created in these TV shows, forensic science – more specifically, but not exclusively, forensic identification science or criminalistics – has come under fierce attack in recent years. Some of the graver miscarriages of justice which have come to light in several countries in the last decades were at least partly associated with inadequate standards of forensic expertise or erroneous interpretations of otherwise correct findings. What were long held to be tried and trusted forensic identification procedures like fingerprint examination and questioned document examination are now said to lack a sound scientific basis, and the traditional claims of forensic identification science have come to be dismissed as logically untenable. Studies like those by Evett and Williams (1996) and recent cases like those of Shirley McKie in Scotland and Sally Clark[1] in England provide further evidence of the present crisis in the forensic arena. At the same time, forensic science is rapidly expanding. DNA profiling, in particular, may fairly be said to have revolutionized forensic science. It not only constitutes a powerful investigative and evidential tool in its own right, but it is, ironically perhaps, also largely as a result of the growing familiarity with the scientific paradigm associated with DNA evidence that traditional identification science is now lying so heavily under siege. More specifically, it could be argued that it is primarily through post-conviction DNA testing, frequently undertaken following actions by initiatives such as the Innocence Project in the USA,[2] that the limitations of traditional forms of evidence, more specifically eyewitness identification but also errors in forensic science testing, have been demonstrated.[3]

Origin and relevance

The examination of material traces such as glass, fibres, tool marks or biological matter is undertaken with a view to answering two questions. The first concerns the presence of a *relationship* between the trace and the incident under investigation; the second addresses the *origin* of the trace. The criminal investigator wants to know who left a particular trace at the crime scene and how certain he or she can be of its origin. The answer to this question is clearly only going to be of interest if it can also be demonstrated that the trace under examination is related to the crime and therefore potentially *relevant* to the question of who committed the crime or how the crime was committed.

For traces that are left at a possible crime scene by persons or objects, the presence of an association with the presumed crime is by no means always a foregone conclusion. If, for example, a finger mark is found on the door-jamb of the living-room in the house of an elderly widow who was found brutally stabbed to death and if this finger mark can be reliably attributed to her tax consultant, as was the case in the Deventer murder, this identification does not in and of itself establish a relationship between the finger mark and the crime, especially if the man subsequently explains that he happened to pay his client a business visit on the day she was believed to have been killed.

The Deventer murder

On Saturday 25 September 1999, a 60-year-old widow, Mrs Jacqueline Wittenberg, was found dead in the living-room of her house at the Zwolseweg in Deventer, the Netherlands. The post-mortem revealed that she was strangled, received five deep stab wounds in the chest and incurred several fractured ribs as well as serious head injury. No murder weapon was found nor was there any damage indicating forcible entry. It appeared, therefore that the perpetrator was known to the widow. Further investigation of the house suggested that the widow was killed two days earlier. It also appeared that only ten days earlier she changed her will, leaving her entire fortune – the equivalent of more than a million pounds – in accordance with the wish of her late husband, to a charitable trust.

Police attention finally fell on the widow's fiscal lawyer, Ernest L, who, at 8.36 p.m. on the evening of the murder, appeared to have been the last person to speak to the widow over the phone. It also appeared that he was the executor of the will and chairman of the trust. When L's fingerprint was found on the door of the victim's living-room, he suggested that he must have left it there during a visit he paid to her on the morning of her murder. L was asked to participate in a so-called 'scent identification test' or human scent line-up. On the Saturday following the murder, a knife had been found in a doorway in the city centre, as well as an umbrella. The result of the scent test, in which only the scent of the knife was used, was positive: for the police and prosecution alike this suggested that Ernest L was the murderer (no consideration was apparently given to the thought that it might be false positive).

Although acquitted by the district court on the grounds of insufficient evidence, L was found guilty by the Arnhem Court of Appeal and sentenced to 12 years' imprisonment. After a revision request was granted by the Dutch Supreme Court, on 9 February 2004, L was once again found guilty by the Court of Appeal in 's-Hertogenbosch and sentenced to 12 years' imprisonment, mainly on the basis of fresh DNA evidence. An examination of the victim's blouse, not previously undertaken because the prosecution originally felt that the knife, in combination with the rest of the evidence, made a strong enough case for conviction, turned up a small blood stain on the inside of the collar. A full 10-locus SGM Plus DNA profile[4] obtained from this material proved identical with the suspect's profile. The random match probability[5] for this profile was reported to be less than one in a billion.

In addition to the blood stain on the collar, partial profiles matching that of the suspect were obtained from samples from the victim's blouse taken from places where this was soiled with a light red substance, possibly make-up from the victim's face, and from stains which showed up under special lighting. It might be argued that these profiles were obtained from biological material deposited via a process of secondary transfer (see later in this chapter) – for example, as a result of biological material from the suspect being transferred from the victim's hand to the victim's blouse after they had shaken hands. In other words, at least two transfer mechanisms could be posited: crime-related intensive contact v. casual business-like contact. For this reason, it was decided to take control samples from places on the blouse where there was no reason to assume the perpetrator would have touched the victim. These yielded no profiles matching the suspect, no profiles at all or (partial) profiles matching the victim. The reasoning behind this approach was that, if the suspect were the perpetrator, the soiled areas were places where he would have touched the blouse in the commission of the crime. Using the standard DNA method (i.e. SGM Plus), matching profiles were to be expected from these samples and none from the control samples, where the perpetrator would not have touched the blouse. If, on the other hand, the biological traces were due to a casual, business-type contact and had been deposited on the blouse through secondary transfer, profiles would either not be obtained anywhere using the standard method, or they would be obtained to the same extent from both types of sample. It should be clear that the findings of the examination are much more plausible under the first of the two possible transfer mechanisms posited (i.e. crime-related intensive contact) than under the second (i.e. casual business contact), thereby lending support to the proposition that the suspect did not merely touch the victim in a casual fashion, as in a businesslike contact but, as Locard (1923) put it, 'avec l'intensité qui suppose l'action criminelle'.[6]

The Putten murder

Although a semen stain found on the thigh of a raped and strangled young woman is not necessarily crime related either, an innocent explanation here is perhaps less easily forthcoming. Yet, in another highly publicized case in the Netherlands, the Putten murder, the prosecution declared a semen stain located in precisely this position to be non-incriminating.

Christel Ambrosius, a 23-year-old flight attendant, was found dead in her grandmother's house. A full nuclear DNA profile was obtained from semen found on the victim's thigh but was declared a non-perpetrator trace by the prosecution when it turned out not to match the profiles of the two main suspects. The men had confessed to raping and killing the woman to the police as well as to the examining judge after they had undergone what later turned out to have been prolonged and somewhat unorthodox questioning by the police. When the men later retracted their confessions both in front of the district court as well as at the appeal court, the police and prosecution stuck to their story. They explained the non-match by arguing that the semen found on the victim's thigh originated from an earlier consensual sexual contact, and that it had been dragged from the victim's vagina to its position on her thigh as a result of the penetration involved in the subsequent involuntary sexual contact with one or both of the suspects.

Largely because it was backed by expert opinion, this argument, which came to be known as the 'drag theory', was accepted by both the district court and the appeal court.[7] The two men were sentenced to ten years' imprisonment. Many years later, the expert retracted his theory, on the grounds that he had not given due consideration to the fact that there was no 'drag trail' on the victim's leg to mark the route the semen had travelled. A retrial was ordered, in which both men were acquitted. They were released in 2002, after serving seven years in prison.

For material traces that are not left at a crime scene but were possibly transferred from the scene by a suspect, a relationship with the incident under investigation tends to be more obvious. A large quantity of glass fragments on a suspect's clothing that are similar to the remnants of glass in a window smashed during a burglary will tend to be taken as an indication that the suspect may have been at the crime scene at the time of the incident (unless, of course, there are plausible alternative explanations for the presence of the glass – e.g. the suspect is a glazier, painter or demolition worker.

If trace material is wrongly attributed to a crime, this may have very serious consequences. An example is the false-positive result of an explosives test that led the prosecution to believe that a number of the suspects in the Birmingham Six case had been handling explosives in the hours before their arrest (see Mullin 1997). Many years later, it was demonstrated that the men may have tested positive because they had been playing cards with a plastic coating before they were arrested.

However important the question of the relationship of traces with a crime may be, this chapter does not address that question but examines how the origin and evidential value of a trace may be determined, irrespective of the existence of a relationship between the trace and a suspected crime.

Individualization: the determination of identity of source

In general, the investigation of a crime focuses on establishing the chain of events that constitutes that crime. The information gathered in this process frequently plays a decisive role in settling the question of guilt and may also influence the nature and magnitude of any sanctions imposed. Primarily, however, the investigation seeks to establish the circumstances of the case, and this is often said to involve answering the seven golden criminalistic 'Wh'-questions. These are questions starting with the words *who, what, where, when, what with, in what way* and, to a lesser extent, *why*. Each of these questions leads, in turn, to a large number of sub-questions. For example, the question *who?* concerns which people may be associated with the crime (i.e. the victim, suspect, witnesses, person reporting the crime, etc.).

Because the answers to these questions require specific, non-legal expertise, these questions may be viewed as criminalistic or forensic questions. A forensic investigation may therefore involve a very wide range of questions, and a significant number of these will focus on the collection and examination of a wide variety of material traces and impression evidence. The analysis of this evidence will involve a large number of forensic methods and techniques. There is, however, one question that all these various forms of forensic examination seek to answer: the origin of the trace material under investigation. Indeed, Kwan (1977), following Kirk (1963a), considers the question of the *identity of source* (i.e. the question of the unique, common origin of objects) as the central question in forensic science.

Identification, classification and individualization

The ultimate form of source attribution is *individualization*: the establishment of an association between a trace and a single unique source. Indeed, the forensic scientist hopes that the traces found will ultimately lead him or her to a single individual or to a single object, to the exclusion of all other possible sources. If two light-to-dark-brown natural fibres and a pink wool fibre from a pair of trousers collected from the suspect's house match those found at the crime scene, as happened in the Putten murder, this evidence may seem to incriminate this suspect. If, however, it is subsequently found that similar fibres are probably quite widely distributed in the area where the incident took place because some years earlier carpets composed of fibres such as these were sold at a local shop, the relevance of these fibres to the investigation would decrease. We would then only be able to conclude that the traces are fibres and that, on the basis of the morphological characteristics observed, they belong to two different classes, each of which comprises all the fibres that have the particular combination of features that defines the class. We would thus have *identified* the traces as fibres and *classified* them as a particular type or subclass of fibre. If, however, we were to be able to demonstrate that the fibres share a unique combination of properties with those found at the crime scene, then we could say – especially because of the combination of the two types of fibre – that we have a strong indication of a link between the suspect and the crime scene. If we can relate a trace to a single, unique source to the exclusion of all other potentially relevant sources, we speak of the 'individualization' of the trace and this, according to Kirk (1963a: 236), is the essence of criminalistics: 'The criminalist does not attempt identification except as a prelude to his real function – that of individualizing. The real aim of all forensic science is to establish individuality, or to approach it as closely as the present state of the science allows. Criminalistics is the science of individualization.'

In the examination of tool marks, shoeprints and firearms, similar situations occur. For example, a shoeprint found at the crime scene may enable us to distinguish the make, type and size of the shoe that left the mark, and therefore to distinguish an Adidas Schwalbe from a Nike Hot Air, but it does not necessarily always show the amount of detail that would enable us to trace the print back to a specific shoe (sole). The examination starts with the identification of the physical evidence as a shoeprint, proceeds to the classification of the type of shoe that caused the mark and may ultimately lead to the individualization of a single, individual and unique shoe.

As already mentioned, the term individualization is primarily associated with Kirk (1963a), who saw this process as the essence of criminalistics. Others, however, such as Kwan (1977) and Inman and Rudin (2000), have pointed out that a forensic analysis does not necessarily lead to individualization: it is sometimes impossible to determine the specific origin of the physical evidence, in which case the forensic scientist will have to confine him or herself to stating a range of possible sources. In many cases, source attribution is not necessary. If the possession of a certain type of object amounts to a criminal offence, the question of the origin of that object is not relevant but, rather, the nature and composition of the object. This is why the analysis of illicit drugs may be confined to establishing that the material is indeed illicit, and why a blood-alcohol test only measures the alcohol concentration in the blood. The question of whether the suspect had a glass of wine and, if so, of what year is not relevant.

Recognition, identification and verification in biometry

In biometry (see Chapter 14, this volume) and in the wider context of pattern recognition, the terms 'identification' and 'verification' are used according to the procedure employed. Identification is used if a person's identity is determined by comparing his or her test sample with the reference samples of *all* persons in the database. In a verification procedure, the test sample is compared only with the reference sample of the person the applicant claims he or she or is thought to be. In either case, it is important to know whether the test material belongs to a member of a population with limited membership (a closed set) or to a member of a population whose size is unknown or indefinitely large (an open class). In criminalistics, both types of populations occur. If we compare a DNA profile from a crime scene with a large collection of profiles in a forensic database, we would be involved in an identification procedure. If, however, we try to establish whether a particular trace originates from a particular suspect by comparing it with reference material from that particular suspect only, we are using a verification procedure. In traditional identification disciplines, such as handwriting or speaker identification (Broeders 1995), verification tends to be the procedure of choice, as the questioned material tends to be compared with the reference material of a single suspect only.

Both the identification and the verification procedures can be applied on an anonymous basis. It is not necessary to know the identity of the person whose fingerprints or handwriting you are examining to find out if they match a particular test sample. This means that the comparison procedure can be 'blind' in the sense that the forensic scientist is unaware of the details of the case so that even a semblance of bias or prosecutorial thinking can be ruled out. It is also possible to compare large numbers of crime scene evidence whose source is unknown with a view to revealing relationships among various incidents, as has been happening for some time now with DNA material in the detection of high-volume crime. For example, burglary scenes may be clustered on the basis of biological material yielding identical profiles of as yet unknown DNA donors. In non-forensic applications, anonymity potentially provides reliable and effective personal identification in a format that complies with regulations for the protection of personal privacy.

In biometric verification procedures, a threshold value is established as a criterion for acceptance or rejection. If the threshold value is reached, the applicant will be accepted; if not, the applicant is rejected. The higher the threshold value, the greater the probability of a legitimate applicant being rejected. Lowering the threshold reduces the number of false rejections, but this also inevitably leads to an increase in the number of non-legitimate applicants being accepted. In identification systems a similar threshold may be used. For an open class, an identification procedure may produce a list of potential candidates ranked in descending order of similarity with the test material. This procedure is typically applied when searching large databases of fingerprints, handwriting samples or speech samples. An additional procedure is therefore subsequently used to decide if any of the candidates qualifies as the donor of the crime scene material.

Relationships between traces and their sources

Traces vary in the way they are related to their source. Often they form part of a larger whole, as in the case of glass, paint, fibre or bullet fragments, or they may arise as a result of the impact of an object on trace bearers. Under this impact, deformations may be created or patterns transferred that mark the origin of the traces, as is also true of impression evidence. For example, the lands and grooves in the barrel of a pistol leave a pattern of parallel striation marks running along the vertical axis of any bullet that is fired through its barrel. (Lands are parallel spiral elevations that are created when grooves are etched into the inside of the barrel of a gun. Lands and grooves cause the bullet to rotate, thereby giving it greater stability in its flight.) The number, nature and direction of the lands and grooves may be used to eliminate certain groups of firearms. There may be four, five or six lands and grooves depending on the firearm make, and they may twist to the left or to the right with reference to the long axis of the barrel. Other parts of the firearm will also tend to leave marks on bullets or cartridge cases, which may be so specific that firearms experts may be able to conclude they were definitely fired with a particular firearm.

Sometimes trace material may allow the national, regional or ethnic origin of an unknown person to be determined, as in the case of written or spoken language material. In other cases, the determination of source concerns the direction and speed of an object, as in the reconstruction of a bullet trajectory or a traffic accident. The analysis of blood-stain patterns in a violent crime may shed light on the place, position or posture of the victim at the time the injury was incurred and, by extension, on crucial issues such as the determination of the manner and cause of death. Analysis of gunshot residue on the victim's clothing, combined with information about the bullet used, may similarly enable the shooting distance to be determined, while an analysis of entry and exit holes in a door, window or clothing, or entrance and exit wounds in body tissue, may allow the shooting direction to be determined.

Apart from the trace bearers, the source material itself may undergo changes after the trace material was created. When such liquids as motor fuel or photo chemicals are mixed, this may give rise to mixtures or blends whose constituent components are hard to determine with any precision after the event. An example of this is the so-called Srebrenica photo film, which emerged entirely transparent from the Dutch Navy Military Intelligence Service developing machine in 1995. The hypothesis that fixative had – inadvertently or otherwise – been added to the developer received some support from the investigation, but it proved impossible to reconstruct the exact composition of the chemicals used.[8]

Traditional forensic identification: the weight of evidence

To determine if physical evidence originates from a particular source or if two or more items of evidence derive from the same common source, a *comparative trace examination* is undertaken. This examination concentrates on the similarities and differences that are to be expected between the trace material and its potential source. The question of how the findings of such a comparative examination are to be reported once the comparison process is completed is one that has always occupied forensic practitioners. Except in fingerprint comparison, the findings of this type of examination do not generally lead exclusively to categorical conclusions. The examination will (as in fingerprint comparisons) show a certain degree of correspondence between questioned material (trace) and reference material (potential source), as well as differences that are not always entirely or necessarily compatible with a common origin. Scales ranging from 1 to 10, from 1 to 7 or from –5 to +5 have been proposed to indicate to what extent the findings support the hypothesis of a common source. Many forensic scientists report their conclusions by means of probability scales, which indicate how (im)probable they consider it for the trace to originate from a particular source.

In recent years, this latter practice has met with increasing opposition on logical grounds, and it is worth noting in this context that the majority of DNA experts do not normally make (positive) source attribution statements about crime-scene DNA samples. However, traditional practitioners still overwhelmingly report their findings as source attribution statements expressed in verbal probability scales. Indeed, the very way in which the police and the judiciary formulate the questions they put to the experts strongly suggests that this is what they expect the experts to be able to do. Depending on the nature of the material submitted, experts do appear quite happy to testify, for example, that a particular signature (probably) was or was not produced by a particular suspect, or that a particular bullet (probably) was or was not fired from a particular firearm.

Verbal or quantitative statements

What controversy there is among practitioners of traditional forensic identification about the way the findings of a forensic examination should be reported tends to concentrate on the use of words *v.* numbers – whether degrees of certainty or probability are better expressed in terms of some range of verbal labels or by means of numbers or percentages. The lack of quantitative data, however, frequently rules out the use of quantifiable parameters, and so verbal statements are by far the most common choice. It is the perceived or estimated *rarity value* (frequency or, in Rose's (2002) terms, typicality) of the similarities observed that determines what item on the probability scale is chosen. If the shared characteristics are held to be (very) rare – and if all relevant differences can be accounted for – this will lead to the conviction that it is (very/extremely) unlikely that the degree of similarity between the questioned material and reference material is purely coincidental, and to the conclusion that the questioned material and the reference material – probably, very probably or with a probability verging on certainty – share a common source.

Although all traditional identification practitioners are aware of the importance of knowing the relative frequency of the features in terms of which questioned material and reference material agree, any frequencies or background statistics they use are almost invariably estimates. Figures based on systematic empirical research are, in most cases, lacking. Autosomal DNA analysis is the one exception to this rule, and it is for this reason that DNA typing is increasingly being held up as a model for other forensic identification disciplines to follow (see Saks and Koehler 2005).

Alternatives to the probability scales: 'consistent with'

Attempts to find alternatives to the probability scales have not always led to greater uniformity, let alone greater accuracy and precision. A favourite term with many forensic scientists is 'consistent with'. Findings (say, in a comparative glass examination) may be reported as 'consistent with' the proposition that trace and reference material have the same source. What remains unclear is how many other traces (in concrete terms, how many other glass fragments) would lead to the same conclusion. The phrasing could therefore rightly be dismissed as highly suggestive, precisely because the latter consideration is not made explicit. As an alternative, the phrase 'not inconsistent with' has been suggested on the grounds that this expresses more appropriately the notion that the identity of the source 'cannot be ruled out'. Other phrases, such as 'could have come from' or 'possibly comes from', are similarly inadequate in that they 1) leave unsaid that there are alternative sources that might reveal – at least – a similar degree of correspondence with the trace material; and 2) do not indicate how numerous these would be. What is lacking in all these cases is a more precise statement of the importance of the similarities and differences observed, preferably on a quantitative basis.

Criticisms of traditional probability scales

In the last ten years or so, the widespread use of statements of the probability of a hypothesis has increasingly been called into question (Evett 1995; Robertson and Vignaux 1995a; for speaker identification, see Broeders 1999; Champod and Meuwly 2000; Rose 2002). The central argument is that a forensic scientist's knowledge may well enable him or her to estimate how likely it is for the physical evidence to take the shape it has, given a particular hypothesis, but that this knowledge does not enable the scientist to pronounce upon the probability of the source of the evidence – i.e. to infer the identity of the source. As a concrete example, the fact that a suspect wears size-14 shoes merely enables us to say that, if he left a shoeprint at the crime scene, it was very probably a size-14. But if we subsequently find a size-14 shoeprint on the crime scene, the shoe size information alone gives us no basis to say that it was the suspect who left it rather than one of the other shoe-size-14 wearers in the area (or beyond). The mere fact that the suspect wears size-14 shoes does not make him more suspect than anybody else with this size shoes. By the same token, the mere fact that we find numerous similarities between the handwriting of the writer of an anonymous bomb-threat letter and the reference material produced by a suspect should not, *on the basis of these similarities alone*, lead us to draw conclusions about the degree of probability that the suspect did in fact write the letter. If we do this, we are guilty of making a fundamental logical error which, in the judicial context, has come to be referred to as the prosecutor's fallacy (Thompson and Schumann 1987), a term which – probably wrongly – suggests that prosecutors are particularly prone to this fallacy. In fact, it is an example of a more general type of error that is often made in the context of probability statements or inverse reasoning, and it has come to be known as the 'fallacy of the transposed conditional'.

For example, although it is correct to say that the street will be wet if it rains long enough, the converse is clearly not true. The single observation that the street is wet does not allow us to infer that it must have been raining. Alternative explanations are possible: the street may have got wet when the police used a water cannon to break up a demonstration, or it is wet because somebody has just been washing his or her car. So we can make a statement about the probability of a particular finding (e.g. a wet street) under a particular hypothesis ('it has been raining') but not about the probability of this same hypothesis merely on the basis of the finding that the street is wet.

Towards a logically correct scale

As we saw in the above example, statements of the probability of a hypothesis are not logically possible on the basis of the findings only. Estimates of the probability of the findings (given a particular hypothesis) are. The latter type of information may therefore provide a basis for a logically correct way of stating the weight of the evidence. This is achieved by means of the likelihood ratio, which is arrived at by calculating the ratio of the probabilities of the evidence for two competing hypotheses – in the context of a criminal case, these are usually the prosecution hypothesis and the alternative, or defence, hypothesis. The figure arrived at can be regarded as a measure of the weight of the evidence. To the extent that the likelihood ratio exceeds 1, the evidence lends greater support to the prosecution hypothesis; to the extent that it is smaller than 1, the evidence supports the alternative (defence) hypothesis.

Suppose a size-14 shoe is worn by one in 30 men and a size-9 shoe by one in 5. The likelihood ratio would then be 30 for the size 14 (the probability of finding a size 14 if the suspect left the mark divided by the probability a random man left the mark – i.e. 1 divided by $1/30 = 30$) and 5 for the size 9 (i.e. 1 divided by $1/5 = 5$). In more concrete terms, this means that the evidential weight of a size-14 match between the suspect's shoe size and the crime scene shoeprint is considerably greater than a size-9 match would be. This makes sense. As there are fewer size-14 wearers than size-9 wearers, all other things being equal, the number of potential candidates for the size-14 print would be smaller, and the occurrence of the match accordingly more significant.

The predictive value of evidence is comparable with the predictive value of a test result, as in a psychological or medical test. The result of a DNA test, an eyewitness line-up or a handwriting examination is therefore essentially similar to that of an HIV test. Unfortunately, the results of medical tests are not always well understood, by doctors and patients alike (Eddy 1982; Gigerenzer 2002; Steurer *et al.* 2002). Suppose a serial monogamist is considering entering into a fresh relationship but his potential partner requires a clean bill of health prior to reciprocating. The man makes an appointment for an HIV test and reports to the testing service some days later for the result. From the brochure he was given when he took the test, he has learnt that the test is extremely sensitive: it will recognize an existing infection in ninety-nine cases out of a hundred. On giving him the result, the doctor says: 'I have good news and bad news. I'm afraid the bad news is that you've tested positive. The good news, is that, apart from high-risk groups, HIV infection is relatively rare in this country.' Even though a positive result increases the probability of HIV infection, it does not do so to the point where it is certain or even probable that the person in question is infected in an absolute sense.

The actual probability of HIV infection is also dependent on the so-called 'prior probability' of infection. For a person who belongs to a risk group or for someone who lives in southern Africa, for example, the prior probability of infection is high, and therefore also the chance that a positive test result is correct. A person who does not belong to a risk group, on the other hand, and whose prior probability is low, is not likely to test positive but if he or she does, this will probably be a false alarm.

The predictive value of a test, therefore, depends on two elements. The first is the quality of the test, often referred to as the diagnostic value of the test. The second is rather less obvious: the prior probability that the person tested for a disease has that disease, or the probability that the person had the disease before the test result was known. The same applies to the result of a forensic test. The comparative examination may reveal a certain amount of similarity between the trace and a possible source. This lends a degree of support to the hypothesis that the shoeprint or finger trace originates from the source. To determine the actual degree of support, we would have to know the diagnostic value of the shoeprint or fingerprint evidence, just as we did in the case of the HIV test. This value is, however, unknown. Moreover, the increase in support is relative: it does not mean that the source attribution hypothesis is probable in absolute terms. To decide whether this is the case, we need to know the prior probability of the shoe or finger leaving the trace, in addition to the weight of the evidence, as expressed in the likelihood ratio.

At present, it is really only for DNA evidence that the diagnostic value can be expressed adequately in quantitative terms. As the frequency of the DNA markers or alleles in various reference populations is known, it is possible to calculate how frequently a particular DNA profile made up of, say, 10 pairs of alleles is expected to occur in a population for which these reference values have been established. In the case of a DNA test we do not normally speak of the diagnostic value but of the likelihood ratio. This, too, is based on the ratio of the probability of a positive result (i.e. finding a matching profile if the biological matter was left by the matching suspect) and the probability of a positive result if the crime scene material was left by someone other than the suspect. In the former case, the probability is 1 (or 100 percent); in the latter, it may be smaller than one in a billion.

In many cases, the correspondence between trace and source will not be perfect. For continuous variables (such as length, weight or the refraction index of glass) which, unlike discrete variables (such as biological gender, blood type or shoe size), do not assume discrete values, there will always be a difference because, in both the trace and the source material, we are dealing with samples that will necessarily deviate somewhat from the true population value (for continuous and discrete variables, and for forensic statistics in general, see Aitken and Taroni 2004). In that case, the number in the numerator of the likelihood ratio is not 1 (or 100 per cent) but, say, .8 (or 80 per cent). The degree of correspondence will then be found on average in 80 per cent of cases when trace and source are identical, or the degree of similarity found will, on average, be 80 per cent for individual cases. The diagnostic value is further determined by the value taken on by the denominator, and this will depend on the probability that the degree of correspondence observed is found in a randomly picked alternative source.

All evidence is probabilistic

It should be clear from the above that neither an expert nor an expert system can provide incontrovertible categorical evidence – i.e. absolute proof that a particular handwriting sample was produced by a particular person or, more generally, that a certain trace originates from a particular source. There is no objective or subjective, scientific or alternative method that will enable us to do this. This holds even for DNA evidence. Even though every individual (barring identical twins, triplets, etc.) is genetically distinct from all other individuals, categorical identification (or, rather, individualization) is not possible because the present method of DNA typing is based on a limited number of class characteristics. Here, too, the only possible statements in a positive sense have a probabilistic character. On the basis of a limited number of observations, we cannot make categorical statements about an open class: a group comprising an indefinitely large membership. The inferential process is one of *induction*. Logically speaking, we can only arrive at a categorical, unique source attribution if we can exclude all alternative sources. In order to do so, we would have to know the entire population of potential sources and that is not, in practice, a feasible option.

The misconception that absolute positive identification evidence can be produced is a result of the way the police and judiciary have traditionally used fingerprint evidence. Although the discriminatory power of fingerprints is very great indeed, there is no method or procedure that will deliver absolute proof that a particular finger mark can be attributed to a particular finger only, and there is, as yet, no scientific method that enables us to calculate how likely this may be in a particular case. If, nevertheless, we do this, we would be reversing the 'if … then' implication discussed earlier in this chapter: we would be making a statement about the probability of the prosecution hypothesis in the light of the findings of the examination, while, logically, we only have data (i.e. the findings of the comparative examination) that will allow a statement of the probability of the findings, given the prosecution hypothesis. In other words, the forensic scientist cannot address $Pr(H \,|\, E)$, where Pr is the probability of a hypothesis (H) given the evidence (E). He or she may, however, address $Pr(E \,|\, H)$, the probability of the evidence (E), given a particular hypothesis (H). Or, as in the case of the shoeprint, the mere fact that the suspect's shoe size (and/or make and model) corresponds with that of the crime scene print does not make him any more suspect than all other men with the same shoe size (and/or make and model). Similarly, the fact that the suspect's DNA profile matches that of the crime scene material does not imply that this material can be attributed to the suspect with absolute certainty. Unlike the case of the shoe print, however, the estimated frequency of a particular profile in the relevant potential perpetrator population may be so small that this finding, combined with other incriminating evidence, may weigh very heavily with the judge or jury. On the other hand, it should always be borne in mind that the possibility of error at any stage of the investigation will limit the value of DNA evidence (Koehler *et al.* 1995; Thompson *et al.* 2003).

A logically correct scale

In response to the logical objections raised about traditional probability scales, a number of proposals have been made in recent years for the introduction of logically correct verbal probability scales (see Sjerps and Biesheuvel 1999). One example is a scale that does not express the probability of a certain hypothesis, given the findings of the forensic examination, but that indicates what degree of support the findings lend to a particular hypothesis. For those occasions when quantification of the results is not possible, this raises the question of what verbal conclusions might be preferable to traditional, logically unsound ones. The British Forensic Science Service uses such formulations as: 'The comparative examination provides ... evidence to support the hypothesis (H_s) that S is the source of the trace (T) material', where the word 'evidence' may preceded by one of the qualifiers 'limited', 'moderate', 'moderately strong', 'strong' or 'very strong' (Evett *et al.* 2000; Champod and Evett 2001). At first this sounds fine, but there is a real danger that these verbal conclusions will also be interpreted as probability statements. Even though the expert is now using a 'logically correct' reporting format, this will not improve the reader's understanding or interpretation of the weight of the evidence. We can only argue that an examination has led to an *increase* or *decrease* in support of a particular hypothesis. If the notion of incremental or decremental support is lacking, the scale will tend to be interpreted as a posterior probability scale, and the unsuspecting reader will very likely equate a conclusion like 'the examination lends very strong support to the proposition that S wrote the letter' with 'the findings of the examination lead to the conclusion that it is very probable that S wrote the letter'.

The Netherlands Forensic Institute (NFI) in The Hague is currently considering a reporting format that seeks to avoid these problems. This format refers explicitly to an alternative hypothesis, and it should not be easily misunderstood as a posterior probability scale. Used primarily in the various forensic identification disciplines, this format is as follows:

The findings of the comparative examination are

equally likely
more likely
much more likely
very much more likely

under the prosecution hypothesis H_p that S is the source of T, as/ than under the defence hypothesis H_d that a random member of the population is the source of the trace material.

In those cases where the forensic scientist arrives at a subjective conviction that the trace material originates from a particular source (as in physical fits of torn paper, or qualitatively superior shoeprints or toolmarks), he or she would still be expressing his or her subjective conviction, but emphasizing that this is precisely that – a subjective conviction, not a scientific fact.

The classical approach: the underlying principles

The traditional forensic process of the inference of identity of source or individualization is based on four principles:

1 The principle of the transfer of evidence.
2 The principle of the divisibility of matter.
3 The uniqueness assumption.
4 The individualization principle.

The last principle, which aims to ascertain the unique identity of a trace, is particularly problematical. As we have seen, logically speaking, the forensic scientist can only make statements about the probability of the evidence given a particular proposition, as happens in forensic DNA analysis. As a result, although criminalistics has had a relatively long and, in many ways, successful history, some of its underlying principles do not stand up to close scientific scrutiny, as appears from such analyses as those by Kwan (1977) and Saks (1998). In spite of their unstable basis, however, these principles have long served to provide forensic practice a degree of scientific legitimacy and respectability. If, on the other hand, traditional forensic identification procedures were demonstrated to lack a sound scientific basis, as has recently been argued perhaps most forcibly by Saks and Koehler (2005), then this would of course reflect upon the scientific status of the entire field.[9]

Uniqueness and identity

Two central notions in criminalistics require some further consideration: uniqueness and identity. From a strictly logical perspective, all objects are unique: two separate objects cannot occupy the same position in time and space. Similarly, no two objects are identical, even though we may not be able to tell them apart. As Wittgenstein (1961) put it: 'roughly speaking, to say of two things that they are identical is nonsense, and to say of one thing that it is identical with itself is to say nothing at all.' At first sight, this would seem the kiss of death for criminalistics – after all, the very purpose of forensic science is that we can say, for example, that a fingermark shows a pattern that is identical to that of the source finger that left it. On closer examination, however, the words 'identical' and 'identity' appear to be ambiguous, to say the least. The sense intended by Wittgenstein is numerical identity: numerically, all objects are unique and different. All entities, by virtue of their very existence, have numerical identity and are numerically distinct. However, objects may be identical in a qualitative sense. A new, mass-produced car, revolver, screwdriver or shoe sole, for example, is numerically different from all other copies of the same make, model and specifications, but, if adequate quality control is maintained, it is qualitatively identical to the other copies in the same production batch or series.

Quantitative identity, then, is descriptive or comparative in nature and it enables us to see an object as belonging to a class with, as yet, a large, undefined membership. Numerical identity, on the other hand, has a referential or definitive character, and it makes it possible for us to refer to a single, specific object: a particular fingermark of an unknown offender or a specific car with a unique chassis number.

Level of analysis for the inference of identity of source

Although the distinction between numerical and quantitative identity is particularly relevant to criminalistics, we are not so much concerned to find out if a trace is unique (in the sense that it has numerical or quantitative identity) as to ascertain whether two traces, or a trace and a reference item, have identity of source. The words 'identical' and 'identity' do not refer to the trace itself, but to its relationship with another object as the source of that trace. The question therefore is not only what the trace material is but also what its source is.

Even though no two objects can ever be completely identical, this term is used regularly in expert reports. In a Dutch publication on fingerprint identification, for example, one possible conclusion is formulated as follows: 'the mark and the reference print are identical and therefore originate from a particular person' (Zeelenberg 1993: 135). Not only will two traces never be exactly the same, but they will also differ in some minor respects, and a trace and its reference material will similarly never be identical, even if they do stem from the same source.

In their book on the interpretation of DNA evidence, Evett and Weir (1998) emphasize that DNA profiles will never be identical either, even if they are obtained from material originating from a single person. DNA profiles may be represented as a set of numbers but, in reality, they are derived from a complex biochemical process in which a certain amount of variation is inevitable. What is meant by the statement that two traces are identical or, more properly, correspond, is that the traces cannot be distinguished *at the level of analysis at which we have decided to look at them*. Or, as Evett and Weir (1998: 239) put it for DNA evidence: 'The fact that we choose to summarize each profile by a set of numbers and that two profiles have the same sets of numbers merely means that they are indistinguishable from each other using the measuring system that we have chosen.'

The notion within forensic science that there is a best level of analysis in the comparative examination of trace material is not new, but it is seldom made explicit. Outside criminalistics, the same principle is at work. It is easier, for example, to recognize the coastline of a country from a plane than from walking along a beach. In this context, Inman and Rudin (2000) have introduced the notion of 'scale of detection' and suggest that this will often be related to the 'scale of manufacture' of the relevant characteristics. Striation marks on bullets or cartridge cases that are hard to distinguish from each other with a comparison microscope will differ beyond recognition when observed with a scanning electron microscope. These differences do not conflict with the proposition that the cartridges were fired by the same pistol because, at the level of observation of the scanning electron microscope, we would not expect to see the reproduction of details.

Tuthill and George (2002: 73) warn of the danger of what they call 'empty magnification': if the amplification is too strong, differences between traces may dominate and similarities may seem to evaporate. Contrary to the familiar notion of a linear or even asymptotic increase in the degree of correspondence observed as a function of more detailed analysis, Uges (pers. comm.) argues that traces with a common origin more frequently show a parabolic or even an upside-down U-shape relationship: beyond a certain level of detail, the analysis will produce more and more differences and the degree of similarity will decrease.

The question, therefore, is not whether the traces are similar but whether they have a common source. Similarity is not necessarily a decisive factor in answering this question. Hairs that have a common source in the sense that they grew on the head of the same person and therefore have identity of source may be very dissimilar indeed. So the critical question in criminalistics is not always that of the identity of a trace as such, nor the qestion of what it is, nor the question of whether it is identical to another trace or even resembles that trace. The real question is that of the identity of source or, as Kirk (1963a: 236) puts it: 'The criminalist is not interested in the similarity of two objects but in their source.'

How trace evidence arises

Before embarking on an exploration of the interpretation of trace material it is useful to look briefly at the mechanisms whereby traces are created – a thorough analysis of the way traces originate may be of considerable importance for the determination of the source of a trace.

The transfer principle: 'every contact leaves a trace'
One of the underlying principles of criminalistics is the notion that, in the commission of both criminal and non-criminal acts, traces will be left. This insight was presumably first formulated by the Frenchman, Edmond Locard, who is universally accepted as one of the founders of criminalistics:

> No one can act with the intensity that the criminal act presupposes without leaving numerous marks in his wake; either the criminal will have left traces of his activity at the scene or, by an inverse action, he will have carried indications of his stay or his action on his body or on his clothing (Locard 1923, trans. author).

What Locard had in mind was presumably the transfer of microscopic traces, such as dust, dirt or nail debris, or fibres left or collected in the commission of violent crimes. However, the transfer principle, as this is now known, is equally applicable to things that can be seen by the naked eye and that arise in the context of less violent crimes. On the other hand, not every act will necessarily yield usable trace material, and trace material present on a large number of trace bearers may pose serious problems to the forensic examiner. This is why it is very important to use a consistent and well reasoned sampling strategy in high-volume DNA analysis in order to ensure the efficient use of resources.

The analysis of contact traces (i.e. latent, patent or plastic impression evidence as widely defined, including fingerprints, tool marks, shoeprints and striation marks on bullets or cartridge cases) is also based on the transfer principle. Here it is not matter that is deposited at or taken away from a scene, but certain patterns or shapes that are transferred from the donor (object) to the recipient (object). In this sense, handwriting and speech could also be regarded as forms of trace evidence because, rather than the content, it is the form of the writing or the speech signal that implies the source. Unlike many other physical traces that may establish an indirect association with a crime, writing and speech often establish a direct relationship between the perpetrator and the criminal act.

Donors and receptors: primary and secondary transfer

As the quotation from Locard suggests, transference may go either way. Therefore the person who leaves trace material at the crime scene may be referred to as the donor of the material, and the person who picks up traces as the receptor. A receptor may subsequently him or herself pass the material collected to a second receptor; in that case we speak of secondary transfer. It is possible, for example, that cell material belonging to person A can be transferred to person C if A and B shake hands and then B shakes hands with C. In a similar fashion, fibres may be transferred from A's clothing to chair B, and thus end up on C's clothing. In principle, forms of tertiary and even quartary transfer may also occur.

The phenomenon described by Locard has come to be known as 'Locard's exchange principle' or the 'transfer principle', and it is viewed as part of transfer theory – a term used to refer to the (almost inevitable) transfer of matter (hairs, fibres, dirt and cell material) and patterns (for contact traces like finger marks or striation marks). These transferences may be used to establish a relationship between a person and a particular time and place. Inman and Rudin (2000: 94) observe that, strictly speaking, the transfer principle is a working hypothesis or axiom: it applies very frequently but it is unclear that it will always apply, as Locard's dictum seems to imply. It would appear to contradict at least one other rule of thumb in forensic work, which says that *absence of evidence is not evidence of absence*: the absence of traces may not be regarded as absolute evidence of the suspect's absence at the crime scene. It may well be that traces were left at or taken from the scene, but that (for whatever reason) these were not collected and were therefore not available for subsequent examination. Moreover, there are actions that, if carried out competently, leave no technically detectable traces, as in the manipulation of digital data (including digital sound and image material).

The principle of the divisibility of matter

Underlying the transfer principle is a more fundamental principle that explains *why* transfer can play such an important role in the generation of traces. Although this principle, as such, is fairly obvious, it is of considerable importance for a thorough understanding of the relationship between the way traces arise and their interpretation. Possibly because it is so obvious, it has taken a long time for this principle to be recognized. The first to do so explicitly were Inman and Rudin (2000: 83–99). In an article entitled 'The origin of evidence', they describe the process of the division of matter and its results as follows: 'Matter divides into smaller component parts when sufficient force is applied. The component parts will acquire characteristics created by the process of division itself and retain physico-chemical properties of the larger piece' (2002: 12).

According to Inman and Rudin, this mechanism has three corollaries that have important implications for the relationship between traces and their sources:

Corollary 1 Some characteristics retained by the smaller pieces are unique to the original item or to the division process. These traits are useful for individualizing all pieces to the original item.

Corollary 2 Some characteristics retained by the smaller pieces are common to the original as well as to other items of similar manufacture. We rely on these traits to classify them.

Corollary 3 Some characteristics from the original item will be lost or changed during or after the moment of division and subsequent dispersal; this confounds the attempt to infer a common source (2002: 12).

Inman and Rudin point out that the principle of the divisibility of matter not only underlies the transfer of traces at the microscopic level but also applies at the macroscopic level. A good example is physical match evidence, which may arise when a piece of paper is torn in half. The rough edges that are created can be regarded as potentially unique features that result from the division process. Together with the characteristics present in the undivided object that are retained in the torn fragments, the rough edges can form the basis for an individualization (i.e. an inference of identity of source). An essential element in this reasoning is the uniqueness assumption (see below) – that replication tests, even with very similar paper, will invariably result in both distinct and distinguishable patterns.

As observed above, the transference of traces is not limited to situations where actual matter is transferred. In many cases, what is transferred is a pattern. For patterns, too, the transfer process itself may interfere with the determination of identity of source because a certain degree of distortion will almost inevitably arise in the transfer process, as in the case of finger marks, ear marks or shoeprints which, as a result of pressure, rotation or movement, will never produce a perfect match with the reference print of the source.

The traditional interpretation of trace evidence

The traditional method of trace identification is based on the assumption that objects may be uniquely identified. In practice, this assumption is frequently regarded as a proven fact. Van der Lugt (2001: 220), writing about the comparative examination of ear marks, has this to offer: 'You need to know and understand the underlying principles. One of these principles is a simple and well accepted one ... All objects in the universe are unique.' Although this assumption may often be used profitably as a working hypothesis for casework, we shall see that it does not, as such provide, an adequate theoretical basis for identification evidence.

Traditionally, forensic scientists have distinguished two types of characteristics in their comparative analyses: class characteristics, which may be used to assign traces to certain categories, and individual characteristics. It is the latter type that are supposed to relate traces to their unique source. A problem here is that it is difficult to formulate objective criteria in order to define a given characteristic as an individual characteristic.

The uniqueness assumption: 'nature never repeats itself'

In addition to the transfer principle, which, combined with the principle of the divisibility of matter, accounts for the creation of traces, there are two more fundamental principles underpinning traditional identification procedures. The first of these lies at the root of the traditional interpretation of traces and says, quite simply, that no two objects are identical. Kirk puts this as follows:

> *Identity* is defined by all philosophical authorities as uniqueness. A thing can be identical only with itself, never with any other object, since all objects in the universe are unique (1963a: 236).
>
> It has been stated that nature never duplicates herself, so that no two objects are ever completely alike. In the most precise terms, this is absolutely true (1953: 9).

Although this statement (as implied by Kirk's appeal to 'philosophical authorities') primarily applies to numerical identity and not to qualitative identity, it nevertheless tends to be interpreted as if it did apply to qualitative identity. Tuthill (1994: 17) and Van der Lugt (2001: 220) reduce Kirk's words to a slogan and state: 'All objects in the universe are unique.' This effectively amounts to the supposition that numerically different objects are not qualitatively identical. No two trees, leaves or ants are the same, no two persons have the same signature or the same fingerprints, no two firearms have the same barrel and no two shards have the same shape. The important implication of this assumption is that all objects can be distinguished in principle (the assumption of discernible uniqueness – see Saks and Koehler 2005). In the words of Kirk and Grunbaum (1968: 289): 'Now most students believe that all items of the universe are in some respect different from other similar items, so that ultimately it may be possible to individualize not only a person but any object of interest. This effort is the heart of criminalistics.'

Perhaps the most useful version so far of the uniqueness assumption is that given by Robertson and Vignaux (1995a: 4): 'Two objects may be indistinguishable but no two objects are identical.' The problem of inference of identity therefore does not so much reside in the theoretical assumption that all objects are unique but in the practical question of whether different objects (more specifically, two traces of different origin) can always be distinguished. Even if we subscribe to the uniqueness assumption and accept that no two fingers have the same friction ridge patterns, it does not even remotely follow that all finger marks can be attributed to the correct finger. And the fact that we do not find differences between separate objects cannot be taken as disproof of the uniqueness assumption. This should, on the other hand, be seen as indicative of the inadequacy of existing discrimination procedures rather than as evidence for the incorrectness or inappropriateness of the principle of uniqueness or individuality.

The individualization principle: 'that cannot be a coincidence'

That the uniqueness principle implies that two traces left by the same object (or a trace and its source) will differ to some extent – as in the case of two signatures by the same person or two marks left by the same finger – is a complicating factor which, at first sight, seems to undermine fatally the explanatory value of this very principle. After all, if every single signature or every single finger mark is unique, how can we ever determine if two signatures or finger marks originate from the same source? The fact that they are all unique does not seem immediately to provide a promising basis. This apparent paradox resolves itself if we consider that it is not so much the unique character of an object but Locard's principle of the transfer of (a unique configuration of) features the trace or trace bearer shares with the source or with another trace from the same source that provides the logical basis for the principle of individualization.

Tuthill (1994) obscures this paradox by applying the uniqueness principle selectively to the source or the traces only, and not to the traces themselves. If all (source) objects have unique features, the traces they produce – which are tacitly assumed to share all these features – can be identified on the basis of these features, so the argument goes. The only question Tuthill, and mainstream criminalists alike, sees is the question of how much similarity must be demonstrable between the trace and the presumed source to be able to decide on individualization. Tuthill's answer (1994: 21) is implied in the classical individualization principle, which says, for example, that an impression mark can be related exclusively to a single source 'by finding agreement of corresponding individual characteristics of such number and significance as to preclude the possibility (or probability) of their having occurred by mere coincidence, and establishing that there are no differences that cannot be accounted for'. As Tuthill indicates, this is a variation on the formulation given by the American handwriting expert, Huber (1959–60). Huber (1959–60: 289) labelled this 'the principle of identification': 'When any two items have characteristics in common of such number and significance as to preclude their simultaneous occurrence by chance, and there are no inexplicable differences, then it may be concluded that they are the same, or from the same source.'

The problem with this approach is that it implies that a criterion ('a sufficient number of characteristics') may be defined that will provide a principled and objective way to determine what the possibility (or probability) that two objects meet this criterion by chance can be excluded (with any differences being accountable). Such a criterion is not only unfeasible (what is 'a sufficient number'?) but also lacks a theoretical basis in that it ignores the induction problem.[10]

Class characteristics and individual characteristics: natural variation and wear

As we have seen, objects that share a number of characteristics constitute an open class, even though there may be differences among them. Kwan (1977) refers to this as the qualitative identity of source: traces that share class characteristics with one another or with a certain source. Objects that share individual characteristics collectively, on the other hand, form a closed set of items, and they all share a common source (e.g. the hairs of one particular person). Kwan calls this the numerical identity of source: the material may be traced back to a single source.

The distinction between class and individual characteristics has traditionally always been made in fingerprint identification where, in addition to similarity in the overall pattern (i.e. in terms of class characteristics), the analysis also focuses on individual characteristics. The overall fingerprint patterns (loops, whorls and arches) are structures formed by what at first sight appear to be parallel ridges on the fingertips and toes, on parts of the palms and on the soles of the feet. The points where these seemingly parallel lines end or split in two potentially qualify as dactyloscopic points or typica.

There are two causes of individual characteristics in traditional forensic science. The first is natural variation and, although the term suggests otherwise, natural variation can account for the presence of (frequently minute) individual differences between mass-produced goods. These minute differences, however, may not always be discernible in the forensic traces objects leave. The second cause is wear. The soles of new shoes of the same make, size and model will, depending on the nature of the material used, show minute variations that will not generally be visible in a print left by the shoe. Once the shoes have seen some wear, in addition to acquiring wear patterns due to the owner's distinct walking style, the soles will incur cuts, tears and gouges that may, to some extent, depend on the use the shoes are put to. Evett et al. (1998: 242) refer to these wear-related features as acquired features. However, as we have already seen, whether a particular feature may be regarded as an individual characteristic is a question that cannot strictly be answered as it requires familiarity with all possible manifestations of the variable within its relevant population – i.e. the population from which the object is assumed to originate.

The fundamental principles of criminalistics revisited

The emergence of DNA evidence has had a major impact on traditional forensic identification practices and on the customers for such evidence – the police and lawyers. As Gigerenzer, Director of the Berlin Max Planck Institute for *Bildungsforschung*, puts it (2002: 183): 'DNA fingerprinting has … put new demands on the legal profession. These include overcoming the illusion of certainty and learning how to understand and communicate uncertainties.' Saks and Koehler (2005) also argue that the emergence of DNA typing as a model for a scientifically defensible approach to questions of shared identity is driving the older forensic sciences towards what they refer to as a new scientific paradigm. The way DNA evidence is presented is indeed very different from what the user of the forensic product is accustomed to. This difference is perhaps most obvious in the way conclusions are formulated in terms of quantitative probabilities, often presented in a frequentist format or within a Bayesian model. Furthermore, the probabilities reported for DNA evidence do not normally directly address the question of whether the suspect can be taken to be the donor of the crime scene material, but state how much more likely or less likely the trace material was left under the hypothesis by the suspect rather than under the hypothesis that it was left by someone else.

What has emerged from the above description of traditional identification procedures is that the premise on which the inference of identity of source is made is similarity or quantitative identity. Kirk (1963b: 368–9 cited by Kwan 1977) tries to resolve the contradiction between the uniqueness assumption and the individualization principle as follows:

> According to an old axiom, nature never reproduces herself exactly; thus no two objects in the universe are ever totally indistinguishable. However, two pieces of the same original object share many properties and are so much alike that, if one piece is of known origin, the origin of the other can be established.

Thornton and Peterson (2002: 149–50, emphasis in original) also discuss the use of class characteristics and individual characteristics for the determination of common origin, if not in an absolute sense:

> In the comparison of physical evidence it is often helpful to make use of the concepts of *class characteristics* and *individual characteristics*. Class characteristics are general characteristics that separate a group of objects from a universe of diverse objects. In a comparison process, class characteristics serve the very useful purpose of screening a large number of items by eliminating from consideration those items that do not share the characteristics common to all the members of that group. Class characteristics do not, and cannot establish uniqueness. Individual characteristics, on the other hand, are those exceptional characteristics that may establish the uniqueness of an object. It should be recognized that an individual characteristic, taken in isolation, might

not in itself be unique. The uniqueness of an object may be established by an ensemble of individual characteristics. A scratch on the surface of a bullet, for example, is not a unique event; it is the arrangement of the scratches on the bullet that mark it as unique.

While this sounds plausible, there is still a major logical problem. Individual characteristics are defined as characteristics that are capable of establishing uniqueness. But uniqueness is defined by a collection of individual characteristics. Whether characteristics are unique is an inductive question, which raises the classic induction problem: we can never be sure that all swans are white until we have seen all swans. Similarly, we can never be sure that a feature or combination of features is unique until we have observed all the relevant objects.

What practitioners of traditional forensic identification sciences really do is perhaps best described by Stoney (1991, emphasis added) who uses the image of the 'leap of faith' as the mechanism whereby the forensic scientist actually establishes individualization:

> When more and more corresponding features are found between the two patterns scientist and lay person alike become subjectively certain that the patterns could not possibly be duplicated by chance. What has happened here is somewhat analogous to a *leap of faith*. It is a jump, an extrapolation, based on the observation of highly variable traits among a few characteristics, and then considering the case of many characteristics … In fingerprint work, we become subjectively convinced of identity; *we do not prove it*.

Dactyloscopists, and all other traditional forensic identification scientists, are ultimately making a subjective judgement in reaching a categorical decision about the identity of source of two traces. They become convinced that the unknown trace and the reference material have the same origin, but there is no logical basis for this conclusion.

The quantification of the frequency of the characteristics involved is often difficult but, even if it is possible (as in the case of DNA typing) and no matter how infrequent we estimate the combined occurrence of the characteristics to be, it will not allow us to individualize – as Stoney so aptly expressed it in the title of his 1991 paper, 'What made us ever think we could individualize using statistics?'

The essence of the individualization problem, therefore, lies in the fact that we cannot avoid induction in inferring identity of source. Logically speaking, we can only arrive at a conclusion of common origin if we can exclude all other sources, and that is impossible. The population from which a finger mark originates is indefinite in size and frequently largely unavailable for examination. The best we can do, therefore, is draw a sample from the potential population and study the distribution of the relevant characteristics. The larger the sample, the more insight we will gain about the distribution of these features and about the probability of finding potential sources who could leave traces that correspond to those of the crime scene. But we will never be able to say, on the basis of a sample only, that we have eliminated all possible sources. This means that, logically, there is no basis for absolute identifications or individualizations. In the words of Champod and Evett (2001:105): 'If we wish to address an open population then probabilistic statements are unavoidable. Indeed, this is the notion of the entire discipline of statistics.' In other words, a population of indefinite size will only allow probabilistic statements.

De Groot (1994: 106, trans. author) observes that single deterministic hypotheses of the type 'all As are B' (all ravens are black' or 'all fingerprints/ears/handwriting styles are different') may be refuted with a single counter-example, but cannot be proved: 'Only by examining the entire universe of A cases can we conclude with certainty that every A is indeed B.' In practice, this is only possible for small closed sets or, in the forensic context, for small source populations.

It is worth noting that, unlike individualization, elimination is based on deductive reasoning, a logical process that leads to a (logically) correct and necessary conclusion. For forensic evidence and for expert evidence in general, this means that, after testing, certain plausible hypotheses or scenarios may be excluded categorically, and certain persons or objects eliminated as sources of a particular trace or as perpetrators. On the other hand, failure to reject a hypothesis should not lead us to infer that the hypothesis has been proved to be true.

Dactyloscopy – the 'positivity doctrine': 'all or nothing'

The fingerprint is one of the oldest and, certainly until recently, by far the most effective forensic means of identification that, over the past century or so, has proved an invaluable arm in the police crime-fighting arsenal.[11] It is, however, also a technique that developed in the practical context of investigative work and it clearly bears the marks of this history. Dactyloscopy was largely developed *by* police officers *for* police officers and what, critics argue, is sadly lacking is a scientific basis for fingerprint identification (see, for example, Saks 1998; Champod and Evett 2001; Cole 2001, to name but a few). Ashbaugh (1999: 4) sums this up as follows:

In the past the friction ridge identification science has been akin to a divine following. Challenges were considered heresy and challengers frequently were accused of chipping at the foundation of the science unnecessarily. This cultish demeanor was fostered by a general deficiency of scientific knowledge, understanding, and self-confidence within the ranks of identification specialists. A pervading fear developed in which any negative aspect voiced that did not support the concept of an exact and infallible science could lead to its destruction and the destruction of the credibility of those supporting it.

The failure of the identification community to challenge or hold meaningful debate can also be partly attributed to the fact that the friction ridge identification science has been basically under the control of the police community rather than the scientific community. In the eyes of many police administrators, friction ridge identification is a tool for solving crime, a technical function, as opposed to a forensic science.

Fingerprint experts differ from almost all other forensic science practitioners in their self-imposed obligation to report absolute identifications and eliminations only (as well as 'inconclusives', if the standard required for identification is not met). Qualified conclusions, such as 'possible' or 'probable', are not allowed under penalty of decertification by the International Association for Identification (IAI), whose membership comprises, in the main, North American fingerprint experts. In 2001 the North American dactyloscopy working group, SWGFAST, (Scientific Working Group on Friction Ridge Analysis, Study and Technology) declared: 'Friction ridge identifications are absolute conclusions. Possible, probable or likely identification conclusions are outside the acceptable limits of the science of friction ridge identification' (McRoberts 2001: 238; see also McRoberts 2004: 346).[12]

Other fingerprint experts are similarly doctrinaire. For example, Zeelenberg (1993: 135), the most authoritative fingerprint expert in the Netherlands, states:

We know that if a finger mark has sufficient quality, we can always state with certainty whether it originates from a particular person. [There are] therefore two conclusions possible:

1 [The fact that] the fingermark has been identified … means … that the mark originates from this person and at the same time cannot originate from anyone else;
2 The mark does not originate from a particular person [sic]. There are then no or insufficient correspondences and there are differences.

Similarly, in an Interpol document released in 2004 and edited by Zeelenberg under the auspices of the European Expert Group on Fingerprint Identification II, the 'positivity doctrine' is vigorously defended. Paragraph 8.13.3 reads: 'Fingerprint evidence should only be stated as absolute and positive conclusions. There is no basis for likely or probable conclusions neither based on statistics nor upon personal judgement.'[13]

The use of a fixed number of dactyloscopic points as an absolute requirement for a fingerprint identification has also come in for considerable criticism in recent years. What empirical research there is, as well as anecdotal evidence, suggests that even very experienced fingerprint experts observe different numbers of dactyloscopic points in the same material (see Evett and Williams 1996). In the Netherlands, the fixed-point requirement is 12 and, in the UK, it was, until mid-2001, 16. However, a decision by the Association of Chief Police Officers (ACPO) has led to the abolition of the UK fixed-number requirement. While the results of the Evett and Williams' (1996) study may have played a role in this decision, it may well also have been taken as a result of the somewhat less orthodox consideration that the abolition of the fixed-number requirement opened the way to declare absolute identifications where this would previously have been impossible (i.e. in those cases where fewer than 16 points were counted but there were no inexplicable differences and the degree of correspondence present was perceived as conclusive).

A major drawback that applies equally to virtually all other forensic identification procedures is the absence of a systematic, principled and logical approach to the question of whether the finger mark and reference exemplar match, and what the meaning of such a match or identification is. Ashbaugh (an opponent of the number of points philosophy) suggests that, in a comparative fingerprint examination, a combination of quantitative and qualitative data should be used (as implied by the title of his 1999 book, *Quantitative-qualitative Friction Ridge Analysis*). A purely quantitative criterion would then be impossible to define. His answer to the question of how much similarity is required for a categorical identification is strongly reminiscent of that of Tuthill discussed earlier:

> A frequently asked question is, 'How much is enough?' The opinion of individualization or identification is subjective. It is an opinion formed by the friction ridge identification specialist based on the friction ridge formations found in agreement during the comparison. The validity of the opinion is coupled with an ability to defend the position, and both are founded in one's personal knowledge, ability, and experience ... but it must be clearly understood that if there is any doubt whether there is sufficient specific detail present to individualize, then an opinion of individualization cannot be formed.
>
> How much is enough? Finding adequate friction ridge formations in sequence that one knows are specific details of the friction skin, and in the opinion of the friction ridge identification specialist that there is sufficient uniqueness within those details to eliminate all other possible donors in the world, is considered enough (Ashbaugh 1999: 103).

Unfortunately, this seems to raise more questions than it answers. The phrase 'sufficient uniqueness' is a case in point. As long as a clear criterion is lacking, dactyloscopy cannot lay claim to the status of a scientific discipline. In fact, an inductive process appears to be at work in which a limited amount of data, in the form of knowledge and experience, is used to make a statement about an entire population. As observed above, such inductive inferences necessarily have a probabilistic character and cannot logically lead to categorical judgements.[14]

In the traditional approach to fingerprint identification, therefore, the probabilistic character of dactyloscopic evidence is ignored twice: first, because all identifications are reported in absolute terms; and secondly, because all evidence that falls short of the required standard (but may nevertheless be highly informative and relevant) is withheld from the judge or jury. And, as we have already seen, unless a qualified judgement is explicitly requested, IAI members risk disciplinary action if they make non-categorical, qualified statements.

Unfortunately, the way in which fingerprint experts present their findings has had a profound effect on the thinking of judges and jury members, as well as on other forensic practitioners. The well-nigh universal application of the so-called 'positivity doctrine' has helped to foster and perpetuate the illusion, both within and outside the forensic arena, that forensic scientific examinations can lead to identifications or, rather, individualizations. As Champod and Evett (2001) point out, this is a misconception. In most forensic investigations we are dealing with an open population of potential offenders, and therefore normally only probabilistic statements will be possible. As Grieve, the editor of the *Journal of Forensic Identification*, said in response to an article by Evett and Williams (1996) about the 16-point rule:

> The argument that any forensic science, particularly the identification process utilized in latent print comparison, is based solely upon deductive logic cannot be substantiated in the face of overwhelming evidence to the contrary. Thus, imposing deductive conclusions of absolute certainty upon the results of an essentially inductive process is a futile attempt to force the square peg into the round hole. As Evett notes, this categorical requirement of absolute certainty has no particular scientific principle but has evolved from a practice shaped more from allegiance to dogma than a foundation in science. Once begun, the assumption of absolute certainty as the only possible conclusion has been maintained by a system of societal indoctrination, not reason, and has achieved such a ritualistic sanctity that even mild suggestions that its premise should be re-examined are instantly regarded as acts of blasphemy. Whatever this may be, it is not science (Grieve 1996: 527–8).

As in virtually all traditional identification procedures, the fingerprint expert comes to his or her decision when he or she has found so many corresponds with such rarity value that the possibility the examination of material from a randomly picked alternative individual or object would yield a similar degree of correspondence is practically non-existent. As Ashbaugh (1999: 109) says: 'there is sufficient uniqueness in the details to eliminate all other possible donors in the world.' From a logical point of view, this line of reasoning is incorrect and, in that sense, unscientific. In fact, the fingerprint expert uses a set of class characteristics and, no matter what statistical sophistication is brought to bear on the situation, these can never, with certainty or even with an absolute degree of probability, lead to a single individual, as DNA evidence shows.

Conclusion

Expert reports may play an essential and sometimes decisive role in settling legal issues both in the criminal and civil context. They may be used by judges and juries to help them determine the facts of a case or to find for one party rather than another. They may, however, also be used to legitimize preconceived convictions that are based on non-scientific evidence. There is a danger, therefore, that forensic expertise (because of its perceived scientific status) may lend an aura of scientific respectability to the legal decision-making process which is not only frequently unjustified but is also at all times undesirable. The legal decision-making process is essentially that – a legal process. Forensic scientists should not be allowed or should not take it upon themselves to usurp the role of the judge but should always be aware that the role of the expert is to pronounce upon the weight of the forensic evidence, not to address the ultimate issue.[15] Unlike traditional reporting formats, the logical model used in the interpretation of DNA evidence is ideally suited to this: it forces the expert to report on the probability of the findings under a particular set of hypotheses and leaves the determination of the probability of the prosecution hypothesis to the judge or jury.

To conclude on a positive note, the critical scrutiny of traditional forensic science procedures is likely to lead to an improved understanding of the nature of scientific evidence, which can eventually only strengthen its position. Despite or rather precisely because of the current critical climate, forensic science is bound to play an increasingly important role in national criminal justice systems, as well as in those associated with international courts and tribunals.

Selected further reading

Aitken, C.G.G. and Taroni, F. (2004) *Statistics and the Evaluation of Evidence for Forensic Scientists* (2nd edn). London: Wiley. A comprehensive introduction to the statistical evaluation of forensic evidence. This book provides a clear explanation of the logical approach to the evaluation and interpretation of trace evidence, such as glass, fibres and DNA.

Broeders, A.P.A. (2006) 'Of earprints, fingerprints, scent dogs, cot deaths and cognitive contamination: a brief look at the present state of play in the forensic arena', *Forensic Science International*, 159: 148–57. A brief but wide-ranging introduction to the underlying assumptions of traditional forensic identification science and to the current debate among forensic practitioners.

Butler, J.M. (2005) *Forensic DNA Typing: Biology, Technology, and Genesis of STR Markers* (2nd edn). Burlington, MA: Elsevier Academic Press. A very comprehensive, well edited, beautifully laid-out and up-to-date treatment of current forensic DNA techniques. This book caters for the needs of the novice as well as the expert.

Faigman, D.L., Kaye, D.H., Saks, M.J., Sanders, J. and Cheng, E.K. (eds) (2006) *Modern Scientific Evidence: Forensics. American Casebook Series* (2006 student edn). St Paul, MN: West Publishing. The two-volume student edition of the four-volume Modern Scientific Evidence (3rd edn, forthcoming) by the same authors. An authoritative and comprehensive introduction to the US law and science of expert testimony.

Inman, K. and Rudin, R. (2000) *Principles and Practice of Criminalistics: The Profession of Forensic Science*. Boca Raton, FL: CRC Press. A stimulating discussion of the underlying principles of forensic science by two prominent DNA experts.

Jackson, A.R.W. and Jackson, J.M. (2004) *Forensic Science*. Harlow: Pearson Education. A comprehensive introduction to forensic science, ranging from the collection of physical evidence to the presentation of findings in a UK court.

Robertson, B. and Vignaux, G.A. (1995) *Investigating Evidence: Evaluating Forensic Science in the Courtroom*. Chichester: Wiley. An introduction to the Bayesian approach to evidence interpretation.

Notes

1 It took Sally Clark, a solicitor from Chester, five years to be cleared of the charge of killing her two baby sons. Forensic experts of various medical persuasions featured prominently both in the first trial and in the later appeal proceedings. What is particularly worrying is the fact that, while expert opinion was clearly divided, this did not stop the jury from finding her guilty, or the judge from administering two life sentences, of which Clark eventually served almost three years. It is now clear that several women suffered a similar fate and that women at the centre of later cases like Trupti Patel and Angela Cannings only narrowly escaped the same fate. Following the acquittal of Angela Cannings early in 2004, a large-scale review of hundreds of cot death convictions was announced. For a brief discussion of some of the forensic aspects of the case, see Richardson (2004). For a full account, see Batt (2004). For details visit www.sallyclark.org.uk or see *R. v. Sally Clark* (2003) EWCA Crim 1020 (case no. 200203824 Y3).

2 The Innocence Project was set up as a non-profit-making legal clinic by Barry C. Scheck and Peter J. Neufeld at the Cardozo Law School of Yeshiva University, New York in 1992. The project only handles cases where post-conviction DNA testing of evidence can yield conclusive proof of innocence. As a clinic, students handle the case work while supervised by a team of attorneys and clinic staff. To date, the project has produced 198 exonerations (see www.innocenceproject.org).

3 Based on case analysis data provided by the Innocence Project, Saks and Koehler (2005) found eyewitness errors in 71 per cent of 86 DNA exoneration cases studied, forensic science testing errors in 63 per cent, police misconduct in 44 per cent, prosecutorial misconduct in 28 per cent and false or misleading testimony by forensic experts in 27 per cent. (Since more than one factor was involved in several cases, the figures do not add up to 100 per cent.)

4 SGM Plus stands for second-generation multiplex, a system for DNA typing that was introduced in forensic casework in 1999.

5 The random match probability is the probability that a random individual who is not related to the suspect has the crime scene profile. It is an estimate of the frequency of occurrence of the profile in the relevant population based on the observed frequency of the markers (alleles) making up the profile in a reference sample of that population.

6 After a series of reports in the Dutch media in late 2005 suggesting that the police had failed to follow up on evidence incriminating an ex-patient of the widow's husband, odd-job-man Michael de J, in an unprecedented move, the Public Prosecutor's Office decided to reopen the investigation, only to conclude that the investigation gave no grounds to end the imprisonment of L.

7 Further support for this scenario was based on the phenomenon of sperm competition, which occurs when sperm from two individuals competes to fertilize eggs. During intercourse, the penis of a more potent male may remove

any semen deposited earlier by a weaker competitor in the female's reproductive tract and replace it with its own (for a detailed treatment, see Birkhead 2000).

8   On 13 July 1995, after the fall of the UN-declared 'safe area' of Srebrenica, a Dutch army lieutenant took pictures in Potocari of nine dead bodies and of the separation of the Bosnian men and women prior to their deportation from Srebrenica. In spite of a ban by the Bosnian Serbs on taking photos, the lieutenant smuggled the film back to the Netherlands. When the film was finally developed, it emerged entirely transparent. A detailed account of the investigation can be found in NIOD (2002: Part IV, ch. 8, s. 4) or at www.213.222.3.5/srebrenica/.

9   The following discussion is based on Tuthill (1994), Inman and Rudin (2000), Faigman et al. (2002), Tuthill and George (2002), Saks and Koehler (2005), Broeders (2006).

10 It is worth noting that, in classical significance testing, a similar, relatively arbitrary and clearly conventional 'coincidence' criterion is used to reject the null hypothesis. Rejection of the null hypothesis takes place if a result is obtained whose probability would be lower than a fixed value (the significance level α) if the null hypothesis were valid, irrespective of the probability of the result under the alternative hypothesis.

11 Burrows and Tarling (2004) found that, while only 3 per cent of all collected tool mark and shoeprint evidence leads to an identification, the score is 25 per cent for fingerprints and 44 per cent for DNA.

12 As with the case of Sally Clark, Detective Constable Shirley McKie was charged with perjury when she denied entering a crime scene where a fingerprint was found that the Scottish Criminal Records Office claimed was hers. Two years later it was pointed out that the latent print did not match the police officer's reference fingerprint and therefore could not be hers (H.M. Advocate v. Detective Constable Shirley McKie; see also www.clpex.com/Articles/McKie). In February 2006, McKie's campaign for rehabilitation ended when she accepted a settlement of £750,000 (Grieve 1999; McKie 2003; www.ShirleyMcKie.com). Similarly, in 2004 Stephen Cowans was released from prison in Boston, MA, after DNA analysis had demonstrated that biological trace material on the baseball hat and sweatshirt of an unknown perpetrator and on a drinking glass used by this same perpetrator could not be Cowans. The three DNA profiles obtained from these objects were identical but they did not match Cowans' profile. It subsequently appeared that a thumb print on the glass which the Boston police had attributed to Cowans did not originate from him either. This fingerprint and an identification from a photo line-up had been the only evidence against him at the time of his conviction. Cowans is the first case in which DNA evidence has led to the release and subsequent exoneration of a suspect whose conviction was based on flawed fingerprint evidence. Cowans, who was convicted for the non-fatal shooting of a police officer with his own gun, spent nearly seven years in prison (Loftus and Cole 2004).

13 An excellent critique of this position is provided by Champod et al. (2004).

14 A more promising approach is that outlined by Champod and Evett (2001) and Champod et al. (2004).

15 For different views on the role of the expert in common law as opposed to continental or civil law systems, see Broeders (2003a, 2003b) and Saks (2003).

References

Aitken, C.G.G. and Taroni, F. (2004) Statistics and the Evaluation of Evidence for Forensic Scientists (2nd edn). Chichester: Wiley.

Ashbaugh, D.R. (1999) *Quantitative-qualitative Friction Ridge Analysis: An Introduction to Basic and Advanced Ridgeology*. Boca Raton, FL: CRC Press.

Batt, J. (2004) *Stolen Innocence: A Mother's Fight for Justice: The Authorised Story of Sally Clark*. London: Ebury Press.

Birkhead, T. (2000) *Promiscuity: An Evolutionary History of Sperm Competition*. London: Faber & Faber.

Broeders, A.P.A. (1995) 'The role of automatic speaker recognition techniques in forensic investigations', in *Proceedings of the XIIIth International Congress of Phonetic Sciences* (Stockholm), 3: 154–61.

Broeders, A.P.A. (1999) 'Some observations on the use of probability scales in forensic identification', *Forensic Linguistics: The International Journal of Speech, Language and the Law*, 6: 228–41.

Broeders, A.P.A. (2003a) Op zoek naar de bron: Over de grondslagen van de criminalistiek en de waarde van het forensisch bewijs. PhD thesis (with a summary in English), Deventer, Kluwer.

Broeders, A.P.A. (2003b) 'The role of the forensic expert in an inquisitorial system', in P.J. van Koppen and S.D. Penrod (eds) *Adversarial versus Inquisitorial Justice: Psychological Perspectives on Criminal Justice Systems*. New York, NY: Plenum.

Broeders, A.P.A. (2006) 'Of earprints, fingerprints, scent dogs, cot deaths and cognitive contamination: a brief look at the present state of play in the forensic arena', *Forensic Science International*, 159: 148–57.

Burrows, J. and Tarling, R. (2004) 'Measuring the impact of forensic science in detecting burglary and autocrime offences', *Science and Justice*, 44: 217–22.

Champod, C. and Evett, I.W. (2001) 'A probabilistic approach to fingerprint evidence', *Journal of Forensic Identification*, 51: 101–22.

Champod, C., Lennard, C., Margot, P. and Stoilovic, M. (2004) *Fingerprints and Other Ridge Skin Impressions*. Boca Raton, FL: CRC Press.

Champod, C. and Meuwly, D. (2000) 'The inference of identity in forensic speaker recognition', *Speech Communication*, 31: 193–203.

Cole, S.A. (2001) *Suspect Identities: A History of Fingerprinting and Criminal Identification*. Cambridge, MA: Harvard University Press.

De Groot, A.D. (1994) *Methodologie* (12th edn). Assen: Van Gorcum.

Eddy, D.M. (1982) 'Probabilistic reasoning in clinical medicine', in D. Kahneman *et al.* (eds) *Judgment under Uncertainty: Heuristics and Biases*. Cambridge: Cambridge University Press.

Evett, I.W. (1995) 'Avoiding the transposed conditional', *Science and Justice*, 35: 127–31.

Evett, I.W., Jackson, G., Lambert, J.A. and McCrossan, S. (2000) 'The impact of the principles of evidence interpretation on the structure and content of statements', *Science and Justice* 40: 233–9.

Evett, I.W., Lambert, J.A. and Buckleton, J.S. (1998) 'A Bayesian approach to interpreting footwear marks in forensic casework', *Science and Justice* 38: 241–7.

Evett, I.W. and Weir, B.S. (1998) *Interpreting DNA Evidence*. Sunderland, MA: Sinauer.

Evett, I.W. and Williams, R.L. (1996) 'A review of the sixteen points fingerprint standard in England and Wales', *Journal of Forensic Identification*, 46: 49–73.

Faigman, D.L., Kaye, D.H., Saks, M.J. and Sanders, J. (2002) *Modern Scientific Evidence: The Law and Science of Expert Testimony*. St Paul, MN: West Publishing.

Gigerenzer, G. (2002) *Calculated Risks: How to Know when Numbers Deceive You*. New York, NY: Simon & Schuster.

Grieve, D.L. (1996) 'Possession of truth', *Journal of Forensic Identification*, 46: 521–8.

Grieve, D.L. (1999) 'Built by many hands', *Journal of Forensic Identification*, 49: 565–79.

Huber, R.A. (1959–60) 'Expert witnesses', *Criminal Law Quarterly*, 2: 276–96.

Inman, K. and Rudin, R. (2000) *Principles and Practice of Criminalistics: The Profession of Forensic Science*. Boca Raton, FL: CRC Press.

Inman, K. and Rudin, R. (2002) 'The origin of evidence', *Forensic Science International*, 126: 11–16.

Kirk, P.L. (1953) *Crime Investigation*. New York, NY: Interscience/Wiley (2nd edn 1985, Malabar, FL: Krieger Publishing).

Kirk, P.L. (1963a) 'The ontogeny of criminalistics', *Journal of Criminal Law, Criminology and Police Science*, 54: 235–8.

Kirk, P.L. (1963b) 'Criminalistics', *Science*, 140: 367–70.

Kirk, P.L. and Grunbaum, B.W. (1968) 'Individuality of blood and its forensic significance', *Legal Medicine Annual*, 289–325.

Koehler, J.J., Chia, A. and Lindsey, S. (1995) 'The random match probability (RMP) in DNA evidence: irrelevant and prejudicial?', *Jurimetrics Journal*, 35: 201–19.

Kwan, Q.Y. (1977) 'Inference of identity of source.' PhD thesis, University of California, Berkeley.

Locard, E. (1923) *Manuel de technique policière*. Paris: Payot.

Loftus, E.F. and Cole, S.A. (2004) 'Contaminated evidence', *Science*, 304: 959.

McKie, I.A.J. (2003) 'There's nane ever fear'd that the truth should be heard but they whom the truth would indite', *Science and Justice*, 43: 161–5.

McRoberts, A.L. (2001) 'Scientific Working Group on Friction Ridge Analysis, Study and Technology', *Journal of Forensic Identification*, 51: 224–98.

McRoberts, AL (2004) 'Scientific Working Group on Friction Ridge Analysis, Study and Technology', *Journal of Forensic Identification*, 54: 342–59.

Mullin, C. (1997) *Error of Judgement: The Truth about the Birmingham Bombings*. Dublin: Poolbeg Press.

NIOD (2002) '"There's nothing on it": a ruined roll of film', in *Srebrenica: a 'Safe' Area*. Amsterdam: Boom.

Richardson, B.A. (2004) 'The Sally Clark case and its implications', *Interfaces*, 38: 6–7.

Robertson, B. and Vignaux, G.A. (1995) *Investigating Evidence: Evaluating Forensic Science in the Courtroom*. Chichester: Wiley.

Rose, P. (2002) *Forensic Speaker Identification*. London: Taylor & Francis.

Saks, M.J. (1998) 'Merlin and Solomon: lessons from the law's formative encounters with forensic identification science', *Hastings Law Journal*, 49: 1069–141.

Saks, M.J. (2003) 'The Dublin trial: expert witnesses in Europe and America', in P.J. van Koppen and S.D. Penrod (eds) *Adversarial versus Inquisitorial Justice: Psychological Perspectives on Criminal Justice Systems*. New York, NY: Plenum.

Saks, M.J. and Koehler, J.J. (2005) 'The coming paradigm shift in forensic identification science', *Science*, 309: 892–5.

Sjerps, M. and Biesheuvel, D.B. (1999) 'The interpretation of conventional and "Bayesian" scales for expressing expert opinion: a small experiment among jurists', *Forensic Linguistics*, 6: 214–27.

Steurer, J., Fischer, J.E., Bachmann, L.M., Koller, M. and ter Riet, G. (2002) 'Communicating accuracy of tests to general practitioners', *British Medical Journal*, 324: 824–6.

Stoney, D.A. (1991) 'What made us ever think we could individualize using statistics?', *Journal of the Forensic Science Society*, 31: 197–9.

Thompson, W.C. and Schumann, E.L. (1987) 'Interpretation of statistical evidence in criminal trials: the prosecutor's fallacy and the defence attorney's fallacy', *Law and Human Behavior*, 11: 167–87.

Thompson, W.C., Taroni, F. and Aitken, C.G.G. (2003) 'How the probability of a false positive affects the value of DNA evidence', *Journal of Forensic Sciences*, 48: 47–54.

Thornton, J.I. and Peterson, J.L. (2002) 'The general assumptions and rationale of forensic identification', in D.L. Faigman *et al.* (eds) *Modern Scientific Evidence: The Law and Science of Expert Testimony*. St Paul, MN: West Publishing.

Tuthill, H. (1994) *Individualization: Principles and Procedures in Criminalistics*. Salem, OR: Lightning Powder Company.

Tuthill, H. and George, G. (2002) *Individualization: Principles and Procedures in Criminalistics* (2nd edn). Jacksonville, FL: Lightning Powder Company.

Van der Lugt, C. (2001) *Earprint Identification*. The Hague: Elsevier.

Wittgenstein, L. (1961) *Tractatus Logico-philosophicus* (trans. P. Spears and B. McGuiness). New York, NY: Humanities Press.

Zeelenberg, A.J. (1993) *Het identificatieproces van dactyloscopische sporen*. The Hague: VUGA.

Chapter 13

Forensic investigation in the UK

Robert Green

Introduction

The main aim of this chapter is to consider what is known about the ways in which forensic science support assists the investigation of volume crime – in particular, the investigation of burglary and vehicle crime – in the 43 police forces of England and Wales. In its course the chapter asks and answers a series of basic questions about the quantity and quality of this assistance. These questions include the following:

- How are scientific support units (SSUs) resourced?
- What proportion of crime scenes are attended and forensically examined?
- What level of forensic material can we expect to recover from crime scenes?
- What are the matching efficiencies of the different types of evidence?
- What investigative output should be derivable from these?
- And what are the factors critical to achieving an effective and efficient level of forensic support?

While the focus of the chapter is on current practice, it begins with a short outline of the historical development of crime scene examination.

Historical background

Until the middle of the last century, and with the exception of highly specialist scientific practice, police detective officers normally carried out the majority of routine trace-evidence collection and fingerprint investigations at scenes of crime. Scientists outside the police service provided more specialist assistance as and when needed. The first forensic laboratory was not established until

1935. Sanctioned by the Commissioner, Lord Trenchard, this laboratory was the brainchild of a Metropolitan Police officer, Cyril Cuthbert. Cuthbert had an interest in the application of science to police investigations and had 'a private collection of scientific apparatus at Scotland Yard' (Fido and Skinner 1999: 95). In the ensuing years, forensic science advanced to the point where, in 1966, the Home Office recommended that:

> in addition to the detective officer in charge of the investigation, all scenes of crimes such as murder, breaking into premises and others where there is a likelihood of fingerprints and/or traces being found (which would assist in detecting the criminal), should be visited by officers skilled in fingerprints, forensic and photographic work (Touche Ross 1987: 7).

The framework within which non-specialist scientific work would be carried out at scenes of crime and the role of the scenes of crime officer (SOCO) were thus established. Some 20 years later, the Home Office commissioned Touche Ross (1987) to undertake a thorough review of forensic support – an area now considered to be a significant element in the investigation of crime, especially serious crime. The key areas studied included scenes of crime departments and fingerprint bureaux, as well as the externally procured forensic services. Touche Ross also scrutinized the provision, financing and structure of the Forensic Science Service (FSS). While their report can be regarded as a milestone in the development of forensic science, it is disheartening to note that, some 19 years on, many of the issues contained within it are only partially resolved or remain unactioned.

Three of the report's key recommendations, however, have had an impact on the organization and staffing of scientific support. The first concerns the recommendation that forces consider the civilianization of their SOCOs. Because those forces that had already civilianized some of their services had encountered no significant difficulties in this, the report suggested that 'a long term aim should be to civilianize all SOCOs [as] civilianization can lead to lower costs and or can free police officers for other operational duties.'[1]

The second key recommendation was the series of proposals for the organization and management of SOCOs. All scientific support departments should have dedicated managers with overall responsibility for this function, in order to standardize its operation across the police service: '[there is] a wide variation in almost every aspect of the organisation and management of scenes of crime. Moreover ... the administration of scientific support, within police forces, is generally inferior with insufficient awareness of the contribution of forensic science' (Touche Ross 1987: 12).

As far as the external provision of forensic science was concerned, Touche Ross (1987) suggested four organizational options for the FSS. To

1 remain within the Home Office;
2 be privatized;
3 be transferred to regional police management; or
4 be transferred to a non-departmental public body.

The report's summary referred to the management of scientific services within the police service (Touche Ross 1987: 38). It recommended the setting up of scientific support units and the appointment of scientific support managers, but recognized that managers should have the appropriate level of support and standing.

The report made specific reference to the provision of fingerprint services. For example, it reviewed the 16-point standard for fingerprint evidence pointing out that the majority of countries have a 12-point requirement for fingerprint identifications and that the UK 16-point standard appeared excessive in comparison. In the event, the 16-point standard was only discontinued some 13 or 14 years later, in 2001. The report also made a number of specific recommendations regarding fingerprints. Among other things, it suggested that more positive steps should be taken to obtain fingerprints from arrested juveniles and cautioned offenders. Significantly, the report's authors recommended that fingerprint officers should be able to achieve expert status within less time than the mandatory five years.

The report went on to suggest that SOCOs should be deployed within individual police forces, their work being co-ordinated by a centrally based scientific support unit manager or management team. In the decades following the report, this model has been realized in various ways. In some instances SOCOs have been devolved to division or basic command unit level, leading some to assert that devolution has resulted in non-standardized practices, low accountability, parochialism and an inability to cope with fluctuations in demand for the service. In addition, it has also been claimed that devolution has reduced the capacity of scientific support managers to influence positively the performance of staff, who may work at dispersed locations under the supervision of police staff who are themselves outside the scientific support structure. The assertion by Touche Ross that SOCOs work most effectively when they are based in divisions close to investigating officers but are co-ordinated and managed centrally has yet to be challenged by subsequent research.

The third important recommendation related to 'appropriate' workloads and the associated levels of performance of individual SOCOs. The report highlighted very significant variations in the workloads of the SOCOs they studied (for example, in the four divisions of one large urban police force, the daily case load per SOCO ranged from a low of four to a high of 17). Although it can be claimed that performance monitoring at the time was rather crude, nevertheless, pressure of work was indeed preventing the proper supervision and management of SOCOs' performance.

The report paved the way for a reconsideration of many aspects of forensic science provision. Most importantly, it laid the foundations for the future funding of (externally provided) forensic support, as well as outlining the organizational options for the FSS. Changes to the 'forensic landscape' now appear settled, with the transformation of the FSS from a Home Office agency to a newly formed government-owned company. Tilley and Ford (1996), however, state that several of the areas suggested by Touche Ross as likely to increase the yields from forensic evidence have not been implemented or have only been partially put into practice.

Since 1987 several other studies have been undertaken of the provision of scientific support, the most important of which was that conducted by the Home Office Police Research group in the mid-1990s. Common themes emerge from this research: a low level of awareness among police officers of forensic science provision and techniques; poor communication; the need to assess the effectiveness of forensic science; and the importance of partnerships – to name but a few. With the benefit of hindsight, the more effective implementation of these findings would have significantly advanced the use of forensic science in both volume and major crimes.

In a review of the police use of forensic science, McCulloch (1996) noted that forces were particularly keen to compare their performance with that of others, but nevertheless pointed to differences in recording practices and missing data. Using data from 1994, McCulloch recommended that a central body should be set up to produce standardized offence categories and definitions for evaluating scores. Furthermore, McCulloch suggested, inter-force comparisons should be made cautiously and selectively. While recommendations are still being voiced several years later, peer group comparison is now well established, with the frequent collection of forensic data by all police forces.

Finally, an important Her Majesty's Inspectorate of Constabulary (HMIC) report (2000) has reiterated the lack of awareness even among senior detectives of Association of Chief Police Officers' (ACPO) policy on forensic science. HMIC reported their frustration about the quality and accuracy of performance data across all aspects of their inspection and criticized the performance data contained in the annual scientific support returns. While in 2002 they accepted that some improvement had occurred since the publication of *Under the Microscope* (2000), some forces were still unable to provide data and, of those that did, the quality was such as to make interpretation unreliable. Concurring with Touche Ross, they recommended that the police should follow guidelines to ensure that proper standards are maintained, and that performance monitoring of scenes of crime and fingerprint personnel should be introduced.

This lack of awareness was re-emphasized by Chief Constable David Coleman who, until recently, held the ACPO portfolio on forensic science. In a speech to the Forensic Science Conference in Newport, Gwent, Coleman posed the question 'do we care enough about forensics?' (Townsley and Laycock 2004). HMIC (2000) have similarly pointed out that the service must face difficulties in finding out what works best, in identifying areas for improvement and in satisfying the demands of best value if data are debatable or missing. In terms of making the best use of forensic science, the HMIC report (2002) highlights that many forces still have great difficulty in turning identifications into detections. Furthermore, they note that timeliness is a matter of concern – timeliness in the significant delays following receipt of the identification and the commencement of the investigative process.

The staffing of scientific support units

In the financial year 2004–5, a total of 4,490 staff were employed in forensic science posts across the police service in England and Wales (annual return data 2005). On 31 March 2004, there were 140,563 full-time equivalent police officers in England and Wales (Christophersen and Cotton 2004). Accepting that a very small number of police officers will also be engaged in forensic duties, the proportion of staff directly employed to undertake forensic work is a little over 3 per cent of the total. Generally speaking, this percentage is the same across all forces.

Figure 13.1 shows the breakdown of forensic staff in England and Wales. From this figure it is clear that most resources are operationally focused. For example, a few forces have chosen not to employ assistant SOCOs to deal with vehicle crimes and with scenes requiring less training and experience. Differences also appear in the degree to which forces have invested in forensic intelligence staff, irrespective of the force's size. Nevertheless, the figure illustrates clearly the dominance of staff engaged in a scenes-of-crime role. This is reasonable in that the forensic process begins with the collection of scientific material from crime scenes. There is, therefore, a significant statistical relationship between crime scenes attended, identifications and detections (from forensic science). The reassurance victims receive from forensic scene attendance should not be underestimated here.

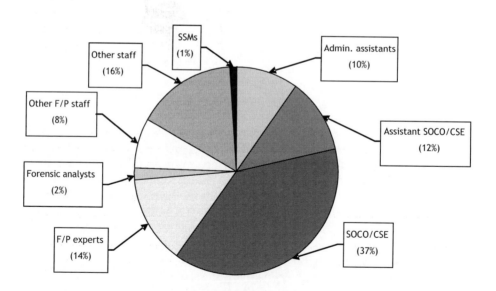

Figure 13.1 Staff engaged in forensic duties (England and Wales, 2004–5)

The volume crime forensic process

An attrition model

The majority of forensic staff assist in the investigation of both serious and volume crimes. A number of attrition models have been proposed for this work, most notably by the FSS in support of the expansion of the National DNA Database (NDNAD) and, more recently, by the Pathfinder Model reported by Burrows *et al.* (2005). This section provides a generic model of the process involved in the forensic investigation of volume crime – the type of investigation that takes up the majority of most SSUs' time and resources. Figure 13.2 represents a simplified outline of this process. The figure shows that the volume crime forensic process begins with attendance at the crime scene and typically ends when DNA, fingerprint or other crime scene evidence can be attributed to an identified suspect. While there may be a number of additional stages in the use of such evidence, the investigative phase of the criminal justice process can be said to end at this point. At each link in the chain there will be attrition: not all scenes attended will result in the recovery of forensic material; not all the material recovered will produce results; not all results will lead to identifications; and not all identifications will be followed up by investigations. This attrition must be managed carefully – there is little point in expending valuable resources if the investigative value of these resources is not optimized.

The next section examines some of the available data on the performance of police forces at each stage of the attrition process. The focus here is on the two most common forms of forensic evidence: biological samples suitable for DNA profiling, and fingermarks. (Footwear is considered in detail later in this chapter.)

Performance

SOCO attendance rates in England and Wales vary to some extent, giving rise to an abnormal data distribution. A median average is therefore used to establish annual SOCO crime-scenes attendance (see Table 13.1). SOCO

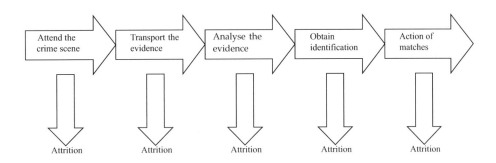

Figure 13.2   The volume crime forensic process

Table 13.1 SOCO crime-scene attendance, 2004–5

Offence type	Attendance rate (median) %
Burglary (dwelling)	88
Burglary (other)	49
Theft of motor vehicle*	49
Theft from motor vehicle	25

Note:
*Not all vehicles will be recovered/are suitable for forensic examination.

attendance rates at dwelling burglaries indicate an average attendance at about five scenes out of every six. Individual force attendance rates, however, vary from a high of 99 per cent to a low of 64 per cent. In one force, for example, the screening policy excludes 36 per cent of scenes from the outset, which means that over 2,000 victims of burglary were not visited.

Attendance rates at vehicle crimes are a function of both the nature of the crime and individual force policy-attendance criteria. In terms of overall vehicle crime, 738,531 offences of theft of and from vehicles were recorded in 2004–05. Of this total, aggravated vehicle taking amounted to 11,121 offences; theft or unauthorized taking of motor vehicles 230,729; and theft from a vehicle 496,681. Some 76,678 offences of vehicle interference and tampering were also recorded.

The most prolific of all vehicle crimes are those categorized as theft from a vehicle. These are followed closely by theft of motor vehicles. In 2001–2 the number of vehicles found after being taken was 69 per cent (Simmons *et al.* 2002).

Attendance policies based on an initial assessment of the crime scene may not be the most effective because of attrition rates in later stages of the forensic process. Thefts from vehicles, for example, have for some time been considered the Cinderella of crime scene attendance yet these offences make up the majority of vehicle crime. How do we know there is little or no evidence to collect? Who makes the decision to task forensic resources, and on what knowledge does he or she base these decisions?

Following attendance, DNA and fingerprints are recovered from volume crime scenes (see Table 13.2). Theft of vehicle scenes are significantly more productive per scene visit than any other volume crime category. However, while vehicle offences are significantly more 'fertile' than all other volume crime scenes, they have significantly lower attendance rates – only one in four of these crime scenes is examined.

If the yield of material is the proportion of scenes visited that result in the collection of forensic material, the forensic process may be measured by a combination of the following:

• *Activity*: what proportion of crime scenes is attended? Does this vary by crime type and/or between BCUs?

Table 13.2 DNA and fingerprint yield, 2004–5

Offence type	Fingerprint yield (median) (%)	DNA yield (median) (%)
Burglary (dwelling)	35	8
Burglary (other)	31	10
Theft of motor vehicle	51	20
Theft from motor vehicle	28	6

Table 13.3 Identification rates, 2004–5

Offence type	Fingerprint identifications (median) (%)	DNA identifications (median) (%)
Burglary (dwelling)	17	36
Burglary (other)	16	44
Theft of motor vehicle	21	37
Theft from motor vehicle	11	47

- *Yield*: having attended the scene, in what proportions is forensic material gathered?

- *Output*: what does this level of collection mean in terms of suspects identified or scenes linked?

- *Investigative outcome*: what is the investigative/intelligence value added by the production of the forensic link? What does it add in terms of offenders brought to justice or the building of a more detailed intelligence picture?

The identification rates in Table 13.3 were calculated from the proportion of those crime scenes where DNA and fingerprint material was gathered. While McCulloch (1996) warns that inter-force comparisons should be made cautiously, these figures do, nevertheless, give a reasonable and conservative estimate of what is achievable.

Following identification, it is necessary to consider the conversion of these identifications to detections. The figures in Table 13.4 represent the conversion rates from those scenes where DNA and fingerprint material was identified. It should be noted that these conversions reflect only primary detections: the total contribution (including all other offences taken into consideration) is far higher than the figures quoted here.

Paradoxically, the most productive scene in terms of investigative contribution appears to be theft from a motor vehicle, followed by burglary (other), burglary (dwelling) and, finally, recovered stolen motor vehicle. While these are not the crime scenes that receive the highest attendance rates, they are the scenes at which examiners are most likely to collect material that can be converted into detections. However, it is one thing to examine the scene,

Table 13.4 Conversion rates, 2004–5

Offence type	Fingerprint conversions (median) (%)	DNA conversions (median) (%)
Burglary (dwelling)	47	56
Burglary (other)	52	59
Theft of motor vehicle	43	34
Theft from motor vehicle	52	78

submit material and obtain a match; it is another to make sure this match is converted into a detection. It is worth while repeating the comments of HMIC (2002):

> Many forces still have a great deal of difficulty in managing the process of turning identifications into detections and this is rooted in a paucity of quality performance. Timeliness is a matter of concern and there are significant delays in most of the forces assessed in commencing an investigation following receipt of the identification.

Questions remain, however, concerning the variable rates at which DNA and fingerprint identifications are converted into detections. While police investigators have very wide discretion over their choices of action, it seems unlikely that this variability can be attributed to this. Why do forensic matches sometimes fail to produce investigative value? And how can we separate discretionary decision-making from other limiting factors? To answer these questions, Barrow (2005) gathered detailed information on the attrition process that occurs between the production of a forensic match and the detection of an offence illuminating.

During the period of Barrow's research, 230 DNA and fingerprint 'packages' were brought to a conclusion. Of these packages, 124 resulted in detections. Of the 106 that had not resulted in detections, the following was established:

- In 26 cases (25 per cent) no further action was taken on the advice of the Crown Prosecution Service (CPS). This represents one in every nine (11 per cent) of the total packages that had been actioned.

- In 32 cases (30 per cent) non-affirmative action was the result of legitimate access. This represents about three in every ten (14 per cent) of the total packages that had been actioned.

- In 15 cases (14 per cent) non-affirmative action was due to 'no crime'. This represents one in every seven (7 per cent) of the total packages that had ben actioned.

- In 33 cases (31 per cent) no further action was taken for unclear reasons. This represents five in every 16 (14 per cent) of the total packages that had been actioned.

This research (summarized in Figure 13.3) provides an insight into the process weaknesses way downstream from the collection of material or the analysis of samples. Rather than accept this attrition at face value, managers should establish the reasons why these cases fail early in the investigative process and should try to account for the variation in performance between BCUs and between individual officers.

Temporal features

The volume crime forensic process should move as quickly as possible from one stage to the next so that the whole process can be completed as speedily as possible. As the Scientific Support Manager for Lincolnshire Police, Michael Carling, comments: 'from the time the crime is reported, we are in a race. A race to attend the scene, find and convey the forensic material, identify and arrest the suspect.' Those who make the decision whether or not to attend a particular scene are expected to follow a maximum (scenes)–minimum (time) procedure. The procedure serves crime scene examiners by giving them the chance to examine the maximum number of scenes possible and by allowing them to get to scenes at the earliest opportunity. On the whole, research has suggested that the more scenes are attended and examined adequately, the more identifications will result, and that there is a reasonable correlation between (volume) scenes attended and primary detections (i.e. the more scenes are attended, the more detections are achieved). It has also been shown that the quicker the scene is examined, the greater the chance of recovering forensic evidence. Speedy attendance is particularly important for vehicle crimes, where the victims often want to repair vehicles as quickly as possible. The service offered to victims is also enhanced if scenes of crime are seen to be examined speedily.

It has been suggested that transporting evidence from the local station to the centre often takes longer than necessary. While the batching of

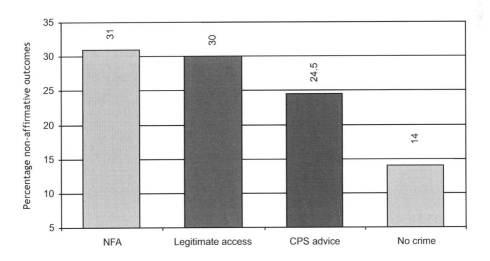

Figure 13.3 Non-affirmative actioning of forensic matches

submissions may be convenient, it can extend the time it takes for samples to arrive for scientific analysis. Once-a-week laboratory submissions have been shown to be inherently inefficient and can, on occasions, cause a six-day delay. Such submissions are now discouraged on the advice of HMIC and the Home Office's Police Standards Unit.

The speed at which forensic outcomes are produced is often a convenient scapegoat for the overall ineffectiveness of the forensic/investigative process. It is not uncommon, for example, for volume crime DNA processes to be completed in five to seven days and fingerprint identifications can be produced in a similar period of time. In order to maximize the benefit of these leads, however, they need to be converted into investigative outcomes promptly on receipt. There is a considerable variation in the time taken by forces to produce intelligence packages, and there can be further delays in passing such packages to police officers for action. In some forces, these packages are put together by centralized intelligence sections within the police service; in others, they are put together by the BCU. From time to time the debate arises as to whether it is better to arrest a suspect rapidly or whether it is better to delay arrest in order to build an 'intelligence picture'. While this is a matter for the investigating officer, in process terms, the quicker the apprehension, the more likely it is to recover stolen property or forensic evidence linking the suspect to the crime.

In practice, therefore, the forensic process may take up to 70 days to complete. For example:

- 1 day to attend the scene.
- 12 days to transport the material to the centre.
- 15 days to analyse the samples.
- 5 days to arrive at an identification.
- 31 days to detain the suspect.

These times are summarized in Figure 13.4, which shows clearly that over half the process time (54 per cent) is taken up by a delay in arresting suspects. It is this stage of the process that perhaps offers the best opportunity for reducing this overall time delay. Indeed, the study on which this section of the chapter is based was able to reduce the overall process to 23 days a reduction of almost 68 per cent.[2]

The use of footwear marks for the investigation of volume crime

It has been argued that the contribution of shoe-mark data to police intelligence, crime detection and prosecution has, for many years, been undervalued (e.g. HMIC 2000). This may be due to the inability to take footwear impressions from suspects in custody and the inability to search these marks against police intelligence databases. More recently, the findings of Home Office research (Rix 2004) suggested the following:

- Most police forces could improve the intelligence and evidence available to them by taking and using shoe-marks more effectively.

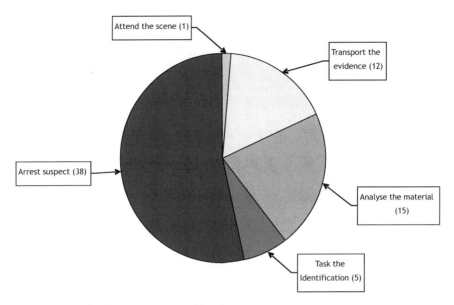

Figure 13.4 The forensic process (days)

- Retrieval rates varied between forces – the best performing force was over ten times more effective than the lowest performing force.

- Shoe-marks were routinely searched against other shoe-mark records in only a minority of forces.

- During the 12-month period of the study (2002–3), forces retrieved shoe-marks from an average of 9 per cent of crime scenes attended by a crime scene examiner.

The same study went on to suggest that shoe-marks have four potential contributions to make to the investigation and detection of crime:

1 Using the marks found at different scenes to link crimes to the same suspect.
2 Providing intelligence for use during interviews so that other crimes can be raised with the suspect.
3 Where an imprint and suspect shoe match, using this as evidence in the prosecution case.
4 Targeting the most prolific offenders. When officers know what shoes prolific offenders wear or have records of their footwear marks, SOCOs can be alerted to watch out for this particular mark.

Figure 13.5 shows the decline in footwear mark recovery between 1998 and 2003 and compared with the patterns for fingerprint and DNA recovery. One reason for the low take-up of footwear marks may be a lack of suspect reference samples. However, the legislative opportunities provided by Part 3 (Police Powers) of the Serious Organized Crime and Police Act 2005 should

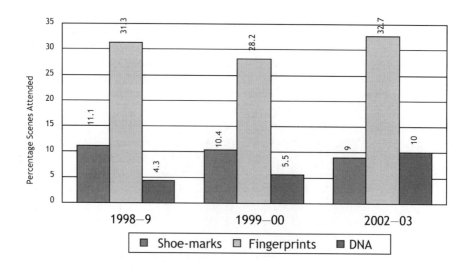

Figure 13.5   Recovery of forensic material
Source: Adapted from Rix (2004)

act as the catalyst to reinvigorate the debate regarding the position and future of footwear intelligence. It is also noticeable that the recovery rates for footwear marks vary widely – more widely than the recovery rates for fingerprints and DNA – between the best and lowest performing forces. Footwear-mark collection at burglary scenes stands at an average of 14.8 per cent or roughly 5 in every 33 scenes attended. Some forces collect material at higher than the national average. Figure 13.5 summarizes these differences in recovery rates from all crime scenes. The median is a little over 9 per cent and, more interestingly, there is a ten-fold variance between the highest-scoring force and the lowest scoring (Rix 2004). Footwear-mark collection, therefore, seems to be concentrated in a small number of forces.

Improving performance

There are four main areas in scientific support operations that have an impact on the productivity of individual officers and, consequently, on the productivity of the units overall. These areas are:

1 *Deployment*: scene examiner attendance policies, and resource allocation and location in relation to peaks in demand.

2 *Effective performance management*: managerial control at all stages of the process.

3 *Effective use of technology*: NDNAD, IDENT 1.

4 *Investigative skills*: officers' differing abilities.

Deployment

First in the order of events are requests for crime scene examinations. What criteria are used in deciding how requests are best answered? Given the contribution forensic science can make to volume crime, limiting scene attendance to particular volume-crime types may be misguided, even though resources may be scarce. Likewise, collection policies may merit a review. For example, non-attendances based on such statements 'this scene is a walk-in theft' or 'the surfaces are damp' are irrelevant nowadays. Offenders do not disappear into thin air and dampness does not preclude a requirement to search for DNA or other forms of contact trace material. Forces that have a rapid and structured attendance response are the ones that invariably get the most evidence.

The way SOCOs are tasked when examining vehicle offences may dramatically affect the recovery of forensic material – ineffective briefing may mislead crime scene examiners into undertaking an inappropriate level of examination. Similarly, an over-reliance on the electronic reporting of vehicle crimes may limit the effectiveness of a forensic examination. Vehicle thefts are often noted and logged at the time of the offence, but the staff manning crime desks and vehicle-crime reporting bureaux have often received little or no forensic-awareness training, even though they are the first point of contact for effective SOCO deployment.

Examination decisions are often based on the category of offence and not on the likelihood of forensic recovery. This may mean that offences normally screened out for SOCO attendance may, in fact, yield valuable forensic clues. Several instances of this have been noted: 'There are serious weaknesses in systems which depend heavily on the judgements of the first officer attending' (Tilley and Ford 1996). Forces that specify a detailed minimum standard of crime scene investigation again generally achieve better results.

Different attendance policies have been noted throughout England and Wales (see, e.g. Taylor and Hirst 1995; ACPO/FSS/Audit Commission 1996; Tilley and Ford 1996). These policies seem to fall broadly into the following categories.

Attend all (target) crimes

There is no screening policy for particular crime types – all crimes are passed to the crime scene examiner. This type of policy may be best suited to forces with lower crime levels, high levels of crime scene examiners or very limited geographical areas. This system may provide the most effective method for deploying forensic resources, but it has to be balanced against the number of crime scene examiners available. Some forces are experimenting with some success with the concept of scene attendance solely by a SOCO. The justification for this is that it releases sworn officers to the conversion end of the forensic process. However, this obviously takes up a considerable amount of SOCO time.

Crime screening by scene examiners

This method depends upon the experienced judgement of competent crime scene examiners. The examiners assess the information in relation to each reported crime and make their own assessment of the benefits of their attendance. This policy may not, however, suit the needs of the force in terms of its crime detection and reduction targets, and it often results in experienced staff devoting their time to call screening/attendance issues. A further concern is that this approach may not be entirely consistent with the tasking and co-ordinating aspects of the National Intelligence Model.

Police officer: first officer attending
This is probably the most common method: all volume crime scenes are attended and the officer routinely conducts a forensic assessment of the scene. In recent years, however, there has been a trend towards central crime reporting, with a reduction in the number of visits to scenes by police officers. This is due largely to the move towards intelligence-led policing and to the need for officers' time to be employed more effectively.

Standardized call scripting
Based on an assessment of the crime type and its location, the caller is asked a series of questions from a checklist (an example is provided in ACPO 2002). These questions range from the very detailed to the fairly superficial. This system can be very effective, providing the assessment and questioning are based on commonly understood principles and not technicalities (for example, 'did the offender enter through a window' rather than 'are there any surfaces around the window that are shiny and non-porous and suitable for a fingerprint examination?'.

Any one of these systems may be appropriate, depending on circumstances, but it is likely that the systems preferred by individual forces have become fixed over time. These may be overdue for a reconsideration – especially in the light of the adoption of the National Intelligence Model.

Performance management

A force's strategic attendance policy must be constantly monitored. In most instances this would fall to the senior scene examiner. These people should report regularly to BCU commanders on the performance of SOCOs. Crime scene examiners are vital to the performance of a force in terms of detected crime. The performance of these individuals is therefore paramount:

• *Performance management*: why does individual performance vary? Why are some SOCOs more likely to obtain a forensic match compared with others? More importantly, how is low performance addressed?

• *Managing the output*: what investigative value is derived from the forensic product? Why does this vary between individuals and between BCUs?

• *Managing the speed of whole process*: What is the impact of the speed of forensic/investigative processes on the offending rates of prolific and persistent offenders (see Leary and Pease 2003).

Effective use of technology

The DNA Expansion Programme commenced in April 2000. Its aim was to supply funding to the police forces in England and Wales so that they could take DNA samples from all known offenders. The project also delivered support to enable the collection of more DNA material left at crime scenes.

The DNA Expansion Programme has made possible a four-fold increase in DNA detections. The annual number of direct DNA detections has more than doubled, from 8,612 in 1999–2000 to 19,873 in 2004–05 (DNA Expansion Programme 2005). In round numbers, each month the DNA database supplies the police with around 3,000 matches. Roughly speaking there were 40,000 matches in 2004–5 (about 109 DNA matches per day) – a figure that testifies to the imagination of all those who were instrumental in the development of DNA as a crime-fighting tool. Over the course of the programme, the number of crime scenes examined increased from 904,560 in 1999–2000 to 995,180 in 2003–4. In 2004–5 the number of scene examinations was 913,717. Although this indicates a decline of 8 per cent, this is consistent with a 7 per cent fall in recorded crime between 2003–4 and 2004–5. The DNA Expansion Programme (2005) investigated 620 cases where a DNA match had been reported. Fifty-eight per cent were noted as detected. Of the 42 per cent that were not detected, one third were still ongoing and therefore could become detected crimes. In 58 per cent of all detected cases, the DNA match was the first link to the offender. In order to get the most from the investment in automated fingerprint technologies, a fundamental review of working practices, shift patterns and demand should be undertaken. For instance, there may be little point in investing in Livescan (with its ability to match suspects' prints with those found at crime scenes) unless real-time identifications can be made. Matching demand with supply is often not well served by traditional working practices and shift patterns: policing is a 24-hour activity and scientific support, in its widest sense, is also required around the clock. Real-time identification, therefore, should be followed by real-time investigation and, where appropriate, arrest.

Investigative skills

Some forces (for example, West Yorkshire Police) have created 'converter teams' that take direct responsibility for forensic identifications. These teams attempt to convert all volume crime forensic output into detections and, hence, convictions. The officers in these teams become skilled in the structured disclosure of scientific links when suspects are being interviewed, but specialist teams such as these may de-skill the general patrol officer who may be required to deal with forensic packages from time to time. Dedicated converter teams may, however, not be appropriate for quiet BCUs but they may have a role to play for those BCUs that wish to pool their resources.

In actioning forensic output, queuing is important: the length of time a forensic match must wait before it is actioned by investigators.

If there are too few investigators to action matches, the number of products in the system will grow. This will have an adverse effect on the detection and arrest of prolific offenders. How long it takes for each forensic package to be converted from output to an investigative outcome, however, can be quantified – we should be able to predict the arrival of a given number of matches per unit of time and schedule accordingly.

It is now well established that suspects should be handled correctly right from the start. For example, where appropriate, suspected burglars should have their clothing, footwear and hair examined immediately upon arrest. Similarly, scientific support specialists should be consulted when preplanned arrests are envisaged. Likewise, consideration should be given prior to executing searches as to what forensic material should be recovered. Forces should ensure that all those charged with or reported for, recordable offences are given DNA mouth-swabs, have their fingerprints taken and are photographed.

Conclusion

There have been many criticisms of the police's performance in the collection and use of fingerprints and DNA profiles in support of volume crime investigation. The figures provided in previous sections of this chapter, however, can be used to demonstrate the impact of the forensic process on the investigation of volume crime nationally – at least as far as these particular forensic technologies are concerned. The national crime statistics for England and Wales for the 12-month period to 31 March 2004 indicate that there were 402,333 recorded offences of dwelling burglaries, 290,657 thefts of vehicles and 598,514 thefts from vehicles (http://www.crimestatistics.org.uk). Of the dwelling burglaries reported, 88 per cent were attended. DNA and fingerprint evidence was collected in 43 per cent of these attendances. Of the thefts of vehicles reported, 49 per cent were attended. DNA and fingerprint evidence was collected in 71 per cent of these attendances (not all vehicles were found). Of the thefts from vehicles reported, 25 per cent were attended. DNA and fingerprint evidence was collected in 32 per cent of these attendances.

These statistics suggest that most forces could improve their performance. For example, simply increasing the percentage of crime scenes attended would improve the number of matches obtained and, hence, the ability to link scenes of crime together. Improving the response time and briefing SOCOs thoroughly before they attend a crime scene may similarly improve the quality and quantity of the evidence collected.

The value of this kind of information should not be underestimated. At present, forensic science is often not considered to be a pivotal component of policing. For example, at a strategic level forensic science does not seem to be included in routine assessments of a force's business – a fact that seems to contradict the calls the public make on the service. The challenge for policing is to move forensic science to centre-stage so that it is part of service delivery at a strategic level. This will require some fundamental questions to be answered. For example, is the resourcing level for forensic science correct when only around 3 per cent of a force's resources are devoted to it? Are the right levels of resources available to guarantee the maximum benefit from the forensic matches delivered? These and similar questions may give direction in the years to come to policy deliberations about the future of forensic support.

Notes

1 Not all forces have followed this recommendation. Some forces continue to have a mix of civilian and sworn-officer SOCOs, arguing that trained policing skills enhance the work of SOCOs. However, others argue that the skills of sworn officers are more effectively deployed in the effort to convert forensic intelligence into investigative outcomes. The Professionalizing Investigative Practice (PIP) initiative may provide an opportunity for better informed deliberations on this issue.
2 In 2004, the Home Office commissioned a performance improvement work package for maximizing the effectiveness and efficiency of forensic processes. This work package was based on a computer simulation model and was developed by Lanner Group Ltd. It will be implemented in all UK SSUs.

References

ACPO (2002) *Investigation of Volume Crime Manual*. London: Association of Chief Police Officers.

ACPO/FSS/Audit Commission (1996) *Using Forensic Science Effectively*. London: HMSO.

Barrow, K. (2005) *Study into Forensic Intelligence Packages – Process Flow Case Study*. London: Home Office.

Burrows *et al.* (2005) *The Forensic Science Pathfinder Project Evaluating Increased Forensic Activity in Two English Police Forces*. Online Report 46/05. London: Home Office.

Christophersen and Cotton (2004) *Police Service Strength in England and Wales*. London: Home Office.

DNA Expansion Programme (2005) *Report*. London: Home Office.

Fido, M. and Skinner, K. (1999) *The Official Encyclopaedia of Scotland Yard*. London: Virgin.

Her Majesty's Inspectorate of Constabulary (2000) *Under the Microscope: Thematic Inspection Report on Scientific and Technical Support*. London: Home Office.

Her Majesty's Inspectorate of Constabulary (2002) *Under the Microscope Refocused: A Revisit to the Thematic Inspection Report on Scientific and Technical Support*. London: Home Office.

Leary, D. and Pease, K. (2003) *DNA and the Active Criminal Population*. London: University College London, Jill Dando Institute of Crime Science.

McCulloch, H. (1996) *Police Use of Forensic Science*. London: Home Office Police Research Group.

Rix, B. (2004) *The Contribution of Shoe-mark Data to Police Intelligence, Crime Detection and Prosecution*. London: Home Office.

Simmons, J. *et al.* (2002) *Crime in England and Wales*. London: Home Office.

Taylor, M. and Hirst, J. (1995) *Initial Scene Visits to House Burglaries*. London: Home Office.

Tilley, N. and Ford, A. (1996) *Forensic Science and Crime Scene Investigation*. London: Home Office.

Touche Ross (1987) *Review of Scientific Support for the Police. Volumes I–III*. London: Home Office.

Townsley, M. and Laycock, G. (eds) (2004) *Forensic Science Conference Proceedings 17, 19 May 2004*. London: Home Office.

Chapter 14

Trace biometrics and criminal investigations

Robin Williams and Paul Johnson

Introduction

> [T]he expanding use of scientific expertise in criminal process is (in both senses) a progressive and irresistible fact of modern life, and […] its impact is likely only to increase for the foreseeable future. Criminal proceedings inevitably reflect their broader social environment (as well as helping to shape that social context in some measure), so it is hardly surprising that, as science and technology have come to exert a pervasive influence on all aspects of modern society, their forensic applications have undergone a correspondingly rapid expansion (Roberts 2002: 254–255).

There is a growing academic literature on the varied, complex and recursive relationships between expert scientific practice and the administration of justice. Prominent recent examples include Roberts and Willmore (1993), Lynch and Jasanoff (1998), Cole (2001), Redmayne (2001), Thompson (2001), Roberts (2002), Faigman *et al.* (2004), Jasanoff (1995; 2004), Lazer (2004). Taken together, these studies constitute a significant contribution to a general understanding of the embrace of science and technology by state agencies in many criminal jurisdictions and of the (often contested) trajectories of the deployment of particular forensic innovations and expertise within criminal justice institutions. However, despite the scholarly interrogation of many scientific, social, legal and ethical issues raised by such an embrace, the predominant focus of this work has been on the deployment and disputation of scientific evidence and expertise within court proceedings.

Another body of literature exists – often called 'criminalistics' in the USA, but more contestably referenced as 'crime scene science', 'crime scene examination' or 'forensic investigation' in the UK – which documents, evaluates and extends the ways in which forensic science disciplines are deployed in efforts to detect crime. The recent and rapid global growth in tertiary education courses in forensic science has fuelled the demand for this

357

instructional literature, both in the dominant form of summary texts, and as research papers and monographs.[1] The main contribution of these teaching and/or research materials has been the provision of detailed accounts of the technical procedures for finding and recovering specific evidence types from scenes of crime (where 'scenes of crime' refers both to the physical environment within which crime relevant actions have taken place and to the bodies, clothes and other material objects relating to victims, suspects and witnesses), alongside commentaries on the scope, validity and reliability of existing or novel methodologies for their visualization and analysis.

Both kinds of work briefly described above provide essential accounts of certain aspects of specific forensic sciences and technologies. However, their focus on the techniques for the production of forensic artefacts, the analysis of such artefacts in laboratories or their final deployment as evidence in courtroom deliberations has meant that they have not contributed to an understanding of the diverse practical ways in which police investigators make use of the wide variety of forensic science disciplines and their associated technologies in the course of both routine and exceptional criminal inquiries. In the main, these studies have not provided any systematic consideration of the temporally and organizationally varied operational uses to which specific technologies are put but, rather, have described their uses in exemplary, prominent, innovative or asserted 'typical' cases. Outline descriptions of what is, and might be, done can be found in a variety of manuals and handbooks designed to encourage or shape the work of both forensic and police investigators.[2] Yet, while such materials are important sources of practical advice to such investigators, their mixture of normative and factual assertions is not derived from a body of rigorously interrogated and directly examinable research data on investigative practice. Equally, while the manner and consequences of the actual uses of forensic science and technology are subject to various forms of professional accountability, performance management and organizational audit, neither the goals nor the methodologies of such scrutiny are necessarily consistent with the standards that inform contemporary social research.

In fact there is a paucity of any detailed data on how specific kinds of forensic resources are actually used by investigators to provide actionable information to direct and support efforts to detect particular instances of crime, regardless of whether or not these uses eventuate in the presentation of physical evidence in the course of a criminal prosecution.[3] This research deficit is all the more remarkable since it exists despite the increasingly frequent assertions of many police commentators of the ability of forensic science to resolve uncertainties by reducing the reliance of investigators and prosecutors on more subjective, less robust, and more easily contestable forms of evidence.

While such assertions of 'closure' and 'authoritative certainty', associated with what Ericson and Shearing (1986) have called the 'scientification of police work', may exaggerate what the collection and interpretation of physical evidence may provide in any individual case, there is clearly a wide range of ways in which such evidence might reduce important uncertainties in individual cases and, in this way, provide support for particular investigative actions. These supports include, at least: the establishment of the identity of victims and suspects; the capacity to infer the presence and sequential actions of individuals at crime scenes; the corroboration or falsification of suspect, witness and victim statements; and the assessment of the significance and promise of alternative lines of inquiry (Townley and Ede 2004: 6). Certainly the growth in financial and human investments in the application of these resources to a rising number and variety of criminal investigations in the UK and elsewhere[4] have rested, in part, on the growth in confidence that forensic science and technology can deliver such benefits. The UK's leading position in many of these global developments is largely attributable to the fact that a number of interconnected state, academic, scientific and commercial institutions have enthusiastically supported and facilitated substantial increases in government investments in forensic science as a central element of contemporary crime control policies.

Significant liaisons have developed between policy-makers, academics, operational scientists, private companies and the police, in the course of which persuasive cases have been made for supporting a range of forensic science initiatives and developments.[5] At the operational level, three national policing organizations – the Association of Chief Police Officers (ACPO), Her Majesty's Inspectorate of Constabulary (HMIC) and the Police Standards Unit (PSU) of the Home Office – have also made significant efforts to challenge and develop existing force practices in the routine and exceptional uses of forensic science in the investigation of both volume and serious crime.[6] Additionally, both the near-monopoly supplier of forensic science services to the police (the Forensic Science Service) and the agency currently responsible for the delivery of police training, including forensic training (Centrex), have participated alongside these other bodies in a range of initiatives to raise both the quality of forensic science support and the awareness of the potential benefits of this support within the police service.

Since July 2002, many of these policy and operational areas have been brought together through the establishment of the Police Science and Technology Strategy Group which has the responsibility to provide the Home Secretary with 'advice on the overall strategic management and funding of science and technology in support of policing' (Home Office 2004: 39). Described as a 'partnership between central Government, the police service, police authorities, industry and academia' (Home Office 2004: 2), the group is chaired by the Director of Policing Policy at the Home Office. It includes among its membership senior Home Office postholders; four ACPO portfolio holders (for 'information management', 'forensic science', 'research and development' and 'technical support'); representatives from a number of specialist national police operational inspection and educational agencies; the Chief Executive Officer of the Forensic Science Service; and two 'independents' from external scientific organizations. The strategy developed by the group encompasses more than forensic science (it includes 'technical support, information management and information technology') since its purpose is to consider the whole range of new technologies used in policing. Nevertheless, forensic science remains at the core of its remit and, accordingly, several forensic science and technology developments (especially in DNA and fingerprinting technologies) have figured prominently in the two annual reviews published since its inception.[7]

Each of the UK stakeholder groups and agencies listed above seeks to shape the uses of existing and emergent forensic technologies in support of criminal investigations (and, in turn, their contribution to crime reduction). However, none of them has yet undertaken or encouraged any detailed analysis of the varied historical trajectories within which such efforts have been undertaken before or elsewhere. Nor have they systematically considered the ways in which new uses of such technologies further effect the development of the technologies themselves, or how their uses both reflect and reconstitute understandings of the subjects whose actions these technologies seek to assist or capture. For the influential members of the Police Science and Technology Strategy Group, for example, social science research in this socio-technical domain should be about the 'human and social factors that are essential to the effective use of science and technology' (Home Office 2004: 6), and this limited view is commonly encountered in many other relevant publications by ACPO and HMIC.[8] However, this remit for social science research constrains rather than facilitates the take-up of available scholarship and research. It fails to encourage consideration of the wider significance of changing political, social and cultural configurations, and its reiteration of the audit theme of 'effectiveness' reflects a particular, and relatively narrow, approach to understanding the relationship of technology to policing in general, and forensic technology to investigative work in particular.

In this chapter, we challenge this narrow understanding of the scope and significance of human science research and scholarship for an understanding of forensic science, and encourage a wider consideration of the relationship between the achievements of forensic scientists and the ambitions of criminal investigators. We do this in relation to only one area of common interest between these two groups, albeit a vital one: the achievement of human identification within investigations. Modern policing relies upon technologies of human identification – both to corroborate the identity of present individuals and to infer the identity of absent suspects – and the history of policing is, as Caplan and Torpey note, 'the source of repeated efforts to rationalize and standardize practices of identification and the systems for storage and retrieval of the expanding documentation this generated' (2001: 9). Yet, while the practical ability to determine and record individuality is rightly recognized to be central to policing, and while identity archives are justifiably celebrated, what is underappreciated is both the ways in which technological developments have been shaped by the practical requirements of policing and, conversely, the ways in which policing itself is shaped by the use of these technologies.[9]

In the following parts of this chapter, we consider the ways in which novel methods for capturing the unique characteristics of the bodies of individual subjects, particularly though the collection of the traces of those bodies left by offenders during the commission of criminal acts, may serve both to enhance and reshape existing methods of criminal investigation. In particular, we focus our attention on the deployment of two particular trace biometric technologies used to infer individual identity from materials recovered from scenes of crime: fingerprinting and DNA profiling.

Recovering physical evidence from scenes of crime

A range of operational and academic authorities have asserted for some years that more evidence is potentially available at crime scenes – including volume crime scenes – than is currently collected. North American criminalistics texts are particularly apt to make this kind of claim, alongside criticism of the continuing lack of interest shown by police investigators in such evidence. For example, in a discussion of the successful prosecution of burglary offenders, Lyman (1999: 360) comments that '[e]xperience has shown that most burglars are convicted on circumstantial evidence. Therefore any physical evidence located on the burglary crime scene will be critical to the case'. Similarly, Osterburg and Ward write that:

> For the purposes of identifying perpetrators and making a case that will hold up in court, a wealth of physical evidence is usually available. Unfortunately, for a variety of reasons, crime scene searches are conducted in only a few cases … Research indicates that most crime scenes contain much more physical evidence than is discovered (2000: 523).

In contrast to these (and similar recent UK texts such as Jackson and Jackson 2004, Langford *et. al.* 2005 and Pepper 2005), social science studies of crime investigation have tended to be more pessimistic about the effectiveness of forensic contributions to the investigation of volume crime. Ericson's (1981) pioneering study of the work of detectives in a Canadian municipal police force examined 295 cases, including 179 cases of property crime, and he (or the detectives he studied) showed limited interest in the production and use of forensic information. Thus according to his account, 86 per cent of the total cases 'involved no physical clues whatsoever' and fingerprint evidence existed in only 1 per cent of cases. When physical evidence was available it was used in about a quarter of such cases 'mainly to assist in identifying a suspect, inducing a confession, and/or as evidence in court' (Ericson 1981: 92, fn. 9). Ericson's detectives argued that its contribution to investigation was much less significant than information provided by uniformed officers, informants and victims.

A later British study of Devon and Cornwall Constabulary (Morgan 1990: 86–9) suggested that fingerprint examinations at scenes of crime (including all crimes) resulted in identifications in about 5 per cent of cases, and characterized its contribution as numerically insignificant since it was 'used' in less than 1 per cent of serious cases. Finally, Coupe and Griffiths' (1996: 38) study of residential burglary investigations by the West Midlands Police confidently asserted that 'Visits by SOCO to burglary victim homes were neither cost-effective, nor did they appear to improve the victims' regard for the police'. The authors reported that 'SOCOs visited the site of about 90% of all the burglaries that were committed. However, forensic evidence was found and tested in only 9 per cent (470) of the c. 5200 burglaries that were visited and it proved useful in under 1 per cent' (1996: 18).[10]

It is against these alternating background assertions that many UK initiatives have been designed to improve the practices of crime scene examination and forensic science support. In particular, there have been efforts to increase the collection of trace artefacts at scenes of crime, to improve the accuracy and speed of their analysis, and to encourage the informed uses of analytical results by investigators. These issues have constantly been engaged in a range of major external reviews of the police use of forensic science (including Touche Ross 1987; Audit Commission 1993; House of Lords Select Committee on Science and Technology 1993; Roberts and Willmore 1993). Several of these early reviews balanced the optimism of the American criminalists with the pessimism of the empirical researchers, largely by commending the willingness of police forces to 'harness the power of science to beat crime', while being critical of aspects of the current methods for the delivery, organization and monitoring of such scientific support.

In response to such observations, several Home Office-funded studies of scientific support to crime investigation published in the mid-1990s (notably McCulloch 1996; Tilley and Ford 1996) undertook more systematic evidence-based examinations of the uses made of forensic information and expertise within the police service. These studies played a central role in advancing the general understanding of the forensic process in crime investigation and were also used to promote 'good practice' in the collection and utilization of forensic information for intelligence and evidential purposes (especially in the ACPO/FSS/Audit Commission Report 1996).

A further substantial number of evaluative studies have shared an underlying commitment to the further development of a model of investigative process and performance (e.g. McCulloch and Tilley 2000; DNA Expansion Programme Evaluation Group 2001; MHB 2001; Burrows *et. al.* 2005; Home Office 2001a, 2001b, 2005). In addition to these, regular HMIC force and basic command unit (BCU) inspections have drawn on and interpreted a restricted range of data on scientific support activity as part of their more general evaluations of force and divisional performance (see Her Majesty's Inspectorate of Constabulary 2002 for a summary statement of emerging findings from the former). Finally, a recent HMIC thematic on scientific and technical support to the detection and reduction of volume crime (Her Majesty's Inspectorate of Constabulary 2000) has been especially influential in further extending critical consideration of this aspect of policing.

The examination of crime scenes: an 'improvised' practice

In order to assess the significance, validity and importance of the varied assertions made by the studies listed above it is crucial to consider the practical aspects of crime scene work. Crime scene examination is achieved through the preservation and construction of a series of physical artefacts alongside a contemporaneous written record of observations made and actions taken during the examination. Any subsequent examinations and interrogations of these artefacts and records are undertaken by other forensic experts (and subsequently by other actors and agencies) against a background of tacit knowledge about the activity of crime scene examination in general and the relevance of particular kinds of information to the trajectory of investigation and the development of a prosecution case. This means that examiners are required to be simultaneously attentive to a series of considerations that relate to their conduct, including the technical adequacy of their search, collection and preservation practices; the organizational adequacy of their records of attendance and actions at the scene; the investigative adequacy of their interpretations of the nature and significance of particular instances of physical evidence; and the legal adequacy of the methods used for the conduct of the examination and the recovery of relevant material artefacts.

A central impulse underlying both routine and exceptional scene examination practice is an orientation to 'reconstruct' the sequence of events that occurred in the course of each crime under investigation. Such a reconstructive impulse requires the interpretation of a variety of material signs of movement and activity within scenes, the application of accumulated knowledge of a repertoire of typified and standardized modus operandi, as well as the use of general background knowledge of crime types. While Locard himself wrote of 'recreating' the criminal from traces left, the seemingly intuitive and fugitive nature of the process has meant that it has been the subject of inadequate research assessment. Scene examiners themselves refer to and formulate it only in the most general way as a matter of accumulated professional expertise. Furthermore, it is normal for report forms to encourage the production of such a reconstructive account of the actions of suspects at the scene without indicating how it was made possible and on what basis it might rest. Scene examiners fully recognize the likely imprecision of their practice while arguing for its usefulness in shaping and focusing each particular examination by reducing what would otherwise be its almost indefinite scope. This is especially important when examiners are making professional judgements about scene searching in the light of their knowledge of scarce resources, the range of alternative demands on their time and a concern with the measurement of individual and group performance by the use of a restricted range of indicators. These judgements are informed both by prior understandings of 'normal' or 'typical' scenes of particular crimes and the constant comparison of such a priori expectations with the emerging details of the particular scene in question.

It can, of course, be argued that all those involved in the process of investigating crime are informed by a similar reconstructive impulse, so it may be useful to distinguish what is distinctive about the way in which the work of examiners subjects this impulse to ongoing reformulation and redirection through the discovery and local interpretation of physical evidence. In particular, their reconstructive accounts are measured against the detailed collection and documentation of physical evidence alongside preliminary and provisional interpretation of such evidence. It can be instructive to compare the reconstructions contained in such examiners' written accounts with the reconstructions offered by other investigators. For example, the (usually uniformed) first officers who attend scenes of crime in response to calls from the public also provide such accounts in their crime reports. However, these accounts are derived largely from interviews with victims (or whoever reported the occurrence) and therefore rest on interviewees' inexpert interpretations of material signs rather than direct inspection. Equally, detectives may subsequently interview victims and other witnesses, as well as visit the crime scene, but their own examination of the scene in question may not take place until the scene has been restored following the completion of the work of scene examiners.

Some scene examiners may re-interview victims or witnesses about their knowledge of the crime (e.g. where they believed the intruder had entered and left the property, what rooms seem to have been entered by the intruder, what was taken away, what disturbed, what they believed to be the timing of the crime and so forth) and triangulate this information with what their own training and experience made visible in the material appearance of the crime scene. This important interaction between the search for physical evidence and the interviewing of victim or witness is a vital resource for the accurate reconstruction of the likely sequence of events, and therefore for the effectiveness and efficiency of the scene examination as a whole. It makes possible and encourages an informal ongoing falsification/verification of hypotheses that serve to give impetus and direction to the developing scene examination.

While manuals, protocols and other exhortations give some structure to the work of examiners, they all have to be interpreted against a background of assumptions derived from the training and experience of such scene examiners, and this makes possible the deployment of such criteria and protocols in a flexible manner appropriate to specific scenic circumstances. Without this, the mechanical application of such guidance would be unlikely to facilitate productive scene examinations.

Collecting fingerprints and DNA

Traditionally, the search for fingerprints has been understood to constitute a primary preoccupation of the work of generic crime scene examiners. The historical reasons for this are interesting, though space does not permit their discussion in this chapter. Tilley and Ford's (1996) study reported (on the basis of interviews with scenes of crime officers (SOCOs)) that an average 70 per cent of the time spent at crime scenes is spent looking for fingerprints, with the remaining 30 per cent being spent looking for other forensic evidence. While this may be a spuriously exact quantification of examination practice, it is certainly the case that most crime scene examiners still treat the discovery and collection of fingerprint marks as a central element in their professional practice. It is also noticeable that a record of the success of examiners in finding fingerprint marks is one of the indicators of individual and collective performance.

The work of finding and recovering fingerprint marks is a skilled task that involves the use of background technical knowledge, a number of interpretative and manual skills, and a willingness to organize and sustain close visual attention to a range of material surfaces over an extended period of time. Nickell and Fischer (1999) describe three kinds of fingerprints or fingermarks (including prints or marks left by other parts of the hand, notably the palm) found at crime scenes. These are 'plastic fingerprints' (impressions left by fingers in dust, soap, putty or other soft material); 'visible fingerprints' (marks left by fingers previously coated with substances like paint, ink, grease or blood); and 'latent fingerprints' (deposits of secretions of the skin which remain relatively invisible until they are enhanced by some relevant technology). In the case of the first two of these, marks are photographed for subsequent searching against a collection of ten print marks held in paper or electronic form within force fingerprint bureaux, and via such bureaux, against a national collection of records. In the case of the third kind of fingerprint (comprising the overwhelming majority of prints discovered during the research), the visibility of such deposits is improved – or 'developed' – before being photographed and/or captured by additional imaging and retention technologies. For each individual fingerprint discovered, the scene examiner makes a series of decisions about the eventual quality of the marks that are likely to be derived since such marks vary in their quality and clarity.

Scene examiners make a series of practical decisions about how to conduct their search for such marks and how to deal with the relative invisibility of latent fingerprints in particular. This is an improvised skill: 'knowing where to look for prints and how to develop them is a fine art learned mostly through experience' (Fisher 1995: 158). Furthermore, the exact placement of fingermarks at a crime scene is something to which examiners give serious and sustained attention in the course of their decisions about which such marks deserve attention and work. They show particular concern with the discovery of marks that they describe – by reference to their location and orientation – but their actions at crime scenes exhibit a permanent and general concern with the interpretative significance of all potentially recoverable fingerprints. After all, it is possible for someone whose fingerprint has been found and identified on the outside of a window to claim that it was left there when the window was touched in passing; similarly that a fingerprint found on a CD casing discarded near the scene of a burglary was the result of the innocent inspection of the CD as a passer-by. Effective and efficient fingerprint-mark collection, then, requires an attentiveness to the possibility of these kinds of responses to discovered matches made by suspects along with the necessity to record and communicate exact details of fingerprint discovery and placement to investigating officers for use in interviews and other inquiries.

A similar interpretative process is applied to the collection of biological materials from which DNA profiles might be obtained. More than any other technological development in human identification the practice of DNA profiling has rendered the human body available to a system of standardized and repeatable techniques. It goes, as David Lyon (2001) puts it, 'under the skin' to capture the very essence of the body itself, bypassing the need to measure any external surface or to engage with the outward aspects of human corporeality. Since DNA is found in almost any cell in the body, there is a variety of sources of material for DNA testing potentially available for recovery at crime scenes. Blood (which might shed by cuts caused when a burglar breaks glass, splinters wood or penetrates his or her skin by the use of a tool) is the most promising type of source. Its relatively easy observability on glass, metal, plastic, wood or painted surfaces combines with straightforward collection and subsequent extraction to result in highly productive DNA profiling. While shed body and head hair (as opposed to hair roots) contains only trace amounts of DNA, specialized 'mitochondrial sequencing' (mtDNA) can be used to obtain more limited information. However, mtDNA is inherited solely through the maternal line so that all relatives linked through the female line will share the same mtDNA as their mother. In addition, the discriminatory potential of mtDNA is radically reduced in comparison with DNA profiling. The overwhelming majority of hair found in the ordinary environment has simply fallen naturally as a result of the routine shedding of dead hair. In cases of volume crime the efficient recovery and analysis of any human hair are made difficult by the inability of scene examiners to be able to make a clear determination of its origin. However, there may be some locations of its occurrence that lead examiners to consider this possibility. For instance, hair caught at a point of entry to a burglary scene or trapped in the ignition cowling of a car may well belong to the offender (and such pulled hair may also contain root material as a better source of DNA).

DNA can be recovered from the nucleated buccal cells that are sloughed off the cheek and other parts of the mouth and shed in saliva. The quantity of such cells contained in any particular saliva deposit is unpredictable. In addition, oral bacteria can degrade the DNA present in such cellular material and this means that recovered items have to be submitted for analysis is soon as possible – or stored frozen until submission. Saliva may be left at crime scenes on a number of possible objects, most frequently on cups, bottles and cigarette butts. Partially eaten food may also contain such material, but the nature of the food itself can cause differing degrees of success at the extraction of analysable DNA (in the case of chewing-gum, for example, success depends in part on the type of gum in question, and the acid in some foods and drinks can damage any DNA left on the object). In 1999, the Forensic Science Service (FSS) reported that SGM™ technology (along with the technical ability to overcome the masking effect of nicotine) was enabling DNA profiles to be obtained from 60 per cent of cigarette butts submitted for analysis, and that this success rate was expected to rise with the introduction of FSS SGMplus™ (by early 2001 the rate had risen to 72 per cent). At the same time, DNA profiles were obtained from saliva on beer or soft drink cans in less than 5 per cent of submissions.

Nasal secretions comprise a good source of DNA and such material can be recovered from used handkerchiefs and paper tissues found at crime scenes. Australian researchers showed in 1997 that genetic profiles can be obtained from human secretions (comprising sweat and skin cells) adhering to objects that had been touched by hands and other bodily surfaces (see van Oorschot and Jones 1997; van Oorschot et al. 1998, 2000), and it has been demonstrated that a range of fingerprinting techniques and reagents do not inhibit the discovery of such profiles. Both urine and faeces can contain shed nucleated cells, but success at DNA profiling with these materials remains uncommon while the latter type of material can also be subject to mitochondrial sequencing.

Material suitable for DNA analysis is collected in four common ways by scene examiners: by the recovery of a discrete item believed to contain DNA; by the swabbing of a visible stain; by scraping a dried stain; and by cutting away the surface of fixed material thought to be stained with a relevant deposit. The recovery of entire items bearing a stain is the FSS preferred method since this means that the stain is less likely to be contaminated by handling and an unstained part of the item will be available to the laboratory for control purposes. However, there are clear practical limits to this practice, especially in the case of volume crimes where the owners of large items such as bedspreads, sofa covers, etc., would be unwilling to lose them in the cause of forensic science. Equally it may not be possible for a scene examiner to suggest cutting away a relevant part of a carpet or the cloth used in soft furnishing. In such situations, scene examiners are more likely to swab the areas of stain, and in cases in which visual inspection suggests the presence of a possible blood stain, it is conventional to test the material in advance of sampling to discover whether or not the examiner's suspicions are justified using a particular kit available for such on-scene determinations.

Whatever decisions examiners make, it is clear that their work is impelled through a series of improvised actions that are framed by organizational rules and procedures. Written manuals give us access to such rules but they fail to tell us anything meaningful about the ways in which daily routines are the outcomes of spontaneous decision-making based on both formal mechanisms and situated doxa. It is this latter aspect of examination that remains under-researched and yet it is the most crucial. Attempts to improve the reliability of crime scene examination continually fail to engage with the highly improvised nature of this work. They fail to account for the ways in which scene examiners themselves construct the parameters of their own practice (what constitutes the limits of the scene itself) and then decide on how such parameters will be measured, assessed, captured and recorded.

Biometric databases and the investigation of crime

Crime scene examination provides a fundamental pillar in the collection of 'body data' that are stored and searched in large police databases, and there have been especially significant efforts to expand both fingerprint and DNA collections in the UK in the last five years. The importance of their investigative significance, and the commonality of their use, is marked by the continual pairing of the technologies in relevant UK legislation as well as in operational practice. Several important legislative changes (Criminal Justice and Public Order Act 1994, Criminal Justice and Police Act 2001 and Criminal Justice Act 2003) have expanded the powers of the police in England and Wales to collect, retain indefinitely and search speculatively fingerprints and non-intimate samples from all arrested individuals.[11] One important justification offered by the government for this expansion is the value of constructing the most extensive identity archives possible for use in policing. There is an inherent assumption that expanding archives *automatically* ensures greater investigative efficiency. Or, as Bramley, the former custodian of the National DNA Database, argued of the expansion of the database: 'We are loading more and more profiles from individuals onto the database and its value is increasing accordingly' (FSS 2005: 2).

Since legislative and technological innovations have allowed the 'speculative searching' of increasingly large collections of DNA profiles and fingerprints, UK government and police promotion of the need for such archives has heightened. It is widely recognized that such searches regularly result in the identification of possible suspects in the absence of any other forms of criminal intelligence. In this way such archives have an increasingly significant inceptive capacity to provide investigative leads and potential lines of inquiry, a capacity which radically supplements the role of fingerprint comparison and DNA profile matching from the reactive testing of existing investigative inferences.

These facets of DNA profiling and databasing are the basis for continuous claims about the absolute value of constructing and expanding DNA profile collections as important elements in criminal archives wherever possible. Where forensic uses of DNA have been incorporated into routine criminal investigations, this has often been claimed to have facilitated and reflected important changes in the organizational practices of policing. Some have gone so far to argue that this technology has not merely enhanced existing police capacity but has even begun to replace 'the slow, tedious and expensive traditional investigative methods of police interviews' (Watson 1999: 325). While this may be an exaggerated claim it is often acknowledged that the introduction of DNA profiling has provided an especially powerful forensic resource for the enhancement of 'intelligence-led' policing in the UK and elsewhere – and part of the enthusiasm for this technology is attributable to the ease of its incorporation into this model of policing.

Such a possibility certainly provided part of the basis for government support of this extensive archive. The 'DNA Expansion Programme', first announced in 1999, provided £241 million to police forces for DNA activity between April 2000 and March 2005. Yet the amount of funding is less important than the commitment to construct an identity archive of this kind and to make it available for policing. The expansion programme has aimed at both extending and intensifying the use of DNA: extension through funding the collection of DNA both from more suspects and more crime scenes; intensification through developing analytical technologies capable of sequencing smaller and more degraded samples. The government commitment to these two aims reflected a general ambition to expand the collection of DNA into the routine investigation of volume crime, an ambition that has now largely been realized.

Prior to the expansion programme, the use of genetic profiling by the police had already produced significant improvements in identification and detection rates. As early as July 1996, when the database had been running for less than one year, the FSS announced that 14,000 'hits' had been made (matches made between either DNA profiles taken from suspects and crime scene stains, or between crime scenes themselves). They also unveiled plans to open a second database unit in London to cope with the large number of criminal justice and crime scene samples provided by the police for DNA sequencing and profile matching. Almost immediately, after it went live, the database promised spectacular results. Since then, the story of the database is one of consistent expansion. Yet this growth, which has produced a continual and dramatic rise in recorded hits made on the database (in July 2003, the FSS claimed that 'in a typical month matches are found linking suspects to 15 murders, 31 rapes and 770 motor vehicle crimes'), has demanded significant investment and planning.

The investigative deployment of fingerprint comparisons has been considerably enhanced in the last decade through the digitization of fingerprint images and the resulting capacity to search large collections of such images electronically. Most recently in the UK the introduction of 'Livescan' technology has allowed the police to obtain digital fingerprints from suspects which can be compared with records already held on the National Automated Fingerprint Identification Service (NAFIS). NAFIS was introduced in 2001 and currently holds more than five million sets of fingerprints and over half a million crime scene marks. The system processes more than 100,000 sets of prints obtained at the point of arrest every month and operates 80,000 searches of the database using marks obtained from scenes of crime. The introduction of computerized searching has reduced the cumbersome process of manually inspecting paper archives to a process that takes a few minutes – although fingerprint examiners are still required to confirm, through visual inspection, a 'match' between prints. NAFIS has been constructed using the previously held paper records of individual police forces which have been digitized through scanning. However, 'Livescan' now allows the entry to be made directly from the body rather than from a paper and ink record. Recent legislation (Serious Crime Act 2005) allows the police in England and Wales to take a fingerprint scan, using portable equipment, from an individual prior to arrest where identity cannot be established by other means. This enables the police to transmit the scan to NAFIS where it can be compared with previously held records with the objective of making an identification – a process which the police term 'live ID'. The same process will, of course, permit the immediate comparison of the scanned print with the set of unmatched crime scene marks also held on NAFIS.

Measuring forensic effectiveness in criminal investigations

Over the past ten years the repertoire of concepts and measures that constitute 'attrition' has stabilized into a standard framework for representing what happens to individual cases as they pass through the criminal justice process. The basis of this representation is a series of summative measurements of the proportion of cases that either proceed or fail to proceed through the investigative 'chain': from the commission of an offence, the reporting of it to the police, the offence being recorded by them, the offender being detected, charged and finally convicted. The simplicity of the model (and the distinctiveness of the stages identified) makes it especially attractive for use within the wider discourse of 'effectiveness' within research on policing. It provides both a forward narrative to describe investigation and a retrospective metaphor to describe the rates at which the police 'clear up' offences.

Thinking about the use of forensic science and technology in this way has been conditioned by the emergence of an 'audit culture' approach to the administration of UK public services (see, for example, Power 1994, 1996, 1997; Clarke *et al.* 2000; Strathern 2000). A recent study of contemporary policing practices in Europe and North America (Garland 2001: 190) argued that an 'economic style of reasoning' is pervasive. Employing a 'ragbag of techniques, models, analogies and recipes for action that are loosely bound up by their appeal to economic rationality', Garland argues that economic rationality is now the basis for both 'doing and representing' policing (2001: 190).

For Garland (2001), this culture already dominates current understandings and discussions of a wide range of state provision, including practices of crime control, and it is best understood as supporting the capacity of government agencies to pursue centrally determined policy objectives. This is certainly exemplified by the current programme of public sector reform in the UK as applied to policing with its complex commitment to the importance of a national framework of standards and accountability, alongside the apparent devolution of power to a local level (to 'enable innovation and development' responsive to particular and different contexts). For example, an early statement of the government's crime reduction strategy (Home Office 2000) commends the beneficial results of the introduction of performance league tables and regular monitoring of performance in other sectors and looks forward to the results expected to derive from the enhanced application of such approaches in the field of policing. In other words, the government's desire is to determine the use of science and technology in policing through the development of measures of the attrition process.

While the PSU now regularly supplies forces with summary statistics that provide a very general picture of forensic science performance, there remains little systematic knowledge of what methods of collecting, recording, processing and using forensic intelligence work most effectively. Particular forces may introduce innovations which seem superficially to be successful, and these are sometimes taken up more widely (e.g. Operation Converter, Operation Cesare), but their proliferation is often accompanied by changes in the details of their implementation, or the enthusiasm with which their arrival is greeted by secondary users. These considerations often mean that what has seemed to have worked well in one context has worked less well in another. A general understanding of these variations requires a detailed specification of the variety of socio-technical actions that comprise forensic investigations as well as the combinatorial tolerances of their joint uses. Available studies have not examined the detail of the organizational arrangements that are involved in routine and exceptional efforts to collect these and other trace materials, even though – as in the majority of the reports referred to in earlier sections of this chapter – an outline sequence of actions may be identified (e.g. as 'scene attended', 'contact trace material collected', 'DNA profile matched', 'fingerprint eliminated', 'crime detected through forensic match', etc.).[12]

The failure to describe the contingencies that surround the collection, analysis and interpretation of forensic artefacts and intelligence – including fingerprint identifications and DNA matches – during the course of individual instances of criminal investigations is visible even in the best studies of the use of forensic science in support of volume crime investigation (e.g. Tilley and Ford 1996; Burrows *et al.* 2005). All such studies have recognized the central role played by those staff who are directly employed by individual police forces to examine crime scenes for the presence of physical evidence. Such personnel record and collect available evidence, assemble specific evidential artefacts and, in cases of serious crimes, work as part of a larger team of investigators comprising detectives, other specialist police officers and, sometimes, more highly qualified forensic scientists. Yet despite the central importance accorded to the work of such 'scenes of crime officers', 'scientific support officers', 'crime scene examiners' or 'crime scene investigators', there exist no adequate formal accounts of the ways in which competent crime scene examination is actually accomplished in and through their use of a repertoire of observational skills, manual competences, logical inferences, technical understandings and other forms of situated practice. Nor are there any rigorous studies of how particular artefacts and information derived from such examinations are deployed by police staff in the course of investigations.

All the reviews, studies and reports listed earlier in this chapter represent selected features of these detailed activities to identify 'good practice' and construct 'models of the forensic process'. However, these representations rest on unexplicated assumptions which gloss over the complexity and contingency of the process and products of forensic examinations. Rather, they favour the identification, grouping, measurement and comparison of atomized units of activity (e.g. volume of scenes attended; percentage of fingermarks collected; positive DNA matches obtained) within and between BCUs and police forces. This analytical restriction is no doubt encouraged by the seeming natural visibility of the standard objects and events within the forensic domain (especially artefacts like latent fingerprints and DNA profiles recovered from scenes of crime as well as the matches achieved when each of these is compared with existing records held by the police). In turn, confidence in the 'obviousness' of such objects and events is reflected in the willingness of a number of researchers and agencies to assert the significance of specific kinds of forensic activity (including some 'pilot' or other innovations) to explain the attrition levels of particular aggregations of cases (usually based on offence types or on BCU or forces' performances).

However, such assertions are inadequate surrogates for detailed research on the situated uses of the wide repertoire of forensic knowledge, technology and inferential practices that are used in and through the course of criminal investigations. This repertoire includes, in the case of trace biometrics, for example, a corpus of relevant natural and human science orthodoxies (including inorganic chemistry and microbiology); a collection of forensic technologies (e.g. fingerprint powers and lifting agents, Luminol application, DNA profiling collection kits); techniques of classification, identification and databasing; the rhetorical endoxa of criminal investigation (e.g. who had the means, motive and opportunity to commit the crime under investigation); and the deployment of commonsense knowledge of human action (e.g. modus operandi).

Research is needed to examine the ways in which selections from this repertoire are used at specific moments to afford a series of 'forensic accomplishments' which in turn contribute to the course of criminal investigations. The precise nature of these varies according to context, but they variously figure as 'categorizations' (what is an object); 'individualizations' (which one is it or whose is it); 'associations' (what may be inferred about contacts between objects and persons); and 'reconstructions' (the temporal and spatial ordering of associations). These are all elements in the lingua franca of forensic investigations and are recurrent discursive themes in investigative talk. Each of them is no more than a placeholder for the complex, heterogeneous and socially facilitated work of forensic examination which deserves careful study. These crucial activities – of recognizing, analysing and interpreting – should be made topics of study in order to ground firmly an understanding of forensic investigations as a routine set of activities accomplished by practitioners in the course of their ordinary work.[13]

To understand properly the work of crime scene examination and its place in supporting criminal investigations – as a series of embodied practices of instructed searching, the use of specific technologies to locate and recover material artefacts, of asking questions, of presenting accounts to others in talk and texts, etc. – we have to set aside statistical measures of the 'outputs' and 'outcomes' of such work. Rather, we need to build up a 'grammar of forensic investigation'. Such a grammar would outline the repertoire of knowledge, actions and inferential processes that makes possible standardized forensic accomplishments and shows the ways in which these accomplishments are integrated into a wider investigative process. In particular, it would show how abstract forms of knowledge are embedded within the 'concerted human reasoning, perception, conduct and communication' (Coulter 1989: 19) that make up the reality of criminal investigations. An adequate account of these matters would provide an important resource for the future training of investigative staff and for the assessment of the value of different organizational arrangements for the delivery of forensic support. It would help answer more general questions concerning the ways in which applications of forensic technologies are shaped by existing police systems and processes, as well as the ways in which the integration of these technologies is driving change in established crime investigation practices.

Writing about recent work concerned to assess the contribution of forensic science to criminal investigations, a recent HMIC report asserted that:

Despite considerable effort from some committed individuals – and sharp prompts from HM Treasury – the Home Office and the [police] service have struggled to develop an agreed mechanism for measuring the relationship between inputs, processes, outputs and outcomes ... The service thus needs to continue working with the grain of efforts to get a better handle on issues such as cost and productivity as well as continuing the search for the ultimate goal of comprehensive qualitative outcome measures (Her Majesty's Inspectorate of Constabulary 2000: para. 5).

While we do not share an interest in 'comprehensive qualitative outcome measures' (whatever they might be), we do share a concern to understand the ways that the expanding availability of forensic intelligence in general, and fingerprint and DNA intelligence in particular, does and may contribute to the effectiveness of investigations. There is a fundamental connection between the inclusiveness of identity archives and the operational uses of the information they provide, but understanding the nature of that connection requires an exploration of the variety of investigative practices that both structure and are structured by their availability.

In place of the currently under-researched assertions of what individuals and groups do, which themselves serve as ad hoc 'explanations' of the statistical regularities of the attrition process, we advocate the need for more detailed studies of the *in situ* collaborative work of crime scene examiners, scientists and other experts, and police investigators. Without such work, there will remain a distinct lack of understanding of how forensic technologies, and the identity archives on which they rely, are shaping, and are shaped by, the process of investigation. As we stated at the beginning of this chapter, the importance of the collection and use of body data for policing is not at issue, nor is the enthusiasm for it across a range of social sites. Yet against a background where new biometric technologies have been eagerly embraced by government, and where claims have been made about their efficiency and authority, we still know less than we should about their impact upon the mundane and daily practices of investigation.

Concluding remarks

The growing fingerprint and DNA databases held in the UK are recent extensions of a long-standing process of the state-sponsored collection of knowledge of the bodies of individuals. As part of a 'bio-surveillance', apparatus to be used to detect past, present and potentially future criminal conduct, such databases can be seen as one of a series of 'centres of calculation' (Latour 1987) whose existence demonstrates the extensive (but seemingly unintrusive) bureaucratic surveillance of individual subjects. In other words, they are just one example of a multiplicity of ways in which modern forms of government seek and use knowledge about their citizens (see, for example, Lyon and Zuriek 1996; Norris *et al.* 1996; Norris and Armstrong 1999; Lyon 1991, 2001; Marx 2002).

Given the very many practical and policy issues surrounding the existence of these biometric technologies and archives, the efficiency of their investigative uses has to be balanced against more general considerations of the ethical issues that surround new forms, or the extension of older forms, of such body knowledge. This is another reason why we need more rigorous understandings of the social processes through which such technologies are deployed in everyday practice as well as the wider social consequences of their uses. For instance, Duster (2003, 2004, 2005) and others have noted the ways in which criminal justice DNA databases reinscribe prior differences in the treatment of minority groups by the police and, in doing so, are capable of posing new threats to those already marginalized and excluded (see also Sankar 1997, 2001; Lazer 2004). If such threats are real then they cannot be assessed by auditing forensic science through currently prevailing methodologies. Rather, an understanding of how the daily uses of forensic sciences intersects with the intricacies of social life is needed.

Factual issues of the effectiveness of technologically enhanced methods of criminal investigation necessarily collide with normative issues of the acceptability and consequences of the collection, retention and use of personal data from a widening category of individuals. Recent legislation on the retention of fingerprints and DNA profiles from individuals has meant that more categories of individuals have their trace biometric data compared with such data collected from an increased number and variety of crime scenes. While at a policy level, recourse is readily made to the rhetorical trope of a 'balance' between public protection and the protection of individual liberties, decisions about how to proceed in the course of particular investigations are more difficult. Certainly, the actions of those involved in particular investigations will often be subject both to the hammer of expectations of effective crime control and to the anvil of human rights legislation. In the UK, this tension is instantiated in the alternating imperatives of the Criminal Procedures and Investigations Act 1996, on the one hand, and those of the Human Rights Act, on the other. This means that however much police forces seek, and are encouraged to seek, to increase the use of trace biometric technologies in support of criminal investigations there are some fundamental moral dilemmas which remain at the centre of this (and of the many other efforts to gather personal information about those who are the perpetrators, victims or witnesses of criminal actions). At the very least, ongoing debates about the appropriate balance for the use of forensic technologies would be significantly enhanced by a more thorough understanding, and more nuanced and detailed accounts, of the role they play in supporting many and varied concrete instances of crime investigation.

Selected further reading

Townley, L. and Ede, R. (2004) *Forensic Practice in Criminal Cases*. London: The Law Society. A guide to the practice and uses of forensic science in England and Wales that provides a good introduction to a range of scientific, investigative and legal issues.

Caplan, J. and Torpey, J. (eds) (2001) *Documenting Individual Identity: The Development of State Practices in the Modern World*. Oxford: Princeton University Press. This collection of papers is a useful overview of the history of recent interest in, and methods for, the verification of identity in contemporary society.

James, S.H. and Nordby, J.J. (eds) (2005) *Forensic Science: An Introduction to Scientific and Investigative Technique*. Boca Raton, FL: CRC Press. An extensive primer on a wide range of forensic technologies with an emphasis on their application to investigative contexts. Accessible to non-scientists.

Bradbury, S.-A. and Feist, A. (2005) *The Use of Forensic Science in Volume Crime Investigations: A Review of the Research Literature. Online Report* 43/15. London: Home Office. An excellent systematic review of the research literature in this field, with particular emphasis on fingerprints and DNA.

Lazer, D. (ed.) (2004) *DNA and the Criminal Justice System: The Technology of Justice.* Cambridge, MA: MIT Press. An authoritative collection of papers on legal, ethical and policy aspects of the uses of genetic information in the criminal justice system. While its focus is on the USA, it raises general issues for all those interested in the effectiveness and intrusiveness of this technology.

Notes

1 Recent UK examples include White (1999), Jackson and Jackson (2004); Langford *et al.* (2005), Pepper (2005) and a range of papers published in *The International Journal of Forensic Science* and *Science and Justice.*

2 Some current examples include publications with varying levels of access within and outside the police community: *Murder Investigation Manual* (ACPO 2000), *Investigation of Volume Crime Manual* (ACPO 2002), *DNA Good Practice Manual* (ACPO 2004), *Practical Advice on Core Investigative Doctrine* (Centrex 2005), *Good Practice Guide on Cold Case Reviews of Rape and Serious Sexual Assault* (PSU 2005), *A Practitioners' Guide to Intelligence-led Mass DNA Screening* (Centrex 2006).

3 Equally, there is no robust knowledge of exactly how jury members evaluate the significance of forensic evidence despite assertions that such evidence is thought to be compelling. Such assertions commonly fail to distinguish between the significance attributed to an idealized form of such evidence in abstract and its evidential weight in any particular case; furthermore, there has been no significant research on the ways in which juries deliberate such evidence.

4 In England and Wales during 2002–3, £402 million was spent centrally on science and technology for use by the police, including £224 million on 'national science and technology projects' which included a large element of forensic science investment, especially on DNA and fingerprint technology. In addition, the 43 police forces of England and Wales spent a further £748 million on science and technology (see Home Office 2004: 25–6).

5 Examples of these include: state-funding programmes designed to increase the routine uses of forensic science and technology as well as substantial investment in research and development; the expansion of relevant education and employment for a range of police and forensic personnel; the establishment of professional bodies to encourage high and improving levels of practice; and the commercial development of specific technological innovations and initiatives to support and extend police investigatory practice. These numerous packages of support have been provided by the Home Office DNA Expansion Programme and investment in the National Automated Fingerprint Identification System (NAFIS); the work of the Department of Trade and Industry Foresight Crime Prevention Panels (Department of Trade and Industry 2000a, 2000b); the establishment of the Engineering and Physical Sciences Research Council Research Programme 'Think Crime' funding initiative; the analysis of forensic science education provision in relation to current and future employer needs (SEMTA 2004); and judicial and government support for the establishment of the Council for the Registration of Forensic Practitioners (see www.crfp.org.uk).

6 See, for example, ACPO/FSS/Audit Commission (1996), Her Majesty's Inspectorate of Constabulary (2000, 2002), Police Standards Unit (2005).

7 The strategy's overall aim of ensuring the effective use of science and technology by the police has in turn shaped the recent development of the Home Office 'Forensic Integration Strategy' (Home Office 2004). This is the most recent government initiative seeking to enhance the ways in which the current range of forensic techniques are used in crime investigation, along with support for the integration of intelligence derived from the application of these techniques within the generic framework for the collection and use of criminal intelligence provided by the National Intelligence Model.

8 While the Home Office spent £36.3 million on social science research in 2002–3, hardly any of this funded work examined the police uses of forensic science and technology. Of the total police spend of £748 million on science and technology during that year, only £75,000 funded 'research and development' (see Home Office 2004: 27).

9 Our assertions here are informed by work by Jasanoff (2004) and others on 'co-production', in this case the ways that both policing and forensic science practices are co-produced as features of social control in contemporary societies.

10 A very useful systematic review of this literature is Bradbury and Feist (2005).

11 'Non-intimate samples' include swabs of check cells from which DNA can be extracted and profiled.

12 There is no reason for surprise at this failure. Strathern (2005: 2) has cogently argued that such 'audit' approaches to these kinds of work processes only take into account the actions that they most want to affect while taking for granted (by both presupposing and reasserting) adequate knowledge of the enabling social processes and surrounding social contexts.

13 In the course of a recent paper on 'crime intelligence analysis', Innes et al. (2005) have pointed to the usefulness of the approach of Knorr-Cetina (1980) and Lynch (2003) in providing analytical resources for such studies. We would add to these science and technology studies the recent work of Jasanoff and her colleagues (2004) which uses the concept of 'co-production' to emphasize the ways in which science and technology 'both embed and [are] embedded in social practices, identities, norms, conventions, discourses, instruments and institutions – in short in all the building blocks of what we term the social' (Jasanoff 2004: 3).

References

ACPO/FSS/Audit Commission (1996) *Using Forensic Science Effectively.* London: HMSO.

Amey, P., Hale, C. and Uglow, S. (1996) *Proactive Policing.* Edinburgh: Scottish Central Research Unit.

Audit Commission (1993) *Helping With Enquiries: Tackling Crime Effectively.* London: HMSO.

Ball, K. (2005). 'Organisation, surveillance and the body: towards a politics of resistance', *Organization,* 12: 89–108.

Barton, A. and Evans, R. (1999) *Proactive Policing on Merseyside Police.* London: Home Office.

Bradbury, S. and Feist, A. (2005) *The Use of Forensic Science in Volume Crime Investigations: A Review of the Research Literature. Home Office Online Report* 43/05. London: Home Office.

Burrows, J., Tarling, R., Mackie, A., Poole, H. and Hodgson, B. (2005) *Forensic Science Pathfinder Project: Evluating Forensic Activity in Two English Police Forces. Home Office Online Report* 46/05. London: Home Office.

Caplan, J. and Torpey, J. (eds) (2001) *Documenting Individual Identity: The Development of State Practices in the Modern World*. Princeton, NJ: Princeton University Press.

Clarke, J., Gewirtz, S. *et al.* (eds) (2000) *New Managerialism, New Welfare?* London: Sage.

Cole, S.A. (2001) *Suspect Identities: A History of Fingerprinting and Criminal Identification*. Cambridge, MA: Harvard University Press.

Cole, S.A. (2004) 'Fingerprint identification and the criminal justice system: historical lessons for the DNA debate'. in D. Lazer (ed.) *DNA and the Criminal Justice System*. Cambridge, MA: MIT Press.

Coulter, J. (1989) *Mind in Action*. Cambridge: Polity Press.

Coupe, T. and Griffiths, M. (1996) *Solving Residential Burglary*. London: Home Office.

Dean, M. (1999) *Governmentality: Power and Rule in Modern Society*. London: Sage.

Department of Trade and Industry (2000a) *Foresight Crime Prevention Panel Consultation Document: Just Around the Corner*. London: DTI.

Department of Trade and Industry (2000b) *Foresight Crime Prevention Panel Report: Turning the Corner*. London: DTI.

DNA Expansion Programme Evaluation Group (2001) 'Evaluation report, phase one' (unpublished report, Home Office).

Duster, T. (2003) *Backdoor to Eugenics*. New York, NY: Routledge.

Duster, T. (2004) 'Selective arrests, an ever-expanding DNA forensic database, and the specter of an early-twenty-first century equivalent of phrenology', in D. Lazer (ed.) *DNA and the Criminal Justice System: The Technology of Justice*. Cambridge, MA: MIT Press.

Duster, T. (2005) 'Race and reification in science', *Science*, 307: 1050–1.

Eastel, S. (1990) 'DNA fingerprinting by PCR amplification of HLA genes', in J. Vernon and B. Sellinger (eds) *DNA and Criminal Justice*. Canberra: Australian Institute of Criminology.

Eco, U. and Sebeok, T.A. (eds) (1983) *The Sign of Three: Dupin, Holmes, Peirce*. Bloomington, ILL: Indiana University Press.

Ericson, R.V. (1981) *Making Crime: A Study of Detective Work*. Toronto: Butterworths.

Ericson, R.V. and Haggerty, K.D. (1997) *Policing the Risk Society*. Oxford: Oxford University Press.

Ericson, R.V. and Shearing, C.D. (1986) 'The scientification of police work', in G. Bohme and N. Stehr (eds) *The Knowledge Society: The Growing Impact of Scientific Knowledge on Social Relations*. Dordrecht: Reidel.

Faigman, D.L., Kaye, D.H., Saks, M.J. and Sanders, J. (eds) (2004) *Science in the Law: Forensic Science Issues*. St Paul, MN: West Group.

Fisher, D. (1995) *Hard Evidence*. New York, NY: Dell.

Forensic Science Service (2005) *Fact Sheet: The National DNA Database*. London: FSS.

Foucault, M. (1977) *Discipline and Punish: The Birth of the Prison*. Harmondsworth: Penguin Books.

Galton, F (1884) 'Measurement of character', *Fortnightly Review*, 36: 179–85.

Galton, F. (1892) *Finger Prints*. London: Macmillan.

Garland, D. (2001) *The Culture of Control: Crime and Social Order in Contemporary Society*. Oxford: Oxford University Press.

Gibson, M. (2001) 'The truth machine: polygraphs, popular culture and the confessing body,' *Social Semiotics*, 11: 61–73.

Gill, P. (2000) *Rounding up the Usual Suspects*. Aldershot: Ashgate.

Heaton, R. (2000) 'The prospects for intelligence-led policing: some historical and quantitative considerations,' *Policing and Society*, 9: 337–56.

Her Majesty's Inspectorate of Constabulary (2000) *Under the Microscope: Thematic Inspection Report on Scientific and Technical Support*. London: Home Office.

Her Majesty's Inspectorate of Constabulary (2002) *Getting Down to Basics: Emerging Findings from BCU Inspections in 2001.* London: Home Office.

Her Majesty's Inspectorate of Constabulary Scotland (2004) *Scottish Criminal Records Office Primary Inspection 2004.* Edinburgh: Scottish Executive.

Higgs, E. (2001) 'The rise of the information state: the development of central state surveillance of the citizen in England, 1500–2000,' *Journal of Historical Sociology,* 14: 175–97.

Home Office (2000) *The Government's Crime Reduction Strategy* (available online at http://www.homeoffice.gov.uk/crimprev).

Home Office (2001a) 'Evaluation of the contribution of shoemark data to police intelligence, crime detection and prosecution' (unpublished report).

Home Office (2001b) 'Evaluation of the impact of the FLINTS software in West Midlands and elsewhere' (draft report).

Home Office (2003) *Police Science and Technology Strategy, 2003–2007.* London: Home Office.

Home Office (2004) *Police Science and Technology Strategy, 2004–2008.* London: Home Office Science Policy Unit.

Home Office (2005) *DNA Expansion Programme, 2000–2005: Reporting Achievement.* London: Home Office.

House of Lords Select Committee on Science and Technology (1993) *Report on Forensic Science.* London: HMSO.

Human Genetics Commission (2002) *Inside Information: Balancing Interests in the Use of Personal Genetic Data.* London: Department of Health.

Innes, M. (2003) *Investigating Murder: Detective Work and the Police Response to Criminal Homicide.* Oxford: Oxford University Press.

Innes, M., Fielding, N. and Cope, N. (2005) 'The appliance of science: the theory and practice of crime intelligence analysis', *British Journal of Criminology,* 45: 39–57.

Interpol (2002) *Global DNA Database Inquiry: Result and Analysis* (available online at http://www.interpol.int/Public/Forensic/dna/Inquiry/InquiryPublic2002.pdf).

Jackson, A.R.W. and Jackson, J.M. (2004) *Forensic Science.* London: Pearson Prentice Hall.

Jasanoff, S. (1995) *Science at the Bar: Law, Science and Technology in America.* Cambridge, MA: Harvard University Press.

Jasanoff, S. (ed.) (2004) *States of Knowledge: The Co-production of Science and Social Order.* London: Routledge & Kegan Paul.

John, T. and Maguire, M. (2003) 'Rolling out the National Intelligence Model: key challenges'. in K. Bullock and N. Tilley (eds) *Essays in Problem-oriented Policing.* Cullompton: Willan Publishing.

Knorr-Cetina, K. (1980) *The Manufacture of Knowledge.* Oxford: Pergamon.

Langford, A., Dean, J., Rooed, R., Holmes, D., Weyers, J. and Jones, A. (2005) *Practical Skills in Forensic Science.* London: Pearson.

Latour, B. (1987) *Science in Action: How to Follow Scientists and Engineeers through Society.* Cambridge MA: Harvard University Press.

Lazer, D. (ed.) (2004) *DNA and the Criminal Justice System: The Technology of Justice.* Cambridge, MA: MIT Press.

Lyman, M.D. (1999) *Criminal Investigation: The Art and the Science.* Englewood Cliffs, NJ: Prentice Hall.

Lynch, M. (1993) *Scientific Practice and Ordinary Action: Ethnomethodology and Social Studies of Science.* Cambridge: Cambridge University Press.

Lynch, M. (2003) 'God's signature: DNA profiling, the new gold standard in forensic science,' *Endeavour,* 27: 93–7.

Lynch, M. and Cole, S. (2005) 'Science and technology studies on trial: dilemmas of expertise', *Social Studies of Science,* 35: 269–311.

Lynch, M.D. and Jasanoff, S. (eds) (1998) 'Contested identities: science, law and forensic practice' (special issue of *Social Studies of Science*, 28).

Lyon, D. (1991) 'Bentham's panopticon: from moral architecture to electronic surveillance', *Queen's Quarterly*, 98: 596–617.

Lyon, D. (2001) *Surveillance Society: Monitoring Everyday Life*. Buckingham: Open University Press.

Lyon, D. and Zureik, E. (1996) 'Surveillance, privacy, and the new technology', in D. Lyon and E. Zureik (eds) *Computers, Surveillance and Privacy*. Minneapolis, MN: University of Minesota Press.

Maguire, M. and John, T. (1995) *Intelligence, Surveillance and Informants: Integrated Approaches*. London: Home Office.

Marx, G.T. (2002). 'What's new about the "new surveillance"? Classifying for change and continuity,' *Surveillance and Society*, 1: 9–29.

McCulloch, H. (1996) *Police Use of Forensic Science*. London: Home Office Police Research Group.

McCulloch, H. and Tilley, N. (2000) 'Effectiveness and efficiency in obtaining fingerprint identifications' (unpublished report, Home Office).

MHB (2001) 'The evaluation of increased forensic activity in GMP and Lancashire' (unpublished report). London: Home Office.

Morgan, J.B. (1990) *The Police Function and the Investigation of Crime*. Aldershot: Averbury.

Nickell, J. and Fischer, J. (1999) *Crime Science: Methods of Forensic Detection*. Lexington, KY: University of Kentucky Press.

Norris, C. and Armstrong, G. (1999) *The Maximum Surveillance Society: The Rise of CCTV*. Oxford: Berg.

Norris, C., Moran, J. and Armstrong, G. (eds) (1996) *Surveillance, Closed Circuit Television and Social Control*. Aldershot: Aldgate.

Osterburg, J.W. and Ward, R.H. (2000). *Criminal Investigation: A Method for Reconstructing the Past* (3rd ed.) Cincinnati, OH: Anderson Publishing.

Pepper, I. (2005) *Crime Scene Investigation: Methods and Procedure*. Maidenhead: Open University Press.

Police Standards Unit (2005) *Good Practice Guide: Cold Case Reviews of Rape and Serious Sexual Assault*. London: Home Office.

Power, M. (1994) *The Audit Explosion*. London: Demos.

Power, M. (1996). 'Making things auditable', *Accounting, Organisations and Society*, 21: 289–315.

Power, M. (1997) *The Audit Society: Rituals of Verification*. Oxford: Oxford University Press.

Rabinow, P. (1992) 'Galton's regret: of types and individuals', in P.R. Billings (ed.) *DNA on Trial: Genetic Identification and Criminal Justice*. New York, NY: Cold Spring Harbour Laboratory Press.

Redmayne, M. (2001) *Expert Evidence and Criminal Justice*. Oxford: Oxford University Press.

Roberts, P. (2002) 'Science, experts and criminal justice', in M. McConville and G. Wilson (eds) *The Handbook of the Criminal Justice Process*. Oxford: Oxford University Press.

Roberts, P. and Willmore, C. (1993) *The Role of Forensic Science Evidence in Criminal Proceedings*. Royal Commission on Criminal Justice Study 11. London: HMSO.

Rose, N. (1996) 'Governing "advanced" liberal democracies', in A. Barry *et al.* (eds) *Foucault and Political Reason: Liberalism, Neo-liberalism and Rationalities of Government*. London: UCL Press.

Rose, N. (1999) *Powers of Freedom*. Cambridge: Cambridge University Press.

Saks, M.J. and Koehler, J.J. (2005) 'The coming paradigm shift in forensic identification science,' *Science*, 309: 892–5.

Sankar, P. (1997). 'Topics for our time: the proliferation and risks of government DNA databases', *American Journal of Public Health*, 87: 336–7.

Sankar, P. (2001) 'DNA-typing: Galton's eugenic dream realised?', in J. Caplan and J. Torpey (eds) *Documenting Individual Identity: The Development of State Practices in the Modern World*. Princeton, NJ. Princeton University Press.

Sekula, A. (1986) 'The body and the archive', *October*, 39: 3–64.

SEMTA (2004) *Forensic Science: Implications for Higher Education 2004*. London: SEMTA.

Spufford, F. and Uglow, J. (eds) (1996) *Cultural Babbage: Technology, Time and Invention*. London: Faber & Faber.

Strathern, M. (2000) 'Accountability and ethnography', in M. Strathern (ed.) *Audit Cultures: Anthropological Studies in Accountability, Ethics and the Academy*. London: Routledge.

Strathern, M. (2005) 'Abstraction and de-contextualisation: and anthropological comment or: e for ethnography' (conference paper for *Virtual Society: The Social Science of Electronic Technologies*, available online at http://virtualsociety.sbs.ox.ac. uk/GRpapers/strathern.htm).

Thompson, T. (2001) 'Legal and ethical considerations of forensic anthropological research', *Science and Justice*, 41: 261–70.

Tilley, N. and Ford, A. (1996) *Forensic Science and Crime Investigation*. London: Home Office.

Touche Ross (1987) *Review of Scientific Support for the Police*. London: Home Office.

Townley, L. and Ede, R. (2004) *Forensic Practice in Criminal Cases*. London: The Law Society.

Valier, C. (1998) 'True crime stories: scientific methods of criminal investigation, criminology and historiography', *British Journal of Criminology*, 38: 88–105.

Van de Ploeg (2005) 'Biometric identification technologies: ethical implications of the informatization of the body' (BITE policy paper available online at http://www. biteproject.org/reports.asp).

van Oorschot, R.A.H. and Jones, M. (1997) 'DNA fingerprints from fingerprints', *Nature*, 387: 767.

van Oorschot, R.A.H., Szepietowska, I., Scott, D.L., Weston, R.K. and Jones, M.K. (2000) 'Retrieval of genetic profiles from touched objects.' Paper presented at the First International Conference on Forensic Human Identification in the Millennium (available online at http://www.forensic.gov.uk/forensic/conference/papers/ genetic_profiles.html).

van Oorschot, R.A.H., Weston, R.K. and Jones, M.K. (1998) 'Retrieval of DNA from touched objects', in *Proceedings of the 14th Annual Symposium of the Forensic Sciences of Australia and New Zealand Forensic Science Society*, Adelaide, 12–16 October.

Watson, N. (1999) 'The analysis of body fluids', in P. White (ed.) *Crime Scene to Court: The Essentials of Forensic Science*. Cambridge: Royal Society of Chemistry.

White, M.D. (ed.) (1999) *Crime Scene to Court: The Essentials of Forensic Science*, London: Royal Society of Chemistry.

Chapter 15

The application of forensic science to criminal investigation

Jim Fraser

Introduction

In circumstances where science and technology contribute to solutions in wider areas of human activity, such as criminal justice, the application of specialist skills knowledge in relation to complex practical problems is rarely delivered directly by specialists without intermediary agents. Such environments are usually complex and with numerous barriers to the optimal conditions for the application of specialist knowledge. These barriers include conflicting or misunderstood organizational policies and aims, financial constraints and cultural differences between different sectors. Such factors are generally overcome by formal or informal co-operative activities based on shared organizational aims or short-term goals. The corresponding level of knowledge of each party in such joint enterprises is rarely extensive or deep but more typically represents what is essential to ensure that problems are dealt with effectively within notional standards and timeframes and that perceived risks are managed.

A key factor in the use of specialist technology is knowledge complementarity: what each party needs to know of the other to work together effectively. Generalists who apply technology via a third party and indirectly to their problems are often unaware of its full potential. Those who provide the technological solution, the specialists, frequently fail to understand the full significance of the circumstances in which their technology is applied. The consequences of this are the development of a set of suboptimal operational activities that meet the needs of stakeholders to varying degrees. It is often the case that applications to a wider range of problems would be beneficial but the barriers described above prevent this.

For the most part the use of forensic science by the criminal justice system is delivered via the police service. They are the largest users of forensic science and are influential in defining and articulating their needs and those of the criminal justice system. In this chapter I wish to explore how knowledge of the investigative use of forensic science grows and is acquired. It is important at this point that we explain what is meant by the term 'knowledge acquisition'. This is used in a very wide sense to include education or training programmes and how changes in practice, methodologies, roles and organizational aims support knowledge growth. This includes practice manuals, guidance notes and policy documents that contribute to the overall changes in the use of forensic science. A particular issue that merits consideration is the growing repository of knowledge, especially evidence-based reports and reviews, that is not incorporated into the practice. For example, the need for formal quality assurance procedures in scenes of crime work was identified almost 20 years ago (Touche Ross 1987) but remains unimplemented in any real sense. In addressing these issues I will describe the agents, agencies, processes, roles, problems and solutions that incrementally contribute to knowledge growth and acquisition.

I will also describe the main influential and historic events in forensic science and police investigation in recent decades and critically review the current position, particularly any implications for the contribution of forensic science to police investigations. These issues are considered from a UK perspective, primarily the jurisdiction of England and Wales. In order to constrain the scope of this theme, I have limited the definition of forensic science to those activities carried out by the current or former public sector laboratories (e.g. the Forensic Science Service) and forensic science functions carried out by the police: fingerprint examinations, crime scene investigation and photography. This excludes forensic medicine and pathology and a number of other highly specialist areas (e.g. forensic entomology).

As in other jurisdictions, forensic science in England and Wales has rapidly developed and expanded, particularly during the past decade. In most countries the influences for these changes have been scientific and technological, primarily developments in DNA profiling. The use of DNA as an intelligence tool, especially when aggregated into a database, is of particular significance. But the growth and impact of the National DNA Database in England and Wales have been on a scale dramatically different from any other country in the world. A comparison of sample numbers of mainland European DNA databases with England and Wales illustrates this point. Of the 2.9 million individuals on DNA databases throughout Europe in 2002, 2.5 million (86 per cent) were on the database in England and Wales (Townsley and Laycock 2004). This is a tangible indicator of the differences in scale. Furthermore, scientific developments have been accompanied by frequent and supportive changes in legislation, resulting in new or modified policies and practices in the use of forensic science in police investigations. These developments have also contributed to a significant restructuring of the forensic science sector, increased expectations of stakeholders and influenced broader political issues, such policy formulation in criminal justice.

The development of forensic science in England and Wales

The primary sources of forensic science to the police in England and Wales from the 1930s onwards were the laboratories of the Home Office

Forensic Science Service (FSS) and the Metropolitan Police Forensic Science Laboratory in London. By the 1960s there were nine laboratories in England and Wales, and forensic science continued to expand steadily on the basis of increased police use and technological developments that improved investigative potential (Gallop 2003). During the 1980s a number of high-profile miscarriages of justice involving forensic science (e.g. the Birmingham Six, the Maguire Seven) ultimately led to a Royal Commission (Royal Commission on Criminal Justice 1993). This recommended a number of important changes in legislation and practices in police investigations that had significant implications for the use and provision of forensic science.

The Police and Criminal Evidence Act (PACE) 1984 radically altered police procedures, roles and responsibilities in criminal investigations. The purpose of these changes was to regulate the actions of investigators, to improve the quality of materials put before the courts and to safeguard the rights of arrestees and those in custody. PACE and its codes of practice provided the police with specified powers balanced with the rights of the individual. The Act sets out practices for the investigation of crime, in relation to search, detention, interviewing and a range of other powers.

One of the main responses to this crisis of confidence by the then Home Office Forensic Science Service was to increase and formalize quality management procedures, which at that time were comparatively novel in forensic practice. Changes to procedures included standardized protocols for examinations and increased numbers of declared and undeclared (blind) trials – a form of internal audit. These trials resulted in closer scrutiny of scientific methods, administrative procedures and interpretations of results within and between different laboratories. This was in addition to new roles specifically responsible for the planning, implementation and evaluation of quality assurance practices in laboratories. The wide-scale introduction of these measures resulted in structural and cultural changes in forensic science laboratories in England and Wales and ultimately the whole of the forensic science sector in the UK. Forensic science continued to grow in the political environment of the 1980s in which a Conservative government strongly favoured the market as a control mechanism for the public sector. Following a House of Commons Home Affairs Committee inquiry, it was recommended that the FSS become an executive agency of the Home Office and that they should commence direct charging of police forces for their services (Gallop 2003). This was seen as a potential mechanism for controlling the spiralling increase in the workload of forensic science laboratories that were effectively obliged at that time to accept and examine virtually all items submitted by the police service. It also meant that the customer (the police) was entitled to instruct any examination that they considered relevant so long as they were willing to foot the bill.

The resulting relationship between user and provider was radically different from traditional public sector provision in most other countries in the world. This new arrangement compelled each party to develop new management structures and procedures to track laboratory examinations and costs to maintain financial control. The FSS developed a price list for products and services and the police were required to implement an authorization process to control laboratory examinations not considered useful or economically viable. The Metropolitan Police Forensic Science Laboratory, the largest laboratory in Europe, remained within the Metropolitan Police until it was merged with the FSS in April 1996. The FSS, as a consequence, became the main supplier of forensic science to the police service in England and Wales with a virtual monopoly of the market.

The former Laboratory of the Government Chemist (LGC) provided a restricted range of services, such as drugs analysis, to law enforcement agencies, primarily Revenue and Customs (formerly Her Majesty's Customs and Excise). The LGC subsequently became an executive agency of the Home Office and was privatized in 1996 (see http://www.lgc.co.uk). This privatization appeared to pass without controversy, perhaps because of their relatively limited involvement in forensic science at that time. In 2005 the LGC acquired Forensic Alliance Ltd, a private company that was set up to provide a wide range of specialist forensic services. With this acquisition the LGC expanded their portfolio of services considerably, enabling them to move from being a primary niche supplier to a strategic supplier according to the typology of Fraser (2003). It is anticipated that the FSS will soon become a private company, thus ensuring competition but with highly limited choice in strategic terms. This privatization has attracted considerable public and political attention, including that of a House of Commons Select Committee (2005).

The increasingly commercialized relationship between law enforcement agencies and forensic science laboratories has resulted in a unique environment in England and Wales. The privatization of forensic science remains controversial and it will take some time before sufficient evidence becomes available to evaluate the benefits and risks it may bring. However, the gradual change in the relationship between the police and forensic scientists, particularly via direct charging, has led to a shift from the expert power of laboratories to that of the police. This has resulted in some tangible benefits to the criminal justice process. One of the main benefits appears to be speed of delivery of forensic analyses. In many instances drugs analysis and DNA profiling are now carried out within a few days of submission by the police and, in a significant proportion of cases, on the same day. This contrasts strongly with the public sector provision of forensic science around the world, which is almost universally characterized by backlogs. In some countries this situation is also compounded by a lack of resources and poor infrastructure. The US Department of Justice (2005) estimated the backlog of cases in US publicly funded laboratories at just over 500,000 – an increase of 70 per cent on their backlogs at the beginning of the same year (2002). The report also estimated the need for an additional 1,900 staff at a cost of $70 million to achieve a 30-day turnaround time. If justice delayed is justice denied, then perhaps there are significant benefits to be gained from a competitive market that are in the interests of justice.

The impact of DNA

In 1995, following new legislation, the world's first DNA database was introduced as a joint venture between the FSS and the Association of Chief Police Officers (ACPO). From a slow start, beset by organizational difficulties, unrealistic expectations and backlogs in processing, the National DNA Database (NDNAD) has led to a revolution in how major and volume crime are investigated. The introduction of a number of novel tactical investigative tools, such as intelligence-led screens (for an overview, see Williams *et al.* 2004) and familial searching (ACPO 2005a), is a direct consequence of the implementation of the NDNAD. Although such techniques are now in use in other jurisdictions, they were pioneered in England and Wales and, as such, England and Wales has led most of the advances in this area of forensic science. The development of the NDNAD also led to DNA and other aspects of forensic science having an increasingly important role in the formulation of criminal justice policy. This is most clearly demonstrated by the investment of £300 million by the Home Office to the DNA Expansion Project (see http://police.homeoffice.gov.uk/police-reform/policing-improvement-agency/). The aim of this project was to have the DNA of every active criminal on the NDNAD. Subsequent changes in legislation have resulted in England and Wales having the most permissive DNA laws in the world.

Further legislative developments

The Criminal Procedures and Investigations Act 1996 was introduced following criticisms of the police in two Royal Commission reports in the 1980s and an Audit Commission report in 1994. Part I of the Act provides specific instructions for the disclosure, recording and retention of materials and directs that retained material is revealed to the prosecutor. This Act requires the prosecution to disclose all material that it relies upon for the prosecution in addition to any other material that may undermine the prosecution case or assist the defence case as set out in the defence statement. This includes all material of a scientific nature and contemporaneous notes, photographs, analytical results, informal reports, discussions and statements. The codes of practice under Part II of the Act also place a general responsibility on the investigator to 'pursue all reasonable lines of inquiry, whether these point towards or away from the suspect'. The codes of practice also make it clear that those who act on behalf of the investigating officer, including civilian specialists such as crime scene investigators, are deemed to be investigators under the Act. This places a distinctive legal duty on those forensic experts acting on behalf of the police to investigate in an inquisitorial manner.

In summary, the forensic science environment in England and Wales is a distinctive and dynamic one with the forthcoming developments in large-scale privatization likely to remain one of its main distinguishing features.

Professional developments in forensic science

While it is the case that science is an international enterprise, forensic science develops and is constrained by the jurisdiction within which it operates. The distinctive trajectory of forensic science in England and Wales is partly a consequence of a particular legal environment. A further recommendation of the Royal Commission on Criminal Justice (1993) which remains unimplemented was the introduction of a 'Forensic Science Advisory Council'. However, a number of proposed roles for this advisory council have been fulfilled following the inauguration of the Council for Registration of Forensic Practitioners (CRFP). The CRFP is a professional regulatory body and non-profit-making company limited by guarantee (see http://www.crfp.org.uk). It is currently funded by pump-priming money from the government via a grant from the Home Office until it becomes self-sufficient. The Royal Commission report (1993) recommended that 'the professional bodies assist the courts in their task of assessment by maintaining a special register of their members who are suitably qualified to act as an expert witness in particular areas of expertise'. On the face of it this recommendation appears reasonable – asking the experts to provide some guidance on who is fit to give evidence in particular disciplines. There was at that time no professional body for forensic science and it was assumed that professional bodies for other scientific disciplines were sufficiently interested and had sufficient understanding of the nature of forensic science to make such recommendations.

Although it is generally the case that scientific expertise and credentials are often equated with forensic science expertise and competence, this can only be to a limited degree. A forensic scientist not only requires knowledge of his or her scientific discipline but also of criminal law and procedure, together with the reasoning skills to evaluate this evidence in the light of the specific case findings and the communications skills to present the evidence in court. In short, equating scientific expertise with forensic science expertise is fallacious. However, the recommendation for a Forensic Science Advisory Council resulted in a novel approach to governing forensic professional practice in the UK. The notorious cases that led to the inquiry had wide-ranging problems that included forensic science, but not all the problems derived from the poor practice of forensic science. Furthermore, the Royal Commission appears to have taken a very narrow view of forensic science – as scientific work carried out in a laboratory environment. This ignored potential problems that may be manifest by scientific analysis (for example, contamination of items) but that have their roots in activities that take place at crime scenes prior to receipt by laboratories. A simple example from current practice illustrates this point. Despite the vast numbers of scientific tests carried out by the NDNAD, errors in the laboratory are extremely rare. The largest source of errors in DNA submissions are administrative mistakes by the police before the sample is submitted to the database.

Setting standards in laboratories in isolation to the rest of the criminal justice process, particularly scene management and forensic aspects of investigations carried out in the police service, is of limited value. The difficulty of how to describe the multiplicity of roles directly involved in processes was resolved by denoting all such roles as 'forensic practitioners'. In addition to introducing the notion of accrediting forensic practitioners, in the debate on the Royal Commission report, Lord Dainton made it clear that registration demonstrating fitness to practise should be 'tested' *irrespective of qualifications and experience*. Registrants of the CRFP are assessed by current practitioners, are required to adhere to a code of conduct and may be subject to disciplinary action that includes removal from the register. This approach is fundamentally different from all other professional bodies that typically use qualifications, experience and references as indicators of competence as opposed to attempting to establish competence directly by assessment. The approach used by the CRFP to accredit practitioners is based on a review of recent cases carried out by the individual, irrespective of his or her discipline or field of expertise, and this adds a further unique dimension to the forensic science environment in the UK.

In order to achieve this, the CRFP has three sector assessment panels: Science, Medicine and Healthcare, and Incident Investigation. We will confine ourselves in this chapter to Science and Incident Investigation. The functions of the assessment panels are to identify the criteria that denote competence in each of their forensic specialities and to develop methods to assess the competence of applicants. They are also responsible for the appointment of assessors in each specialty, all of which must be registered. Some examples of specialty areas in science include drugs, firearms, human contact traces, incident reconstruction, marks, questioned documents and toxicology. The CRFP has strong but not universal support from the police and the forensic science profession. Approximately 70 per cent of laboratory-based scientists are currently registered, but the figure for fingerprint experts and crime scene investigators is under 50 per cent (Horne, pers. comm. October 2005).

The Forensic Science Society

The Forensic Science Society (FSSoc) was founded in 1959 in response to a perceived need by forensic scientists for a forum to promote discussion and the advancement of forensic science. Until recently the FSSoc acted as a traditional learned society, arranging conferences and publishing a wide range of materials of relevance to forensic scientists. Despite previous involvement at governmental level, such as select committees, the influence of the FSSoc steadily waned throughout the 1990s. This was possibly due to the many structural changes in forensic science in England and Wales and the heavy involvement of employers in setting standards in forensic science via quality management and organizational accreditation. The advent of the CRFP also raised the question of the relevance of a professional body if the CRFP were to be successful in becoming the benchmark of competence in forensic practice. Prior to the development of the CRFP, the FSSoc was perceived by many as the logical locus for any register of practitioners. However, this did not take place. Increasingly, the membership of the FSSoc became concerned that they had no professional association by which to address the potential difficulties that the changing shape of the sector, and in particular, the market, may have presented. Furthermore, the burgeoning of academic forensic science courses (many of which were considered to be of little relevance to forensic science practice) increasingly became a matter of concern to practitioners.

In 2004, therefore, the FSSoc was formally launched as a professional body, a development that was widely supported by the membership and recognized as significant in the sector (see http://www.forensic-science-society.org). The significance of this development will take some time to be known. The functions and activities of the FSSoc now mirror those of a typical professional body. The FSSoc has around 2,500 members in over 58 countries, with the vast majority of these in the UK. Furthermore, over 90 per cent of UK members are laboratory-based scientists as opposed to police personnel. The recent change in status has raised the profile of the FSSoc and it is now represented on a number of national committees, such as the Forensic Science Sector Strategy Group (an employers' group). It was also invited to give evidence at the House of Commons select committee inquiry on forensic science (2005).

Forensic science in the police service

The primary source of forensic science knowledge and expertise in the police service resides with the scientific support departments (SSDs). The term 'scientific support' derives from a Touche Ross report (1987) and is not used outside the UK. Touche Ross recognized the need for the effective management of a range of forensic science activities within police organizations. The report recommended the recruitment of managers – scientific support managers (SSMs) – skilled and experienced in general management to rectify the difficulties described in the report. The exact role, structure and composition of SSD vary widely, although most have delegated responsibility for the investigation and management of the forensic aspects of crime. Scientific support is also the day-to-day source of advice and expertise in ongoing investigations and on matters of policy, practice and standards. However, although SSDs have extensive knowledge of the investigative applications of forensic science, they rarely have the detailed scientific knowledge that is available within forensic science laboratories that may be required in some investigations and for the development of policy and practice. The role of the SSM, according to HMIC (2000):

should encompass the following core responsibilities:

- The development of strategy for scientific support and input into the overall force strategy regarding crime
- The development of policy for all forensic activity including fingerprint bureaux and chemical laboratories
- The development of monitoring systems
- Quality control processes
- Identification and dissemination of good practice
- Inspectorate/Best Value.

Each police force and most police organizations in England and Wales have an SSD, the core activities of which are crime scene investigation, fingerprint examination and photography. Although they carry out similar functions, there is considerable variation in the designations of these departments, including forensic investigation, scientific investigation and scientific or forensic services.

The role of crime scene investigation is the routine examination of crime scenes as determined by individual force policy. There are considerable differences in crime scene investigation practices between police organizations that remain unexplained, despite recommendations from external organizations such as Her Majesty's Inspectorate of Constabulary (HMIC) and the Police Standards Unit (PSU). Crime scene examination consists mainly of the examination of stolen vehicles and burglaries for evidence and intelligence such as shoe-marks, tool-marks, fingerprints, blood and other body fluids containing DNA. This work is carried out by volume crime scene examiners (VCSEs) or crime scene investigators (CSIs). There is no agreed terminology for either of these roles, and variants include volume crime scene investigator and assistant scenes of crime officer, for the former, and scenes of crime officer (SOCO), crime scene examiner and forensic investigator for the latter. In serious or major incidents such as sexual offences, robbery or homicide, a senior crime scene investigator, crime scene manager or crime scene co-ordinator is likely to be involved. These roles bring higher levels of skill and knowledge to bear in more serious investigations, in addition to co-ordination and planning. Crucially, one of these roles will, on behalf of the senior investigating officer (SIO), be a direct link to an external forensic science laboratory and will play an influential part in the development of a forensic strategy for an investigation.

The fingerprint bureau, department or unit provides specialist skills in fingerprint recovery, examination and comparison. The identification of individuals is central to the criminal justice process, and fingerprint experts are responsible for the identification of offenders and victims of crime. The implementation of the National Automated Fingerprint Identification Service (NAFIS) in 2000 has resulted in fingerprints roles that are increasingly standardized nationally. Fingerprints experts – those who by virtue of their training, knowledge and expertise give evidence as expert witnesses – are the largest group of experts in forensic science within the police service. Most police forces also have a chemical development laboratory, the function of which is to use a number of routine chemical and physical processes to develop latent (i.e. invisible) fingermarks on items of interest. The size of these laboratories varies considerably, with only the largest metropolitan forces having more than a few personnel.

Photography and imaging is the third main component of SSDs which fulfils an essential aspect of forensic work: the recording of crime scenes and incidents using still and moving images. These units in most police forces are the repository of specialist knowledge in the capture, storage, printing and transmission of still images from traditional 'wet' photography and in developing digital techniques. In relation to moving images (analogue or digital), the position is less clear cut. However, most SSD photography/

imaging units have some expertise in relation to video images. In most police organizations, image capture (still and moving) at crime scenes is routinely carried out by CSIs, senior CSIs or their equivalent.

Training of scientific support

Prior to 1990, training for the police service in the functions that would generally be considered those of a typical SSD was patchy and fragmented. This was provided by three regional training centres in the Metropolitan Police, West Yorkshire Police and Durham Constabulary. In 1990, following a recommendation in the Touche Ross (1987) report, the National Training Centre for Scientific Support to Crime Investigation (NTC) was set up. Currently there are two main scientific support training centres in the Metropolitan Police and the NTC in Durham. The training provision of both these organizations is becoming increasingly harmonized, the aim being to develop a consistent national approach. Training provided by the NTC includes:

- all aspects of crime scene investigation;
- crime scene management and co-ordination;
- all aspects of fingerprint examination; and
- a range of specialist courses (e.g. fire investigation, digital photography, facial identification).

These are in addition to two academic diploma programmes in fingerprints and crime scene examination, accredited by the University of Durham. A small number of forces (for example, Kent Police) continue to train their own scientific support staff.

The most significant recent development in police training was the establishment of the Central Police Training and Development Authority (Centrex), the aim of which is 'to help drive a modernising agenda by creating and delivering career long learning, and by providing a centre of policing excellence and support' (see http://www.centrex.org.uk). Following a recommendation by HMIC (2000), the NTC became part of Centrex. Part of the rationale for this recommendation included the need for the NTC to act as a truly national centre, with appropriate financing and resources that could not be made available from within an individual police force.

Investigative development in the police service

A key interface between the police service and forensic science laboratories is the investigation of serious major crime (e.g. sexual offences, robbery and homicide). Historically, homicide has been at the forefront of developments and difficulties in many aspects of investigation, including forensic science. This has resulted in significant and continuous improvements in overall investigative knowledge and standards in homicide in recent decades.

Following the widely publicized failures in the 'Yorkshire Ripper' investigation and a report by Sir Lawrence Byford, significant changes to the methodology and administration of major investigations were recommended. For the most part – such as the use of computer databases (e.g. HOLMES – Home Office Large Major Enquiry System) – these are now embedded in current practice. A key recommendation was the implementation of investigative reviews (Home Office 1982). ACPO subsequently introduced a policy that recommended the review of all murders that remained undetected after four weeks. This review process is of considerable value in establishing variations in practice and knowledge acquisition. In 1998 further guidance on reviews (ACPO Crime Committee 2000) was introduced into the *Major Incident Room Standardised Administrative Procedures* (*MIRSAP*) manual to ensure that investigations met nationally agreed standards.

The *Murder Manual* (1999) was published by ACPO with the aim of setting a national standard in homicide investigations. The *Murder Manual* (*MM*) was the first attempt to set out standards and guidance in serious investigations that went beyond checklists and procedures by developing a model for effective investigation that included not only relevant aspects of process but also conceptual aspects of investigation. The *MM* addressed specific aspects of forensic science, but only to a limited extent.

The National Centre for Policing Excellence (NCPE) was founded in April 2003 to increase the professional capacity of the police by identifying and disseminating evidence-based practice. The NCPE, part of Centrex, has three key business areas: doctrine development, operational support and specialist training. The need for doctrine development derives from the legal obligations placed on Centrex by the Police Reform Act 2002 to develop draft regulations and codes as commissioned by the Home Secretary. The NCPE also receive requests from ACPO and Home Office policy units for guidance and practice advice. Operational support falls into three categories: uniformed support, crime support and the serious crimes analysis section. The key document produced by the NCPE with respect to investigation and therefore forensic science is the *Core Investigative Doctrine* (ACPO 2005b). This provides definitive national guidance on the principles of criminal investigation. The Core Investigative Doctrine (CID) also supports the Professionalizing Investigation Programme (PIP), a tripartite ACPO, Home Office and Police Skills and Standards Organization (now known as Skills for Justice) project. The purpose of this project is to examine, develop and make recommendations to professionalize investigation. At the heart of the CID is a model of investigation that describes the activities, decisions and outcomes in criminal investigations and that sets out, in a comprehensive manner, the legal, ethical, procedural and conceptual aspects of criminal inquiries. Central to this, following a range of new legislation (particularly the Criminal Procedure and Investigations Act (CPIA) 1996), is the need for an 'inquisitorial investigator'. These developments in investigation and in the use of forensic science should be seen in a broader context of the shared expectations of the Home Office and police service in the use of science in investigations as presented in the Police Science and Technology Strategy (Home Office 2004). The purpose of the Police Science and Technology

Strategy (PSTS) is 'To ensure the police service is equipped to exploit the opportunities in science and technology to deliver effective policing as part of a modern and respected criminal justice system' (Home Office 2004).

The strategy identifies key priorities, all of which are relevant to the investigative use of forensic science:

- Maximizing the value of evidence.
- Effective management of investigations, including the use of intelligent systems to assist decision-making.
- Effective location and recovery of evidence.

The PSTS (Home Office 2004) goes on to state:

> If the benefits of science and technology are to be realised then training is essential and not only for those in specialist roles, but for all officers and support staff. Centrex (NCPE) and other training providers play a key role in ensuring that all staff can make the most of science and technology. The NCPE in cooperation with ACPO, Association of Police Authorities (APA), HMIC and the Police Standards Unit, (PSU) will play an important part in the identification, capture and dissemination of good practice in operational policing.

In April 2006 a new organization of relevance was due to commence operations. The National Policing Improvement Agency (NPIA) was created 'to support self improvement across the police service and to drive forward the Home Secretary's national critical programmes outlined in the national policing plan' (see http://police.homeoffice.gov.uk/police-reform/policing-improvement-agency/). It is anticipated that, with the creation of the NPIA, the number of staff employed at national level in Centrex, the Police Information and Technology Organization (PITO) and parts of the Home Office will reduce to at least half the current levels. A core function of the NPIA is 'improving professional practice', and it is anticipated that a single new organization will be more effective than the multiple organizations that appear currently to share this aim. The NPIA will also have major implications for ACPO, the APA and the HMIC.

The role of ACPO

The effective management of developments in forensic science and investigation requires a wide range of specialist stakeholders in a rapidly changing environment. Within the police service this role is carried out by ACPO. ACPO is a company limited by guarantee and funded jointly by the Home Office and 44 police authorities that acts on behalf of the police service (see http://www.acpo.police.uk). ACPO was set up 50 years ago in order that policy development could be made in one place as opposed to in 43 separate forces. According to the ACPO website: 'the nature of modern crime, with an increasingly international dimension, and the ever present

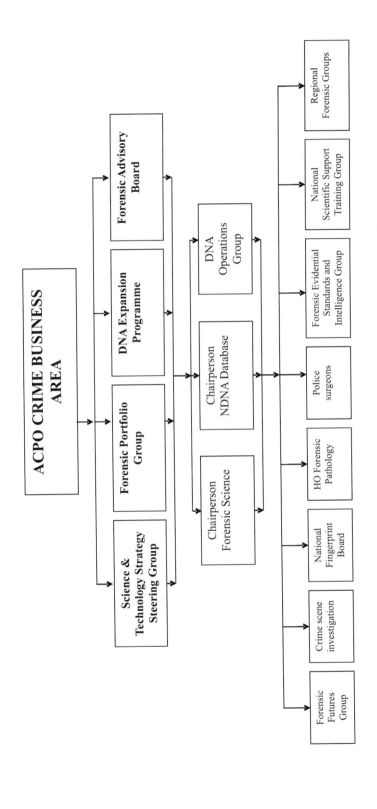

Figure 15.1 Association of Chief Police Officers' forensic management portfolio

need to use public resources to best effect, places a voluntary duty on forces to work together, employing common policies, strategies and methods wherever possible.'

Figure 15.1 illustrates the committee structure of ACPO for the management of the forensic science portfolio. In addition to senior officers and specialists from the police service, these committees include representatives from the Home Office Forensic Science and Pathology Unit, the PSU, the Human Genetics Commission, the FSS, the PITO, Centrex, the NTC, the NCPE and occasionally external consultants and advisers.

Forensic science training by laboratories

There are two major strategic suppliers (LGC and the FSS) of forensic science to the police service who provide training on a commercial basis. The provision of this training is therefore dependent on a perceived customer need from individual police organizations as opposed to being a formal aspect of national police training. These organizations contribute to knowledge growth and acquisition in two ways: directly as training providers and indirectly by a range of other means, such as during individual case investigations. They are also involved in a range of advisory roles in the development of policy and guidance via specific committees. The FSS provided 737 training courses to over 60 law enforcement agencies in 2004–5 (Hands, pers. comm. January 2006). In terms of developing their own staff, they ran over 14,000 training days in all subjects in the same year.

Forensic science education

Until recently there was limited direct connection between higher education and police investigative knowledge of forensic science. The majority of forensic scientists in England and Wales were recruited into scientific organizations as graduates, and the comparatively small number of graduates recruited into scientific support or the police more generally had no specialist training in forensic science. There have been considerable developments in this arena in the past decade or so. The first educational programme in forensic science in the UK was implemented by the University of Strathclyde in 1967. This was followed in the mid-1980s by King's College London, who introduced an MSc in Forensic Science. In 1989, the University of Strathclyde introduced the first undergraduate programme, a BSc in Forensic and Analytical Chemistry, following the success of their Masters course. Since then there has been a virtual explosion of programmes badged as 'forensic', with around 50 institutions providing over 350 courses (SEMTA 2004). This is a global not just a UK phenomenon. A similar expansion of forensic programmes is taking place in North America and Australasia, but less so in continental Europe. The Science, Engineering and Mathematics Alliance (SEMTA) is a government-funded organization whose role is to link employers' needs to higher education. Following increasing concerns expressed by forensic science organizations and the FSSoc, SEMTA reviewed the provision of 'forensic science' higher education programmes. Their report identified highly variable content in courses in addition to a diversity of potentially misleading titles. Although most of these programmes were science degrees, some had very little formal scientific content. The review examined the scientific and 'forensic' content of a number of programmes. The highest science content was identified as '85 per cent', but some courses were considered to be '100 per cent forensic'. It is far from clear what '100 per cent forensic' means other than that there is no scientific content. Most students gave their reason for studying forensic courses as to gain employment as forensic scientists, crime scene investigators or fingerprint experts. This is despite the fact that graduate numbers will soon exceed demand by employers at least fourfold, and that many of the qualifications do not meet the needs of employers. Most scientific employers cited a preference for science degrees as opposed to forensic science degrees, and were sceptical of the ability of higher education institutions to deliver their needs. They also expressed the view that there was a major disparity between the skills required and those being provided by educational institutions. Police representatives consulted in the review suspected that they were being approached by some universities to add credibility to their courses.

The enormous growth in students who wish to study forensic science is hard to explain. The popular reason cited by the media and some educational institutions is the 'CSI effect' – that is, a number of TV drama series have inspired thousands of students to seek careers in this type of work. Whatever their merit as drama, most of these programmes are inaccurate, some fantastically so, in their portrayal of forensic science, the legal process and police investigation. Therefore large numbers of students may be embarking on studies with false perceptions of the subject and very limited prospects of a career in their chosen area of interest. A further aspect of the growth in forensic courses, given that most institutions in the review cited income as 'an important factor', is that universities are using these courses to maintain student numbers against a decline in popularity in more traditional subjects. The contribution of these courses to knowledge growth and acquisition will take some time to assess.

Law, science and investigation

Forensic science is applied, and develops, at the interfaces of three powerful and influential areas of human activity: law, science and policing. Each of these spheres of activity has distinctive traditions, structures, cultures and professional dimensions. However, to some degree all three sectors are influenced by general environmental factors, such as the political or economic climate. The combination of such diverse spheres of activity results in a distinctive cultural web (Johnson and Scholes 1997), creating a unique arena of activity for forensic science. The interface of science and law has been the subject of scrutiny from observers in the social sciences, such as Jasanoff (1995) in the USA. Although Jasanoff largely confines herself to science and the law, with the issues of investigation or policing not explicitly addressed, these are implicit for as we have seen, the police are key intermediaries in forensic science use by the criminal justice system.

Jasanoff makes a number of original and insightful observations on the relationship between science and law that are relevant to an understanding of how knowledge is shaped and acquired in the context we are considering. Two of these observations merit further exploration. The first is that the law and science are continually involved in conflicts over knowledge – the traditional preserve of science – and responsibility – the traditional preserve of the law. These conflicts are continually shaping and reshaping science and the law but not necessarily to each other's satisfaction. A good example of this is the development of case law and scientific practice in relation to the 'prosecutor's fallacy'. The central issue in the 'prosecutor's fallacy' is confusion of the DNA match probability (a matter for the scientist) with the probability of guilt or innocence (a matter for the jury). An increasingly complex series of disputes over the interpretation of DNA statistics in the English courts ultimately led to definitive judgments.[1] Although this clarified the issue in many respects, the judgments replaced standard and universally agreed statistical terminology with legal phraseology that was unsatisfactory to scientists and statisticians.

Secondly, Jasanoff cites effectiveness as a key issue in the legal process: the right for citizens to be dealt with to an acceptable standard and for outcomes to be reasonable, explicable and fair. There are clear implications here for scientific and investigative practices. If effectiveness means in essence getting it right, how does one go about getting forensic science right in the context we are considering? How does one establish acceptable standards and, in the more specifically managerial sense, good practice?

Given the dynamic nature of the sector as it is currently configured and described by Jasanoff, it is perhaps appropriate at this stage to consider the centrality of forensic science knowledge to policing as a whole. The management literature (Grant 1995; Johnson and Scholes 1997) contains extensive references to the concepts of core competences or distinctive competences and explores the idea of organizational capabilities. Such matters have a bearing on our consideration of knowledge growth and acquisition. The term 'core competency' was coined by Prahalad and Hamel (1990) to distinguish those capabilities that are fundamental to an organization's performance and strategy from those that are more peripheral. Is knowledge of forensic science a core competency of policing? Although forensic science may be peripheral to public order policing, roads policing and community policing, it is central to the investigation of crime and other incidents, such as mass disasters. In some instances, such as supply of drugs, one cannot determine if a crime has been committed without the identification of the relevant substances, as this information is fundamental to the formulation of the charges involved.

Increasingly in volume crime, forensic science is being presented as the most effective means of detection, with cited rates for cases in which DNA has been recovered being up to seven times those of cases with no DNA (Forensic Science Service 2004). However, a note of caution is required here. Although

DNA is likely to be a more effective means of detection, the true causal relationship between DNA and crime detection is yet to be clearly established. In serious and major crime such as homicide, there appears to be a strong case for arguing that forensic science is central to any investigation. This does not mean that it necessarily always produces significant intelligence or evidence in individual cases but that, with rare exceptions, it must be considered in every case and is therefore a core aspect of police knowledge. One can gain some perspective of the police view of the importance of forensic science to crime investigation from the *MM*:

> As professional investigators, SIOs must be able to optimise the benefits of forensic science. This can only be achieved if the SIO not only understands the significance of material that may be found at crime scenes but is also able to access its potential and interpret the findings. The SIO can only hope to maximise forensic potential if they harness their own knowledge of the subject with other experts; for example, SOCOs, Scientific Support Managers and Forensic Scientists (ACPO 1999: 41).

What emerges from the guidance in the *MM* on the use of forensic science is the essential need for its integration within the investigation, and the means by which this can be achieved. The effective use of forensic science requires a multidisciplinary forensic management team which may include a number of specialists – typically, the deputy SIO, an exhibits officer, a forensic scientist, pathologist and crime scene manager. The purpose of the forensic management team is to ensure that there is effective consideration of the potential for forensic science to contribute to the investigation and that all who can contribute are given the opportunity. This is achieved by addressing a number of specific objectives that are typically encountered in a murder investigation and by developing strategies for optimizing forensic outcomes in relation to laboratory submissions and analysis, the arrest of the suspect, and the search and management of the crime scene. Forensic strategy, scene strategy, arrest strategy, search strategy and forensic management team represent a new vocabulary describing processes and concepts that aid the integration of science with investigation and the sharing and acquisition of knowledge. This approach is extended in the CID, which details some of the issues that ought to be considered in developing a forensic strategy:

- The clarification of the involvement and activities of suspects and witnesses.
- The elimination of individuals from an inquiry.
- The use of forensic intelligence, such as partial DNA or partial finger-marks.
- The use of inceptive intelligence for the identification of individuals from DNA or fingerprints.
- The corroboration of events.
- Establishing the sequence of events.
- Ensuring scientific evidence is set in context.

This last point is probably the single most important breakthrough in the use of forensic science by the police: the growing understanding that evidence can only be interpreted in relation to the specific circumstances of the case. Given the attention paid to forensic science in the *MM* and other similar publications, one is compelled to conclude that, although it forms a very small part of policing overall, the effective use of forensic science is a core capability. If forensic science is a core capability of policing, then the identifiable components, structures and mechanisms by which this capability is maintained and developed ought to be identifiable within the police service and in some of the organizations we have described above.

The current state of knowledge

Published audits from a number of sources consistently highlight a poor knowledge of forensic science in the police service. This is the case not only in general terms but also in high-risk areas such as homicide investigation. *Using Forensic Science Effectively* (ACPO/FSS/Audit Commission 1996) is a seminal document published over a decade ago. It found that 'awareness of scientific support is poor and often insufficient for purpose' and that there was 'almost a complete absence of forensic science content in probationer [constable] or refresher training'. Four years later, HMIC (2000) carried out a thematic inspection of scientific support only to find that 'despite repeated reminders in successive reports from diverse sources, there is no national policy that operational staff receive "awareness" training'. And: 'Despite several revisions of the content of training for inspectors or sergeants ... national supervisory training does not at present provide any input on scientific and technical support.' The Appendix of *Under the Microscope* (HMIC 2000) reinforced this message by including a summary of *Using Forensic Science Effectively*, outlining its methodology, findings and recommendations. A follow-up thematic inspection by HMIC (2002) later found that improvement was very patchy: 'A recurrent theme of the inspection was the lack of awareness [of forensic science] at all levels, particularly the operational level, of what could be achieved.' It was also directly critical of ACPO: 'The lack of full engagement amongst Chief Officers was reflected in many of the responses from the forces assessed in this revisit.' Although both *Using Forensic Science Effectively* and *Under the Microscope* referred to good practice, this appears to be more by way of assertion than on the basis of evidence.

In a thematic inspection on training by HMIC (2004), good practice was defined on the basis of the European Framework of Quality Management. This requires a process of evaluation before good practice can be identified and recommended. As a consequence, no examples of good practice were cited in the HMIC publication, but instances of 'noteworthy practice' were. In this extensive review of national police training, the word 'forensic' is only used once, in passing, in the entire document. Nor does forensic science feature anywhere in the 31-week national training programmes for probationer constables described in the Annexe to the document.

Nicol *et al.* (2004) identified among six main areas of failure in homicide reviews 'forensics (exhibit management and submission)'. They go on to identify forensic science as an area of particular concern, as there was a routine failures to comply with standard procedures as well as a number of cases where potential forensic evidence had been completely overlooked and not submitted for laboratory examination.

A joint initiative between the FSS and PSU (FSS 2005) that commenced in January 2004 confirmed the poor use of forensic science in serious cases. In 213 unsolved cases in which DNA was present but had previously only been analysed by now out-of-date technology, 76 usable DNA profile were obtained resulting in 31 matches from the NDNAD. These results were subsequently central to the conviction of a number of individuals. It seems clear that not only is knowledge of forensic science very poor in the police service but also that the response to processes one would normally expect to detect poor practice (i.e. audit and review) were failing to improve the situation.

Despite the rather pessimistic assessment that emerges from formal audit, it is clear that the growth and acquisition of knowledge by a number of mechanisms continue to take place. The sources of this knowledge include published manuals and policies; the implementation of new roles; investigative use in individual cases; formal reviews of investigations; and the implementation of new scientific techniques and technologies.

The *MM* and CID are supplemented by a continuous stream of policy and practice guidance from ACPO. For example, the *DNA Good Practice Manual* (ACPO 2005a) provides extensive guidance on the use of DNA, including the use of partial matches, intelligence-led screens and familial searching. Furthermore, effective forensic strategies in individual cases require continuous high-quality interaction and communication resulting in knowledge transfer on a range of procedural issues in policing and forensic science. These include improved knowledge of the processes, stages, scientific disciplines, timescales and the potential evidential value of forensic strategies. The introduction of direct charging has led to the monitoring of the volume and outcome of specific areas of forensic analysis that can be used to judge the cost effectiveness and efficiency of testing. Together with the DNA Expansion Programme, direct charging has resulted in the development of new roles that support a closer focus on performance management issues that should enable the evaluation of evidence-based good practice.

However, the absence of specific aspects of scientific knowledge within the police service strongly suggests that, in some key areas, there is no current mechanism for developing certain important areas of knowledge. There are very few practising scientists within the police service, despite the growing importance of science to policing. This situation is exacerbated by the current physical, methodological and conceptual gulf between forensic science as practised in laboratories outside the police service and fingerprints, which operates mainly within the police service. This has led to some obvious gaps in knowledge that could present future risks if not addressed. The Touche Ross (1987) report recommended the introduction of formal quality-assurance mechanisms. Formal quality assurance in forensic science is now routine and is embedded within UK laboratories, but there has been very limited implementation in the police service. Fingerprint laboratory work carried out in the police service that is not formally scientifically accredited presents an increasing risk, as this will inevitably be compared with that work provided by external scientific laboratories that do have independent accreditation. This is distinct from the more general quality assurance of fingerprints, which does not require accredited scientific standards.

A second important gap in core knowledge relates to the methods of evidence evaluation now widespread in forensic science. Bayesian evaluation (Robertson and Vingaux 1995) of evidence is now the norm in most areas of forensic science. As scientific laboratories become more involved in fingerprint examinations as part of the external market, it is increasingly likely that they will evaluate their findings differently from fingerprint experts. Fingerprint evidence is generally presented as categorical identifications (i.e. unique matches to the exclusion of all other possibilities). This contrasts with scientific evidence, which is generally presented in probabilistic terms. This has significant implications for handling fingerprint intelligence from 'partial' matches. Forensic science routinely deals with probabilistic non-categorical identifications, but the fingerprint community is unfamiliar with this approach and suspicious of recommendations that it could provide a better means of providing evidence and intelligence.

The role of Centrex

Fundamental to the issue of knowledge growth and acquisition is Centrex as the national police training organization. We have already considered the basic (probationer) police training, and I would now like to deal with some aspects of specialist police training that are provided by Centrex (in particular, the NTC). Given that most forensic specialists in police forces are trained by the NTC, its role in knowledge growth and acquisition is crucial. One might also expect this issue to figure highly on the Centrex agenda in terms of the strategic development of knowledge and of the organization that sets the agenda and business targets for the NTC. In the 2002–3 and 2003–4 Centrex annual reports, there is virtually no mention of the NTC and there are no aims, objectives or references of any kind that address the clear need for forensic science training. Nor is there any direct mention of the NTC in the Centrex 2003–8 corporate plan (see http://www.centrex.org.uk). Centrex has never seen the need for any specific aims or objectives in relation to forensic science training in the police service and does not anticipate any for the foreseeable future.

Conclusion

The growth and acquisition of knowledge in the investigative use of forensic science take place in an incremental and fragmented manner, despite the increasing importance of forensic science to the criminal justice system.

Although there is ample evidence of major gaps in knowledge that can only be remedied by extensive training and education, there is no evidence that this is being addressed as a strategic issue by national police-training organizations. The forthcoming privatization of forensic science in England and Wales and the profusion of higher education 'forensic' programmes can only make this situation more complex and confusing. According to Sir David Phillips (ACPO 2005b), the challenge that faces the police service is clear, but this may prove to be beyond reach: 'The real test for policing will be our ability to provide investigators of such credibility that they resemble in every respect the best forensic scientists.'

Selected further reading

ACPO/FSS/Audit Commission (1996) *Using Forensic Science Effectively*. London: HMSO. The seminal report on how forensic science is used, which is still fundamentally accurate despite significant changes in technology and legislation.

Her Majesty's Inspectorate of Constabulary (2000) *Under the Microscope: Thematic Inspection Report on Scientific and Technical Support*. London: Home Office. Her Majesty's Inspector of Constabulary (2002) *Under the Microscope Refocused*. London: Home Office. Two major audits of scientific support usage and effectiveness following the implementation of the National DNA Database. These two publications continue to explore many of the issues encountered in *Using Forensic Science Effectively*.

ACPO (2005) *Practice Advice on Core Investigations Doctrine*. London: ACPO/Centrex. The definitive national guidance on investigative practice. A sophisticated and comprehensive source of relevant information, including an extensive bibliography.

Note

1 *R v. Doheny* (1996) Court of Appeal, Criminal Division; *R v. Adams* (1996) Court of Appeal, Criminal Division.

References

ACPO (1999) *Murder Manual*. London: ACPO.

ACPO (2005a) *DNA Good Practice Manual* (2nd edn.) London: ACPO.

ACPO (2005b) *Practice Advice on Core Investigative Doctrine*. London: ACPO/Centrex.

ACPO Crime Committee (2000) *Major Incident Room Standardised Administrative Procedures*. London: ACPO.

ACPO/FSS/Audit Commission (1996) *Using Forensic Science Effectively*. London: HMSO.

Forensic Science Service (2004) *Annual Report 03/04: The National DNA Database*. Forensic Science Service.

Forensic Science Service (2005) 'Operation Advance: a joint initiative with the Home Office Police Standards Unit (PSU)' (press release).

Fraser, J.G. (2003) 'Delivery and evaluation of forensic science', *Science and Justice*, 43: 127–30.

FSSoc (2004) 'Forensic Science Society launched as a professional body', *Interfaces*, 40: 1.

Gallop, A.M.C. (2003) 'Forensic science coming of age', *Science and Justice*, 43: 55–9.

Grant, R.M. (1995) *Contemporary Strategy Analysis* (2nd edn). Oxford: Blackwell.

Her Majesty's Inspectorate of Constabulary (2000) *Under the Microscope: Thematic Inspection Report on Scientific and Technical Support*. London: Home Office.

Her Majesty's Inspector of Constabulary (2002) *Under the Microscope Refocused*. London: HMIC.

Her Majesty's Inspector of Constabulary (2004) *Training Matters*. London: HMIC.

Home Office (1982) *The Investigation of a Series of Major Crime* (Circular 114/82). London: Home Office.

Home Office (2004) *Police Science Technology Strategy, 2004–2009*. London: Home Office.

Home Office (2005) *DNA Expansion Programme, 2000–2005: Reporting Achievement*. London: Home Office.

House of Commons Science and Technology Committee (2005) *Forensic Science on Trial: Seventh Report of Session 2004–05*. London: HMSO.

Jasanoff, S. (1995) *Science at the Bar: Law Science and Technology in America*. Cambridge, MA: Harvard University Press.

Johnson, G. and Scholes, K. (1997) *Exploring Corporate Strategy*. Hemel Hempstead: Prentice Hall.

Nicol, C., Innes, M., Gee, D. and Feist, A. (2004) *Reviewing Murder Investigations: An Analysis of Progress Reviews from 6 Forces. Home Office Online Report 25/04*. London: Home Office.

Prahalad, C.K. and Hamel, G. (1990) 'The core competencies of the corporation', *Harvard Business Review*, May–June: 79–91.

Robertson, B. and Vignaux, G.A. (1995) *Interpreting Evidence: Evaluating Forensic Science in the Courtroom*. Chichester: Wiley.

Royal Commission on Criminal Justice (1993) *Report* (Cm 2263). London: HMSO.

SEMTA (2004) *Forensic Science: Implications for Higher Education*.

Touche Ross (1987) *Review of Scientific Support for the Police*. London: Home Office.

Townsley, M. and Laycock, G. (2004) *Beyond DNA in the UK: Integration and Harmonisation*. London: Home Office.

US Department of Justice (2005) *Census of Publicly Funded Forensic Crime Laboratories, 2002*. Washington, DC: Bureau of Justice Statistics.

Williams, R., Johnson, P. and Martin, P. (2004) *Genetic Information and Crime Investigation*. Durham: University of Durham.

Part 4

Investigative sources
and processes

The chapters in this part of the book look at such issues as covert surveillance and informant handling, the treatment of victims and witnesses, investigative interviewing, offender and geo-demographic profiling. David Carson's opening chapter examines different approaches to the task of investigation. He questions the extent to which it is appropriate to think of investigation as a scientific process and examines the nature and reliability of expert evidence. Carson analyses decision-making processes and, following a number of other contributors, notes that there is now a balance to be struck between analyses of evidence and the assessment of risk. The rise of risk-based assessment, at least as a basis for the management of investigation, has been paralleled by the emergence of an audit-based approach to criminal investigation. This focuses on the quality, and by implication, cost-effectiveness, of the 'fact-finding' processes. In the event, Carson favours such a model, largely for its potential to enhance not only the investigative process but also the status and reputation of such work.

One area of growing importance in criminal investigation concerns the use of covert surveillance and human intelligence. Dennis Clark examines both these features of contemporary investigation. Both are illustrative of the shift towards more proactive policing techniques, in contrast to what he describes as traditional approaches to investigation. Such traditional policing was based, he argues, on three main approaches: crime scene preservation and examination; the search for witnesses; and the evaluation of information. For a number of reasons, there has been a shift away from reactive styles of policing towards the use of covert techniques and other forms of intelligence gathering. Among the key reasons appear to be the development of new information technologies; the potential for high-quality evidence provided by new surveillance techniques; and the promise of the speedier resolution of cases. Of course, such approaches raise a host of practical, financial and ethical questions, and the regulation of such behaviour is a key issue in contemporary investigative practice and, indeed, in the politics of policing.

Clark takes the reader through the ins and outs of the Regulation of Investigatory Powers Act 2000 as it applies to policing, and also to the growing human rights discourses that surround such policing practices – an area of key concern for the future of police investigation.

Just as there are formal protocols covering police work with informants so, similarly, considerable attention has been paid recently to the 'handling' of victims and witnesses. Nicholas Fyfe and Kevin Smith lead us through this territory and, in particular, examine the ways in which the role of witnesses has altered somewhat in criminal justice policy. There has been a huge array of policy initiatives which have sought to enhance the role of witnesses and to protect those considered to be vulnerable or open to intimidation (an apparently increasing problem). Though significant progress appears to have been made in a number of areas, policing practice remains somewhat variable. The development of specialist witness protection officers has both improved the service provided to witnesses and relieved an important burden hitherto shouldered by investigating officers. However, some problems remain and a key issue emerges, once again, from the growing dominance of risk-based approaches. Fyfe and Smith argue that many witness initiatives are situational in approach – looking to manipulate environments so as to improve the situation of witnesses (via screen, CCTV or relocation). However, at heart these put the needs of the criminal justice system first, are concerned with risk minimization and fail to deal with the fundamental concerns raised and felt by witnesses. There is an important lesson for all public services here.

A related issue is that of 'investigative interviewing'. The term was introduced, Gudjonsson notes, to indicate the shift that has taken place over the last decade or two in which evidence gathering has been prioritized over securing confessions. Gudjonsson outlines a number of investigative interviewing techniques – the most widely used of which is the 'Reid technique' – as well as identifying their shortcomings. He identifies seven principles underlying contemporary practice in the UK, including that the fundamental objective should be the collection of accurate and reliable accounts from victims, witnesses and suspects, and that officers should approach interviews with an open mind. Once again, one would be hard pressed to recognize such approaches in contemporary fictionalized accounts of police work. Gudjonsson goes on to consider the particular case of interrogation in terrorist cases and the very current concerns over the use of coercive techniques. There is much that can go wrong in interrogation, not least in the search for confession, though as yet it appears that the process of confession is still not especially well understood. Gudjonnson concludes by outlining a model of the interrogative process and considering the issue of false confessions. It appears that both successful interviewing and the likelihood of securing a confession rest fundamentally on the quality and strength of the evidence obtained and utilized. Where evidence is weak or flawed there is an increased chance of false confessions and of miscarriages of justice.

The final two chapters in this section consider profiling. The first, by Laurence Alison, Clare McLean and Louise Almond, considers offender profiling. This is arguably the area of contemporary investigative practice that generates the greatest interest and, probably, the greatest inaccuracy. Alison and colleagues provide a detailed account of the nature of different approaches to offender profiling, together with their strengths and limitations. Rather like earlier discussions of forensic science, Alison and colleagues point to the difficulties of making firm statements when the best that can be done is to outline possibilities on the basis of calculating probability. Even this is problematic given the relatively thin evidence base that profilers often have to work with. Nevertheless, used appropriately, offender profiling can help in detectives' decision-making processes, in the processes of investigative interviewing, in the handling of informants and in the prioritization of suspects. Criminological research in recent times has highlighted such issues as repeat victimization and repeat offending. Essentially, researchers have found that not only is crime often concentrated geographically – within particular communities – but often there are 'hotspots' that centre around particular offenders, or groups of offenders, and that people who have been victimized once have an increased risk of future victimization. As a consequence, there is much that can be done to prioritize police work using information about the location of previous crimes, the whereabouts and patterns of behaviour of certain offenders, and the location of victims (of, say, burglary). Plotting such information is undertaken using geographic information systems and other emerging software. David Ashby and Max Craglia take the reader through the history of such approaches and their current development. Their conclusion, after a thorough analysis of existing and emerging techniques, is that 'in the collection, retrieval, display, sharing and analysis of data in a variety of contexts, GIS can enable the investigator to integrate better diverse information sources and target spatially both proactive and reactive policing responses'. The use of geodemographic tools based on huge datasets drawn from the public and private sectors, such as census data and commercial transactions, can provide a profile of neighbourhoods down to the post-code level. Ashby and Craglia provide examples of their potential for assisting investigations and interpreting crime databases. The use of such analytical tools is another indication of the trend towards investigators as knowledge workers. Alongside other developing technologies and techniques, it appears modern criminal investigation is undergoing some potentially very startling changes.

Chapter 16

Models of investigation

David Carson

There are no procedures which can embody truth and fairness (or justice) without sacrificing one to the other, and both to cost (Nobles and Schiff 1997: 299).

This volume flows from a growing interest in, and concern about, investigations. And this chapter flows from a concern that this growing interest will take the nature of investigations for granted or be limited to current policing perspectives, such as proactive or reactive, intelligence led or problem centred, etc. (Newburn 2003). It is particularly concerned with the relationship between investigations, proof and trial – albeit, as the chapter emphasizes, this is very unusual. We have had investigations from time immemorial so that we tend to take things about them for granted, indeed reify them. So this chapter begins by challenging some of these assumptions. It then identifies a number of models, or paradigms, with which investigations might be associated. The chapter will be criticized for being impractical but, it would be replied, this sort of review is a necessary precursor to proposals for appropriate reforms.

Contrasting with the belief that miscarriages of justice are rare aberrations, Nobles and Schiff (1997, 2000) argue that we are condemned to an imperfect system:

Any real life system of criminal justice has to accept that resources are limited, and that society has to do other things with them. So criminal trials are institutions in which the truth is traded off against fairness, and both against considerations of cost. These trade-offs are constantly disguised so that, for example, traditional mechanisms can be presented as if, by being fair, they are also contributing to the pursuit of truth (1997: 297).

But perceived imbalances, affecting the possibility of truth finding, can lead to changes or trade-offs, such as in the rules relating to pre-trial disclosure of evidence (Criminal Procedure and Investigations Act 1996) or the admissibility of prior convictions at trial (Criminal Justice Act 2003). Many of these and other changes, or trade-offs, provoke considerable controversy (Kennedy 2005). Are the problems intrinsic to investigations and the trial and proof systems within which they are located?

Investigating assumptions: what is typical?

The typical criminal justice investigation does not exist, in the sense of a most common example (ACPO 2005), because the norm is no inquiry. The government's Justice Gap Task Force for England and Wales (n.d. but inferred 2002) noted that from 12.9 million offences committed, and 5.17 million recorded, there were 0.62 million prosecutions. So the vast majority of crimes are not investigated and processed to trial in any sense that corroborates the popular image and expectation. Thirty-seven per cent of sexual offences, 10 per cent of criminal damage offences and 9 per cent of burglary offences may be 'brought to justice' but that is – as it can only be – based on crimes known to the police and relates to number of trials rather than convictions. A higher proportion than average of murders may lead to prosecution and conviction (Nicol *et al.* 2004) but other very serious offences, such as rape, have a frighteningly low rate (Her Majesty's Inspectorate of Constabulary and Her Majesty's Crown Prosecution Service Inspectorate 2002; Kelly 2002; Westmarland 2004). A third of the average 3,500 deaths on roads in England and Wales each year is related to speeding (Department for Transport 2004). Consider that there were, in 2004–5, some 2,181 deaths in 'patient safety incidents' in NHS hospitals (National Audit Office 2005: 1). Not only is the popular image of a police inquiry, leading to a contested trial, atypical, but investigations are atypical of crime. For all the writings about modern life involving a 'risk society' (e.g. Wright 2002), with government and policing (e.g. Ericson and Haggerty 1997) preoccupied with removing, distributing or managing risk, the norm is for the consequences of such risks, relating to crime, to go without remedy or remark. But then we focus on the atypical in our criminal justice system. For example, the Royal Commission on Criminal Justice, chaired by Lord Runciman (1993), had broad terms of reference to examine the criminal justice system generally, and miscarriages of justice in particular, but limited themselves almost exclusively to Crown Court trials with juries.

Investigating: at what cost?

How much justice can we afford? The very notion that justice might have a price tag or budget offends popular sensibilities and is rarely highlighted in academic discourse about criminal justice. For example, while Wright (2002) does briefly mention the cost of investigations in his text, the only two finance-related words or phrases in the index to his book are to the interactional costs of crime and the Financial Management Initiative, which requires the police to give 'value for money'. Similarly, in Newburn's (2003) 700-plus-page *Handbook of Policing*, there are no index references to the cost or financing of policing or investigations.

Media representations of policing, particularly of serious crime, imply that cost is not a relevant consideration. Prosecutions are represented as failing because there is insufficient admissible evidence, rather than for insufficient resources. The Justice Gap Task Force's analysis and proposals (2002) note government plans to increase the number of police officers but do not identify resources as either a problem or a solution. Their preferred strategy assumes that more skilful investigators and efficient use of existing resources, such as by focusing on prolific offenders, will solve the problem. But police clear-up rates, on a like-for-like basis, have fallen from 40 per cent in 1980 to 24 per cent in 2000 (Home Office 2001: para. 1.15).

The Audit Commission (2002) identified considerable wastage and inefficiencies in the criminal court system, including over £80 million in adjournments, delays and cracked trials. But it did not challenge the cost of trials, in particular, the large differential between magistrates' (£0.36 billion in 2001–2) and Crown Courts (£0.27 billion), even though the former deal with 95 per cent of cases. It does not consider investigations that never reach court. But those cases have 'costs' for the system. Victims of crime who do not see their violators apprehended and punished are surely less likely to be to be a witness or motivated juror in other cases. Without willing witnesses we cannot begin to have investigations. The sufficiency of resources for undertaking existing and more investigations has not been a focal point in recent official documents on the criminal justice system, even though detection reduces crime (Home Office 2001: para. 3.141; 2004: 8) and resources are a problem, even in better resourced murder inquiries (Nicol *et al.* 2004). Do courtroom investigations need to cost so much? Could as many, as likely to be accurate, decisions be made by other trial investigation methods, according at least equivalent levels of protection and participation? We appear to be intellectual prisoners of traditional analyses and expectations.

Investigating rational competence

Is investigative expertise rationally and efficiently distributed? Just how good a detective and judge do we need to investigate and then try a case? The principal rule for deciding which level of criminal court will hear a case is the nature of the crime. Lord Justice Auld (2001), in his report for the government on the criminal courts of England and Wales, recommended a unified courts system. Adoption of his proposals would have led to significantly different arrangements for trials, but they would not have challenged the philosophy that perceived seriousness of offence should determine the forum. For example, he recommended that only the most serious cases should be reserved for the High Court judges who go on circuit to leading Crown Courts around the country, rather than to the resident judges (2001: 248).

Crown Court judges are, effectively, divided into four levels by the types of crime they can try. For example, murder and treason are in the top level, manslaughter and rape in the next (Auld 2001: 233). Is perceived offence seriousness the most appropriate criterion? Should murders routinely be allocated to more senior investigators? Surely the complexity of an investigation, whether at police or court level, has more to do with fact finding, fact presentation and fact testing than with articulating the law to a jury. Many murders are relatively straightforward to investigate and to prove (Innes 2003). Complex issues relating to the admissibility of different forms of evidence are not restricted, logically or practically, to cases perceived to be serious. Correctly directing the jury on the applicable law has been simplified and made more consistent by the creation of specimen directions by the Judicial Studies Board (2005). And the association between seriousness of offence and severity of penalty possible ought not to justify the present assumptions. First, sentencing is subject to its own system of precedent. Secondly, there is supposed to be an assumption of innocence until guilt is clearly demonstrated. Choosing a more senior judge or court because he, she or it has greater sentencing powers ought to be impermissible reasoning. Indeed, given that greater resources (financial, time and skill) are likely to have been invested in the investigation, preparation and presentation of a case perceived to be serious, the argument ought to be that less skilled and experienced judging could be accorded. A rational system, such as that which – hopefully – applies in health care, would ensure allocation according to need. Senior registrars may appropriately remove appendices in uncomplicated cases; hopefully, consultants are at least immediately available to take control in more difficult cases. Indeed, if that were not the position, those surgeons might get sued if harm resulted. It is as if we are determined to avoid key issues in relation to investigations by not challenging our assumptions.

Investigating for what?

Another implicit assumption relates to the focal stage for the investigation. The current paradigm, it is submitted, focuses on the product, the prosecution and conviction, rather than the process, investigating. In so many ways this is so unremarkable. Why undertake an investigation if it is not to achieve an outcome? But the point trying to be made relates to the consequential implications. This approach assumes that it is the perceived fairness of the conclusion, rather than the process, that matters. As criminal evidence scholars, such as Roberts and Zuckerman (2004) note, the common law has opposed rejecting evidence at trial (product) merely because it was improperly obtained (process). The House of Lords has decided that it is not the courts' responsibility to discipline or regulate police investigations by rejecting evidence improperly obtained (*Morris v. Breadmore* (1981)).[1] They would only draw the line at oppression or trickery. Section 78 of the Police and Criminal Evidence Act 1984 authorizes trial judges to reject prosecution evidence that would have such an effect on the fairness of the proceedings that it ought not to be admitted. However, it is only used in practice for 'significant and substantial' abuses (Roberts and Zuckerman 2004). Article 6 of the European Convention on Human Rights may, eventually, have a more profound effect as case law has developed the notion that a fair trial, to which the convention refers, requires a fair police investigation (*Teixeira de Castro* v. *Portugal* (1988);[2] Roberts and Zuckerman 2004).

Process is important, and we should be able to identify problems for the credibility of investigations from developing trends. For example, Hillyard and Gordon (1999) have noted a dramatic increase in police use of arrest – between 1981 and 1997 it increased by 54 per cent (1999: 509) – although there has been a decline in numbers prosecuted. They argue that this supports Choong's (1997) 'social discipline' model. A 'shadow' criminal justice system is developing where the police act against crime, but not always with prosecution in mind. Their focus is on 'process' rather than 'product'. Arrest is used to enforce the law rather than a prelude to prosecution and conviction (see also Bayley 1994). This need have nothing to do with improper motives or the 'noble corruption' of yore. They may believe that they do not have sufficient resources to obtain sufficient evidence to satisfy a court. Alternatively, they may know or believe there is not going to be sufficient evidence, particularly where offenders are aware of simple means of minimizing the forensic traces they leave. They may believe that prevention or disruption is a better, and cheaper, strategy to waiting for a complete, or inchoate, crime to be committed. This is fed by investment in intelligence-led policing. More crimes may be disrupted but not to the standards of proof required. Even if judges were to reject more prosecution evidence that was improperly obtained it would have no impact on the standards and practices in this shadow criminal justice system. If we wish to effect structural and cultural change, for example in the extent to which people are prepared to participate in the criminal justice system as witnesses, jurors, etc., and to trust prosecution evidence, then we cannot afford to ignore informal justice systems.

Investigating which miscarriages?

Wrongful acquittals, although the requirements of the standard of proof are deliberately skewed in their favour, are not commonly considered to be miscarriages of justice. 'Wrongful' in this context does not necessarily involve error. Insufficient evidence is sufficient justification for an acquittal. Our courts do not 'do' innocence. 'Miscarriage' does not include errors made earlier in the investigation and trial process. And those who obviate a thorough investigation because they plead guilty (perhaps in the belief that although innocent they are liable to be found guilty and/or the reduction in sentence for an early plea is attractive; Dell 1971; Gudjonsson 2003) are not considered victims of a miscarriage. Once again the focus is on the atypical and on the final product rather than decision-making processes.

Of course, being wrongly or unsafely convicted and sentenced to several years' imprisonment is many times more serious than being wrongly arrested and detained for a few hours. And, perhaps, it is inappropriate to consider multiplying a small miscarriage by the many people who experience it in order to argue it is a major problem. But if we want to improve decisions, should we not be looking at the decisions? There will always, necessarily, be more examples of 'errors' at earlier stages in the criminal justice process. So why do we not focus on decision-making and systems problems when and where they are most likely to arise? There will be more examples to study and improvements should have a quantitatively greater impact. If we are concerned about the quality of investigations and decisions in our criminal justice system, then the end is not always the best place to begin.

Investigating errors and failure

A cause of several miscarriages of justice has been identified as precipitous decision-making. Maguire and Norris suggested in 1992 that police investigations were characterized by case construction rather than truth finding. Case construction suggests that, as soon as someone is suspected, the investigation becomes a search for information that will support that suspicion rather than a continuing search focused on what happened. The process, it has been argued (McBarnet 1981), extends into the courts. Indeed, legislative intervention has sought to minimize or prevent this problem. Section 23 of the Criminal Procedure and Investigations Act 1996 requires publication of a Code of Practice (Secretary of State for the Home Department 2005) which, in turn, insists that all reasonable inquiries, whether for or against the suspect, are pursued. These provisions are, effectively, trying to legislate for an open mind.

Maguire (2003) concedes that case construction theory does not explain how the investigators came to identify that suspect out of a range of possible candidates. There has to be, outside corrupt practices, an interaction with the evidence collected before suspicion can settle on an individual (Innes 2003; ACPO 2005). Attention, it is submitted, should be focused on this interaction rather than case construction, which is a natural part of our accusatorial process. Fact finding, and the preparation of evidence, necessarily involves abductive reasoning (Twining 2003). We need procedures and reflective practices that encourage this. Unfortunately the law of evidence is concerned with a much later stage, with what may be said, shown, etc., in trials (e.g. Roberts and Zuckerman 2004). Fortunately a new evidence scholarship is refocusing attention on to the earlier, and thereby more fundamental, processes of inference and decision-making about disputed facts (see, in particular, Anderson et al. 2005).

Identifying premature conclusions, as a problem, is unhelpful. It tells us no more than what we already know; there was a mistake. There cannot be a miscarriage of justice, in the strong sense of wrong person convicted, without there having been a premature conclusion as to the apt suspect. No miscarriage; no premature conclusion. Similarly, effective senior investigative officers (SIOs) may be those who: 'were able to make decisions based on what is relevant to the investigation, rather than making decisions on the basis of unsubstantiated assumptions. This involved SIOs keeping an open mind and retaining flexibility within the investigative process' (Smith and Flanaghan 2000: 36). But, again, what was 'relevant', 'unsubstantiated', let alone what is 'open minded' and 'flexible', cannot be determined in advance but only after the investigation. If there was a miscarriage, then the SIO, by definition, was not effective in those terms.

It is too easy to condemn someone for making a premature decision when, at the time that decision was being made, that person was, properly, seeking to be efficient in using the available information (perhaps being actuarial in considering offenders known to have that modus operandi) and minimizing costs. Investigators could be helped by further elaboration of argumentation systems (e.g. Prakken 2004) and by the identification of the ways in which abductive and defeasible reasoning (e.g. Pollock 1987) would help. It is self-evident at the time a miscarriage is demonstrated that more time and other resources should have been employed on that investigation, at the time. Investigations involve decision-making under pressure, with time and other restraints. We need to be able to identify failures in perception, reasoning and resource allocation before they occur.

Jackson (2004), by developing contrasting models of investigation and prosecution, demonstrates the importance of broadening such debates to consider the roles (within established legal systems) of judges, prosecutors and the police. In our system the police and prosecution are required to come forward with a positive hypothesis that X is guilty. They are not entitled to present X, Y and Z, saying they believe that one of them is guilty, but they will leave the choice to the court. They can only do their current job by nominating a suspect, or by admitting defeat and allowing the crime to go unsolved and/or unpunished. Premature decision-making is a natural by-product of our system. If it never happened it would mean that the police were being inefficient, were using more resources than necessary.

When a system fails (for example, insufficient investigations lead to convictions), it may be more appropriate than blaming those involved to 'move up a level' in the analysis (Chapman 2004). A broader, more encompassing system might be identified. Law making and law enforcement might be seen as parts of a single system, rather than as separate systems. For example, legislators could accept more responsibility for structuring and defining crimes in ways that would make investigation and prosecution more realistic. Alternative methods of achieving goals might be considered. For example, at the time of writing (and after considerable delay), the government is consulting on its proposals for a new corporate manslaughter law (Home Office 2005). But, if we are really concerned about deaths at work, why not consider attacking the necessarily bigger problem of injuries at work, from which death is often an accidental consequence (Clarkson 2005)?

Chapman (2004: 36) distinguishes 'messes' and 'difficulties':

A difficulty is characterised by broad agreement on the nature of the problem and by some understanding of what a solution would look like, and it is bounded in terms of the time and resources required for its resolution. In contrast, messes are characterised by no clear

agreement about exactly what the problem is and by uncertainty and
ambiguity about how improvements might be made.

In these terms our criminal justice and investigation systems constitute messes,
rather than mere difficulties. It is not a time for timid thinking. Assumptions
need challenging. There isn't the time to develop ideas here but, for example,
why do we not challenge the criminal versus civil distinction? Most crimes
are also torts, civil wrongs. Victims can sue. If police investigators cannot
secure a conviction, shouldn't they pass the evidence collected to victims
for them to use? Of course there are counter-arguments, just as there are
lots of victims of crime not receiving remedies leading to a spiralling loss of
confidence in our criminal justice mess.

Alternative models

Hopefully the preceding discussion has contributed towards a more
questioning approach to investigations. One way forward is to consider
other models or guiding principles for investigations.

Science

Contemplating investigations as a science produces images of the detective
as a scientist exploring alternative hypotheses with dispassion, neutrality,
objectivity and rigour (e.g. Jackson and Jackson 2004). But the police
investigator is more of a co-ordinator of others, and should 'scientific'
describe the investigator or the methods adopted? Being able to describe
evidence (or an induction from some collected facts) as 'scientific' gives it
'weight' and prestige. In social settings, including courts, we are more likely
to acquiesce in arguments that are presented as being 'scientific'. But it is
an error to think of scientific as a dichotomous rather than relative quality.
For example, DNA evidence has been presented in fallacious ways in court
(Balding and Donnelly 1994). The presence of scientific evidence does not
make the investigation, itself, scientific.

   Even if police investigations become more scientific, can and will this be
appreciated at the courtroom stage? Judges, magistrates and jurors rarely
have scientific knowledge or skills, particularly across the range of disciplines
that could be involved in a particular case. They rely upon expert evidence.
The Supreme Court of the United States of America has developed tests for
federal judges to use when acting as gate-keepers over the admissibility of
scientific evidence.[3] The courts in the UK say that they are permissive with
regard to admitting a wide range of forms of scientific evidence, while being
rigorous about how it is applied (*Robb* (1991);[4] Dennis 2002). But even if
that is achieved it is an uneasy compromise. For example, both science and
the law share the concept of probability; but criminal trials require proof
beyond reasonable doubt. That, it is submitted, is as much an emotional as
an intellectual test. Defence lawyers are, perfectly correctly within the current
rules, entitled to worry jurors about possibilities. The emotional should be

inimical to the rational scientific but it has a place in legal decision-making. So even if criminal investigations become more scientific there is still the trial, which is not.

Perhaps we could and should work towards measures of the comparative quality of different forms of evidence. Rationally it should always be the quality and quantity of the evidence in the particular case, covering all salient points, which determine the outcome. Quality of evidence has a lot to do with its provenance, testing and storage. The courts have, effectively, devised checklists to help in the assessment of eyewitness evidence (*Turnbull* (1977)).[5] They could adopt similar approaches to the comparative qualities of different forms of evidence. They could decide, for example, that admissions made in suspect interviews, demonstrably undertaken in accordance with the principles of investigative interviewing (Clarke and Milne 2001), are more reliable, in the absence of evidence to the contrary, than interviews undertaken in other ways.

Hammond (1983) developed a 'cognitive continuum' (see also Hamm 1988). This identifies six 'levels' of knowledge with those later in the sequence manifestly deserving more credibility because of their nature. From least to most credible they are intuitive judgement, peer-aided judgement, system-aided judgement, quasi-experiment, controlled trial and scientific experiment. While he was concerned with how clinicians do, and should, make their decisions, it is submitted that the basic idea could be appropriated for use in relation to trial evidence. What is the knowledge claim being made for each piece of evidence? A witness's memory for a face or event could only be an 'intuitive judgement' but, if corroborated, deserves more respect as 'peer aided'. Participation in a system designed to minimize errors, such as an identification parade, while highlighting both positive and negative results, deserves being trusted as more reliable than mere recognition. Being able to identify the defendant with the same key variables as those tested in a large study, better still if double-blind, deserves (unless special contrary reasons are identified) to be rated as very powerful evidence. The reliability of different forms of evidence, particularly where there have been scientific advances, has changed over time and must continue to do so. Courts need aids and guidance in how to assess differentially different forms of evidence. Relying on 'the good sense' of the jury is a mere rhetorical appeal to an intuitive judgement.

Expert evidence

The appeal of expert evidence as a model for investigations is very similar to that of scientific evidence, given that that is what it is supposed to be. But it allows an emphasis to be placed upon the expert's expertise rather than the science. Expert evidence is an exception to the general rule that only factual evidence may be given (Dennis 2002). People with knowledge or experience beyond that of a judge or jury may state opinions. But the rule is based upon a series of false premises. Facts and opinions do not arise from a neat dichotomy. And how are judges and juries to know what they do not know, without knowing it? Courts have been anxious that juries might be too impressed with the expert's credentials (Tapper 1985). That can cause many problems. The expert may, indeed, be an expert within his or her special topic but be incompetent as a witness, or the converse. An expert witness with extensive academic credentials might be inappropriately preferred over a professional witness who may lack comparative knowledge of the research but have extensive practical experience that the academic lacks.

There are at least two ways in which expert evidence might identify a distinctive type of investigation. First, this model would recognize that there are certain topics where, at least contemporaneously, the best we can do is rely upon expertise. We do it in our daily lives when we get on planes and enter hospitals as patients. A classic example would be the recent 'cot death' cases in England (Batt 2004) where there was extensive reliance upon a few experts. Upon appeals deciding that the evidence, particularly statistical, was improper and misleading, several miscarriages of justice were declared. Such cases tend to be cited against the greater involvement of expert witnesses, but was the problem the expert's evidence or the lawyers' and adversarial system's inability to identify it? The flawed statistical evidence was actually challenged soon after it was given (Nobles and Schiff 2005). The lawyers might have been more skilled in their questions. Is a major part of the problem that modern legal education is so narrow that lawyers are ill equipped to investigate the quality of scientific claims, or to know how to have others do it for them?

Secondly, a model based upon expertise could focus on how the expert's evidence is given and used. Take, for example, an area where research is being undertaken – such as credibility assessment (e.g. Vrij 2000) – but the state of contemporary knowledge is considered insufficiently robust to merit consideration by a court. While the police and other investigators may use this knowledge to help them identify a suspect, they must then rely on other evidence to convince a court. Why should evidence that is useful for one investigation not be useful (note it is not suggested it should determine the issue) for another? All evidence does not have to pass the 'beyond all reasonable doubt' test. Some may have the role of corroboration, be it circumstantial or reinforcement.

Since one of the concerns (Tapper 1985) about expert evidence is that decision-makers will give too much credit to the reputation of the witness rather than his or her evidence, why not move towards an alternative explanatory paradigm? The expert could teach the judge, jury or lawyers how to use the evidence. Research into statement-based content analysis suggests that it is possible to distinguish truthful from lying statements on the basis of what is said (Vrij 2000). One test relates to whether the witness changes his or her account of the incident. Superficially that appears to be a sign of unreliability, if not lying; the witness is changing his or her story. But, given that we do not experience the world and events over time with explanatory labels attached, we have to choose which words will be accurate enough and sufficient enough to describe our observation. It ought not to be surprising that a witness will find better, albeit different from the original, words to describe what he or she saw when repeating the description. So 'changing your evidence' rather than sticking to it rigidly could be a sign of truth telling rather than the converse. The prosecuting lawyer ought to be able to explain this, as an exercise in persuasion, to the jury without requiring any reference to science or expertise. The expert's role could move to educating the decision-makers (Imwinkelreid 1997). Educating can help people avoid known errors and consider points that might otherwise be ignored, even if it cannot pronounce the correct answer.

Risk

Juries reach verdicts and judges make judgments; neither takes risks. But is that just a preferred way of describing essentially the same thing? Risks are decisions taken under uncertainty (e.g. Yates and Stone 1992); so are trials. Criminal investigations require many risk decisions: which is the correct hypothesis, story or suspect to investigate; when is it the correct time to move from investigation to proof? Risks have elements (their outcomes and their likelihood) and dimensions (e.g. degrees of reliability of information, resources and opportunities to control). There is a risk that the defendant will be found guilty, although actually innocent, or be found innocent, although guilty. There is a risk that the prosecution will not present sufficient evidence. So the concept of risk seems to provide a neat fit with criminal investigations and trials, although it is usually applied, in relation to criminal justice, in a much broader sense (e.g. Ericson and Haggerty 1997; Johnston 2000; Kemshall 2003).

How is a risk model relevant to trials and investigations? There is a risk that the verdict will be wrong. That is dichotomous, either guilty or not guilty. Most risk decisions in the real world concern relative outcomes – for example, degrees of dangerousness (from killing to scratching). But when they come into a legal context they get squeezed into a dichotomous decision: is the offender dangerous, or not; is there a serious risk, or not? But proof of guilt is a relative issue. Perhaps the risk is not so much the decision as its significance. For example, the risk of wrongly being found guilty and given 12 years' imprisonment is significantly higher than wrongly convicted and given 12 months' imprisonment. This approach would mandate greater protection and investment during investigation and trial against such an error. In some senses that is already provided. There is a correlation, discussed above, between types of trial, levels of court and judge involved, and the seriousness of the offence measured in terms of the potential punishment for the most serious offence charged. However, alternative perspectives on the outcome (for example, the significance – on the victims – of a failure to gain any convictions) are not recognized in this approach. And there is no direct correlation between the difficulty of proving a case and its seriousness in these terms.

Most importantly for this risk model, the other key element of risk, likelihood, is not utilized. Whether the charge is murder or travelling on public transport without a ticket, the degree of likelihood required is the same, proof beyond reasonable doubt. If we could cast off centuries of tradition, education and socialization, would we not think that it would be more rational to vary the degree of likelihood of guilt along with the seriousness of the outcome? Perhaps this actually happens; we just do not like to recognize it. 'Beyond reasonable doubt' may, in practice, consciously or unconsciously, mean something very different to magistrates asked to decide charges that they perceive to be relatively minor (e.g. where the punishment is limited) as opposed to charges where the punishment could lead to incarceration for a quarter of a person's life.

Risk may also be a useful construct for examining investigations and trials, with reference to broader conceptions. A five-'level' model of risk has been developed with reference to mental health contexts (Carson 1997). Perhaps some of these levels may also apply within the criminal justice context. First, there is the risk 'in' the nature of the investigation (e.g. violent serial offences). Secondly, there is risk in the context of the investigation (e.g. absence of, or too much, media attention). Thirdly, there is the risk in the decision-making process. Here the focus is on the competence of the person making the risk decisions, the investigator. The lack of competence may not be blameworthy; he or she may not have been trained to recognize the common causes of decision errors, for example. Fourthly, the investigators may be very competent, as such, but not be provided by their managers with the most useful or sufficient information, nor with the aids they need to cope with so much information and pressure. And, fifthly, the danger may not be 'in' the offender, the setting, the decision, the support provided by managers, but within the system that everyone has to operate in. For example, the system may demonstrate preoccupation with management by target setting, which may distort a more rational system of priorities (Chapman 2004).

For example, compare the number of homicides occurring during the first year of life with that experienced by elderly people (Cotton 2003). Is that entirely a reflection of fact – the reality of differential risks – or is it a reflection of the quality of existing systems for identifying homicides? The quantity and quality of services available for observing children during their first year of life may be considerably more powerful in ensuring homicide is detected in comparison with systemic protections for elderly people. Thinking of trials and investigations as risks (for example, the likelihood and significance of errors) might enable us to be both more honest about their nature and to apply some of the growing intellectual sophistication in risk analysis and management to them.

Decision-making quality

Doctors, dentists and other professionals know that, if their decisions are poor and lead to harm, they may be sued for negligence; but not detectives. A prerequisite of liability for negligence is the existence of a duty of care. Doctors, etc., owe such a duty to their patients (Healy 1999). But the courts are extremely reluctant to impose such a duty on investigators. The police can be, and have been, sued for negligent handling of detained people. Indeed they would have been liable in *Vellino* v. *Chief Constable of Greater Manchester* (2002)[6] had the prisoner not escaped from custody and thereby removed their duty of care. There was a duty to supervise a drunken prisoner in a cell properly in *Karen Orange* v. *Chief Constable West Yorkshire Police* (2001),[7] but the facts demonstrated they did not breach the resulting standard of care. The existence of a duty is explicable in such cases because of the directness of the relationship; the individual is (or was not, in *Vellino*) under their control. But investigations are treated very differently.

The mother of a victim of the Yorkshire Ripper (a serial murderer) sued the police for negligent investigation of the crimes. Whether the police were negligent or not was never decided because the claim was dismissed, without a trial of the facts. It was decided that the police did not owe the victim a duty of care so there could be no question of liability for negligence. The House of Lords agreed in *Hill* v. *Chief Constable of West Yorkshire* (1989).[8] As a matter of public policy, they decided, it is inappropriate to subject investigators to a legal duty that could compromise the quality of their professionalism. The distinction is between managing someone arrested and investigating a crime.

In a later case a father was killed while seeking to protect his son from a former teacher who had formed an improper interest. The few publicly known facts about the case suggest considerable negligence by the Metropolitan Police (see Hoyano 1999), although court records suggest there might have been good reasons for their conduct. Again we do not know because it was again decided that the police did not owe a duty of care, in the law of negligence, even though they knew the identity of the suspect and were on their way to arrest him, at the time of the killing, for a motoring offence. The Court of Appeal agreed, in *Osman and another* v. *Ferguson and another* (1993),[9] and the House of Lords declined to hear an appeal, because of their earlier decision.

The European Court of Human Rights (ECtHR) decided that British law broke convention requirements, specifically Article 6(1) (*Osman* v. *UK* (2000)).[10] However, it does not follow that police investigators now owe a duty of care in the law of negligence. The ECtHR decision has been criticized (Hoyano 1999) for opaque reasoning. In essence the court objected to the blanket decision that public policy is always against individuals' rights to obtain a remedy. They could only accept that public policy would prevent a duty of care in most cases (Hoyano 1999). However, the ECtHR decision has made little difference to the House of Lords, who have again decided that the police do not owe a duty of care when investigating a crime (*Brooks* v. *Commissioner of Police for the Metropolis and Others* (2005)),[11] although permitting the applicant to argue that public policy should not prevent him having a remedy. The case was brought by Duwayne Brooks. He was with Stephen Lawrence when he was killed in a racially motivated attack. The investigators were roundly criticized by an independent inquiry (Macpherson 1999).

Do investigators need this protection? Does it help or hinder the development of high standards in investigations? Indeed, do British police investigators know that they are protected in this way? Yes, they need protection from frivolous claims; but so do doctors and other professionals. It is difficult to bring a case that does not have a realistic chance of succeeding. It is argued that investigators can do without constantly having to look over their shoulder and worry about someone suing them for an erroneous decision. But that is misconceived. Just as with every other occupation, there could only be liability for a negligent decision – that is, one which would not be supported by a responsible body of colleagues (*Bolam* v. *Friern HMC*

(1957)).[12] That standard of care permits a great deal of variety; it does not require the best decision or even what most co-professionals would have done. Following the guidance and advice produced by the National Centre for Policing Excellence, and approved by the Association of Chief Police Officers (ACPO) in their *Practice Advice on Core Investigative Doctrine* (2005), would be sufficient. There is no such restriction on suing in, for example, Canada (i.e. *Jane Doe* v. *Metropolitan Police of Toronto* (1998)),[13] France, Germany and South Africa (Hoyano 1999; see also Markesinis *et al.* 1999).

Audit

A model that could combine the best features of those outlined above could be described as 'audit'. Such an approach would focus on the assurance of quality of fact-finding processes, the differential quality of the resulting evidence and the manner in which hypotheses were imaginatively created and rigorously tested. A virtue is that it is, in some respects, more or less explicitly acknowledged in current practice. For example, recent developments in policing have emphasized the importance of improving the quality of investigations (e.g. ACPO 2005). But the approach has not been worked through in the sense that neither the problems of inferential reasoning in relation to generating hypotheses (or suspects) nor all the potential advantages have been articulated or realized. In particular, demonstration of improved investigative techniques has not led to greater confidence in the evidence identified. Investigative interviewing is adopted because approved (ACPO 2002) rather than because the courts accord its product greater credibility. There used to be extensive concern about police officers 'verballing' or misstating what suspects told them in interviews. The requirements, under the Police and Criminal Evidence Act 1984, for tape-recording of suspect interviews have caused a transformation. Such claims are now very rare. Tapes may be wrongly transcribed – meanings can be misrepresented such as by not allowing for tone of voice or when imposing a grammatical structure – but the reliability of reports of suspects' statements is, implicitly, rated much higher since that Act. Should it not be possible to have similar effects with other forms of evidence which, because of the way in which they have been collected and assured, are properly considered more credible? For example, jurors and magistrates should be expected to accord greater reliability to information produced in an interview which followed current best practice, including the establishment of a good rapport before questioning begins, which empowered the witness to say what he or she wants and the avoidance of interruptions and questions until late in the interview.

Instead of judges determining what is, and is not, admissible as evidence, they could give guidance on how it should be weighed. Judges should investigate whether evidence has been collated and preserved according to current good practice (contributing to critiques of those standards so that they improve over time), advising juries of their finding. This should lead to investigators focusing on the quality of the processes they use, not just the products. This should assure trial courts that the facts 'found' and interpreted have been subjected to both congruence (interpretation) and matching (demonstration) approaches towards proof. It would focus on the quality of decisions and encourage more scientific approaches.

Conclusion

But the main reason why we need to adopt an 'audit' approach is its potential impact upon investigations generally, their reputation, the status and motivation of investigators and the consequential response of future victims and witnesses. Police investigators and prosecutors should be required both to prove guilt and to disprove innocence. They should not just be encouraged by codes to consider alternative possible explanations. They should also demonstrate that all reasonable (decided pre-trial by a judge if necessary) alternative stories (including those suggested by the defence) lack reasonable credibility. This would encourage investigators to see themselves as, and to be seen by others as, closer to neutral scientists than the current system allows. The rigour of their investigations should be demonstrable through the production of documents that identify how each essential element in the alleged crime may be substantiated by audited evidence. This should involve investigators demonstrating the use of the most current approved methods to test evidence as well as to collate and preserve it appropriately. This may involve a move towards continental investigatory systems but, it is submitted, we are already moving in that direction (Jörg et al. 1995).

Having a pre-trial investigatory system, with adversary thereafter, is not only feasible but would give judges a role in determining both that sufficient evidence has been adduced (rather than waiting for a 'no case to answer' application at the end of the prosecution's evidence) and that all reasonable requests by the defence for the investigation of alternative stories have been undertaken. Judges would audit guilty pleas to ensure that defendants do not plead guilty for improper reasons. If prosecution evidence has been audited against contemporary standards, and defence requests for alternative lines of inquiry have been undertaken (perhaps by a different group of investigators), then, over time, the reliability and credibility of investigations are likely to increase. More defendants are likely (safely) to plead guilty, given both the quantity and quality of evidence produced and sentencing discounts for pleas. And as audited evidence and the additional duty to disprove innocence gain in credibility, it should become more difficult for suspects and defendants not to provide information to investigators. In this way a 'virtuous circle' of greater credibility of investigations should be possible.

But, as stressed at the start, very few police investigations reach fruition in the sense of get to court, let alone realize a conviction. That reality must be expected to continue, but it does not follow that victims should be without a remedy. Individuals could be empowered and encouraged to use the civil legal system even if, indeed largely because, the vast majority of such cases are dealt with before they get to court and because alternative dispute resolution continues to develop there. If we are to have any hope of tackling the crisis in our criminal justice system, we need to be prepared to consider imaginative alternatives, both at the level of individual cases and whole systems.

Selected further reading

Anderson, T., Schum, D. and Twining, W. (2005) *Analysis of Evidence* (2nd edn). Cambridge: Cambridge University Press. A most important book that addresses issues ignored by traditional studies of evidence, such as how we do (and should) infer from facts, and how we seek to test and 'prove' such inferences in court.

Hoyano, L.C.H. (1999) 'Policing flawed police investigations: unravelling the blanket', *Modern Law Review*, 62: 912–36. This article describes the English law on whether police investigators can be sued for undertaking negligent investigations. If they can be sued in other countries, why not in the UK?

National Audit Office (2005) *A Safer Place for Patients: Learning to Improve Patient Safety*. London: HMSO. A comparatively rare example of a systems approach being developed to tackle a problem. What would a similar report on police investigations contain?

Notes

1 *Morris* v. *Breadmore* [1981] AC 446.
2 *Teixeira de Castro* v. *Portugal* (1988) 28 EHRR 101.
3 *Daubert* v. *Merrell Dow Pharmaceutical Inc.* 579 US 563 (1993); *General Electric Co* v. *Joiner* 522 US 136 (1997); *Kumho Tire Ltd.* v. *Carmichael* 526 US 137 (1999).
4 *Robb* (1991) 93 Cr App R 161.
5 *Turnbull* [1977] QB 224.
6 *Vellino* v. *Chief Constable of Greater Manchester* [2002] 1 WLR 218.
7 *Karen Orange* v. *Chief Constable West Yorkshire Police* [2001] EWCA Civ 611.
8 *Hill* v. *Chief Constable of West Yorkshire* [1989] 1 AC 53.
9 *Osman and another* v. *Ferguson and another* [1993] 4 All ER 344.
10 *Osman* v. *UK* (2000) 29 EHRR.
11 *Brooks* v. *Commissioner of Police for the Metropolis and Others* [2005] 2 All ER 489.
12 *Bolam* v. *Friern HMC* [1957] 2 All ER 118.
13 *Jane Doe* v. *Metropolitan Police of Toronto* (1998) 160 DLD (4th) 697.

References

ACPO (Association of Chief Police Officers) (2002) *Investigative Interviewing Strategy*. Bramshill: Centrex.
ACPO (Association of Chief Police Officers) (2005) *Practice Advice on Core Investigative Doctrine*. Cambourne: National Centre for Policing Excellence.
Anderson, T., Schum, D. and Twining, W. (2005) *Analysis of Evidence* (2nd edn). Cambridge: Cambridge University Press.
Audit Commission (2002) *Route to Justice: Improving the Pathway of Offenders through the Criminal Justice System*. London: Audit Commission.
Auld, Lord Justice, Rt. Hon. (2001) *A Review of the Criminal Courts of England and Wales*. London: HMSO (available online at: http://www.criminal-courts-review.org.uk).
Balding, D.J. and Donnelly, P. (1994) 'The prosecutor's fallacy and DNA evidence', *Criminal Law Review*, 711–21.
Batt, J. (2004) *Stolen Innocence: The Sally Clark Story – a Mother's Fight for Justice*. London: Ebury Press.

Bayley, D.H. (1994) *Police for the Future*. Oxford: Oxford University Press.

Carson, D. (1997) 'A risk management approach to legal decision-making about "dangerous people"', in R. Baldwin (ed.) *Law and Uncertainty: Risks and Legal Processes*. London: Kluwer Law International.

Chapman, J. (2004) *System Failure: Why Governments Must Learn to Think Differently* (2nd edn). London: Demos.

Choong, S. (1997) *Policing as Social Discipline*. Oxford: Clarendon Press.

Clarke, C. and Milne, R. (2001) *National Evaluation of the PEACE Investigative Interviewing Course*. London: Home Office.

Clarkson, C.M.V. (2005) 'Corporate manslaughter: yet more government proposals', *Criminal Law Review*, 677–89.

Cotton, J. (2003) 'Homicide', in C. Flood-Page and J. Taylor (eds) *Crime in England and Wales, 2001/2002. Supplementary Volume*. London: Home Office.

Dell, S. (1971) *Silent in Court: The Legal Representation of Women who Went to Prison*. London: Bell.

Dennis, I.H. (2002) *The Law of Evidence* (2nd edn). London: Sweet & Maxwell.

Department of Transport (2004) *Tomorrow's Roads – Safer for Everyone*. London: Department for Transport (available online at http://www.dft.gov.uk/stellent/groups/dft_rdsafety/documents/downloadable/dft_rdsafety_028169.pdf).

Ericson, R.V. and Haggerty, K.D. (1997) *Policing the Risk Society*. Oxford: Clarendon Press.

Gudjonsson, G. (2003) *The Psychology of Interrogations and Confessions: A Handbook*. Chichester: Wiley.

Hamm, R.M. (1988) 'Clinical intuition and clinical analysis: expertise and the cognitive continuum', in J. Dowie and A. Elstein (eds) *Professional Judgment: A Reader in Clinical Decision Making*. Cambridge: Cambridge University Press.

Hammond, K.R. (1983) 'Teaching the new biology: potential contributions from research in cognition', in C.P. Friedman and E.F. Purcell (eds) *The New Biology and Medical Education: Merging the Biological, Information, and Cognitive Sciences*. New York, NY: Josiah Macy, Jr, Foundation.

Healy, J. (1999) *Medical Negligence: Common Law Perspectives*. London: Sweet & Maxwell.

Her Majesty's Inspectorate of Constabulary and Her Majesty's Crown Prosecution Service Inspectorate (2002) *A Report on the Joint Inspection into the Investigation and Prosecution of Rape Offences in England and Wales*. London: HM Inspectorate of Constabulary and HM Crown Prosecution Service Inspectorate (available online at http://www.hmcpsi.gov.uk/reports/jirapeins.pdf).

Hillyard, P. and Gordon, D. (1999) 'Arresting statistics: the drift to informal justice in England and Wales', *Journal of Law and Society*, 26: 502–22.

Home Office (2001) *Criminal Justice: The Way Ahead*. London: HMSO.

Home Office (2005) *Corporate Manslaughter: The Government's Draft Bill for Reform*. London: Home Office.

Hoyano, L.C.H. (1999) 'Policing flawed police investigations: unravelling the blanket', *Modern Law Review*, 62: 912–36.

Imwinkelreid, E.J. (1997) 'The next step in conceptualizing the presentation of expert evidence as education: the case for didactic trial procedures', *International Journal of Evidence and Proof*, 1: 128–48.

Innes, M. (2003) *Investigating Murder: Detective Work and the Police Response to Criminal Homicide*. Oxford: Clarendon Press.

Jackson, A.R.W. and Jackson, J.M. (2004) *Forensic Science*. Harlow: Pearson.

Jackson, J.D. (2004) 'The effect of legal culture and proof in decisions to prosecute', *Law, Probability and Risk*, 3: 109–31.

Johnston, J. (2000) *Policing Britain: Risk, Security and Governance.* Harlow: Longman.

Jörg, N., Field, S. and Brants, C. (1995) 'Are inquisitorial and adversarial systems converging?', in P. Fennell *et al.* (eds) *Criminal Justice in Europe: A Comparative Study.* Oxford: Oxford University Press.

Judicial Studies Board (2005) *Criminal Law: Specimen Directions* (available online at: http://www.jsboard.co.uk/criminal_law/cbb/index.htm).

Justice Gap Task Force (2002) *Narrowing the Justice Gap: Framework.* London: Home Office (available online at http://www.cjsonline.org.uk/njg/documents/njg-framework.pdf).

Justice Gap Task Force for England and Wales (n.d. but inferred 2002), *Narrowing the Justice Gap: Framework.* London: Home Office.

Kelly, L. (2002) *A Research Review on the Reporting, Investigation and Prosecution of Rape Cases.* London: HM Crown Prosecution Service Inspectorate (available online at http://www.hmcpsi.gov.uk/reports/Rapelitrev.pdf).

Kemshall, H. (2003) *Understanding Risk in Criminal Justice.* Maidenhead: Open University Press.

Kennedy, H. (2005) *Just Law: The Changing Face of Justice – and Why it Matters to Us All.* London: Vintage.

Macpherson of Cluny, Sir W. (1999) *The Stephen Lawrence Inquiry: Report of an Inquiry.* London: HMSO.

Maguire, M. (2003) 'Criminal investigation and crime control', in T. Newburn (ed.) *Handbook of Policing.* Cullompton: Willan Publishing.

Maguire, M. and Norris, C. (1992) *The Conduct and Supervision of Criminal Investigations. Royal Commission on Criminal Justice Research Study 5.* London: HMSO.

Markesinis, B.S., Auby, J.-B., Coester-Waltjen, D. and Deakin, S.F. (1999) *Tortious Liability of Statutory Bodies: A Comparative and Economic Analysis of Five English Cases.* Oxford: Hart.

McBarnet, D.J. (1981) *Conviction: Law, the State and the Construction of Justice.* London: Macmillan.

National Audit Office (2005) *A Safer Place for Patients: Learning to Improve Patient Safety.* London: HMSO.

Newburn, T. (ed.) (2003) *Handbook of Policing.* Cullompton: Willan Publishing.

Nicol, C., Innes, M., Gee, D. and Feist, A. (2004) *Reviewing Murder Investigations: An Analysis of Progress Reviews from Six Police Forces.* Home Office Online Report 25/04 (available online at http://www.homeoffice.gov.uk/rds/pdfs04/rdsolr2504.pdf).

Nobles, R. and Schiff, D. (1997) 'The never ending story: disguising tragic choices in criminal justice', *Modern Law Review,* 60: 293–304.

Nobles, R. and Schiff, D. (2000) *Understanding Miscarriages of Justice.* Oxford: Oxford University Press.

Nobles, R. and Schiff, D. (2005) 'Misleading statistics within criminal trials', *Significance,* 2: 17–19.

Pollock, J.L. (1987) 'Defeasible reasoning', *Cognitive Science,* 11: 481–518.

Prakken, H. (2004) 'Analysing reasoning about evidence with formal models of argumentation', *Law, Probability and Risk,* 3: 33–50.

Roberts, P. and Zuckerman, A. (2004) *Criminal Evidence.* Oxford: Oxford University Press.

Runciman, Lord (1993) *Royal Commission on Criminal Justice: Report* [(Cm 2263)]. London: HMSO.

Secretary of State for the Home Department (2005) *Criminal Procedure and Investigations Act 1966: Code of Practice under Part II.* London: Home Office.

Smith, N. and Flanaghan, C. (2000) *The Effective Detective: Identifying the Skills of an Effective Detective.* London: Home Office.

Tapper, C. (1985) *Cross on Evidence* (6th edn). London: Butterworths.

Twining, W. (2003) 'Evidence as a multi-disciplinary subject', *Law, Probablity and Risk*, 2: 91–107.

Vrij, A. (2000) *Detecting Lies and Deceit: The Psychology of Lying and the Implications for Professional Practice*. Chichester: Wiley.

Westmarland, N. (2004) *Rape Law Reform in England and Wales. University of Bristol School for Policy Studies, Working Papers Series, Paper 7* (available online at http://www.bristol.ac.uk/sps/downloads/working_papers/sps07_nw.pdf).

Wright, A. (2002) *Policing: An Introduction to Concepts and Practice*. Cullompton: Willan Publishing.

Yates, J.F. and Stone, E.R. (1992) 'The risk construct', in J.F. Yates (ed.) *Risk-taking Behaviour*. Chichester: Wiley.

Chapter 17

Covert surveillance and informer handling

Denis Clark

The process of criminal investigation

Criminal investigation is the process undertaken to establish whether an act, intention to act or omission may be labelled a crime and, if it is so labelled, the collection of evidence to determine those responsible and how they will be dealt with in the criminal justice system (Clark 2004). There are two broad categories of investigative processes – namely, reactive and proactive. To these categories should be added a third area of activity: intelligence gathering that is not part of an investigative strategy but that is ostensibly subject to similar legal controls. All investigation consists of the gathering of information and, for policy reasons, investigators seek to separate that which they label *intelligence* from that which they label *evidence*. It is because of the tensions that exist between these two types of information that the third category of investigative process has emerged. These categories are often interchangeable and should be viewed as overarching styles, comprising a range of investigative techniques and strategies.

Reactive investigation

The traditional style of investigation is reactive: a search for evidence following an allegation of, or the discovery of circumstances which amount to, a crime. The primary focus is on identifying the suspects, and there is a basic sequence to this style of investigation:

- *Crime scene preservation and examination*: a systematic examination of the location and vicinity for trace evidence, marks, items of property and so on that may have evidential value.

- *The search for witnesses*: obtaining witness accounts from victims and people who may have knowledge of issues relating to the crime.

- *Information evaluation*: the consultation of data in information systems, the matching of witness accounts and an analysis of the available evidence.

This demand-led style of investigation combines the skills of the historian with those of the scientist, but experts may also be used, such as crime scene specialists, forensic scientists and psychologists. It is heavily reliant on accurate information and its effective analysis. If suspects are identified, the techniques involved may become proactive in the sense that the investigator employs strategies that are associated with the proactive style of investigation.

Proactive investigation

This style of investigation has been the guiding principle for work on serious crime. It arose as a result of an Audit Commission (1993) report, which sought to refocus the police and other investigative agencies' attention on criminals rather than on crimes. It proposes that investigations should be intelligence led, making use of information gleaned from informants and from profiling techniques, such as crime pattern analysis. Information is evaluated systematically, which leads to the more efficient use of resources, and investigative effort is put into such activities as surveillance and undercover operations. In recent years this style of investigation has focused on the recovery of the financial benefits of crime.

Proactive investigation has proved to be particularly effective in dealing with terrorism and organized crime. However, its effectiveness is dependent on the secrecy of its methods, and there is a tension between fair trial rights and keeping these methods secret, in the public's interest.

Preventative intelligence gathering

This category of investigation has emerged as a result of legislation such as the Crime and Disorder Act 1998, and the Sex Offenders Act 1997, and as a result of the inquiries into the death of Victoria Climbie and into the murders of Jessica Chapman and Holly Wells in Soham, Cambridgeshire. The failures of data sharing revealed by these inquiries led to the Bichard Inquiry (*The Times* 18 December 2003). Preventative intelligence gathering represents a category of investigation whereby information is gathered and then stored for the public's protection. In essence, it is a recognition of the importance of information in terms of public protection and is a consequence of legislation that encourages multi-agency solutions to crime and disorder.

Covert policing

Marx (1988) distinguishes between four broad categories of police work. First, there is work that is overt and non-deceptive. Conventional police work (where the police act in response to reports of crime by victims, witnesses and so on) falls into this category. Secondly, there is police work that is overt and deceptive, as when, for example, a suspect is tricked by police officers into providing a confession. Thirdly, police work may be covert and non-deceptive (for example, passive surveillance operations). Finally there is police work that is covert and deceptive, and this is the category into which most undercover operations fall. This chapter is concerned with the third and fourth categories.

Taylor (2003) has identified a number of reasons why investigative agencies have moved towards techniques of surveillance and covert operations:

- The development of information technologies that provide a new site for policing activities.
- The trend away from reactive to proactive policing strategies.
- The statutory scheme that governs covert operations is less well established than the Police and Criminal Evidence Act (PACE) 1984.
- Surveillance techniques can provide high-quality evidence that is tantamount to a confession, without the need to interview.
- Covert operations can bring speedy results.

These factors have been supplemented by an increasing reluctance among members of the public to give evidence and the growth of organized crime and terrorism, which have required law enforcement agencies to enhance their investigative capabilities (see Home Office 2004).

A number of issues must be considered when deciding whether or not undercover tactics are justified. Marx (1988) suggests the following:

- The seriousness of the crime.
- Non-deceptive methods have been tried and have failed.
- Undercover activities have been subject to some democratic decision and have been announced publicly.
- The strategy is consistent with the spirit as well as the letter of the law.
- The eventual goal is to invoke the criminal justice system so that the deception can be made public.
- They are proposed for crimes that are clearly defined.
- There are reasonable grounds for concluding that the targets are engaged in the commission of equivalent offences, regardless of the tactic used.
- There are reasonable grounds to suspect that a crime will be prevented.

In the UK these issues have been addressed on a case-by-case basis, and a body of common law has thus developed. The principles issuing from the common law were incorporated into the code of practice on undercover operations published by the police and Customs in 1999, and now largely superseded by the Regulation of Investigatory Powers Act (RIPA) 2000. The Association of Chief Police Officers and Her Majesty's Customs and Excise also published a number of policy manuals and guidance. These are classified as 'restricted' and now incorporate the provisions of RIPA.

The regulation of covert policing

Prior to RIPA, the gathering of information via secretive means (such as surveillance, listening devices, the interception of communications and the use of informants) was not subjected to sufficient safeguards and led to a series of embarrassing judgments against the UK government in the European Court of Human Rights. The turning point was *Malone (John)* v. *United Kingdom*,[1] which brought about the enactment of the Interception of Communications Act 1985.

Subsequently, a series of piecemeal measures was introduced to cover other areas of authorized secret intrusions, among them the Data Protection Acts 1984 and 1998, the Police Act 1997 and the Intelligence Services Act 1994. Prior to this, too much reliance had been placed on informal non-statutory mechanisms, such as Home Office guidelines (for a discussion, see Lidstone and Palmer 1996).

The demands of compliance with the European Convention on Human Rights (ECHR) provided the central impetus for change.[2] Existing laws were inadequate and did not provide sufficient safeguards against possible abuse by the state. Since the introduction of the Human Rights Act 1998, the government has sought to avoid future problems by passing RIPA.

The purpose of the Act was:

> to make provision for and about the interception of communications, the acquisition and disclosure of data relating to communications, the carrying out of surveillance, the use of covert human intelligence sources and the acquisition of the means by which electronic data protected by encryption or passwords may be decrypted or accessed; to provide for Commissioners and a tribunal with functions and jurisdiction in relation to those matters, to entries on and interferences with property or with wireless telegraphy and to the carrying out of their functions by the Security Service, the Secret Intelligence Service and the Government Communications Headquarters; and for connected purposes.

It regulates:

> The use of a range of investigative powers by a variety of public authorities. It updates the law on the interception of communications to take account of technological changes such as the growth of the internet. It also puts other intrusive techniques on a statutory footing for the very first time; provides new powers to help combat the threat posed by rising criminal use of strong encryption and ensures that there is independent oversight of the powers in the Act.

The general scheme of the Act is to seek to provide legality within a framework of accountability. The powers contained within it permit interference with a person's right to a private and family life, as guaranteed by Article 8 of the ECHR. This interference will be justified if it is authorized for one or more of the purposes provided for in Article 8(2) and if the action is necessary and proportionate to the ends sought to be achieved.

The Act is in five parts, which provide powers in relation to specific investigative techniques or in relation to establishing systems of scrutiny, oversight and redress, as follows:

- *Part I*: the interception of communications and the acquisition and disclosure of communications data.
- *Part II*: the use of covert surveillance, agents, informants and undercover officers.
- *Part III*: the investigation of electronic data protected by encryption.
- *Part IV*: the independent oversight of the powers in the Act.
- *Part V*: miscellaneous and supplemental matters, such as consequential amendments, repeals and interpretation.

RIPA does not provide a complete framework for covert investigation and thus must be supplemented by, *inter alia*, codes of practice issued under s. 71, a series of statutory instruments and the Police Act 1997, which makes property interference lawful if properly authorized. There are codes of practice on the following:

- The interception of communications.
- Property interference.
- Covert surveillance.
- Covert human intelligence sources.

Oversight of RIPA is the responsibility of the Chief Surveillance Commissioner and the Interception of Communications Commissioner, both of whom must also have held high judicial office. Their responsibility is to keep under review the performance of functions under Part III of the Police Act 1997 and the performance of the powers and duties conferred, or imposed, by or under Parts I–III.

In addition to the commissioners, a tribunal has been established under RIPA s. 65 to deal with complaints under s. 7(1)(a) of the Human Rights Act 1988 (proceedings for actions incompatible with convention rights); to consider and determine any complaints made to them; to consider and determine any reference to them by any person who claims to have suffered detriment as a consequence of any restriction or prohibition under s. 17; and to hear and determine any other proceedings as may be allocated by order. Section 67 requires the tribunal merely to exercise a form of judicial review. A tribunal will simply state whether the determination is favourable or not. Its structure is complex, with several different commissioners covering activities that could, logically, be the province of a single body. The government preferred this scheme in order to ensure that expertise prevailed and to maintain – what they considered to be – a higher standard of scrutiny.

Covert human intelligence sources (informants and undercover police)

Background

Many successful investigations and prosecutions of criminal offences have involved the use of an informant. Typically, the informant will be a criminal who comes to police notice and who is able to negotiate a trade-off for information in the form of an indemnity from prosecution or a financial reward. Of necessity these types of individuals operate in a murky hinterland that is only superficially regulated by a façade of rules and principles.

The use of informants must be put into its historical context, and therefore an understanding of the development of the police is essential. Prior to the creation of the full-time uniformed police in the nineteenth century, the responsibility for providing information and accusations of criminal conduct (and even apprehending offenders) lay with those who were, by definition, members of the civilian community (Radzinowicz 1956). Prosecution might be taken in the name of the Crown, but the modern distinction between 'informer' – the person who supplies information to the police – and 'informant' – the person who makes the formal accusation – was blurred. Long before the invention of police forces, English law accommodated arrangements for obtaining information from persons who were themselves suspected of participating in criminal offences with others. In *Chitty*,[3] the following is to be found:

> The law confesses its weakness by calling in the assistance of those by whom it is broken. It offers a premium to treachery and destroys the last virtue which clings to the degraded transgressor. Still, on the other hand, it tends to prevent any extensive agreement among atrocious criminals, making them perpetually suspicious of each other.

In 1975, an indemnity given to Bertie Smalls (armed robber and police informant par excellence) attracted criticism in the Court of Appeal from Lawton LJ:

> The spectacle of the Director of Public Prosecutions recording in writing, at the behest of a criminal like Smalls, his undertaking to give immunity from further prosecutions, is one which we find distasteful. Nothing of a similar kind must happen again. Undertakings of immunity from prosecution may have to be given in the public interest. They should never be given by police. The Director should give them most sparingly.

Modern practice is to give those who assist the police and who are subsequently convicted a discounted sentence, which reflects their contribution to criminal detection. Such individuals are regarded as essential to law enforcement but are not without risk to the integrity of the trial process.

The use of informants in criminal investigation has a long history. Informants are regarded as an effective source of information by those in law enforcement and, nowadays, are not confined to the most serious offences that threaten the fabric of society: they have become sufficiently commonplace to be a regular practice. RIPA now provides the statutory controls for the use and conduct of informants, who have been given the somewhat bureaucratic label of covert human intelligence sources (CHISs).

Essentially, the CHIS is a witness who is afforded special status and protection on the grounds of public policy. The transition from witness to CHIS rarely follows a smooth path and presents law enforcement agencies with a multiplicity of ethical and organizational concerns. The RIPA regime is intended to deal with issues of legality, which require a delicate balance of ethical management and control (for a more detailed consideration of associated issues, see Billingsley *et al.* 2001). Before this is considered, the regulatory regime should be examined.

Definitional issues

It was not RIPA alone that served as the catalyst to regularize the use of informants – a number of controversies surrounded their use. An example is the case of Delroy Denton who, while registered by the Metropolitan Police as an informant, raped and murdered Marcia Lawes (*Guardian* 16 July 1999). Similarly, a working party consisting of representatives from the Police Complaints Authority, the Metropolitan Police, the National Crime Squad and members of community consultative groups was set up in 1997. This working party made suggestions for minimum national standards to be established that took into account human rights and an assessment of an informant's value. The working group also stressed such issues as public confidence and the seriousness of the crimes involved. Finally, while an investigation conducted by Sir John Hoddinott, Chief Constable of Hampshire, could not establish sufficient evidence to prosecute any of the officers involved in the investigation, it did reveal instances of mismanagement and illegality.

Prior to RIPA, the regulation of informants was set out in guidelines. The police defined an informant as:

> an individual [because of] whose very existence and identity the law enforcement agencies judge it essential to keep confidential and who is giving information about crime or about persons associated with criminal activity or public disorder. Such an individual will typically have a criminal history, habits or associates, and will be giving the information freely whether or not in the expectation of a reward, financial or otherwise (ACPO 1999).

Dunnighan and Norris (1996) found that it was not possible to run informants according to the guidelines in existence in 1996. There were a number of risks attached to law enforcement agencies employing individuals who came within the above definition. There was a need, therefore, for strong evidence of their utility.

According to Billingsley *et al.* (2001), 'about one third of all crimes cleared up by the police involve the use of informants'. Informants can be classified as follows:

- Witnesses who wish to remain anonymous.
- People who give information to Crimestoppers.
- Confidential sources.
- Registered CHISs.
- 'Supergrasses.'

The witness who wishes to remain anonymous becuase he or she is in 'fear' may be able to do so as a consequence of the hearsay provisions in ss. 23–26 of the Criminal Justice Act 1988. Those who call Crimestoppers to give information about criminal activity always remain anonymous. 'Supergrass' is the derisory name given to those who give Queen's evidence and who are given a reduced sentence for their co-operation. It is, however, the overlap between 'confidential contacts' (who are not subject to the RIPA regime) and the CHIS (defined below) that has the potential to circumvent the law. The National Criminal Intelligence Service (ACPO) (1999) define a confidential contact as 'an individual or member of an organization who discloses information to the police from which an individual can be identified and there exists personal, professional or other risks by their doing so'. The fundamental difference between the two categories is that confidential contacts do not establish or maintain a personal or other relationship 'for the purpose of gathering information'.

There is considerable difficulty in labelling sources, and so investigative agencies have to exercise great care. The differences are very fine and similar principles apply however they are labelled. In cases of doubt, the RIPA procedures should be followed. Under RIPA s. 26(8), a person is a source if:

a he establishes or maintains a personal or other relationship with a person for the covert purpose of facilitating the doing of anything falling within Code (b) or (c);
b he covertly uses such a relationship to obtain information or to provide access to any information to another person; or
c he covertly discloses information obtained by the use of such a relationship or as a consequence of the existence of such a relationship.

The definition is drawn in very broad terms ('relationship' is not defined, and the words 'personal or other relationship' could cover most situations) (Gillespie and Clark 2002). The purpose of the relationship is to obtain 'information' or 'any information', which contrasts with the obtaining of 'private information' in relation to intrusive and directed surveillance. 'Covert' is given the same self-evident meaning as elsewhere in the Act: 'a purpose is covert, in relation to the establishment or maintenance of a personal or other relationship, if and only if, the relationship is conducted in a manner that is calculated to ensure that one of the parties to the relationship is unaware of the purpose.'

'Use' and 'conduct' are key terms within the Act and require separate consideration before authorization. The use of a source involves inducing, asking or assisting a person to engage in the conduct of a source or to obtain information by means of the conduct of such a source – this is what the law enforcement agency does in connection with the source. The conduct of a source is any conduct falling within RIPA s. 29(4) or which is incidental to anything falling within s. 29(4) – in other words, what the source does to fulfil the task given to him or her or what he or she does that is incidental to the task.

Authorization procedures

Under RIPA s. 29(3), an authorization for the use or conduct of a source may be granted by the authorizing officer when he or she believes that the authorization is necessary:

- In the interests of national security.
- For the purpose of preventing and detecting crime, or of preventing disorder.
- In the interests of the economic well-being of the UK.
- In the interests of public safety.
- For the purpose of protecting public health.
- For the purpose of assessing or collecting any tax, duty, levy or other imposition, contribution or charge payable to a government department.
- For any other purpose prescribed in an order made by the Secretary of State.

The authorizing officer must also believe that the authorized use or conduct of a source is proportionate to what is sought to be achieved by that use or conduct (Code 4.8). Significantly, there is no requirement for an authorizing officer to have reasonable suspicion that the target(s) has committed or is about to commit a criminal offence.

The public authorities entitled to authorize the use or conduct of a source are those listed in Schedule 1 to RIPA. Responsibility for authorizing the use or conduct of a source rests with the authorizing officer, and all authorizations require the personal authority of the authorizing officer. An authorizing officer is the person designated under RIPA s. 29 to grant an authorization for the use or conduct of a source. The Regulation of Investigatory Powers (Prescriptions of Offices, Ranks and Positions) Order 2000 designates the authorizing officer for each different public authority and the officers entitled to act only in urgent cases. In certain circumstances, the Secretary of State will be the authorizing officer (see RIPA s. 30(2)).

The authorizing officer must give authorizations in writing. In urgent cases, however, they may be given orally by the authorizing officer or the officer entitled to act in urgent cases. On such occasions, a statement that the authorizing officer has expressly authorized the action should be recorded in writing by the applicant as soon as is reasonably practicable. A case is not normally regarded as urgent unless the time that would elapse before the authorizing officer was available to grant the authorization would, in the judgement of the person giving the authorization, be likely to endanger life or jeopardize the operation or investigation for which the authorization was being given. An authorization is not to be regarded as urgent where the need for an authorization has been neglected or the urgency is of the authorizing officer's own making.

Authorizing officers should not be responsible for authorizing their own activities (e.g. those in which they, themselves, are to act as the source or in tasking the source). However, it is recognized that this is not always possible, especially in the case of small organizations. Where an authorizing officer authorizes his or her own activity, the authorization should highlight this, and the attention of a commissioner or inspector should be drawn to it during his or her next inspection.

The authorizing officers in the police, the NCIS and the National Crime Squad (NCS) may only grant authorizations on application by a member of their own force, service or squad. Authorizing officers in Her Majesty's Revenue and Customs (HMRC) may only grant authorizations on application by a customs officer. On 31 March 2005, there were 4,452 CHIS authorizations in place to law enforcement agencies and 53 to local authorities (Office of the Chief Surveillance Commissioner 2005).

Information to be provided in applications for authorization

An application for the authorization of the use or conduct of a source should be in writing and should record the following:

- The reasons why the authorization is necessary in the particular case and on the grounds (e.g. for the purpose of preventing or detecting a crime) listed in RIPA s. 29(3).
- The reasons why the authorization is considered proportionate to what it seeks to achieve.
- The purpose for which the source will be tasked or deployed (e.g. in relation to an organized serious crime, espionage, a series of racially motivated crimes, etc.)
- Where a specific investigation or operation is involved, the nature of that investigation or operation.
- The nature of what the source will be tasked to do.
- The level of authority required (or recommended, where that is different).
- The details of any potential collateral intrusion and why the intrusion is justified.
- The details of any confidential information that is likely to be obtained as a consequence of the authorization.
- A subsequent record of whether authority was given or refused, by whom and the time and date.

Additionally, in urgent cases, the authorization should record (as the case may be):

- the reasons why the authorizing officer or the officer entitled to act in urgent cases considered the case so urgent that an oral instead of a written authorization was given; and/or
- the reasons why it was not reasonably practicable for the application to be considered by the authorizing officer.

Where the authorization is oral, the detail referred to above should be recorded in writing by the applicant as soon as reasonably practicable.

Duration of authorizations

A written authorization will, unless renewed, cease to have effect at the end of a period of 12 months, beginning with the day on which it took effect. Urgent oral authorizations or authorizations granted or renewed by a person who is entitled to act only in urgent cases will, unless renewed, cease to have effect after 72 hours, beginning with the time when the authorization was granted or renewed.

Reviews

Regular authorization reviews should be undertaken to assess the need for the continued use of a source. This review should include the use made of the source during the period authorized, the tasks given to the source and the information obtained from the source. The results of a review should be recorded on the authorization record. Authorizations where the use of a source provides access to confidential information or involves collateral intrusion should, in particular, be reviewed.

In every case the authorizing officer in each public authority should determine how often a review should take place. This should be as frequently as is considered necessary and practicable.

Renewals

Before an authorizing officer renews an authorization, he or she must be satisfied that a review has been carried out about the use of a source. If at any time before an authorization ceases to have effect the authorizing officer considers it necessary for the authorization to continue for the purpose for which it was given, he or she may renew it in writing for a further 12 months. Renewals may also be granted orally in urgent cases, and these last for a period of 72 hours.

A renewal takes effect from the time the authorization would have ceased to have effect but for the renewal. An application for renewal, therefore, should not be made until the authorization period is due to draw to a close. Any person who is entitled to grant a new authorization can renew an authorization. Authorizations may be renewed more than once, if necessary, provided they continue to meet the criteria for authorization. The renewal should be recorded as part of the authorization process.

All applications for the renewal of an authorization should record the following:

- Whether this is the first renewal, or every occasion on which the authorization was renewed previously.
- Any significant changes to the information in Code 4.14.
- The reasons why it is necessary to continue to use the source.
- The use made of the source in the period since the grant or, as the case may be, since the latest renewal of the authorization.
- The tasks given to the source during that period and the information obtained from the conduct or use of the source.
- The results of regular reviews of the use of the source.

Cancellations

The authorizing officer who granted or renewed the authorization must cancel it if he or she is satisfied that the use or conduct of the source no longer satisfies the criteria for authorization or that satisfactory arrangements for the source's case no longer exist. Where the authorizing officer is no longer available, this duty will fall on the person who has taken over the role of authorizing officer or the person who is acting as authorizing officer (see the Regulation of Investigatory Powers (Cancellation of Authorizations) Order 2000). Where necessary, the safety and welfare of the source should continue to be taken into account after the authorization has been cancelled.

Management of sources

Tasking

Tasking is the assignment given to the source by the persons defined in RIPA, ss. 29(5)(a) and (b). Tasking involves asking the source to obtain information, to provide access to information or to otherwise act, incidentally, for the benefit of the relevant public authority. Authorization for the use or conduct of a source is required prior to any tasking where such tasking requires the source to establish or maintain a personal or other relationship for a covert purpose.

The person referred to in RIPA ss. 29(5)(a) as the source handler has the day-to-day responsibility for:

- dealing with the source on behalf of the authority concerned;
- directing the day-to-day activities of the source;
- recording the information supplied by the source; and
- monitoring the source's security and welfare.

The person referred to in RIPA ss. 29(5)(b) as the source controller is responsible for the general oversight of the use of the source.

In some instances, the tasking given to a person will not require the source to establish a personal or other relationship for a covert purpose. For example, a source may be tasked with finding out purely factual information about the layout of commercial premises. Alternatively, a trading standards officer may be involved in the test purchase of items that have been labelled misleadingly or are unfit for consumption. In such cases, it is for the relevant public authority to determine where, and in what circumstances, such activity may require authorization.

It is not the intention that authorizations be drawn so narrowly that a separate authorization is required each time the source is tasked. Rather, an authorization might cover, in broad terms, the nature of the source's task. If this changes, then a new authorization may need to be sought.

It is difficult to predict exactly what might occur each time a meeting with a source takes place, or the source meets the subject of an investigation. There may be occasions when unforeseen actions or undertakings occur. When this happens, the occurrence must be recorded as soon as practicable after the event and, if the existing authorization is insufficient, it should either be updated and reauthorized (for minor amendments only) or it should be cancelled and a new authorization should be obtained before any further such action is carried out.

Similarly where it is intended to task a source in a new way or in a significantly greater way than previously identified, the persons defined in RIPA ss. 29(5)(a) or (b) must refer the proposed tasking to the authorizing officer, who should consider whether a separate authorization is required. This should be done in advance of any tasking, and the details of such referrals must be recorded.

Management responsibility

Public authorities should ensure that arrangements are in place for the proper oversight and management of sources, including appointing individual officers as defined in RIPA ss. 29(5)(a) and (b) for each source. The person responsible for the day-to-day contact between the public authority and the source will usually be of a rank or position below that of the authorizing officer.

In cases where the authorization is for the use or conduct of a source whose activities benefit more than a single public authority, responsibilities for the management and oversight of that source may be taken up by one authority or can be split between the authorities.

Security and welfare

Any public authority deploying a source should take into account the safety and welfare of that source when carrying out actions in relation to an authorization or tasking, and any foreseeable consequences to others of that tasking. Before authorizing the use or conduct of a source, the authorizing officer should ensure that a risk assessment is carried out to determine the risk to the source of any tasking and the likely consequences should the role of the source become known. The ongoing security and welfare of the source (after the cancellation of the authorization) should also be considered at the outset.

The person defined in RIPA s. 29(5)(a) is responsible for bringing to the attention of the person defined at s. 29(5)(b) any concerns about the personal circumstances of the source, in so far as they might affect:

- the validity of the risk assessment;
- the conduct of the source; and
- the safety and welfare of the source.

Where deemed appropriate, concerns about such matters must be considered by the authorizing officer, and a decision taken on whether or not to allow the authorization to continue. Public authorities have a duty of care to those who are affected by surveillance. This includes surveillance operatives and CHISs. Civil liability may arise if the duty of care is breached. In the context of the duty of care to a CHIS, in *Swinney* v. *Chief Constable of Northumbria Police*[4] the details of an informant were contained in a briefcase that was stolen from a car. Public authorities have a duty 'to take reasonable care to avoid unnecessary disclosure to the general public of the information which X had given to the police'. In *Swinney* there had been no breach of the duty of care because, compared with the duty to suppress crime, the risk of the car being broken into was small, and sensible steps had been taken to prevent the theft of the briefcase. Where a CHIS voluntarily wishes to sacrifice his or her own anonymity, he or she is not precluded from doing so under the principle of public interest immunity.[5]

Sources and undercover officers involved in the commission of crime

There are conflicting views as to the legality of the criminal conduct sources engage in during an 'infiltration'. The deployment of sources who participate in criminal activity with the authority of the law enforcement agency that deploys them is a recognized tactic in detecting serious crime. While RIPA does not give authority for such activity, Code 1.4 of the *Covert Human Intelligence Sources Code of Practice* states: 'Neither Part I of RIPA 2000 or the Code of Practice is intended to affect the practices and procedures surrounding criminal participation of sources.'

Where the source has acted in accordance with the terms of the authorization, the law enforcement agency relies on its prosecutorial discretion and does not prosecute. There are are a number of difficulties with this approach. First, it is not the agency's province to decide against prosecution – that is the Crown Prosecution Service's province. Secondly, authorizations are vaguely worded, which means it is likely that the extent of the criminal activity will be outlined, despite the intentions of the authorizing officer. Finally, the deployment of sources in these circumstances may not be 'in accordance with the law'.

Fair trial values and disclosure of evidence

No matter what strategies are used in the investigative process, the public's interest lies in compliance with the law. Criminal investigation consists of policy-making and specific actions as part of a staged process. Investigations are regulated by the requirement to maintain accurate records and, in due course, to be accountable to the courts if a prosecution takes place. It is essential, therefore, that investigations are conducted ethically and that investigators approach their task in a methodical and scientific manner. This is recognized by the courts.

The judges have developed a common law duty for the prosecution to disclose the evidence it has at its disposal to the defence, in an effort to achieve both a fair trial and 'equality of arms'. This is now the subject of a statutory regime set out in the Criminal Procedure and Investigations Act (CPIA) 1996, supplemented by a code of practice issued under the Act. 'Criminal investigation' is defined in s. 1(4) as follows: 'an investigation which police officers or other persons have a duty to conduct with a view to it being ascertained whether (a) a person should be charged with an offence, or (b) whether a person charged with an offence is guilty of it.' In the case of covert investigations, it may be difficult to ascertain the boundaries of the investigation, and the starting point used by the prosecution in presenting evidence may be artificial and inaccurate.

The investigator must draw to the prosecutor's attention any material that might undermine the prosecution's case and, after disclosure by the defence, must look again at the material in the light of the defence statement and draw to the prosecutor's attention material that might reasonably be expected to assist the defence. These are onerous responsibilities. A schedule listing material that has been obtained but that is not part of the prosecution's case must be prepared. Sensitive material will frequently be gathered during the course of an investigation, and the investigator may believe it is not in the public's interest to disclose such material (e.g. material relating to national security, material given in confidence and material relating to informants and undercover officers). This type of information must be included in a separate schedule.

Such evidence may not be tested in open court, and a jury will therefore not be aware of it because of the doctrine of public interest immunity. In these circumstances, the public's interest lies in protecting the identity of the informant/undercover officer and/or of the particular investigative technique. However, if the defence are able to produce evidence involving an informant that may prevent a miscarriage of justice, this may outweigh the public's interest in protecting the informant.[6]

RIPA and the codes of practice issued under the Act have been designed to ensure that informants operate lawfully. Ethically, the use of informants may be justified on utilitarian grounds (Williamson and Bagshaw 2001). It is in terms of the fairness of the trial that the use of informants should be considered, as well as the extent to which it is possible for a defendant to have a fair trial when an informant or undercover officer has been deployed. The central dilemma in these cases is that, in most cases, the evidence of CHISs remains untested because of disclosure rules and because of the principle of public interest immunity.

Human rights and the doctrine of proportionality

Under the ECHR there are three principal levels of rights. First, there are absolute rights, such as those under Article 2 (the right to life) and Article 3 (the right not to be subjected to torture, or to inhuman or degrading treatment). Derogation from these rights is not permitted under any circumstances.

Second are those rights contained in Articles 5 and 6, which are the rights most frequently raised in criminal proceedings. Third are the qualified rights – those under Articles 8–11, where the rights are declared along with the circumstances in which interference with those rights is permitted. The practical difference between these categories of rights is that restriction in the public's interest can be justified, but only on the grounds expressly provided for in the articles themselves. According to case law, a limitation or restriction on these rights can only be justified in the following circumstances:

- The limitation or restriction must be 'prescribed by law'. This means the law must be readily accessible and must be formulated with sufficient precision to enable individuals to regulate their own conduct. The Privy Council in *de Freitas* v. *Ministry of Agriculture*[7] said that the fundamental issue in these circumstances is the principle of legal certainty (*per* Lord Clyde).

- The limitation or restriction must be for the pursuit of a legitimate aim (i.e. one of the aims specifically listed in the article).

- The limitation or restriction must be necessary in a free society. In respect of the third category of rights, this means it must be shown that the limitation or restriction fulfils a pressing social need and is proportionate to the aim of responding to that aim.

- The limitation or restriction must not be discriminatory. Differences in treatment that do not have objective or reasonable grounds cannot be justified.

The exercise of every investigative power must therefore be shown to be lawfully in pursuit of a legitimate aim, necessary and proportionate to the end it seeks to achieve. 'Necessity' is not defined in the convention. However, it has been interpreted as not synonymous with 'indispensable', and not as flexible as 'ordinary, useful or desirable'.[8] Proportionality occupies a central position in the exercise of investigative powers. It is considered a vehicle for conducting a balancing exercise, and it balances the nature and extent of the interference against the reasons for interfering. A number of questions must be considered:

- Would it have been possible to achieve the legitimate aim by less intrusive means?[9]

- Does the interference deprive the right-holder of the very essence of the right?[10]

- Is the right of sufficient importance that particularly strong reasons are required to justify any interference?[11]

- Does the interference cause harm to the right-holder that is serious enough to outweigh any benefit the interference might achieve in furthering a legitimate aim?[12]

- Are there sufficient safeguards against abuse?[13]

The elements of proportionality were formulated by the House of Lords in *R (Daly)* v. *Secretary of State for the Home Department*[14] as follows. That:

- the objective of the interference is sufficiently important to justifying limiting the right;
- the measures designed to meet the objective are rationally connected with it;
- the means used to impair the right are no more than is necessary to accomplish the objective; and
- the interference does not have an excessive or disproportionate effect on the individual concerned.

Articles 6 (the right to a fair trial) and 8 (the right to a private and family life) are directly relevant to the deployment of CHISs.

Article 6: the right to a fair trial

Article 6 states:

> (1) In the determination of his civil rights and obligations or of any criminal charge against him, everyone is entitled to a fair and public hearing within a reasonable time by an independent and impartial tribunal established by law. Judgment shall be pronounced publicly but the press and public may be excluded from all or part of the trial in the interest of morals, public order or national security in a democratic society, where the interests of juveniles or the protection of the private lives of the parties so require, or to the extent strictly necessary in the opinion of the court in special circumstances where publicity would prejudice the interests of justice.
>
> (2) Everyone charged with a criminal offence shall be presumed innocent until proved guilty according to law.
>
> (3) Everyone charged with a criminal offence has the following minimum rights:
>
> > (a) to be informed promptly, in a language which he understands and in detail, of the nature and cause of the accusation against him;
> >
> > (b) to have adequate time and facilities for the preparation of his defence;
> >
> > (c) to defend himself in person or through legal assistance of his own choosing or, if he has not sufficient means to pay for legal assistance, to be given it free when the interests of justice so require;
> >
> > (d) to examine or have examined witnesses against him and to obtain the attendance and examination of witnesses on his behalf under the same conditions as witnesses against him;
> >
> > (e) to have the free assistance of an interpreter if he cannot understand or speak the language used in court.

The right to a fair trial involves observing the principle of 'equality of arms' under which the defendant must have 'a reasonable opportunity of presenting his case to the court under conditions which do not place him at a substantial disadvantage vis-à-vis his opponent'.[15] The principle of equality of arms under Article 6(1) overlaps with the specific guarantees in Article 6(3), though it is not confined to those aspects of the proceedings.

Article 6(1) does not require the adoption of any particular rules of evidence since this is, in principle, a matter for domestic law. However, the admission of certain types of evidence may render the trial as a whole unfair. It is in relation to entrapment and agents provocateurs that the use of CHISs is at its most problematic. The right to a fair trial will be violated where police officers have stepped beyond an 'essentially passive' investigation of a suspect's criminal activities and have 'exercised an influence such as to incite the commission of the offence'.[16]

In *R. v. Looseley*,[17] the House of Lords gave guidance on the application of Article 6 to cases of alleged entrapment. By recourse to the principle that courts have an inherent power and duty to prevent abuse of their process, the courts should ensure that executive agents of the state do not misuse the coercive law-enforcement functions of the courts and thereby oppress citizens of the state. Entrapment is an instance where such misuse may occur. It is simply not acceptable that the state, through its agents, should lure its citizens into committing acts forbidden by the law and then seek to prosecute them for doing so. The role of the courts is to stand between the citizen and the state and to make sure this happens. A useful guide to identifying the limits of acceptable police conduct is to consider whether the police did no more than present the defendant with an unexceptional opportunity to commit a crime. The yardstick was, in general, whether the police's conduct before the commission of the offence was no more than might have been expected from others in the circumstances. If that was the case, then the police were not to be regarded as inciting or instigating crime. Since they did no more than others might be expected to do, they were not creating crime artificially. However, the provision of an opportunity to commit a crime should not be applied in a random fashion or used for wholesale virtue testing. In general, the greater the degree of intrusiveness involved in a particular technique, the closer would the court scrutinize the reason for using it.

Proportionality had a role to play in this. The ultimate consideration was whether the law enforcement agency's conduct was so seriously improper as to bring the administration of justice into disrepute. The use of proactive techniques was more likely to be necessary, and hence more appropriate, in some circumstances than in others. The secrecy and difficulty of detection and the manner in which the particular criminal activity was carried on were relevant considerations, but the gravity of an offence was not, in itself, sufficient justification. The police were required to act in good faith.

In general, it would not be regarded as a legitimate use of police power to provide people not previously suspected of being engaged in a particular criminal activity with the opportunity to commit a crime. The only proper purpose of police participation is to obtain evidence of criminal acts they suspect someone is about to commit or in which he or she is already engaged. Its purpose is not to tempt people to commit crimes in order to expose their bad characters and then to punish them. However, a reasonable preexisting suspicion is not always necessary. The police might, in the course of a bona fide investigation, provide an opportunity for the commission of an offence that is taken by someone to whom no suspicion previously attached. In deciding what is acceptable, regard has to be taken of the defendant's circumstances, including his or her vulnerability. In general, the accused's predisposition to commit an offence or his or her previous criminal record would be irrelevant unless it was linked to other factors grounding a reasonable suspicion that the accused is currently engaged in the alleged criminal activity.

Specifically, Lord Hoffman stated that: 'the only proper purpose of police participation is to obtain evidence of criminal acts which they suspect someone is about to commit or in which he is actively engaged.' There will be circumstances, notwithstanding authorization, where the activity of a CHIS is in breach of Articles 6 and/or 8 or amounts to incitement, and is therefore unlawful. The difficulty with these principles may be that evidence of the transaction that constitutes the offence itself may be emasculated by mechanisms designed to protect both the covert technique and the identity of the CHIS.

Article 8: the right to a private and family life

Article 8 states:

> (1) Everyone has the right to respect for his private and family life, his home and his correspondence.
>
> (2) There shall be no interference by a public authority with the exercise of this right except such as is in accordance with the law and is necessary in a democratic society in the interests of national security, public safety or the economic well-being of the country, for the prevention of disorder or crime, for the protection of health or morals, or for the protection of the rights and freedoms of others.

The concept of private life is broadly defined.[18] It includes not only personal information, but also an individual's relationships with others, including (in certain circumstances) business relationships.

The right to respect for a person's home includes the right to peaceful enjoyment free from intrusion.[19] The concepts of a person's home and private life may, in some circumstances, extend to professional or business activities or premises.[20] Correspondence includes both written communications and telephone calls.[21] It also extends to modern means of electronic communication, provided the person concerned can reasonably expect that his or her communications would be private.

A criminal prosecution constitutes an 'interference by a public authority' for the purposes of Article 8(2).[22] The mere threat of a prosecution may be sufficient if it interferes directly with private life.[23] Article 8(2) sets out the circumstances whereby an interference with the right to a private and family life will be justified. Activities are justified provided it can be shown that:

- the interference is in accordance with the law;[24]
- it is for one of the purposes specified in Article 8(2); and
- the interference is necessary and proportionate.

Intrusive surveillance constitutes an interference with the rights protected by Article 8.[25] It can, in principle, be justified in the interests of national security or for the prevention of crime, and provided it is 'in accordance with the law'. The term 'in accordance with the law' has a special meaning in this context. The law must give an adequate indication of the circumstances in which, and the conditions under which, such surveillance can occur.[26] The rules must define with clarity the categories of citizens liable to be the subject of such techniques, the offences that might give rise to such an order, the permitted duration of the interception and the circumstances in which recordings are to be destroyed.[27] There must, in addition, be adequate and effective safeguards against abuse.[28] While it is desirable that the machinery of supervision should be in the hands of a judge, this is not essential, providing the supervisory body enjoys sufficient independence to give an objective ruling.[29] The deployment of a CHIS constitutes an interference with the rights protected by Article 8.

The doctrine of proportionality and a human rights model of policing mean that authorizing officers must be satisfied that these requirements are met before a CHIS is deployed. However, it cannot be safely concluded that these requirements are met in all cases. The Chief Surveillance Officer stated the following in his 2004–5 annual report: 'Bad practice points [include] insufficiently specific applications authorizations ... Exceeding the terms of authorizations, codes of practice not readily available to practitioners, and inadequate RIPA training and education' (Office of the Chief Surveillance Commissioner 2005: para. 8.8).

The potential for abuse

The potential for abuse by informants is well documented (Marx 1988; Billingsley *et al.* 2001; Sharpe 2002). The role of the CHIS in criminal investigations has been described as 'the untidy phase of police work, a distasteful but vitally important ingredient in the chemistry of man hunting' (Purvis 1936).

The majority of undercover investigations rely to some degree on individuals of dubious integrity for information; for technical advice; for contacts; and for opportunities to confirm the law-breaking credentials of undercover police officers. For example, in cases of conspiracy, the police must depend on people whose professional lives routinely involve deceit and concealment, and who have a motive to lie. The types of problems that emerge are going beyond the legal or ethical guidelines issued by authorizing and/or tasking officers; exaggerating and concealing crimes; the informant taking control of the officer; and corruption between informants and police officers (for a discussion of corruption, see Clark 2001).

Informants often have strong incentives to ensure that others break the law: they may be financially rewarded and they may receive a sentencing discount if they are prosecuted in the future.[30] Evidence that has been obtained unlawfully may also be reconstructed to make it appear untainted (Johnson and Rowe 2000).[31]

The admissibility of evidence

A fundamental aspect of policing in the human rights era is respect for individual autonomy. New technology, however, has challenged this principle. Until recently, it was possible to argue (with a fair degree of certainty) that everything was lawful that was not specifically prohibited. This is no longer true: the courts will vigorously scrutinize investigative techniques. This is especially so of covert policing because it reflects the state's power and because of the idea that the use of intrusive techniques must be proportionate to the legitimate aim of preventing and detecting crime. Whatever the nature or extent of the regulation of investigative techniques, a question arises concerning the admissibility of evidence if the relevant regulatory procedures have not been complied with or if the means used to obtain the evidence are challenged as unlawful or unfair. However, the discretionary nature of the regulatory regime, the Office of the Chief Surveillance Commssioner's *post hoc* review of procedures and public interest immunity limit the effect of such challenges.

Of particular concern is the fact that authorizations for the use of a CHIS under RIPA Part II may be given without there being reasonable suspicion that the target(s) has committed or is about to commit an offence. Thus it is possible for evidence obtained in breach of both Articles 8 and 6 to be inadmissible because the exercise of powers gave rise to an abuse of process or to such unfairness that the evidence should be excluded under PACE s. 78.

Conclusion

It is surely healthy to maintain at least a sceptical attitude towards the use of covert policing techniques, and informants in particular. Not to adopt this attitude would lead to overconfidence and complacency. There will always be dangers lurking beneath the surface, and the policy-makers in a democratic society must be alert to the risks. In the UK, informants are employed without independent supervision, and reliance is placed on oversight after the event, which, some would argue, is unsatisfactory. The extent to which such regulation is appropriate is worthy of further consideration if we are serious about maintaining the balance between the public's interest in the prevention of crime and avoiding unjustifiable intrusions into privacy and protecting fair trial values.

There are many factors that indicate that the deployment of informants represents a high level of risk, both to the organizations that use such tactics and to the integrity of criminal trials. There is abundant research which shows that weak constraints on discretion allow considerable scope for misuse (for a fuller discussion, see Sanders and Young 2003). RIPA and the codes of practice leave room for such discretion and for the possibility of misuse, leading to the exclusion of evidence as well as to the undermining of fair trial values. The potential for the corruption of law enforcement officials is great indeed, and informants may be motivated to operate beyond the terms of their deployment because of financial or other rewards. Oversight is random, *post hoc* and primarily concerns the checking of documentation.

Notwithstanding these concerns, CHISs have proved to be effective and will continue to be deployed as an essential tactic in criminal investigations. Governments and law enforcement agencies are prepared to accept the risks and are convinced that the benefits outweigh these risks. Policy-makers consider the RIPA accountability regime both appropriate and effective.

Selected further reading

Billingsley, R., Nemitz, T. and Bean, P. (2001) *Informers: Policing, Policy, Practice.* Cullompton: Willan Publishing. An overview of many of the issues associated with the use of covert human intelligence sources, including risk assessment and rewards.

Clark, D. (2004) *The Law of Criminal Investigation.* Oxford: Oxford University Press. An analysis of all aspects of procedure relating to criminal investigation, including evidential admissibility.

Harfield, C. (2005) *Covert Investigation.* Oxford: Oxford University Press. A practical guide with case studies and examples.

Wright, A. (2002) *Policing: An Introduction to Concepts and Practice.* Cullompton: Willan Publishing. A very useful introduction to policing written in an accessible style. This book provides the background to police methods.

Notes

1 Malone *v* United Kingdom (1985).
2 Halford *v.* United Kingdom (1997); Hewitt and Harman *v.* United Kingdom.
3 (1826). Chitty on Contracts 29th edn (2006) London: Sweet and Maxwell.
4 Swimey *v* Chief Constable of Northumbria Police (1997) QB 464.
5 Savage *v.* Chief Constable of Hampshire (1997) 1 WLR 1061.
6 R *v.* Agar (1994).
7 (1999).
8 Silver *v.* United Kingdom (1983).
9 Campbell *v.* United Kingdom (1993).
10 Rees *v.* United Kingdom (1987).
11 Jersild *v.* Denmark (1994).
12 Dudgeon *v.* United Kingdom (1982).
13 Klass *v.* Germany (1978).
14 (2001).
15 Neumeister *v..* Austria.
16 Teixeira de Castro *v.* Portugal; Lüdi *v.* Switzerland.
17 Attorney-General's Reference (No. 2 of 2000) [2002].

18 Niemietz *v.* Germany.
19 Lopez-Ostra *v.* Spain.
20 Niemietz *v.* Germany; Chappell *v.* United Kingdom.
21 Klass *v.* Germany (1978); Malone *v.* United Kingdom.
22 Dudgeon *v.* United Kingdom (1982); Modinos *v.* Cyprus.
23 Norris *v.* Ireland.
24 Halford *v.* United Kingdom (1997).
25 Klass *v.* Germany (1978); Malone *v.* United Kingdom.
26 Malone *v.* United Kingdom.
27 Huvig *v.* France; Kruslin *v.* France.
28 Klass *v.* Germany (1978); Malone *v.* United Kingdom.
29 Klass *v.* Germany (1978).
30 R *v.* Piggot (1994); R *v.* X (1999).
31 R *v.* Davis.

References

ACPO (1999) *National Standards for Covert Policing.* London: ACPO.
Akdeniz, Y. Taylor, N. and Walker, C. (2001) RIPA 2000: BigBrother.gov.uk: state surveillance in the age of information and rights, *Criminal Law Review*, 73.
Ashworth, A. (2005) *The Criminal Process* (3rd edn). Oxford: Oxford University Press.
Audit Commission (1993) *Helping with Enquiries: Tackling Crime Effectively.* London: Audit Commission.
Bean, P. (2002) *Drugs and Crime.* Cullompton: Willan Publishing.
Billingsley, R. Nemitz, T. and Bean, P. (2001) *Informers: Policing, Policy, Practice.* Cullompton: Willan Publishing.
Brown, D. (1997) *PACE Ten Years on: A Review of the Research.* HORS 135. London: HMSO.
Clark, D. (2004) *The Law of Criminal Investigation.* Oxford: Oxford University Press.
Clark, D. (2006) *The Law of Covert Investigation.* London: Routledge-Cavendish.
Clark, R. (2001) 'The ethics of informer handling', in R. Billingsley *et al.* (eds) *Informers: Policing, Policy, Practice.* Cullompton: Willan Publishing.
Colvin, M. (1998) *Under Surveillance – Covert Policing and Human Rights Standards.* London: Justice.
Cousens, M. (2004) *Surveillance Law.* London: Lexis Nexis Butterworths.
Dixon, D. (1992) 'Legal regulation and police practice', *Social and Legal Studies*, 1: 515–41.
Dixon, D. (1997) *Law in Policing.* Oxford: Clarendon Press.
Dorn, N. Murji, K. and South, N. (1992) *Traffickers: Drug Markets and Law Enforcement.* London: Routledge.
Dunnighan, C. and Norris, C. (1996) 'The narks game', *New Law Journal*, 146.
Dunnighan, C. and Norris, C. (1999) 'The detective, the snout and the Audit Commission: the real costs of running informants', *Howard Journal of Criminal Justice*, 38: 67–86.
Ericson, R. (1981) *Making Crime: A Study of Detective Work.* Toronto: Butterworths.
Gill, P. (2000) *Rounding up the Usual Suspects.* Aldershot: Dartmouth.
Gillespie, A. and Clark, D. (2000) 'Using juvenile test purchasers', *Journal of Civil Liberties*, 7.
Greer, S. (1995) *Supergrasses.* Oxford: Clarendon Press.

Greer, S. and South, N. (1998) 'The criminal informant: police management, supervision and control', in S. Field and C. Pelser (eds) *Invading the Private? New Investigation Methods in Europe.* Aldershot: Ashgate.

Home Office (2004) *One Step Ahead: A 21st Century Response to Organised Crime.* London: Home Office

Justice (2000) *The Regulation of Investigatory Powers Bill: Briefing Paper.* London: Justice.

Keegan, J. (2004) *Intelligence in War.* Croydon: Pimlico.

Lidstone, K. and Palmer, C. (1996) *Bevan and Lidstone's Criminal Investigation* (2nd edn). London: Butterworths.

Maguire, M. and John, T. (1995) *Intelligence, Surveillance and Informants: Integrated Approaches.* London: Home Office.

Marx, G. (1988) *Police Surveillance in America.* Berkeley, CA: University of California Press.

Neyroud, P. and Beckley, A. (2001) *Policing, Ethics and Human Rights.* Cullompton: Willan Publishing.

Newburn, T. (2003) *Handbook of Policing.* Cullompton: Willan Publishing.

Office of the Chief Surveillance Commissioner (2005) *Annual Report of the Chief Surveillance Commissioner, 2004–05.* London: House of Commons.

Purvis, M. (1936) *American Agent.* New York, NY: Garden City Publishing.

Radzinowicz, L. (1956) *A History of the Criminal Law and its Administration from 1750. Vol. 2. The Clash between Private Initiatives and Public Interest in the Enforcement of Law.* London: Stevens.

Rowe and Davis *v* UK (2000) 30 EHRR 1 [2000] Crim LR 584.

Sanders, A. and Young, R. (2003) 'Police powers', in T. Newburn (ed.) *Handbook of Policing.* Cullompton: Willan Publishing.

Sharpe, S. (2002) 'Covert surveillance and the use of informants', in M. McConville and G. Wilson (eds) *The Handbook of Criminal Justice Process.* Oxford: Oxford University Press.

Williamson, T. and Bagshaw, P. (2001) 'The ethics of informer handling', in R. Billingsley *et al.* (eds) *Informers: Policing, Policy, Practice.* Cullompton: Willan Publishing.

Wright, A. (2002) *Policing: An Introduction to Concepts and Practice.* Cullompton: Willan Publishing.

Chapter 18

Victims and witnesses in criminal investigations

Nicholas Fyfe and Kevin Smith

Introduction

> Without witnesses, the rudiments of prosecution, such as identifying the accused and establishing the requisite nexus between the accused and the crime, would become insurmountable obstacles to conviction, and the criminal justice system would cease to function (Harris 1991: 1285).

> Witnesses are 'the cannon fodder of the system' (Spencer and Stern 2001: 11).

These two comments capture something of the paradoxical position witnesses find themselves in within the criminal justice system. On the one hand, their role in assisting police investigations and giving evidence in court is crucial to the success of criminal prosecutions. As Spencer and Stern (2001: 17) note, crime is rarely hidden from public view: 'Whether it is a pub brawl, vandalism, shoplifting, burglary or domestic violence, someone frequently sees or knows the offence is taking place.' On the other hand, the participation of witnesses in the criminal justice system has, until quite recently, largely been taken for granted. Research evidence suggests that their experiences at court are typically characterized by a mix of inconvenience caused by delays in the trial process; indifference on the part of criminal justice agencies; and feelings of intimidation due to the unfamiliar environment of the court and the legal process as well as the presence of the accused and his or her associates (see Rock 1991; Fyfe 2001).

Over the last ten years, however, there have been significant changes in UK policy and practices with respect to how witnesses are treated within the criminal justice system. In this chapter, we examine these changes and assess their impact and implications for criminal investigation. In particular, we argue that the vital role played by witnesses hinges not just on how the police interact with witnesses during an investigation but also on witnesses' broader experiences of the criminal justice process as a whole because it is this wider context which strongly influences whether someone is prepared to be a witness again. To explore these issues we begin by briefly reviewing some key pieces of existing research which identify why people decide to become, or not to become, a witness. This material helps highlight some of the key challenges faced by the criminal justice system in terms of providing appropriate support and protection for witnesses. These challenges have only recently been addressed, and the second section briefly traces the history of how witnesses were once the 'the forgotten soul' of the criminal justice system but are now viewed as 'vital voices'. The third section then uses evaluative research to assess the impacts and implications of recent initiatives designed to encourage witnesses to come forward and assist police investigations and deliver evidence in court. We should also add at the outset that throughout this chapter we use the term witness to embrace both victim and non-victim witnesses, recognizing that not all victims are witnesses and not all witnesses are victims.

To be or not to be a witness?

Like the decision to report a crime, the decision to become a witness and assist police in the investigative process is subject to a complex set of influences. These include the perceived seriousness of an offence and the immediate context in which it occurs but also relate to people's broader perceptions and previous experiences of the legal process as well as their perceptions of community reaction to their involvement with the criminal justice system. In terms of the influence of the perceived seriousness of the incident, a survey of witness motivation carried out for the Institute for Public Policy Research (Spencer and Stern 2001) found that 88 per cent of respondents said they were 'very likely' to come forward as a witness to a murder, while 78 per cent were 'very likely' to come forward if they witnessed a mugging in the street. For other types of crime covered by the survey, including vandalism at a bus stop, shoplifting, and screaming and shouting from neighbours, less than half the respondents said they were 'very likely' to come forward as a witness, falling to less than a third of those who witnessed a brawl in the street. In attempting to understand these differences, the research highlights an important tension between an 'instinct to steer clear of trouble' and individuals doing what they perceived to be 'right' (Spencer and Stern 2001: 37). How such tensions are resolved depends partly on the perceived severity of the crime but also on the immediate social and geographical context in which it occurs. People were less likely to come forward if they felt an incident happened in a location where they felt responsibility lay elsewhere, for example in a shop with CCTV cameras and security staff. Similarly, respondents said they were less likely to report incidents that occurred in private or domestic space for fear of being perceived as interfering. Even if an incident happened in public space, however, there was a range of reasons why people might not come forward as a witness (Spencer and Stern 2001: 39). These include 'audience inhibition' (where being in public makes people less likely to act), 'social influence' (where the failure of others to respond leads individuals to conclude that indifference is an appropriate response) and 'diffusion of responsibility' (where the presence of others reduces the pressure on any one person to act).

The immediate circumstances of an offence are, however, only one factor in the decision to become a witness. As recent surveys of witness satisfaction reveal, more than half of witnesses are worried about appearing in court, with victim-witnesses more likely than non-victims to be worried because of anxieties about seeing the defendant as well as concerns about possible repercussions from either the defendant or the defendant's family or associates (Whitehead 2001: 11). Women and young people are also particularly likely to have concerns and to be worried about meeting the defendant, especially in sexual offence cases where cross-examination tends to be more severe. More generally, however, people have concerns about going to court because, as Burton *et al.* (2006: 1) observe:

> The Anglo-American common law system poses particular problems for victims and witnesses. Common law systems are adversarial and rely far more than inquisitorial systems ... on the provision of oral evidence in prosecutions. Not only do witnesses generally have to give evidence orally, which can be an ordeal for many people, but ... this can be challenged by the side against whom evidence is being given. Challenge, in the form of cross-examination, can be robust, making the giving of evidence even more of an ordeal in many cases.

This has been vividly illustrated through Rock's (1991, 1993) observational research in an English crown court. Confronted by defence agents who will often attempt 'to make witnesses appear so inconsistent, forgetful, muddled, spiteful, or greedy that their word cannot be safely believed' (1991: 267), witnesses frequently leave the witness box 'angrily and in tears'. In addition, simply being in the witness box makes witnesses vulnerable to verbal abuse and threats shouted from the public gallery, or being stared at by the accused. Moreover, when trials end or adjourn, suspects, victims and witnesses may all move out of the court room into public waiting areas where further intimidation may occur (Rock 1991; Maynard 1994; Fyfe 2001).

These experiences at court are significant because they strongly influence the willingness of witnesses to assist with criminal investigations in the future. For many witnesses, however, intimidation often begins before they ever reach the courtroom. In the communities where they live witnesses may be vulnerable to intimidation aimed at discouraging them from reporting crime or coming forward with evidence. Measuring the extent of such intimidation, like crime more generally, is notoriously difficult. Official criminal statistics need to be interpreted with caution because not only does much intimidation go unreported and unrecorded but even if it is reported it is hidden under headings such as assault or criminal damage. In 1993, however, growing anecdotal evidence of the intimidation and harassment of witnesses prompted the Home Office to commission the first in-depth UK study of witness intimidation (Maynard 1994). This research examined the experiences of witnesses on four high-crime housing estates and provided quantitative evidence of the extent of the problem in these areas. It revealed that 6 per cent of crimes experienced by victims and 22 per cent of crimes mentioned by other witnesses were never reported to the police because of intimidation. When crimes were reported, the research found that 13 per cent of crimes reported by victims and 9 per cent reported by other witnesses led to intimidation. Maynard concludes that fear of intimidation deters a greater number of witnesses than victims from reporting crimes, whereas actual intimidation is directed at more people who have been the victim of an initial crime than a witness to one (1994: 12–14). In addition, this research also showed how the timing and location of intimidation can partly be linked to police actions in investigating the initial crime. Police visits to witnesses' homes after an offence has been committed may help potential intimidators to identify witnesses. There was also evidence of police asking witnesses to identify suspects without the use of screens, which can place witnesses in a vulnerable position.

Witness intimidation is often, however, linked to a more general fear about the consequences of having contact with the police or others in authority. Evans et al.'s (1996) ethnographic study of crime in inner-city Salford in the UK revealed a local culture of 'no grassing' (i.e. of not communicating with the police or others in authority) sustained by the pressure and influence of gang activity which meant that many victims of and witnesses to crime were not prepared to report offences. Similarly, Fyfe's (2001) study of witness intimidation in Glasgow also found that the stigma of being labelled a 'grass' in the large local-authority housing schemes in and around the city was often sufficiently strong to dissuade victims or witnesses from ever coming forward to assist the police with the investigation of crime. Discussing the reluctance of witnesses to come forward, one social worker interviewed for the Glasgow study commented:

> I think part of it is fear and part of it is intimidation but a lot of it is just culture ... You just don't do it, no matter how bad things are; you just don't grass your own kind ... It tends to be a generational thing that is passed down from your grandparent to parent to child: you just don't talk to the police and you certainly don't grass anybody (cited in Fyfe 2001: 37).

From these studies, a broad distinction emerges between two main types of witness intimidation. On the one hand there is community-wide or perceived intimidation comprising victim and non-victim witnesses whose perception of the possibility of intimidation means they are not prepared to come forward and give evidence to the police. On the other hand, there is case-specific intimidation involving actual physical assaults or damage to property to deter a person from reporting a crime or giving evidence in court. These two types of intimidation are, however, inter-related with each example of case-specific intimidation helping to reinforce 'community-wide' intimidation. A third type of intimidation, typically linked to drugs and other forms of organized crime, involves serious, even life-threatening, intimidation of witnesses and their families. The numbers of people believed to be at such high risk are relatively small compared with the other forms of intimidation. Nevertheless, a growing number of police forces in the UK (and internationally; see Fyfe and Sheptycki 2006a) increasingly need to be able to offer high levels of protection to such witnesses, typically involving their secret relocation and a change of identity, in order to facilitate witness co-operation in serious and organized crime investigations (Fyfe 2001).

From 'forgotten soul' to 'vital voices': the changing position of witnesses in criminal justice policy

From the evidence discussed in the previous section, securing the participation of witnesses in criminal investigations and any subsequent legal proceedings is a process fraught with challenges. Witnesses may be reluctant to come forward for reasons ranging from indifference to fears of intimidation. Attempts to address such challenges are, however, relatively recent. Up to and including the early 1980s, witnesses were largely taken for granted: 'the forgotten soul of the criminal justice system', to use Harris' (1991: 1376) evocative phrase. The 1981 Royal Commission on Criminal Procedure in England Wales was typical of this lack of interest. It contained only a single reference to witnesses related to a concern that delays in trials might cause distress and inconvenience (see Rock 1993: 3). Several overlapping reasons contributed to this situation. According to Rock, witnesses were largely 'invisible' to the Home Office:

> When it is recalled that witnesses were not voicing audible demands, ... that the Home Office was very generally 'reactive' rather than 'proactive' in its policy-making, and that fiscal prudence was being urged insistently and continuously by government, it will be appreciated how very little inducement there was for the Department to embark unilaterally on a major spate of policy-making for the prosecution witness (1993: 294).

Furthermore, it was the Lord Chancellor's Department rather than the Home Office which had a more immediate responsibility for witnesses because of its role in relation to the administration of courts, yet this department had to ensure it was seen to be neutral in relation to the different participants in a trial. As a result, Rock notes, 'Proposals to aid the prosecution witness alone were ... innately uncongenial to the Department' (1993: 295).

From the mid-1980s to the mid-1990s, however, witnesses gradually moved from the periphery of the mental maps of criminal justice policy-makers to occupying a much more central position. A key factor in initiating this change came not from government, however, but from the increasingly important role played by the voluntary organization, Victim Support. Their volunteers offered not just short-term crisis intervention, but longer-term support and in many cases accompanied victims to court. Here it became clear that victims and other prosecution witnesses frequently had to endure

Table 18.1   Key government initiatives affecting witnesses 1998–2006

Date	Initiative
1998	*Speaking up for Justice: Report of the Interdepartmental Working Group on the Treatment of Vulnerable or Intimidated Witnesses in the Criminal Justice System* (Home Office)
	Towards a Just Conclusion: Vulnerable and Intimidated Witnesses in Scottish Criminal and Civil Cases (Scottish Office)
1999	*Youth Justice and Criminal Evidence Act*: contains 'special measures' to assist vulnerable and intimidated witnesses give evidence in court in England and Wales, including the use of screens, a live TV link to outside the courtroom and giving evidence-in-chief via a prior video-recording.
2002	*Justice for All* (Home Office)
	Vital Voices: Helping Vulnerable Witnesses Give Evidence (Scottish Executive)
	Achieving Best Evidence in Criminal Proceedings: Guidance for Vulnerable and Intimidated Witnesses, including Children (Home Office)
2003	*Criminal Justice Act*: allows use of live video links for witnesses
	No Witness No Justice: Towards a National Strategy for Witnesses (Home Office): recommends establishment of 'witness care units' staffed by the police and the Crown Prosecution Service
	A New Deal for Victims and Witnesses: National Strategy to Deliver Improved Services (Home Office)
2004	*Vulnerable Witnesses (Scotland) Act*: contains 'special measures' to assist vulnerable and intimidated witnesses give evidence in court in Scotland, including the use of screens, a live TV link to outside the courtroom and giving evidence-in-chief via a prior video-recording
	National roll-out of witness care units
	Domestic Violence, Crime and Victims Act: creates new post of Parliamentary Commissioner for Victims and Witnesses
	Cutting Crime, Delivering Justice: Strategic Plan, 2004–08 (Office of Criminal Justice Reform)
2005	*The Code of Practice for Victims of Crime* (Office of Criminal Justice Reform): sets out the services to be provided to direct victims of criminal conduct by a range of organizations, including the police and the joint police/Crown Prosecution Service witness care units
	The Witness Charter Consultation Document: sets out the key commitments of criminal justice agencies and defence lawyers to support witnesses from the time of reporting a crime through to giving evidence at court
	Serious Organized Crime and Police Act: establishes legislative framework for witness protection arrangements in cases involving serious organized crime
2006	Recruitment of a new Commissioner for Victims and Witnesses and of 'victim and witness intermediaries'

unexplained delays and were often at risk from unplanned encounters with the accused or his or her associates. Responding to this situation, Victim Support established a working party in 1986 to examine the experiences of witnesses at court in more detail which in turn led to a Home Office-funded pilot project to provide support services to victims and witnesses at court. Following a successful evaluation of this project, a Crown Court Witness Service provided by Victim Support had been established in every crown court in England Wales by 1996.

This increased profile for witnesses was sustained by several other policy developments. In 1989 the Pigot Report (Home Office 1989) on video evidence made several important recommendations in relation to the giving of evidence by child witnesses, suggesting similar measures be introduced for adult witnesses who are vulnerable to intimidation. Special measures to assist children in giving evidence, such as the use of pre-recorded evidence and the giving of evidence via CCTV, were also introduced from the late 1980s onwards. In relation to most cases of intimidation, the 1990s also saw growing recognition among some police forces of the need to improve their response to witnesses who are at risk of serious injury or life-threatenining intimidation, typically linked to serious and organized crime investigations. Following the lead of the Metropolitan Police, which had established a specialist witness protection unit in 1978, six other forces in England and Wales and one in Scotland had, by 1998, formed their own witness protection programmes. Officers from these programmes were trained to manage the secure and permanent relocation of witnesses and their families away from their home area and, if necessary, provide with them with new identities (Fyfe 2001).

From the late 1990s onwards, policy activity with respect to witnesses gathered momentum and the result has been a wide-ranging set of initiatives aimed at securing the participation of witnesses in the criminal justice system (see Table 18.1). From being the 'forgotten soul', witnesses were now the 'vital voices' (Scottish Executive 2002) of the criminal justice system.

The immediate catalysts for this renewed activity were the two interdepartmental working groups (one for England and Wales and the other for Scotland) established by the newly elected Labour government in 1997 to examine the treatment of vulnerable and intimidated witnesses in the criminal justice system. The establishment of these working groups reflected a specific Labour Party manifesto commitment to provide greater protection for victim-witnesses in rape and serious sexual offence trials. However, the remit of the working groups was made much broader so that they could examine measures at all stages of the criminal justice process (from pre-trial to post-trial) which could improve the treatment of vulnerable witnesses, including those likely to be subject to intimidation. As the Home Office working group explained in the Introduction to their report (Home Office 1998: 1), this broader focus was necessary and overdue:

> While measures are in place to assist child witnesses, many adult victims and witnesses find the criminal justice process daunting and stressful, particularly those who are vulnerable because of personal circumstances, including their relationship to the defendant or because

of the nature of certain serious crimes, such as rape. Some witnesses are not always regarded as capable of giving evidence and so can be denied access to justice. Others are in fear of intimidation, which can result in either failure to report offences in the first instance, or a refusal to give evidence in court.

Comprising representatives from various government departments, the courts, the prosecution service, chief police officers and Victim Support, the working groups' terms of reference focused on identifying measures 'at all stages of the criminal justice process which will improve the treatment of vulnerable witnesses, including those likely to be subject to intimidation' (Home Office 1998; Scottish Office 1998). Between them the two reports of the working groups – *Speaking up for Justice* (Home Office 1998) and *Towards a Just Conclusion* (Scottish Office 1998) – contained over one hundred recommendations and led directly to two key pieces of legislation: the Youth Justice and Criminal Evidence Act 1999 for England and Wales and the Vulnerable Witness (Scotland) Act 2004. This legislation identified five categories of vulnerable and intimidated witnesses (VIWs): children; adults with learning disabilities; adults with a mental disorder; adults with a physical disability or disorder; and adults suffering from fear or distress as a result of the crime or intimidation. The legislation then defined certain 'special measures' that should be available for VIWs. These include the use of screens to shield the witness from the accused and the public gallery, video-recorded evidence, live television links, clearing the public gallery of the court, removal of wigs and gowns in court, allowing witnesses to use communication aids, video-recorded pre-trial cross and re-examination, and the use of intermediaries (Hamlyn *et al.* 2004). A witness will only be eligible for special measures if the court is satisfied that the quality of his or her evidence would be diminished if he or she were not given access to one or more of these measures. In addition, other measures were introduced which required administrative action and training, including pre-court familiarization visits, the presence of a supporter in court, escorts to and from the court, and the provision of separate waiting areas for prosecution and defence witnesses.

Other significant developments since 1997 include the 'No Witness, No Justice' Programme. This is a partnership between the Crown Prosecution Service (CPS) and the Association of Chief Police Officers (ACPO) which aims to deliver a new model of victim and witness care. The police assess the needs of a victim or witness when he or she is first interviewed and then he or she should have the continued support of a witness care officer (based in established witness care units) from the point of charge through to his or her appearance at court and in the immediate post-court period. The intention is that witness care officers will ensure that victims and witnesses are kept better informed of progress in their case and have the necessary court-day support (such as the special measures discussed above) to enable them to give their best evidence in court. Five pilot areas appointed new police and CPS witness care officers in 2003 and the roll-out of the whole programme across England and Wales was completed by 2006.

In the most serious cases of witness intimidation, where the lives of witnesses and their family may be at risk, the Serious Organized Crime and Police Act 2005 contains provisions for the 'protection of witnesses and other persons' involved in investigations related to organized crime. Such protection typically involves the police in managing the process of the secret and permanent relocation of witnesses away from their home area and establishing them in new communities with, in some cases, a new identity. Those eligible for such protection will be assessed in terms of the nature of the risks they face, the cost of protecting them, their ability to adjust to their change in circumstances (given the challenges associated with relocation and possible changes to their identity) and the importance of their testimony (see Fyfe and Sheptycki 2006a: 330).

Finally, it is interesting to note that one potential measure that has been considered for use in serious organized crime cases – witness compellability – has not, at the time of writing, been introduced into the UK (Fyfe and Sheptycki 2006b). Witness compellability has also been considered in the context of domestic violence cases which, like organized crime, typically involve close relationships between witnesses and the accused (Cretney and Davis 1997). As Cretney and Davis (1997) have shown, however, the arguments 'for' and 'against' compellability are finely balanced. In terms of humanitarian considerations, compellability might be taken to represent the 'real interests' of a complainant by helping secure punishment of the accused but equally the removal of choice about whether or not to be a witness could be seen as a grave infringement of civil liberties.

Similarly, in relation to pragmatic considerations, compellability might reduce the reluctance of the police and other criminal justice agencies to investigate and prosecute crime where witness co-operation might be difficult to secure, yet forcing a witness to give evidence may lead a witness to become hostile to the prosecution, making the chance of achieving convictions by compelled evidence quite low (Cretney and Davis 1997).

Impacts and implications

To what extent are the policy initiatives introduced over the last ten years making a difference to witness participation in criminal investigation? Drawing on recent evaluative research, this section provides some insights into the impacts and implications of this policy activity.

Keys findings from the Witness Satisfaction Surveys

Improving the satisfaction of witnesses with their treatment by the criminal justice system has been one of the key performance targets set by government in the wake of the initiatives described in Table 17.1. In order to measure this, a national baseline Witness Satisfaction Survey was carried out in 2000 (Whitehead 2001) followed by a second survey in 2002 (Angle et al. 2003). These surveys provide important information on the nature and consequences of witnesses' contacts with the police. In the 2002 survey, 95 per cent of victim witnesses, 91 per cent of other prosecution witnesses and just over half of defence witnesses had contact with the police, and nearly all had made an evidential statement. Among those who gave evidence, just under half volunteered information, while the remainder were asked by the police for help. The main reasons given for volunteering information were that they were the victim (27 per cent), 'it was the right thing to do' (17 per cent), 'they saw what happened' (13 per cent) or 'they wanted justice done' (13 per cent) (Angle *et al.* 2003: 8). Among those who had been in contact with the police, almost 90 per cent were satisfied with their treatment, with no clear differences in terms of age, gender, ethnicity or social class. Of crucial importance in terms of influencing levels of satisfaction was whether or not they were treated in a courteous manner by the police and whether they were given clear information.

Also of relevance to criminal investigation is the fact that these surveys provide important insights into the factors which determine the willingness or unwillingness of witnesses to be a witness again in the future. From the 2002 survey, two thirds of witnesses said they would be happy to be a witness again, a 6 per cent increase since the baseline survey, while 80 per cent would be likely to be a witness again if required, indicating that even if some witnesses were not happy to participate they would repeat the experience out of a sense of 'public spiritedness' (Angle *et al.* 2003: 49). The strongest predictors of unwillingness to be a witness again were how appreciated a witness felt by the agencies he or she came in contact with and whether he or she felt intimidated by either the legal process or by the defendant or his or her associates.

The impacts of 'special measures' for VIWs

The 'special measures' for VIWs introduced by the Youth Justice and Criminal Evidence Act 1999 and the Vulnerable Witnesses (Scotland) Act 2004 are clearly focused on what happens at court rather than during the criminal investigation. Nevertheless, the introduction of such 'special measures' does have important direct and indirect implications with respect to the investigative process. The opportunity to present video-recorded evidence-in-chief, for example, means that the police may have to make arrangements to video-record the evidence of a witness during an investigation. More generally, as research carried out for the Home Office (Burton *et al.* 2006) clearly shows, the police have a crucial role as the main 'gatekeepers' to special measures given that they have the initial responsibility for identifying VIWs. Other agencies, including the CPS, the Witness Service and the courts, are then largely dependent on the police to provide accurate information about VIWs in order to assess the need for 'special measures'. Indeed, the CPS rarely identified witnesses as vulnerable or intimidated unless they had already been identified as VIWs by the police. Within the police, responsibility for identifying VIWs normally lies with the investigating officer, with the support of individuals with specialist expertise. Before the implementation of special measures, just under half of all the police forces surveyed for the study by Burton *et al.* (2006) had officers who were trained to give advice to colleagues about the identification of VIWs. After implementation, the situation had improved markedly with most forces having trained officers, particularly with respect to child witnesses, victims of domestic violence and victims of sexual assault. Even so, police effectiveness in identifying VIWs appears quite variable. They found it easiest, not surprisingly, to identify child witnesses but had more difficulty in identifying victims of sexual assault and domestic violence as VIWs, and had the greatest difficulty with those VIWs with mental disorders or learning difficulties and those fearing or experiencing intimidation. As Burton *et al.* (2006: 25) observe, 'Officers are heavily reliant on self-identification, particularly in the case of witness intimidation. Concealment may be deliberate or unwitting and occurs for a variety of reasons. Some police respondents stated that the pride of witnesses sometimes leads them to conceal their difficulties.'

Once identification has been carried out, the police still have a crucial role in terms of providing VIWs with pre-trial support. Under *The Code of Practice for Victims of Crime* (introduced by the Domestic Violence, Crime and Victims Act 2004) for example, the police have a clear duty to victim witnesses in relation to providing information about special measures:

> Where a vulnerable or intimidated victim may be called as a witness in criminal proceedings, and may be eligible for assistance by way of special measures ... the police must explain to the victim the provision about special measures in the [Youth Justice and Criminal Evidence] Act and record any views the victim expresses about applying for special measures (Office of Criminal Justice Reform 2005: 5).

The police must also provide the CPS with the information on which they can base an application for special measures. Research conducted before implementation revealed an important distinction between the expertise held in specialist units and that of generalist police officers. While the former worked well, the information provided by generalist officers was 'often insufficiently detailed to establish the particular nature of the difficulties experienced by the witness and to identify measures to assist them' (Burton *et al.* 2006: 39). After implementation of special measures, this distinction was less important but it was still apparent that many police officers had little understanding of how many of the special measures operated in practice and were therefore unable to provide VIWs with detailed information. This is significant because an explanation of 'special measures' might encourage some witnesses to give evidence in court in circumstances where they might not have otherwise done so.

The importance of this relationship between police and VIWs is underlined in research examining the views of VIWs themselves (Hamlyn *et al.* 2004). In particular, VIWs who said the police had given them enough support were more likely to feel satisfied with the overall experience of going to court to give evidence. According to a 2003 survey of VIWs, 77 per cent of those who felt the police gave them sufficient support felt satisfied with the overall experience, compared with 38 per cent of those who felt they were not given sufficient support. Similarly, 48 per cent of those who said they had received sufficient support when giving their statement said they would be happy to be a witness again, compared with 24 per cent of those who felt they did not have sufficient support from the police. As Hamlyn *et al.* (2004: 27) conclude: 'support from the police at this initial stage is an important factor in overall satisfaction and willingness to be a witness again.' More generally, the 2003 survey of VIWs also found that nearly 80 per cent of those satisfied with the police were also satisfied with their overall experience of being a witness (2004: 90), underlining the crucial role played by the police in the likelihood of someone who has been a VIW being willing to be a witness again in the future.

Witness protection

What are the impacts and implications of the witness protection arrangements established by many police forces for those cases where the lives of witnesses and their families may be at risk? Research carried out by one of the authors (Fyfe and Mackay 2000a, 2000b; Fyfe 2001) evaluating the Strathclyde Police Witness Protection Programme has highlighted several important issues. For the police, a key benefit has been that responsibility for protecting witnesses is taken away from the limited resources of an investigating team. In the past, investigating officers have often found themselves (in the words of one officer) 'baby-sitting these people [witnesses and their families]'. The use of specialist witness protection officers has helped relieve this pressure on investigative resources and overcome two other difficulties. First, in cases where local detectives attempted witness relocation they often relied on ad hoc, informal arrangements with housing and other agencies which were often insecure. Secondly, where investigating officers looked after witnesses, they risked claims by the defence during the trial that they had coached a witness and assisted him or her to give good evidence. The use of a specialist witness protection programme has not only brought a professionalism to witness protection matters which has helped ensure a higher level of security for protected witnesses, but also, because witness protection officers have no connection with the cases witnesses are involved in, they are less likely to be accused of coaching them.

For the witnesses interviewed for this study of the Strathclyde Witness Protection Programme, their overall assessment of the assistance provided by the police was very positive. Many stated that they did not think that they would have given the evidence that they gave, or were prepared to give, if they had not had the support and assistance of the police. Indeed, in some of the most serious cases, the witnesses were convinced that, were it not for the protection programme, they would have been killed to prevent them giving evidence. As one witness observed 'I think we could have ended up dead. Someone would have ended up dead. [The police] helped us get there ... I don't think we would have got as far with the court case because someone would have killed someone; it was getting out of hand' (cited in Fyfe and Mackay 2000a: 297). Nevertheless, relocated witnesses also face enormous challenges in relation to their sense of mental and social well-being. While relieved to have found a place of safety, witnesses must rebuild their lives without the immediate support of family and friends and there is evidence from the USA that many relocated witnesses go on to suffer higher-than-average rates of depression, anxiety and even suicide (Koedam 1993).

Conclusions: 'gems' and 'grasses'

The formal role and responsibilities of witnesses within the criminal justice process are well established. 'A witness to a crime', the Home Office declares, 'is expected, as a civic duty, to report the crime to the police ... At a later date the witness may be asked to give oral evidence in court about what they have seen, and answer questions during cross-examination by the defence' (1998: 19). Nevertheless, it is only relatively recently that research has highlighted the complex range of factors that shape witnesses' decisions to assist in the investigation of crime and give evidence at court. Perceptions of the seriousness of the offence, the social context in which it occurs and concerns arising from past experiences of going to court, all impact on whether or not a witness will assist a criminal investigation. Recognition of these issues has prompted a period of intense policy activity with respect to witnesses as government tries to secure higher levels of witness participation in the criminal justice system. While such policy activity is clearly to be welcomed, there are also important limitations with the current policy agenda. First, in terms of the timing and location of most of the measures that have been implemented, the main emphasis has been on the period of the trial and what happens in the courtroom. While this is important, this chapter has presented evidence to show that what happens at the investigation and pre-trial stage is also crucial to being able to bring cases to court. As Burton *et al.* (2006: viii) observe:

> The focus of policy and practice [has] tended to be the courts, as successful court cases are the ultimate objective of most criminal justice processes ... [E]ffort must now be directed at the investigation and pre-trial processes as much as at court processes, for these court cases to be successful.

Indeed, this point was also made back in 1998 in the report *Speaking Up for Justice*, which noted that 'vulnerable witnesses are likely to need assistance at earlier stages in the criminal justice process and require the adoption of special measures both during the investigation and during the pre-trial period as at the trial itself' (Home Office 1998: 20).

A second and related point is that policy in relation to witnesses, particularly with regard to intimidation, appears to favour what is essentially a situational approach, focused on the management and manipulation of specific environments which help reduce the vulnerability of witnesses to intimidation, such as the courtroom use of screens and CCTV or witness relocation. While the availability of such 'special measures' might help at the investigative stage in terms of encouraging witnesses to give statements, such measures tackle symptoms not causes. They are concerned with risk minimization, rather than addressing the underlying concerns of witnesses. If progress is to be made in terms of tackling some of these anxieties, then more emphasis needs to be placed on social rather than situational approaches. One example of this is the Community and Police Enforcement (CAPE) initiative in Newcastle. This is attempting to confront a local culture of 'no grassing' by getting residents to provide support for one another if they report an incident to the police or if the case is taken to court. The support is low level, such as keeping in touch with the witness or attending court in support of another resident, but the impact has been encouraging in terms of reducing a fear of crime among residents involved in the initiative and promoting a sense of solidarity (Hetherington and Maynard 2000). Arguably, such social, community-based strategies correspond more closely with the long-term needs of witnesses and their communities than situational approaches.

Against this background it is vital that future policy activity in this area addresses the ways in which witness involvement in the criminal justice process is understood in broader terms than simply the immediate circumstances of providing an evidential statement and attending court. In the past, criminal justice policy has tended to abstract the witness from his or her local social environment, viewing him or her simply as an object required for the legal process. Indeed, this process of abstraction is often reinforced at an informal level through the subcultures of criminal justice agencies. It is not untypical, for example, for police officers to talk about witnesses as 'gems', objects of great value to an investigation which need to be carefully looked after. By contrast, there will be some witnesses who view themselves as 'grasses' because the communities in which they live view assisting the police and other criminal justice agencies as transgressing local cultural norms about not assisting those in authority. While much progress has been made in the UK in recent years in addressing the anxieties of the 'reluctant witness' (Spencer and Stern 2001), recognizing and responding to the fact that witnesses are embedded in particular social contexts which strongly shape their decision-making with respect to co-operating with police investigations and, at a later stage, giving evidence in court, remain crucial challenges for UK criminal justice policy.

Selected further reading

Fyfe, N. (2001) *Protecting Intimidated Witnesses*. London: Ashgate. Based on research with Strathclyde Police in Scotland, this book examines witnesses' experiences of intimidation and provides an in-depth critical analysis of a witness protection programme from the perspectives of both the police and the witnesses who have been relocated by it.

Home Office (1998) *Speaking Up for Justice: Report of the Interdepartmental Working Group on the Treatment of Vulnerable and Intimidated Witnesses in the Criminal Justice System*. London: Home Office. This report acted as the catalyst for a series of policy measures designed to assist vulnerable and intimidated witnesses to give evidence at court. It therefore provides crucial insights into how policy-makers viewed this problem and what they believed would be appropriate solutions.

Rock, P. (1993) *The Social World of an English Crown Court: Witness and Professionals at the Crown Court Centre in Wood Green*. Oxford: Clarendon Press. This is an excellent examination of the social environment of a crown court, providing a vivid picture of witnesses' experiences while giving evidence before the introduction of the 'special measures' discussed in this chapter.

Spencer, S. and Stern, B. (2001) *Reluctant Witness*. London: Institute of Public Policy Research. An important study of the motivations of witnesses in terms of the decisions they make about whether to assist police investigations or to give evidence in court.

References

Angle, H., Malam, S. and Carey, C. (2003) *Witness Satisfaction: Findings from the Witness Satisfaction Survey 2002*. London: Home Office.

Burton, M., Evans, R. and Sanders, A. (2006) *Are Special Measures for Vulnerable and Intimidated Witnesses Working? Evidence from Criminal Justice Agencies*. London: Home Office.

Cretney, A. and Davis, G. (1997) 'The significance of compellability in the prosecution of domestic assault', *British Journal of Criminology*, 37: 75–89.

Evans, K., Fraser, P. and Walklate, S. (1996) 'Whom can you trust? The politics of "grassing" on an inner city housing estate', *Sociological Review* 44: 361–80.

Fyfe, N.R. (2001) *Protecting Intimidated Witnesses*. Ashgate: Aldershot.

Fyfe, N.R. and McKay, H. (2000a) 'Police protection of intimidated witnesses: a study of the Strathclyde Police Witness Protection Programme', *Policing and Society: An International Journal of Research and Policy*, 10: 277–99.

Fyfe, N.R. and McKay, H. (2000b) 'Desperately seeking safety: witnesses' experiences of intimidation, protection and relocation', *British Journal of Criminology*, 40: 671–87.

Fyfe, N.R. and Sheptycki, J. (2006a) 'International trends in the facilitation of witness co-operation in organized crime cases', *European Journal of Criminology*, 3: 319–55.

Fyfe, N.R. and Sheptycki, J. (2006b) *Facilitating Witness Cooperation in Organised Crime Investigations: An International Review*. London: Home Office.

Hamlyn, B., Phelps, A., Turtle, J. and Sattar, G. (2004) *Are Special Measures Working? Evidence from Surveys of Vulnerable and Intimidated Witnesses*. London: Home Office.

Harris, R.J. (1991) 'Whither the witness? The Federal Government's Special Duty of Protection in Criminal Proceedings after *Piechowicz v United States*', *Cornell Law Review*, 76: 1285–316.

Hetherington, S. and Maynard, W. (2000) *Community and Police Enforcement in Newcastle*. London: Home Office.

Home Office (1989) *Report of the Advisory Group on Video Evidence*. London: Home Office.

Home Office (1998) *Speaking Up for Justice: Report of the Interdepartmental Working Group on the Treatment of Vulnerable and Intimidated Witnesses in the Criminal Justice System*. London: Home Office.

Koedam, W.S. (1993) 'Clinical considerations in treating participants in the federal witness protection program', *American Journal of Family Therapy*, 21: 361–8.

Maynard, W. (1994) *Witness Intimidation: Strategies for Prevention*. London: Home Office.

Office of Criminal Justice Reform (2005) *Code of Practice for Victims of Crime*. London: Office of Criminal Justice Reform.

Rock, P. (1991) 'Witnesses and space in a Crown Court', *British Journal of Criminology*, 31: 266–71.

Rock, P. (1993) *The Social World of an English Crown Court: Witness and Professionals at the Crown Court Centre in Wood Green*. Oxford: Clarendon Press.

Scottish Executive (2002) *Vital Voices: Helping Vulnerable Witnesses Give Evidence*. Edinburgh: Scottish Executive.

Scottish Office (1998) *Towards a Just Conclusion: Vulnerable and Intimidated Witnesses in Scottish Criminal and Civil Cases*. Edinburgh: Scottish Office.

Spencer, S. and Stern, B. (2001) *Reluctant Witness*. London: Institute of Public Policy Research.

Whitehead, E. (2001) *Witness Satisfaction: Findings from the Witness Satisfaction Survey 2000*. London: Home Office.

Chapter 19

Investigative interviewing

Gisli H. Gudjonsson

Introduction

Many governmental and local agencies are involved in conducting investigative interviews, including the police, Her Majesty's Revenue and Customs, the military and the security services. The focus of this chapter is on investigative interviews of suspects for the purpose of potential prosecution. There will be some references made to the importance of obtaining 'reliable' (the term 'valid' is more commonly used among psychologists) accounts from victims and witnesses, because accurate accounts from them can influence whether or not guilty suspects decide to confess (Kebbell *et al.* 2005). Similarly, an inaccurate account can result in the wrong suspect being arrested, questioned and, on occasions, wrongfully convicted (Gudjonsson 2003a).

This chapter reviews the relevant literature on investigative interviewing, describes some of the main techniques and their effectiveness and potential dangers in the investigative and judicial process, and discusses the role and importance of expert psychological evidence in court in cases where confession evidence is being disputed. Finally, it suggests steps that can be taken to minimize the risk of miscarriages of justice.

Two fundamental assumptions are made in this chapter. First, that interviews, whether of victims, witnesses or suspects, are an essential part of the investigative and judicial process. Secondly, it is the quality and fairness of these interviews that determine whether or not justice is served.

Victims, witnesses and suspects

The term 'investigative interviewing' was introduced in England in the early 1990s to represent the shift of focus that had appeared in police interviewing philosophy away from confessions and towards general evidence gathering (Williamson 1993). Traditionally, of course, the main aim of interviewing suspects was to obtain a confession to secure a conviction (Gudjonsson 2003a).

The term 'interrogation' implies a confrontational process and is used in the context of suspect interviews, typically involving both accusation and active persuasion (Buckley 2006). The person interviewed is usually in custody, has been read his or her legal rights, and the interview is structured. In contrast, victims and witnesses are 'interviewed', which implies that their interviews are relatively free of confrontation and accusation. They need not necessarily be interviewed at the police station. However, the distinction between an 'interview' and an 'interrogation' may not always be so clear cut. For example, as a part of a strategy, suspects may be interviewed first in a non-accusatory manner to gather general information and establish rapport and co-operation that could assist with the interrogation that follows the interview. For example, this strategy is an important part of the so-called 'Reid technique of interviewing and interrogation' (Buckley 2006).

Victims, witnesses and suspects are all potentially important factual witnesses in the investigative and judicial process. However, there are some salient differences between them. First, witnesses and victims are required to recall events they observed, whereas suspects, when involved in the offence, would be expected to focus more on their actions and intentions. Innocent suspects would not be in a position to give details of the offence unless they had observed it or details had been communicated to them by the police or somebody else. The so-called 'special knowledge', which is commonly used by police and prosecution as a powerful form of corroboration of guilt, is sometimes later proved to have originated from the police (Gudjonsson 2003a).

Another salient difference between suspects and other witnesses involves the circumstances and nature of the interview with the police. Unlike other witnesses, suspects are thought to be implicated in a criminal offence and the likelihood of self-incrimination is high. It is for this reason that they are cautioned against self-incrimination, have the right to legal advice and, if mentally disordered or young persons, they are in England and Wales entitled to the presence of an 'appropriate adult' to assist them at the police station. The person acting in this capacity has to be at least 18 years of age and he or she cannot be a police officer or the suspect's solicitor. In the case of a youth, a parent is most commonly called to act as an appropriate adult. In the case of an adult who is suffering from mental disorder, the social services are most commonly approached by the custody officer (Medford et al. 2003).

Following the introduction of the Police and Criminal Evidence Act 1984, interviews with suspects are tape-recorded and this has made it much easier to observe and understand what goes on in the interview room (Baldwin 1993; Pearse and Gudjonsson 1999; Gudjonsson 2003a). No such parallel mandatory requirement exists in the case of victims and witnesses, although the memorandum for good practice does provide guidance (see Chapter 18, this volume). However, s. 27 of the Criminal Evidence Act 1999 allows the video-taping of interviews with vulnerable witnesses, which can subsequently be used as evidence-in-chief of that witness.

Clarke and Milne (2001) provided the first large-scale evaluation of interviews with victims and witnesses. These interviews were found to be less proficient than those conducted on suspects. The authors point to the absence of proper guidelines in relation to the taking of witness statements and the lack of audio or video-recording of many such interviews.

Investigative interview techniques

A number of police interview manuals have been written (e.g. Royal and Schutte 1976; Walkley 1987; MacDonald and Michaud 1992; Rabon 1992, 1994; Stubbs and Newberry 1998; Inbau *et al.* 2001). The following quotation provides the philosophy behind most of these manuals:

> Practical interrogation manuals are generally based on the extensive experience of interrogators and offer allegedly effective techniques for breaking down suspects' resistance. The authors of these manuals argue that most criminal suspects are reluctant to confess because of the shame associated with what they have done and the fear of the legal consequences. In their view, a certain amount of pressure, deception, persuasion and manipulation is essential if the 'truth' is to be revealed. Furthermore, they view persuasive interrogation techniques as essential to police work and feel justified in using them (Gudjonsson 2003a: 7).

Interrogation manuals have a long history in the USA commencing in the 1940s (for a review, see Leo 1992, 1994). Since his (1942, 1948) 'lie detection and criminal investigation model', Inbau joined forces with Reid (Inbau and Reid 1953, 1967) and, more recently, with Buckley (Inbau *et al.* 1986) and Jayne (Inbau *et al.* 2001). In the 1986 publication, Inbau and his colleagues introduced a nine-step method, which was intended to break down the resistance of reluctant suspects and make them confess. This is known as the 'Reid technique'. It was a more sophisticated method of interrogation and came under some criticism because of its psychologically manipulative nature and failure to address risks associated with false confessions (Gudjonsson 1992). The most recent edition of their book (Inbau *et al.* 2001) builds on the previous work of the authors, updates it and introduces new topics, such as false confessions, guidance to courtroom testimony and responses to defence experts' criticisms of their work. Buckley (2006) outlines the current application of the Reid technique and suggests factors that he considers potentially important in evaluating the credibility of the suspect's confession. The Reid technique relies heavily on psychological manipulation, including deliberately lying to suspects, which would not be allowed in English and Welsh courts, but would be admissible evidence in US courts (Gudjonsson 2003a). The Reid technique is undoubtedly the most widely used interrogation technique in the USA. According to the website of John E. Reid and Associates (http://www.reid.com), over 300,000 interviewers have been trained in the Reid technique since 1974.

Gudjonsson (2003a), Kassin and Gudjonsson (2004) and Kassin (2006) provide critique of the Reid technique, and other similar techniques, and point to inherent dangers (e.g. being a guilt-presumptive process, over-reliance on behavioural signs as indicators of deception and the use of trickery, deceit and theme development, which does on occasions result in false confessions). Authors of police interrogation manuals generally ignore the possibility that their recommended techniques could, in certain instances, make a suspect confess to a crime that he or she had not committed, and even argue that they 'don't interrogate innocent people' (Kassin and Gudjonsson 2004: 36). The problem is that many of the deception indicators recommended in interrogation manuals are not based on scientific evidence and are actually factually wrong (Vrij 2000). As a result they may wrongly assume guilt, resulting in 'tunnel vision' and pressuring innocent suspects to confess (Gudjonsson 2003a).

Walkley (1987) wrote the first interrogation manual for British police officers. It was written after the Police and Criminal Evidence Ace (PACE) 1984 and provides extracts from the new Act. However, this manual appears to have been greatly influenced by the American interrogation manuals, such as those of Inbau and his colleagues. It never gained national support in Britain. The most likely reason is that many of the 'persuasive ploys' recommended were in breach of PACE and its codes of practice. For example, in the concluding chapter, the following is recommended after the interviewer is satisfied that the suspect is lying:

> The interviewer will first deal with the lie-telling denials which the suspect is making and convince him that they have little or no value to him, possibly even may have certain penalties. He will hint that confession on the other hand has certain advantages. Whenever the suspect takes steps away from lie telling, he will be rewarded by suitable reinforcement ploys (Walkley 1987: 109).

The English and Welsh courts are likely to be very critical of such manipulative ploys and exclude confession evidence obtained by such methods (Gudjonsson 2003a).

In spite of the importance of police interview training, it was not until 1992 that there was formal interview training for officers, and they mainly learnt from watching others carry out interviews (Walkley 1987). In the first published research on police interviewing, Irving and Hilgendorf (1980: 52) stated:

> Training in interrogation is not a major feature in the training of English police officers. The evidence from the Association of Chief Police Officers of England, Wales and Northern Ireland to the Royal Commission comments that 'police officers receive no formal training in the art of interrogation. They are given some advice, in addition to instruction on the law, at training school and by colleagues by and large skills developed through experience' (Part I, para. 7.9). Training in interrogation is widely practised in the United States.

Current interview practice in England

The first formal approach to investigative interviewing was implemented in England in 1992 through a national committee, which consisted of collaboration between police officers, psychologists and lawyers (Williamson 2006). The committee produced a set of seven principles, focusing on searching for the truth, which were circulated to all police forces in Home Office Circular 22/1992. The seven principles can be summarized as follows (see Williamson 2006):

1 The objective of the investigative interview is to obtain accurate and reliable accounts from victims, witnesses and suspects in order to discover the truth about the subject matter under investigation.

2 The officer should approach the interview with an open mind and test the information obtained against what is already known or what can be reasonably established.

3 The interviewer must always act fairly in the circumstances of each case.

4 The interviewer is not obliged to accept the first answer given and persistent questioning does not have to be seen as unfair.

5 The officer has the right to put questions to the suspect, even in cases where the suspect chooses to exercise his or her rights to silence.

6 During interviews officers are free to ask questions to ascertain the truth, except in cases of child victims of sexual or violent abuse, which are to be used in criminal proceedings.

7 Victims, witnesses and suspects who are vulnerable must always be treated with special consideration.

The Home Office circular represented the beginning of a national training programme on investigative interviewing. This was followed by Home Office Circular 7/1993, where a new training package for basic interviewing skills was introduced. Two booklets on interviewing were produced (CPTU 1992a, 1992b). These were issued to all 127,000 operational police officers in England and Wales (Bull 1999). The booklets were supplemented by the setting up of one-week training programmes. The booklets, and the interview model on which they are based, became nationally agreed guidelines on interviewing for victims, witnesses and suspects.

The mnemonic 'PEACE' was used to describe the five distinct parts of the new interview approach:

P *Preparation and planning.* This includes knowledge of the case, what is required to be proved legally, arranging the interview and ensuring attendance and suitable facilities.

E *Engage and explain.* This is the opening phase of the interview where introductions formally take place, legal requirements (e.g. reading the suspect his or her legal rights) are met and an explanation of the interview and its process takes place.

A *Account.* Interviewees are asked to provide their account of events, which may require clarification and challenges.

C *Closure.* This involves the interviewer summarizing the main points from the interview and providing the suspect with the opportunity to correct or add anything.

E *Evaluate.* The account and evidence obtained during questioning need to be evaluated. The performance of the interviewers should also be evaluated.

There are two methods taught for eliciting an account from the interviewee. These are known as the 'cognitive interview' and 'conversation management'. The former is based on the work of Fisher and Geiselman (1992) and the latter on the work of Eric Shepherd (see Mortimer and Shepherd 1999). The cognitive interview involves a memory-facilitating process based on psychological principles. It is more commonly used with victims and witnesses, but it can also be used with co-operative suspects. In contrast, conversational management is recommended when the co-operation from the suspect is insufficient for the cognitive interview techniques to be applied satisfactorily.

The national training programme is a mandatory part of the training of all police officers in England and Wales (Williamson 2006). The Association of Chief Police Officers has conducted a national review of the one-week training programme and recommended further training to take place at five levels or tiers (Williamson 2006):

1 Training of recruits (or probationary officers).

2 Training for investigators of volume crime.

3 Training for investigators of serious crime or those conducting specialist interviews with children and other vulnerable interviewees.

4 Availability of supervisors who act as line managers and are able to supervise the interview process.

5 Availability of interview co-ordinators who form a national nucleus of highly trained and experienced professionals, who can provide advice to investigative teams.

Since its introduction in 1992, the PEACE model has undergone some minor changes to take into account changes in legislation (Mortimer and Shepherd 1999; Ord and Shaw 1999), including the introduction of the five-tier system and advanced 'interview training', which forms an integral part of Tier 3 (Griffiths and Milne 2006).

A number of studies have attempted to evaluate the impact and effectiveness of the PEACE model. McGurk *et al.* (1993) evaluated the effectiveness of the one-week PEACE training. They found that the training improved the knowledge and skills of the interviewers and the improvement was evident at a six-month follow-up. However, at the time concerns were expressed about the lack of quality of management and supervision of police interviews (Stockdale 1993; Williamson 1994).

A detailed national evaluation of PEACE to date (Clarke and Milne 2001) has raised concerns about the apparent lack of sufficient effectiveness of the national training in improving officers' interview skills. It seemed clear that training alone does not assist officers in developing new skills. Planning and basic communication skills remained relatively poor, although some improvement has been noted since the introduction of the national training programme. About 10 per cent of the interviews evaluated in the study were rated as possibly being in breach of the PACE codes of practice. However, according to Griffiths and Milne (2006), the original one-week PEACE interview course focused on improving interviewers' skills in meeting legal requirements (i.e. preventing interviews that were coercive and in breach of PACE). Unfortunately there was no significant improvement in interviewing skills and in obtaining a detailed and probing account from witnesses and suspects (Clarke and Milne 2001; Griffiths and Milne 2006). There is now available an advanced three-week training course, labelled Tier 3, which builds on the foundation taught on the basic one-week course. The focus is more on interviewing suspects in serious cases, such as murder and rape. The outcome of the advanced training appears promising in terms of improved overall interviewing skills, but these skills deteriorate to a certain extent over time in complex areas, and refresher courses may need to be attended (Griffiths and Milne 2006).

It is evident from the above that, in addition to increased interviewing training, interviewing has become more specialist orientated, where the priority is to select the right interviewer for specific interviews (e.g. sex crimes, murders, child victims). This suggests increased professionalism. In Canada, highly specialist teams have been set up to provide interviewing services to investigators (Woods 2002). In addition, forensic psychologists and other professionals are employed to assist with the development of an interview strategy.

Interrogation of terrorist suspects

Terrorist suspects in England who are detained under the Terrorism Act 2000 are subject to special provisions (Home Office 2004), which means that their detention can be extended to up to 14 days. The government is currently implementing a 28-day detention for terrorist suspects, which includes a provision to detain suspects for the purpose of questioning for intelligence purposes.

Interrogation for the purpose of intelligence gathering has become much more prominent following the terrorist attacks on the USA on 11 September 2001 (Arrigo 2003; Mackey and Miller 2004; Gelles *et al.* 2006; Pearse 2006; Rose 2004, 2006; Williamson 2006). Concerns have been raised about the treatment of prisoners by the military and security service in Afghanistan and Guantánamo Bay in Cuba (Rose 2004). One experienced American military interrogator stated: 'But one of the most crucial weapons in the war on terrorism may be the abilities of a relative handful of soldiers and spies trained in the dark art of getting enemy prisoners to talk' (Mackey and Miller 2004: xxii). The same authors claim that 'Fear is often an interrogator's best ally' (p. 8) and 'By the time of our departure from the baking, arid plains of Bagram, we could boast that virtually no prisoner went unbroken' (p. xxv). In the remainder of the book they describe how psychological manipulation and coercive techniques are used to break down the resistance of terrorist suspects.

The techniques described by Mackey and Miller (2004) of current practice by the military are clearly highly coercive and oppressive in nature. The effectiveness and utility of these techniques for obtaining reliable information for intelligence gathering are unknown. The occasional elicitation of apparently useful information for intelligence gathering may reinforce this approach and is commonly used as a justification for its use, irrespective of the amount of irrelevant and unreliable information obtained.

Williamson (2005) argues that interrogation techniques used by the military are based on Survival, Evasion, Resistance and Escape (SERE) training courses. These courses were developed by the US military to show troops how to cope with interrogation by enemy forces. Interrogation techniques based on SERE function to humiliate and disorientate detainees. Williamson (2005) recommends that any training programme used for interviewers of terrorist suspects should be humane and its effectiveness in eliciting valuable information should be demonstrated. He argues that harsh interrogation techniques can be counterproductive in overcoming terrorist threats.

Arrigo (2003) argues that, following the September 2001 terrorist attacks on the USA, the use of torture for the interrogation of terrorists has gained increased public support. This public support is mainly based on the 'ticking bomb' scenario, where torture interrogation of key terrorists will allegedly prevent terrorist plans of mass destruction and save lives at minimal costs to civil liberties and the democratic process. Arrigo explores three causal models of how torture leads to people telling the truth. The main objectives of the torture models are to instil obedience and make the person talk by the use of physical or psychological intimidation. The models are labelled the 'animal instinct model' (i.e. people comply with the commands from the torturer to escape pain or death), the 'cognitive failure model' (i.e. the stress of torture renders the person mentally incompetent to master deception or his or her interpretation of pain) and the 'data processing model' (i.e. torture provokes people to yield information on an opportunistic basis). In addition there are 'non-causal models' ('rogue models', where torture is emotionally, culturally or historically inseparable from other methods, or is just one method among several in a disorganized approach). Each model is susceptible to failure. For example, the animal instinct model fails when the physiological changes from the pain impair the detainee's ability to tell the truth. Similarly, the cognitive failure model fails when the tortured person is unable to distinguish truth from falsehood, or becomes unduly suggestible or compliant. For example, it is known that prolonged sleep deprivation increases people's susceptibility to suggestions and particularly their ability to resist interrogative pressure (see Gudjonsson 2003a for a review of the relevant studies). The data processing model fails when analysts become overwhelmed by data, and torture motivates new terrorists into action. Failures of the rogue models are attributed to the biases and ulterior motives of the torturers, which invalidate the results, or when the tactics empower competing political or criminal entities.

From a historical perspective, Arrigo argues that the initial gains from the use of torture interrogation are soon lost through national and international moral opposition, through demoralization or through corruption of the torture interrogators and their organizations. Ultimately it has damaging social consequences for a number of key institutions, including the police, the military, health care and the judiciary.

When there is an increased threat to national security and public safety, governments are expected to respond and reduce the risks. What is evident is that serious terrorist threats influence the public governments' perceptions of what is legitimate in terms of interrogation procedures, practices and detention. This is perhaps most evident in relation to the setting up of Guantánamo Bay and the moral, legal and political complications that have arisen since the arrival of the first detainees in January 2002 (Maddox 2006; Rose 2006).

Gelles *et al.* (2006) outline a 'rapport' or a 'relationship-based' approach for interviewing terrorist suspects, particularly Middle Eastern al-Qaeda-affiliated detainees. This is a non-coercive approach where the emphasis is on obtaining reliable information. The key to successful interrogation is the understanding of the cultural background, motivation and the communication strategies of the detainee. In order to conduct an effective interrogation of a subject with extremist ideology and one who is committed to jihad, the interview must have some understanding of the subject's ideology and 'the history associated with his thinking, commitments and beliefs' (2006: 29–30). First, there has to be a careful building up of rapport and trust, where the interviewer is sensitive to the needs of the subject, and gradually moving from the general (non-threatening) to the more specific and detailed form of questioning. 'Theme development', where the subjects are provided with possible excuses and justifications for their behaviour, is used in a modified form to fit in with the subjects' particular cultural idiosyncrasies.

Gelles *et al.* (2006) suggest that Middle Eastern Arab males think 'associatively' (e.g. jumping from point to point depending on what associations are triggered) rather than in a 'linear' fashion (i.e. goal directed and following points in a logical order). Linear thinking is more commonly seen in Western cultures (Nydell 2002 cited in Gelles *et al.* 2006). The interrogator needs to understand this different way of communicating, in order to avoid misunderstanding (e.g. mistakenly interpreting it as evasiveness).

How interrogation can go wrong

There are a number of ways in which interrogation can go wrong. Gudjonsson (2003a) highlights the following consequences:

1 A confession, even if true, is ruled inadmissible during *voir dire* (a 'trial within a trial', a 'suppression hearing') due to the coercive nature or unfairness of the interrogation and custodial confinement.

2 The eliciting of a false confession and a miscarriage of justice.

3 Unfair pressure resulting in resentment and causing the suspect to retract the confession, even if true, and failing to co-operate with the police in the future.

4 Pressure or coercion resulting in the suspect developing a post-traumatic stress disorder.

5 The undermining of public confidence in the police due to publicized cases of miscarriages of justice.

6 Poor interviewing resulting in suspects failing to give a confession when they would otherwise do so (e.g. suspects who would have confessed in their own time refuse to confess when they feel they are being rushed or unfairly treated by the police).

7 Suspects who have already confessed may retract their confession when they feel they are pressured too much to provide further information. This phenomenon is known as 'the boomerang effect' (Gudjonsson 2003a).

Confessions

Kebbell *et al.* (2005) argue that confessions to police have two main advantages for the criminal justice system. First, they greatly increase the likelihood that defendants are going to be convicted. Secondly, they often mean that victims and witnesses do not have to give evidence in court. An early guilty plea will have the same effect. It saves court time, reduces the burden on victims and witnesses and, in addition, can be used to mitigate sentence. It is therefore not surprising that police officers are motivated to obtain a confession in cases where they feel reasonably sure of a suspect's guilt. Does this mean that investigative interviews with suspects are inherently guilt presumptive? Generally, they are, because the interviewer is often seeking information that confirms his or her suspicions (Kassin and Gudjonsson 2004). However, a good interviewer will also consider and test out the alternative hypothesis – namely, that the suspect is actually innocent of the crime he or she is accused of.

It is difficult to compare meaningfully the confession rate in different studies because confessions are defined in a variety of ways. In a broad sense a confession may be construed as 'any statements which tend to incriminate a suspect or a defendant in a crime' (Drizin and Leo 2004: 892).

This includes denials, which can be proved as lies (Gudjonsson 2003a). A better operational definition is found in *Black's Law Dictionary*, where a 'confession' is defined as 'a statement admitting or acknowledging all facts necessary for conviction of a crime' and an 'admission' as 'an acknowledgement of a fact or facts tending to prove guilt which falls short of an acknowledgement of all essential elements of the crime.' (cited in Drizin and Leo 2004: 892).

A self-incriminating admission, which does not amount to the suspect accepting responsibility for the crime and giving a detailed narrative account of his or her actions, is not a proper confession. For example, a suspect admitting to having been in the vicinity of the crime may be making a highly incriminating admission, but this must be distinguished from a confession. A comment, such as 'I did it', without a detailed explanation, should be treated as an admission rather than a confession.

Theories of confessions

Confessing to a crime that one has committed has potentially serious consequences for the individual concerned. The more serious the crime the more severe the consequences are likely to be. Offenders' integrity is often adversely affected, they are at risk of being deprived of their liberty and there may be other penalties (e.g. a financial penalty). In some countries the death penalty may be imposed (Ofshe and Leo 1997a). In view of this it is perhaps surprising that a substantial proportion of all suspects confess during custodial interrogation (i.e. in England the confession rate has remained about 60 per cent for more than 25 years; see Gudjonsson 2003a). Why should this be the case? There are a number of theories available to explain why suspects confess to crimes they have committed. These assist us in understanding why suspects confess to crimes they have committed and in generating hypotheses that can be tested empirically.

Gudjonsson (2003a) provides a review of six different models of confession: 'decision-making model' (Hilgendorf and Irving 1981), the 'Reid model' (Jayne 1986), 'psychoanalytic models' (e.g. Reik 1959), an 'interactional model' (Moston *et al.* 1992), 'cognitive-behavioural model' (Gudjonsson 2003a) and the 'Ofshe–Leo model' (Ofshe and Leo 1997a).

A decision-making model of confession

Hilgendorf and Irving (1981) developed an important decision-making model of suspects during custodial interrogation. The model was developed by Hilgendorf and Irving after they had been commissioned by the Royal Commission on Criminal Procedure to provide a comprehensive review of the interrogation process (Irving and Hilgendorf 1980). The model is closely linked to the legal concepts of voluntariness and oppression.

The basic premise of the model is that, during interrogation, suspects become engaged in a demanding decision-making process. First, the suspect has to make some basic decisions, such as the following:

- Whether to speak or remain silent.
- Whether to make self-incriminating admissions or not.
- Whether to tell the truth or not.
- Whether to tell the whole truth or only part of the truth.
- How to answer the questions asked by the police interrogator.

According to Hilgendorf and Irving, the suspect's decision-making process is determined by:

- the courses of action perceived by the suspect to be available at the time;
- the perceived 'subjective' probabilities of the likely occurrence of various consequences attached to these courses of action; and
- the gains or utility values attached to these courses of action.

Suspects have to consider what options are available to them and then evaluate the likely consequences attached to these different options. For example, if they insist on their innocence, is the interrogation likely to continue and their detention be prolonged? If they confess to the offence, are they likely to be charged with it?

The suspect's decision-making is determined by the subjective probabilities of the occurrence of the perceived consequences (i.e. it is what the suspect *believes* at the time to be the likely consequences that influence his or her behaviour rather than the objective reality of the situation). For example, an innocent suspect may confess under the misguided belief that, because he or she is innocent of the alleged crime, no court will convict him or her and somehow the truth will eventually come out (Gudjonsson 2003a).

The suspect has to balance the potential consequences against the perceived value ('utilities') of choosing a particular course of action. For example, will the confession lead to cessation of interrogation and will the suspect be allowed to go home? Hilgendorf and Irving argue that threats and inducements can markedly influence the suspect's decision to confess because of the perceived power the police have over the situation and the apparent credibility of their words.

Hilgendorf and Irving argue that there are many *social, psychological* and *environmental* factors that can influence the suspect's decision-making during police interrogation. Sometimes these factors can undermine the reliability of the suspect's confession when police interrogators:

- manipulate the apparent social and self-approval utilities during interrogation in order to influence the suspect's decision-making;

- manipulate the suspect's perceptions of the likely outcome concerning certain actions (e.g. by minimizing the seriousness of the alleged offence and by altering perceptions of the 'cost' associated with denial, resistance, and deception); and

- impair the suspect's ability to cope with effective decision-making by increasing anxiety, fear and compliance.

The Reid model of confession

Jayne (1986) offers a model for understanding suspects' resistance and how to break down denial during interrogation. The model builds upon the 'nine steps' of interrogation proposed by Inbau *et al.* (1986).

Within this model, interrogation is construed as the psychological undoing of deception. The focus is police-induced confessions, where a confession follows a denial. The model assumes that people are reluctant to confess because of the perceived consequences of making a confession. This motivates them to deceive the interrogator. A suspect confessor is said to confess when the perceived consequences of a confession are more desirable than the anxiety generated by the deception. The interrogator can readily manipulate the perceived consequences and perceived anxiety associated with denial. There are four essential criteria for changing the suspect's expectancies and beliefs:

1 The credibility and sincerity of the interrogator (i.e. the building up of rapport and trust).

2 Understanding of the suspect's attitudes and identifying weaknesses that can be used in psychological manipulation to break down resistance.

3 The suspect needs to agree with the interrogator's suggestions, which means that the more suggestible the suspect, the easier it is to obtain a confession from him or her.

4 The interrogator has to check whether or not the suspect is accepting the theme suggested, whether the suspect needs be placed under more pressure and if the timing of the presentation of an alternative theme is right.

Persuasion is essential to this process, and it is a dynamic process that needs to be regulated according to the suspect's strengths and weaknesses. According to Jayne, it is difficult to elicit a confession from suspects with high tolerance for anxiety and guilt manipulation. There are a number of ploys that can be used by interrogators to reduce the perceived consequences of confessing during interrogation. This is achieved by presenting the suspect with themes that increase self-deception and self-justification ('minimization') while increasing perceived anxiety over denials – for example, by emphasizing or exaggerating the evidence against the suspect ('maximization').

The model predicts that the outcome of interrogation will depend on the extent to which the interrogator is able to identify the suspect's vulnerabilities, exploiting them to alter the suspect's belief system and perceptions of the consequences of making admissions, and persuading him or her to accept the interrogator's version of the 'truth'. This is a potentially powerful way of breaking down resistance during interrogation. Inbau *et al.* (2001) argue that it results in an 80 per cent success rate, although the authors provide no objective evidence for this claim.

Psychoanalytic models of confession

Psychoanalytic models (e.g. Reik 1959; Berggren 1975; Rogge 1975) stipulate that feelings of remorse and the need to elevate it are the fundamental causes of confessions. Reik (1959) argues that the unconscious compulsion to confess plays an important part in religion, myths, art, language and other social activities, including crime. Reik relies on Freud's concepts of the id, ego and super-ego, where a confession is seen as 'an attempt at reconciliation that the superego undertakes in order to settle the quarrel between the ego and the id' (1959: 216). The super-ego is seen to play an important role in the individual's need to confess. A punitive super-ego is associated with proneness to strong feelings of guilt and the need for self-punishment, resulting in a 'compulsion' to confess and, on occasions, false confession.

The development of the feeling of guilt after transgression and the unconscious need for self-punishment are seen as universal. It is only after the person has confessed that the ego begins to accept the emotional significance of the deed. A confession serves the function of relieving the person from the feeling of guilt and is inherently therapeutic. A similar argument is put forward by Berggren (1975), who argues that a confession produces a sense of relief and, for a satisfactory cathartic effect to occur, the confession has to be to a person in authority, such as a priest or police officer.

However, it is important to distinguish cause and effect in relation to the reporting of feelings of guilt. Kebbell et al. (2005) argue from their experimental study of 40 undergraduate students questioned about a mock crime that the act of confessing may make suspects experience the need to explain their confession in terms of guilt rather than the feeling of guilt facilitating them to confess. This is a good point. However, their interpretation was based on the finding that subjects who had been presented with accurate eyewitness evidence during questioning felt under greater pressure to confess and also reported greater feelings of guilt.

An interaction process model of confession

Moston et al. (1992) produced a model that helps us explain how a suspect's background and case characteristics influence the interrogator's style of questioning, which in turn affects the suspect's behaviour and the outcome of the interview. The model postulates that the suspect's initial response to an allegation is influenced by the interaction of three main groups of factors:

1 Background factors relating to the suspect and the offence (e.g. type of offence, the severity of the offence, age and sex of suspect, and the suspect's personality).

2 Contextual characteristics (e.g. legal advice, the strength of the police evidence). The authors draw a distinction between the suspect's initial reaction to the accusation and his or her subsequent responses.

3 The interviewer's questioning technique.

The model's strength is its emphasis on looking at the interaction of variables, rather than viewing each of them in isolation. The outcome of the interview is dependent upon an interaction process of several factors. The implication of the model is that the suspect's background characteristics and the case, in conjunction with contextual factors, influence the interrogator's beliefs, attitudes and style of questioning, which in turn influence the suspect's behaviour. Recently, there has been a growing interest in the influence of the interrogator's personality and attitude and how these impact on the interview process and outcome (Gudjonsson 2002). Case characteristics may also strongly influence the behaviour of *both* the suspect and the interrogator. The limitation of the model is that it does not focus on the suspect's mental state and cognitive processes.

A cognitive-behavioural model of confession

This model was described by Gudjonsson (1989) and expanded in *The Psychology of Interrogations, Confessions and Testimony* (Gudjonsson 1992). Here confessions are best construed as arising through the existence of a particular relationship between the suspect, the environment and significant others within that environment. In order to understand that relationship one has to look at the *antecedents* and the *consequences* of confessing behaviour within the framework of behavioural analysis:

*   *Antecedents* are events that occur prior to interrogation. These may trigger or facilitate a confession. A number of different factors may be relevant, such as state of shock, fatigue, illness, deprivation of food and sleep, stress, social isolation, feelings of guilt and bereavement.

*   There are two main types of *consequence*: 'immediate' (or 'short term') and 'long term'. The immediate or short-term consequences occur within minutes or hours of the suspect's confessing to the alleged crime. The long-term consequences usually take place within days, weeks or years of the suspect's confessing. The types of consequence, whether immediate or delayed, depend on the nature and circumstances of the case and the psychological characteristics of the individual concerned.

Antecedents and consequences are viewed in terms of *social* (e.g. isolation from one's family and friends, the nature of the interrogation), *emotional* (e.g. uncertainty and distress associated with the arrest and confinement, feelings of guilt and shame), *cognitive* (i.e. the suspect's thoughts, interpretations, assumptions and perceived strategies of responding to a given situation), *situational* (e.g. the circumstances of arrest, length and nature of the confinement) and *physiological* (e.g. physical pain, headaches, increased heart rate, blood pressure, rate and irregularity of respiration, perspiration) events.

The Ofshe–Leo model

This model is based on the work of Ofshe and Leo (1997a, 1997b) into disputed and false confessions. Their classification of confessions, according to the authors, applies equally to true and false confessions. There are five levels of confession (voluntary, stress-compliant, coerced-compliant, non-coerced-persuaded and coerced-persuaded), categorized into two groups (true or false). Each type of confession can be either true or false, depending on the circumstances of the individual case. This means that there are ten possible outcome scenarios. The focus of this model is on the interrogation process itself (i.e. what the police say and do) and a psychological description of the type of confession elicited. The model postulates that confessions are chiefly elicited due to police pressure or legally defined coercion, and individual differences and interactive processes are of relatively minor importance. This model is most relevant to coerced confessions (i.e. where the police have made threats or offered inducements), irrespective of the suspect's guilt or innocence.

Comments on the models

Each model makes different assumptions about why suspects confess to the police during questioning (e.g. outcome of a decision-making process; the undoing of deception; feelings of remorse; interactions between the background and the characteristics of the suspect, the nature of the case and contextual factors; the nature of the relationship between the suspect, the environment and significant others within that environment; and interrogative pressure and coercion).

Taken together, the models suggest that suspects confess when they perceive that the evidence against them is strong, when they need to relieve feelings of guilt, when they have difficulties coping with the custodial pressure (i.e. interrogation and confinement) and when they focus primarily on the immediate consequences of their actions rather than the long-term ones. The suspect's personality and psychological strengths and weaknesses are considered important in some of the models (i.e. the Reid model, the cognitive-behavioural model) in producing confessions and denials. However, the nature of the specific vulnerabilities and traits is not well articulated, except in relation to suggestibility and compliance (Gudjonsson 2003a).

A model of the interrogative process

Gudjonsson (2003b) describes a model of the interrogation process that assists with the evaluation of cases of disputed confessions. The 'interaction model' shows the kind of factors that should be considered when evaluating individual cases. The three layers are labelled 'police factors', 'vulnerabilities' and 'support'.

Police factors

These are associated with the custody itself (e.g. the nature and duration of the confinement, sleep deprivation), the interrogation (i.e. the techniques or tactics used by the interrogator, their intensity, the duration and number of interviews) and the personality, attitudes and behaviour of the interrogator (e.g. Gudjonsson 2002; Woods 2002).

Case characteristics, such as the seriousness and notoriety of the crime and the responses of the suspect to the detention and interrogation, closely interact with the custodial and interrogative factors. The police's behaviour is influenced by the nature of the crime they are investigating and how the suspect initially reacts to the detention and interrogation. If a suspect gives an apparently frank confession to the police at the beginning of an interview, then there is usually no need for confrontation and challenges. However, if the police do not believe the suspect, then there may be confrontation, robust challenges and psychological manipulation, which are aimed at overcoming the resistance and denials (Pearse and Gudjonsson 1999; Inbau *et al.* 2001).

Holmberg and Christianson (2002) found that interviews rated as 'dominant' were associated with denials, whereas interviews marked by 'humanity' were more commonly associated with admissions. This suggests that the style of interviewing influences the outcome of the interview. Holmberg and Christianson speculate that, when guilty suspects feel they are treated humanely, they are more likely to confess, particularly when interviewed in relation to sensitive crimes, such as sexual offences and murder.

It would be expected that some offences are more frequently associated with confessions than others. For example, one would expect that the highest rate being found for offences is where the strength of the evidence against the suspect is likely to be high (e.g. being stopped and found driving while intoxicated, being found in the possession of drugs, being caught shoplifting or committing a burglary). There is some empirical evidence for this (Sigurdsson and Gudjonsson 1994). However, as the offence becomes more serious the stakes in terms of perceived and real punishment rise, and this may inhibit some suspects from confessing (Phillips and Brown 1998). Conversely, it is in the most serious cases (e.g. murder, rape) where the duration and dynamics of the interview become more demanding and the risk of coercive interviewing style increases (Pearse and Gudjonsson 1999).

St-Yves (2006) recently reviewed the contradictory evidence relating to the confession rate of sex offenders and argues that there are two main factors that reduce the likelihood of sex offenders confessing to their crimes. These are feelings of shame and humiliation, on the one hand, and the negative attitude of some interviewers towards their crimes, on the other. Gudjonsson (2006) argues that some sex molesters have a strong need to talk about their crimes due to feelings of guilt, and this gives the police an advantage. However, they also find it difficult to be open and honest when interrogated due to feelings of shame, which act to inhibit them from confessing. This means that they are torn between feelings of guilt, which encourage them to confess, and feelings of shame, which inhibit them from confessing. Their feelings of shame need to be overcome during the interrogation. This means that sex offenders need to be interviewed sensitively and skilfully. Challenges will need to be presented in a 'soft' or 'gentle' fashion and with apparent understanding of the perpetrator's perspective and emotional needs.

Research has shown that, the more serious the offence, the more likely the police are to use persuasive techniques to break down resistance (e.g. Irving and McKenzie 1989; Evans 1993; Leo 1996; Pearse and Gudjonsson 1999). Leo (1996) found four interrogation tactics were particularly effective in eliciting a confession from suspects:

1 Appealing to the suspect's conscience.
2 Identifying and pointing out contradictions in the suspect's denial and story.

3 Offering moral justification or psychological excuse for the crime.
4. Using praise and flattery.

Leo also found a significant relationship between the length of the interrogation and the number of tactics used and the number of confessions obtained. Therefore, the more time and effort the interviewer puts into the interrogation process, the greater the likelihood that a confession will be elicited.

Whether or not suspects confess or deny the offence is related to the strength of the evidence against them. For example, Moston *et al.* (1992) found that, where the evidence against suspects was rated as 'weak', 76.6 per cent denied the offence, in contrast to 66.7 per cent who made self-incriminating admissions where the evidence was rated as 'strong'. Research among convicted criminals (Gudjonsson and Sigurdsson 1999) shows that there are three main reasons why suspects confess to crimes they have committed: first, the suspect's belief in the strength of the evidence against them; secondly, the internal need to confess, particularly in violent and sex crimes; and, thirdly, custodial and interrogative pressures. The findings suggest that suspects confess due to a combination of these three factors, but the single most important reason is the suspect's perception of the evidence against him or her (Gudjonsson 2003a).

Kebbell *et al.* (2005) have demonstrated experimentally that the accuracy of the eyewitness information presented during interrogation is associated with confessions (i.e. accurate evidence increases the likelihood of a confession, whereas inaccurate evidence increases denials). The implication is that interviewers should be careful in the way they present evidence to suspects. It is the accuracy of the information that seemed to be more important than the details of the evidence.

Vulnerabilities

Suspects may be 'vulnerable' or disadvantaged during custody or interrogation for a variety of reasons. These may relate to the suspect's physical or mental health, as well as more specific psychological vulnerabilities, such as suggestibility, compliance, acquiescence, anxiety and anti-social personality traits (Gudjonsson 2003a). Children and juveniles (Drizin and Colgan 2004; Redlich *et al.* 2004) and people with mental disorders (Fulero and Everington 2004) are thought to be susceptible to giving unreliable accounts of events if not carefully interviewed.

When mentally disordered people and juveniles are interviewed in England and Wales there are special legal provisions available to ensure that their statements to the police are reliable and obtained properly and fairly. Undoubtedly, the single most important protection is the presence of an 'appropriate adult' during police questioning (i.e. a person who is independent of the police and is not his or her lawyer). The current legal provisions are detailed in the codes of practice (Home Office 2003) which accompany and supplement PACE. Even in cases where the police adhere to all the legal provisions, a judge may consider it unsafe and unfair to allow the statement to go before the jury (Gudjonsson 2003a). The crucial issue here is whether or not the defendant was 'fit' when interviewed by the police (i.e. whether the suspect was sufficiently physically or mentally well to cope with the questioning and give reliable answers). It is only recently that established criteria have been developed for determining 'fitness for interview', which could be applied by forensic medical examiners (FMEs, also known as police surgeons), psychiatrists and psychologists when assessing suspects at police stations (Gudjonsson 2005). 'Fitness for interview' is not a term that appears within PACE. It was first introduced formally into the current codes of practice (Code C, Annex G), which became effective on 1 April 2003.

A suspect may be found unfit for interview when his or her physical or mental condition is severe or disabling, or when combined with certain other factors, such as lengthy and demanding interrogation, the suspect may be found to be unfit for interview (Gudjonsson 2005). When this occurs the interview needs to be either postponed until the person is fit for interview or suspended altogether. In exceptional cases the suspect may never be deemed fit for interview.

In a real-life observational study at two English police stations, over 170 suspects were psychologically assessed by clinical psychologists prior to their being interviewed by the police (Gudjonsson et al. 1993). All tapes of interviews with the suspects were subsequently analysed to discover what factors were associated with denial and confessions (Pearse et al. 1998). Most of the interviews were very short, the confession rate was 58 per cent, there was little interrogative pressure in the tactics used and very few suspects moved from a denial to a confession (see Gudjonsson 2003a). Logistic regression analysis was performed on the data. The dependent variable was confession versus denial. The independent variables included the suspect's age, ethnicity, mental state, intelligence, suggestibility, illicit drug taking, criminal history, police interview tactics and presence or absence of a legal adviser. The strength of the evidence against the suspect was not measured in this study.

Two factors were highly predictive of a denial (i.e. the presence of a legal adviser and a previous history of imprisonment). Only one variable predicted a confession (i.e. whether the suspect had told the researcher that he or she had taken illicit drugs within 24 hours of arrest). The main implications of the findings are that, in run-of-the-mill English cases, there is little interrogative pressure; the great majority of suspects who confess do so right at the beginning of the interview; psychological vulnerabilities, apart from illicit drug taking, are of little relevance; and having a legal representative and previous experience of imprisonment are strongly associated with a denial. However, in the more serious cases, psychological vulnerabilities and police pressure become much more important (Gudjonsson 2003a).

Support

The presence or absence of a lawyer or an appropriate adult during the interrogation needs to be evaluated as a part of the overall custodial environment. The impact of the presence of a solicitor on suspects' behaviour during interrogation is well established (Gudjonsson 2003a). There is evidence from our current work at police stations that the presence of an appropriate adult in an interview, even if he or she does not interact directly in the interview process, influences positively the behaviour of the police and solicitors (Medford *et al.* 2003). Medford *et al.* (2003) found that the presence of an appropriate adult increased the likelihood that a solicitor would also be present in an interview, there was overall less interrogative pressure in the interview and the solicitor took a more active role in the interview. Medford *et al.* (2003) raised concern about the apparently poor interview skills found in interviews with juveniles.

False confessions

Evidence that some people are vulnerable to giving a false confession during questioning comes from three main sources: 1) anecdotal cases histories (e.g. Gudjonsson 2003a; Drizin and Colgan 2004); 2) self-report studies among prisoners and college student samples (Gudjonsson 2003a); and 3) laboratory paradigms (Kassin and Kiechel 1996).

False confessions do happen on occasions for a variety of reasons (see Gudjonsson 2003a for a review), and they are generally classified into three psychological types (Kassin and Wrightsman 1985): 'voluntary', 'coerced-compliant' and 'coerced-internalized', although a number of authors have attempted to refine the classification (see Gudjonsson 2003a, for a review).

The vulnerability of making false confessions can be separated into 'personal' and 'situational' factors (Kassin and Gudjonsson 2004). Personal risk factors are those associated with the suspect's individual characteristics, such as low intelligence, personality (e.g. suggestibility and compliance), youth and psychopathology. In contrast, situational risk factors include physical custody and isolation, the nature of the interrogation techniques used, the process of confrontation and the social support system available to the suspect during the custody and interrogation. Sleep deprivation has been found to increase psychological vulnerability to giving in to suggestions and interrogative pressure (Blagrove 1996).

Following the innovative study of Kassin and Kiechel (1996), a number of studies have demonstrated that the presentation of false evidence can lead some vulnerable people to make a false admission of guilt (e.g. to crashing a computer, to internalizing responsibility for this act and to confabulating details about it) (Redlich and Goodman 2003; Forrest *et al.* 2006). These laboratory paradigms, although having limited similarities to real-life interrogations, show that false confessions can be readily elicited from many apparently normal individuals by using subtle manipulations.

A number of high-profile cases of false confessions have been reported (Gudjonsson 2003a; Kassin and Gudjonsson 2004), but these are likely to represent 'only the tip of a much larger iceberg' (Drizin and Leo 2004: 919). The focus of these studies is on the most serious of cases, such as murder, rape and terrorist offences, and they usually consist of cases where people have been wrongfully convicted (i.e. cases of a miscarriage of justice). Here the interrogative and custodial pressures are likely to be much greater than in the minor cases, increasing the risk of false confessions (Gudjonsson 2003a).

In cases of miscarriage of justice, psychological vulnerabilities (such as borderline learning disabilities, personality disorder, high compliance and suggestibility, anxiety problems and low self-esteem) are often found to be relevant to the legal issues in the case (Gudjonsson 2003a). There is a host of factors that can adversely influence the ability of the person to cope with the custody and interrogation. Each case needs to be evaluated on its own merits (Gudjonsson 2003b).

A number of large-scale studies into false confession rates have been carried out in Iceland. Gudjonsson and Sigurdsson (1994) and Sigurdsson and Gudjonsson (1996) asked Icelandic prison inmates if they had ever confessed falsely to the police. In both studies, 12 per cent claimed to have made a false confession to the police at some time in their lives. Sigurdsson and Gudjonsson (2001) carried out a discriminant function analysis of 62 false confessors and 447 other prison inmates using 17 psychological and 16 criminological and substance misuse variables. The findings suggested that anti-social personality traits and the extent and severity of criminal behaviour, as judged by number of previous imprisonments, were the best predictors of false confessions being made during custodial interrogation. This suggests that, among these Icelandic prison inmates, false confessions appeared to be a part of their offending lifestyle. However, the 'coerced-internalized' false confessors were found to be more suggestible and had a greater tendency to confabulate than the other type of false confessors (Sigurdsson and Gudjonsson 1996). This suggests that the type of false confession needs to be taken into consideration when understanding the psychological vulnerabilities of the false confessor.

In two community studies among Icelandic college and university students who reported that they had been interrogated by the police, 3.7 and 1.2 per cent, respectively, claimed to have made a false confession (Gudjonsson et al. 2004a, 2004b). In a recent study involving 10,472 students in further education in Iceland, a false confession rate of 7.3 per cent was found for those interrogated by police, which gave a false confession rate of 1.6 per cent for the total sample (Gudjonsson et al. 2006).

Gudjonsson et al. (2006) also investigated the association of making a false confession with variables relating to mental state and well-being (anxiety, depression, anger, self-esteem, attitude towards school and parental support), involvement in delinquent behaviours and the extent of the delinquent behaviour of friends. The false confessors reported more anxiety, depression and anger problems; poorer self-esteem; less parental support; more delinquency during the previous year; and more delinquency among friends. This means that they were more delinquent and emotionally disturbed than the other participants.

Conclusions

Interrogation (i.e. investigative interviews of suspects) involves a process of social influence, which is generally guilt presumptive (Kassin and Gudjonsson 2004). Investigators' blind faith in their ability to detect deception by verbal and non-verbal means, and tunnel vision during the investigation, including the interrogation, is a recipe for a miscarriage of justice. Approaching investigations and interviews with an open mind is the current philosophy behind interview training in England and Wales.

It is evident from this chapter that, in addition to increased interviewing training, interviewing has become more specialist orientated, where the priority is to select the right interviewer for specific interviews (e.g. sex crimes, murders, child victims). This suggests increased professionalism. Psychologists are also being increasingly brought in to assist police with interviewing strategy.

The empirical evidence available suggests that there are three main reasons why suspects confess: perceptions of the strength of the evidence against them; internal pressure; and custodial and interrogative pressure (including techniques using deceit, trickery and psychological manipulation). Suspects typically confess for a combination of reasons, but perceptions of the strength of evidence is the single most important reason. This has important implications for investigators. There is an increased risk of false confession in cases where the evidence against the suspect is weak, flawed or misleading. Investigators should know that false confessions do occur on occasions, for a variety of reasons, including suspects wanting to protect somebody else, not being able to cope with the interrogative and custodial pressures, and psychological vulnerabilities (Gudjonsson 2003a).

Selected further reading

Gudjonsson, G.H. (2003) *The Psychology of Interrogations and Confessions: A Handbook.* Chichester: Wiley. This book provides a comprehensive account of the scientific and legal development relating to police interviewing and confessions. It combines academic and practitioner perspectives.

Gudjonsson, G.H., Clare, I., Rutter, S. and Pearse, J. (1993) *Persons at Risk during Interviews in Police Custody: The Identification of Vulnerabilities* (Royal Commission on Criminal Justice). London: HMSO. This is the first and only study conducted where detainees were assessed psychologically before police interviewed them. It provides a excellent insight into the psychological vulnerabilities of suspects detained at two police stations in the London Metropolitan area.

Lassiter, G.D. (ed.) (2004) *Interrogations, Confessions, and Entrapment.* New York, NY: Kluwer Academic/Plenum Publishers. This provides a interesting collection of papers by international, mainly American, experts on interrogation and confessions. Its strength is that it focuses on the interrogation of children as well as of adult suspects.

Williamson, T. (ed.) (2006) *Investigative Interviewing: Rights, Research, Regulation.* Cullompton: Willan Publishing. This book originates from an international

conference on police interviewing held in Canada in 2004. The strength of this
book it that it provides important chapters on recent developments in the areas of
investigative interviewing in a variety of contexts (including terrorist interviews),
from police, legal, research and expert witness perspectives.

Kassin, S.M. and Gudjonsson, G.H. (2004) 'The psychology of confessions: a review
of the literature and issues', *Psychological Science in the Public Interest*, 5: 33–67. This
article provides a succinct but comprehensive scientific review of the psychological
aspects of confessions.

References

Arrigo, J.M. (2003) 'A consequentialist argument against torture interrogations of
terrorists.' Paper presented at the Joint Services Conference on Professional Ethics,
30–31 January, Springfield, VA (available online at http://www.au.af.mil/au/awc/
awcgate/jscope/arrigo03.htm).
Baldwin, J. (1993) 'Police interviewing techniques. Establishing truth or proof?', *British
Journal of Criminology*, 33: 325–52.
Berggren, E. (1975) *The Psychology of Confessions*. Leiden: E.J. Brill.
Blagrove, M. (1996) 'Effects of length of sleep deprivation on interrogative
suggestibility', *Journal of Experimental Psychology: Applied*, 2: 48–59.
Buckley, J.P. (2006) 'The Reid technique of interviewing and interrogation', in
T. Williamson (ed.) *Investigative Interviewing*. Cullompton: Willan Publishing.
Bull, R. (1999) 'Police investigative interviewing', in A. Memon and R. Bull (eds)
Handbook of the Psychology of Interviewing. Chichester: Wiley.
Clarke, C. and Milne, R. (2001) *National Evaluation of the PEACE Investigative
Interviewing Course. Police Research Award Scheme Report* PRAS/149. Portsmouth:
Institute of Criminal Justice Studies, University of Portsmouth.
CPTU (1992a) *The Interviewer's Rule Book*. London: Home Office, Central Planning
and Training Unit.
CPTU (1992b) *A Guide to Interviewing*. London: Home Office, Central Planning and
Training Unit.
Drizin, S.A. and Colgan, B.A. (2004) 'Tales from the juvenile confessions front',
in G.D. Lassiter (ed.) *Interrogations, Confessions, and Entrapment*. New York, NY:
Kluwer Academic.
Drizin, S.A. and Leo, R.A. (2004) 'The problem of false confessions in the post-DNA
world', *North Carolina Law Review*, 82: 891–1007.
Evans, F.J. (1993) *The Conduct of Police Interviews with Juveniles. Royal Commission on
Criminal Justice Research Report* 8. London: HMSO.
Fisher, R.P. and Geiselman, R.E. (1992) *Memory Enhancing Techniques for Investigative
Interviewing: The Cognitive Interview*. Springfield, IL: Thomas.
Forrest, K.D., Wadkins, T.A. and Larson, B.A. (2006) 'Suspect personality, police
interrogations, and false confessions: maybe it is not just the situation', *Personality
and Individual Differences*, 40: 621–8.
Fulero, S.M. and Everington, C. (2004) 'Mental retardation, competency to waive
Miranda rights, and false confessions', in G.D. Lassiter (ed.) *Interrogations,
Confessions, and Entrapment*. New York, NY: Kluwer Academic.
Gelles, M.G., McFadden, R., Borum, R. and Vossekuil, B. (2006) 'Al-Qaeda-related
subjects: a law enforcement perspective', in T. Williamson (ed.) *Investigative
Interviewing*. Cullompton: Willan Publishing.

Griffiths, A. and Milne, B. (2006) 'Will it all end in tiers? Police interviews with suspects in Britain', in T. Williamson (ed.) *Investigative Interviewing*. Cullompton: Willan Publishing.

Gudjonsson, G.H. (1989) 'Compliance in an interrogation situation: a new scale', *Personality and Individual Differences*, 10: 535–40.

Gudjonsson, G.H. (1992) *The Psychology of Interrogations, Confessions and Testimony*. London: Wiley.

Gudjonsson, G.H. (2002) 'Who makes a good interviewer? Police interviewing and confessions', in M. Bockstaele (ed.) *Politieverhoor en Personality-Profiling*. Brussels: Uitgeverij Politeia nv.

Gudjonsson, G.H. (2003a) *The Psychology of Interrogations and Confessions: A Handbook*. Chichester: Wiley.

Gudjonsson, G.H. (2003b) 'Psychology brings justice: the science of forensic psychology', *Criminal Behaviour and Mental Health*, 13: 159–67.

Gudjonsson, G.H. (2005) 'Fitness to be interviewed', in J. Payne-James *et al.* (eds) *Encyclopaedia of Forensic and Legal Medicine. Volume 2*. London: Elsevier.

Gudjonsson, G.H. (2006) 'Sex offenders and confessions: how to overcome their resistance during questioning', *Journal of Clinical Forensic Medicine*, 13: 203–7.

Gudjonsson, G.H., Clare, I.C.H., Rutter, S. and Pearse, J. (1993) *Persons at Risk During Interviews in Police Custody: The Identification of Vulnerabilities. Royal Commission on Criminal Justice*. London: HMSO.

Gudjonsson, G.H. and Sigurdsson, J.F. (1994) 'How frequently do false confessions occur? An empirical study among prison inmates', *Psychology, Crime and Law*, 1: 21–6.

Gudjonsson, G.H. and Sigurdsson, J.F. (1999) 'The Gudjonsson Confession Questionnaire-Revised (GCQ-R): factor structure and its relationship with personality', *Personality and Individual Differences*, 27: 953–68.

Gudjonsson, G.H., Sigurdsson, J.F., Asgeirsdottir, B.B. and Sigfusdottir, I.D. (2006) 'Custodial interrogation, false confession and individual differences: a national study among Icelandic youth', *Personality and Individual Differences*, 40: 795–806.

Gudjonsson, G.H., Sigurdsson, J.F., Bragason, O.O., Einarsson, E. and Valdimarsdottir, E.B. (2004a) 'Confessions and denials and the relationship with personality', *Legal and Criminological Psychology*, 9: 121–33.

Gudjonsson, G.H., Sigurdsson, J.F. and Einarsson, E. (2004b) 'The role of personality in relation to confessions and denials', *Psychology, Crime and Law*, 10: 125–35.

Hilgendorf, E.L. and Irving, B. (1981) 'A decision-making model of confessions', in M. Lloyd-Bostock (ed.) *Psychology in Legal Contexts: Applications and Limitations*. London: Macmillan.

Holmberg, U. and Christianson, S.-A. (2002) 'Murderers' and sexual offenders' experiences of police interviews and their inclination to admit and deny crimes', *Behavioral Sciences and the Law*, 20: 31–45.

Home Office (2003) *Police and Criminal Evidence Act 1984 (s. 66): Codes of Practice* (A–E revised edn). London: HMSO.

Home Office (2004) *Police and Criminal Evidence Act 1984 (s. 66): Codes of Practice* (A–F edn). London: HMSO.

Inbau, F.E. (1942) *Lie Detection and Criminal Detection*. Baltimore, MD: Williams & Wilkins.

Inbau, F.E. (1948) *Lie Detection and Criminal Detection* (2nd edn). Baltimore, MD: Williams & Wilkins.

Inbau, F.E. and Reid, J.E. (1953) *Lie Detection and Criminal Detection* (3rd edn). Baltimore, MD: Williams & Wilkins.

Inbau, F.E. and Reid, J.E. (1967) *Criminal Interrogation and Confessions* (2nd edn). Baltimore, MD: Williams & Wilkins.

Inbau, F.E., Reid, J.E. and Buckley, J.P. (1986) *Criminal Interrogation and Confessions* (3rd edn). Baltimore, MD: Williams & Wilkins.

Inbau, F.E., Reid, J.E., Buckley, J.P. and Jayne, B.C. (2001) *Criminal Interrogation and Confessions* (4th edn). Gaithersberg, MD: Aspen.

Irving, B. and Hilgendorf, L. (1980) *Police Interrogation: The Psychological Approach – a Case Study of Current Practice.* London: HMSO.

Irving, B. and McKenzie, I.K. (1989) *Police Interrogation: The Effects of the Police and Criminal Evidence Act.* London: Police Foundation of Great Britain.

Jayne, B.C. (1986) 'The psychological principles of criminal interrogation', in F. Inbau *et al.* (eds) *Criminal Interrogation and Confessions* (3rd edn). Baltimore, MD: Williams & Wilkins.

Kassin, S.M. (2006) 'A critical appraisal of modern police interrogations', in T. Williamson (ed.) *Investigative Interviewing.* Cullompton: Willan Publishing.

Kassin, S.M. and Gudjonsson, G.H. (2004) 'The psychology of confessions: a review of the literature and issues', *Psychological Science in the Public Interest*, 5: 35–69.

Kassin, S.M. and Kiechel, K.L. (1996) 'The social psychology of false confessions: compliance, internalization, and confabulation', *Psychological Science*, 7: 125–8.

Kassin, S.M. and Wrightsman, L.S. (1985) 'Confession evidence', in S.M. Kassin and L.S. Wrightsman (eds) *The Psychology of Evidence and Trial Procedures.* London: Sage.

Kebbell, M.R., Hurren, E.J. and Roberts, S. (2005) 'Mock-suspects' decision to confess: the accuracy of eyewitness evidence is critical', *Applied Cognitive Psychology*, 19: 1–10.

Leo, R.A. (1992) 'From coercion to deception: the changing nature of police interrogation in America', *Crime, Law and Social Change: An International Journal*, 18: 35–59.

Leo, R.A. (1994) Police interrogation in America: a study of violence, civility and social change.' Unpublished PhD thesis, University of California at Berkeley.

Leo, R.A. (1996) 'Inside the interrogation room', *Journal of Criminal Law and Criminology*, 86: 266–303.

MacDonald, J.M and Michaud, D.L. (1992) *Criminal Interrogation.* Denver, CO: Apache.

Mackey, C. and Miller, G. (2004) *The Interrogator's War: Inside the Secret War against Al Qaeda.* London: John Murray.

Maddox, B. (2006) 'Guantanamo Bay. He is dressed in a tan tunic: I don't want this court, he says', *The Times*, 28 April: 44–5.

McGurk, B., Carr, M. and McGurk, D. (1993) *Investigative Interviewing Courses for Police Officers: An Evaluation. Police Research Group Paper 4.* London: Home Office.

Medford, S., Gudjonsson, G.H. and Pearse, J. (2003) 'The efficacy of the appropriate adult safeguard during police interviewing', *Legal and Criminological Psychology*, 8: 253–66.

Mortimer, A. and Shepherd, E. (1999) 'Frames of mind: schemata guiding cognition and conduct in the interviewing of suspected offenders', in A. Memon and R. Bull (eds) *Handbook of the Psychology of Interviewing.* Chichester: Wiley.

Moston, S., Stephenson, G.M. and Williamson, T.M. (1992) 'The effects of case characteristics on suspect behaviour during questioning', *British Journal of Criminology*, 32: 23–40.

Nydell, M. (2002) *Understanding Arabs: A Guide for Westerners* (3rd edn). Yarnmouth, MA: Intercultural Press.

Ofshe, R.J. and Leo, R.A. (1997a) 'The decision to confess falsely: rational choice and irrational action', *Denver University Law Review*, 74: 979–1122.

Ofshe, R.J. and Leo, R.A. (1997b) 'The social psychology of police interrogation. The theory and classification of true and false confessions', *Studies in Law, Politics and Society*, 16: 189–251.

Ord, B. and Shaw, G. (1999) *Investigative Interviewing Explained: The Operational Guide to Practical Interviewing Skills*. Woking: New Police Bookshop.

Pearse, J.J. (2006) 'The interrogation of terrorist suspects: the banality of torture', in T. Williamson (ed.) *Investigative Interviewing*. Cullompton: Willan Publishing.

Pearse, J. and Gudjonsson, G.H. (1999) 'Measuring influential police interviewing tactics: a factor analytic approach', *Legal and Criminological Psychology*, 4: 221–38.

Pearse, J., Gudjonsson, G.H., Clare, I.C.H. and Rutter, S. (1998) 'Police interviewing and psychological vulnerabilities: predicting the likelihood of a confession', *Journal of Community and Applied Social Psychology*, 8: 1–21.

Phillips, C. and Brown, D. (1998) *Entry into the Criminal Justice System: A Survey of Police Arrests and their Outcomes*. London: Home Office.

Rabon, D. (1992) *Interviewing and Interrogation*. Durham, NC: Duke University Press.

Rabon, D. (1994) *Investigative Discourse Analysis*. Durham, NC: Duke University Press.

Redlich, A.D. and Goodman, G.S. (2003) 'Taking responsibility for an act not committed: the influence of age and suggestibility', *Law and Human Behavior*, 27: 141–56.

Redlich, A.D., Silverman, M., Chen, J. and Steiner, H. (2004) 'The police interrogation of children and adolescents', in G.D. Lassiter (ed.) *Interrogations, Confessions, and Entrapment*. New York, NY: Kluwer Academic.

Reik, T. (1959) *The Compulsion to Confess: On the Psychoanalysis of Crime and Punishment*. New York, NY: Farrar, Straus & Cudahy.

Rogge, O.J. (1975) *Why Men Confess*. New York, NY: Da Capo Press.

Rose, D. (2004) *Guantánamo: America's War on Human Rights*. London: Faber & Faber.

Rose, D. (2006) 'American interrogation methods in the war on terror', in T. Williamson (ed.) *Investigative Interviewing*. Cullompton: Willan Publishing.

Royal, R.F. and Schutte, S.R. (1976) *The Gentle Art of Interviewing and Interrogation: A Professional Manual and Guide*. Englewood Cliffs, NJ: Prentice Hall.

Sigurdsson, J.F. and Gudjonsson, G.H. (1994) 'Alcohol and drug intoxication during police interrogation and the reasons why suspects confess to the police', *Addiction*, 89: 985–97.

Sigurdsson, J.F. and Gudjonsson, G.H. (1996) 'Psychological characteristics of "false confessors": a study among Icelandic prison inmates and juvenile offenders', *Personality and Individual Differences*, 20: 321–9.

Sigurdsson, J.F. and Gudjonsson, G.H. (2001) 'False confessions: the relative importance of psychological, criminological and substance abuse variables', *Psychology, Crime and Law*, 7: 275–89.

Stockdale, J. (1993) *Management and Supervision of Police Interviews. Police Research Group Paper* 4. London: Home Office.

Stubbs, C. and Newberry, J.J. (1998). *Analytic Interviewing*. Queensland: Australian Institute of Analytic Interviewing.

St-Yves, M. (2006) 'Confessions by sex offenders', in T. Williamson (ed.) *Investigative Interviewing*. Cullompton: Willan Publishing.

Vrij, A. (2000) *Detecting Lies and Deceit: The Psychology of Lying and the Implications for Professional Practice*. Chichester: Wiley.

Walkley, J. (1987) *Police Interrogation: A Handbook for Investigators*. London: Police Review Publication.

Williamson, T.M. (1993) 'From interrogation to investigative interviewing. Strategic trends in the police questioning', *Journal of Community and Applied Social Psychology*, 3: 89–99.

Williamson, T.M. (1994) 'Reflections on current police practice', in D. Morgan and G. Stephenson (eds) *Suspicion and Silence: The Rights of Silence in Criminal Investigations*. London: Blackstone Press Ltd.

Williamson, T.M. (2005) 'Anti-terror laws must be humane', *Police Review*, 15: 14.
Williamson, T.M. (ed.) (2006) *Investigative Interviewing*. Cullompton: Willan Publishing.
Woods, G. (2002) 'The selection of the right interrogator', in M. Bockstaele (ed.) *Politieverhooren en Personality-Profiling*. Brussels: Uitgeverij Politeia nv.

Chapter 20

Profiling suspects

*Laurence Alison, Clare McLean
and Louise Almond*

What is offender profiling?

There is no universally accepted definition of offender profiling (Gudjonsson
and Copson 1997). The term is given to a collection of various scientific and
psychological theories and techniques that attempt to draw inferences about
an offender's characteristics by examining the behaviour exhibited in a crime
scene. The contents of an offender profile may, however, vary. Ault and Reese
(1980) provide a list of what components may be included:

1 The perpetrator's ethnicity.
2 The perpetrator's gender.
3 Age range.
4 Marital status.
5 General employment.
6 Reaction to questioning by police.
7 Degree of sexual maturity.
8 Whether the individual will offend again.
9 The possibility that he or she has committed a similar previous offence.
10 Previous convictions.

A brief history of profiling

Although the Federal Bureau of Investigation (FBI) can lay claim to have
invented the term and to the widely recognized 'conventional' acceptance of
offender profiling, there are a number of earlier salient examples where 'pen
portraits' of offenders have been constructed for crime scene investigators. In
what many consider to be the first offender profile, in 1888 Dr Thomas Bond
attempted to profile the personality of Jack the Ripper. He stated that all five

crimes had been committed by the same person, and that the offender was physically strong, composed and daring. The assailant would be quiet and of unexceptional appearance. He might be middle aged and would probably be wearing a cloak to hide the victims' blood. He would be a loner, without a steady occupation, eccentric and mentally unstable. Bond believed that the offender had no anatomical knowledge and was unlikely to be a surgeon or a butcher.[1] Bond speculated that he might even suffer from a condition called 'satyriasis', which is today referred to as hypersexuality. Needless to say, we may never know how accurate Bond was since the identity of Jack the Ripper remains a mystery.

In 1943, during the Second World War, the US government asked Dr Walter Langer, a psychoanalyst, to develop a 'profile' of Adolf Hitler, to aid their strategic planning. This resulted in a 135-page profile, which was later published in the book, *The Mind of Adolf Hitler* (Langer 1972). Langer's profile noted that Hitler suffered from an Oedipal complex, the result of which was manifest in his need to prove his manhood to his mother. He was described as fearing syphilis, germs and moonlight, and that he loved severed heads. He also showed strong streaks of sadism and tended to speak in long monologues rather than have conversations, and he had difficulty establishing close relationships with anyone. Langer correctly predicted Hitler's determination to fight to the end, his worsening mental condition and, ultimately, his suicide. Dr Murray (one of several psychoanalysts who worked with Langer) also compiled a profile in which he surmised Hitler's alleged femininity as a boy, his aversion to manual work, his annoying subservience to superior officers as a young soldier and, as a man, his nightmares suggestive of homosexual panic. Murray argued that Hitler's commitment to genocide as a solution to the 'Jewish problem' stemmed, in part, from a desperate loathing of his own submissive weakness, and the humiliations of being beaten by a sadistic father.[2]

Profiling rose to prominence in 1956 when the New York Police asked a psychiatrist, Dr James Brussel, to assist them in their investigation of a serial bomber who had been terrorizing the city by planting bombs in public places. Brussel suggested that the offender would be a heavy, middle-aged man who was unmarried, but perhaps living with a sibling. He would be a skilled mechanic from Connecticut, a Roman Catholic immigrant and, while having an obsessional love for his mother, would harbour a hatred for his father. Brussel noted that the offender would have a personal vendetta against the city's power company, the target of the first bomb. His alleged prediction that, when the police apprehended the offender, the bomber would be wearing a double-breasted suit, fully buttoned, has entered profiling folklore. The police managed to track down George Metesky, a disgruntled former employee of the power company, who, when told by the police to get dressed, went into his bedroom and returned wearing a double-breasted suit, fully buttoned. The profile was remarkably accurate, the single variation being that Metesky lived with two siblings and not one (for full details of the profile, see Brussel 1968).

Recent history

The modern offender profiling approach primarily originated in the 1970s, based on the techniques developed by the Behavioural Science Unit (BSU) at the FBI's Academy at Quantico, Virginia, which was set up in response to an apparent increasing trend in serial killing in the USA. This specialist unit trained 'professional criminal personality profilers' who were called upon with increasing frequency to assist in apparently motiveless murders, often committed across various jurisdictions, which were especially troublesome for local law enforcement agencies. Profiling was originally intended to assist investigators in either narrowing down an overwhelming list of suspects to a small subgroup or by providing new avenues of inquiry. Reiser (1982 cited in Blau 1994) indicated that these profilers have a unique opportunity for direct involvement in police work and investigations by applying psychological knowledge and experience in a variety of unusual policing circumstances.

The BSU produced a crime scene classification system by studying the crime scene, victim and forensic information, as well as in-depth interviews of 36 incarcerated murderers. Ressler *et al.* (1986: 291) claim that 'facets of the criminal's personality are evident in his offence. Like a fingerprint, the crime scene can be used to aid in identifying the murder.' This behavioural 'fingerprint' took one of two distinct forms – either organized or disorganized – a dichotomy widely accepted as a conceptual tool at the heart of offender profiling and one of the most widely cited classifications of violent, serial offenders. Although first introduced to examine lust and sexual sadistic murders (Ressler *et al.* 1986), the *Crime Classification Manual* (Douglas *et al.* 1992), a handbook of offender profiling issued by the FBI, allows the organized/disorganized distinction to differentiate sexual homicides and types of arson. In it, Douglas *et al.* (1992: 21) explain that 'the crime scene is presumed to reflect the murderer's behaviour and personality in much the same way as furnishings reveal the homeowner's character'. The organized/disorganized model of offence behaviour assumes that each type will have a consistent method of committing a crime (see Table 20.1 for the crime scene characteristics of organized/disorganized offences).

Table 20.1 Crime scene characteristics

Organized	Disorganized
Planned offence	Spontaneous offence
Controlled conversation	Minimal conversation
Scene reflects control	Scene is random/sloppy
Demands submissive victim	Sudden violence to victim
Restraints used	Minimal use of restraints
Aggressive prior to death	Sex after death
Body hidden	Body left in vi
Weapon/evidence absent	Weapon/evidei
Transports victim	Body left at scei

Source: Burgess *et al.* (1985).

Table 20.2 Organized and disorganized perpetrator characteristics

Organized	Disorganized
High intelligence	Below average intelligence
Socially adequate	Socially inadequate
Sexually competent	Unskilled occupation
Lives with father	Low birth-order status
High birth order	Father's work unstable
Harsh discipline	Harsh/inconsistent discipline
Controlled mood	Anxious mood during crime
Masculine image	Minimal use of alcohol during crime
Charming	Lives alone
Situational cause	Lives/works near crime scene
Geographically mobile	Minimal interest in media
Occupationally mobile	Significant behaviour change
Follows media	Nocturnal habits
Model prisoner	Poor personal hygiene
	Secret hiding places
	Usually does not date
	High-school drop-out

Source: Burgess *et al*. (1985).

Burgess *et al*. (1985) argued that these two 'styles of offending' corresponded with two equally distinct offender types, organized and disorganized (see Table 20.2 for perpetrator characteristics). Thus, an FBI profiler could evaluate a crime scene and determine whether it was an organized or disorganized offence, allowing him or her to make inferences about the characteristics of the offender. For example, if an offender had controlled conversations with the victim, used restraints and hid the body, then the FBI profiler would infer that the offender would be of high intelligence, be socially adept, be sexually competent, etc.

Pinizzotto and Finkel (1990) argued that profiling involves a series of inferential steps. They stated that professional profilers 1) assess the type of criminal act with reference to individuals who have committed similar acts previously; 2) thoroughly analyse the crime scene; 3) scrutinize the background of the victim and possible suspects; and 4) establish the likely motivations of all individuals involved. Finally, a description of the perpetrator is generated. The steps described above can be represented in the question sequence 'What'? 'Why'? 'Who'? (Pinizzotto and Finkel 1990). On the basis of crime scene material (*what*), a particular motivation for the offence behaviour is attributed to the perpetrator (*why*) and this, in turn, leads to the description of the perpetrator's likely characteristics (*who*). This simple *what, why, who* inference assumes that the supposed specific motivations that result in an offence occurring are consistently associated with specific types of offender characteristics (if motivation X, then characteristics A, B, C and D). More recently, Alison (2005) has reviewed a host of reasons why this process is problematic, in that profilers do not make it clear how these deductions are made, commonly do not specify what, if any, behavioural or psychological principles they rely on and fail to take into account the powerful influence of context on offender behaviour. However, despite these counterarguments, these sorts of contributions to the field still hold popular appeal, as illustrated by the many autobiographical accounts written by famous offender profilers about their successes (typically ex-FBI officers in the USA).

Undeniably, these individuals have considerable experience of working on a large number of cases, thereby allowing them to give potentially very well informed opinions. However, they fail to benefit from a systematic approach or a set of theoretical behavioural models that would assist in their guidance. A close examination of Douglas and Olshaker's (1997) profiles reveals how, in many cases, the 'basis' of any given profile comprises very general characteristics – i.e. has problems with women, lives in the area of the crime, has few close relationships and has previous convictions. In addition, the profiles often include characteristics that are very difficult to test directly or to disconfirm subsequent to the offender's capture (i.e. the offender is 'unsure of himself' or has 'poor heterosocial skills').

Similar qualities are present in Paul Britton's (1997) UK bestseller, *The Jigsaw Man*. In his book, Britton uses a device to help convince readers of his profiling expertise – by separating two clearly related points within a list of characteristics, Britton gives the impression that they are independent contributions. For example, stating that an individual is sexually immature also implies that he has few, if any, girlfriends. Yet, in presenting 'lists' of characteristics, the simple separation of these two comments in the list could lead the reader to believe they are separate contributions.

The autobiographical accounts of many of the previous generation of profilers are reflected in the way offender profiling is frequently portrayed in Hollywood blockbusters such as *Silence of the Lambs* and TV dramas such as *Cracker*. The idea of an expert who has special insight into the minds of killers and who can, through the examination of the crime scene, draw conclusions about the type of person who committed it is an enticing prospect, and perhaps the reason why this approach is the one most frequently represented in the media. The 'archetype' of the 'visionary' crime fighter, succeeding where the rest of the inquiry team has failed, seems to have a very firm grip on the public's imagination.

Traditionally, therefore, profiling has involved the process of predicting the likely socio-demographic characteristics of an offender based on information available at the crime scene. Alison (2005) has referred to this approach as 'traditional trait-based' (TTB) profiling and has criticized it for its naïve view of human behaviour and its lack of operational utility beyond what might reasonably be expected of any competent detective. Consequently, there has been a gradual decline in the frequency with which police investigators use TTB, at least in the UK (Alison 2005). In the last ten years, a broader definition of offender profiling has emerged, which recognizes the range of fruitful, reliable, tested and transparent evidence-based methods by which psychologists might provide advice to the police during investigations. This has, more recently, involved practitioners adopting the less loaded term, 'behavioural investigative advice'. Extending well beyond attempts to set suspect parameters or explain the behaviour of offenders in one-off critical incidents, advisers can now assist on issues such as media strategy, interview strategy, DNA intelligence-led screens, risk assessments, strategies for identifying the whereabouts of an offender (geographic profiling) and whether a crime appears to be part of a series. Thus, as Adhami and Browne (1996: 1) point out, 'offender profiling, in all its guises, is [now] viewed as a means of improving crime detection practices'.

Traditional assumptions

TTB relies on inferring characteristics of offenders from clusters or combinations of crime scene behaviours and subsequently classifies these clusters as representative of distinct 'types' of offenders. Perhaps the most popular example of this style of profiling is the supposed distinction between 'organized' and 'disorganized' killers, which we described earlier. Criminal behaviour, however, is very much more complex than this simple dichotomy. Alison and Ogan (2006) have described it as follows:

> Let us consider an analogy: If we think about the behaviour of people we know we might be able to say whether they kept a reasonably tidy house or not ('organized' or 'disorganized' house owners). We might even find that there were some very basic differences in the way these people think. Thus, we might want to measure the extent to which individuals who keep their house in pristine condition are more particular in the organisation of their office space. We might also measure the extent to which their level of organization related to other behaviours such as punctuality. The former measure would tell us how consistently tidy they were in different environments and the latter measure would be one indication of how their organization of their house marries up (or not) with other behaviours that we might hypothesize are 'organized' behaviours. Both of these are plausible hypotheses (although similar efforts have not been tested or examined in relation to offence behaviour). However, it is a far more ambitious psychologist who would argue that all of the people that we know who keep their house very tidy are all of a narrowly defined age range and all of exactly the same social competence and all drive exactly the same type of car. Although there might be some loose associations (with younger individuals tending towards the less tidy end of the spectrum) it is probable that there is considerable variation between individuals and that this variation does not neatly marry up with socio demographic features (age, gender, ethnicity etc).

Alison and Ogan go on to argue that such characteristics are probably dimensional rather than categorical, with a range of *levels* of tidiness, and that most people would not fall at extreme ends of the spectrum. Finally, one would have to be sure that, in visiting a friend, one had enough representative visits to take an accurate measure of how generally tidy that person was. If, for example, one visited straight after a dinner party, one may have a less clear idea of how tidy that person was, because the situation had a powerful impact on the behaviour. Therefore, because behaviours normally fall on continua, because psychological processes rarely map on to demographics such as age and because situations often have a powerful influence on behaviour, this simple twofold system is naïve of research on human behaviour.

Canter and Alison (1999) have argued that 'organization' might more fruitfully be considered a continuum rather than an either/or system. While Burgess's original system concedes that hybrids exist (i.e. contain both organized and disorganized elements), we have found that a majority of examples contain *both* elements and, as such, the utility of the two discrete types loses its discriminatory power (Canter *et al*. 2004). Indeed, there is some suggestion that most offenders are relatively organized, but it is the nature of their 'type' of disorganization that varies.

Consistency and homology

The belief that profilers can accurately predict an offender's background and demographic characteristics depends on two major assumptions: 1) consistency and 2) homology. For profiling to 'work', perpetrators have to remain consistent across a number of crimes. If on the first crime an offender gags and binds the victim, on the second he kisses and compliments the victim and on the third he punches and stabs the victim, then clearly it would be impossible to claim that certain clusters of behaviours are closely associated with certain clusters of offender backgrounds. Encouragingly, there is a fair amount of research that suggests that offenders *are* somewhat consistent. This has been demonstrated in rape, burglary and, more recently, serial murder (Salfati and Bateman 2005). The second assumption (homology), however, is more controversial (see Mokros and Alison 2002 for a review). Homology assumes that where two different offenders have the same personality, they will commit a crime in the same way. Similarly, if two crime scenes are similar, then the same *type* of person will have committed them both.

While there is some evidence that certain crime scene behaviours *are* associated with certain background characteristics, there is no compelling evidence that *clusters* of behaviours can be closely matched with particular *clusters* of background characteristics. There is a subtle but very important distinction between the claim that clusters of behaviours are related to clusters of background characteristics *compared* with the claim that single behaviours are related to single characteristics. To further elucidate, take two examples:

1 The offender did not leave any fingerprints at the rape crime scene. It is therefore my assertion that this offender is likely to be a prolific burglar.

Research by Professor X (1987) indicates that 76 per cent of offenders who do not leave fingerprints have more than seven previous convictions for burglary.

2 This offence demonstrates the offender is a 'planner' rapist – there are no fingerprints, the crime scene is tidy, there is no ransacking and he has only stolen electrical goods and children's clothes (both of which can be easily sold on for gain). 'Planner' rapists are between the ages of 25 and 30, feel no remorse, are likely to be in a semi-skilled job and are likely to be married.

The first is called a 'one-to-one relationship' and typifies the sorts of claims made by profilers who may refer to themselves as crime analysts or behavioural advisers (these individuals might be considered the 'new generation' of contemporary profilers). The second example reflects the more traditional method of profiling and is in line with the previous work of some FBI agents (most of whom are now retired) who advised in the early days of profiling in the 1970s, as well as an increasingly dwindling selection of individuals from a variety of backgrounds who appear to be happy to put themselves forward as expert profilers.

Traditional profiling methods (as in point 2) make far more ambitious claims than those offered by the behavioural adviser approach. Indeed, what is so enticing is the seeming promise of a rich and detailed character assessment or 'pen portrait' of the offender. However, this approach assumes that offenders' behaviours are a product of stable personality traits (consistency) and that all offenders who share a particular personality (a 'planner type') will all behave in the same way (homology). Thus, the traditional view makes a number of inferential 'leaps' from which it derives a 'type' from a cluster of behaviours and a cluster of background characteristics from those different 'types'. Several studies, however, have now tested this process and consistently failed to find these sorts of relationships (see, for example, House 1997; Davies *et al.* 1998; Mokros and Alison 2002).

Unfortunately, it has taken some time for science to catch up with and question the methods that had previously been relied upon. Furthermore, science is only just beginning to develop more reliable bases upon which to advise (issues that we shall consider shortly). However, despite its more laboured journey, the scientific method is gradually weeding out the bogus approaches and providing more fruitful, reliable, tested and transparent evidence-based methods for assisting the police. Part of the contribution lies in a change of focus, from the exclusive concentration on the killer and his likely 'psychological profile' to contributions that consider the way the police collect information, make decisions and direct and lead a team that they must motivate during times of stress, often with difficult challenges that require them to deal effectively and sensitively with the community they serve and often rely upon. Thus, behavioural advisers and profiles are now realizing that their contribution may lie more productively in a greater appreciation of the myriad issues that are involved in investigating crime.

How can profiling assist a criminal investigation?

The remit of psychological profiling and behavioural advice is developing more productive areas of research, such as assisting in:

- detective decision-making;
- intelligence-led policing;
- investigative interviewing;
- informant handling; and
- suspect prioritization.

Profilers can therefore offer advice that will render the investigation more efficient than it would otherwise have been – for example, by:

- reducing the time spent on wholly irrelevant suspicions. Given increasing police pressures to meet performance targets, this will always be welcomed;

- providing police officers with a view of the style in which an offence has been committed, by presenting pertinent information in the conventional visual display of the plot. Several police officers have stated that such material can assist in developing interview strategies;

- assisting in the construction of databases and decision-support systems as well as in advising on how data might be most fruitfully collected, stored and utilized;

- assisting in the production of base rates to indicate how unusual or distinct a case is. This has, on occasion, been used in court as a part basis for similar fact evidence;

- advising on interview strategies by preparing police officers or tactical interview managers (TIMs) for what they might expect psychologically from a given offender; and

- assessing the credibility of statements, evaluating interviewer performance and advising on what aspects of the account might most fruitfully be challenged or explored in more detail.

Furthermore, by taking advantage of profiling advice and maximizing these benefits, police forces can demonstrate a continuing commitment to intelligence-led policing and the policing of risks. This is in line with national policing initiatives.

Crucially, however, if investigators do choose to embrace the contribution from psychologists, they should retain a healthy scepticism. As Canter and Alison (1999: 39) noted: 'One must check and treat with caution all opinions and not simply assume that because it is said with great conviction by someone with experience that it must be true.' Because police officers should not be expected to have a full and comprehensive knowledge of the scientific method, it can prove difficult for any given individual to know which of the expert's qualities he or she should be looking to evaluate. Moreover, police officers are unlikely to know the range of issues that psychologists and others may assist with since there is currently no formal checklist of the range of contributions. However, the National Centre for Policing Excellence (NCPE) does have an accredited list of profilers, as well as a list of their in-house behavioural investigative advisers and those analysts working within the Serious Crime Analysis Section. This range of expertise can be drawn upon for any or all of the above contributions and, recently, a more formal procedure has been developed for 1) selecting individuals for the list; and 2) for keeping checks on the advice provided in terms of its timeliness, appropriateness, transparency and detail. Though, as we shall discuss, this system is (in our view) far from perfect, it does at least recognize the importance of other experts as responsible for 'policing' the quality of advice, and it has doubtless resulted in a system that will minimize some of the previous failings and (hopefully) eradicate the worst excesses of one or two earlier, poorly conducted contributions.

How should profiling advice be presented?

How a profiler presents the advice is critical in ensuring that it is clearly interpreted and used judiciously. Currently, as far as we are aware, there are no agreed specific standards or a 'house style' that must be adhered to. However, in Appendix 1 we suggest how a high-quality profiling report might be structured and set out the issues that a police officer might expect it to cover. It is intended to serve as a checklist for assessing the 'soundness' of such reports, although we are not proposing this is the *only* set of criteria that should be considered.

Our checklist is one proposal for a format in the absence of a commonly agreed 'house style', but it does come from several years' experience in working with the police and within an empirical framework in part guided by British Psychological Society codes of conduct and the American Psychological Association. There are, however, no strict rules on what a profiling report should include, and nor is there a universally agreed format. Thus, while experts within the NCPE evaluate profilers' reports each year, as far as we are aware, there is no definite way of ensuring that all individuals on the accredited list provide all (or any) of the reports that they have conducted. Further, the feedback to individuals on the list is not very detailed and is (necessarily) constrained by virtue of having only two experts evaluate all the reports.

There are no easy answers with regard to improving this process but one objective of this chapter is to encourage the individuals involved in criminal investigations to consider their *own* 'checklist' of quality criteria, as assisted by our recommendations. However, a report should not be dismissed simply because it does not conform exactly to the suggested template. Rather, the relative importance of the sections should dictate the level of concern raised by their omission. For example, while a missing contact address is little cause for alarm, failure to specify bases for statements and to indicate the extent to which they can be relied upon is a serious flaw which strikes at the integrity of a report. Unfortunately, it may also be one of the most common shortcomings of profiling advice. For example, in a small-scale study of European and American offender profiles from the last decade, Alison *et al.* (2003) established that nearly half the opinions in these reports contained advice that could not be verified post-conviction (e.g. 'the offender has a rich fantasy life'); that over a fifth were vague or open to interpretation (e.g. 'the offender has poor social skills'); and that in over 80 per cent the profiler failed to provide any justification for the advice proposed (i.e. he or she did not clarify what his or her opinion was based on). Alison *et al.* conceded that their sample was small, somewhat outdated and did not represent the current standard (a more contemporary analysis is currently being conducted by the authors). None the less, these shortcomings were very pronounced and are certainly something that police officers should guard against, since reports of this nature carry a high risk of material being interpreted erroneously by the inquiry team.

In particular, Alison *et al.* (2003) have argued that this lack of clarity can lead to difficulties similar to the 'Barnum effects' operating in social psychology. The latter refers to the established tendency to accept vague and ambiguous personality descriptions as uniquely applicable to oneself, without realizing that the same description could be applied to just about anyone (Forer 1949). In a criminal investigation this may manifest as a readiness selectively to fit ambiguous, unverifiable information from the profile to a given suspect. For example, there is a danger that, after a suspect is apprehended, or if the investigating officer has a 'type' of offender in mind, the inquiry team may engage in an inferential process 'invited' by the ambiguity of the profile. The risk of this is further heightened by the facts that:

- the individual providing the profile is likely to be presented to the team as an expert in his or her field, thereby increasing the credibility of the advice, irrespective of content;

- profilers may not always write down the information, resulting in police officers relying on their memory of the advice; and

- there may exist considerable pressure on an inquiry team to yield results, thereby resulting in a more favourable view of the advice.

Not all claims are equal

Given these pitfalls, it is absolutely crucial that an inquiry team is able to evaluate systematically profiling advice and to weed out those statements that are unverifiable and/or open to misinterpretation. Alison *et al.* (2003) reviewed how Toulmin's (1958) work on the structure of arguments could provide a valuable framework within which to do this. The strength of the 'Toulminian' approach, they argue, lies in its ability to deconstruct arguments into their constituent parts, thus allowing for close scrutiny of the strengths and weaknesses of various aspects of the argument.

Toulmin suggested that arguments contain six inter-related components: 1) the claim; 2) the strength; 3) the grounds; 4) the warrant; 5) the backing; and 6) the rebuttal. In terms of profiling advice, a claim is a statement made by the profiler about the case (e.g. 'the murderer is under 30 years old'). In order to substantiate this claim, certain components must be present (see Figure 20.1):

- *Strength*: this indicates the extent to which the inquiry team should rely on the claim being true. Strength may be described in modal terms such as 'probably', 'possibly', 'certainly' or as a statistical probability (i.e. 'an 87 per cent chance that ...').

- *Grounds*: the grounds are the support for the claim – that is, the specific aspect of the case which has led the profiler to make the claim (i.e. 'because this is the murder of a 23-year-old woman').

- *Warrant*: this authorizes the grounds – that is, it describes why a specific aspect of a case has led to the profiler to make a particular claim (i.e. 'the majority of offenders who murder women less than 25 years old are themselves less than 30 years old').

- *Backing*: this is the formal support for the warrant and it comes in the form of a citation to a specific example(s) of research (i.e. 'research by X (date)').

- *Rebuttal*: this sets out the conditions under which the claim ceases to be likely or must be adjusted (i.e. 'unless other indications suggest he has returned to the scene').

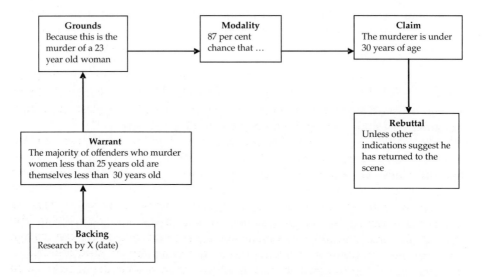

Figure 20.1 Toulmin's structure of argument using a hypothetical 'profiling' example.
Source: Alison *et al.* (2003)

The evaluation of profiling advice in terms of these components will enable the swift identification of unsound claims and help ensure police officers are aware of the weight and significance that can be attached to any inference or conclusion. It should also assist in increasing the likelihood of reports standing up to the strict standards of evidentiary reliability and relevancy afforded to court procedures. The latter is particularly salient given the increasing pressure on investigating officers and profilers to consider carefully the potential legal ramifications of employing such advice in their inquiries (Ormerod 1999).

Below are two examples of claims that might be found in a profiling report:

Statement A
Identical DNA traces were found at the two crime scenes. Research by Prof. X concludes that it is extremely rare for two DNA traces to be exactly alike. Therefore, unless other indications suggest the forensic material was contaminated, there is a 99.7 per cent chance that the two offences are linked.

Statement B
The offender is probably a black male with behavioural problems who feels no remorse.

Statement A has all the components of a sound claim, whereas statement B has only one of five ('strength'), and is therefore (in its current form) unsound. An inquiry team in receipt of a report containing several statements such as in B should contact the profiler and ask for further clarification. In some instances, it may be that the profiler is simply speculating on the basis of his or her tacit knowledge of the field – a perfectly reasonable strategy as long as it is made clear that he or she is speculating. For example, in a rape case a profiler may claim, without reference to relevant research, that there is a reasonable chance that the offender is particularly dangerous because his behaviour is sexually experimental. One cannot be expected to know all relevant literature on every aspect of every case and, not infrequently, there is a paucity of empirical research on specific aspects of a case (e.g. how bogus 999 calls may differ from genuine ones).

Once the report has been considered according to the above process, and any weaknesses satisfactorily addressed by the profiler, the risk of misinterpretation will be substantially reduced. However, police officers should be on guard for other potential pitfalls. In particular, they should be alert to the risk that, in hiring a profiler, they may be likely to be provided with information that the profiler perceives them as wanting to hear. The urge to go along with the expectations of the senior police officer can emerge as a product of wishing to please, relative immaturity or inexperience. At a more subtle level, small details of the way in which the inquiry team presents the information can influence the way in which the information is understood. Furthermore, there is always a danger that profilers will not in fact respect the standards of their discipline, but might become biased and perceive themselves to be a part of the prosecution team, rather than an objective and impartial voice. Inquiry teams must be vigilant to these difficulties, and where there is concern that the profiler is not taking an objective, neutral approach, steps should be taken to address the situation immediately. In extreme cases, this may involve hiring an alternative profiler.

How to check a profiler's credentials

There is a process of accreditation that assists the police in selecting behavioural investigative advisers. Professional standards are developed and maintained through the scrutiny of reports and through advice issued by an Association of Chief Police Officers' board, which includes two professors of forensic psychology. A list of accredited profilers is available from the NCPE. In terms of knowing whether one has the 'right person for the job', it may be helpful for police officers to check who has previously used the services of any given profiler and ask them for the 'inside' view on how useful his or her advice was. A danger here, though, is that one is basing an opinion on a single perspective and a single case. Another strategy may be for officers to avail themselves of the Internet. One obvious method is to consult the British Psychological Society website under the Chartered Psychologist search engine (http://www.bps.org.uk/e-services/find-a-psychologist/directory.cfm). Here, one can search on the basis of topic and on the geographical location of the expert. A more thorough search on the individual can then be conducted through Google or another generic search engine by specifying the name and institutional affiliation.

Another aspect that adds to the confusion is whether an individual has a clinical background or not. Non-clinical forensic psychologists are *less* likely to be competent in conducting analyses or evaluations of individuals (i.e. they are less likely to engage in interviewing clients or in conducting a psychometric test – e.g. IQ tests, etc.), while many non-clinical academic psychologists may be better able to base their opinions on statements and archival sources, as well as advise on investigative strategies. There is also a range of educational and professional backgrounds within the advisory team at the Serious Crime Analysis Section and within the behavioural investigative advisers at the NCPE, and officers should feel free to ask what specialist knowledge any given adviser or analyst has. In practice, each expert will have been drawn towards different types of cases and different methods of working, but it is useful for the officer to be aware of what those working practices are so that both expert and police officer can be sure that they have a common understanding of what the final report will look like. Finally, it may be useful for officers to take advantage of the many conferences that emerge in relation to specialist areas (interviewing, profiling, etc.) so that they may network with and gain a basic understanding of the relevant fields.

What legal and ethical concerns are there?

The trial of Colin Stagg in the UK is a stark example of how dangerous inappropriate and unclear profiling can be, and how it can take a police investigation in entirely the wrong direction if the psychologist and inquiry team have a poor understanding of one another's roles, abilities and boundaries. Briefly, the use of offender profiling led to the identification of Colin Stagg as the primary suspect in the apparently sexually related murder of a young woman in one of London's public parks. The profiler's ensuing advice was used to direct a police 'undercover' operation focused on obtaining either guilty knowledge or a confession from Stagg. This was never forthcoming, and nor was there any compelling evidence against Stagg. Furthermore, other, possibly more compelling, suspects were not focused on with the same verve. The subsequent prosecution of Stagg was thrown out of court at the earliest stages of trial, with the judge, Justice Ognall, severely criticizing the use of 'profiling' and behavioural advice in the investigation. His comments referred in part to profiling's lack of scientific foundations and the apparent unquestioned intuition on which it was based (Britton 1997). He classified the case as an example of 'misconduct of the grossest kind'.

In order to avoid a similar fate, inquiry teams should consider several legal and ethical issues when consulting an offender profiler.

Legal issues

While there are no strict rules concerning the use of profiles in criminal investigations, police officers must bear in mind that, under the Criminal Procedure and Investigations Act 1996, they have specific duties to investigate the crime and not the suspect. This includes an obligation to pursue lines of inquiry pointing away from the suspect.

There are, however, rigid rules governing the use of expert evidence in criminal trials. Thus, if it is to be received by the court, profiling evidence must satisfy the legal tests of relevance and admissibility, as well as the rules concerning the reception of expert opinion evidence. The latter relate to the expert's qualifications, the perceived helpfulness and reliability of the evidence, and, in the case of profiling, its potential categorization as a novel technique. Each of these issues is discussed in detail in Ormerod and Sturman (2005). Generally, the degree of difficulty that the rules will pose depends on the purpose that the profiling evidence is intended to serve. As Ormerod and Sturman point out, where their purpose is to identify the defendant, profiles are likely to be excluded (in England and Wales at least) as insufficiently relevant, unreliable, prejudicial and unscientific. However, where their purpose falls under one of the following categories, they may be deemed admissible (again in England and Wales):

1 The profiler may be able to testify about the crime scene.
2 Profiles may be admitted as comparative crime scene analysis.
3 The accused seeks to establish his or her own personality and its incompatibility with the police profile.

4 A profile might be admitted where the question is whether it is more likely that defendant A rather than defendant B committed the crime with which they are both charged.

Ultimately, however, police should be prepared for the fact that 'any attempt to adduce an offender profile as evidence will see the court systematically deconstruct the material' (Ormerod and Sturman 2005).

Ethical issues

The Colin Stagg inquiry brought the ethical dangers of practising offender profiling improperly to the fore. Stagg was manipulated for many months during the undercover investigation, having his personal weaknesses played upon by the inquiry team. He then spent a year on remand in prison (Ormerod and Sturman 2005). Furthermore, the undercover officer, 'Lizzie James', successfully sued the police for the psychological damage she suffered during the investigation. Finally, the effect on the victim's family is beyond comprehension. The emotional costs of the case are immeasurable.

Despite these dangers, however, neither the British Psychological Society (BPS) nor the American Psychological Association (APA) has devoted special attention to the ethical, legal or professional issues raised by psychologists' involvement in criminal investigations. Rather, their codes of conduct set out general principles to which psychologists must adhere in all their professional endeavours.[3] However, Appendix 2 draws out those points that are particularly salient in relation to offender profiling.

These generic principles are extremely useful in reining in the worst excesses of improper advice, but there are several, more specific concerns and loopholes that are relevant within the profiling arena, where profiling is not a recognized subdiscipline of forensic psychology. However, the following APA statement gives the general overview of what is expected: 'In those emerging areas in which generally recognized standards for preparatory training do not yet exist, psychologists nevertheless [should] take reasonable steps to ensure the competence of their work and to protect clients/patients, students, supervisees, research participants, organizational clients, and others from harm.'

The utility of this statement lies in the direct specification of the range of individuals that the psychologist may have an influence over, specifically in relation to the term 'organizational clients'. Within a law enforcement environment, profilers and other advisers must have at the forefront of their mind that profiling is often ill-understood by the client group that has actioned the advice. This is through no fault of the police or other organizations who are often working at the very limits of their resources and who have little to no time to engage in reading round the subject or 'mugging up' on the current state of the literature. Instead there is a professional, ethical and moral obligation for the experts involved in the profiling arena to provide a variety of routes through which the role of their expertise is made clear in an effective range of formats. This includes publication (in a variety of outlets that are not necessarily embedded within arcane and difficult-to-access journals), attendance at conferences (that are not necessarily academic but, rather, are practitioner friendly), training packages delivered in-force (i.e. contributions to already-existing in-force training), clear and unambiguous statements during the interaction with the inquiry team, and clear and transparent reports that do not over-extend expectations and that clearly set out the parameters of how the advice might best be used.

Appendix 1: how a profiling report should be presented

Section: what should be included?	Why is it important?
A Introductory section	This information is important
1 *Title Page* Does the report have a title page with: The title of the report? The names and addresses of the authors? The contact details of the officer who has instructed the profiler? The date the report was provided?	For the inquiry team, as they must have a point of contact for the authors, particularly in case of the need for clarification of statements made in the report; For the courts, as they must be able, if they so wish, to scrutinize the authors' credentials, and to assess the impact of the report on the investigation with reference to the date on which it was provided.
2 *Executive summary* Has the profiler: Summarized the key points of the report? Made it clear that the executive summary must not be used as an alternative to the full report?	Summarizing the key points at the outset: Assists the inquiry team's interpretation of the main body of the report; Provides a useful aide-memoire for the team in the course of the investigation.
3 *Clarification* Has the profiler: Expressed a willingness to clarify any points in the report? Recommended that, after the provision of the report, the senior police officer and his or her team should meet the profiler to be verbally briefed on the report? Made it clear that he or she will carefully document all clarification and briefing discussions, and that he or she will then provide these as an addendum to the original report?	Misinterpretation of profiling advice may have significant legal and ethical repercussions. Thus, profilers should always make themselves available to clarify any points in the report, should help ensure that information is communicated accurately and should make sure that the rationale for any suggested lines of inquiry is clearly articulated. Finally, to avoid subsequent misinterpretation, to ensure the inquiry team works with a complete unambiguous profile and to ensure the courts can be made aware of all inter-actions and information exchanges between the profiler and the inquiry team all clarifications and briefing discussions should be documented and attached as an addendum to the original report.

Appendix 1 continued overleaf

Appendix 1 continued

Section: what should be included?	Why is it important?
4 *Instructions*	Reiterating the agreed parameters and purpose of the requested advice assists in ensuring:
Has the profiler set out the precise details of what he or she has been asked to do?	
It is often useful for the profiler to meet with officers about a case and agree a list of bullet points on which he or she feels he or she might be able to contribute.	That the inquiry team is clear about what to expect from the report; That, for the purpose of the courts, the motives for the request for advice can be clearly scrutinized.
5 *Caveats*	
Has the profiler clearly outlined the limitations of what are possible, precisely specifying:	Statistically driven profiles can only consider generalities, and correlations and frequencies are rarely clear cut.
How the report *can* be used?	Thus, reports cannot make definitive
How the report *cannot* be used?	statements beyond what is already
Which aspects of the current case may not follow statistical trends?	known about the case. Emphasising these limitations in the report will assist
The confidentiality of the report?	in ensuring that the inquiry team does not become too optimistic about the
Specifically, the profiler should include a caveat articulating the legal implications of how the report is used and the limitations of the statistical information.	profiling advice. Furthermore, the report should not be available to anyone beyond the inquiry team.
6 *Competence*	
Has the profiler provided details of the qualifications, background and case-specific training of all the authors of the report? Demonstrated that these are relevant to the case at hand?	It is crucial that profilers have the necessary competence and relevant expertise to provide investigative advice. Ethically, British and American psychologists are bound by their
Indicated previous key cases on which the authors have provided profiling reports, and illustrated the relevance of these to the case at hand?	respective professional bodies' codes of conduct to work within the boundaries of their competence. Furthermore, if the report is to be received in court, the profiler's qualifications must stand up to the rules on the admissibility of expert opinion evidence. Also, if the report is admitted, it is highly likely that both sides will draw out the background of the profiler(s) who provided it. Thus, the profiler's competence and expertise must also stand up to cross-examination within the courts (in the British and American adversarial systems).

Appendix 1 continued

Section: what should be included?	Why is it important?
7 *Feedback* Has the profiler: Requested that officers complete a copy of a feedback form attached to the report once the investigation and prosecution are complete? Considered gaining some feedback at the post-report debriefing?	Critical to any progression and development of good practice is detailed feedback. Feedback forms completed after an investigation and prosecution are a valuable tool for evaluating how useful the report was to the inquiry team. Such critical feedback may then enhance subsequent reports.
8 *Sources of inferences* Has the profiler: Described the material upon which many of the statements in the report are based? Indicated how transferable these data are to the case at hand (for example, distances travelled by offenders in the USA are much further than in the UK).	This information will assist the inquiry team's interpretation of the report and guide their use of the report, in terms of the limitations of the data – for example, by exercising caution when interpreting the relevance of data sets across different cultures.
9 *Case summary and evaluation* Has the profiler: Clearly set out those details of the case known to him or her at the time of writing? Listed the materials provided to him or her by the relevant police constabulary? Specified any assumptions on which the report is based?	This is to ensure that the court is clear about what information was available to defend a statement based on the knowledge that was available, thereby circumventing the allegation that the expert should have come to a different conclusion if only he or she had considered (for example) statements inconsistent with the other evidence.
B Main body of report In sections (1) to (5) below has the profiler: Made clear and unambiguous statements? Indicated which statements are opinions, based on experiential, tacit knowledge, and which are based on empirical research? Supported each empirically based statement with reference to relevant literature? Indicated, where there are multiple authors, what aspect of the advice has been generated by which author?	In order to avoid the risk of mis-interpretation, and the associated ethical and legal pitfalls, each of the profiler's statements must be clear and unambiguous. Making a clear distinction between experience-based opinion and well documented research enables both the inquiry team and the court to evaluate the certainty and strength of any given statement. The provision of references to relevant literature serves this purpose further with regard to empirically based statements, enabling the inquiry team and the court if they so wish, to refer to the original piece(s) of supporting

Appendix 1 continued overleaf

Section: what should be included?	Why is it important?
	research. Furthermore, where different authors have different types of expertise, indicating what aspect of the advice has been generated by which author will help the courts in deciding whether they require more than one of the experts in court to determine the validity of any given statement. This also presents a more honest and transparent process on the part of the expert.
1 *Behavioural analysis* Has the profiler provided a descriptive behavioural analysis of the case?	This should be based on assessment of crime scene information; information about the context of the crime (accessing relevant research literature and relevant databases); discussions with academics and practitioners, including forensic advisers. A descriptive behavioural analysis discusses the style of offending, including the possible aetiology and motivation, and can be used to assist in profiling and/or interviewing. In this section, the profiler will develop and clearly articulate working hypotheses about the inferred actions of the offender.
2 *Socio-demographic analysis* Has the profiler discussed the likely socio-demographic characteristics of the offender, including age, relationship to victim, location, marital status, employment status and previous criminal convictions? This analysis normally considers single behaviours, setting out the socio-demographic characteristics with which each is associated. Importantly, advice that links clusters of behaviours with clusters of characteristics should be treated cautiously as this method of profiling has been shown to be controversial.	This section provides the basis for many of the other elements of the report – recommending lines of inquiry, prioritizing suspects and areas for leaflet drops of DNA screening, linking offences and/or risk assessment. It is the section that one typically thinks of when considering profiling but really is only one of the pieces in a much larger picture.
3 *Offence linking* Where a series of offences is being considered, has the profiler specified the likelihood that the offences are linked?	Can assist in gathering further evidence/information. The Serious Crime Analysis Section at the NCPE provides this specific service.
4 *Geographic analysis* Has the profiler provided a geographical analysis of the offence(s)?	Often *the* most reliable and most robust form of analysis. Can be provided

Appendix 1 continued

Section: what should be included	Why is it important?
	through computational models or through some more basic analysis set against the known literature.
5 *Temporal analysis* Has the profiler provided a temporal analysis of the offence(s)?	It is important that the profiler understands the timeline. It is often very helpful for the inquiry team to provide a clear temporal summary of the offences.
6 *Investigative recommendations* Has the profiler suggested practical and achievable lines of inquiry that assist in the search for further relevant information and evidence? These may cover such issues as prioritization of suspects, leaflet drops, media strategy, strategy for interviewing suspects, team management, risk management, decision-making.	These should be based on what has been highlighted in the report so far and emerge as a logical extension of what has been generated about the possible characteristics of the offender. In many cases, the inquiry team may have already been considering these suggestions. Nevertheless, for the sake of completeness and with the potential for reinforcing previously considered strategies (or challenging strategies inconsistent with the report), they provide a useful addendum for the team.
C Concluding section 1 *References* Has the profiler provided a complete reference for each piece of literature cited in the report?	The provision of references to relevant literature assists the inquiry team and the court in evaluating the certainty and strength of empirically based statements, by enabling them, if they so wish, to refer to the original piece(s) of supporting research.
2 *Appendices* Where the profiler has included appendices, do these: Relate clearly to the content of the report? Assist interpretation and understanding of the content of the report?	Appendices should complement the report and assist with its interpretation. Where they do not serve this purpose, they may cloud the key issues and thus increase the risk of the report being misinterpreted or misused.
3 *Feedback form* Has the profiler: Included feedback forms for members of the inquiry team to complete post-investigation? Provided clear instructions as to how these should be completed? Indicated where these should be returned to? Specified how they will be used, including a statement regarding confidentiality?	As noted, detailed feedback is critical to the progression and development of good practice, and may enhance subsequent profiling reports. The provision of clear instructions for completion and return, along with a breakdown of how the information will be used and an assurance of anonymity, will help to maximize the number of forms filled in and sent to the profiler.

Appendix 2: codes of conduct salient to offender profiling

Codes of conduct (BPS and APA)	Offender profiling
Boundaries of competence 'recognise the boundaries of their own competence and not attempt to practise any form of psychology for which they do not have an appropriate preparation or, where applicable, specialist qualification' (BPS).	If a profiler does not have the expertise required to work on a particular case, he or she should not offer advice on it.
Limits of evidence 'value and have respect for all relevant evidence and the limits of such evidence when giving psychological advice or expressing a professional opinion' (BPS).	Profilers should not make claims that go beyond the limits of what is possible.
Clarification of roles 'Psychologists delivering services to or through organizations provide information ... about (1) the nature and objectives of the services, (2) the intended recipients, (3) which of the individuals are clients, (4) the relationship the psychologist will have with each person and the organization, (5) the probable uses of services provided and information obtained, (6) who will have access to the information, and (7) limits of confidentiality' (APA).	When preparing a report, profilers should set out exactly what they have been asked to do, by whom, and for what purpose. They should also specify how the report can be used, and list those who are permitted to access it.
Benefit and avoidance of harm 'shall hold the interest and welfare of those in receipt of their services to be paramount at all times ... refrain from improper conduct in their work as psychologists that would be likely to be detrimental to the interests of recipients of their services' (BPS).	Profilers should avoid making unclear and unsupported claims, since these will not be of benefit to/in the interests of the inquiry team and may cause substantial harm to the defendant, complainant or victims, inquiry team or the public.
Record keeping and confidentiality 'maintain adequate records, but they shall take all reasonable steps to preserve the confidentiality of information acquired through their professional practice or research and to protect the privacy of individuals or organisations about whom information is collected or held' (BPS).	Profilers should document all discussions/clarifications with the Senior Investigating Officer, inquiry team and others involved with the investigation. They should also impress on the inquiry team the importance of the confidentiality of the report.
Legal issues When assuming forensic roles, psychologists should be/become 'reasonably familiar	This may be interpreted to mean that profilers should have a basic knowledge of fundamental principles governing the

Codes of conduct (BPS and APA)	Offender profiling
with the judicial or administrative rules governing their roles' (APA).	reception of profiling evidence in the courts.
Professional reputation and public confidence 'In all their work psychologists shall conduct themselves in a manner that does not bring into disrepute the discipline and the profession of psychology' (BPS). Furthermore, psychologists should not, through their conduct, 'inappropriately undermine public confidence in their ability or that of other psychologists and members of other professions to carry out their professional duties' (BPS).	Profilers should not practise offender profiling in such a way as to bring about these effects. (The media and public response to the collapse of Colin Stagg's trial illustrates how improper profiling can undermine public confidence in both psychology and law enforcement, and bring the professions into disrepute.)

Notes

1 There was speculation at the time that the Ripper might have had anatomical knowledge.
2 For the interested reader, Murray's profile can be viewed online at www.lawschool. cornell.edu/library/donovan/hitler.
3 The codes can be viewed in full at http://www.bps.org.uk/the-society/ethics-rules-charter-code-of-conduct/code-of-conduct/code-of-conduct_home.cfm; http://www.apa.org/ethics/code2002.html.

References

Adhami, E. and Browne, D.P. (1996) *Major Crime Enquiries: Improving Expert Support for Detectives. Police Research Group Special Interest Series Paper* 9. London: Home Office.

Alison, L.J. (2005) 'From trait based profiling to psychological contributions to apprehension methods', in L. Alison (ed.) *The Forensic Psychologists Casebook: Psychological Profiling and Criminal Investigation.* Cullompton: Willan Publishing.

Alison, L.J. and Ogan, J. (2006) 'Offender Profiling', in McNulty, D. and Burnette, M. (eds) *Sex and Sexuality Vol. 3. Sexual Deviation and Sexual Offences.* Westpoint, CT: Praeger Publishing.

Alison, L.J., Smith, M.D., Eastman, O. and Rainbow, L. (2003) 'Toulmin's philosophy of argument and its relevance to offender profiling', *Psychology, Crime and Law,* 9: 173–83.

Alison, L.J., Smith, M.D. and Morgan, K. (2003) 'Interpreting the accuracy of offender profiles', *Psychology, Crime and Law,* 9: 185–95.

Ault, R. and Reese, J. (1980) 'A psychological assessment of crime profiling', *FBI Enforcement Bulletin,* 49.

Blau, T. (1994) 'Psychological profiling', in T. Blau (ed.) *Psychological Services for Law Enforcement.* New York, NY: Wiley.

Britton, P. (1997) *The Jigsaw Man*. London: Bantam Press.

Brussel, J. (1968) *Casebook of a Crime Psychiatrist*. New York: Bernard Geis Associates.

Burgess, J., Douglas, J. and Ressler, R. (1985) 'Classifying sexual homicide crime scenes', *FBI Law Enforcement Bulletin*, 54: 12–17.

Canter, D. and Alison, L.J. (1999) *Profiling in Policy and Practice*. Dartmouth: Ashgate.

Canter, D., Alison, L.J., Alison, E. and Wentink, N. (2004) 'The organized/disorganized typologies of serial murder: myth or model?', *Psychology, Public Policy and Law*, 10: 7–36.

Davies, A., Wittebrood, K. and Jackson, J.L. (1998) *Predicting the Criminal Record of a Stranger Rapist. Special Interest Series Paper* 12. London: Home Office, Policing and Reducing Crime Unit.

Douglas, J.E., Burgess, A.W., Burgess, A.G. and Ressler, R.K. (1992) *Crime Classification Manual: A Standard System for Investigating and Classifying Violent Crime*. New York, NY: Simon & Schuster.

Douglas, J. and Olshaker, M. (1997) *Mindhunter: Inside the FBI Elite Serial Crime Unit*. London: Mandarin Paperbacks.

Forer, B. (1949) 'The fallacy of personal validation: a classroom demonstration of gullibility', *Journal of Abnormal and Social Psychology*, 44: 118–23.

Gudjonsson, G. and Copson, G. (1997) 'The role of the expert in criminal investigation', in J. Jackson and D. Bekerian (eds) *Offender Profiling: Theory, Research and Practice*. Chichester: Wiley.

House, J.C. (1997) 'Towards a practical application of offender profiling: the RNC's criminal suspect prioritization system', in J.L. Jackson and D.A. Bekerian (eds) *Offender Profiling: Theory, Research and Practice*. Chichester: Wiley.

Langer, W. (1972) *The Mind of Adolf Hitler*. New York, NY: Basic Books.

Mokros, A. and Alison, L. (2002) 'Is profiling possible? Testing the predicted homology of crime scene actions and background characteristics in a sample of rapists', *Legal and Criminological Psychology*, 7: 25–43.

Ormerod, D. (1999) 'Criminal profiling: trial by judge and jury, not criminal psychologist', in D.V. Canter and L.J. Alison (eds) *Profiling in Policy and Practice*. Aldershot: Ashgate.

Ormerod, D. and Sturman, J. (2005) 'Working with the courts: advice for expert witnesses', in L. Alison (ed.) *The Forensic Psychologists Casebook: Psychological Profiling and Criminal Investigation*. Cullompton: Willan Publishing.

Pinizzotto, A. and Finzel, N. (1990) 'Criminal personality profiling: an outcome and process study', *Law and Human Behaviour*, 14: 215–33.

Ressler, R., Burgess, A., Douglas, J., Hartman, C. and D'Agostino, R. (1986) 'Murderers who rape and mutilate', *Journal of Interpersonal Violence*, 1: 273–87.

Salfati, G. and Bateman, A. (2005) 'Serial homicide: an investigation of behavioural consistency', *Journal of Investigative Psychology and Offender Profiling*, 2: 121–44.

Toulmin, S. (1958) *The Uses of Argument*. Cambridge: Cambridge University Press.

Chapter 21

Profiling places: geodemographics and GIS

David Ashby and Max Craglia

Geographic information systems: introduction

The increasing importance of geographical location as a way to analyse social and environmental phenomena stems, on the one hand, from advances in technology and the availability of digital data linked to a specific place and, on the other, by the recognition that society is becoming ever more complex and that multiple analytical perspectives are needed to make sense of it, to identify possible action, to target resources and to monitor outcomes. The increased use of geographic information systems (GIS) – that is, of computerized systems specifically designed to analyse geographic data – is clearly an important component of this trend, and for this reason we devote much of this chapter to this technology and its applications for crime analysis. Nevertheless, it is also important to highlight the broader picture in order to understand future directions, to exploit opportunities and to reduce possible threats. As an example, the rapid development of companies providing location-based services, such as maps (e.g. www.multimap.com), routing (e.g. www.viamichelin.com), neighbourhood information (www. upmystreet.com) and, more recently, Google Earth, which provides high-definition satellite imagery and 3D urban models for many urban areas around the world (http://earth.google.com) (see Figure 21.1), is witness to the popularization of geography as a way to view the world and to publish, search and access information. Above all, these services point to a paradigmatic shift from computer systems used by specialists in the close bounds of their offices to web-based services enabling information access, analysis and use by the public at large, anytime, anywhere. This offers many opportunities but also raises many organizational, technical, ethical, security and educational challenges, as we discuss in this chapter.

Definitions

Prior to any detailed discussion of the various aspects of criminal investigation linked to GIS and related issues, it is worth clarifying the definition of

Figure 21.1. High-resolution imagery from Google Earth of the Home Office and New Scotland Yard, London
Source: http://earth.google.com

some key terms, to avoid any potential confusion. The term 'geographic information' (GI), or 'geospatial information', refers to any information record that has a reference to the earth's surface or near-surface. It does, therefore, include information on underground networks and geological features as much as objects and features on the earth's surface, such as land parcels, buildings, rivers, transport networks, and urban and rural settlements. The term 'spatial information' or 'spatial data' is broader in the sense that it applies also to non-geographic spaces such as the cosmos, the space of the human body and the internal design of buildings.

The terms 'data' and 'information' are often used as synonyms, but they are not. 'Data' refers to raw facts or observed values in numbers, text or other symbols. 'Information' implies the application of knowledge to organize, select and interpret the data to make sense of them. Information is therefore derived, and requires some prior knowledge and expertise acquired through education, training and experience. For this reason, information is often expensive to obtain – more so than raw data. The elaboration, synthesis and abstraction of information contribute to the further development of knowledge. Although this may appear little more than an academic argument, it does have important implications for the dissemination and sharing of resources, especially in contemporary society that has such wide access to data over the Internet. It is often not enough to share data; it is also necessary to share the context that enables us to make sense of the data and to derive the information required. Moreover, the process of data gathering, information acquisition and knowledge development is not linear. Hence it is not the case that 1,000 times more data deliver 1,000 times more information and even less 1,000 times more knowledge. We return to this issue in the context of data infrastructures.

GIS include the combination of hardware, software, people, skills and organizational processes necessary to handle GI, including data collection, display, integration, analysis, use, dissemination and output. We deliberately take a broad definition of GIS to include more than just hardware and software because the major challenges and costs of introducing GIS into an organization are related to data acquisition and integration, staffing with the right skills, workflow organization and so on, rather than the technology *per se*. (See Longley *et al.* 2005 for a detailed discussion of GIS and science, which includes a range of applications relevant to crime, policing and criminal investigation.)

The evolution of GIS from system to infrastructure

The development of GIS goes back some 40 years to the system set up for the Canadian Department of Agriculture in the early 1960s to manage the forest inventory and associated survey data. From then on, we can divide the development of GIS into three main periods.

The early years
During the 1960s–1980s, many of the concepts of GIS were put in place, including the methodologies for data analysis. These methodologies were heavily influenced by geographers and urban planners seeking to exploit computers to develop comprehensive land-use and transportation models. Such models focused on methods rather than the graphical quality of the output, which was typically via line printers (where patterns were made out of lines of 0 and X). Mapping agencies, on the other hand, concentrated on automating map production, particularly on the creation of maps that had the same quality as traditional paper maps. The convergence of these two streams of development led, in the 1980s, to the development of commercial GIS software, which in many ways already had most of today's characteristics (for participants' accounts of this early period, see, for example, Tomlinson 1988; Antenucci and Brown 1989). In spite of these

major developments, the diffusion of GIS was hampered by the high costs of the computing equipment, which still made it the reserve of large public-sector organizations and research institutions. Moreover, most of the data had to be entered manually by digitizing paper maps, which increased costs significantly.

GIS and the personal computer
During the late 1980s and the 1990s, the emergence of cheap personal computers and the increasing availability of digital data ready for use (such as the TIGER files in the USA by the Census Bureau) caused a major change in the employment of GIS by central and local government and the private sector. For example, a comprehensive survey of all 514 local authorities in Britain in 1991 showed that the overall take-up of GIS was 16 per cent, and this by the larger authorities only (Campbell and Masser 1991). By the end of the decade, however, the situation had changed dramatically, with all but a few small local authorities having one or more GIS. The take-up of the technology was also significant in health authorities, emergency services and other public sector organizations. Similar patterns were reported by studies in the USA (e.g. French and Wiggins 1989) and continental Europe (e.g. Masser and Craglia 1996).

An order of magnitude of the overall growth of the market for GIS and related services was provided by Daratech, which estimated the overall global market revenue at US$ 1.6 billion in 2003 as against an estimated figure of US$ 216 million in 1987 (see Probert and Wolfkamp 2004). This growth had been largely fuelled by the much increased availability of digital geographic data worldwide. In the UK, for example, the completion in 1995 of the national digital topographic database by the Ordnance Survey (OS) led to the marketing of topographic data to major customers exclusively in digital form, and to the formation of a series of service-level agreements with local government, the utilities, the higher education sector and central government, which enabled users to have free access to OS data. From here, it was only a matter of time before the majority of users started visualizing their own data to use in their decision-making.

GIS and the Internet
The third 'era' of GIS is the current one. The Internet has been a major driver for change, allowing the sharing of information in general, and of geographic information in particular, to an unprecedented degree. As an example, Nielsen-Netrating (http://www.nielsen-netratings.com), a leading provider of market intelligence on the Internet, have shown that online map websites are one of the fastest-growing Internet sectors in Europe, supporting a host of industries (particularly leisure and travel). The recent arrival of online mapping services by leading rival Internet companies (see http://maps.google.com; http://virtualearth.msn.com; http://maps.yahoo.net) pays testament to this. With the increased ability to share information came the recognition that transferring data among different proprietary GIS systems was, at best, difficult and resulted in a loss of information due to incompatible formats and standards. As a result many major industrial players, government

agencies and research institutions in the USA, Europe and beyond have come together in the Open Geospatial Consortium, the mission of which is 'to lead the global development, promotion and harmonization of open standards and architectures that enable the integration of geospatial data and services into user applications and advance the formation of related market opportunities' (www.opengeospatial.org). In practical terms, this means that the industry and users collaborate to define open standards that enable not only the sharing of data among different systems but also the development of new web-based services that, to a large extent, perform some of the basic GIS functions without requiring the users to have a GIS on their desktop. A related area of development is 'interoperability' – i.e. 'the capability to communicate, execute programs, or transfer data among various functional units in a manner that requires the user to have little or no knowledge of the unique characteristics of those units' (ISO 2005). A great deal of work is being done in this area in the USA and Europe to address the complexity of sharing not just data but information which, as argued earlier, requires a much deeper understanding of the structure and meaning of data (i.e. its semantics) (see, for example, Kuhn 2003). Such concepts and research are of direct relevance to both the local and the international partnership work necessary in criminal investigation.

In parallel with these developments, there have been in recent years a growth in the use of the Internet calls, and to reuse public sector information (PSI) (GI in particular). In Europe, the 'Information Society' represents the policies and initiatives that, since the early 1990s, have sought to increase competition, eliminate monopolies and stimulate both the demand and supply of service and content providers, the overall aim being to encourage the market, increase job opportunities and competitiveness, and improve governance (Craglia and Blakemore 2004). Hence many European countries have adopted freedom of information and data-protection legislation and, from 1 July 2005, all EU countries had to adopt legislation supporting the reuse and commercial exploitation of PSI following a European Directive of 2003 (CEC 2003). GI is an important component of PSI, contributing over half its economic value (CEC 2000). Moreover, GI underpins policy formulation, monitoring and evaluation at all level of government and in all those policy areas in which spatially targeted intervention is important (such as housing, crime prevention, health and environmental protection). For this reason most governments in the world have initiated the development of spatial data infrastructures (SDIs) – frameworks of policies, institutional arrangements, technologies, data and people that enable the sharing and effective use of GI. From an investigator's view point, such developments signal a paradigm shift: information is not only shared across different departments but also across different agencies and jurisdictions in an effort to support intelligence gathering and evaluation.

Despite these positive developments, Europe remains characterized by the very variable quality and extent of its data coverage; by missing documentation so that it is difficult to know what already exists, who has it and what the conditions for access are; by incompatible spatial data sets and services; by different standards; and by barriers to data sharing and reuse. As far as spatial information is concerned, the European goal of the free movement of people, goods and services is still far from being a reality. With this in mind, in 2001 the European Commission launched an initiative to develop an SDI in Europe focused, in the first instance, on environmental policy – INSPIRE (The INfrastructure for SPatial InfoRmation in Europe) http://www.ec-gis.org/inspire). A directive was adopted in 2004 that is expected to be approved by the European Parliament and Council. INSPIRE is articulated around the following agreed principles:

- Data should be collected once and maintained at a level where this can be done most effectively.
- Spatial data from different sources should be combined seamlessly so that it can be shared between many users and applications.
- Spatial data should be collected at one level of government and shared between all levels.
- Spatial data needed for good governance should be available under conditions that do not restrict their extensive use.
- It should be a relatively straightforward matter to establish which spatial data are available, to evaluate their fitness for purpose and to discuss which conditions apply for their use.

In practice, INSPIRE will build upon existing SDIs established and operated by member states. Its added value lies in establishing a common framework with respect to the following:

- Harmonized spatial data specifications.
- The increased availability and searchability of meta-data (i.e. of the documentation of existing resources, be they data or services).
- Network services to facilitate data discovery, viewing, downloading, transformation and an ability to invoke additional services.
- Agreed measures facilitating the sharing and reuse of spatial data and services between public authorities that prevent the distortion of competition.
- Measures to co-ordinate the implementation and development of the infrastructure and to monitor its performance.

The primary target of INSPIRE is public administrations across Europe. As the infrastructure develops, it is envisaged that further policy areas will be addressed, including security (which is already one of the pillars of common European policy) and Global Monitoring for Environment and Security (www.gmes.info), the aim of which is to facilitate, primarily, public bodies' access to data from satellite and related services. This will, in turn, link to GALILEO, a programme that involves the launch of 30 satellites to provide accurate positioning for civilian use, thus complementing the Global Positioning System managed by the USA. Identified key applications include transport (vehicle location, route searching, speed control, guidance systems, etc.), social services (e.g. aid for the disabled or elderly), the justice system and customs services (location of suspects, border controls), public works (GIS) and search and rescue systems and leisure (direction finding at sea or in the mountains, etc.).

These developments in GIS offer opportunities to address many of the communication failures that have come to light in recent years, particularly in social services, health authorities, and the police (e.g. Lord Laming's inquiry into the death of Victoria Climbie). Information sharing, however, is not just a matter of technology: it requires clear policies on information acquisition, storing, managing and access, as highlighted, for example, by the Bichard Inquiry into the Soham murders (http://www.bichardinquiry. org.uk). Given the extent to which the locations of events, individuals or houses are crucial to information searching, integration and analysis, it is clear that new information systems and practices should include GIS.

Crime mapping

The importance of GIS to crime analysis and the strategic and tactical deployment of forces has been increasingly recognized in both the USA and the UK. This was forcefully endorsed by former New York Mayor, Rudolph Giuliani, during his visit to London in February 2002:

> Senior police officers are keen to learn from the New York experience while Mr Giuliani visits London. In the eight years he was mayor of New York crime plunged. The success was credited to CompStat, the computerised system which keeps track of week-by-week crime figures for each precinct, the basic division of the city's police department. Each week's figures are available to the public within a week, meaning locals can track crime trends. (*Guardian* 14 February 2002).

CompStat is, of course, only part of a wider strategy of crime reduction, but it makes the point that the regular analysis of crime for small geographical areas is crucial for the effective deployment of resources, for monitoring and evaluating impacts, for public accountability and for sharing intelligence. The increased emphasis by successive Home Secretaries in the UK on increasing detection rates by concentrating police resources into selected hotspot areas supports this general notion. It is also worth noting that communicating crime information and trends to the public is an important component of a strategy that aims to involve communities more in maintaining social order. This is reflected by the increasing focus on public accountability and the neighbourhood/reassurance policing agendas in the UK.

The ability to visualize and analyse data geographically is at the heart of GIS. These types of systems are already widely used in the UK, but there are significant variations among police forces in the extent and purpose of their use. There are, therefore, opportunities for using GIS more and better, with a stronger integration into forces' crime reduction strategies and as part of the wider Crime and Disorder Partnerships.

The importance given to GIS in the USA for crime analysis was most clearly demonstrated by the establishment by the National Institute of Justice in 1997 of the Mapping and Analysis for Public Safety (MAPS) programme (http://www.ojp.usdoj.gov/nij/maps/index.html), formerly known as the

Crime Mapping Research Center. The MAPS programme supports research into spatial aspects of crime, spatial data analysis, and mapping and analysis for evaluating programmes and policy, as well as the development of mapping, data-sharing, and spatial analysis tools. MAPS also sponsors conferences and workshops and publish reports. The International Crime Mapping Research Conference has now held its eighth annual event and it provides an important forum for researchers and practitioners to meet and develop the field. This emerging interdisciplinary community is also supported by a mapping listserve (http://www.ojp.usdoj.gov/nij/maps/listserv.html) to share information and practical advice. This is particularly useful as it ensures that each criminal justice agency can learn from the best practice, and indeed the mistakes, of others.

Surveys undertaken in the late 1990s (Crime Mapping Research Center 1999; Police Foundation 2000), supplemented by one undertaken at the University of Sheffield in 2001 through web searches and personal contact via the listserve indicate that, in the USA, ESRI products and MapInfo software are the more commonly used by police departments.

The significant point here, therefore, is the extent to which commercial off-the-shelf software is the choice of US forces rather than bespoke systems. Using such mainstream software enables easier data transfer between systems and access to help from an established user community – a community that is much larger than just that of law enforcement agencies. Another important development in the USA is the extent to which police departments are increasingly publishing local-level crime statistics on the Web (see Figure 21.2).

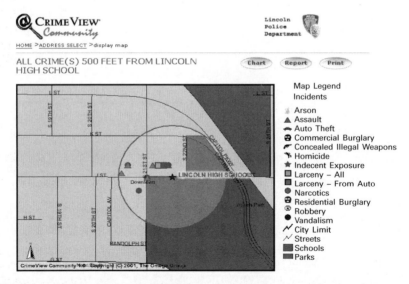

NOTE: Due to both stacked incidents (those located at the same address) and some incidencts of which did not geocode, the number of incidents identified in the table may not be fully reflected in the map above. Data displayed randomly to 100 Block.

Figure 21.2 Local-level crime data provided on a weekly basis by Lincoln Police Department, Nebraska.
Source: http://ims.lincoln.ne.gov/CrimeViewCommunity/wizard.asp

The situation in the UK is not dissimilar to the USA in the sense that there has been an increasing awareness of the importance of GIS to support crime analysis, as is shown by the growing participation at the annual National Mapping Conference organized by UCL's Jill Dando Institute of Crime Science (http://www.jdi.ucl.ac.uk). The recent focus on the importance of crime mapping has also been highlighted by central government in their publication of crime-mapping guidance for practitioners (PSU 2005). The starting point for most forces has been the use of GIS to visualize calls in the 999 incidence room – i.e. for command and control functions – while data analysts are familiar with using large and complex databases without spatial analysis capabilities. This is starting to change, however, and there are more and more calls to train analysts to work with spatial data and GIS. Compared with the USA, however, the publishing of crime data on the Web is still rare.

Visualizing and exploring the data[1]

In any form of spatial analysis, the fist step is to visualize the data (for example in the form of pin-point mapping). Before this can be achieved, however, the data must be properly referenced to location (georeferenced) at the point of recording the event. Although this may sound a purely technical matter, it is in fact an organizational one: it must become routine to report the location of crime events as accurately as possible and against a standard gazetteer of locations. Not all forces have adopted such practice, so it may therefore be necessary not only to encourage this practice but also to assign co-ordinates at past crime data locations to provide the spatial context for analysis. Mapping data can act as a first check on the quality of the reporting, and can alert the user to possible misinterpretations in subsequent analysis. As an example, while burglary data are often reported with an accurate location, car theft may not – it may be assigned to arbitrary street segments, thus resulting in false hotspots. Visualizing the data is also helpful as it allows the analyst to make a hypothesis about the apparent distribution of the data. However, while pin-point mapping has much value at the neighbourhood level and for operational policing, attempting to map large areas (at, say, city levels) has little value; such maps become crowded and often reflect little more than underlying population trends and land use. It is therefore necessary to aggregate the data at some user-defined area level (police beat, census area, Crime and Disorder Reduction Partnership, police force) and to define ratios (e.g. number of offenders per population) or rates (e.g. observed number of offenders/expected number of offenders, the latter perhaps being defined as the number of residents in the area multiplied by the city, or the region-wide average number of offenders). For example, Figure 21.3 shows the ratios and rates for offenders in South Yorkshire over the period 1998–2003. The regional average rate is 100, so less than 100 is less than expected and a rate of 200 would indicate twice the expected rate.

Specialized products are freely available (e.g. GeoDa: https://geoda.uiuc.edu) that combine mapping and statistical software, thus allowing the user to explore the observed data distributions. For example, the use of a boxplot

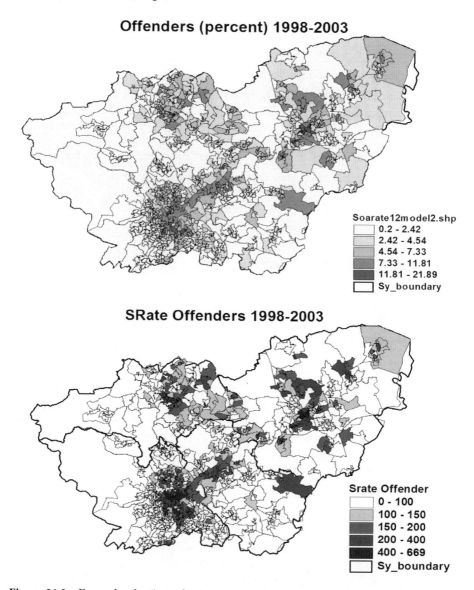

Figure 21.3 Example of ratio and rates at super-output area

helps to identify statistical outliers, while the map spatially locates these
data in the study area (see Figure 21.4). While aggregation over user-defined
areas is useful, particularly to retrieve relevant denominators for the ratios,
the larger the unit of analysis (e.g. wards, basic command units, super output
areas – see the section 'Classifying neighbourhoods' below), the more the
analysis smoothes the details, resulting in maps where the variations within
an area might be greater than between areas. In addition, administrative and
census boundaries have the tendency to become increasingly large as one
moves from the central areas to those more sparsely populated. As a result,

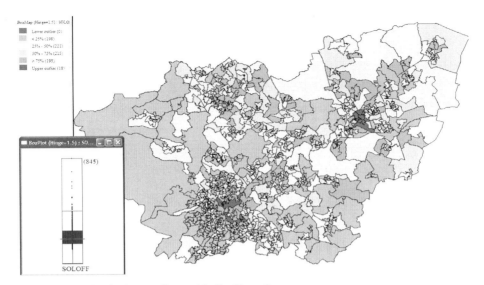

Figure 21.4   Analysing outliers with GeoDa software

such maps tend to deceive because they make the larger areas stand out, even though there are very few people living in them.

One way to address this is to use regular grids. In the UK, Royal Mail post codes (with a grid reference to the nearest 100 m) offer an excellent opportunity to build a grid of 100 × 100 m in which each cell has the true number of residential and non-residential delivery points. From this you can estimate fairly accurately the resident population. This layer not only allows the development of maps that more accurately reflect the distribution of the underlying population but also has the major advantage of being updated every quarter by the Royal Mail, rather than every ten years, as is the case with the census. Figure 21.5 shows the difference between displaying the offender rate by super output area and displaying the same data in a 1-hectare grid.

Strategic mapping: detecting change

GIS can support crime analysis and resource deployment at various levels: operational (i.e. for short-term decisions); tactical (over the medium term); and strategic (over the longer term). Using a 1-hectare grid, Figure 21.6 shows the ratio of burglaries to dwellings for the period 1998–2000. Those areas that have seen a significant increase (hotspots) or significant decrease (cold spots) over the three-year period have been identified.

Temporal analysis

Police records attach a start and an end time to each crime event. This is to highlight the uncertainty that exists over exactly when an offence occurred. Most current analytical methods tend to employ some measure of the middle point between the start and end times. A more accurate method – termed

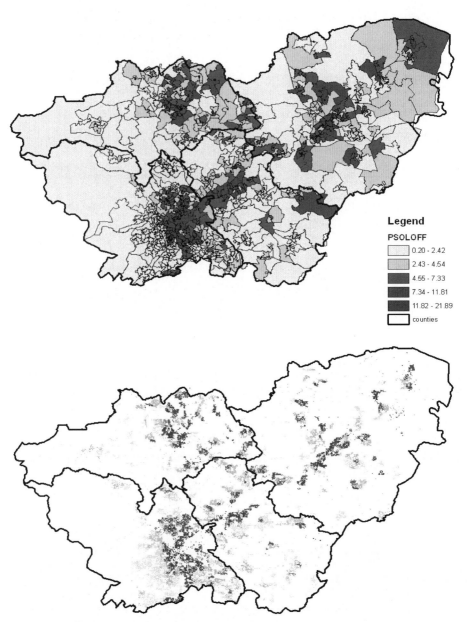

Figure 21.5 Different representations of the same data, by super output and 1-hectare grid

'aoristic search' – considers that the offence might have occurred at any point between the start and end times. It does this by applying some form of probabilistic function to the entire time range (see Ratcliffe and McCullagh 1998 for further details). The greater the uncertainty about the exact time, the more aoristic analysis becomes desirable. Software developed at the University of Sheffield – Crime Map Analysis (CMA) – with funding from

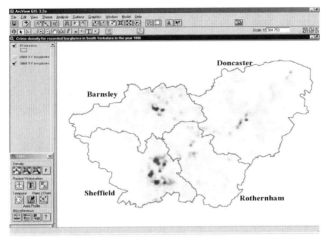

Burglaries in 1998

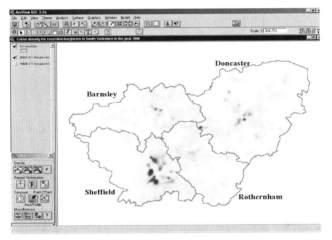

Burglaries in 2000

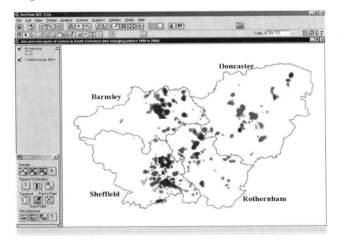

Summary review; area of significant increase or decrease 1998–2000

Figure 21.6 Hot and cold spots for burglaries, South Yorkshire, 1998–2000

529

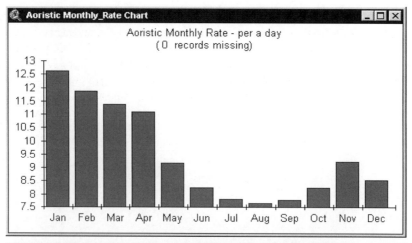

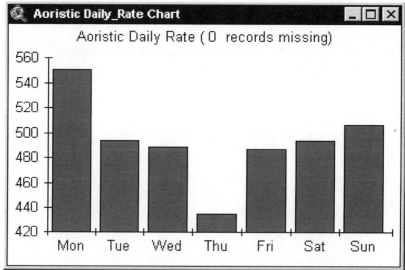

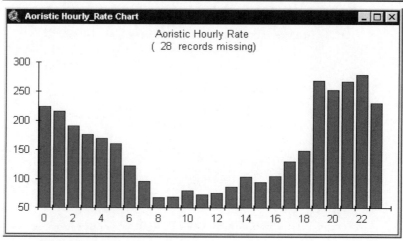

Figure 21.7   An example of aoristic temporal analysis

the Home Office, uses aoristic analysis to assess the probability of a crime occurring at a particular point in time. For example, a crime that may have occurred on Monday or Tuesday (e.g. between 8 pm on Monday and 4 am on Tuesday) would have a probability of 0.5 assigned to both Monday and Tuesday. However, if the crime occurred between 10 pm on Monday and 4 am on Tuesday, in the absence of any further relevant information, we might assume that it was twice as likely to have occurred on Tuesday and, hence, a probability of 0.66 is allocated to Tuesday and 0.33 to Monday. This function allows the user to calculate and graph the number of crimes that occurred each month, day of the week or hour (see Figure 21.7), in a way that better reflects the uncertainty associated with the data than the 'middle-point' approach.

Repeat victimization

According to Farrell and Pease (1993), 10 per cent of the victims of crime account for up to 40 per cent of the crimes in a given year. However, defining repeat cases is notoriously difficult. As an example of the value of GIS, the CMA software uses two different functions to identify repeats: spatially or textually defined. When performing a search for spatial repeats, the program examines a set of points to find those with the same geo-coordinates. This detects repeats at the same place. The user can search for points that are in close proximity to others (radius) or can search for 'clusters' where numerous offences have been committed in a limited geographical space (for example, within 50 or 100 m of the identified location) (see Figure 21.8). To investigate

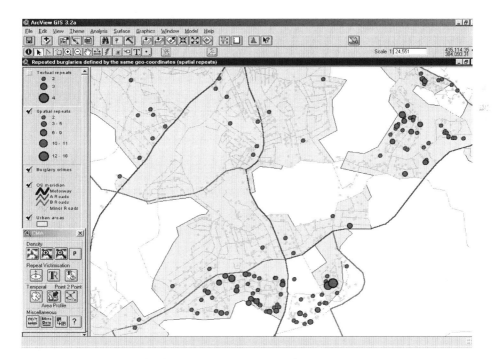

Figure 21.8   An example of repeat victimization analysis

repeats for the same person (such as a vehicle owner) or entity (such as a vehicle registration), a textual repeat finder can be employed that searches for identical text strings within a field. This is, of course, a standard facility in any database package, but the advantage of this method in a GIS package is that the outcome is immediately localized on a map. This function can be extended to explore the spatial patterns of offences based, for example, on a description of the offender. This would be of particular value in a priority programme, such as the recent UK initiative to reduce street crime.

Origin–destination analysis

This function is useful for the analysis of travel to crime or vehicle thefts. It identifies the most likely direction of travel by dropping points along a hypothetical line from an origin (for example, where a vehicle was stolen) to a destination (where the vehicle was abandoned), thereby 'connecting' the two sites. CMA then measures the distance between the pairs of points and constructs a surface density of the lines, as illustrated in Figure 21.9. The resulting map does not show where people have travelled but simply represents the orientation they took. In the example in Figure 21.9 we are not certain which road the stolen cars were predominantly driven along, but we can see that the majority of thieves who stole cars from the town of Stocksbridge (where the darker colour is) travelled to Sheffield, in a south-easterly direction. This may help in deciding the more probable route taken and where to locate Automatic Number Plate Recognition equipment.

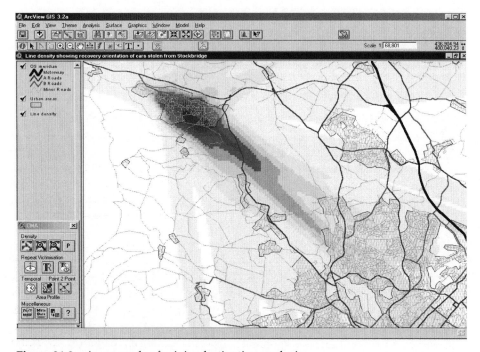

Figure 21.9 An example of origin–destination analysis

Multi-agency analysis

As mentioned earlier in this chapter, a great deal of intelligence can be gathered from the analysis of data collected by different agencies. For example, a project undertaken at the University of Sheffield in 2000 used data from a number of different sources to support the preparation of a three-year plan for young children's services. This project identified those areas in Sheffield with the greatest number of children in need (Craglia and Signoretta 2002). The research was linked to a Home Office project on how to define, in an objective way, high-impact areas – i.e. difficult-to-police areas characterized by a large number of offenders, intimidation of residents and a high incidence of violent and drug-related crime (Craglia *et al.* 2001). The research demonstrated that, in some instances, the high-impact areas identified were also those with the highest number of children at risk. Unfortunately, neither the police nor the children's services appeared to be aware of each other's information, and it was only the informal arrangements made with the university that enabled the sharing of this information. In this example it was not the robustness of the analysis that mattered but the opportunity created by GIS to think spatially and to connect different organizations serving the same areas and people. This requires organizational and collaborative thinking so that each agency's own data or analysis can be linked with those of other agencies. This is particularly important in the profiling of neighbourhoods.

Profiling social context

From an investigator's perspective, the significance of social context may not be immediately apparent. However, geographic profiling (of which social context may be a constituent part) has now become commonplace in high-profile crimes – for example, to help locate serial killers, rapists, arsonists, etc. – and is increasingly employed in volume crime investigations. Geographic profiling uses the geographic locations of a known series of crimes to help identify the most likely area where the perpetrator of those crimes lives (Rossmo 2000). Geographic profiling histories, methodologies, examples and software products are now widely available.[2]

This section focuses on one aspect of geographic profiling – the assessment, examination and comparison of neighbourhood traits. Such analyses may provide information about the level and nature of the support an investigator may receive in different neighbourhoods, and about how best to engage with particular communities.

Social profiling has attracted interest for over a century; indeed, Charles Booth's celebrated *Maps Descriptive of London Poverty* (1898–9) are often cited as the foundation of contemporary neighbourhood classifications (e.g. Harris *et al.* 2005). In Booth's London poverty maps, each street was coloured to indicate the income and social class of its inhabitants (see http://booth.lse.ac.uk/). Significantly, Booth's 'lowest class' contains an explicit reference to criminality (see Table 21.1) which suggests that the relevance to crime

Table 21.1 Booth's seven classes

Black	Lowest class. Vicious, semi-criminal
Dark blue	Very poor, casual. Chronic want
Light blue	Poor, 18s. to 21s. a week for a moderate family
Purple	Mixed. Some comfortable, others poor
Pink	Fairly comfortable. Good ordinary earnings
Red	Middle class. Well-to-do
Yellow	Upper-middle and Upper classes. Wealthy

and policing of mapping and analysing neighbourhoods and individual residences has long been recognized. Spatial studies of crime have been undertaken for nearly two hundred years (Chainey and Ratcliffe 2005), and environmental criminology (the study of criminal activity, victimization and how the contributing factors of space and place may influence offenders, victims and crime patterns) is admirably summarized elsewhere (see Bottoms and Wiles 2002). Many of the spatial theories of crime that provide the foundation for crime mapping and GIS are discussed by Chainey and Ratcliffe (2005). Suffice to say here that the spatial analysis of criminal activity has developed significantly in recent decades and now supports a large and growing community of crime analysts.

Classifying neighbourhoods

Before discussing those classification tools and data sets that enable the user to profile social context, it may be helpful to outline the development of urban studies research. Booth's study is often cited as one of the principal antecedents to much of the pioneering research of the 'Chicago School' (see, e.g., Pfautz 1967). In the 1920s, sociologists at the University of Chicago tried to establish general principles about the internal spatial and social structure of cities (Harris et al. 2005: 37). Burgess's concentric rings model of the city (1925) remains one of the most enduring outputs of the Chicago School. Subsequently, Shaw and McKay (1942) endeavoured to map juvenile delinquency in the city relative to Burgess's zonal model. Thus the study of the relationship between the spatial distribution of criminal activity and generalizable aspects of social structure was truly founded. Shaw and McKay's research on juvenile delinquency is still read today, and their contribution to environmental criminology, in the form of social disorganization theory, remains the subject of much debate (see Bottoms and Wiles 2002).

The Chicago School, therefore, has undoubtedly had a profound influence on urban studies research, which progressed through social area analysis and factorial ecology (see Longley 2004 for further detail) to those areal analyses and classifications in use today. The remainder of this section of the chapter outlines these analyses and classifications from a UK perspective, although equivalent data sources and classifications exist for other countries.

The Census of Population is a valuable resource for small area analyses. It is the most comprehensive survey of the UK population targeting all people from all households and achieving some 98 per cent coverage in 2001. In the 2001 census, new output areas were introduced. The UK was divided into 175,434 such areas, each one comprising approximately 125 households. These areas were constructed so that each one had basically the same social structure (Rees *et al.* 2002). These Output Areas therefore provide the most comprehensive snapshot available of small area variations in the UK population. Furthermore, access to the main results of the census is free and unrestricted.

The deprivation indices produced by the Office of the Deputy Prime Minister include a 2004 Index of Multiple Deprivation. This contains seven categories of deprivation: income; employment; health and disability; education, skills and training; barriers to housing and services; living environment; and, most significantly here, crime. Each category contains a number of subcategories. For example, crime contains 33 subcategories under four major headings: burglary, theft, criminal damage and violence. These indices are based on Super Output Areas – the Output Areas of the census are combined to produce areas with an average of 1,500 residents and 400 households. These areas, therefore, do not represent 'neighbourhoods' but, rather, stable statistical reporting units from which deprivation information can be obtained for the formulation of public-service policy. These indices rank from the most to the least deprived. They do not attempt to discriminate between the relative level of deprivation in Super Output Areas; they measure the level of deprivation within each Super Output Area only. Finally, measures of deprivation take into account only those people who are judged to be unsuccessful or 'deprived' – a distinction between 'deprived/undeprived' would be of little use in analysing levels of fear or anxiety, the propensity to inform the police or the level of social capital in a community.

While valid criminological analyses can be undertaken using, for example, census data and indices of deprivation, for an intervention-specific approach such data may prove inadequate (Ashby 2005; Ashby and Longley 2005; Williamson *et al.* 2005). For example, if a police force was having problems with bogus utility-meter readers and decided to distribute awareness-raising crime prevention literature, using data from a deprivation index is unlikely to be an effective way of targeting the population at greatest risk of such criminals (e.g. the elderly). The use of data alone will not lead to intelligence-led policing: for this, 'geodemographics' (or neighbourhood typologies) developed by the commercial sector for direct-marketing and consumer-profiling purposes may be employed. Geodemographics has been defined as 'the analysis of people by where they live' or 'locality marketing' (Sleight 2004) and the term is generally considered to refer to small-area typologies that discriminate between neighbourhood types and 'consumer' behaviour (Brown 1991; Batey and Brown 1995; Birkin 1995; Harris *et al.* 2005). The phrase 'birds of a feather flock together' is used to characterize neighbourhoods and to anticipate their behavioural patterns. Geodemographics, therefore, involves the classification and analysis of small areas through a combination of geographic, socioeconomic and demographic variables.

Geodemographic classifications are based on social similarity rather than locational proximity and are created using a wide variety of sources, such as the census, market research data, lifestyle surveys, financial surveys, family expenditure surveys, credit data, etc. A wide range of geodemographic products is now available (see Sleight 2004) including Mosaic (Experian) and ACORN (CACI), academic research tools and the new National Statistics Area Classification (http://www.statistics.gov.uk/about/methodology by theme/area classification/default.asp). What these products have in common is fine spatial granularity that permits users to discriminate differences at scale that is likely to reflect residents' perceptions of their neighbourhoods. This fine spatial granularity is achieved by using unit post-codes, comprising on average 15 households – far fewer than the 125 households in the census Output Areas or the 400+ households in the Index of Multiple Deprivation.

Geodemographic profiling at such areal units as electoral wards or basic command unit is a valuable method of intelligence gathering for policing purposes. Ward-level summary statistics are freely available through the National Statistics' Neighbourhood Statistics programme, and such indicators are commonly used with census data to provide small-area analyses. However, these units often fail to highlight the differences present within wards or even within the smaller census output areas (see Ashby 2005). The finer spatial granularity afforded by geodemographic profiling, however, promotes a fuller understanding of a local 'community'. Furthermore, the lifestyles data and visualization tools provided with geodemographic products offer further insight into the dominant characteristics of neighbourhoods.

An example proprietary geodemographic classification is Mosaic UK, developed by Experian Business Strategies (http://www.business-strategies. co.uk/Content.asp?ArticleID=629). The neighbourhood classifications used by this system maximize between-group variance and minimize within-group variance across an extensive range of small-area demographic and socioeconomic indicators. Approximately 400 data variables are used in the clustering process, 54 per cent of which have been derived from the 2001 census, with the remainder gathered from administrative and commercial data sources (e.g. shareholders' registers, consumer credit databases, postal address files, council tax records, edited electoral rolls and lifestyle surveys) (Experian 2003). The resulting typology classifies each one of the UK's 1.75

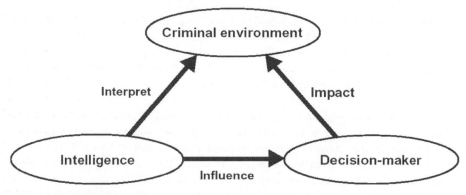

Figure 21.10 An intelligence-led policing and crime reduction process
Source: Ratcliffe (2003: 3)

million unit post codes (each one containing approximately 15 households) into one of 61 different neighbourhood types (labelled 01–61) and into aggregate neighbourhood groups (labelled A–K).

Geodemographics can help in such areas as intelligence-led policing, strategic resource management, neighbourhood policing and criminal investigation. For example, Ratcliffe's three Is model of intelligence-led policing (see Figure 21.10) stresses the importance of a detailed knowledge of the criminal environment. Geodemographics is one information tool that can assist the police in acquiring this knowledge. Similarly, a detailed knowledge of the local policing environment is essential for community policing and, indeed, for targeting and assisting in investigations.

Crime and neighbourhoods

Environmental criminology is the study of crime, criminality and victimization as they relate, first, to particular places and, secondly, to the way individuals and organizations adjust their activities spatially and, in so doing, are in turn influenced by place-based or spatial factors (Bottoms and Wiles 2002: 620). In this section we explore what can be learnt about the relationships between neighbourhoods, communities and crime through the analysis of recorded crime datasets.

A recent police-reform white paper calls on the police service to devise effective community-engagement strategies. To achieve this, the police service will require a 'detailed, neighbourhood level understanding of the demographics of the community it serves' (Home Office 2004: 67). Such a detailed appreciation of local populations is, however, largely lacking in UK policing. Moreover, although the public may reasonably expect their local police to have a detailed knowledge of crime hotspots, evidence suggests that police perceptions are usually at odds with evidence-based, computer-generated hotspot maps (Ratcliffe and McCullagh 2001: 336). Ashby (2005) promotes geodemographic profiling as a supplementary intelligence source in public-service resource determination and performance assessment. Geodemographic profiling, however, can also be of value to the criminal investigator.

Geodemographics has highlighted variations in victimization and offender rates in different neighbourhood types. Table 21.2 illustrates such variations in the 11 aggregated Mosaic UK neighbourhood groups in a Devon and Cornwall police division. These values have been standardized to 100 so that the average or expected rate is equal to 100. A value of 200, therefore, would indicate twice the expected propensity, and a value of 50 only half. The table shows that, for the neighbourhood group 'Symbols of Success', the standardized offender rate observed is only one fifth of the expected rate, whereas in 'Municipal Dependency' it is four times the expected rate – a ratio of 24:1. Similarly, the variation in victim rates across different neighbourhood groups is also marked. However, of most interest to the criminal investigator, perhaps, are the detection rates. Detection rates are disproportionately better in neighbourhood groups F and G – a trend that is borne out in similar studies of police force areas (see Ashby and Webber 2006).

Table 21.2 Summary profiles for the North and East Devon BCU segmented by Mosaic UK neighbourhood groups
Source: Ashby (2005: 454)

Share of population	Neighbourhod group		Victims	Offenders	Successful detections
2.5	A	Symbols of Success	73	18	94
8.3	B	Happy Families	85	100	95
11.1	C	Suburban Comfort	69	43	74
13.3	D	Ties of Community	172	183	124
5.5	E	Urban Intelligence	186	129	98
1.4	F	Welfare Borderline	300	372	166
2.1	G	Municipal Dependency	168	439	130
8.8	H	Blue Collar Enterprise	117	217	109
2.9	I	Twilight Substance	88	115	95
24.1	J	Grey Perspectives	68	45	78
20.2	K	Rural Isolation	68	38	73

The 'Successful detections' column shows the clear-up standardized rates of all crimes by neighbourhood group. The police are performing somewhat better than expected in those neighbourhoods that experience high crime rates ('Municipal Dependency', 'Welfare Borderline') but are underperforming in those areas that generally experience less crime and call on the police less frequently (e.g. 'Rural Isolation', 'Grey Perspectives'). Furthermore, when such analyses are compared with levels of public satisfaction with the police service as reported in the British Crime Survey, it is precisely those neighbourhoods that experience higher detection rates that are most dissatisfied and those neighbourhoods with below expected detection rates that are generally most satisfied with the police service (Ashby and Webber 2006; Williamson *et al.* 2006).

In the same way that Clarke and Eck (2003) consider the 80–20 rule, geo-demographics can be used to ascertain the extent to which crime, offenders, victims and attitudes are disproportionately concentrated in certain areas. For example, if the offender rates in Devon and Cornwall are segmented by the 61 Mosaic types, it can be seen that neighbourhood types that account for only 20 per cent of the population co-ordinally account for some 55 per cent of all offenders (Figure 21.11). Similarly, those neighbourhood types that account for some 40 per cent of the population account for well over three quarters of all offenders. While geographic profiling in the form of 'jeopardy surfaces' (Rossmo 2000) may be of most value in the investigation of high-profile crimes, geodemographic segmentation may assist in the investigation of volume crime and in the subsequent targeting of resources and preventative measures.

National datasets (such as the British Crime Survey) are also of potential value to the criminal investigator. Using the British Crime Survey (BCS) for the year 2000, the residential location of survey respondents was recorded and coded by the Mosaic UK typology. All the responses from the 25,000 participants were then collated and segmented by geodemographic

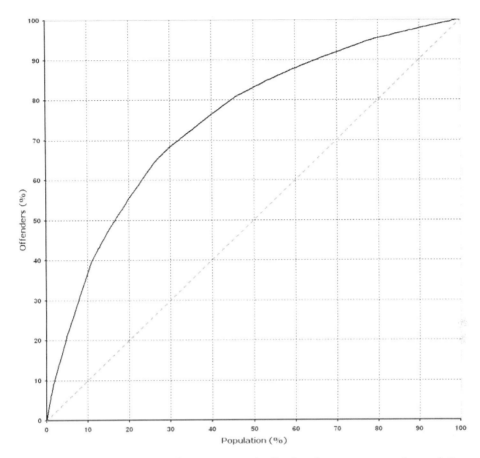

Figure 21.11 Lorenz curve of percentage of offenders by percentage of population (North and East Devon BCU)

neighbourhood type. This classification can then be used to calculate the average propensity to reply to a question in a certain way. For example, Table 21.3 summarizes the response propensities to a number of questions on the BCS (again, all the values are standardized to 100).

Such profiles were used in Devon and Cornwall as part of a policing reassurance strategy. Geodemographics was employed to identify those sectors of the community that, according to the BCS, have:

- the highest fear of burglary, rape and violence from strangers;
- the highest reported victimization rate immediately outside their homes; and
- the lowest opinion of the police response.

The locations of these 'at risk' neighbourhood types were mapped, which immediately highlighted the fact that they were all located on direct access routes from pubs and clubs to taxis and late-night take-aways. Unsurprisingly,

Table 21.3 Geodemographic profiles of selected BCS variables
Source: After Williamson *et al.* 2006.

Neighbourhood group	Do neighbours generally help each other or go their own way?	Is this area a nice place to live?	Common problems in local area	Common problems in local area	Rating of police	The police response
	Help each other	Bad	Homes in bad condition	Noisy neigh-bours	Very good	Police found offender
A: Symbols of Success	123	8	21	43	111	89
B: Happy Families	92	35	54	61	108	119
C: Suburban Comfort	117	31	42	54	105	83
D: Ties of Community	92	151	145	120	85	99
E: Urban Intelligence	63	100	103	132	109	83
F: Welfare Borderline	64	305	210	224	89	124
G: Municipal Dependency	74	284	220	155	71	137
H: Blue Collar Enterprise	85	114	104	111	102	116
I: Twilight Subsistence	112	78	61	74	118	85
J: Grey Perspectives	126	24	38	64	128	76
K: Rural Isolation	170	12	21	26	125	108

an analysis of recorded crime data showed that these neighbourhoods suffered high levels of criminal damage, late-night anti-social behaviour and burglary. Geodemographic profiles of these neighbourhoods demonstrated an above-average use of public transport, and so posters concerning the reassurance strategy were displayed in a number of bus-shelters in these neighbourhoods (see Scott 2005). In providing a fuller picture of a community's composition, geodemographic profiling can be a very valuable investigative tool. For example, Figure 21.12 illustrates the extent to which neighbours may be expected to help one another in different neighbourhood types. Williamson *et al.* (2006) developed this as a measure of the social capital in an area – a notion that is inherently difficult to evaluate quantitatively.

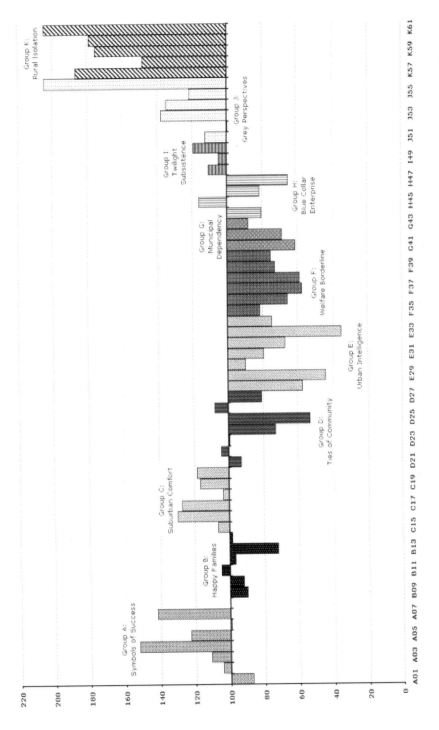

Figure 21.12 Index values segmented by Mosaic UK type for the BCS response 'in the local area neighbours tend to help each other'
Source: Williamson *et al.* (2006)

Conclusions: how criminal investigation may benefit from geodemographics

A study by Rossmo *et al.* (2004) of the geodemographics of stranger rapists may help to demonstrate the benefits of this type of analysis to criminal investigation. This study used data from solved rape cases held on the Serious Crime Analysis Section database at the National Centre for Policing Excellence, which is required to conduct comparative case analyses of murders, rapes and abductions for the UK police forces. A stranger rape was defined as rape or serious sexual assault where no prior relationship existed between the victim and the offender. In order to test proprietary geodemographic databases, the study used three major systems available in the UK: Mosaic, Acorn and PriZM.

There were 310 addresses for offenders that could be georeferenced to the post-code level. Rossmo *et al.* (2004) found that stranger rapists' home addresses were eight times more likely to be in the neighbourhoods described as 'Graffitied Ghettos'. Comparing the offence location with the offender's home address, it was found that there was a strong relationship in four neighbourhood types. For an offence that occurred in locations referred to as 'Council Flats', for example, the offender was six times more likely also to live in a 'Council Flats' area, and twice as likely to reside in an area described as 'Mortgaged families'.

Where the offence was against a street prostitute, it was found that there were concentrations of offenders in three geodemographic groups – 'Victorian Low Status', 'Low Rise Council' and 'Blue Collar Owners' – and that these post codes accounted for two thirds of offenders in all reported prostitute rapes. It was concluded that relationships appear to exist between offence site and offender residence, and that this information could be of benefit to both investigators and crime analysts. The analysis also found a relationship between geodemographic profile and distance from the crime.

Commenting on the limited use made of geodemographics by investigators and analysts, Rossmo *et al.* (2004: 41) observe:

> To date the use of demographic information in geo-profiling has been more ad hoc and qualitative than systematic and quantitative. The current research adds an important dimension to geographic profiling by incorporating knowledge about the demographic landscape – the 'who' as well as the 'where'. In serial rape cases, high offender likelihood ratio geodemographic codes may be used to further refine the geoprofile output.

As we have demonstrated in this chapter, geodemographic profiling has a wide application across a range of crime types. We are currently only at the beginning of the application of geodemographics to criminal investigation, and we are confident that investigators and analysts will be able to mine a great deal from the rich vein of geodemographics if they begin to employ it in their analyses and if they georeference all data and intelligence that are is captured and recorded. Geodemographics, spatial analysis and geoprofiling are likely to become a critical part of the investigative toolkit for knowledge-based policing.

Selected further reading

Ashby, D.I. and Webber, R. (2006) *High Crime. High Disorder Neighbourhoods: Spatial Analysis and Geodemographics* (report submitted to the Audit Commission). London: UCL (available online at www.spatial-literacy.org/index.php?p=crime&s+audit). A detailed and comprehensive geodemographic analysis of ten selected 'high crime' neighbourhoods from a neighbourhood-policing context. A range of supporting information is available from the Audit Commission at www.audit-commission. gov.uk/neighbourhoodcrime.

Chainey, S. and Ratcliffe, J. (2005) *GIS and Crime Mapping*. Chichester: Wiley. The most recent and accessible textbook, providing a comprehensive outlook on crime mapping: fundamental theory of mapping and criminology; scientific methodologies; analysis and design techniques; applications; and examples of best practice.

Harris, R., Sleight, P. and Webber, R. (2005) *Geodemographics, GIS and Neighbourhood Targeting*. Chichester: Wiley. An excellent introduction and overview of the methods, theory and classification techniques that provide the foundation of neighbourhood analysis and geodemographic products. Particular focus is given to the presentation and use of neighbourhood classification in GIS and spatial analysis.

Longley, P.A., Goodchild, M.F., Maguire, D.J. and Rhind, D.W. (2005) *Geographic Information Systems and Science* (2nd edn). Chichester: Wiley. The pre-eminent textbook in the field of GIS and spatial analysis, this is an essential companion for newcomers to spatial analysis and experienced GI practitioners alike. It is written in a fluent and lucid style and covers foundations, principles, techniques, analysis, and management and policy.

Notes

1. This and the following sections are based on a portfolio of work undertaken by the Centre for Geographic Information and Spatial Analysis at the University of Sheffield funded by South Yorkshire Police, the Home Office and other agencies.
2. See, for example, Canter and Alison 1999; Rossmo 2000; Canter 2003; Chainey 2003; Chainey and Ratcliffe 2005. Rigel – http://www.geographicprofiling.com/rigel/index.html; Dragnet – http://www.i-psy.com/publications/publications_dragnet.php; CrimeStat – http//www.icpsr.umich.edu/CRIMESTAT/; and the recent geoprofiling discussions facilitated by the US National Institute of Justice MAPS programme – http://www.oip.usdoj.gov/njj/maps/gp/html.

References

Antenucci, C.J. and Brown, K. (1989) 'An interview with Jack Dangermond', *URISA Journal*, 1: 50–2.

Ashby, D.I. (2005) 'Policing neighbourhoods: exploring the geographies of crime, policing and performance assessment', *Policing and Society*, 15: 413–47.

Ashby, D.I., Irving, B. and Longley, P. (2007) 'Police reform and the new public management paradigm: matching technology to the rhetoric' (submitted).

Ashby, D.I. and Longley, P.A. (2005) 'Geocomputation, geodemographics and resource allocation for local policing', *Transactions in GIS*, 9: 53–72.

Ashby, D.I. and Webber, R. (2006) *High Crime: High Disorder Neighbourhoods. Spatial Analysis and Geodemographics* (report submitted to the Audit Commission). London: UCL.

Bailey, N.T.J. and Gatrell, A.C. (1995) *Interactive Spatial Data Analysis*. Harlow: Longman.

Batey, P. and Brown, P. (1995) 'From human ecology to customer targeting: the evolution of geodemographics', in P. Longley and G. Clarke (eds) *GIS for Business and Service Planning* Cambridge: GeoInformation International.

Birkin, M. (1995) 'Customer targeting, geodemographic and lifestyle approaches', in P. Longley and G. Clarke (eds) *GIS for Business and Service Planning*. Cambridge: GeoInformation International.

Bottoms, A.E. and Wiles, P. (2002) 'Environmental criminology', in M. Maguire *et al.* (eds) *The Oxford Handbook of Criminology*. Oxford: Oxford University Press.

Brown, P.J.B. (1991) 'Exploring geodemographics', in I. Masser and M.J. Blakemore (eds) *Handling Geographical Information*. London: Longman.

Burgess, E.W. (1925) 'The growth of the city', in R.E. Park *et al.* (eds) *The City*. Chicago, IL: University of Chicago Press.

Campbell, H. and Masser, I. (1991) 'The impact of GIS in local government in Britain', in *Proceedings of AGI'91 Conference*, Birmingham, 20–22 November.

Canter, D. (2003) *Mapping Murder: The Secrets of Geographical Profiling*. London: Virgin Books.

Canter, D. and Alison, L.J. (eds) (1999) *Offender Profiling Series. Volumes I–IV*. Aldershot: Ashgate.

Chainey, S. (2002) 'Geographic profiling of serial offences', *Criminal Justice Management*, September.

Chainey, S. and Ratcliffe, J. (2005) *GIS and Crime Mapping*. Chicester: Wiley.

Clarke, R.V. and Eck, J. (2003) *Become a Problem-solving Crime Analyst (in 55 Small Steps)*. London: Jill Dando Institute of Crime Science.

Commission of the European Communities (2000) *Commercial Exploitation of Europe's Public Sector Information: Executive Summary*. PIRA International Ltd, University of East Anglia and Knowledge View Ltd. (available online at http://www.ftp://ftp.cordis.lu/econtent/docs/2000-1558.pdf).

Commission of the European Communities (2003) *Directive 2003/98/EC of the European Parliament and of the Council of 17 November 2003 on the Re-use of Public Sector Information* (OJ L 345/90 31.12.2003).

Craglia, M., Haining, R. and Signoretta, P. (2001) 'Modelling high-intensity crime areas in English cities', *Urban Studies*, 38: 1921–42.

Craglia, M. and Signoretta, P. (2002) 'Joined-up government in practice: a case study of children's needs in Sheffield', *Local Government Studies*, 28: 59–76.

Experian (2003) *Mosaic United Kingdom – the Consumer Classification for the UK*. Nottingham: Experian Ltd.

Farrell, G. and Pease, K. (1993) Once Bitten, Twice Bitten: Repeat Victimisation and its Implications for Crime Prevention. *Police Research Group: Crime Prevention Unit Series, Paper 46*. London: Home Office.

French, S.P. and Wiggins, L.L. (1989) 'Computer adoption and use in California planning agencies: implications for education', *Journal of Planning Education and Research*, 8: 97–108.

Haining, R. (2003) *Spatial Data Analysis: Theory and Practice*. Cambridge: Cambridge University Press.

Harris, R., Sleight, P. and Webber, R. (2005) *Geodemographics, GIS and Neighbourhood Targeting*. Chichester: Wiley.

Home Office (2004) *Building Communities, Beating Crime: A Better Police Service for the 21st Century. Home Office White Paper* (Cm 6360). London: HMSO.

ISO (2005) *Geographic Information – Services* (ISO19119:2005). International Organization for Standardization, Geneva.

Kuhn, W. (2003) 'Semantic reference systems', *International Journal of Geographical Information Science*, 17: 405–9.

Longley, P.A. (2004) 'Urban studies', in K. Kempf-Leonard (ed.) *Encyclopedia of Social Measurement*. San Diego, CA: Academic Press.

Longley, P.A. (2005) 'Geographical information systems: a renaissance of geodemographics for public service delivery', *Progress in Human Geography*, 29: 57–63.

Longley, P.A. and Batty, M. (1996) *Spatial Analysis: Modelling in GIS Environment*. Cambridge: Geoinformation International.

Longley, P.A., Goodchild, M.F., Maguire, D.J. and Rhind, D.W. (2005) *Geographic Information Systems and Science* (2nd edn). Chichester: Wiley.

Masser, I. and Craglia, M. (1996) 'A comparative evaluation of GIS diffusion in local government in nine European countries', in I. Masser *et al.* (eds) *GIS Diffusion*. London: Taylor & Francis.

Pfautz, H. (1967) 'Sociologist of the city', in H. Pfautz (ed.) *On the City: Physical Patterns and Social Structure (Selected Writings of Charles Booth)*. Chicago, IL: University of Chicago Press.

Probert, M. and Wolfkamp, A. (2004) 'Key players in Europe', in M. Craglia *et al.* (eds) *Geographic Information in the Wider Europe* (available online at http://www.ec-gis.org/ginie/doc/book/ch6.pdf).

PSU (2005) *Crime Mapping: Improving Performance. A Good Practice Guide for Front Line Officers*. London: Policing Standards Unit/Home Office.

Ratcliffe, J.H. and McCullagh, M.J. (1998) 'Aoristic crime analysis', *International Journal of Geographical Information Science*, 12: 751–64.

Ratcliffe, J.H. and McCullagh, M.J. (2001) 'Chasing ghosts? Police perception of high crime areas', *British Journal of Criminology*, 41: 330–41.

Rees, P., Martin, D. and Williamson, P. (eds) (2002) *The Census Data System*. Chichester: Wiley.

Rossmo, D.K. (2000) *Geographic Profiling*. Boca Raton, FL: CRC Press.

Rossmo, K., Davies, A. and Patrick, M. (2004) *Exploring the Geo-demographic and Distance Relationships between Stranger Rapists and their Offences. Special Interest Series Paper 16*. London: Home Office.

Scott, R. (2005) 'Targeting resources using geodemographic profiling.' Paper presented at the Third National Crime Mapping Conference, London: (available online at http://www.jdi.ucl.ac.uk/news_events/conferences/third_mapping_conference/third_nat_map_programme.php).

Shaw, C.R. and McKay, H.D. (1942) *Juvenile Delinquency and Urban Areas*. Chicago, IL: University of Chicago Press.

Sleight, P. (2004) *Targeting Customers: How to Use Geodemographic and Lifestyle Data in Your Business* (3rd edn). London: WARC.

Stark, R. (1987) 'Deviant places: a theory of the ecology of crime', *Criminology*, 25: 893–09.

Tomlinson, R.F. (1988) 'The impact of the transition from analogue to digital cartographic representation', *American Geographer*, 15: 249–61.

Williamson, T., Ashby, D.I. and Webber, R. (2005) 'Young offenders, schools and the neighbourhood: a new approach to data-analysis for community policing', *Journal of Community and Applied Social Psychology*, 15: 203–28.

Williamson, T., Ashby, D.I. and Webber, R. (2006) 'Classifying neighbourhoods for reassurance policing', *Policing and Society* 16(2): 189–218.

Part 5

Governance of criminal investigation

As with all areas of police activity, questions of governance, accountability and ethics are among the most important. Given what we had to say in the Introduction to this book about the less than entirely happy history of police criminal investigation, there can be little doubt about the importance of such issues in this area. In the opening chapter, Peter Neyroud and Emma Disley look at some of the issues involved in the management, supervision and oversight of criminal investigation. They identify four dimensions: the co-ordination of the elements and processes of an investigation; the supervision and leadership of police officers and staff conducting investigations; performance management; and, finally, the systems of oversight of such investigatory activity. Some of these areas have been the subject of relatively limited academic inquiry. However, all four have recently been the subject of considerable policy development. Almost certainly, what is now required is further systematic research on the effectiveness of the new systems and procedures that Neyroud and Disley outline.

As the Stephen Lawrence case demonstrated only too clearly, major incidents can have catastrophic consequences for all parties if handled badly. As a result, significant attention has been paid in recent years to the management of critical incidents. John Grieve, Jonathan Crego and Bill Griffiths examine the nature of 'critical incidents' and outline the assessment of risk that should be undertaken as part of a community impact assessment in order to try to identify the needs of families and others caught up in such incidents. Crucially, they argue, officers need to be trained for such eventualities. According to the authors, there has clearly been much progress in this area in recent years. However, as the shooting at Stockwell tube station in 2005 and the police operation in Forest Gate in 2006 demonstrate, this is an area in which considerable expertise is required.

Alan Wright then outlines what arguably is one of the core developments across policing in recent years – that of the nature and role of ethics in the governance of policing practice. The police service has long been subject to extensive legal regulation and, with the Human Rights Act 1998 and related legislation, this has increased. Additionally, however, there is a need to consider the normative and ethical structures that should guide day-to-day policing, including investigative practice. There is now a considerable literature on misconduct and corruption, much of it suggesting that police detective/investigative activity is close to what has been called the 'invitational edge' of corrupt activity. As a consequence, as Wright concludes, 'moral responsibility remains the key to professional conduct in criminal investigation'. Nevertheless, there are sadly numerous instances of serious wrongdoing.

Stephen Savage and Becky Milne's exploration of miscarriages of justice attempts to draw important lessons from them. They begin by unpicking the term and argue that, rather than 'wrongful convictions', we might better think of 'questionable convictions', together with 'questionable actions' by the police, and 'failures to respond' (as in the Stephen Lawrence case). Exploring a number of major cases, such as those involving the 'Guildford Four' and the 'Birmingham Six', Savage and Milne describe criminal investigation as the 'golden thread' running through the recent history of miscarriages of justice. Their conclusion that police investigative practice has historically been a root factor in a great many miscarriages of justice leads them to argue that greater emphasis should be placed upon *professionalizing* the investigative process.

This is precisely the subject taken up by Peter Stelfox in the concluding chapter in this part. He outlines the Professionalizing Criminal Investigation Programme (PIP) launched by the Association of Chief Police Officers in September 2005. This is a core part of the government police reform agenda and, although at the time of writing elements of the reform programme appear to have stalled, there is no reason to believe that PIP, and its core objectives, will not be pursued quickly. The core 'investigative doctrine' focuses on three facets of the investigator's toolkit: knowledge, skills and understanding. 'Knowledge' encompasses legal knowledge, local and national policies and investigative principles. 'Skills' cover crime scene management; forensic investigation; searching; victims and witness management; intelligence management; passive data management (e.g. CCTV, telephone billing data and financial records); elimination inquiries; communication; covert policing; and suspect management. Finally, 'understanding' refers to the broader social and community context in which knowledge and skills are deployed and being able to demonstrate that one can apply such knowledge and skills in difficult operational circumstances. As in some other areas, Stelfox argues that one of the current difficulties with such a professionalizing programme is the relative absence of a strong evidence base. Indeed, this is arguably true of most aspects of investigation and, moreover, policing as a whole. One of the core challenges for the newly established National Policing Improvement Agency, therefore, will be to attempt to stimulate the development of just such a research and information base. Another challenge for the police service, as Stelfox outlines, will be to 'ensure that those [officers and staff] who are not able to carry out criminal investigations to the highest standard are not allowed to practise'.

Chapter 22

The management, supervision and oversight of criminal investigations

Peter Neyroud and Emma Disley

Introduction

In this chapter we explore four dimensions of the management, supervision and oversight of criminal investigations: the co-ordination of the elements and processes of an investigation; the supervision and leadership of police officers and staff conducting an investigation; performance management; and the forms of oversight of criminal investigations. These four areas have been chosen because we consider them to be particularly pertinent to a basic, descriptive understanding of this topic and because they provide a framework for analysis which enables us to highlight what we consider to be the important, emerging trends in the management of investigations. What ostensibly appears to be (and has often been discussed in the literature as) mere bureaucratic or managerial change in fact has significant implications for the governance and conduct of policing and reflects broader trends within policing which are discussed throughout this volume.

Academic literature offers surprisingly little commentary on or analysis of the management of criminal investigations. The study by Maguire and Norris (1992) of investigations conducted by the criminal investigation department (CID) provides valuable insight into the nature of crime investigation and the challenges posed for its management. However, the age of this research and its focus on investigations carried out by CID limit the contribution it can make to an analysis of contemporary practices. Official inquiries into the deaths of Stephen Lawrence (Macpherson 1999) and Victoria Climbie (Laming 2003) provide a more recent insight into investigative practices, but given the pace of change in this area of policing we cannot rely on these to provide an accurate account of current processes. Further, these reports look at very serious, high-profile homicide investigations in which the police were criticized for not abiding by official investigative standards. This chapter hopes to offer an up-to-date analysis of officially accepted procedures: the implications of doing things by the book, rather than the lessons to be learnt from investigative failure. We will look critically at the day-to-day issues of managing and supervising investigations into volume crime as well as major crime.

Two themes underlie our discussion in this chapter. The first stems from the multiplicity of complicated, overlapping targets, requirements and auditable standards with which managers of criminal investigations must comply; targets and requirements which are decided upon and imposed from different levels of governance, ranging from the national and supranational to the very local, and which are set by parties with widely divergent roles and interests in policing, including government ministers and departments, national professional organizations and lobby groups, inspectorates, pressure groups and local organizations. The tensions which arise from this must be negotiated by managers of criminal investigations. The second theme relates to the changing boundaries and relationships between the police, other criminal justice agencies and social care agencies such as social services, housing and drugs services, which mean that criminal investigations are increasingly supervised and managed in an interagency way. We think that the management and supervision of criminal investigations can helpfully be conceptualized as being conducted within and through a 'laminate' approach, consisting of intersecting layers of scrutiny and monitoring. Managers of criminal investigations must find ways of reconciling these multiple and sometimes conflicting demands.

The co-ordinating function: managing the processes and elements of an investigation

In this section we look at the co-ordinating function which managers of investigations must fulfil. By this we mean the role of bringing together the different processes and stages so as to construct a coherent and effective investigation which complies with the strictures of the law and with the extensive guidance and standard operating procedures which specify how the processes of an investigation should be managed. This co-ordinating role has been affected by the growth in the amount and detail of guidelines, specialization within policing and the increasing involvement of non-police agencies, all of which add to the diversity of the elements which must be drawn together to form an effective investigation.

Establishing investigative priorities

Criminal investigations can be categorized according to the nature and seriousness of the criminality they deal with – namely, volume crime, serious crime, critical incidents, terrorism or cross (force) border criminality. Superimposed on to this, the management of investigations can be further classified according to the level of seniority at which decisions about investigations are taken: at the strategic, operational or tactical level. To this, we could also add that investigations could be conducted proactively or reactively.

In the broadest sense, the management of all investigations begins when strategic decisions are made at the force or national level by chief officers and ministers. Ministers have official responsibility for setting the overarching, national priorities and powers for policing and for setting national budgets, which, with the addition of locally raised council tax precepts, provide the funding for local forces. Chief officers (chief constables, deputy chief constables and assistant chief constables) must make their decisions and set priorities within these bounds. The meaning and implication of these high-level, strategic decisions are perhaps most vividly manifested through the process of call handling. All reports of crime and calls for assistance which the police receive from the public are screened and prioritized for attention in accordance with strategic priorities; some reports of alleged criminal offences are allocated for investigation by the police and others are not (Amey *et al.* 1996). There is considerable controversy in the notion of balancing the public's demand that the police respond to every reported offence with the capacity of the police to meet this demand, yet this is exactly what strategic decision-makers must do (Home Office 2005: 7). As well as establishing strategic priorities, chief officers will have direct involvement in the management of the most serious and high-profile investigations, or those that span force boundaries. Generally, however, their management function will be undertaken through performance management (further discussed later in this chapter).

Operational management generally happens at the level of the basic command unit (BCU). It is here where responsibility for managing and conducting volume crime investigation rests (Audit Commission 2001; HMIC 2001). Like chief officers, operational managers (generally chief superintendents and superintendents) will be directly involved only in larger or more serious investigations, managing the majority of investigations through local performance management. It is at the tactical level where detailed, day-to-day management of investigations occurs, including the supervision of individual officers dealing with investigative case loads, the management of individual investigations and working with other criminal justice agencies in the preparation and management of individual cases. The different tactical, management and supervisory roles are carried out by officers of all ranks below superintendent.

Managing a criminal investigation

The management of an individual investigation is, therefore, located within the structure created by strategic, operational and tactical decisions. Each investigation is a complex process, involving many different stages, from call handling and the initial response, to crime scene assessment, to assessing incoming information, selecting appropriate lines of inquiry, evidence gathering, managing the involvement of witnesses, suspect handling and post-charge case management (Smith and Flanagan 2000; NCPE and ACPO 2004). Investigative managers must not only co-ordinate these different stages, but also the input to the investigation by staff from a range of disciplines. In a major crime investigation it has long been the case that a number of specialist teams and functions are involved. For example, the investigation into the death of Dr David Kelly by Thames Valley Police involved major crime investigators, local beat officers, pathologists, a forensic investigator, psychologists and a variety of different scientific disciplines including archaeology (Hutton 2004). The drives for efficiency, a performance culture and the increasing professionalization and specialization within policing mean that it has also become the norm for similar numbers of specialist teams to be involved in volume crime investigations (FitzGerald *et al.* 2000). To those specialist areas listed above we might add administrative support units which prepare prosecution case files, and any one of a range of 'para-professionals' now employed by the police, such as civilian case investigators, introduced under the Police Reform Act 2002, who carry out routine inquiries and conduct post-charge interviews, and specialist investigators who are involved in cases where there is the possibility of an application to recover the proceeds of crime.

In the case of a major crime investigation there is extensive guidance specifying how investigations should be conducted. Guidance in this area was first drawn up in response to recommendations made by the Byford review into the murders committed by the Yorkshire Ripper (Byford 1981). Since then, guidance has become more detailed, more specific to the type of investigation and, consequently, has become both an important resource for those co-ordinating the investigation and a form of control, imposing a structure within which they must work. Today there are two main sources of guidance: the first, the *Major Incident Room Standardised Administrative Procedures* manual (*MIRSAP*) (Centrex 2005), specifies, in detail, the routines which must be followed inside an incident room.[1] It sets out a systematic approach which attempts to ensure that all lines of inquiry are covered and all information coming in is appropriately assessed and acted upon. The *MIRSAP* should be read alongside the ACPO *Murder Investigation Manual* (ACPO 2000), which provides guidelines for the conduct of the investigation outside the major incident room – for example, as to the use of house-to-house and forensic teams.

In the future, it is likely that we will see existing guidance being continually updated and improved (for example, *MIRSAP* was amended in light of findings of the Soham Inquiry) and also the emergence of new guidance, probably coming from the National Centre for Policing Excellence and, subsequently, the National Policing Improvement Agency.

Moves to standardize the way major crime investigations are managed have more recently been replicated in relation to volume crime. Guidance from the National Centre for Policing Excellence sets out an Active Investigation Management (AIM) model (Centrex 2004), which requires detailed plans to be drawn up for the conduct of the investigation, in the hope of achieving a systematic exploration of the lines of inquiry and allowing close supervision of an investigation. As well as following guidance like AIM, managers of criminal investigations must comply with local force policies and have an in-depth knowledge of the criminal law and the legislation which regulates the process of investigation. The changing landscape of regulation has had a large effect on the management of both volume and major crime investigation: the Police and Criminal Evidence Act (PACE) 1984 has become a crucial aspect of any investigation in England and Wales (Maguire and Norris 1992: 27; Brown 1997), and the Regulation of Investigatory Powers Act (RIPA) 2000 has transformed covert investigations from the arcane and unregulated pursuit of a small group of detectives to a highly regulated process, subject to detailed formal codes, substantial national guidance and oversight and inspection by the Office of the Surveillance Commissioners (Billingsley *et al.* 2001; Neyroud and Beckley 2001). Moreover, covert policing now forms part of the overall structure of the National Intelligence Model (National Crime Intelligence Service 2000), which describes the tactics and managerial disciplines of intelligence and prescribes the accreditation and qualification of key players in the process. The Criminal Procedure and Investigations Act 1996 and the Criminal Justice Act 2003 regulate the disclosure of evidence between defence and prosecution.

The manager as a co-ordinator

One way in which the police have sought to meet the demands of co-ordinating an investigation is through the use of technology. IT systems are available to log the progress of the investigation and the activities of investigative officers, and to manage the information collected during an investigation (Chan 2001; Bichard 2004). The well-known HOLMES system (now updated to HOLMES 2) is used nationally in the UK to enable comprehensive storage and retrieval of information collected during a major crime investigation. Storage and retrieval systems akin to HOLMES can enhance the ability of the senior investigating officer to follow the progress of an investigation and review documentation connected with the inquiry, which in turn makes it easier for him or her to make effective judgements about whether the investigation is being properly pursued. It is because of this that they are increasingly used in volume crime investigation – the AIM model relies on IT systems which log investigative activity and decisions.

These systems, however, cannot analyse evidence or make decisions about the direction which an investigation should take. These functions must be undertaken by managers after considering and co-ordinating the various elements of an investigation. The complexity of this co-ordinating task and the need for investigations to be open to scrutiny have led to the creation of an extensive and growing body of national guidance and standards, designed to help officers manage investigations. This guidance presents a highly structured model for the management of an investigation and it seeks to rationalize what is, in reality, a highly complex, 'messy' task (Innes 2002: 685), which requires managers to think creatively rather than merely follow a preconceived, generic framework (NCPE and ACPO 2005: 23). Managers of major investigations and, increasingly, of volume crime investigations, must reconcile this reality with the demands for auditable investigative practices, by fitting the multiple strands of an investigation into the bureaucratic models imposed upon investigation management (Innes 2002: 679).

Supervising investigating officers

Police officers and civilian staff who are involved in the conduct of an investigation need leadership, supervision and management, just like the employees of any other organization,[2] yet this is not something in which the police, as an organization, have excelled. Significant failures have been identified in police leadership, management and supervision. This chapter does not discuss police management and leadership in general.[3] Our discussion will focus on supervision and leadership within the context of criminal investigations. We will describe some of the inherent problems of supervising investigating officers and consider some developments which we think might address these difficulties.

It is helpful to think about who, within the police, is being called on to perform supervisory and leadership roles. In Table 22.1 we set out the supervisory structure for investigating officers, which shows that the majority of investigations are carried out by police constables or detective constables whose case loads are usually separated by seriousness and complexity. The police workforce is becoming increasingly differentiated and specialized, and good practice in volume crime investigation encourages forces and their BCUs to create specialist teams of officers to investigate burglary, car crime and robbery. Alongside this, the drive for efficiency has extended and broadened the role of 'para-professional' civilian investigators, particularly in volume crime investigation.

Table 22.1 The supervisory structure for investigating officers

Rank	Supervisory responsibilities	Supervised by
Constable/ detective constable	A case load	Detective sergeant/ sergeant
Sergeant/ detective sergeant	A case load and a team	Inspector
Inspector/ detective inspector	A team of detective sergeants/detective constables	Detective chief inspector/ chief inspector
Chief inspector/ detective chief inspector	A whole local unit	Superintendent
Superintendent	A BCU	Chief superintendent
Chief superintendent	A BCU	Assistant chief constable
Assistant chief constable	The force's crime team	Deputy chief constable/ chief constable
Deputy chief constable	Performance	Chief constable
Chief constable	Police force	Police authorities
Civilian case investigators	A case load	Detective sergeant

Difficulties inherent in supervising investigating officers

In research carried out as part of the Royal Commission on Criminal Justice, Maguire and Norris (1992) identified problems which they considered to be inherent in trying to supervise officers conducting a criminal investigation. Given that their research is now over a decade old and that their focus was on the supervision of officers in the CID, we draw on this research to signpost potential, persisting problems rather than as a descriptive account of the current state of affairs.

We identify five such inherent problems from Maguire and Norris's work. First, officers conducting investigations were out of the station, out of direct contact with their supervisors and in situations where they must use their discretion. Secondly, sergeants (and this goes for other supervisory ranks) were often based in the station, doing paperwork (Maguire and Norris 1992: 23) and commonly had their own investigative case load (1992: 25). Not only did this distract them from supervising lower-ranking investigating officers, but it also meant that they lacked distance from their supervisees, sharing as they did the problems of their front-line staff. Thirdly, the very nature of criminal investigation means that investigating officers must interact with criminals, thus allowing opportunities for corruption in the forms of officers colluding with criminals and infringing the rights of suspects (Maguire and Norris 1992: 24).[4] Fourthly, the focus of supervision was on the end product of the investigation – whether there was a detection or not – rather than on the quality of the day-to-day conduct of the investigation (1992: 23). Fifthly, as a result of these factors, supervision within the CID was of a charismatic rather than bureaucratic style, based on trust and personality rather than on following procedures (1992: 24).

There is a lack of recent research about whether these problems persist. What recent research there is (and given the pace of change within policing, this is not recent enough to be relied upon as a description of the current state of affairs) suggests that management and supervision of investigation are still poor (FitzGerald *et al.* 2000: 121–5). The report into the death of Stephen Lawrence criticized the ineffectiveness of senior investigating officers (Macpherson 1999) and the review of events in Soham commented on the lack of management experience among senior investigating officers in smaller forces, a point which was been powerfully reinforced by the review of protective services (HMIC 2005). Despite this less than optimistic picture, we think we can point to a few developments and changes within policing which suggest the potential for improvements in the supervision of investigations.

A new debate about leadership and professionalization

In the time since Maguire and Norris did their research, a discussion about police leadership has emerged and flourished among academics (Long 2003), policy makers (Smith and Flanagan 2000; Dobby *et al.* 2004) and professional organizations (ACPO 2004). There has also been a change of terminology; while Maguire and Norris contrasted bureaucratic and charismatic supervision styles, the debate about police leadership today has adopted terms from management theory, contrasting 'transactional' and 'transformational' leadership (Drodge and Murphy 2002). A broad consensus is emerging, calling for a more value-centred style of management, which emphasizes skills and learning (FitzGerald *et al*. 2000: 141; Wright 2000; Neyroud and Beckley 2001; Long 2003: 629–30). The emergence of this debate is inextricably linked with the emergence of a discussion about the professionalization of policing, and signifies a new conceptualization of investigative supervision as a role in its own right, rather than an add-on to the day job of a detective sergeant or detective inspector (Smith and Flanagan 2000: 53). There is a recognition, at least at the level of rhetoric, that officers must be trained in management and leadership skills in order to improve the quality and success of investigations (Smith and Flanagan 2000; HMIC 2002: 4; McFarlane and Mould 2002; Home Office 2004b: 48). Examples of this thinking extending beyond rhetoric into tangible policies and change can be identified. Standards for the training and accreditation of officers who manage and supervise investigations are being created in a Core Leadership Development Programme, established to provide training to officers of all ranks in the nature and qualities of leadership and supervision (Police Leadership Development Board 2003). An initiative called 'Professionalizing the Investigation Process' (see Chapter 26, this volume), launched by the Home Office in response to the 2001 white paper (Home Office 2001), seeks to improve investigation management, along with all other parts of the investigative process, through reviewing and revising existing investigation procedures and providing training and assessment. A National Policing Improvement Agency will be established in April 2007, mandated to develop a 'culture of continuous improvement' (Home Office 2003).

The dispersal of management roles

Moves during the 1990s to de-tier and flatten out the rank structure (Sheehy 1993) are well documented in the literature (Mawby and Wright 2003) and, although the recommendations of the Sheehy Report were never fully implemented, there are now fewer officers occupying management and senior manager ranks (such as superintendents and chief inspectors) than there were ten years ago. This trend has coincided with strong encouragement to devolve management responsibility to the BCU level and below (HMIC 2001). Many responsibilities previously conferred upon chief officers are now being dealt with at a much lower level in the organization (Long 2003: 639); whether an officer has leadership, management or supervisory responsibility is becoming less dependent on his or her rank and increasingly defined by the role which that officer occupies (Wright 2000: 298; Adlam and Villiers 2003). Chief officers are taking an increasingly strategic role, managing criminal investigation through a performance management model reinforced by performance contracts and performance-related pay, rather than through more direct, hands-on ways.

Both the diffusion of leadership and management functions right through the policing organization and moves towards professionalization are in the early stages of development, but they constitute the beginnings of changes to the way that investigations are supervised, which could in turn address some of the problems identified by Maguire and Norris, through producing more skilful and professional managers throughout the ranks, who identify supervision as being at the heart of their role.

New forms of supervision

New methods of measuring performance and effectiveness, which are currently being developed within policing, broaden the focus of supervision to include the quality of officers' actions as well as the end results, and might go some way to addressing Maguire and Norris's criticism that the focus of supervision fell too heavily on the product of police action and neglected the way that officers undertook their work. We will mention two such methods here: professional development reviews and activity analysis.

In an increasing number of forces each officer and civilian member of staff has his or her own professional development review (PDR). This is essentially a record where staff can collate evidence of good performance and competence in their role, set objectives for themselves and identify skills which they need to develop in order to perform their role better. It forms the basis for an annual review meeting between an officer and his or her supervisor. The motives behind the introduction of PDRs lie in the spread of performance culture and the drive for professionalization and accountability, as the process of PDR focuses an officer's mind on the performance targets and strategic objectives set for the force or BCU, and clarifies what he or she should do to contribute to the achievement of these. At the same time, however, PDR encourages a closer, more formalized and focused form of supervision. It might not have an effect on how investigating officers are supervised during a particular investigation but it has the potential to make managers of investigations more aware of the detail of officers' work, and the skills and qualities they demonstrate or lack.

As yet, there has been little evaluation of the effectiveness of PDR. One study suggested that such a system might focus on what was done, rather than how it was done, and would not provide an independent assessment of ability or skill (FitzGerald *et al.* 2000: 122). HMIC found that links between the high-level strategy for a BCU and the objectives set within PDRs were weak (HMIC 2001: 21). These problems, however, do not necessarily rule out the ability of PDR to provide a new form of supervision of investigating officers. We are not suggesting that PDR can provide a comprehensive solution to the problems identified by Maguire and Norris, but we do think that it might have a more general and subtle effect upon supervision, and it is certainly part of a trend towards closer and more attentive supervision of investigating officers.

The other method of supervision we would like to mention is activity analysis. This requires every member of staff to make a detailed log of his or her activities over a specified 48-hour period and is usually conducted within a force about once a year. The driving purpose behind its introduction is the desire to measure the cost of police activities and identify where efficiency savings might be made. There are reasons to be both pessimistic and optimistic about the effect of activity analysis. The pessimist might point to early indications that costing activities such as activity analysis are a poor method of measuring the contribution made by a member of staff to the totality of service delivered by a force (Butler 2000: 315). There is also a danger that activity analysis will judge effectiveness according to whether officers spend their time undertaking tasks that improve performance against targets which, rather than increasing the supervision of the quality of an investigating officer's work, might create yet another pressure to focus on end results. Yet, the optimist might counter that activity analysis has the potential to provide close supervision of investigating officers, providing supervisors with a snapshot of investigating officers' actions, perhaps making them better informed about the quality of their supervisee's work.

The prospects for better supervision of investigations

A new debate has emerged about police leadership and management. Policy and professional rhetoric suggest that in the near future the management of criminal investigations is likely to become a role performed by officers of all ranks, a role which requires specific training to ensure managers meet national competencies and standards, and a role which will be conducted by officers who have training and skills in leadership according to a transformational style. We have yet to see whether this vision will be realised, whilst national competency standards are being developed, evidence suggests that, in practice, police management still suffers significant failings (Adlam 2002: 17).

Other developments might also push against the realization of changes to supervision. The strength of performance culture reduces, rather than increases (Maguire and Norris 1992), the detachment between supervising and investigating officers, who all feel the same pressure to perform, especially given the dispersal of management responsibilities to lower ranks. It is also difficult for supervisors to motivate officers to achieve targets which are perceived to be set arbitrarily (FitzGerald et al. 2000: 140). While the rhetoric calls for transformational leadership, the reality is that those managing investigations are being called on to possess and move between different leadership styles, managing the criminal investigation in a way that complies with the bureaucratic standards and procedures, but also inspiring officers to improve their skills and abilities (Long 2003).

Managing the performance of criminal investigations

The growth of new approaches to performance management – notably the rise and rise of Compstat – has been one of the most significant changes in the management of criminal investigation in recent years. In skeleton form, performance management is the frequent collection and analysis of data, most often quantitative statistics, which indicate how the police are performing against a number of measures and benchmarks. To this have been added managerial techniques (like Compstat, discussed further below) which add personal accountability to rigorous data capture and scrutiny.

The resulting performance culture signifies the dominance of performance management as the primary method of managerial accountability (Loveday 1999: 21; Long 2003: 637; Home Office 2004b).

In this section we describe the main features of performance management as it relates to criminal investigations and consider the implications of this for the management of criminal investigations.

Measures of investigative performance

There are two performance measures which are directly relevant to criminal investigations: the number of offences brought to justice (OBTJ) and the detection rate. Our discussion focuses on these measures, but it should be noted that performance management of investigation does extend beyond this, separating criminal investigation into its constituent parts (for example, pre-arrest processes of gathering intelligence or the management of forensic services) and subjecting these to individual performance measurement and targets which are nationally defined and monitored.

The detection rate measures the percentage of all offences recorded by the police in which the police find out who committed the offence. It is the enduring measure, not only of investigative performance, but has long been seen as a proxy for the overall performance of the police (Audit Commission 1993: 1). Today the detection rate takes the more regulated form of the 'sanction detection'. Sanction detections are those offences reported to the police that result in a charge, an offence taken into consideration at the time of conviction (TIC), a caution or a fixed penalty notice (FPN). The adoption of the sanction detection represents a major shift in the meaning of 'detection' – a shift that was a reaction against the situation in the 1980s where detection rates were crucially underpinned by either pressing a charge regardless of the likelihood that it would result in a successful prosecution, or by the administrative means of a prison visit or post-charge write-off. Concern about how the detection rates were generated was voiced in the 1990s, and forces were asked to classify detections as primary (which involved police activity such as arrest or caution) or as secondary (such as a prison interview or TICs) (Loveday 2000). Secondary detections were seen as 'artificially boosting' detection rates because they did nothing to improve the effectiveness of the police in crime investigation (Loveday 1999: 22). The sanction detection rate is a more rigorous and regulated measure of how successful the police are, not only in catching offenders but also in building cases which are likely to succeed in the criminal justice system.

An OBTJ is an offence recorded by the police, which results in a caution, conviction or TIC. Whereas sanction detections are measured as a percentage of all recorded offences, OBTJs are measured as an absolute number – for example, 1.15 million offences were brought to justice in 2004 (Home Office 2004a). OBTJ is not just a measure of police investigative performance: it is a measure of the performance of the whole criminal justice system, towards which criminal investigation contributes by playing a first, crucial stage. Moves towards joint performance management reflect both the increase in multi-agency working in criminal justice (Crawford and Jones 1995) and a shift in the mission of policing from one of crime fighting to one of raising public confidence in the criminal justice system (Office for Criminal Justice Reform 2004: 7; Neyroud 2006). This shift has implications for managers of criminal investigations and for management accountability more generally in criminal justice. The managers of criminal investigations must now routinely work with their colleagues in the Crown Prosecution Service (CPS), courts and correctional services and must consider the effect of their actions on later stages in the criminal justice process. The broader implications are that if a desired outcome of a criminal investigation is a satisfied witness and a confident public, this might be best achieved through a framework of interdependence and collaboration between agencies, rather than the existing system where agencies manage the performance of their own bit of the process. New structures are created, such as local criminal justice boards, which provide a forum for joint performance management.

The contemporary landscape of performance management

The sanction detection and OBTJ rates are the key measures used in the performance management of criminal investigations, and each force and BCU will agree a target with central government for OBTJ and sanction detections to be achieved over the course of a year. Throughout the 1980s and 1990s, central government had only shown interest in police performance when the figures were published, which usually happened four times a year. The situation now is totally different, with data on sanction detections and OBJT available from iquanta, an Internet-based system that presents statistical information about police performance across a wide number of measures (Home Office 2004b). The data on iquanta are available very quickly (for example, the sanction detection rate during January will be reported in February) and are very detailed, allowing forces, BCUs and crime and disorder reduction partnerships (CDRPs) to be ranked and compared in league tables according to their sanction detection and OBTJ rates. Iquanta can be accessed by managers within the police and within CDRPs, and, of course, by central government. Performance data receives intensive scrutiny from central government and we mention three sources of this scrutiny by way of example.

The Police Standards Unit (PSU) (now called the Police Crime and Standard Directorate) created in 2001, is a national body with the power to intervene in forces and individual BCUs which are judged, on the basis of iquanta data, to be poorly performing. The PSU has shown a specific interest in the performance management of crime investigation and in improving the performance of forces in detecting crimes. The PSU's approach to poor performance involves drawing up detailed action plans to deal with problems systematically, reinforcing a culture of disciplined performance management in the forces and BCUs which are subject to intervention. Another form of scrutiny by central government comes through the Police Performance Steering Group, a part of the Home Office which monitors changes in the performance of forces, BCUs and CDRPs on a month-by-month basis. If there is deterioration in performance, the group will intervene. The form of this intervention can vary, depending on the degree of deterioration, from mere correspondence to more direct intervention to improve performance.

Performance in crime investigation is included as one of seven key 'performance areas' in the Police Performance Assessment Framework (PPAF), which is a set of standards against which all police forces are assessed and graded (Home Office 2005). Standardized assessments, such as PPAF, look likely to extend their scrutiny to new areas of policing. The review of protective services, which includes important areas of criminal investigation, recommended the development of a measurement framework to assess the capacity of forces to provide protective services, and the capability, experience and accreditation of managers to deliver the range of specialist protective services which the report thought were critical to public confidence and to the ability to cope with the threat posed by organized crime and terrorism (HMIC 2005).

The response to performance culture

How have managers of criminal investigation, at BCU and force level, responded to the pressure to meet targets and to the intense scrutiny of performance? One way in which some forces have responded, which we would like to mention specifically, is through the implementation of Compstat. Compstat has been described as 'a goal-oriented strategic management process that uses computer technology, operational strategy and managerial accountability to structure the manner in which a police department provides crime-control services' (Walsh 2001: 347). What this means, when applied to the context of UK policing, is that Compstat is a tool for presenting performance data and holding managers to account for performance against targets – usually BCU commanders being held to account by chief officers. For example, if a BCU has a low sanction detection or OBJT rate, chief officers will ask BCU commanders and senior managers to account for this and to show that a plan is in place to improve performance. Compstat is strongly founded on principles of performance management: a belief that intense managerial oversight of performance figures can lead to improvements in policing, including in crime investigation.

We await formal evaluation of Compstat to see whether it can improve performance. In the absence of research evidence, we offer some points of speculation as to the implications of Compstat for the management of investigations. First, the proper use of Compstat requires officers to be trained in analysing data, problem-solving and management. These qualities are increasing likely to be found among the more senior management ranks, such as superintendents and chief superintendents, but there is little evidence that lower-ranking officers, who have responsibility for volume crime management, have these skills (Walsh 2001: 357). The consequences of Compstat being used by untrained managers are not clear, but it is at least possible that it might result in attention being focused on inappropriate performance measures (Chan 2001: 144).

While Compstat is heralded as supporting the dispersal of supervisory roles throughout the ranks and empowering middle managers, there are concerns that the hierarchical structures of Compstat, far from enhancing transformative systems of leadership, in fact encourage unhealthy competition between officers and focus management and supervisory attention on the outcomes of investigations, rather than on the quality of their conduct (Loveday 2000; Walsh 2001: 356). Compstat claims both to ensure adherence to high-level performance targets and to allow managers some flexibility in how they achieve those targets, but there is a sense in which it glosses over the complexity of criminal investigation; while it can highlight conflicts between targets and priorities, it cannot necessarily resolve them. Compstat is a process of review, not a substitute for active investigation management; it is primarily a strategic management tool; and it is potentially useful to chief officers and tactical-level managers in identifying good or poor performance and setting priorities. It cannot offer operational and supervisory officers much assistance in addressing the problems discussed earlier in this chapter.

Implications of performance management for criminal investigations

While we have set out many of the challenges and problems which come with the introduction of a performance culture to criminal investigation management, we do acknowledge the benefits which can stem from the creation of a framework of aims and objectives for policing and transparent systems for assessing the work of the police (Butler 2000: 308). Our concern lies not with performance culture *per se*, but with the rather aggressive form it can take in contemporary policing. Chief officers and BCU commanders are pressured by central government and this is passed on to managers throughout the organization; performance management is no longer the preserve of chief officers and BCU commanders, but is expected of officers of every rank, and this is specifically a pressure to reach performance targets.

To conclude this section we offer three examples of how tensions can arise between meeting targets and managing an individual investigation and consider some of the effects of performance targets on how front-line policing is conducted. The first example is an investigation which could be resolved informally (i.e. without achieving a charge, caution, conviction, TIC or FPN). Since this form of resolution does not count towards the OBTJ target, managers of criminal investigations are discouraged from using mediated solutions such as anti-social behaviour contracts or restorative approaches falling short of a formal caution, even if they are the most appropriate way to resolve a particular investigation.

The treatment of domestic violence cases provides a second example. When the police receive a report of domestic violence, current government and police policy strongly favours intervention. This can take the form of undertaking a risk assessment as to the likelihood and extent of future violence (ACPO and NCPE 2004), making an arrest or deciding to charge. Choosing to intervene contributes to sanction detection and OBTJ targets. However, there is evidence that arrest and prosecution can themselves trigger further violence (Sherman *et al.* 1992). Thus a decision by the manager of an investigation to arrest and charge may have the perverse effect of increasing the probability of reoffending, even if it contributes to the sanction detection and OBTJ targets. A third and final example is where the pressure to meet targets encourages managers to focus on volume crime investigations which are less resource intensive, at the expense of proper investigation of more serious crimes (Loveday 2000: 25–6). The sanction detection and OBJT rate does not take into account how difficult a crime was to investigate, or whether it increased investigating officers' skills (Reiner 1998: 71–2). These problems have not gone unnoticed; they were highlighted in relation to the detection rate over a decade ago (Maguire *et al.* 1991) and there have been attempts to develop more sophisticated measures of performance which attend to the quality of policing (for example, the Operational Policing Review in the early 1990s). However, there is some evidence of 'soft targeting' to drive up detection figures (HMIC 1999) and the so-called new performance management frameworks have been found to suffer from many of the ills of the old ones – in particular, the failure to take account of qualitative measures of policing (Moore 2002).

In the above three examples, the pressure to meet targets is effectively determining police priorities. Another effect which performance management can have on the management of criminal investigation occurs in the event of a conflict between targets. There is some conflict between OBTJ, expressed in absolute terms, and crime reduction targets, which are measured as a percentage; if there is a percentage reduction in crime, the OBTJ target becomes proportionally harder to achieve. The unintended consequences of performance targets are also troubling – for example, in the last two years the police have responded to intense pressure from central government to improve sanction detection rates and, consequently, more people have been charged. This has created such an increased workload for the CPS, courts, probation service and youth offending teams as to result in delays and backlogs at these later stages of the criminal justice system. In this chapter we have pointed to evidence of the existence of cross-agency performance management, but this example hints at some disjuncture between the rhetoric of central government policy and the reality of joined-up performance management on the ground.

The oversight of criminal investigations

The oversight of criminal investigations has changed quite dramatically in both quantity and quality in the course of the last 25 years. There are now more sources of oversight, more aspects of investigation that are subject to oversight and a strong element of independence and publicity to the current oversight structure. In this final section we highlight four key features of the current oversight regime as it relates to criminal investigation. It is increasingly standardized; it is becoming more local in focus; it is public and independent; and it is cross-agency.

Standardization in the oversight of investigations

Her Majesty's Inspectorate of Constabulary (HMIC) is probably the most visible and active overseer of criminal investigation. The approach and methods of HMIC have become increasingly standardized and rationalized;

standardized in that the methodology of inspection has been comprehensively set out and is uniformly applied to all inspections, and rationalized in that HMIC focuses its efforts where inspection is most needed. HMIC has, itself, been under pressure from central government to adopt an inspection regime which accords with the government's agenda for professionalization and the reform of policing (Hale *et al.* 2004: 294), and as such is both a product of the changes to policing and a driving force behind further change.

HMIC is said to take a 'diagnostic' approach to inspection through its baseline assessment process. A baseline assessment is a self-assessment conducted by each police force, which requires a force to grade its performance according to a variety of indicators. Criminal investigation is directly or indirectly the subject of several of these indicators. For example, the baseline assessment looks at the investigation of hate crime, at volume crime investigation, at the management of forensic services, criminal justice processes, call management and leadership and performance management. The outcome of a baseline assessment is that a force is graded 'excellent', 'good', 'fair' or 'poor', and this grading will determine how HMIC will inspect that force. A poorly performing force will be subjected to a full, formal inspection. Where the baseline assessment reveals only a few areas of concern, HMIC can inspect just those specific areas, and where the baseline assessment reveals good performance, HMIC might only conduct a paper-based assessment, without visiting the force at all.

Whether it is conducting a full or partial inspection, HMIC will conduct its work in accordance with a number of inspection protocols. These set out how particular aspects of policing should be inspected and, as in the baseline assessment criteria, criminal investigation features heavily. There are protocols on the investigation of specific types of crime, on the investigation of major crime and on the various specialist teams which are involved in criminal investigation. HMIC advertises the fact that it makes professional judgements about the qualtity of a force, rather than just scrutinizing quantitative performance figures, but we can see that the whole inspection process is highly formalized, so that each inspection will look at the same aspects of criminal investigation. As a result of this standardization forces are more easily ranked according to inspection outcomes.

The oversight of criminal investigation might also be thought of as standardized due to the presence of significant oversight by central government, which uniformly scrutinizes all forces in line with national policies and guidelines. There has been a near constant shifting in the balance between local and national oversight of criminal investigations. The Police and Magistrates Courts Act 1994 gave police authorities enhanced powers to hold chief constables to account (Jones and Newburn 1997), and these powers were further strengthened by the creation of the Policing Plan and the Best Value Review (BVR) process. BVR gave police authorities the ability to set the priorities for a force – including for crime investigation – and to review the effectiveness of the force's practice. However, authorities appeared slow to use these oversight powers, and the 2001 white paper (Home Office 2001) implicitly criticized the ability of police authorities to hold chief constables to account by creating the PSU, a national organization with a strong oversight function. Police authorities are themselves overseen, according to national standards, by inspections of the BVR process by HMIC and the Audit Commission.

Standardization in the oversight of criminal investigations can be seen in the growth in national guidance which sets down a uniform approach to overseeing the conduct of particular investigations. For example, in every force, a major homicide investigation or critical incident will be monitored and overseen by a 'gold group'. This is a group which convenes to give the senior investigating officer advice and guidance on the direction of the investigation. A gold group will usually be chaired by a chief officer, with the membership of the rest of the group depending on the expertise called for by the particular investigation. The group can include professionals from outside the police – for example in cases where the suspect is being supervised by the probation service, a senior member of the service will be invited to join. The gold group will perform strategic oversight functions, forming the head of a command structure which consists of 'silver command' at the tactical level and 'bronze control' at the operational level.

Local and detailed

At the same time as there have been increases in national level oversight, there have been equally strong moves towards local oversight. The 2004 white paper (Home Office 2004a) proposed that local people should be given the power to 'trigger' the police to respond to persistent problems such as anti-social behaviour. These forms of local oversight could have major implications for the investigation of crimes like drug dealing and street robbery which are likely to be the focus of citizens' scrutiny.

In 2001, HMIC conducted the first round of inspections of individual BCUs. This new, local focus was driven by the idea that 'policing is essentially a local service' (HMIC 2001: 4), and by concern about variance in the performance of different BCUs. Performance in criminal investigation is scrutinized in these inspections through the sanction detection and OBTJ figures for the BCU, and through more qualitative assessments. Inspectors will specifically look at the skill and experience of senior investigating officers, the use of forensic techniques, whether investigation complies with national guidelines and at the effectiveness of investigative resource use (HMIC 2001: 70). Significantly, HMIC encourages the use of Compstat-style approaches within a BCU (HMIC 2001: 66) and thus encourages both management responsibility and performance culture right the way through the organization. Inspection below the strategic surface of the force means that it is not the chief officers who are exposed to scrutiny, but their local commanders and senior crime managers.

A new, local source of oversight is to be found in the power to review cases of domestic homicide. The purpose of these reviews, introduced under s. 9 of the Domestic Violence, Crime and Victims Act 2004, is to examine the circumstances which lead to a domestic homicide. The reviews will be convened by multi-agency CDRPs, and a significant part of the review will be the scrutiny of how the police responded to and investigated earlier reports of domestic violence.

Public and independent scrutiny

In the 1980s the vast majority of criminal investigations were conducted out of sight of the public and with very little external involvement or supervision. Calls for independent and public scrutiny were first voiced in the Byford Report (1981), which recommended measures to make criminal investigation amenable to scrutiny such as standard procedures for investigations, and recommended scrutiny itself through a process of review at key stages of an investigation. The Association of Chief Police Officers (ACPO) now recommends that any major inquiry should be subject to review by another force while the investigation is ongoing and, after the Macpherson Report, it is standard practice for a major investigation to be reviewed after 28 and 90 days, with both reviews made available to the public. As well as these reviews, the investigation into the murder of Damilola Taylor was subject to retrospective review by a semi-independent oversight panel. Macpherson also led to the introduction of independent advisory groups (IAGs). These are informal, non-statutory groups, whose role is to challenge police policies and practices, including in criminal investigation. IAGs have been given substantial licence to see and advise on all aspects of policing and have the potential to impact on police practice, opening it up to scrutiny (Bowling 1999). Since the conduct of criminal investigations can have a significant effect on the confidence which different communities have in the police, this is certainly an aspect of policing of interest to IAGs.

The Independent Police Complaints Commission (IPCC) has a vitally important oversight role in individual cases where any aspect of the investigation is deemed to have gone wrong. Reports by the IPCC will be published and open to the public and will look at the minutiae of an investigation. Investigations in high-profile cases, such as the investigations into the deaths of Victoria Climbie and Stephen Lawrence, can also be subject to a public inquiry (Macpherson 1999; Laming 2003). The public inquiry into the death of Dr David Kelly (Hutton 2004) was conducted at the same time as the police investigation, scrutinizing the investigation as it went along.

There are many other independent forms of oversight of criminal investigations: coroners can now undertake wide-ranging inquiries into deaths, including looking at the police investigation, and can make detailed recommendations (Home Secretary 2003); if there is any doubt about the security of a conviction stemming from an investigation, the Criminal Cases Review Commission can re-examine it; since the *Victims' Code of Practice*, became law in April 2006, victims can make a formal complaint to the Parliamentary Ombudsman if they feel the code has been breached during the course of a criminal investigation (Office for Criminal Justice Reform 2005). There is also the possibility of oversight from the civil courts through the application of the Human Rights Act 1998, and the Freedom of Information Act offers a more limited, but none the less important, source of oversight, empowering citizens to discover the details of a criminal investigation.

Cross-agency oversight of investigations

At several points in this chapter we have highlighted the involvement of non-police agencies in the management of criminal investigations. HMIC now undertakes joint area inspections with the inspectorates of other criminal justice agencies, such as Her Majesty's Crown Prosecution Service Inspectorate (HMCPSI), Her Majesty's Inspectorate of Courts Administration (HMICA) or Her Majesty's Inspectorate of Probation (HMIP). Joint inspections can look nationally at a single, cross-agency theme (HMIC and HMIP 2005) or can look at how local criminal justice agencies are co-operating and working together in their local criminal justice boards (HMIC *et al.* 2005). The focus of these inspections is on how agencies are performing in achieving OBTJ targets and how agencies are working together to improve the level of public confidence in the criminal justice system. The proposal to create a single Inspectorate for the Criminal Justice System (Criminal Justice System 2005) is the clearest example of the growing importance of cross-agency oversight. The police service has expressed concerns about this development, arguing it could result in a focus on the end results of the criminal justice system, thus neglecting the quality and process aspects of investigations.

We are not questioning the need for democratic accountability and independent oversight of policing, but would like to highlight the quite astounding number of organizations having some role in overseeing investigations. New ways of conducting criminal investigations, ranging from the influence of new technology, to the involvement of more non-police agencies, to the growth in neighbourhood policing, create a need for new methods of oversight. The investigators of the next decades will have to hold their own in a variety of fora, ranging from the scrutiny committee of the local authority to the floor of a public inquiry.

Conclusions

In this final section we would like to look at two current government policies that tie together the discussion and the themes of this chapter: the Charging Scheme and the Prolific and Other Priority Offender Strategy.

The Criminal Justice Act 2003 made changes to the way that the decision to charge is made. The CPS now gives pre-charge advice to the police and while the decision to charge formally lies in the hands of CPs, the giving of advice means that decisions about charge are taken in a much more collaborative way than in the past, necessitating cooperation between the CPS charging lawyer and the custody sergeant or officer in the case, leaving the police as the sole decision-maker only in the most straightforward cases. Under the Charging Scheme the prosecutor essentially plays a part in managing and directing a criminal investigation, for the very simple reason that prosecutors can see gaps in evidence which officers must fill by conducting further inquiries. The Charging Scheme unquestionably pushes the police to professionalize and standardize the process of prisoner handling and investigation. It introduces a new kind of interagency working, where both agencies have a clear and equally strong role in the charging process and have an equally strong interest in good performance. The CPS is a national agency, accountable directly to a government minister, but the Charging Scheme has been performance managed through local criminal justice boards, thus reflecting the duality of national and local control.

Under the Prolific and Other Priority Offender Scheme, central government requires CDRPs and local criminal justice agencies to identify, together, the most persistent offenders in an area and take steps to stop them reoffending. This can either be through making the criminal justice process more efficient for these people, so they are caught, convicted and sentenced more quickly, or through offering persistent offenders help to deal with problems such as drugs, housing and employment, which drive their offending. The implications of this for criminal investigation are complicated: the identification of persistent offenders is itself a multi-agency process, conducted by all the agencies including the police, who sit on CDRPs. Once identified, persistent offenders are a priority for police investigation, so we can see how the strategic management of investigations – the stage at which priorities for investigations are set – is now influenced by non-police agencies. Secondly, in effect, the scheme requires the police to play a part in the broader management of these offenders, along with other criminal justice agencies and social care agencies (Mawby and Worrall 2004). This introduces the potential for significant conflicts; if a persistent offender is doing well in drug treatment or training it might be counterproductive (in terms of preventing reoffending) to investigate and prosecute him or her and disrupt this treatment, even though this might be the best course of action for the police in terms of achieving short-term targets for sanction detections and OBTJs.

Writing over 20 years ago, Smith and Gray (1985) found that they did not know enough about the management of investigations to examine and comment on the process. These comments seem inapplicable to how investigations are managed, supervised and overseen today, where every role is defined, every action logged and every decision externally accountable.

Selected further reading

Maguire, M. and Norris, C. (1992) *The Conduct and Supervision of Criminal Investigations.* London: HMSO. Although now 15 years old, this is an excellent starting point for further reading, offering a thoughtful and clear exposition of the issues at stake in conducting and supervising criminal investigations.

Innes, M. (2003) *Investigating Murder: Detective Work and the Police Response to Criminal Homicide.* Oxford: Oxford University Press. A sociologically informed analysis of the stuff of criminal investigations, this book considers how investigators co-ordinate lines of inquiry and make sense of vast amounts of information. As such, it is essential reading.

Smith, N. and Flanagan, C. (2000) *The Effective Detective: Identifying the Skills of an Effective SIO. Police Research Series Paper* 122. London: Home Office. There is not, yet, much written on the meaning and implication of moves to professionalize the police workforce, which has been an important theme in this chapter. This paper offers a comprehensive treatment of the skills and qualities required of investigators and provides some insight into the need and direction of professionalization.

Long, M. (2003) 'Leadership and performance management', in T. Newburn (ed.) *Handbook of Policing*. Cullompton: Willan Publishing. This chapter provides an excellent overview of the issues involved in the leadership of policing.

Adlam, R. and Villiers, P. (eds) (2003) *Police Leadership in the Twenty-first Century: Philosophy, Doctrine and Developments*. Winchester: Waterside Press. This edited collection offers a detailed treatment of the critical questions facing police leadership.

Neyroud, P. (2006) 'Ethics in policing: performance and the personalization of policing', *Journal of Legal Ethics*, 9: 16–34. A recent analysis of performance management in policing.

Notes

1 The incident room is the location from which a major investigation is managed. It is made up of a number of officers who each fulfil a role defined in the *MIRSAP*.
2 We appreciate that each of these terms can be said to have very separate meanings (see Smith and Flanagan 2000; Long 2003: 628).
3 Although there is much to say about this; see McLaughlin and Murji (1997); Macpherson (1999); FitzGerald *et al.* (2000); Wright (2000); Long (2003); Mawby and Wright (2003); Howlett-Bolton *et al.* (2005).
4 Also relevant here is the issue of how to supervise officers who are dealing informants, which space prevents us discussing (but see Dunnighan and Norris 1999).

References

ACPO (2000) *Murder Investigation Manual*. London: ACPO.

ACPO (2004) *Response to Closer to the Citizen*. London: ACPO.

ACPO and NCPE (2004) *Investigating Domestic Violence*. London: ACPO.

Adlam, R. (2002) 'Governmental rationalities in police leadership: an essay exploring some of the "deep structure" in police leadership praxis', *Policing and Society*, 12: 15–36.

Adlam, R. and Villiers, P. (eds) (2003) *Police Leadership in the Twenty-first Century: Philosophy, Doctrine and Developments*. Winchester: Waterside Press.

Amey, P., Hale, C., Uglow, S. and Laycock, G. (1996) *Development and Evaluation of a Crime Management Model. Police Research Series Paper*. 18. London: Home Office.

Audit Commission (1993) *Helping with Enquiries: Tackling Crime Effectively*. London: HMSO.

Audit Commission (2001) *Best Foot Forward: Headquarters Support for Police Basic Command Units*. London: Audit Commission.

Bichard, M. (2004) *The Bichard Inquiry Report*. London: HMSO.

Billingsley, R., Nemitz, T. and Bean, P. (eds) (2001) *Informers: Policing, Policy, Practice*. Cullompton: Willan Publishing.

Bowling, B. (1999) *Violent Racism: Victimization, Policing and Social Context*. Oxford: Clarendon Press.

Brown, D. (1997) *PACE 10 Years On. Home Office Research Study* 123. London: Home Office.

Butler, T. (2000) 'Managing the future: a chief constable's view', in F. Leishman *et al.* (eds) *Core Issues in Policing*. Harlow: Longman.

Byford, L. (1981) 'The Yorkshire Ripper case: review of the police investigation of the Case.' HMIC, unpublished.

Centrex (2004) *Management of Volume Crime.* Harrogate: Centrex.
Centrex (2005) *Major Incident Room Standardised Administrative Procedures.* Harrogate: Centrex.
Chan, J. (2001) 'The technological game: how information technology is transforming police practice', *Criminal Justice,* 1: 139–59.
Crawford, A. and Jones, M. (1995) 'Inter-agency co-operation and community based crime prevention', *British Journal of Criminology,* 35: 17–33.
Criminal Justice System (2005) *Inspection Reform: Establishing an Inspectorate for Justice and Community Safety: Consultation.* London: Criminal Justice System.
Dobby, J., Anscombe, J. and Tuffin, R. (2004) *Police Leadership: Expectations and Impact. Home Office Online Report 20/04.* London: Home Office.
Drodge, E. and Murphy, S. (2002) 'Police leadership as a transformational social process', *International Journal of Police Science and Management,* 4: 198–212.
Dunnighan, C. and Norris, C. (1999) 'The detective, the snout, and the Audit Commission: the real costs in using informants', *Howard Journal,* 38: 67–86.
FitzGerald, M., Hough, M., Joseph, I. and Qureshi, T. (2000) *Policing for London.* Cullompton: Willan Publishing.
Hale, C., Heaton, R. and Uglow, S. (2004) 'Uniform styles? Aspects of police centralization in England and Wales', *Policing and Society,* 14: 291–312.
HMIC (1999) *Police Integrity: Securing and Maintaining Public Confidence.* London: Home Office Directorate.
HMIC (2001) *Going Local: The BCU Inspection Handbook.* London: Home Office.
HMIC (2002) *Emerging Findings from BCU Inspections in 2001.* London: Home Office.
HMIC (2005) *Closing the Gap.* London: HMIC.
HMIC, HMCPSI, HMICA, HM Inspectorate of Prisons and HMIP (2005) *The Joint Inspection of the Merseyside Criminal Justice Area* (available online at http://inspectorates.homeoffice.gov.uk/hmic).
HMIC and HMIP (2005) *Managing Sex Offenders in the Community: A Joint Inspection on Sex Offenders* (available online at http://inspectorates.homeoffice.gov.uk/hmic).
Home Office. (2001) *Policing a New Century Blueprint for Reform.* London: HMSO.
Home Office (2003) *Policing: Building Safer Communities Together.* London: Home Office Communications Directorate.
Home Office (2004a) *Building Communities, Beating Crime.* London: Home Office.
Home Office (2004b) *Managing Police Performance: A Practical Guide to Performance Management.* London: Home Office.
Home Office (2005) *Police Performance Assessments, 2004/5.* London: HMSO.
Home Secretary (2003) *Death Certification and Investigation in England, Wales and Northern Ireland: The Report of a Fundamental Review.* London: HMSO.
Howlett-Bolton, A., Burden, A., Caplin, T., Ramsbotham, D., Rutherford, K., Woodhead, C. et al. (2005) *Policing Matters: Recruitment, Training and Motivation.* London: Politeia.
Hutton, L. (2004) *Report of the Inquiry into the Circumstances Surrounding the Death of Dr David Kelly, C.M.G.* London: HMSO.
Innes, M. (2002) 'The "process structures" of police homicide investigations', *British Journal of Criminology,* 42: 669–88.
Jones, T. and Newburn, T. (1997) *Policing After the Act: Police Governance After the Police and Magistrates' Courts Act 1994.* London: Police Studies Institute.
Laming, H. (2003) *The Victoria Climbié Inquiry.* London: HMSO.
Long, M. (2003) 'Leadership and performance management', in T. Newburn (ed.) *Handbook of Policing.* Cullompton: Willan Publishing.
Loveday, B. (1999) *Managing the Police: A New Paradigm for Policing. University of Portsmouth Institute of Criminal Justice Studies Occasional Paper 10.* Portsmouth: Institute of Criminal Justice Studies, University of Portsmouth.

Loveday, B. (2000) *Managing Crime: Police Use of Crime Data as an Indicator of Effectiveness.* University of Portsmouth Institute of Criminal Justice Studies Occasional Paper 12. Portsmouth: Institute of Criminal Justice Studies, University of Portsmouth.

Macpherson, W. (1999) *The Stephen Lawrence Inquiry.* London: HMSO.

Maguire, M., Noakes, L., Hobbs, R. and Brearley, N. (1991) *Assessing Investigative Performance.* Cardiff: Cardiff University Press.

Maguire, M. and Norris, C. (1992) *The Conduct and Supervision of Criminal Investigations.* London: HMSO.

Mawby, R. and Worrall, A. (2004) '"Polibation" revisited: policing, probation and prolific offender projects', *International Journal of Police Science and Management,* 6: 63–73.

Mawby, R.C. and Wright, A. (2003) 'Police organization', in T. Newburn (ed.) *Handbook of Policing.* Cullompton: Willan Publishing.

McFarlane, P. and Mould, C. (2002) *Report of the Review of Senior Officer Training and Development.* London: Home Office.

McLaughlin, E. and Murji, K. (1997) 'The future lasts a long time: public policework and the managerialist paradox', in P. Francis *et al.* (eds) *Policing Futures: The Police, Law Enforcement, and the Twenty First Century.* Basingstoke: Macmillan.

Moore, M.H. (2002) *Recognizing Value in Policing: The Challenge of Measuring Police Performance.* Washington, DC: Police Executive Research Forum.

National Crime Intelligence Service (2000) *The National Intelligence Model.* London: National Criminal Intelligence Service.

NCPE and ACPO (2004) *Management of Volume Crime: Practice and Advice for the Implementation of a Volume Crime Management Model* (available online at www.acpo.police.uk).

NCPE and ACPO (2005) *Practice Advice on Core Investigative Doctrine.* Cambourne: ACPO.

Neyroud, P. (2006) 'Ethics in policing: performance and the personalization of policing', *Journal of Legal Ethics* 9(1) 16–34.

Neyroud, P. and Beckley, A. (2001) *Policing, Ethics and Human Rights.* Cullompton: Willan Publishing.

Office for Criminal Justice Reform (2004) *Cutting Crime, Delivering Justice: A Strategic Plan for Justice, 2004–08.* London: HMSO.

Office for Criminal Justice Reform. (2005) *The Code of Practice for Victims of Crime.* London: Criminal Justice System.

Police Leadership Development Board (2003) *Getting the Best Leaders to Take on the Most Demanding Challenges: Project Report.* London: Home Office.

Reiner, R. (1998) 'Process or product? Problems of assessing individual police performance', in J.-P. Brodeur (ed.) *How to Recognize Good Policing: Problems and Issues.* Thousand Oaks, CA and London: Sage.

Sheehy, S.P. (1993) *Inquiry into Police Responsibilities and Rewards.* London: HMSO.

Sherman, L., Schmidt, J. and Rogan, D. (1992) *Policing Domestic Violence: Experience and Dilemmas.* New York, NY: Free Press.

Smith, D. and Gray, J. (1985) *Police and People in London: The PSI Report.* Aldershot: Gower.

Smith, N. and Flanagan, C. (2000) *The Effective Detective: Identifying the Skills of an Effective SIO. Police Research Series Paper* 122. London: Home Office.

Walsh, W.F. (2001) 'Compstat: an analysis of an emerging police managerial paradigm', *International Journal of Police Strategy and Management,* 24: 347–62.

Wright, A. (2000) 'Managing the future: an academic's view', in F. Leishman *et al.* (eds) *Core Issues in Policing.* Harlow: Longman.

Chapter 23

Critical incidents: investigation, management and training

John Grieve, Jonathan Crego and Bill Griffiths

Introduction

Policing has had to respond to many complex political, economic, social, technological, ethical and legal developments. Managing critical incidents (such as terrorist attacks, murders, rapes and child abuse cases) involves making and communicating difficult decisions in complex, uncertain and dynamic environments. Officers must motivate large teams and work in concert with other agencies that may have competing agendas, and they must adhere to strict legal and organizational priorities and policies. Much has been learnt from the management of critical incidents in non-policing areas, and the police have developed their own new approaches that have been tested in recent high-profile investigations in England and Wales. This chapter examines the changes to investigative doctrine, processes and accountability that have arisen as a result of the police's experience of critical incidents. These changes are recent: five years ago many of the tools described here, which are now being used routinely, would not even have been considered.

A complex policing environment

We are living in a world that is changing rapidly and in which new risks emerge that are unprecedented historically. The degree of complexity when a critical incident is in progress often startles outside observers, but is quickly forgotten after the event unless it is recorded at the time. According to the German sociologist, Ulrich Beck (1992), these changes are resulting in a global 'risk society'. Risks are identified and instantly made public as a result of global mass media, which gives rise to uncertainty and to new (sometimes aggressive) policing challenges. In response, new ways of managing risk have been developed involving new actors and this at a time when the old structures formed during the industrial society are fast disappearing (Wright 2002). It is self-evident that mass mediation brings with it greater accountability. Once a risk has been identified, the media, politicians, lawyers and others (sometimes in powerful alliances) will demand to know who is responsible and, more importantly, who is to blame. Leishman and Mason (2003) describe the myths, fictions, facts and factions of this many-sided media feast of 'infotainment', spiced as it is with blame and scandal, conspiracy and cover-up.

This culture of accountability is exacerbated by the best-value regime, a legislative requirement of the Local Government Act 1999 now central to police management and public sector governance (Dobson 2000). Accountability has led to an agenda shared with the media of naming, shaming and blaming. Although this can be traced back to the Thatcher era (Clarke and Newman 1997; Leishman *et al.* 2000), the present government has continued this agenda (McLaughlin 2001).

Added to this is an emotional ingredient of fear or hope, satisfaction or anxiety, which is inevitable in such critical circumstances. Blame is assigned not necessarily by subsequent reviewers of the decisions that were made at the time but by media commentators. Emotional intelligence may be seen as a weakness, and this does not help the officer responsible to shed his or her sense of personal blame. What is needed is a methodology for debriefing the incident that teases out the complexities of decision-making within an emotionally safe framework. The skills acquired through such a process should then be tested in an equally safe learning environment.

The Policing Skills and Standards Organization (now Skills for Justice) has recognized that, in the next five years or so, there is likely to be a severe shortage of individuals who have the necessary skills to take on the task of managing critical incidents: 80 per cent of officers now involved with major inquiries have less than five years' experience (PSSO 2002). In order that the police service fully recognizes this issue, a research agenda must be developed that is devoted to harnessing the existing wealth of knowledge and experience for the benefit of future generations of critical incident managers (Crego and Spinks 1997; Crego and Harris 2002).

This chapter, therefore, considers developments in 'practical cop things to do' (Parekh 2000: 124) in response to complex twenty-first century problems:

- Providing community policing responses to a spectrum of risks.
- Protecting communities.
- Dealing with blame.

Good communication, as in all police investigations, lies at the heart of all such responses.

Institutional failure, blame and racism

The Stephen Lawrence Inquiry described institutional racism as:

> The collective failure of an organisation to provide an appropriate and professional service to people because of their colour, culture or ethnic origin. It can be seen or detected in processes, attitudes and behaviour which amount to discrimination through unwitting prejudice, ignorance, thoughtlessness and racist stereotyping which disadvantages minority ethnic people (Macpherson 1999: para. 6.34).

Policing failures characterized as unwitting prejudice, ignorance, thoughtlessness and stereotyping can not only be applied to hate or sectarian crimes but also to other forms of bigotry. Institutional incompetence is a useful concept when considering whether people learn from their mistakes. Once a failure has been pointed out, is it now possible to claim the defence of unwitting prejudice, ignorance or thoughtlessness? Is it now more likely to allege that the prejudice was deliberate? Another excuse proffered for institutional racism is that, in the complexity of the investigation, racism goes unrecognized or is ignored. Foster *et al.* (2005: 96) conclude that the term 'institutional racism was the single most powerful message that police officers received from the Stephen Lawrence Inquiry but it did not prompt police forces to consider the issues fully'. We hold that critical incident thinking produces an intelligence- or knowledge-led learning organization.[1] Such an approach has been described as the opposite of stupidity-led policing (Reiner 2000 pers. com.).

Emotional intelligence and 'wicked' problems

There are two dimensions to critical incidents in the context of policing. Emotional intelligence (popularized by Daniel Goleman 1996, 1998, 2000) involves understanding and controlling one's emotions – key to health and success in life. It has been suggested that there are four critical components to emotional intelligence:

1 An accurate understanding, perception, expression and response to emotions.
2 An ability to access, manage, regulate and generate emotions in the service of thinking and problem-solving.
3 Understanding emotions and emotional meanings.
4 Being able to manage and regulate one's emotions appropriately (Mayer *et al.* 2000).

Emotional intelligence has an impact on decision-making and leadership styles. Traditionally, policing skills are often taught in a sterile environment that ignores emotions, and decision logs and policy files are largely written in abstract scientific, even mechanistic, style.

Decision-making can create what have been called 'wicked problems' that test the emotional intelligence of the officer involved:

- Was he or she scared?
- Did he or she think that this was a career-limiting decision?
- Did he or she believe he or she would be supported by his or her managers or the police force?

- Would the team work with him or her?
- What would they think of him or her after the decision had been made?

These are all questions that are considered in the heat of the critical incident and sometimes in the blink of an eye. Gladwell (2005) suggests that rapid decisions are much more complicated than is often assumed. Drawing on neuroscience and psychology, he shows that the difference between good and bad decision-making has nothing to do with how much information we can process quickly, but on the few particular details on which we focus. How and on what we focus depends on our previous experiences. Critical incident training allows participants to experience the complexity of the situation and the emotions involved in the decision-making when dealing with such 'wicked problems'.

Structures for responding to critical incidents

A 'critical incident' is defined as 'Any event where the effectiveness of the policing response is likely to have a significant impact on the confidence of the victim, their family or the community' (MPS 2002b: 3). Critical incident thinking is both tactical and strategic and is appropriate at different levels of investigation management:

- First responders, for example, constables and their supervisors (sergeants and inspectors).
- Middle managers, borough command unit commanders[2] and senior investigating officers.
- Chief officers and the groups they work with at the strategic level.

All three levels interact in the management and investigation of the incident and therefore the same considerations apply.

Critical incidents can occur in either the external operational or internal organizational policing environment. An external critical incident might be a racist or sectarian murder; an internal critical incident may involve a grievance by a police officer on race, gender or sexual orientation grounds that mirror tensions in the community. A critical incident may also develop from events that have already taken place, perhaps years before, or may also involve 'continuing events in action' which have the potential to become critical at some point, or that may be ongoing and need constant revisiting. These latter types are sometimes be called 'slow burning' critical incidents.

Key management tools

There are a number of tools that can be used in the policing of critical incidents:

- Family liaison officers.
- Community impact assessments.

- Risk assessments.
- Management structures, with minimum standards for supervision and perhaps a role for lay advisers.
- Decision logs for recording the decisions taken and the reasons why.
- Debriefing.

The difficulties in managing critical incidents may be exacerbated by communications failures with the victim, community or family, or by real or perceived investigative failure. This problem can be alleviated by the appointment of trained family liaison officers.

Family liaison officers[3]

A quarter of the recommendations of the Stephen Lawrence inquiry refer to families and their relationships with communities.[4] It will come as no surprise, therefore, that the primary tool for crafting solutions to the policing of critical incidents is the family liaison officer (FLO).

Since 1999 this role has grown enormously and has been widely welcomed by police officers (Foster *et al.* 2005: 75). FLOs are specialists, who need a high level of communication skills. They are investigators but they also maintain open dialogues with families, their support networks and communities. This allows them to carry out their primary investigative task of enabling the flow of evidence and intelligence while, at the same time, assisting the families of victims to steer the best possible course through what can be a terrible series of events.

Because of the potential stress of such a role, FLOs have a support structure. Coordinators guard their welfare, which is outlined in a manual of guidance. FLOs were deployed, to international acclaim, in New York in the aftermath of 11 September 2001.

FLOs maintain detailed logs of their partnerships, communications, service delivery and activities. They increasingly operate with representatives or advocates working on behalf of the family or victim. It is important that the police recognize these relationships as opportunities rather than as threats: 'an issue for the family is an issue for the police'. Some families, lawyers, single-issue pressure groups (e.g. racial-incident monitoring groups) and street agencies have become extremely adept at understanding the nature of critical incidents. Meetings with families, therefore, are often of vital importance as incidents develop or become less critical.

Community impact assessments

Early intervention in a crime or series of events can often forestall a critical incident. Indeed, most critical incidents do not progress beyond the first responders attending the scene – what is known as the 'golden hour'. A greater awareness of how critical incidents develop is achieved by robust methods of recording and analysing events, actions, allegations and problems. As a result of this process the unique nature of the critical incident can be assessed as well as its impact on the local community.

Community impact assessment derives in part from Chapter 10 of the *Major Incident Room Standardised Administrative Procedures* (*MIRSAP*) manual[5] (ACPO 2000). While there are different assessment formats, they all include sections that cover analysis of the incident risk management and accountability. One developed by Thames Valley Police has the following structure:

- Brief details of the critical incident contained in a summary of events. The assumption here is that if you can précis the events you understand what the issues are.

- Details of the consultation (communities and individuals): internally within the service and externally with agencies large or small or with other institutions and individuals.

- The investigation strategy and the operational strategy. These strategies are at the heart of the assessment. The investigation team outline how the investigation involved communities and their concerns (for example, a faith location); the operational officers identify existing local mechanisms and contacts that are hopefully already in place and the way they dealt with the investigative issues.

- A risk and impact assessment of issues within and beyond the control of the police and management concerns deriving from the above analysis (the likelihood of specific risks occurring; their consequences; description of control strategies and activities for these impacts, risks and consequences).

- The community impact assessment: an overall analysis of the options and consequences and the steps taken to deal with them.

- The community and race relations officer's information/advice to the process.

- Approval/authority for action. The document is presented to, agreed by and signed off by the relevant senior officers.

Risk assessments
One of the effects of the Human Rights Act, the Stephen Lawrence Inquiry (Macpherson 1999) and the Damilola Taylor Inquiry (Metropolitan Police Service 2002) was the need for the police to learn from and advise local leadership and communities on the emerging risks attached to certain kinds of decisions. Confidence is closely related to community impact assessment and this, in turn, is an ingredient of the risk assessments required by both human rights legislation and health and safety regulation and monitoring.

As Richards (2003) has pointed out 'risk' can be measured as follows:

- *Standard*: there is no current indicators of risk.
- *Medium*: there are indicators of events with a potential impact. A change or trigger has the potential to raise the position to high risk.
- *High*: there is a likelihood of the trigger event happening. The impact of this event is probable, serious and possibly imminent.

Impact assessments require consultation with the local community. They can be prepared by intelligence officers, community and race relations officers or community safety staff. Richards (2003) goes on to explain how risks can be managed by structured judgements and activity:

- Reducing the impact, threats or hazards, possibly by using intervention strategies such as interviews, publicity, safety planning.
- Avoidance – taking steps to bypass particular risks, such as changing the venue of an event or the potential ingredient of a critical incident.
- Removing the problem completely, such as rehousing some vulnerable parties.
- Accepting the risk but with continuing assessment in the absence of other options.

Practical street-level solutions and skills are therefore at the heart of responding to community risks. The response has to be consistent – any inconsistencies will soon be picked up. For example, mistakes admitted privately but not in public can undermine the whole critical incident approach. For this reason communications specialists need to be full members of the team.

Management structures
Critical incidents should be managed by a 'gold support group' (also called a 'critical incident support group'). This group provides leadership and sensitivity in what can be very complex and difficult operational circumstances. These teams are analogous to the 'dream teams' suggested by Flin (1997) following her analysis of the Piper Alpha disaster on a North Sea oil rig. They have been used in policing since the counter-terrorist campaigns of 1997 and 1998.

The gold support group supports the borough team, the investigative team or the tactical arm of the police response by providing strategic direction, guidance, resources, advice and analysis. Group membership will vary from incident to incident and across communities, but in general it will consist of the local and investigative command teams' representatives, information/media specialists, intelligence officers, diversity and community liaison support and independent advisers. One of its primary tasks is to monitor the regularly updated community impact assessment and to consider or mediate in the often competing needs of the family, community, senior investigating officer and borough commander, sometimes within a national context (for instance, when there is a terrorist dimension or a national public-order concern).

These needs of the victim, family, community, the nation and the task in hand are part of the group's strategic terms of reference. These terms of reference will help dictate group membership but, as mentioned above, there are no hard-and-fast rules. However, there should always be available independent advice, legal advice, specialist internal or external communications staff and representatives from the borough police management, the investigation team, family liaison co-ordinators and staff associations. Where they are available, police minority-group staff associations have been found to be hugely helpful. Critical incidents are frequently fast moving, so the gold support group needs to operate at a strategic level where it can consider the long-term consequences and the post-incident strategies.

Independent involvement

Independent involvement is a vital instrument in the communication, trust-building and confidence-inspiring measures of an active consultation process for impact assessment. Independent advisers can provide sensitivity and understanding in dealings with communities and, although they are never mediators with families and communities, they do facilitate communications. Although they are advisory, they may take up some executive roles on behalf of their communities. They are, however, never held to account for police activity although they may be, and frequently are, seen to be 'standing up and being counted' as, for instance, in the aftermath of the first Damilola Taylor murder trial. Independent advisers are a long-term development of partnership and multi-agency thinking and another product of the Stephen Lawrence Inquiry deliberations.

Independent involvement also avoids misunderstandings where the police have developed a particular approach to an event to the exclusion of all others. Therefore, while independent advisers are an outward and visible sign of openness and accountability, they can also challenge police mindsets and assumptions. This helps to build confidence and trust between police, families and communities.

Independent advisers should not be selected in the white heat of an acrimonious confrontation where something has already gone wrong. They have an important contribution to make from the beginning and are not there just for post-event validation of policing tactics. The earlier they are involved the better. Indeed, they should ideally be in existence and have an understanding of policing processes and challenges. There should be an established dialogue between potential independent advisers and the police prior to a critical incident occurring. In this way they have been found to be most effective. There is now an Association of Chief Police Officers - sponsored national network of local advisers, with terms of reference, a national conference and a training programme to ensure some consistency, co-ordination and continuity.

Because independent advisers are involved in a wide range of activities, it is probably easier to describe what independent advice is not, rather than what it is. It is not about mediation, not about being police informers or stooges, and independent advisers are not investigators, family mediators or lay liaison officers. Paying close attention to the terms of reference for independent advisers, maintaining records of their involvement, their briefing and debriefing and their welfare can avoid many problems. Their role (in the light of some cases) has been crucial in avoiding what could be termed 'institutional incompetence' and, like other processes, needs to be properly managed. It does not just happen.

It is vital that, although they will sometimes be paid from the public purse, independent advisers are seen to remain separate and independent of the police. They must not become involved in evidence giving, mediating or negotiating. In areas of tension or conflict this can lead to unhelpful participation, either as a witness or as an alleged agent of the police. Again, careful preparation of the terms of reference can avoid this blurring of tasks. However, independent advisers can help the police with community impact assessments and, in particular they provide a perspective on community concerns, particularly with the gold support group. They have been found to be core to effective decision-making and to the resolution of complex, potentially disastrous critical incidents.

Decision logs

Article 13 of the European Convention on Human Rights requires that records be kept of the rationale for decisions involving risks or threats to families and victims, to their human rights or to the human rights of others. This means citizens must have access to information if they are to make effective challenges, possibly using the Freedom of Information Act. These records used to be known as policy files (Metropolitan Police Service 2002b) or, interestingly, policy and progress files, with no mention of setbacks. Since the Stephen Lawrence Inquiry (Macpherson 1999) and the Home Secretary's action plan (Home Office 1999a) policing decisions must now be accountable (in practice, this means written records) as well as legal, proportionate and necessary. This is so that policing decisions can be audited and shown as not to be in breach.

It must also be shown that decisions were taken on the best information (BI) available. Decisions, therefore, should be based on a process known as PLAN BI:

Proportionate
Legal
Accountable
Necessary
and acting on the **B**est **I**nformation.

John Sentamu, a member of the Stephen Lawrence Inquiry, has reviewed policing developments since the inquiry's report was published. He concluded (2002) that much progress had been made although there is still a long way to go before society as a whole comes to recognize where bias, prejudice and stereotyping occur in communities.

The argument that there were neither sufficient police resources nor sufficient police skills to record all those things demanded by human rights legislation or the time available to avoid every injustice has been held to be inadequate. A shortage of resources is, therefore, inadequate grounds not to investigate every case thoroughly, rigorously, competently or comprehensively.

To be thorough and comprehensive, the Crown Prosecution Service has held that an inquiry must be led by someone with the appropriate skills and knowledge. This person must be capable of investigating the crime, be professional and must apply an appropriate level of supervision. This includes managing those elements that constitute a critical incident. Such supervision should include a separate review of the inquiry and should ensure the complete documentation of all activities and decisions. In other words, it is not enough to be successful; there has to be a record of how the decisions that lead to the success were reached.

Preparing people for critical incident management

It has been argued (Grieve 1998) that comparing case studies and academic research is an important part of intelligence-led policing. Analysis and critical and creative thinking will generate innovative solutions to complex problems (for example, illicit drug use (Grieve 1998) and hate crimes (ESRC Travis 2001; Hall 2005)). This might suggest the attributes and skills we would hope to find in individuals and, particularly, teams investigating and managing critical incidents.

These skills and attributes have been described by Irving and Dunningham (1993) as 'fundamental to the investigator'. They can be summarized as follows:

- Fairness, proactivity and an ability to use knowledge effectively.
- A focus on outcomes.
- Community awareness.

To these may be added the following:

- Investigative interviewing skills (including statement-taking from witnesses and victims) (Shepherd and Milne 1999).

- Leadership abilities (see, for example, Grieve 2002).

- Communication skills.

- Planning ahead to prepare for challenges.

- Integrity.

- Resilience (including the ability to introduce dissent from a received or directed decision)

- Co-operate with (not just keep in touch with) others.

- An understanding of communities and families.

- Detailed knowledge of the law, especially concerning evidence and exhibits.

- Being able to learn from positive outcomes rather than 'blamestorming' (i.e. discussing why an operation went wrong and who is to blame).

- Being an intelligent customer of services. The intelligent customer knows what questions to ask, how to integrate and analyse different kinds of intelligence, information and knowledge, and does not immediately start crying 'intelligence failure' when things do not go according to plan (Grieve 2004).

The Victoria Climbie Inquiry (Laming 2003) concluded that we need teams and individuals with decision-making experience and competences that we can equate to the investigative skills and attributes considered here:

- *Healthy scepticism*: leadership; vigilance; resilience (including emotional resilience); a cunning, proactive, intelligent and well founded interpretation of salient features.

- *Open minded*: thinking skills, breadth of view, flexibility, integrity, fairness, using knowledge effectively, perceptual discrimination, acuity.

- *Investigative approach*: information gathering and classification; structured logic; decision and choice; investigative interviewing; communication skills; working with others; respect for and co-operation with communities and families; outcomes focus; evidence preserved and compiled into well managed case files.

These are the skills and attributes required of critical incident investigators. Experts, however, behave differently from novices: experienced decision-makers recognize much earlier the possibility that a problem will become a critical incident, and may generate effective strategies and apply tactics that will have a positive impact on the problem. Training provides an opportunity for gaining this experience, both as an individual and as a team.

10,000 volts

One of the key techniques used in the training programme developed by the authors is 10,000 Volts (Crego and Harris 2002).[5] It is based, in part, on approaches to training in the aviation industry. Aviation training uses information collected in two different ways. First, there is information reported by pilots and other aviation professionals, in a safe and blameless way, about any occurrences that endangered air safety and, perhaps more significantly, any incident that had the potential to endanger air safety. The second type of information is a repository of essential knowledge: a collection of data from air-accident investigations including, where possible, actual recordings from black boxes and news and other footage.

The 10,000 Volts technique uses similar information. The participants sort, assess and prioritize the information, working as an electronic focus group (Crego and Allison 2003), which allows every participant's contribution to be captured anonymously on individual laptops. The technique can be applied to an actual operation, a siege, a murder investigation or a missing person's inquiry. In effect, it is a virtual public inquiry, trial or coroner's court, and everyone gets to answer every complex question. Each session includes an evaluation of the participants' performance, but the real test of its value is in the workplace, on the street or in the incident room.

Conclusion

Critical incidents often receive continuous and intense public and peer scrutiny, and peer or higher-ranking officers will examine all decisions as part of a review process. In some cases, this review is conducted by a public inquiry (Runciman 2004; Foster *et al.* 2005). The impetus for this examination is often failure, or perceived failure, of the investigative team or, more drastically, perceived organizational shortcomings.

However, the possibilities of learning from successes as well as failures are now being considered. It must not be forgotten that the vast majority of critical incident management is successful. A recent assessment of the impact of the Stephen Lawrence Inquiry concluded that there was universal agreement that there was a need to liaise with 'communities in response to events that had the potential for "critical impact"' (Foster *et al.* 2005: 52) – a fact now well established in critical incident management. Every critical incident training course results in long lists of positive and useful experiences, some of which we have noted here. Immersion learning, debriefing and the analysis of comparative cases and experiences will lead to an evolving menu of options for investigators. Acquiring this understanding, adopting these structures and using these skills will enable police agencies to deal better with the complexity, accountability and tendency to blame that are part of late modernity.

Selected further reading

Flin, R. (1997) *Sitting in the Hot Seat: Leaders and Teams for Critical Incident Management*. Chichester: Wiley.
Hall, N. (2005) *Hate Crime*. Cullompton: Willan Publishing.
TSO (1999) *Stephen Lawrence Inquiry*. London: Home Office.

Acknowledgements

The authors would like to express their thanks to Carol Bewick, Jeff Brathwaite, Joe Chowdry, Ron Cuthbertson, Dave Field, Howard Gosling, Ian Johnston, Steve Kavanagh, Duncan McGarry, Pat McLoud, Denis O'Connor, George Rhoden, John Sutherland among many others.

Notes

1 The emphasis here is on the word 'learning'. 'Intelligence-led learning' (as opposed to intelligence-led strategies, tactics and operations) leads to knowledge (Sims 1993; Crandon 1997; Grieve 2004).
2 The Metropolitan Police District is divided into geographic divisions that are co-terminus with the London boroughs, and so these divisions are known as borough commands. They are led by officers of chief superintendent rank who are referred to as borough command unit commanders.
3 The thinking behind this role first came from Avon and Somerset Police. FLOs were subsequently taken up by the Metropolitan Police as part of its response to the findings of the Stephen Lawrence Inquiry. It is unfortunate they are not

known as Stephen Lawrence officers as the role is directly related to the family's experiences and drive and to the recommendations of the inquiry.

4 Critical incident management techniques are not specific recommendations of the inquiry but many of the solutions are derived from the report, the daily transcripts and commentary. It is regrettable that little credit is ever given to Mr and Mrs Lawrence and the inquiry for these watershed operational techniques and for their huge contribution to communities and policing. It is similarly regrettable that the folk memory of the inquiry is 'police found guilty of institutional racism' rather than 'policing took a giant leap forward'.

5 The training programme, which has been run over 60 times, is a three-day immersion learning course. The course consists of three phases: strategic preparation, strategic application and strategic review. What is distinctive about the course are the detailed records participants keep about their decision-making, the participation of independent critical friends and the immediate visibility of the mistakes participants make.

References

ACPO (2000) *Major Incident Room Standardised Administrative Procedures*. London: ACPO.

Beck, U. (1992) *Risk Society: Towards a New Modernity*. London: Sage.

Clarke, J. and Newman, C. (1997) *The Managerial State: Power, Politics and Ideology in the Remaking of Social Welfare*. London: Sage.

Crego, J. and Alison, L. (2003) *Development of the Centre for the Study of Critical Incident Decision Making* (available online at http:/www.incscid.org).

Crego, J. and Harris, C. (2002) 'Training decision making by team based simulation' in R. Flin and K. Arbuthnot (eds) *Incident Command: Tales from the Hot Seat*. Aldershot: Ashgate.

Crego, J. and Spinks, T. (1997) 'Critical incident management simulation', in R. Flin *et al.* (eds) *Decision Making under Stress*. Aldershot: Ashgate.

Department of Health (2003) *The Victoria Climbie Enquiry*. London: HMSO (available online at http://www.victoria-climbie-inquiry.org.uk/finreport/finreport.htm).

Dobson, N. (2000) *Best Value, Law and Management*. Bristol: Jordan.

ESRC (2001) Alan Travis. Partners in Crime. Policemen (sic) and Academics. The Edge. *Journal of Economic and Social Research Council and Policy Forum for Executive Action*. Issue 8, November 2001, 12–14.

Flin, R. (1997) *Sitting in the Hot Seat: Leaders and Teams for Critical Incident Management*. Chichester: Wiley.

Foster, J., Newburn, T. and Souhami, A. (2005) *Assessing the Impact of the Stephen Lawrence Inquiry*. Home Office Research Study 294. London: Home Office Research, Development and Statistics Directorate.

Gladwell M. (2005) *Blink: The Power of Thinking without Thinking*. London: Allen Lane.

Goleman, D. (1996) *Emotional Intelligence*. London: Bloomsbury.

Goleman, D. (1998). 'What makes a leader?' *Harvard Business Review*, November–December.

Goleman, D. (2000). 'Leadership that gets results', *Harvard Business Review*, March–April.

Grieve, J. (1998). 'Intelligence as education for all? Government drugs policies, 1980–1997', in L. O'Connor *et al.* (eds) *Drugs Partnerships for Policy, Prevention and Education*. London: Cassell.

Grieve, J. (2002) 'The mask of police command' in R. Adlam and P. Villiers (eds) *Police Leadership in the Twenty-first Century*. Winchester: Waterside Press.

Grieve, J. (2004) 'Developments in UK criminal intelligence' in J.H. Ratcliffe (ed.) *Strategic Thinking in Criminal Intelligence*. Canberra: Federation Press Australia.

Hall, N. (2005) *Hate Crime*. Cullompton, Devon, UK. Willan Publishing.

Irving, B. and Dunningham, C. (1993) *Human Factors in the Quality Control of CID Investigations*. Research Study 21 (Royal Commission on Criminal Justice). London: HMSO.

Laming, Lord (2003) *The Victoria Climbie Inquiry* (Cm 5730). London: HMSO.

Leishman, F., Loveday, B. and Savage, S. (2000) *Core Issues in Policing*. (2nd ed.) Harlow: Pearson.

Leishman, F. and Mason, P. (2003). *Policing and the Media: Facts, Fictions and Factions*. Cullompton: Willan Publishing.

Mayer, J.D., Salovey, P. and Caruso, D. (2000) 'Models of emotional intelligence', in *Handbook of Intelligence*, Cambridge: Cambridge University Press.

McLaughlin, E. (2001) 'The permanent revolution: New Labour, new public management and the modernisation of criminal justice', *Criminal Justice* 1: 301–18.

Metropolitan Police Service (2002) *The Damilola Taylor Murder Investigation Review*. Report of the Oversight Panel. Chaired by Right Reverend John Sentamu. London, UK. Metropolitan Police Authority.

Metropolitan Police Service (2002a) *The Damilola Taylor Murder Investigation Review*. London, U.K.: MPS (available online at http://image.guardian.co.uk/sys-files/Guardian/documents/2002/12/09/damilola.pdf).

Metropolitan Police Service (2002b) *Guide to the Management and Prevention of Critical Incidents (Version 5)*. London: MPS.

Parekh B. (Chair) (2000) *The Future of Multi-ethnic Britain* (the Parekh Report). London: Profile Books.

Police Skills and Standards Organisation (2002) *Police Skills Foresight Report*. Sheffield: PSSO. (available online at (http://www.psso.co.uk/publications/Final%20Report%202002.pdf).

Richards, L. (2003) *Risk Assessment: A Model for Domestic Violence*. London: Metropolitan Police and Home Office.

Runciman, W.G. (ed.) (2004) *Hutton and Butler: Lifting the Lid on the Working of Power*. Oxford: Oxford University Press.

Sentamu, J. (2002) 'After Stephen Lawrence', *Toynbee Journal*, 3.

Shepherd, E. and Milne, R. (1999). 'Full and faithful: ensuring quality practice and integrity in outcome in witness interviews', in A. Heaton-Armstrong *et al.* (eds) *Analysing Witness Testimony*. London: Blackstone Press.

Sims, J. (1993) 'What is Intelligence?' in A. Shulsky and J. Sims (eds) *What is Intelligence? Working Group on Intelligence Reform*. Washington, DC: Consortium for the Study of Intelligence, Georgetown University.

Travis, A. (2001) 'Partners in crime: policemen (sic) and academics – the edge', *Journal of Economic and Social Research Council and Policy Forum for Executive Action*, Issue 8.

Wright, A. (2002) *Policing: An Introduction to Concepts and Practice*. Cullompton: Willan Publishing.

Chapter 24

Ethics and corruption

Alan Wright

This chapter reviews four main themes that are relevant to an ethical approach to criminal investigation. First, it examines the importance of ethics to investigative practice and argues that law, statements of rights and rules of procedure are not sufficient in themselves to ensure good professional conduct. Secondly, it analyses the moral dilemmas that face investigators, including those which derive from conflicting loyalties and competing value systems. Thirdly, it examines the corrosive effect of corrupt investigations on society, on the legitimacy and effectiveness of investigating organizations and on individual investigators.

Finally, it argues that good investigators need to demonstrate a range of technical and ethical virtues. In addition to being technically competent, they need to have a strong ethical conception of investigation if they are to be successful. Investigators and those who supervise them must effectively manage ethical issues, just like any other aspect of investigation.

The relevance of ethics

Ethical principles are important to criminal investigation for several reasons. Investigations are often complex endeavours, involving large numbers of people with conflicting views as to the facts and differing opinions about possible courses of action. Serious or protracted investigations involve the marshalling of a wide variety of resources. Because of potential and actual conflicts over the right ways to proceed, decisions about the deployment of these resources have moral implications as well as organizational ones. In some cases, it is not possible for investigators to resolve choices between courses of action by recourse to technical solutions alone. 'Doing the thing right' is often a technical issue but 'doing the right thing' may not be established by technical means.

Criminal investigation also requires the collation and presentation of a wide range of 'facts'. Although investigations may bear similarities, differing contexts mean that perspectives on facts vary from case to case. For this reason, the selection and arrangement of facts are not as straightforward as they may sometimes appear. They have emotive and evaluative content. Their context and the ways in which different audiences might interpret the case will influence their evaluation.

Although they clearly have legal relevance, facts often require qualification. This gives them an ethical 'edge'. For example, the fact that my fingerprints are on the gun that killed a man certainly has relevance in proving who killed him. However, other facts may throw further light on why they are there, such as the fact that I am a gun-smith who handled the weapon during its repair. Contemporary interpretations of such things as the 'battered wife' or the 'shaken baby' syndromes give a case a moral texture far beyond a simple responsibility to identify 'the facts'. Although objectivity is important, facts alone can never establish whether an investigator should take a particular investigative action or adopt a particular policy. These are moral (and sometimes political) judgements.

Criminal investigations are also highly susceptible to extreme pressures to achieve results within limited timescales. Some may involve sensitive issues which provoke high levels of public and media interest. As discussed earlier in this volume, investigators need to regard such cases as 'critical incidents', upon which the future reputation of the investigating agency may depend. How investigators handle these cases is laden with ethical significance. As Kleinig (1995: 213) suggests in relation to policing more generally, the novelty, complexity and time-bound nature of criminal investigation mean that it is necessary to understand the ethical context of cases and to assess the impact that moral issues may have on outcomes and on the minds of the investigators.

Although ethical considerations are important to criminal investigation, they have not often figured prominently in debates about the subject. Nor, with the limited exception of courses for senior investigation officers in some places, has the professional training that investigators receive highlighted them extensively. In many cases, the management of investigations has ignored ethical issues in favour of legal or technical considerations. And yet many of the problems that have arisen in failures of criminal investigation have not been due to an absence of technical skills or a lack of knowledge of law and procedures. All too often, inappropriate conduct by otherwise highly skilled and knowledgeable people has brought these failures about. They are frequently the result of ethical difficulties of one kind or another rather than lack of competence.

Ethical considerations have not been predominant in the thinking of those responsible for maintaining the accountability of investigators. The prevailing ethos of the so-called 'new public management' means that the focus has generally been upon the instrumental effectiveness of action aimed towards achieving planned objectives, rather than upon ethical propriety. This structural myopia has contributed towards the failure of investigative ethics as much as has malpractice by groups and individuals.

Ethical concepts and practice

What is investigative ethics? The first concept the meaning of which we need to establish is that of 'ethics' itself. Ethics or morals are the set of beliefs, values and standards by which people regulate their conduct. The roots of these terms are in Greek and Latin. 'Ethics' is derived from the Greek *ethos* ('habit' or 'custom') of the community. It is associated, in relation to individuals, with a way of life, with a disposition to act or with character that guides conduct (Urmson 1990). 'Moral' from the Latin *morale*, also emphasizes the normative nature of human conduct. 'Normative', in the sense in which we use it here, means something that establishes or encourages a norm or standard.

Ethics therefore deals with values: with good or bad, with right or wrong. A large number of controversial debates have arisen over the subject, including whether there are any absolute or universal principles which should guide our conduct; whether ethical judgement is simply relative to the position in which individuals find themselves; or, at the extreme, whether it is simply a matter of personal choice. These debates are extensive.[1]

In this chapter, however, we are interested in 'applied ethics', rather than in the study of ethical theory for its own sake. Again, we need to be careful how we use this terminology. One sense of 'applied ethics' refers to the application of ethics to the problems, decisions or dilemmas of human life. Thus, we can talk about applied ethics in relation to such things as poverty, the environment, abortion, equality and discrimination, politics, and crime and punishment.

However, the most relevant sense of the term 'applied ethics' to this current chapter is the application of normative ethics to the distinctive set of problems of a workgroup, occupation or profession. We can discuss applied ethics in relation to medicine, the law and other professional activities, including criminal investigation. 'Applied ethics', therefore, is central to the concerns of this chapter.

It is clear from our earliest days that we develop a personal ethics. We learn to distinguish right from wrong in the family and in the social and cultural settings in which we develop. Although our early years, our gender and our social and economic position greatly influence the acquisition of values, ethical development continues to some extent throughout life. The world of work provides an important influence. The prevailing *ethos* of the immediate workgroup and of the organization to which people belong has a considerable influence on the growth of ethical beliefs during adult life.

Police work of all kinds (including criminal investigation) has a powerful impact upon the ethical beliefs of its practitioners. Fielding (1988) has noted the influence of police culture on attitudes in this respect, with the dominant cultural biases of authoritarianism and scepticism affecting organizational behaviour. Investigative practice (in the public police and in other investigative bodies) develops its own culture and attitudes, both formal and informal. Sometimes they develop positively, in the sense that both organizational policies and personal beliefs express an ethos of care and compassion, thoroughness and tenacity. In other cases, more negative attitudes may be evident (for examples, see Young 1991).

This distinction between individual and organizational ethics is an important one. At the individual level, we make judgements about behaviour, drawing on moral concepts. We apply these to the conduct of others and (sometimes) to ourselves. At the organizational level, an institution also has high a degree of moral responsibility in its collective conduct. Clearly, if we wish to say more about the ethics of criminal investigation in terms of the people and institutions that carry them out, we need to clarify the difference between individual and organizational levels of responsibility.

Let us test this argument by supposing that ethics is only about malpractice committed by an individual practitioner. Let us assume that an individual investigator has behaved corruptly and has committed what amounts to a criminal offence. Where such cases are straightforward, as in cases of individual greed or malevolence, we may have little difficulty in making a moral judgement about individual behaviour. In this sense, we define 'malpractice' as a form of improper professional conduct, which is outside the recognized 'practice' of an institution. On the other hand, where the corruption is widespread, we cannot simply assess individual behaviour in the analysis of the problem. In such cases, the negative norms which promote (or at least permit) conduct which the wider community would regard as wrong subvert the positive norms which promote good ethical conduct.

To grasp this more clearly, we need to understand the idea of a 'practice' as the key concept which enables us to make judgements about conduct at the organizational level. The concept of a practice refers to a specific range of types of institutional activity. It does not simply refer to the infinite number of transactions that examples of individual behaviour may represent. Important though they are, such individual transactions are only possible because of more durable relations that are not themselves transactions but are the context of all such transactions (Oakeshott 1975: 54 cited in Wright 2002). In this sense, practice is the 'set of considerations, manners, uses, observances, customs, standards, maxims, principles, rules and offices specifying useful procedures or denoting obligations which relate to human actions and utterances' (Oakeshott 1975: 55).

This may seem complicated but all it does is to affirm that investigative practice (properly understood) is the set of formal and informal rules, procedures and values that configure investigative conduct. Investigative practice is the context within which an indeterminate range of behaviour may take place: some good, some bad. Investigative ethics, therefore, is not about judgements on individual behaviour taken outside this context. It is concerned with professional practice and conduct, understood as a legal, moral, social and political category (Wright 2002: 39–44).

We can, under these circumstances, begin to separate the behaviour of individual investigators as ordinary ethical agents from their conduct as members of an investigating institution. It is the fact that an individual acts against the practice norms of the institution that provides the basis for moral judgement. However, the reverse is not necessarily true. Individual *malpractice* does not necessarily condemn a practice as a whole.

Referring to the investigation of the murder of Stephen Lawrence, the subsequent inquiry criticized the behaviour of a number of officers. It criticized aspects of police action at the scene of the crime and the subsequent investigation. More importantly, it ascribed these failures to 'institutional racism', which it defined as:

> The collective failure of an organization to provide an appropriate and professional service to people because of their colour, culture or ethnic origin. It can be seen or detected in the processes, attitudes and behaviour which amount to discrimination through unwitting prejudice, ignorance, thoughtlessness and racist stereotyping which disadvantage minority ethnic people (Macpherson 1999: 28).

This suggests that the institution itself did not conform to the rules and procedure of its own practice and thereby failed in its performance. However, this does not mean a total condemnation of the actual practice of policing or of criminal investigation *per se*. Macpherson (1999) does not suggest that the police should stop policing or discard criminal investigation as a practice. However, it does serve to emphasize the crucial role of institutions in ensuring the professional integrity of their practice *and* of their practitioners. The idea of *mal*-practice elevates the question of 'investigative ethics' beyond that of individual misbehaviour.

It is also important to remember that neither the individual nor the institutional aspects of investigative ethics are simply an internal affair. Members of the public may also have strong views on the subject. As Mawby describes elsewhere in this volume debates in the press and on television generally mediate these views. They also have practical consequences. Adverse public attitudes can produce extreme pressures for investigators, sometimes negatively affecting the decision-making process.

The combined implication of personal, organizational and public obligations means that it is necessary to manage ethical conduct like any other organizational issue. In contrast to simply making judgements about individual behaviour, criticism of investigative practice at the organizational level encourages us to ask a new range of ethical questions. The most important of these are concerned with how senior practitioners manage the organization in terms of its collective moral standards and how this affects the behaviour of its individual personnel. We return to the question about the relationship between individual moral responsibility and failures of institutional practice later in this chapter.

Law, codes of conduct and human rights

Because the courts test many aspects of criminal investigation, some commentators maintain that this alone is sufficient to assure ethical accountability. The predominant model of investigative accountability which operates in the British criminal justice system is one which insists upon following the due process of law. The courts regard compliance with the formal rules as paramount to avert miscarriages of justice. They rule evidence as inadmissible where there is non-compliance and cases often fail under such circumstances.

Legislation therefore provides the primary control upon investigators. For all investigators in the UK, the Police and Criminal Evidence Act (PACE) 1984 sets out comprehensive rules and guidelines for dealing with persons suspected of crime. The implications of this legislation for such things as the detention of suspects and investigative interviewing are subject to extensive discussion elsewhere in this volume.

In addition to the requirement to adhere to the law, police conduct (including that of investigators) is subject to other rules and sanctions. From the beginning of the modern police, written orders had a primary role in preventing police misconduct. Although many of these orders dealt with such things as minor incivility or drunkenness on duty, others dealt with more serious matters. The large volumes of police general orders and instructions, which have expanded until recent times, are simply catalogues of past mistakes (Wright and Burke 1995). The current *Police Code of Conduct* came into force in 1999 (as Schedule 1 to the *Police (Conduct) Regulations* 1999). It provides the means for controlling the conduct of police officers and for dealing with those who disregard their requirements. It applies to all investigators employed by the public police and similar disciplinary codes apply to investigators from other institutions.

The code demands (among other things) that police officers should demonstrate honesty, integrity, fairness and impartiality and should avoid discreditable conduct. However, invoking the sanctions associated with the code is often the last resort in the day-to-day management of police conduct. Most discipline charges against police officers derive from complaints by the public. They do not arise because supervisors initiate them. In this sense, the code of conduct does not provide a flexible tool for management. At best, it is a deterrent; at worst, a blunt instrument leading to punishment.

The fact that the Home Office converted the earlier 'police discipline code' into a 'code of conduct' may reflect an increased emphasis on ethics rather than on regulation (see Neyroud and Beckley 2001: 190–1). Certainly, the Association of Chief Police Officers (ACPO) has long considered developing a code of ethics to help improve professional standards. Policy guidelines, such as the *ACPO Statement of Common Purpose and Values* (1990), have attempted to provide an ethical framework for managing police conduct, although many police officers regarded them as unnecessary or (at worst) insulting to their professionalism. The creation by ACPO of a Quality of Service Committee in 1991 showed the rise in the strategic importance of quality control in policing. This committee pursued the initiative to produce a code of ethics. However, progress towards defining the code was slow. The draft circulated within the police service during 1993 did not reach the status of an approved statement. There was no public sign of the results of the consultation procedure that followed the publication of this draft. However, the subsequent development of a *Code of Police Ethics* by the Council of Europe goes some way towards redressing the need for an explicit ethical framework (see below).

Investigators also have a moral and an explicit legal responsibility to respect human rights. Human rights are important to investigation because they affect the legal and moral accountability of investigators in democratic states. International human rights instruments, therefore, have exceptional ethical and legal significance for criminal investigation, not least because they provide the standards against which observers may judge their conduct. Although they should act as a check on their conduct in the real-world contexts within which they operate, investigators rarely make overt reference to them.

An important development in this field was the adoption by the United Nations in 1948 of the Universal Declaration on Human Rights. In adopting the declaration, the UN General Assembly claimed that it was 'a common standard of achievement for all peoples and all nations' (United Nations 1995). The adoption of the European Convention on Human Rights (1951) in the wake of the UN declaration is important because it provides a framework for adjudication and compensation of great relevance to investigators in Europe. The convention sets out the rights and freedoms that it protects in a series of articles which specify the nature of the right and any exemptions or restrictions to that right. All European states have incorporated it into their domestic law or their constitution. Surprisingly, the UK was among the last to do so. Although the UK ratified the convention in 1950, almost 50 years passed before English law gave it effect in the Human Rights Act 1998.

A number of articles of the convention are particularly relevant to criminal investigation. Article 2 of the convention protects a person's right to life. This article is of great importance for policing in general and for criminal investigation in particular. The European Court of Human Rights applies the tests of necessity and proportionality to such cases. Proportionality refers to the need to strike a balance between individual rights and the interests of the community. In effect, the authorities are not entitled to 'use a sledge-hammer to crack a nut' in this respect. This means that any restriction on substantive rights (for example, by arrest and detention) must be necessary and proportional to the legitimate aim being pursued (case of *Handyside v. United Kingdom* (1976)).[2] The use of force must also be strictly necessary and proportional to the achievement of the aims set out in Article 2 (2). In addition to considering the actual actions of agents of the state, the court will also take into account all the surrounding circumstances. These include the planning and control of the actions under examination (Council of Europe 1998: 20, 27). The mnemonic 'PLAN' is useful to remind practitioners of their responsibilities to ensure that the concepts of proportionality, legality and necessity are considered and respected.

Article 3 of the convention prohibits torture or inhuman or degrading treatment. This, unlike articles of the convention that are qualified by means of exceptions, is an absolute right. Again, this is of great importance for criminal investigation. Inhuman treatment means treatment that deliberately causes severe mental and physical suffering. Torture is an aggravated form of inhuman treatment, which has a purpose such as the obtaining of information or confessions or the infliction of punishment. Police investigations have provided a number of examples of violations of this article of the convention. An important case before the European Court of Human Rights was that of *Ireland* v. *UK* (1978).[3] Here, the Republic of Ireland brought allegations against the UK government of torture and inhuman treatment in contravention of Article 3. In this case, the UK authorities in Northern Ireland used interrogation methods aimed at producing psychological disorientation. The European Court of Human Rights held that this was inhuman and degrading because of the pattern of treatment which aroused feelings of fear, anguish and inferiority capable of humiliating and debasing them and breaking their physical or moral resistance (see Beddard 1993: 148–9). Later jurisprudence in the European Court of Human Rights, including *Selmouni* v. *France* (1999),[4] has consolidated these principles.

Article 5 secures the right to liberty and security of the person. The article permits the authorities to derive a person of his or her liberty by arrest or detention if it is in accordance with the law. This includes the arrest or detention of a person to bring that person before a competent legal authority on reasonable suspicion of having committed an offence. The measures enacted under PACE cover much of this ground.

Article 6 secures the right to a fair and public trial by an independent and impartial tribunal in the determination of rights and obligations or of any criminal charge. It also enshrines the principle that the courts shall presume that everyone charged with a criminal offence is innocent until proved guilty. The case of *Osman* v. *UK* (1998)[5] also has important implications for criminal investigation. In *Osman*, the European Court of Human Rights ruled that the policy which protects police from actions for negligence in investigations was a violation of Article 6. Clearly, this could have the effect of making police liable in cases where it is possible to show negligence in carrying out criminal investigations. Although this case has been affected by other judgments in cases before the House of Lords, it challenges previous UK case law in *Hill* v. *Chief Constable of West Yorkshire* (1989)[6] (see Coppell 1999: 243).

The European Court of Human Rights has also consistently upheld the right to silence as an important factor in the presumption of innocence under Article 6. In *Funke* v. *France* (1993),[7] the court held that the state infringed the right to silence when it sought to compel the defendant to produce bank statements. Similarly in *Saunders* v. *UK* (1996),[8] the validity of the requirements of s. 2 of the Criminal Justice Act 1987, relating to the requirement to provide information and documents to the Serious Fraud Office, has also come into question.

Article 8 of the convention provides the right to respect for private and family life, home and correspondence. In the case of *Malone* v. *UK* (1984),[9] the European Court of Human Rights found a breach of this article. Malone was an antique dealer whom the police suspected of handling stolen goods. In accordance with the procedures then in place in the area where he lived, the police intercepted his telephone calls. Because the procedures were administrative rather than under statute, the European Court was not satisfied that they were satisfactory. This case led to legislation in the form of the Interception of Communications Act 1985, which sought to rectify the anomalies. The court adjudicated on similar violations against France in the cases of *Kruslin* v. *France* (1990)[10] and *Huvig* v. *France* (1990).[11] A further case, *Halford* v. *UK* (1997),[12] held that the monitoring of calls on an office telephone was also a violation of Article 8. As in *Malone*, the decision turned on the lack of legal regulation. The Regulation of Investigatory Powers Act (RIPA) 2000 and *Code of Practice for Intrusive Surveillance* under s. 101(3) of the Police Act 1997 now deal with policies in this field.

The important lesson from these cases is that they seriously affect real-world investigation in democratic states that claim to adhere to the rule of law. They are not merely of theoretical interest. They affect many aspects of investigations, especially those relating to covert surveillance. In the UK, they have implications for potential challenges to police decisions under the Human Rights Act 1998.[13]

In addition to the human rights instruments discussed above, two other measures provide guidance for police and investigators as to their conduct. The UN *Code of Conduct for Law Enforcement Officials* (1979) sets out basic standards for all policing agencies across the world (United Nations 1996). It requires law enforcement officials to respect and protect human dignity and to maintain and uphold the human rights of all persons. In particular, it requires them to recognize the rights set out in the UN Universal Declaration and other international conventions.

The Council of Europe Declaration on the Police (1979) provides a series of rules with which the police in Europe should comply. Drawing upon the principles of the 1979 UN *Code for Law Enforcement Officers*, the European declaration provides basic standards for the operation of legitimate law enforcement, although it is not directly applicable in law. It should, however, indirectly inform both the laws of most member states of the Council of Europe and the Justice and Home Affairs Pillar (Pillar 3) of the Treaty of European Union (Maastricht Treaty). For all practical purposes, the Council of Europe *Code of Police Ethics* (Council of Europe 2001) sets out a wide range of policies on ethical policing with which European police forces should comply, superseding the 1979 European declaration.

International measures to protect human rights have a great influence on public policy. However, if nation-states are fully to apply their principles, it is necessary to give them effect in domestic law. In the UK, the Human Rights Act 1998 provides a source of law on which the courts can draw. The Act has two parallel purposes. The first is to ensure that UK domestic legislation is compatible with convention rights. The second is to provide individuals with a domestic remedy for breaches of convention rights, rather than requiring them to take their case to Strasbourg (Cheney *et al* 1999: 14–15).

Section 6(1) of the Act provides that 'It is unlawful for a public authority to act in such a way which is incompatible with a convention right'. Although a 'public authority' is not defined in the Act, in the debates in Parliament the Lord Chancellor said:

> In many cases it will be obvious to the courts that they will be dealing with a public authority. In respect of government departments, for example, or police officers, or prison officers, or immigration officers, or local authorities, there can be no doubt that the body in question is a public authority (cited in Cheney *et al.* 1999: 19).

Section 6 provides a clear duty for police and for investigators who fall into the category of a 'public authority' under the Act. This section applies to all acts of public bodies, whether they regard their acts as public or private. The courts will exercise their judgement about other investigative bodies (for example, commercial security companies), where the status of their work may be of a 'public' nature. Only in cases where public authorities could not have acted differently, because they were enforcing legislation without an option to act otherwise, would their action not be unlawful.

Their role as a 'public authority' under the Act puts new responsibility on the UK police and to other investigating institutions to ensure compliance with the convention and the Act. The application of the principles of proportionality, legality and necessity to all aspects of policy and planning means continuing scrutiny of investigative systems is required. Covert surveillance, stop and search, arrest, searching suspects and premises, questioning, the right to silence, interception of communications, legal representation, disclosure of evidence and fair trial, are all likely to feature in future claims of violation of rights.

Going by the book? The limitation of rules and codes

Research by McConville *et al.* (1991) suggests that the police play a structurally pernicious role in the construction of criminal prosecutions. This includes a prejudicial definition of the suspect population; placing suspects in a hostile environment after arrest; dictating the terms of interviews; and manipulating the paper reality in order to authenticate cases. The effect of these habits is that conviction or acquittal is determined early in the process by informal rules, not in the criminal justice system by due process. Although McConville *et al.* carried out the fieldwork for this research during the late 1980s, against this background it is not surprising that efforts to ensure compliance with the rules have become the predominant tool in trying to influence individual conduct and investigative practice as a whole.

Apart from training, most attempts to improve conduct focus on the prevention of malpractice by a progressive tightening of the rules and ensuring compliance with human rights principles. As suggested above, PACE effectively tightened the rules which govern the detention and questioning of suspects. This Act was important because it put into place new procedures to make the police more accountable. The Human Rights Act 1998 has placed upon policing and criminal investigation the responsibility to conform to the articles of the European convention. If it is true that this tightening of the law and procedure can be effective in regulating some aspects of behaviour, why not counter all potential misconduct simply by enforcing compliance with the rules?

Some commentators have argued that that is precisely what must happen. The consequences of failing to do so are serious both for individual prosecutions and for the criminal justice system as a whole. In court cases which breach procedural rules, the doctrine of the so-called 'fruit of the poisoned tree' will apply, resulting in all the evidence being excluded (Zander 1994). This emphasis on compliance with the rules rather than the search for truth which has emerged in British criminal justice has been evident in the US courts for some years.

Given the requirements of law, procedures and international human rights instruments, what should be the response to someone of a positivist frame of mind who insists that investigation is simply about applying the law and following the appropriate codes of conduct rather than worrying about something as conceptually unclear as investigative ethics? There can be little doubt that following the law and applying the codes are *necessary conditions* for good professional conduct in investigation. If an investigator follows the rules, we might suppose, the ethics will look after itself.

However, the very nature of criminal investigation means that they are not *sufficient conditions*. The problem with seeing investigative ethics simply as a matter of compliance with the formal rules is that investigators often operate with strong discretionary concepts of justice that they believe they share with the public at large. In cases where the law or the 'official' rules seem to work against these informal concepts of justice, there is a danger that investigators may act in a quasi-judicial way and reinterpret them to achieve what they perceive to be just ends.

Here we need to look at aspects of policing and investigation to understand why the temptations of non-compliance can be strong. Research by Skolnick (1966) suggests that the 'working personality' of police officers may be stronger than due process in deciding on appropriate courses of action. According to Skolnick, who carried out extensive sociological studies of the subject, both street policing and detective work involve a kind of 'craftsmanship' that is geared towards peace-keeping and informal concepts of justice rather than simply to enforcing the law. The strict following of law and legal principle is not, therefore, the only underpinning 'ethic' of police work and investigation.

Similarly, Bittner (1970) is sceptical about the kind of ethics which police are required to adopt. Given the nature of police work, prejudice is unavoidable. He says: 'Because the preponderant majority of police interventions are based upon mere suspicion or on merely tentative indications of risk, policemen would have to be expected to judge matters prejudicially, even if they personally were entirely free from prejudice' (Bittner 1970: 11). For Bittner, therefore, police work is a 'tainted occupation', exhibiting ethical norms which are set by the discretionary and potentially prejudicial character of the occupation rather than by the rule of law and legal principle.

So although adherence to law, codes of conduct and human rights provides the necessary conditions for good investigative conduct, investigating institutions need to do more to provide the sufficient conditions for regulating the conduct of investigators. Sufficient conditions for good ethical conduct include ethical leadership and effective management. Only by taking account of rules and by active management of informal processes is an organization likely to achieve high standards of professional conduct.

Investigative decision-making and moral dilemmas

Investigative decision-making involves gathering and interpreting the facts and evaluating their impact in the relevant ethical context. However, the controversial nature of criminal investigation often produces moral dilemmas for investigators. A moral dilemma, in the sense in which we use the term here, relates to circumstances which confront the investigator with equally repugnant or equally unavoidable courses of action. This may include such things as conflicts between personal values and those of the organization; conflicts over the need to follow the law and the need to obtain justice for victims; and conflicts between the need to do one's duty and the need to get results.

Research by Wright and Irving (1996) showed that the dilemmas police officers experience in their work strongly affect their ethical attitudes. The research revealed a range of problems across a number of areas. These included dilemmas in criminal investigation; in dealing with death and trauma; in meeting the requirements of the criminal justice system; and in ensuring justice for victims. Conflicts of loyalty to the organization ('the job'), to colleagues, to friends and family were also common. Respondents mentioned clashes between individual and organizational values in most of the cases they reported. Personal values were set against those derived from the operating culture, which emphasized the need to look after one's colleagues, the need to get the job done and to achieve justice in spite of, rather than through, the application of due process.

The dilemmas and value conflicts revealed during research showed that 72 per cent of the cases concerned problems over the occupational culture or the job itself. Some 56 per cent concerned relations with colleagues; 40 per cent were concerned with conflicts between the formal requirements of law and informal pressure to ensure justice; 24 per cent were concerned with conflicts with the public world outside the police; and 16 per cent related to issues concerning friends and family. Some scenarios included conflicts in more than one category. Figure 24.1 shows the web of interaction between the self and the various categories of problem. These problems signify very

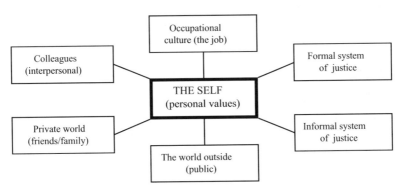

Figure 24.1 A simplified model of the interaction between internal and external values

deeply held commitments which, when they come into conflict, are primary causes of stress (which psychologists will recognize as a form of cognitive dissonance). The key point is the moral ambiguity which they appear to entail, particularly when a practitioner thinks that the rule of law or the requirements of procedure do not predominate over the need for loyalty.

Regrettably, it is too late to remedy the problem after the conflict of loyalty has arisen. This is particularly the case in dealing with loyalty to a colleague who may have used excessive force or in conflicts between the formal requirements of the law and a perceived need to ensure a just outcome. These cases are impossible to remedy after the event because in many cases the attempt to ensure 'justice' involves assaults, 'system-bending' or the creative reconstruction of events. It is very unlikely that police officers will be willing to discuss these problems because to do so could end a police career or even result in prosecution.

Frustration at being unable to achieve a 'just' outcome in a criminal case is a major problem. Some investigators who find difficulty in getting people convicted of a crime within the criminal justice system may think that a resort to 'dirty' methods is justified. 'Noble-cause corruption' is the name often given to this phenomenon. In general, there is little difficulty in dealing with it as malpractice. However, when there are serious dilemmas about ends and means, including the need to save life, the problem is more complex.

The so-called 'Dirty Harry problem' (from the 1970s film portraying Harry Callahan, a fictional American detective) is an extreme example of this kind of moral tale. In this example, the ends Callaghan seeks to achieve are urgent and unquestionably good. However, only a resort to 'dirty' means will achieve them. In one scene from the film, Callaghan is trying to prevent the death of a kidnapped girl and resorts to torture of the suspected perpetrator to find out where he has hidden her. Of course, this is against the principles of the UN declaration and the UN *Code of Conduct for Law Enforcement Officials*. Yet, if he wants to save the girl's life, what is he to do?

In Harry's case, the problem is the difficulty of reconciling ends and means, as shown in Figure 24.2. Klockars (1980) discusses this case extensively. He illustrates four possibilities:

1 Where the ends and means are both morally good, no problems arise (sector A).

2 Similarly, we have no difficulty in understanding that morally bad ends are corrupt when we use bad means to achieve them (sector D).

3 That we sometimes only secure bad ends despite the use of good means may simply be because of unpredictability or because of our incompetence. We often have to live with such unintended consequences (sector C).

4 The real difficulty arises when the ends are undoubtedly good but where we feel we must use questionable means to achieve them (sector B).

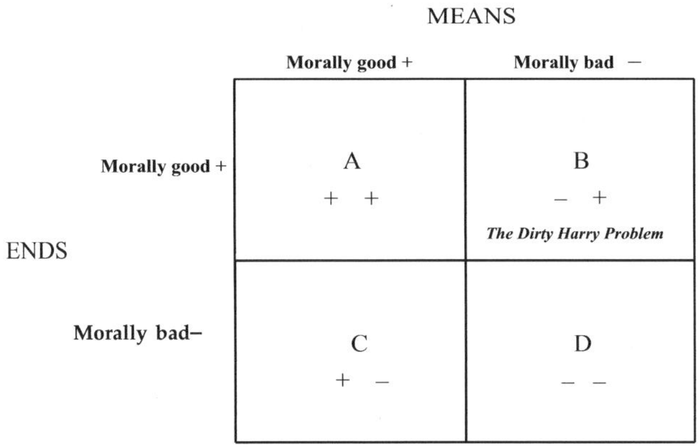

MEANS

	Morally good +	Morally bad −
	A + +	B − + *The Dirty Harry Problem*
	C + −	D − −

Morally good + (ENDS top row), Morally bad− (ENDS bottom row)

Figure 24.2 The Dirty Harry problem

Clearly, the use of bad means in such cases works strongly against the rules, especially against those protecting human rights. Responsibility to rise above these ordeals rests with the individual investigator but the organization also has a role. Although it is important for investigators to develop strength of character to deal with such situations, it is also necessary to recognize that this is not only a matter for the individual. The quality of training, supervision and support also plays an important role.[14]

Dilemmas of other kinds arise in relation to the pressure on investigators to improve their 'performance'. In 1983, the government required police forces to set objectives and to rationalize the use of their resources (Home Office 1983). This put considerable pressure on the police to achieve results. Since the mid-1990s, governments have increased this pressure by requiring the police to meet objectives that reflect political, as well as local, priorities. This way of thinking produces a number of ethical problems. Effectiveness, when we think of it in these terms, is a purely utilitarian concept. It is primarily concerned with ends rather than means. Although it has a degree of moral respectability when concerned with achieving the greatest good of the greatest number of people, in its most crass form, it is totally uninformed in relation to ethical content.

Research on value conflicts has shown that the requirement to concentrate on the 'figures' is both dysfunctional and stressful (Wright and Irving 1996). At the extreme, some detectives have been tempted to 'massage' the figures or even to fabricate results. According to Young (1991: 323–6, 385), the reasons for this are deeply embedded in the detective culture, which is geared towards achieving 'results'. For example, a Kent police officer revealed that detectives from that force had falsified clear-up figures by getting prisoners to admit to crimes they had not committed (Young 1991: 378). These improper practices are a form of 'performance crime'. Sharpe (1995) suggests that the nature of the organization and the requirements of the performance culture provide a form of structural coercion which encourages such malpractice.[15]

Another source of moral dilemmas for investigators is that of secrecy and deception. In some cases, investigators feel compelled to conceal or disguise information which may tend to compromise an investigation. For example, press releases may not include the full details of a murder method which would then only be known to the investigators themselves and to the true offender. This is sometimes used to identify those who might come forward with false confessions as a result of publicity. In other cases, investigators may regard the tactic of disinformation as a legitimate weapon in convincing organized criminal or terrorist groups that the attention of investigations is focused elsewhere. In both cases, these tactical decisions may be in conflict with ethical imperatives to ensure transparency and openness in investigation. As in other cases, the moral dilemma between concealment and publicity is not easily resolved without a deeper understanding of the ethical issues that such conflicts involve.

We can identify the underlying problem in moral dilemmas of all kinds in the conflicts between ends and means; between utility and principles. The danger arises when we give too much power to either. Accordingly, in making judgements about the right way to proceed, it is necessary to apply both a 'test of utility' (to the ends) *and* a 'test of universality' (to the means). The utility test enables us to balance the good or harms to the greatest number of people that we might do by choosing a scenario based upon utilitarian principles. In each case, we should pose (at least to ourselves) the question: 'Who will be harmed and who will benefit?' The test of universality requires us to ask the question, 'What if everyone did that?' in relation to the means we use to achieve our ends. If the answer is logically self-contradictory, or clearly against a duty of care or other obligation, we should seriously question whether the course of action is the right one. A comparison of the results of these tests enables us to understand how each dimension affects our ethical decision-making.

Although they apply to all criminal investigations, the test of utility and the universality test become highly important in terrorism cases. For example, in the use of torture as a supposed aid to investigation, if we allow its use (even the repugnant concept of so-called 'torture lite'), we may in fact be willing it to be used against ourselves, regardless of the ostensibly good results that it achieves. Using torture, therefore, certainly serves to defeat us at the categorical (duty-related) end of the ethical spectrum. Similarly, if everyone corrupted their assessment of performance, thinking that they were serving the ends of utility, they would destroy the very basis of judgement about what they should be trying to achieve. In summary, investigative decisions should be as much about duties as they are about being effective.

Typologies of corruption

The corruption of public bodies is an important problem. Corruption is very damaging to such bodies because it undermines their legitimacy and reduces their effectiveness. It is insidious because it corrodes public confidence. Although this applies to all public bodies, corruption is particularly problematic for criminal investigation because it undermines relationships between investigators and the public. Ultimately, it destroys any pride which investigators might feel in doing their job.

We have argued that the study of investigative ethics applies both to individual action and to the idea of a 'practice'. We defined '*mal*-practice' as a form of improper professional conduct, which is outside the normal practice of an institution. Initially, in the case of corruption, it seems that we may be rather straightforward in condemning such malpractice. However, if organizations are to be effective in tackling it, they need to recognize the complexity of the individual and organizational contexts within which it takes place. This means that they need to understand both the motivations of individuals who commit such malpractice and the organizational factors that surround it.

What is corruption? Many criminologists have attempted to define the concept. Barker and Roebuck (1973) define police corruption as: 'any type of prescribed behaviour engaged in by a law enforcement officer who receives or expects to receive, by virtue of his official position, an actual or potential unauthorised material reward or gain.' Similarly, Goldstein (1977: 188) defines corruption as: 'the misuse of authority by a police officer in a manner designed to produce personal gain for the officer or for others.'

For Punch (1985), we can analyse corruption in five dimensions. These include the acts and the actors involved; the norms they violate; the degree of support from the peer group; the extent to which the deviant practices are organized; and the reaction of the police department. He suggests that the corruption can cover both profiting from the abuse of power as well as the actual abuse of power itself. Newburn (1999) makes use of these typologies and lists the types and dimensions of police corruption shown in Table 24.1.

According to Sherman (1985), the road to corruption is often a gradual one. The officer starts by accepting small gratuities and moves on to larger forms of corruption. The need for acceptance by peers and the advice of more experienced practitioners who show newcomers 'how things are done on the street' may reinforce this behaviour. Other commentators reject this idea. They suggest that it is unrealistic to believe that low-level corruption will inevitably lead to bribery or worse. According to Feldberg (1985), most police officers know where to draw the line between petty gratuities and bribery. However, according to Bonifacio (1991), low level corruption, including the acceptance of bribes and gratuities, tends to validate an officer's status and to show that citizens recognize his or her power and authority. The officer enjoys the feeling of power that comes from believing him or herself to be above the law.

It is particularly noticeable that much of the corruption that has historically been associated with investigation has been at the so-called 'invitational edge' of investigative work – such as work by squads of detectives investigating drugs, pornography, vice or organized crime. Investigators are particularly vulnerable to temptation in cases where they have to act like criminals in the groups they are penetrating; where they are using informants; where they may act as agents provocateurs; or where they are operating in illicit markets which are not regarded as 'real crime' (Manning and Redlinger 1977). Corruption may also be evident in areas where the law is weak, such as in the policing of pornography (Cox et al. 1977).

Table 24.1 Typologies of corruption

Type	Dimension
Corruption of authority	When an officer receives some form of material gain by virtue of his or her position as a police officer without violating the law *per se* (e.g. free drinks, meals and services)
'Kickbacks'	Receipt of goods, services or money for referring business to particular individuals or companies
Opportunistic theft	Stealing from arrestees (sometimes referred to as 'rolling'), from traffic accident victims, crime victims or the bodies or property of dead citizens
'Shakedowns'	Acceptance of a bribe for not following through a criminal violation (i.e. not making an arrest, filing a complaint or impounding property)
Protection of illegal activities	Police protection of those engaged in illegal activities (prostitution, drugs, pornography) enabling the business to continue operating
'The fix'	Undermining criminal investigations or proceedings, or the 'loss' of traffic tickets
Direct criminal activities	A police officer commits a crime against person or property for personal gain in clear violation of both departmental and criminal norms
Internal payoffs	Prerogatives available to police officers (holidays, shift allocations, promotion) are bought, bartered and sold
'Flaking' or 'padding'	Planting or adding to evidence (argued by Punch 1985 to be particularly evident in drugs cases)

Source: Adapted from Newburn (1999).

Marx (1988) also suggests that there is often a link between drugs police work and corruption. The very conditions in which narcotics officers carry out their work are likely to cause corruption. Isolation, secrecy and the use of deception can lead to an undercover investigator becoming like the criminal he or she portrays. In such cases, bribery and corruption do not occur simply because of the fallibility of individuals. They arise in particular contexts that diminish the normal 'distance' between investigators and suspects (Waddington 1999: 125).

Sherman (1974) develops a way of classifying corruption that enables us to made judgements of its character according to the extent to which it is *organized* or *pervasive*:

- At the lowest level of organizational collusion, *disorganized* corruption is like the 'rotten apples' in a barrel. Not all the apples in the barrel, however, are contaminated. Corruption of this type is characterized by individual acts of misconduct, which are unconnected to others.

- At a higher level, *disorganized pervasive* corruption implies a more widespread range of corrupt activities embedded in the operating culture (all or most of the apples are rotten), but still at an individual level.

- *Organized pervasive* corruption includes a still wider degree of collusion and structure, which often involves top management. In such cases, the corruption is so extensive that we can regard the barrel itself as rotten.

Corruption, therefore, is frequently not just an individual act. We may regard it as malpractice guided by a contradictory set of group norms that operate within the organization of which the corrupt individual is a member.

Controlling corruption

There is no doubt that, due to its clandestine nature, investigative corruption is difficult to evaluate and to control. Corrupt investigation departments usually have informal rules that govern the behaviour of their members. These informal rules minimize the chances of external bodies discovering the corruption and reforming the department (Sherman 1978). For this reason, Sherman suggests that corruption is both a crime and a management problem. An effective control policy must deal with both simultaneously. In practice, a mixture of *internal* and *external* measures has characterized the control of police corruption worldwide.

Types of internal control aimed at tackling police corruption include anti-corruption strategies, regulations to control police discipline and codes of professional ethics. Methods in use in the USA are mainly internal control systems but there is also considerable pressure for better civilian oversight of the police. Many forces now use various form of integrity testing. The New York Police Department (NYPD) has for many years operated an integrity control system. Local precincts have integrity control officers whom the force specially appoints to carry out this work. They also make use of proactive measures, including 'sting' operations, which provide opportunities for corrupt investigators to implicate themselves in criminal activity. Here, internal affairs departments use all legitimate means, including covert surveillance, to investigate officers whom they suspect of corruption. Improvements in human resource management, training and career development are also effective tools against corruption. Some UK police forces have now adopted these methods.

The evidence shows that there is no single effective method for controlling police corruption. In some jurisdictions, because police corruption has been widespread, the authorities have found it necessary to introduce systems based primarily on external measures to control it. Anti-corruption commissions have been developed to reduce corruption in the police and in other public departments.

In Hong Kong, for example, until the mid-1980s, government sources estimated that large numbers of employees in government departments were corrupt. In consequence, the government launched a massive clean-up campaign. It raised the salaries of civil servants and police to discourage bribe taking. It also created an Independent Commission against Corruption (ICAC) with widely ranging investigative powers (Huberts 1999).

In Australia, and in some parts of Africa and South America, governments have adopted the ICAC approach. This model encourages the relentless investigation of corruption so that it becomes a crime with a very high risk of detection and punishment. In Australia, similar commissions have been set up to help eliminate corruption from within the government itself. These bodies also offer corruption prevention services to private sector companies (Urquhart 1998).

The control of police corruption in England and Wales is a mixture of *external* and *internal* controls. In the external dimension, the Independent Police Complaints Commission and the Crown Prosecution Service independently investigate cases that reveal criminal offences. The police service also uses professional standards departments to ensure a degree of internal control, often making use of proactive approaches to overcome the weaknesses in relying upon a complaints-based system. A proactive approach ensures that corrupt elements cannot continue to act with impunity.

In England and Wales as a whole, the authorities generally regard police corruption as under control. However, by early 1999, 19 of the 43 police forces in England and Wales had officers (100+) facing dishonesty or corruption charges. The courts have dealt severely with some officers. For example, one officer has received eight years' imprisonment for corruption for selling details from a police computer system. The report of HM Inspector of Constabulary on police integrity provides a considerable amount of contemporary detail and advice on this subject (HMIC 1999).

It is evident that most police organizations across the world are susceptible to corruption. There are common areas relating to the causes of corruption and its control. The evidence shows the following:

- There is a link between police corruption and the prevailing social, economic, political and cultural conditions.

- There are at least two distinct levels of corruption, namely low-level 'mooching' and a more serious level linked to drugs, vice and organized crime.

- Recruitment and selection of police officers are crucially important. Likewise the training of police officers, both of newly appointed officers and those whose careers are more established.

- Human resource management approaches are crucial to the prevention of corruption. These include continuing professional development, appraisal, ongoing monitoring and promotion systems, police officers' pay, terms and conditions of service, and effective management and supervision of officers.

- Integrity testing or monitoring of 'at-risk' officers is crucial.

- Defusing corruption involves breaking the code of silence while maintaining the team ethos (changing the police culture). The protection of 'whistle-blowers' is an important element in this respect.

In summary, although there is no consensus in the debate about definitions, there is wide agreement that abuse of power for personal gain is an important element in police corruption. However, individual motivation is not the only element the authorities need to take into account. Researchers also agree that organizational factors are an important influence on the level and type of police corruption. Effective control measures may be either internal or external or a mixture of the two. Investigative authorities, however, need to tailor their strategies to the problem and not to apply either internal or external measures in a doctrinaire way.

The good investigator: virtue and moral luck

Most practitioners rightly regard investigative ethics as a 'minefield'. It is especially so for the inexperienced. Experienced investigators (almost by definition) are survivors of a considerable number of value conflicts. This is not simply a matter of luck. Such practitioners survive because they have developed strategies to cope with the ethical problems they encounter during their work. They recognize the importance of consistency and constraint. They understand that the ethical minefield is more likely to punish those who are insensitive to moral issues.

According to Wright and Irving (1996), the development of ethical virtue and survivability has three key elements. First, because so much of the work of police officers and investigators is about conflicts between values, they need to learn early in their careers about the value systems within which they operate. They may already have extensive training in the knowledge and skills that they require but when newly trained people reach the 'real world' of investigation, they need to acquire a set of behaviours to enable them to cope with the job. They should therefore be encouraged, as part of their early professional training, to develop a repertoire of positive strategies to deal with the value conflicts they will experience.

Secondly, behavioural change is a long-term process. It requires a clear understanding of the pervasive culture of criminal investigation work and the individual and collective need it fulfils. Only a long-term career development programme will enable practitioners to cope with this and enable them to face the extraordinary ethical difficulties they will meet in the course of their work.

Thirdly, for a professional development programme to be successful it must meet a need that is at least as powerful as that expressed by the informal culture. It must be powerful enough to provide investigators with strategies on which they can draw when they meet difficult circumstances in their professional careers. Such an approach must respond to the 'compliance agenda' but must also be highly credible to experienced practitioners and address the real difficulties inherent in the job.

While long-term success is more likely to accrue to an investigator who recognizes the importance of developing an ethical understanding alongside legal knowledge and technical skills, the ethos of the organization within which he or she works is also of crucial importance. It is therefore highly important for an investigative organization to develop checks and balances to ensure its ethical health. Because criminal investigation is complex, there is great value in the development of a logical framework for ethical analysis and audit. According to Clutterbuck and Snow (1990), ethical audits are necessary to answer the organization's need for information on where it is and where it ought to be in terms of its values. Such audits should cover policies, systems and standards and should include the means for monitoring and analysing performance in the areas of ethics, human rights and social responsibility. Unless investigating organizations ask these questions in the course of routine planning, their commitment to ethical and human rights principles will only be superficial. They will not be able to gear them to the real business of running the organization.

Regular monitoring of the conduct of individuals and the activities of their workgroups is also required. In many cases, however, individuals keep their problems and fears to themselves. They are reluctant to discuss them with their supervisors or their colleagues. To do so may reveal criminal or disciplinary offences. To discuss them would spread the responsibility. This perceived need for secrecy is an undoubted barrier to the defusing of explosive situations by means of official counselling. If an investigator admits malpractice, even under a promise of confidentiality, the hearer may feel obliged to take it further. For a supervisor to keep such an issue confidential raises a further dilemma for the supervisor concerned. In this sense, 'A problem shared is a problem doubled'.

Because of this, effective managers should develop their own sensors in investigative workgroups. Awareness of the problems of staff is a day-to-day requirement. Managers need to develop their own tactics and to make clear the acceptable limits of conduct. These are not remedial measures for some kind of sickness. They are simply commonsense ways in which management can help investigators to follow certain patterns of behaviour (such as fairness, honesty and the use of minimum force). Even so, there are dilemmas from which they cannot easily escape because of the nature of their work.

Moral responsibility remains the key to professional conduct in criminal investigation. The managerial approach to investigative ethics will not eradicate the dilemmas that are a major source of failures to reach the ideals set out in the law and in regulations. It will, however, help practitioners to avoid their worst consequences and to develop a degree of 'moral luck'. For this reason, only a judicious mixture of personal commitment, ethical audit, monitoring, team management and career development is likely to be successful in the long term.

Selected further reading

Klockars, C.B. (1980) 'The Dirty Harry problem', in T. Newburn (ed.) *Policing: Key Readings*. Cullompton: Willan Publishing. A seminal paper setting out a rigorous analysis of the types of value conflict of relevance to investigators.

Newburn, T. (1999) *Understanding and Preventing Police Corruption: Lessons from the Literature. Police Research Series Paper* 110. London: Home Office. An excellent overview of issues in police corruption.

Neyroud, P. and Beckley, A. (2001) *Policing, Ethics and Human Rights.* Cullompton: Willan Publishing. A wide-ranging discussion of policing ethics, providing an excellent overview of the moral and organizational context within which criminal investigation operates.

Wadham, J. and Mountfield, H. (2003) *Blackstone's Guide to the Human Rights Act 1998* (3rd edn). London: Blackstone Press. A detailed and accessible guide to the intricacies of human rights law.

Notes

1 Interested readers should refer to standard works on the subject, such as Singer (1993), if they wish to study its theoretical complexity.
2 *Handyside* v. *United Kingdom* (1979–80) 1 EHRR 737.
3 *Ireland* v. *UK* (1978) 2 EHRR 25.
4 *Selmouni* v. *France* (2000) 29 EHRR 403.
5 *Osman* v. *UK* (1998) 29 EHRR 245
6 *Hill* v. *Chief Constable of West Yorkshire* [1989] 1 AC 53.
7 *Funke* v. *France* (1993) 16 EHRR 297.
8 *Saunders* v. *UK* (1996) 23 EHRR 313.
9 *Malone* v. *UK* (1985) 7 EHRR 14.
10 *Kruslin* v. *France* (1990) 12 EHRR 547.
11 *Huvig* v. *France* (1990) 12 EHRR 528.
12 *Halford* v. *UK* (1997) 24 EHRR 523.
13 The text of the convention is accessible through a number of sources. For commentary on this subject, see Crawshaw *et al.* (1998), Wright (2000) and Neyroud and Beckley (2001: 54–70). For the full text of the convention, see Wadham and Mountfield (2003).
14 Readers who wish to investigate this model further should refer to Klockars (1980), from which Figure 24.2 is drawn.
15 For arguments for and against the performance culture, see Neyroud and Beckley (2001: 94–123).

References

ACPO (1990) *Strategic Policy Document: Setting the Standards: Meeting Community Expectations.* London: ACPO.

Barker, T. and Roebuck, J. (1973) *An Empirical Typology of Police Corruption.* Springfield, IL: Bannerstone House.

Beddard, R. (1993) *Human Rights and Europe.* Cambridge: Grotius Publications.

Bittner, E. (1970) *The Functions of Police in Modern Society.* Chevy Chase, MD: National Institute of Mental Health.

Bonifacio, P. (1991) *The Psychological Effects of Police Work*. New York, NY: Plenum Press.

Cheney, D., Dickson, L., Fitzpatrick, J. and Uglow, S. (1999) *Criminal Justice and the Human Rights Act, 1998*. Bristol: Jordan Publishing.

Clutterbuck, D. and Snow, D. (1990) *Working with the Community*. London: Weidenfeld & Nicholson.

Coppell, J. (1999) *The Human Rights Act 1998*. Chichester: Wiley.

Council of Europe (1998) *Human Rights and the Police: A Workbook for Practice Oriented Teaching*. Strasbourg: Human Rights Information Centre.

Council of Europe (2001) *Code of Police Ethics*. Recommendation Rec (2001)10 adopted by the Committee of Ministers of the Council of Europe, 19 September 2001. Strasbourg: Council of Europe Publishing.

Cox, B., Shirley, J. and Short, M. (1977) *The Fall of Scotland Yard*. Harmondsworth: Penguin Books.

Crawshaw, R., Devlin, B. and Williamson, T. (1998) *Human Rights and Policing*. The Hague: Kluwer Law International.

Feldberg, M. (1985) 'Gratuities, corruption and the democratic ethos of policing: the case of the free cup of coffee', in F.A. Elliston and M. Feldberg (eds) *Moral Issues in Police Work*. Totowa, NJ: Rowman & Allanheld.

Fielding, N. (1988) *Joining Forces*. London: Routledge.

Goldstein, H. (1977) *Policing a Free Society*. Cambridge, MA: Ballinger.

HMIC (1999) *Police Integrity: Securing and Maintaining Public Confidence*. London: HM Inspectorate of Constabulary.

Home Office (1983) *Manpower, Effectiveness and Efficiency in the Police Service* (Circular 114/83). London: Home Office.

Huberts, L. (1999) 'Dilemmas in anti-corruption strategies: some lessons from Hong Kong.' Paper presented at the ICAC Silver Jubilee Conference 'Fighting corruption in the 21st century', Free University, Amsterdam.

Kleinig, J. (1995) 'Ethical questions facing law enforcement agents', in B. Almond (ed.) *Introducing Applied Ethics*. Oxford: Blackwell.

Klockars, C.B. (1980) 'The Dirty Harry problem', in T. Newburn (ed.) (2005) *Policing: Key Readings*. Cullompton: Willan Publishing.

Macpherson of Cluny, Sir W. (1999) *The Stephen Lawrence Enquiry* (Cm 4262-1). London: HMSO.

Manning, P.K. and Redlinger, J. (1977) 'Invitational edges of corruption', in P.K. Manning and J. van Maanen (eds) *Policing: A View from the Street*. New York, NY: Random House.

Marx, G.T. (1988) *Undercover Police Surveillance in America*. Berkeley, CA: University of California Press.

McConville, M., Sanders, A. and Leng, R. (1991) *The Case for the Prosecution*. London: Routledge.

Newburn, T. (1999) *Understanding and Preventing Police Corruption: Lessons from the Literature*. Police Research Series Paper 110. London: Home Office.

Neyroud, P. and Beckley, A. (2001) *Policing, Ethics and Human Rights*. Cullompton: Willan Publishing.

Oakeshott, M. (1975) *On Human Conduct*. Oxford: Clarendon Press.

Punch, M. (1985) *Conduct Unbecoming*. New York, NY: Tavistock.

Roebuck, J. and Barker, T. (1974) 'A typology of police corruption', *Social Problems*, 21: 423–37.

Sharpe, A.N. (1995) 'Police performance crime as structurally coerced action', *Police and Society*, 5: 201–20.

Sherman, L.W. (1974) *Police Corruption: A Sociological Perspective*. Garden City, NJ: Anchor Press.

Sherman, L.W. (1978) *Scandal and Reform: Controlling Police Corruption*. Berkeley, CA: University of California Press.

Sherman, L.W. (1985) 'Becoming bent: moral careers of corrupt policemen', in F.A. Elliston and M. Feldberg (eds) *Moral Issues in Police Work*. Totowa, NJ: Rowman & Allanheld.

Singer, P. (1993) *A Companion to Ethics* (1st paperback edn). Oxford: Blackwell.

Skolnick, J. (1966) *Justice without Trial*. New York, NY: Wiley.

United Nations (1995) *The United Nations and Human Rights, 1945–1995. UN Blue Books Series*, Vol. VII. New York, NY: UN Department of Public Information.

United Nations (1996) *International Human Rights Standards for Law Enforcement: A Pocket Book on Human Rights for the Police*. New York, NY and Geneva: United Nations.

Urmson, J.O. (1990) *The Greek Philosophical Vocabulary*. London: Duckworth.

Urquhart, P.D. (1998) 'The Police Integrity Commission in New South Wales.' Paper presented at the 13th World Conference of the International Association for Civilian Oversight of Law Enforcement, Seattle, October.

Waddington, P.A.J. (1999) *Policing Citizens*. London: UCL Press.

Wadham, J. and Mountfield, H. (2003) *Blackstone's Guide to the Human Rights Act 1998* (3rd edn). London: Blackstone Press.

Wright, A. (2000) 'An introduction to human rights and policing', *Police Journal*, 73: 193–209.

Wright, A. (2002) *Policing: An Introduction to Concepts and Practice*. Cullompton: Willan Publishing.

Wright, A. and Burke, M. (1995) 'The Greater Manchester Police Blue Book', *Policing*, 11: 331–41.

Wright, A. and Irving, B. (1996) 'Value conflicts in policing: crisis into opportunity: making critical use of experience', *Policing and Society*, 6: 199–211.

Young, M. (1991) *An Inside Job*. Oxford: Clarendon Press.

Zander, M. (1994) 'Ethics and crime investigation by the police', *Policing*, 10: 39–47.

Chapter 25

Miscarriages of justice

Stephen P. Savage and Becky Milne

Introduction

Criminal investigation and miscarriages of justice are in many ways joined at the hip. From the fictional depiction of detectives 'fitting up' hapless suspects, to the widely publicized abuses committed by police investigators in notorious cases such as the 'Birmingham Six' (Mullin 1990), the association in the public mind between miscarriages of justice and police investigation remains strong. This association is even stronger in the academic criminal justice literature, where the investigative process has been identified in many ways as the 'golden thread' connecting a whole series of miscarriages of justice. Although the responsibility for miscarriages of justice ranges far and wide, from poor legal representation to questionable 'expert evidence' (Walker 1999), it would seem that police conduct in undertaking criminal investigations bears much of the blame for this particular form of system failure.

Although the role of police conduct in miscarriages of justice had attracted public attention as long back as the mid-1970s (in relation to the 'Confait' case, examined later), it was the miscarriages of justice associated with Irish terrorism, which only came to light in the late 1980s, that above all turned the spotlight on police conduct and its relationship with miscarriages of justice. This began with the case of the 'Guildford Four', involving the conviction of Gerald Conlon, Paul Hill, Carole Richardson and Patrick Armstrong in 1975 for the murder of five people killed in the bombing of the Horse and Groom public house in 1974. The case for the prosecution relied almost totally on confession evidence, and at the trial the Four claimed that confessions had been extracted from them by force by the Surrey Police. In 1989 the then Home Secretary, Douglas Hurd, referred the case back to the Court of Appeal, after a lengthy campaign by supporters of the Four, including church leaders. In preparation for the appeal process the case was investigated by the Avon and Somerset Police, and one of the detectives involved found typed notes, heavily edited by hand, from the police 'interview' with Armstrong, whose confession was central to the conviction. The problem was that these amended notes corresponded with the notes presented to the trial as evidence and, it was claimed, they were notes taken during the police interview. The implication was that the police had manipulated the notes after the 'interview' to fit in with the case they wished to present (Rozenberg 1994: 303–4). These findings led the Crown to concede that the case against the Guildford Four could not be sustained and the convictions were quashed later in 1989.

The miscarriages of justice in the case of the Birmingham Six also pivoted around the extent to which police conduct was a factor in generating injustices (Mullin 1990). In 1975 Hugh Callaghan, Patrick Hill, Gerry Hunter, Richard McIlkenny, Billy Power and Johnny Walker were convicted of the 21 murders which arose out of two pub bombings, associated with Irish terrorism on the British mainland, in Birmingham the previous year. Again, confession evidence was central to the case against the Six, and, as with the Guildford Four, allegations were made about maltreatment by the police (in this case the West Midlands Police) – although scientific evidence was also critical. After another lengthy campaign the case was referred to the Court of Appeal in 1990 (the convictions having been upheld at two previous appeals). Electrostatic analysis of interview transcripts suggested that one of the interviews had not been recorded contemporaneously with the police interview, as claimed at the trial. This, together with concerns over the scientific evidence used in the original convictions, caused the Crown to concede that evidence against the Six was not reliable. In 1991 the Court of Appeal duly quashed the convictions of the Birmingham Six (Rozenberg 1994: 310–14).

It is difficult to overstate the shock to the justice system which the Guildford Four and the Birmingham Six cases created. In particular, the cases pointed an accusing finger at the police as being 'confession oriented' and willing to turn to questionable means in order to obtain such confessions. Ironically, the exposures of past police practices in these two miscarriages of justice came at a time when legislation which would lead to significant controls on police investigations and conduct, the Police and Criminal Evidence Act 1984 (legislation which, as we shall see later, was itself driven in part by a miscarriage of justice), was beginning to bed down. This is further evidence of the inter-relationship between miscarriages of justice and the police investigative process.

The aim of this chapter is to examine further this relationship between miscarriages of justice and the police investigative process. In part it will draw from empirical research relating to a wider project (Savage et al. 2007) involving semi-structured interviews ($n = 37$) with a range of individuals associated with miscarriages of justice. Interviewees included representatives from campaigning organizations, lawyers, journalists, victims and relatives of victims of miscarriages of justice. The research aimed to determine both the 'critical failure points' across a range of past cases of miscarriages of justice, and the 'critical success factors' in campaigns against miscarriages of justice. The focus of this discussion will be on two primary issues, which in a sense make up the symbiotic nature of the relationship between miscarriages of justice and the investigative process. First, it will consider the role of police investigative processes in the *causation* of miscarriages of justice and, in particular, whether the established focus on the police treatment of *suspects* is adequate as a basis for understanding miscarriages of justice. Secondly, it will examine the role of miscarriages of justice in *shaping* the investigative process itself. The exposure of key cases of miscarriages of justice has set in motion change agendas for the police investigative process which have in due course involved legislative and/or policy reforms. Thus, not only does the process of criminal investigations contribute to miscarriages of justice but miscarriages of justice also contribute to the ways in which criminal investigations themselves, given the passage of time, are conducted. This discussion will lead us to finally consider some of the major features of current attempts to 'professionalize' criminal investigation in directions that, among other things, will hopefully militate against future miscarriages of justice. As a basis we need to begin by considering what is meant by 'miscarriages of justice'.

Categorizing 'miscarriages of justice'

When the term 'miscarriages of justice' is used it is most typically identified with what are called 'wrongful convictions'. For the purposes of this discussion, however, the reduction of miscarriages of justice to 'wrongful convictions' only is doubly troublesome. To begin with, the term 'wrongful convictions', as Nobles and Schiff (2000) have argued, is problematic in the sense that it is often taken to mean that where 'miscarriages of justice' have taken place there has somehow been a 'denial of the truth'. In other words a miscarriage of justice has occurred when an 'innocent' person is convicted because the 'correct' verdict had not been reached. The very notion of *wrongful* conviction is laced with this notion of 'truth' as the mirror opposite of 'error', both of which are almost impossible to demonstrate unequivocally. Nobles and Schiff challenge this notion of an absolute 'truth' standing outside the justice system which is distorted as a result of malpractice, lack of professionalism or simple mistakes within the justice system. They offer the more relativistic notion of miscarriages of justice as occurring when there is a gap between the values claimed for the criminal justice system – due process, obedience to rules, rights of suspects and so on – and its actual procedures and practices (Nobles and Schiff 2000: 35). In this respect we would argue that it is more appropriate to use the term *questionable convictions* than wrongful convictions, by which we mean convictions based on grounds which appear to conflict with the rhetoric of criminal justice and which are as such open to challenge by others.

However, the definition of miscarriages of justice as relating to questionable convictions is itself only partly adequate. There has been an increasing awareness that 'miscarriages of justice' can also occur when there is *no action or inaction*, in the sense that an act has taken place (an offence against a victim) but no action or insufficient action has followed. Indeed, each time a questionable conviction is exposed, another 'miscarriage of justice' is exposed at one and the same time, in the sense that the revelation of a questionable conviction leaves an offence for which no one stands identified. While much of the research on miscarriages of justice – and indeed most of the media attention – has focused on 'wrongful convictions', miscarriages based on *failures to act*, perhaps increasingly, also warrant attention.

This is particularly the case when discussing the role of police investigative processes in miscarriages of justice. There has been more controversy in recent years surrounding the failures of the police to do anything or anything appropriate in response to the investigation of serious crimes than over the police role in wrongful/questionable convictions. Nowhere is this better illustrated than in the Stephen Lawrence case. Lawrence was the victim of a racist murder attack committed by a group of white youths in 1993. Information on their identity was readily available from members of the local community and indeed was passed on to the police very soon after the murder was committed. However, as a result of a catalogue of questionable investigative decisions and actions (perhaps better termed *inactions*), the police failed to bring anyone to account for the crime (Macpherson 1999). The 'miscarriage of justice' in this case related to the failure of the police to conduct an investigation effectively and to the satisfaction of the murder victim's family.

For these reasons and for the purposes of this discussion the term 'miscarriages of justice' will cover two sets or processes. On the one hand are *questionable convictions*, convictions which are made on grounds which appear to run contrary to the processes, procedures and principles stated to govern the justice process. On the other hand are *questionable actions*, the decisions and non-decisions, actions and inactions associated with law enforcement and justice agencies and which can be held responsible for failures to respond. As we shall see, police investigative processes play a key role in relation to both types of miscarriages of justice.

Criminal investigation: the 'golden thread' of miscarriages of justice?

Miscarriages of justice stem from a range of sources and stages in the law enforcement, investigative and justice processes. Walker, in his review of the miscarriages of justice literature, provides a useful summary of 'recurrent forms of miscarriage of justice' (1999: 52–5) from which we might take the following as being the basis of questionable convictions in the past: the fabrication of evidence; unreliable identification of an offender by the police or witnesses; unreliable expert evidence; unreliable confessions resulting from police pressure or the vulnerability of suspects; non-disclosure of evidence by the police or prosecution; the conduct of the trial (due mainly to the judge's role in the proceedings); and problems associated with appeals procedures (including limited access to legal funds). In this respect it is evident that the investigative process is a hugely significant factor, what might even be termed the 'golden thread', in the generation of injustices. This section of the chapter will examine the actions – and inactions – within the investigation process which, it could be argued, are directly or indirectly responsible for miscarriages of justice.

The dominant theme in the literature and research on miscarriages of justice, in so far as the investigative process is concerned, relates to the confession culture which has seemingly governed the ethos of police investigations, at least in the past. Traditionally, the primary concern of police investigators has been to extract or elicit a confession from the primary suspect, the confession being seen by officers to be the bedrock of a 'successful' investigation and the predominant means by which a conviction can be secured (Maguire 2003; Sanders and Young 2003). This ethos has spawned approaches to police investigation, particularly at the stage of interviewing suspects in police detention, which have relied on oppressive questioning to gain confessions (Rozenberg 1994). Specific examples of this seem evident in the questionable convictions of Stephen Downing (Hale 2002) and the 'Cardiff Three' (Sekar 1997). Short of oppressive questioning, investigators, wittingly or otherwise, have at least taken advantage of the psychological vulnerability, and suggestibility, of suspects subjected to questioning under conditions of detention (Gudjonsson *et al.* 1993) (this area of analysis is dealt with extensively in Chapter 19, this volume). Of more direct concern to this discussion is the question of *why* confessions could have become such a focal concern of the investigative process. This leads us to the issue of what has been called the problem of 'premature closure' of police investigations (Shepherd and Milne 1999).

Premature closure is a concept that has been applied particularly to the interview stage of police investigations. In this context it has been defined as 'the disposition to draw pre-emptive conclusions from information processed prior to conducting an interview' (Shepherd and Milne 1999: 126). However, the notion of premature closure can also apply to the investigative process overall. Investigations which may start with a degree of 'openness' and a willingness of investigators to consider a variety of potential lines of inquiry, at some early stage in the process, close around a particular 'thesis' and a particular suspect or suspects. As one interviewee, an investigative journalist with a track record of campaigning about miscarriages of justice, expressed it:

> If you know a case really well, you know that the police change in their approach to witnesses, from when they are trying to find out what happened to when they "know" what happened and they want to prove it.

Another campaigner, who had written extensively on miscarriages of justice, argued in a similar vein:

> I found over and over again that the plain clothes police got it into their heads early on who they thought the perpetrator of the crime was and having done that they tailored the evidence to suit that theory. That's how most miscarriages of justice in my view came about.

In the academic literature one interpretation of this process of premature closure is that it operates around the logic of 'case construction', summarized nicely by Sanders and Young (2003: 368):

once a person becomes a suspect, he or she is placed into an adversarial relationship with the police rather than one in which the latter seek 'the truth' in a neutral and 'objective' fashion. Thereafter, detectives, starting from a premise of guilt, selectively weave together available pieces of information, or statements by suspects and witnesses, to produce a simplified and coherent story of 'what happened'.

In the context of miscarriages of justice, the process of case construction has in some ways moved further, beyond just building up the case against the suspect; notoriously, the suppression of counter evidence has come into play (Rozenberg 1994: 303 ff.), most notably in relation to the miscarriages of justice associated with Irish terrorism in the 1970s (Mullin 1990). This pushes the 'closed mindset' of investigators to the extreme – not so much 'closure' but the veritable exclusion of all that does not fit the initial narrative.

We would, however, make two qualifications to the, now well established, case of premature closure and exclusion. First, that investigative closure is not just a problem for miscarriages based on questionable convictions, but is also a feature of that other area of miscarriages of justice – what we have called questionable actions. Closed mindsets have been found to be responsible for critical shortcomings in police investigations where a failure to act is the issue. The Stephen Lawrence case, again, is the classic example of this. Among the many deficiencies identified in the public inquiry that, in due course, followed the murder of Stephen Lawrence (Macpherson 1999), were those associated with police inaction due to what the inquiry report famously labelled as 'institutional racism'. This was reflected in the way in which investigators failed to consider the murder as a racially motivated one and to gather evidence with this in mind (Macpherson 1999: 23). This included the failure to treat Stephen's friend, Duwayne Brooks, who was with Stephen when the attack took place, as a victim and also as someone with valuable information. In this respect a 'closed mind' to the possibility that a crime might be racially motivated seemed to be at issue. Another example of this seems to be the case of Ricky Reel, an Asian youth who was found drowned a week after his failure to return home. Despite his family's insistence to the police that his failure to come home was cause for grave concern, the initial police response was to treat the disappearance as harmless. One interviewee associated with the Reel campaign recalled one interchange with the police: '[The police officer said] as it happens in Asian culture parents try to find a girl for their children and he said, well because of that maybe he has run away with his girlfriend.'

What was even more significant was that many months after the death and despite evidence to the contrary, police investigators held to the view that this was not a racially motivated crime but rather an 'accident'. If in the Lawrence case the 'closed' mentality was relatively short lived (but with long-term costs to justice), in the Reel case closure in this sense was much more deeply ingrained. In both cases, however, the link between closed mindsets in the investigative process and miscarriages of justice is evident. In this context we might extend the notion of 'case construction' to include almost its mirror opposite: *case denial*.

The second qualification to the notion of premature closure takes us back to questionable convictions. The notion of 'case construction' in principle applies to the whole investigative process; however, the focus of actual research and debate in this area has tended to be on the police treatment of suspects. We would argue that, in terms of miscarriages of justice, police investigation in terms of dealings with victims and witnesses now warrants fuller attention, as it is this area which may be increasingly likely to be associated with miscarriages of justice. This is particularly the case regarding police interviews. The Police and Criminal Evidence Act (PACE) 1984 has undoubtedly changed the climate of police interviews with suspects, notwithstanding the fact that questionable convictions in cases such as the 'Cardiff Three' were based on interviews conducted under PACE (Sekar 1997). Nevertheless, Clarke and Milne (2001) have argued that both the implementation of PACE and the introduction of training initiatives such as the PEACE interviewing approach have rendered interviews of suspects far less likely to result in miscarriages of justice than has been the case in the past. This leaves the interviewing and handling of victims and witnesses.

Strong indications that 'victim' testimony can contribute to miscarriages of justice have been provided by the questionable convictions of care workers in child sexual abuse cases. After a number of individuals previously convicted in such cases had their convictions quashed, the Home Affairs Select Committee conducted an inquiry into the investigative practices associated with those convictions. The committee focused on the investigative processes of 'trawling', whereby the police contacted whole cohorts of past residents of care homes to elicit evidence of past abuse, and on the ways in which 'victims' were interviewed. The committee reported in 2002, arguing that: 'a new genre of miscarriages of justice has arisen from the over-enthusiastic pursuit of these [child abuse] allegations' (House of Commons 2002: 5). The committee expressed concerns about the conduct of police interviews with witnesses and in particular the role of 'leading questions' in police interviews. The report quotes the view of Curtis-Thomas, MP, which fits closely with the 'case construction' thesis but in this context applies to the treatment of witnesses: 'The police will plant suggestions producing narratives that fit their case rather than the truth. What happens ... is a kind of indirect collusion which develops through witnesses' unrecorded contact with members of the same police team' (House of Commons 2002: 16).

It is of concern that adult witness interviews are not required by law to be digitally recorded and may thus lack integrity, especially if the witness was unreliable and/or compliant, as there is currently no record of the interviewing process for adult witnesses. The Youth Justice and Criminal Evidence Act 1999 (s. 17) and the Criminal Justice Act 2003 (s. 137), should help rectify this. When (and if) these sections are enacted work fully, more interviews with adult witnesses should be video-interviewed as a matter of course, especially those deemed 'intimidated' witnesses. Until that transpires interviews with adult witnesses/victims will remain recorded through contemporaneous note-taking. This is a serious problem for any investigation relying on witness evidence as a key part of the prosecution case. This is because research has shown that even adult memory is malleable: it can be altered, changed and edited through many factors (see Milne and Bull 1999 for a review). One primary cause of erroneous information being elicited from adults is the use of leading questions, and research has shown that police officers, when interviewing adult witnesses, use such questions too frequently (Clarke and Milne 2001). To add to this problem, further research has shown that the handwritten records of interviews with witnesses and victims, which become statements of evidence, are often incomplete, inaccurate and do not represent what the witnesses remembered at all; instead they can become a reflection of what the officer wanted to hear (see Milne and Shaw 1999, Shepherd and Milne 1999 and Milne and Bull 2006 for a review of the statement-taking process). This is governed in part through officers using what they already know/suspect about the case and as a result shaping their questioning around the 'key' topic areas; they may also frame the written statement itself in accordance with the investigative hypotheses (Shepherd and Milne 1999; 2006).

Having made these connections between investigative practices and processes, on the one hand, and miscarriages of justice on the other, it should not be assumed that police investigation is driven by simple malice or a wilful disregard for the 'truth'. It is also important to have some sense of the pressures placed on the police to get 'results'. At times this pressure can be almost irresistible and can create a climate where the investigation can become ends rather than means oriented. As one interviewee, associated with a campaigning TV series, put it:

> for me the most important driver for miscarriages of justice is the combination of the need to find a guilty party and the presence of the usual suspects ... There's huge pressures on the investigating officers either because this is a famous case or gruesome case ... if you think of every case where people have started to worry about it being a miscarriage of justice, it has been where there has been a rush to get someone fast and I think that's what frames the mindset of officers ... effectively having to sort out who the usual suspects might be and then having to build a case around them.

The investigative process, unfortunately, is not immune from the environmental pressures which surround law enforcement and criminal justice more generally (Savage 2003). Such pressures may create some of the conditions for system failure which in the policing context is often reflected in misconduct (Punch 2003). However, those pressures can also work in a positive as well as negative direction. In this respect it evident that, while the investigative process plays a major part in the genesis of miscarriages of justice, miscarriages of justice themselves can also shape the investigative process.

Miscarriages of justice and the shaping of investigative processes

System failure can often be a spur for reform. Miscarriages of justice, particularly if they become high profile and enjoy the full glow of media attention, can act as archetypical examples of system failure. They can expose abuses of authority and power and undermine the trust that is vested in those that enforce the law or administer justice. This gives miscarriages of justice the potential of being formative chapters in policing and criminal justice reform. The link between miscarriages of justice and reforms of investigative practices is rarely direct. Most typically, it is the official inquiry – public or private – which can follow cases of miscarriages of justice that acts as the catalyst for change. Official inquiries tend to use the specific set of events which are the focus of the inquiry as a platform for more general reviews of practices and procedures around the field in question. We shall cite two notable examples of the linkage between miscarriages of justice, official inquiries and reforms of the investigative process. The first relates to questionable convictions which were to bring about reforms of police powers; the second relates to questionable actions (or failures to act) which have generated reforms of investigative practices.

The first case arose out of the murder of Maxwell Confait in 1972. Confait was strangled in a flat in London which was subsequently set alight (the time lapse between the two events would become a crucial issue in the trial processes that would follow). Two boys were convicted of the crime in 1972, Colin Lattimore and Ronald Leighton, both of whom confessed in writing to the murder of Confait and arson of his flat, as had a third boy, Ahmet Salih, although the murder charge against him was withdrawn before the trial, leaving a charge of arson. Lattimore and Leighton both pleaded not guilty to the murder, claiming that their confessions were made under duress, or worse. Nevertheless, Leighton was convicted for murder and Lattimore for manslaughter on the ground of diminished responsibility; both, together with Salih, were also convicted of arson. Leighton was 16 years old, but had a reading age of a 10-year-old (Fisher 1977: 47). Lattimore was 19 years old, but was estimated to have a mental age of a 14-year-old (Fisher 1977: 53).

The boys' application for leave to appeal was refused by the Court of Appeal in 1973 but, after subsequent investigations carried out on the order of the Home Office in 1974, their case was referred to the Court of Appeal. The court quashed both the murder and manslaughter convictions, together with other convictions of arson which were attached to the original conviction. The prosecution case rested on there being only a matter of minutes of time between the strangling of Confait and the starting of the fire and this is what their confessions amounted to. However, the court agreed that expert pathological evidence now pointed to a time of death more than two hours before the fire started. This not only contradicted the confession evidence but it also opened up an alibi defence, most strongly in favour of Lattimore, who had witnesses to him being at a youth club throughout the time period of Confait's murder. On quashing the convictions as unsafe and unsatisfactory, the court's judgment also made damning comments about the confessions, stating: 'There are ... a number of very improbable matters in the confessions, and some striking omissions from them' (cited in Fisher 1977: 250).

In the circumstances the Home Secretary ordered an official inquiry into the circumstances leading to the trial of the three boys, to be held primarily in private, under the aegis of Sir Henry Fisher, which reported in 1977. The Fisher Report became a landmark dossier documenting system failures throughout the conviction process, providing what has since become a familiar catalogue of factors contributing to miscarriages of justice (see above and Walker 1999). One of these was the role of expert evidence, whereby the pathologist appointed by the coroner was thought to have failed to carry out the appropriate tests which would have more accurately estimated the time of death, and who then proceeded to give testimony at the trial which failed to remedy the consequences of this failure (Fisher 1977: 21–2). The report also found the prosecution decision-making and evidential processes wanting (1977: 19–21). However, it was the police investigative processes which took much of the blame for the miscarriages of justice in the Confait case. The Fisher Report highlighted wide-ranging failures in the conduct of the investigation of the murder, most particularly in relation to the 'interrogation' process – a term which has significantly fallen out of favour in discourse on police investigation in the UK. What the report identified as failure points in this regard set the agenda for the Royal Commission on Criminal Procedure (Phillips 1981 – known as the 'Phillips Commission') which followed in the wake of the Fisher Report, and PACE, which saw through many of the key recommendations of the Royal Commission (Zander 1995). In this respect the report was hugely predictive. Aspects of the investigative process identified as in need of procedural reform included the following:

- *Protections for persons under interview*: the report raised the issue of the appropriate balance between 'police effectiveness' and individual rights – with a clear steer towards the latter – and the need for the codification of criminal procedure (Fisher 1977: 13). Both were to become pivotal concerns of the Phillips Commission and subsequently PACE (Zander 1995).

- *Rights to communicate with a solicitor*: the report alluded both to the need for access to legal advice to become a formal right for suspects under 'interrogation' and to the need for the development of a duty solicitor scheme to guarantee such access (Fisher 1977: 14–16). Via the Phillips Commission, this proposal found its way into the revisions on police powers of detention contained in PACE.

- *The recording of interviews with suspects*: as the report argued: 'The Confait case lends support to the argument for the introduction of tape-recording for interviews in police stations and the taking of written statements … Apart from the additional protection afforded to the individual, tape-recording would constitute a valuable protection for the police themselves' (1977: 16). As with access to legal advice, the recording of interviewing of suspects was to become a central element of PACE and, arguably, a milestone in the reform of police investigative practice – although, as has already been noted above, the subsequent miscarriage of justice in relation to the 'Cardiff Three' case (Sekar 1997) demonstrated that much remained to be done to make this provision fully effective.

- *The fair treatment of young people and mentally disordered persons*: the report raised serious concerns about investigations involving the interview of young or mentally disordered suspects conducted in the absence of parents or guardians and, in particular, the reliability of confessions gained under these circumstances (Fisher 1977: 18–19). Again, this was highly predictive of the shape of things to come in PACE.

In addition to these specific aspects of problematic investigative processes, the Fisher Report also made some telling comments about the need for police investigations to remain open even when confessional statements have been made (Fisher 1977: 29–30) which in ways constituted a case for what, much later, would become known as investigative interviewing. In that sense the miscarriages of justice associated with the Confait case provoked, in due course, legislative reform of police powers and contributed to a longer-term process of the reorientation of investigative 'philosophy' towards greater openness.

Our second example of a miscarriage of justice impacting upon investigative practice relates not to questionable convictions but to failures to act and to perhaps the most notable example of this category of injustice, the Stephen Lawrence case. The police response to the murder of Stephen Lawrence in 1993 eventually became one of the most widely publicized examples of system failure in recent British history. As a result, the impact of the case in terms of policy influence and legal reform has been widespread (Savage *et al.* forthcoming). Stephen Lawrence was stabbed to death by a gang of young white men, in what was by all accounts a racially motivated attack (Macpherson 1999: 1). Although the identities of those responsible are virtually a matter of public record – those identities were available almost immediately after the murder – nobody has been convicted for the crime. After a campaign headed by Stephen's family, the Home Office set up a public inquiry under Sir William Macpherson into the 'matters arising from the death of Stephen Lawrence, in order particularly to identify the lessons to be learned for the investigation and prosecution of racially motivated crimes' (Macpherson 1999: Foreword). The Macpherson Inquiry reported in 1999 and quickly became a landmark document for British public policy in general and policing in particular. We shall draw from the wide range of issues raised by the Lawrence case a number of themes of most significance to the investigative process.

Institutionalized racism and the investigative process

The most widely publicized matter identified in the Macpherson Report related to the role of 'institutionalized racism' in the system failures surrounding the policing response to the murder and its aftermath. In terms of the investigative process itself, institutionalized racism, according to Macpherson, was evident at various stages of the investigation of the murder, from initial response – in the failure to recognize the crime as racially motivated (what was referred to above as case denial) – to the handling of witnesses and the subsequent treatment of the Lawrence family. As the report states:

The failure of the first investigating team to recognise and accept racism and race relations as a central feature of their investigation ... played a part in the deficiencies in policing which we identify in this Report ... a substantial number of officers of junior rank would not accept that the murder ... was simply and solely 'racially motivated'. The relevance of the ethnicity and cultural status of the victims ... was not properly recognized (Macpherson 1999: 23).

The policy recommendations which fell out of this area of concern took a number of forms, including three in particular. First, that the definition of a 'racist incident' should be clarified, the proposed definition being 'any incident which is perceived by the victim or any other person' (Macpherson 1999: 328). From the investigative perspective this served to shift the 'judgement' as to whether an incident was to be deemed 'racially motivated' from the investigator (as an outcome of the investigation) to the victim, or others (as a premise of the investigation) – a shift that could, in principle, work to reorient the whole ethos of a criminal investigation (but see Hall 2005: 198–9). Secondly, that the Association of Chief Police Officers, as a key generator of general policing policy (Savage *et al.* 2000), be charged with devising a national 'good practice guide' for the police response to racial incidents (Macpherson 1999: 329). This was initially reflected in the *Action Guide to Identifying and Combating Hate Crime* (ACPO 1999) and, in due course, in *Hate Crime: Delivering a Quality Service* (ACPO 2005). What emerged in this context was guidance on the definition and classification of hate crimes (ACPO 2005: 9–12), approaches to gathering 'community intelligence' (ACPO 2005: 15–17), initial investigations (ACPO 2005: 38–43) and the treatment of witnesses and victims by investigating teams (ACPO 2005: 24–32). Thirdly, that police training be reformed to reflect more effectively racism awareness and valuing cultural diversity, in the context of which the training of officers specializing in criminal investigation becomes particularly significant. We shall return to this issue later in this chapter.

Family liaison and the process of criminal investigation

One of the most disturbing features of the Lawrence case was the way in which Stephen Lawrence's family were treated by the police, in the immediate aftermath of the murder and subsequently in terms of liaison between the family and the police. As the Macpherson Report states:

the family liaison in sensitive and difficult cases of this kind has to be handled with great care and understanding. Things obviously went wrong from the start, and it was the duty of the senior officers in particular to take their own steps to ensure that alternative methods were followed in order to see that the family were kept properly informed and that their relationship with the investigation team was a healthy one. This they signally failed to do (1999: 117).

The report proceeded to make a number of recommendations about family liaison, including the need to establish the role of family liaison officer as a dedicated role with specialist training, that senior investigating officers take formal responsibility for ensuring best practice in family liaison and that family preferences and needs should take a full role in investigative decision-making (Macpherson 1999: 330). Since Macpherson the critical role of family liaison in the investigative process has been widely accepted, not least in national guidance on responding to hate crime (ACPO 2005: 27–9). This is not to say that the critical role of family liaison had not been recognized before – the Avon and Somerset Constabulary had shown the way by developing specialist training in this area the year before Macpherson reported (see Grieve and French 2000). However, what the national guidelines signal is that family liaison has moved from the periphery of criminal investigation – as something which took place alongside, or even after, the investigative process – to become an integral feature of the investigation itself. It also places family liaison as something which not only supports families through the process of conducting an investigation, but also values families as sources of intelligence around which an investigation might be managed. As expressed in the Association of Chief Police Officer's guidance on hate crime: 'In cases where lifestyle, friends and associates of the victim may hold the key to identifying witnesses or suspects, the family liaison role *is pivotal to the success of the investigation*' (ACPO 2005: 27, emphasis added). Of course, there is the potential that the provision of support to families and the pursuit of information from them might not always be compatible exercises, and the message from Macpherson is that the care of families should be the primary concern. In this context, the investigative process should ideally be oriented to reducing the degree of suffering by victims as a central goal and in this respect the support role of family liaison is critical. Nevertheless, as a result of Lawrence and Macpherson, family liaison has now attained high status in the 'mindset' and practice of criminal investigation in Britain.

Review and oversight of the investigative process

What was often downplayed in the aftermath of the publication of the Macpherson Report was that a central concern of the inquiry was with the actual quality of the investigation into the murder of Stephen Lawrence. In part this related to the competency or otherwise of the key players in the investigation, of which Macpherson had much to say. However, it also related to the 'quality assurance' measures at work, or more accurately not at work, throughout the Lawrence investigation. If mistakes or miscalculations have been made at one or more stages of a criminal investigation, it is important that procedures are available and deployable to remedy them at later stages in the process. This was clearly not the case with Lawrence.

It is now accepted that a means of challenging the 'premature closure' of an investigation – or in this case its parallel, case denial – and of maintaining a degree of openness in the investigation is to conduct case reviews. Reviews have traditionally been used to reinvestigate 'unsolved' major crimes (see Macpherson 1999: 195). In the Lawrence case, some four months after the murder and the initial investigation, a review was conducted which became known as the 'Barker Review'. The Barker Review involved an assessment of the way in which the initial investigation and subsequent decisions were made, and it concluded that 'The investigation has been progressed satisfactorily and all lines of inquiry correctly pursued' (cited in Macpherson 1999: 199), although it did acknowledge weaknesses in the liaison between the investigating team and the Lawrence family. The review was heavily criticized by Macpherson as being 'uncritical', 'anodyne', guilty of 'factual errors' and overall as 'flawed and indefensible' (Macpherson 1999: 200–3). The report concluded that 'Failure to acknowledge and to detect errors [in the investigation] resulted in them being effectively concealed' (Macpherson 1999: 320).

The Macpherson Report made two recommendations relating to review of investigations: first, that 'ACPO devise Codes of Practice to govern Reviews of investigations of crime, in order to ensure that such Reviews are open and thorough'. Secondly, that the Metropolitan Police Service 'review their internal inspection and accountability processes' (Macpherson 1999: 329–30). The message from Macpherson was that a rigorous staged review of criminal investigations should be a key feature of the quality assurance of an investigation and the decision-making which an investigation involves. Significantly, this was also a key message of the Byford Inquiry into the 'Yorkshire Ripper' murders in the 1970s (Byford 1982), although not one, apparently, fully appreciated. In effect, Macpherson was calling for greater openness in criminal investigations and countering the problem of 'premature closure' as discussed above.

Following the publication of the Macpherson Report, Her Majesty's Inspectors of Constabulary (HMIC) conducted a review of the Metropolitan Police Service's approach to major crime investigation, including murder review procedures. This process eventually extended to all other police forces in England and Wales (see Nicol *et al.* 2004: 9). A momentum had gathered in the wake of Macpherson, which eventually culminated with the Association of Chief Police Officers updating their policy guidance on major crimes in the form of the *Murder Investigation Manual*, a document which aimed in part to institutionalize periodic review of investigations; in turn this has found its way into force-level policy on major crime investigations (National Centre for Policing Excellence 2005).

In practice, reviews range from 'informal reviews' where the Senior Investigating Officer (SIO) reports on progress to the Head of Criminal Investigation and/or another SIO, through 'self-inspection' or 'peer review' – where another SIO checks on progress – through to a 'concluding review', a full re-examination of the evidence and decision-making after all lines of inquiry are completed. Of course, since well before Macpherson, there has also been a practice of one police force reviewing investigations conducted by another, where there are reasons to warrant it. Indeed, this happened in the Lawrence case with the reinvestigation of the murder by Kent Police in 1997. However, this sort of review takes place when there are grounds to believe something may have 'gone wrong' – the thrust of the Macpherson case for institutionalized review of investigations is to avoid them going wrong in the first place.

The final point to make about the Lawrence case is that this particular miscarriage of justice has also played a critical role in the reform of police governance relating to oversight of policing, including oversight of the investigative process. One of the key recommendations of Macpherson is that consideration be given to a fully independent system for the investigation of complaints against the police (Macpherson 1999: 333). The Home Secretary pledged to adopt this recommendation and in due course the Police Reform Act 2002 established the Independent Police Complaints Commission (IPCC), which went 'live' in April 2004. This mirrored the establishment of the Police Ombudsman for Northern Ireland in 2000, which followed in the wake of the Patten Report (Patten 1999) (a model that was also later to follow by the formation of the Garda Siochana Ombudsman Commission). What is particularly interesting about these developments is not only that police investigative processes would now come under external scrutiny as never before, but also that a new body of 'investigators' has come into being, working alongside the police service. Historically, police opposition to the idea of independent investigation of complaints reflected a logic that 'only police officers' possessed the skills set effectively to investigate complaints or major police incidents. A challenge which the IPCC and the Police Ombudsman presents is whether 'non-police' investigators can demonstrate that the investigative process is as, if not more, safe in their hands than it is with police investigators themselves. If that proves to be the case, it opens up the prospect of a form of 'lay investigative' element which might, perhaps as part of the review of investigations, serve to improve the quality of the investigative process overall. It is on this issue of quality and the question of the professionalization of the investigative process that we shall conclude this discussion.

Conclusion: professionalizing the investigative process?

A central concern of this chapter has been with the role of the investigative process in the genesis of miscarriages of justice, whether defined in terms of questionable convictions and failures to act or act appropriately. In this respect it has been argued that the process of premature closure, either in the sense of 'case construction' or 'case denial', is a root factor in many cases of miscarriages of justice. We have also considered how some of the measures to challenge premature closure, such as formalized case review, have themselves been forced through, at least to an extent, as a result of key cases of miscarriages of justice. There is now, however, evidence that improving the quality of criminal investigation in the direction of greater 'openness' has become a more institutionalized concern and not simply one trailing in the wake of the system failures characteristic of miscarriages of justice.

As well as the IPCC, another initiative that arose out of the agenda of the Police Reform Act 2002 was the Professionalizing the Investigative Process (PIP) programme, which was formally launched by the Association of Chief Police Officers in 2005. The aim of PIP (see Chapter 26, this volume) is to enhance the investigative process through training and development of those involved in criminal investigation. As mapped out in what is known as the *Core Investigative Doctrine*, this is to be achieved by providing training and work-placed assessment based on an integrated competency framework that is supported by practice advice (National Centre for Policing Excellence 2005). Interestingly, the practice advice document also examines many of the issues discussed in this chapter, including 'investigative mindset and investigative and evidential evaluation ... which will assist investigators in making accountable decisions and minimise the chance of errors' (National Centre for Policing Excellence 2005: 7). For example, the doctrine discusses that, when applying the investigative mindset, 'investigators must keep an open mind and be receptive to alternative views or explanations. Investigators should never rush to premature judgements about the meaning of any material or the reliability of its source' (National Centre for Policing Excellence 2005: 63). These messages, now institutionalized as national policing guidelines on the conduct of criminal investigation, could hardly be more evocative of the lessons provided by miscarriages of justice over the years.

However, the effectiveness or otherwise of PIP and other attempts to enhance the quality of investigation may depend on a greater understanding, and an issue perhaps for future research, of what it is that makes a 'good detective', or what it is that makes a 'good investigation'. Is it a matter of meticulous attention to detail, of 'creativity', or some combination of both? The *Core Investigative Doctrine* refers to the need for an investigator to 'think creatively', defined as requiring 'the investigator to look at the problem in another way, to question any assumptions that may have been made and to query the validity of all information. Investigators must continually question whether there may be another possible explanation for the material gathered' (National Centre for Policing Excellence 2005: 23). A danger in the linkage between investigative work and 'creativity', however, is that it may reinforce the image of detective work as an 'art' or 'craft', more exposed to officers' discretion and as such less subject as such to regulation and accountability, whereas, in a sense, a 'quasi-scientific' approach might be more appropriate. Indeed, the doctrine also encourages investigators to adopt an appropriate use of 'hypothesis testing' (National Centre for Policing Excellence 2005: 72–3). Instead of the traditional tendency for investigators to seek evidence that would support one hypothesis (as in 'case theory' discussed above), a message of the PIP programme and training is to encourage investigators to create multiple hypotheses and 'test the null hypothesis' – i.e. seek to disprove a theory.

The question is whether such attempts to forge the 'investigative mindset' in the direction of more openness and critical reflection will overcome the more deeply ingrained elements of 'cop culture' which point in many ways in the very opposite direction (Foster 2003). It might be argued that it is at the level of investigative work where 'cop culture' is at its most resilient and where attitudes such as 'cynicism' and 'solidarity' (Reiner 2000: 89–95) are more likely to flourish, than in, for example, community-based police work, where officers are more exposed to an environment which challenges those attitudes (Fielding 1995). So-called 'noble cause corruption' (Reiner 2000: 89) is one, exaggerated and acute, consequence of 'cop culture', in which investigators have allowed ends to over-ride means and where miscarriages of justice have followed as a result. The setting out of a 'doctrine' might be a necessary, but not sufficient, basis for forging the form of 'investigative mindset' which effective and fair investigation requires.

In these respects miscarriages of justice might play another role in the ongoing reform of the investigative process. The PIP programme lays great emphasis on training as a means to professionalize and enhance criminal investigation. Perhaps if a core feature of that training was to be a study of miscarriages of justice and the lessons to be learnt from them, the professionalization of investigation might be even more achievable.

Selected further reading

Heaton-Armstrong, A., Shepherd, E., Gudjonsson, G., and Wolchover, D. (2006). *Witness testimony: Psychological, Investigative and evidential perspectives.* Oxford: Oxford University Press.

Kebbell, M. and Davies, G. (eds.), *Practical psychology for forensic investigations.* Chichester: Wiley.

Milne, R. and Bull, R. (1999) *Investigative Interviewing: Psychology and Practice.* Chichester: Wiley.

Milne, R., and Bull, R. (2006) Interviewing victims, including children and people with intellectual disabilities. Chapter in Kebbell, M. and Davies, G. (eds.), *Practical psychology for forensic investigations.* Chichester: Wiley.

Nobles, R. and Schiff, D. (2000) *Understanding Miscarriages of Justice: Law, the Media and the Inevitability of a Crisis.* Oxford: Oxford University Press.

Shepherd, E., and Milne, R. (2006) Have you told the management about this?: Bringing witness interviewing into the 21st Century. In A. Heaton-Armstrong, E. Shepherd, G. Gudjonsson and D. Wolchover (eds.). *Witness testimony: Psychological, Investigative and evidential perspectives.* Oxford: Oxford University Press.

Williamson, T. (2005) Investigative interviewing: Rights, research, regulation. Cullompton: Willan Publishing.

References

ACPO (1999) *Action Guide to Identifying and Combating Hate Crime.* London: ACPO.

ACPO (2005) *Hate Crime: Delivering a Quality Service.* London: ACPO.

Byford, L. (1982) *The Yorkshire Ripper Case: A Review of the Police Investigation of the Case.* London: HMSO.

Clarke, C. and Milne, R. (2001) *National Evaluation of the PEACE Investigative Interviewing Course.* London: Home Office.

Fielding, N. (1995) *Community Policing* Oxford: Oxford University Press.

Fisher, Sir H. (1977) *The Confait Case: Report.* London: HMSO.

Foster, J. (2003) 'Police cultures', in T. Newburn (ed.) *Handbook of Policing.* Cullompton: Willan Publishing.

Grieve, J. and French, J. (2000) 'Does institutional racism exist in the Metropolitan Police Service?', in D. Green (ed.) *Institutional Racism and the Police: Fact or Fiction?* London: Institute for the Study of Civil Society.

Gudjonsson, G., Clare, I., Rutter, S. and Pearse, J. (1993) *Persons at Risk during Interviews in Police Custody.* London: HMSO.

Hale, D. (2002) *Town without Pity.* London: Century.

Hall, N. (2005) *Hate Crime.* Cullompton: Willan Publishing.

House of Commons (2002) *The Conduct of Investigations into Past Cases of Abuse in Children's Homes.* London: House of Commons.

Macpherson, Sir W. (1999) *The Stephen Lawrence Inquiry.* London: HMSO.

Maguire, M. (2003) 'Criminal investigation and crime control' in T. Newburn (ed.) *Handbook of Policing.* Cullompton: Willan Publishing.

Milne, R. and Bull, R. (1999) *Investigative Interviewing: Psychology and Practice.* Chichester: Wiley.

Milne, R. and Shaw, G. (1999) 'Obtaining witness statements: best practice and proposals for innovation', *Medicine, Science and the Law,* 39: 127–38.

Mullin, C. (1990) *Error of Judgement: The Truth about the Birmingham Bombings.* Dublin: Poolbeg.

National Centre for Policing Excellence (2005) *Practice Advice on Core Investigative Doctrine.* Wyboston: NCPE.

Nicol, C., Innes, M., Gee, D. and Feist, A. (2004) *Reviewing Murder Investigations: An Analysis of Progress from Six Police Forces.* London: HMSO.

Nobles, R. and Schiff, D. (2000) *Understanding Miscarriages of Justice: Law, the Media and the Inevitability of a Crisis.* Oxford: Oxford University Press.

Patten, C. (1999) *A New Beginning: Policing Northern Ireland.* Norwich: HMSO.

Punch, M. (2003) 'Rotten orchards: "pestilence", police misconduct and system failure', *Policing and Society,* 13.

Reiner, R. (2000) *The Politics of the Police* (3rd edn). Oxford: Oxford University Press.

Royal Commission on Criminal Procedure (1981) *The Investigation and Prosecution of Criminal Offences in England and Wales: The Law and Procedure* (the Phillips Commission). London: HMSO.

Rozenberg, J. (1994) *The Search for Justice.* London: Sceptre.

Sanders, A. and Young, R. (2003) 'Police powers', in T. Newburn (ed.) *Handbook of Policing.* Cullompton: Willan Publishing.

Savage, S. (2003) 'Tackling tradition: reform and modernisation of the British police', *Contemporary Politics,* 9.

Savage, S., Charman, S. and Cope, S. (2000) *Policing and the Power of Persuasion.* London: Blackstone Press.

Savage, S., Grieve, J. and Poyser, S. (2007) 'Putting wrongs to right: campaigns against miscarriages of justice', *Criminology and Criminal Justice,* 7 (1): 83–105.

Sekar, S. (1997) *Fitted in: The Cardiff Three and the Lynette White Inquiry.* London: The Fitted in Project.

Shepherd, E. and Milne, R. (1999) 'Full and faithful: ensuring quality practice and integrity of outcome in witness interviews', in A. Heaton-Armstrong *et al.* (eds) *Analysing Witness Testimony: A Guide for Legal Practitioners and other Professionals.* London: Blackstone Press.

Shepherd, E., and Milne, R. (2006) Have you told the management about this?: Bringing witness interviewing into the 21st Century. In A. Heaton-Armstrong, E. Shepherd, G. Gudjonsson and D. Wolchover (eds) *Witness testimony: Psychological, Investigative and evidential perspectives.* Oxford: Oxford University Press.

Walker, C. (1999) 'Miscarriages of justice in principle and practice', in C. Walker and K. Starmer (eds) *Miscarriages of Justice: A Review of Justice in Error.* London: Blackstone Press.

Walker, C. (2002) 'Miscarriages of justice and the correction of error', in M. McConville and G. Wilson (eds) *The Handbook of the Criminal Justice Process.* Oxford: Oxford University Press.

Zander, M. (1995) *The Police and Criminal Evidence Act 1984* (3rd edn). London: HMSO.

Chapter 26

Professionalizing criminal investigation

Peter Stelfox

Introduction

In September 2005, the Association of Chief Police Officers of England, Wales and Northern Ireland (ACPO)[1] launched a national training and development programme which is intended 'to enhance the crime investigation skills and ability of police officers and staff involved in the investigative process and to drive through new standards of investigation at all levels' (NCPE 2005b: 1). The Professionalizing Criminal Investigation Programme (PIP) is a key feature of the government's police reform agenda (Home Office 2004a: 88) and is one of the milestones in the National Policing Plan 2004–2007 (Home Office 2004b).

Underlying PIP is the development of a professional practice of criminal investigation in which investigators can be trained and developed (Phillips 2002: 5). The professional practice, sometimes also called the expert knowledge, of any occupational group consists of 'the particular competences, specialised knowledge and practices used by occupations claiming autonomy and authority to solve specific types of problem' (Flynn 1999: 34). It is generally contained in a literature written specifically for practitioners and has to be mastered before one can be considered to be professionally competent. Such competency is usually recognized by a qualification or by entry on to a professional register, both of which function 'as a trademark does, promising a certain level of performance to those who rely on it' (Davis 2002: 4). Professional practice of this sort has been slow to develop within the police service because the specialized knowledge and practice required by investigators have generally been developed 'on the job' and so have tended to be subject to local and individual variation. This 'craft model' of criminal investigation was viable when criminal investigation was lightly regulated and required low levels of technical and procedural competence. However, the process is now highly regulated and involves the use of technologies and procedures that require considerable competence from investigators. This chapter examines the development of the professional practice of

628

criminal investigation which underpins PIP. It argues that the emerging model is incomplete because it lacks a capacity to systematically evaluate the operational effectiveness of professional practice. There is also a limited research and development capacity in the police service when compared with other occupational groups which have a professional practice. Finally, some of the wider implications for the police service of professionalization will be explored. The chapter concludes that PIP presents the service with an opportunity to fundamentally change the way it does business by investing in the skills of the workforce. If the full benefits of this professionalization are to be realized, there needs to be a change in management culture to accommodate not only new working practices, but also a new relationship between professionally qualified staff and those who manage them. Without such a change, it is unlikely that professionalization will deliver the level of change promised.

Historical perspective

Criminal investigation was not traditionally viewed by the police as an activity that was sufficiently distinct from general policing to require a separate professional practice. The police role in general was not considered to be complex (Dale 1994: 211). It was thought to require the application of a commonsense approach to the wide range of situations that the police were faced with, but little specialist ability. The model was that of the 'omni-competent' constable who was able to deal with all policing problems equally well and criminal investigation had no special status within this range of problems.

The model of the omni-competent constable was supported by the fact that, until relatively recently, the process of criminal investigation was not subject to specific legislation. The view of the police as 'citizens in uniform' who had few powers above and beyond those available to any member of the community meant that the role of the police in investigating crime was poorly defined by legislation simply because their role in general was not regarded as being legally distinct. The position was summarized in the report of the 1929 Royal Commission on Police Powers: 'The police of this country have never been recognized, either in law or by tradition, as a force distinct from the general body of citizens' (cited in Hitchens 2003: 51). In carrying out a criminal investigation and presenting evidence to courts the police were being paid to do what, in theory at least, anyone could have done and so they required little specialist knowledge to do it. The regulation that did exist, such as the Judges' Rules, was not difficult to understand or apply and the consequences of non-compliance were negligible for the individual.

The view that the investigation of crime required few skills additional to those of policing in general was reinforced by research carried out in the late 1970s and early 1980s. This showed that, as a general rule, crimes are solved because members of the public supply the police with the necessary information during the early stages of the investigation. Where this information is not available, it is unlikely that the crime will be detected by additional police activity (Zander 1979; Steer 1980; Bottomley and Coleman 1981; Banton 1985; Burrows and Tarling 1987; in the UK; Greenwood *et al.* 1977; Eck 1983 in the US). The implication usually drawn from these studies is that because detections are primarily determined by the willingness of the public to pass information to the police, changes in police activity or an increase in resources make little difference (Burrows and Tarling 1982: 14).

As a consequence of the above, the police service did not develop a professional practice of criminal investigation which could be taught to officers. Some work was done by individuals, usually located in force training schools, but this was uncoordinated and was not subject to any formal evaluation to ensure its quality. Even where training was provided, it did not lead to any specific qualification by which individuals could demonstrate competence.

The drivers for change

There appear to be three main reasons why criminal investigation has now come to be seen by the police service as an activity that requires its own professional practice:

1 Changes to the legal framework of criminal investigation.
2 Technological and procedural changes to the investigation process.
3 Concerns over police effectiveness and conduct in criminal investigation.

None of these factors has occurred in isolation and they sit in a complex relationship to one another. For example, changes to the legal framework were largely influenced by concerns over police effectiveness in investigating major crime which arose from a series of miscarriages of justice and many technological and procedural changes were driven by a desire to improve effectiveness. However, these three headings provide a convenient way to discuss the range of factors involved.

Changes to the legal framework of criminal investigation

The series of miscarriages of justice which were uncovered during the 1970s and 1980s, and the two subsequent Royal Commissions which they gave rise to, triggered a series of legislative changes to the process of criminal investigation. These were aimed at defining the rights of suspects and others, delimiting the powers of the police and assuring the quality of evidence through procedural compliance. A consequence of these developments was to introduce a specialist body of law which has to be mastered before criminal investigations can be conducted with any competence.

The main legislative changes and the effect they have on the criminal investigation process are shown in Table 26.1. Taken together these developments clearly envisage the role of criminal investigation as one of gathering material about the crime in a non-partisan, inquisitorial way and

Table 26.1 Legislative changes to criminal investigation

Date	Legislation	Change to the investigation process
1984	Police and Criminal Evidence Act (PACE)	Defined police powers, laid down investigative procedures and defined suspects' and others' rights.
1985	Prosecution of Offences Act	Established the Crown Prosecution Service to take over responsibility for prosecution from the police.
1996	Criminal Procedure and Investigations Act (CPIA)	Provided a legal definition of criminal investigation and the role of investigator. Placed a duty on investigators to investigate impartially. Provided statutory disclosure process.
2000	Regulation of Investigatory Powers Act (RIPA)	Defined processes of investigation and placed them within a regulatory regime.
2003	Criminal Justice Act	Gave the Crown Prosecution Service responsibility for selecting charges (they previously reviewed police charges).

making it available to both the prosecution and the defence who argue the case according to the adversarial procedures of a criminal trial. The overall effect has been to create a complex legal framework within which investigations are carried out. As a result, when the police are investigating crime they no longer have the role of 'citizens in uniform', exercising a general set of duties and responsibilities that apply to all members of society. They are now implementing an investigative process which has been designed specifically with them in mind.

Technical and procedural changes

Developments in DNA and other forensic evidence, the availability of material from CCTV cameras, telephone data, automatic number plate recognition, Internet traffic, improved intelligence analysis and more provide investigators with sources of material that their predecessors could only dream of. Furthermore, developments in legislation such as those covering the right to silence contained in the Criminal Justice and Public Order Act 1994 also mean that older techniques, such as interviewing suspects, are now a richer source of material. These developments require investigators to expand the range of investigative techniques they are able to use in order fully to exploit the possibilities that are open to them.

There has also been a growth in the number of specialists involved in criminal investigation and it is now likely that even in the most straightforward of cases, investigators will have to co-ordinate the work of a range of specialists such as crime scene examiners, forensic scientists and intelligence analysts. In more complex cases, the list of specialists and experts may be considerable. Investigators must know what specialists are available to them, how they can contribute to the investigation, what information is required to deploy them and how to use the material they provide. They must also have the management skills necessary to co-ordinate the work of all the specialists used in the investigation.

One of the ironies of the professionalization process is that while the police service has not viewed investigation by police officers as requiring a separate professional practice, it has embraced the professionalization of many of the subprocesses of investigation. Thus, for example, crime scene examination, behavioural sciences, forensic sciences, media management and intelligence analysis are now commonly accepted as encompassing a distinct professional practice in which people must be trained and accredited. In addition, some hitherto general investigation techniques, such as interviewing or conducting searches, are becoming increasingly specialist. This increase in the professionalization of the subprocesses of criminal investigation has not been accompanied by any parallel professionalization of investigators themselves. This situation is to be found in most countries and is increasingly becoming untenable.

Concerns over police effectiveness in investigation

The third factor that has helped to define the need for a professional practice of criminal investigation is concern over police effectiveness in the investigation of both major crime and volume crime. The investigation of major crimes, such as murder, is seen by the public as an index of police competence overall (Innes 2003: 276). It is also seen within the police service as a model for the way in which other investigations should be conducted. Her Majesty's Inspector of Constabulary (HMIC 2000: 115) has stated that 'the investigation of murder should set clear standards of excellence that all other criminal investigation can follow'. But the police have not always succeeded in living up to public expectations or their own aspirations in this area. Corruption scandals, miscarriages of justice and organizational and individual blunders have occurred in major crime investigations throughout the history of the police service (Maguire 2003: 375). These failures are generally followed by the introduction of new procedures aimed at ensuring that they do not reoccur. Recent research suggests that, for homicide at least, the service's best defence against failure in investigation is not the introduction of such procedural measures but rather improving the skills of investigators. This is because the high level of variation in the way in which individual homicides are committed makes it difficult for the police organization to lay down hard-and-fast rules about the type of activity that may be effective in any given case. Investigators must adapt to the unique circumstances that each case presents them with. This means that their competence in the techniques of homicide investigation, their experience of applying these techniques to a wide range of cases and their ability to process information and make relevant decisions are the key components of investigations, more so even than the organizational structures or procedures that facilitate them (Stelfox 2005: 308). Management structures and procedures do of course need to be adequate, and Bowling and Phillips (2002: 155) make the valuable point that often too little attention is paid to them when seeking to understand the outcomes of police work, particularly adverse outcomes such as racism. However, the evidence points to the competence of investigators as being the key determinant in the success of homicide investigation. The police service has already identified that there is a lack of senior detectives with the necessary skills to carry out the role of senior investigating officer (SIO) in more serious crimes (Flannery 2004: 26) and making improvements in this area was one of the original drivers behind PIP.

In addition to its role in relation to major crime, criminal investigation is also viewed as an important element in the drive to reduce crime in general: 'Detecting, convicting and punishing criminals appropriately are at the heart of long-term crime reduction' (Home Office 2001: 17). In pursuing this policy the government set a target of 1.2 million 'offences brought to justice' by the year 2005–6. Detections were the key police input to these targets but it was estimated that some forces needed to improve detections by an average of almost 13 per cent and, in some cases, by 28 per cent if they were to be met (Flannery 2004: 25). In responding to government targets, forces introduced performance regimes which provided evidence that in some areas there was a lack of adequate investigative skills among patrol officers (Flannery 2004: 26). This was graphically illustrated by Chief Constable Michael Todd of the Greater Manchester Police who, after reviewing the quality of interviews of suspected burglars conducted by his officers, concluded that 'Some of them would have been better off being interviewed by someone who has watched *The Bill* or *Inspector Morse*' (*Independent* 13 August 2003). This lack of basic skills was not confined to patrol officers. Her Majesty's Inspector of Constabulary (HMIC) found that their managers did not understand the processes of investigation and did not check that the routine procedures of investigation were carried out adequately (Flannery 2004: 26).

Changes to the legislative framework of criminal investigation, developments in the techniques and procedures used to carry them out and concerns over the effectiveness of criminal investigation have, between them, served to identify criminal investigation as an area of policing that requires the development of a professional practice which can be taught to investigators and against which they can be tested. As HMIC (2004: 173) has noted:

Policing is now highly complex and spans a massive spectrum of activities requiring a similarly extensive range of skills and competences in those taking up the challenge. The omni-competent officer has been a traditional icon and supposed mainstay of the service. It is debatable whether effective omni-competence has ever actually been achieved but it is now abundantly clear that such an aim is no longer viable, or indeed appropriate, for 21st century policing needs.

Other occupational groups which have traditionally been seen as having a broad and ill-defined public service remit have developed such a professional practice, for example nursing (Bernhard and Walsh 1995; Benner 1984; Laurenson 1995) and social work (Davies 1994; Malin 2000). Now that the police service has recognized the need to professionalize the process of investigation, there is no reason why it cannot do the same.

Developing the professional practice of criminal investigation

Professional practice is usually developed and regulated by bodies which are independent of those who employ individual practitioners. The result of this arrangement is that practices can be developed that are in the best interests of clients and the public good rather than in the best interests of the employers, who may be more interested in issues of profitability, productivity or minimizing expenditure in training rather than the maintenance of professional standards.

Table 26.2 lists some of these professions and their respective professional bodies that develop their professional practice. This division between the bodies that develop professional practice and employers has not always been seen in a positive light. The claim of professionals to know what is right for customers has been increasingly questioned (Exworthy and Halford 1999: 5) and professional bodies have sometimes been seen to be more concerned with protecting their professional position than serving the public good (Flynn 1999: 19).

The police service has no single body which defines professional practice independently of chief constables or the Home Office. The most common way in which practice has been developed for the service is through working groups of ACPO, through research commissioned by the Home Office or through the efforts of individual forces. In addition, a range of bodies including HMIC, the Policing Standards Unit (PSU), the National Centre for Policing Excellence (NCPE) and the Police Information Technology Organisation (PITO), among others, develop professional practice for areas of policing within their remit. In many cases these organizations have no full-time staff dedicated to the role and so it is done by working groups of individuals in addition to their other duties. Despite the difficulties, a great

Table 26.2 Professions and professional bodies

Profession	Professional body
Medical doctors	General Medical Council
Chartered accountants	Association of Chartered Certified Accountants
Nurses	Nursing and Midwifery Council
Social workers	General Social Care Council
Solicitors	Law Society
Barristers	General Council for the Bar
Psychologists	British Psychological Society

deal of policy, guidance and advice for practitioners has been produced. Examples include the *Murder Investigation Manual* first published by the ACPO Homicide Working Group in 1998, *Vulnerable Witnesses: A Police Service Guide* produced by the Home Office in 2001 and *Domestic Burglary: National Good Practice and Tactical Options Guide*, published by the Policing Standards Unit in 2003. Many more examples could be given. Even so, this body of work does not amount to a comprehensive professional practice of the sort that would be recognized by other occupational groups. This is because there is no central method of validating it and no systematic method of updating it in light of changes to legislation or developments in technology or practice. In addition, it is not co-ordinated and so there are some gaps in the guidance available to practitioners.

The range of agencies producing guidance has been described by the Home Secretary as a 'vast alphabet soup' (Home Secretary's speech to the ACPO Annual Conference 2005). He has put forward proposals to establish a National Police Improvement Agency (NPIA) with a view to reducing the number involved. The NPIA will become operational in 2007. At the time of writing it has not been decided which elements of the 'alphabet soup' will become part of the NPIA, but it is clearly envisaged that the new agency will take a lead in the development of professional practice through 'good practice development – refinement and codification of core policing processes and competencies' (Home Office 2004a: 112).

At present, the professional practice most closely associated with PIP is the Core Investigative Doctrine developed by the NCPE. The NCPE was established in 2003 with a remit to provide operational support in serious crime inquiries, specialist training and policing doctrine. The term doctrine has not met with universal approval. Some believe that its militaristic overtones are inconsistent with the civilian ethos of the police service and there are those who think that it may lead to the development of a 'simplistic view that there is one single right answer to solving policing problems' (Jones 2004: 191). However, in this context doctrine is synonymous with professional practice in that it encapsulates the collective knowledge of the service into a coherent set of guidance. This is published in the form of a manual written specifically for practitioners and is often also accompanied by a training programme. The Core Investigative Doctrine was produced to support PIP by providing national guidance on the key principles of criminal investigation. It draws on the experience of practitioners and academics, the literature and existing guidance. It also refers investigators to sources of further information on investigating particular types of crime or the use of specialist techniques.

The Core Investigative Doctrine focuses on the knowledge, skills and understanding that investigators need to be operationally competent.

Knowledge

The knowledge required for professional practice is generally produced by an academic community with strong links to practitioners and is contained in a professional literature. In comparison with other occupational groups, investigators have a relatively modest professional literature and there is a pressing need to develop this further. It should contain all of the knowledge investigators need to make sense of the wide variety of situations they are presented with (Ormerod *et al.* 2005: 1). It is likely to draw on a diverse academic literature. In describing what she calls 'crime science', Laycock (2005: 6) draws an analogy with the medical profession, which uses the disciplines of chemistry, biology, physics, epidemiology, biochemistry, etc., to provide a body of knowledge which is described as 'medical science'. A literature for investigators is likely to be multi-disciplinary and will include the criminal law, psychology, the forensic sciences, sociology, criminology, operations management and the media, among others. The NCPE Core Investigative Doctrine divides the knowledge required by investigators into three basic areas, each of which has leanings towards different academic disciplines.

Legal knowledge

Investigators are expected to take action to secure relevant material in operational situations when 'they must depend on instinct, habit, or memory, rather than library research' (Davis 2002: 187). In order to do this they need a working knowledge of the legislation that governs the conduct of investigations, together with the main types of offences they are likely to have to investigate. Lack of this knowledge could lead them to take action that is unlawful or to gather material in ways that make it unlikely that it will be accepted as evidence. Of all the areas of knowledge required by investigators, the literature on criminal law is perhaps the most developed and readily accessible. Online access to the Police National Legal Database is available to all officers and there are a number of publications written specifically for them (Wilson 2004; English and Card 2005; Johnston and Hutton 2005). NCPE have also produced guides to specific areas which are judged to be problematic, for example *The Use of Immigration Powers* (2005c), *Part 4 of the Anti-social Behaviour Act 2003* (2005d) and *Evidence of Bad Character* (2005e).

National and local policies

The local structure of policing and the complexity of its strategic remit leads to the development of a great deal of national and local policy. The reasons for producing policy include:

- ensuring compliance with the law;
- procedural good practice;
- improving service delivery;
- resource management;
- managing interagency co-operation.

Many of these policies impact on criminal investigation and so investigators need to know those that are relevant to the type of investigations they are involved in. This enables them to comply with legislation, follow procedure and gain access to the most appropriate resources or level of interagency cooperation required to carry out an investigation.

Investigative principles

There is no tradition in the police service of recording the experience of investigators or of analysing the reasons for success or failure (West 2001: 13). As a consequence, no overarching principles of criminal investigation have developed which would serve to guide practitioners and empirical research has not focused on comparing and evaluating criminal investigation techniques. For example, it would be difficult to determine from the literature what the conditions are under which house-to-house inquiries will be most effective or the measures that can be taken to improve the chances of success if the technique appears not to be working. The range of practice involved in searching people, vehicles, premises and open spaces and the relative success rates achieved by each would be similarly difficult to establish. Individual investigators will of course have a view on each of these points based on their own experience, although whether they are right or not cannot be tested. That this situation exists in such fundamental areas as locating witnesses and searching is indicative of the scale of the problem and is typical of most investigative activities.

There is one exception to this general rule, which shows what can be achieved. In the area of investigative interviewing there is an active group of practitioners and academics which promotes research and develops practice. Research, such as that by Milne and Bull (1999) and Bull and Milne (2004), has been developed into practice in the *ACPO Investigative Interview Strategy* (2001) and guidance for practitioners in the *Practical Guide to Investigative Interviewing* (2003). There are now national training courses in investigative interviewing and an ongoing programme of evaluation of the effectiveness of the technique. Those involved in these developments believe that the key to success has been the existence of a national infrastructure under the leadership of the ACPO National Investigative Interviewing Strategic Steering Group which is supported by regional coordinators and lead officers within each force.[2] The work done by this group provides a model of what can be achieved in relation to investigative principles.

Skills

In addition to knowledge, investigators also need a range of practical skills in carrying out the techniques of investigation and in investigative decision-making.

The techniques of criminal investigation

The Core Investigative Doctrine has identified that investigators require to be skilled in the following techniques:

- Crime scene management.
- Forensic investigation.
- Searching.
- Victims and witness management (which includes interviewing and care, as well as techniques for locating witnesses and managing them through the criminal justice system).
- Intelligence management.
- Passive data management (that is, data gathered by automated systems such as CCTV, telephone billing systems, Internet providers, financial records, computer audits, etc.).
- Elimination inquiries.
- Communication.
- Covert policing.
- Suspect management.

Each of these areas can be further subdivided into specific techniques and, as investigators progress to more complex investigations, new techniques will be needed. The basics of these practical skills can be taught, but competence in their use can only really be developed by using them in operational settings. As noted above, there is some guidance in some of these areas but it falls short of being a comprehensive professional practice.

Investigative decision-making

Criminal investigation is a knowledge-based, information-processing activity which relies heavily on the decision-making abilities of investigators. Where investigations remain undetected or miscarriages of justice occur, it is often through flawed decision-making (see, for example, the Byford Report 1982; the Macpherson Report 1999; the Shipman Inquiry Third Report (Smith 2003); Nicol et al. 2004). Such failures of decision-making are not confined to major investigations or difficult cases. A study carried out in 1992 for the Royal Commission on Criminal Justice found that the most common type of error in crime investigation in general was that of decision-making (Irvine and Dunningham 1993: 37).

Investigators are increasingly required to document their decision-making, for example in SIO decision logs and on applications to the Surveillance Commissioners under the Regulation of Investigatory Procedures Act 2000. While this makes it easier to hold investigators to account for their decision-making there has been little research aimed at helping them to do it better. What there is suggests that they rely on a set of rules which they develop from their own experiences of conducting investigations or which they learn from colleagues (Adhami and Browne 1996; Smith and Flannigan 2000; Saunders 2001). These heuristics enable investigators to make sense of the situations they are faced with and provide a framework which helps them to understand the material they gather. They are an efficient means of decision-making and are common to many occupational groups. But the strong tradition in the police service of 'learning on the job' means that the repertoire of working rules that investigators have access to is highly dependent on their personal experience. As a consequence, even apparently experienced investigators may have gaps in their repertoire when they are faced with situations they have not encountered before. An investigator's ability to make decisions may therefore be limited by the extent of their past experience and the degree to which they are able to adapt it to any given situation. To the limitations of investigators' heuristics can be added the common, and well documented, problems of human cognition which are as likely to affect investigators as everyone else (Stelfox and Pease 2005: 192). The Core Investigative Doctrine provides guidance to investigators in avoiding these common problems and a decision-making model aimed at enabling them to better evaluate the material gathered during an investigation.

Decision-making is not simply a question of processing information and making choices about the course of action that is most likely to be effective in getting the job done. How those choices are made and the types of outcomes they may lead to for individuals, communities and society as a whole are held by most occupational groups to be of some importance. As a result, most professional practice includes a code of ethics which seeks to guide the decision-making of practitioners.

The police are often required to take action on limited, incomplete or contested information where the outcomes can have significant implications for the liberty and well-being of individuals and the wider social good. In the UK, the importance of ethics to guide the choices that the police make has been the subject of some interest (Neyroud and Beckley 2001) and in the *Police Service Statement of Common Purpose*, ACPO provides a number of principles which seek to set a broad ethical framework for policing. In addition, some police forces, such as the Police Service of Northern Ireland (PSNI), have developed a Code of Ethics which lays down the standards of behaviour expected of officers and provides an ethical framework within which decisions and actions should be taken. The Core Investigative Doctrine seeks to contribute to the ethical framework of criminal investigation by proposing a number of principles which are 'designed to ensure that investigations are conducted in ways which are ethical and encourage community support'. They are as follows:

- When a crime is reported, or it is suspected that one may have been committed, investigators should conduct an effective investigation.

- The exercise of legal powers should not be oppressive and should be proportionate to the crime under investigation.

- As far as operationally practical and having due regard to an individual's right to confidentiality, investigations should be carried out as transparently as possible; in particular, victims, witnesses and suspects should be kept updated with developments in the case.

- Investigators should take all reasonable steps to understand the particular needs of individuals including their culture, religious beliefs, ethnic origin, sexuality, disability or lifestyle.

- Investigators should have particular regard for vulnerable adults and children.

- Investigators should respect the professional ethics of others. This is particularly important when working with those whose role it is to support suspects (NCPE 2005: 20).

Developing effective and ethical decision-making practice for investigators is far from complete but, as with the knowledge and techniques needed by investigators, the Core Investigative Doctrine has at least put the issue on the agenda so that further work can be done.

Understanding

Knowledge and skills alone are an insufficient basis for professional practice. Investigators need to understand how best to apply their knowledge and skills in operational situations. A wide variety of behaviour is deemed to be criminal and it can occur in a range of circumstances. The way in which victims, witnesses and offenders respond to crimes and the way they interact with the police are influenced by a multitude of factors. Different communities will view crime and the police response to it in different ways. An understanding of these factors and the complex relationship between them is essential if investigators are to make sense of the situations they are faced with (Alison and Barrett 2004: 68) and if they are to take effective action which has the support of the public. While there is a criminological and sociological literature that is relevant in this area, it is rarely written for or accessed by practitioners and ways need to be found of making it more accessible to them.

Some progress has been made in this area, mainly through diversity training. In addition, the Home Office Research Development and Statistics Directorate (RDS) publishes papers that are relevant to practitioners and publications such as those produced by NCPE in relation to domestic violence (2004) and child abuse (2005) make use of the literature to give investigators a better understanding of the phenomenon they are investigating, but more needs to be done.

The Professionalizing Investigation Programme (PIP)

The Core Investigative Doctrine and procedural manuals such as the ACPO *Murder Investigation Manual* and the ACPO *Investigative Interview Strategy* form the basis of the professional practice underpinning PIP. The term 'professionalizing' appears to have been deliberately chosen by those designing PIP to signal that it will bring about improvements in criminal investigation through training and development rather than through alternative strategies, such as re-engineering business processes or improving management systems. While there is little agreement in the general literature on the meaning of terms such as professional or the attributes that define a particular occupational group as a profession (Beckley 2004: 92), the term professionalization is widely used within the police service as shorthand for improved training and development (Perrier 1978: 212; Allgood 1984: 676; Small 1991: 315; Phillips 2003: 5) and it is in this sense that it is used by those designing PIP.

The training of investigators, like most police training, has been based on a craft model where officers receive some basic formal training but learn the majority of what they know 'on the job'. In addition, and possibly because of the above, the police service has never formally examined the competence of investigators against an objective standard. Judgements about competence have generally been made by line supervisors based on their experience of working with the individual, usually once a year during formal performance appraisal. This system is heavily reliant on the experience of the individual supervisor who may have difficulty in explaining the standards used.

PIP seeks to address these shortcomings by providing a cradle-to-grave training curriculum for investigators that takes them from the basic levels of investigation through to the most complex. PIP originated in the South Wales Police which introduced a system of training and accreditation in investigation for all officers in 2002 (Griffiths 2003: 23). This followed recognition that the quality of some investigations was poor and that it 'needs to be professionalised' (Evans 2002: 18). PIP was subsequently adopted by ACPO as a national model for improving standards in criminal investigation. The PIP programme focuses on the qualities of investigators at four levels, shown in Table 26.3. Following training, investigators will have a period of workplace development intended to provide them with the experience

Table 26.3 PIP investigative levels

Investigative level	Example role	Description of typical investigative activity
Level 1	Patrol constable/ police staff/ supervisors	Investigation of anti-social behaviour and volume crime
Level 2	Dedicated investigators (e.g. CID officer)	Investigation into more serious and problem offences, including road traffic deaths
Specialist investigative roles	Child abuse investigation, Special Branch, Family Liaison, major crime	Child abuse investigations, Special Branch, Family Liaison, Force Intelligence Bureau
Level 3	Senior investigating officer	Lead investigator in cases of murder, stranger rape, kidnap or complex crimes

Source: NCPE (2005b:1).

necessary to apply their knowledge and skills in operational settings. They will then be subject to independent assessment against the National Occupational Standards (NOS). NOS have been developed by Skills for Justice, which is an organization funded by the government to identify learning needs in criminal justice organizations and to link these to qualifications. The NOS describe competent performance in relation to the outcomes of investigations and the knowledge, skills and understanding investigators need to perform effectively. They, therefore, provide a benchmark against which an individual investigator's competence to practise can be tested. Assessment will have three elements: competent performance of investigations against the NOS; proving the required level of understanding of the specialist knowledge of criminal investigation; and demonstrating appropriate core behaviours, including community relationships and diversity (NCPE 2005b: 10). Individual forces will nominate their own assessors who will be subject to national training and quality control. The assessment of level 1, 2 and specialist investigators will be verified at force level but verifying the assessment of level 3 investigators will be done nationally. Those who fail to achieve the required standard will be subject to their force's normal personal development review system which will enable them to receive the support required to gain registration. It is anticipated that continued failure to achieve registration will be dealt with under existing competence procedures. Investigators will undergo periodic reassessment and mechanisms will exist to suspend the registration of those who are found not to be competent.

PIP is aimed at ensuring that the professional practice of criminal investigation being developed by the service is backed up by a training and development programme and, perhaps most importantly, by a means of assessing the competence of investigators. The programme is only just being rolled out and so there is as yet no data on how this is feeding through to improvements in performance, although a formal evaluation is planned. Whether PIP does deliver the intended benefits will depend to a large extent on the rigour with which the assessment process is applied. If applied with rigour, it is highly likely that raised standards of investigation will be reflected in improved outcomes. If, on the other hand, assessment becomes another box to tick in the HR paper chain, then PIP is unlikely to deliver the outcomes that the service is looking for.

Shortcomings in the professionalization model: the research gap

The model of professionalization which is emerging in relation to criminal investigation already has some strong elements. The service has a capacity to develop professional practice, albeit one that is spread throughout a variety of agencies with little co-ordination between them. The proposed NPIA seems likely to bring about improvements in this area by reducing the number of agencies involved and by providing leadership in the development of professionalization. The NOS produced by Skills for Justice are an established means of setting a performance benchmark for investigators and have been incorporated into PIP. PIP itself provides a comprehensive means by which investigators can be trained and can develop their investigative techniques in operational settings. It also enables them to be tested against the NOS.

There are some elements of the professionalization process that are not so well developed. A comprehensive body of professional practice should be supported by a strong evidence base, continual evaluation of existing practice and ongoing review of the knowledge, skills and understanding needed by practitioners. What is required is the capacity to carry out research and development which will produce a specialist literature upon which evidence-based practice and policy can be developed. These elements should combine with those already discussed to provide a cycle of continually improving professional practice within the service, as shown in Figure 26.1.

The two final elements of this cycle, ongoing evaluation and the capacity to produce a research literature, are not well developed in relation to criminal investigation. If the benefits of professionalization are to be fully realized, capacity will need to be developed in these two areas. The police service is not alone in this: 'Whichever part of the public sector one is concerned with, one observation is clear: the current state of research based knowledge is insufficient to inform many areas of policy and practice' (Nutley *et al.* 2002: 4). Some of this capacity does exist. For example, the Home Office and ACPO both commission research into various areas of policing but the co-ordination required for the creation of an evidence base to inform policy and development of best practice is missing from the equation.

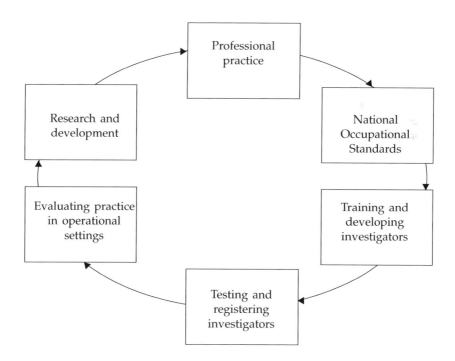

Figure 26.1 A cycle of continuously improving professional practice

How this gap in the cycle of professional practice might be filled is beyond the scope of this chapter, but it seems likely that it must involve forging stronger links between the service and those universities which have developed expertise in the study of policing. These universities are already involved in the kind of evaluation, research and development which is required and are experienced at working closely with the police service. But there is often a gap between what is of interest to researchers and what the police service needs, or thinks it needs (Laycock 2001: 2). Bringing the interests of these two groups into closer alignment would go a long way towards filling the gap in the professional practice cycle. But university research does not come cheap and one of the major challenges of professionalization may be finding ways of funding the level of research required to support it.

The challenges of professionalization

While professionalism clearly has potential benefits for the police service in terms of improving the skills and abilities of investigators, delivering it is likely to present a number of difficulties in such a hierarchical organization. In the USA, four areas have been identified by police leaders as the risks arising from professionalization:

1) It leads to greater functional autonomy.
2) It is associated with individuals formulating their own role definitions.
3) It can be associated with loyalty to one's career rather than loyalty to the organization.
4) It poses a threat to the tradition of secrecy in the police service (Price 1977, cited in Steinman and Eskridge 1985: 27).

The potential for these to arise in the UK is reviewed below.

The functional autonomy of investigators

The structure of the police service is highly bureaucratic and assumes that those of higher rank are in a better position to determine the correct course of action in any given instance. But investing the professional practice of investigation in the individual implies a high level of practitioner autonomy at the point of service delivery (Price 1979: 96). In general, these high levels of practitioner autonomy can prove to be incompatible with modern performance culture, where managers are more concerned with achieving organizational outcomes than promoting professional practice (Flynn 1999: 30). There are a number of very good reasons why chief officers may wish to delimit the discretion of their investigators in order to achieving a particular organizational goal. For example, the investigation of murder may require individuals to subjugate their judgements to those of managers who are co-ordinating the collective effort. In future, situations such as this may lead to tensions between those claiming greater professional autonomy and those managing them. After all, as Dale (2002: 187) points out, 'You cannot have both the advantages of someone's judgement and completely control what they decide.' What may turn out to be a significant factor in negotiating these tensions is the professional status of managers. In other occupational groups this has often been found to be crucial to their credibility with those they are seeking to manage (Causer and Exworthy 1999: 89). This may not present too much difficulty in the case of PIP level 1, where by definition all supervisors and managers will be able to lay claim to the same professional status as those they are managing. Above this level, as the training of investigators becomes more specialized and accreditation becomes more difficult to achieve and maintain, things may not be so easy. At present the police service tends towards the view that competency in management is transferable throughout the organization. This is consistent with the public sector as a whole, where management practices imported from the private sector tend to value personal qualities and generic management competencies above the knowledge of specific professional rules or procedures (Exworthy and Halford 1999: 7). In the police service, this may mean that as practitioners become more professionally qualified, managers will have to 'move away from the military style, command and control hierarchy of today's police organisation. We must leave police room for (something like) professional judgement' (Dale 2002: 187).

Formulation of role definitions

As investigators invest more in the development of their professional competence, they may also take a greater interest in how their roles are defined within the organization. This may be particularly so at the higher PIP levels where achieving registration is likely to require a considerable commitment from the individual. Registered SIOs may not feel that their role should involve non-investigative functions such as organizational management. This is in direct contrast to the present situation where it is common for senior detectives to have management responsibility for business units in addition to their role as investigators. This is not as common in other professional groups. Nurses and doctors do not generally manage hospitals, pilots don't as a rule manage airlines and barristers don't manage chambers. This is because their role definition is focused on the delivery of the professional service rather than the management of the organization that exists to support them in doing that.

If this model develops within the police service, it may be that ways will have to be found to enable professional investigators to be rewarded in ways other than through the present rank structure which is focused on matching ranks to levels of organizational management responsibility. Other professional groups have achieved this. For example, nurse practitioners are paid enhanced salaries based on their professional competence rather than the span of management responsibility they hold within the organization.

There may also be implications for police staff associations arising out of professionalization. At the moment police staff associations are rank based but this may come to be seen as anachronistic by those who identify their interests in terms of their professional qualification rather than their rank. They may come to view functional staff associations as a preferable alternative.

Career loyalty over organization loyalty

Investigators seeking promotion are currently dependent on being successful under the systems in use in their force. As there is no national system, these vary. PIP may mean that investigators become less dependent on their own police forces for career advancement because they will be able to market their professional skills to a range of employers against objective national criteria. The shortage of experienced senior investigators that has already been noted by HMIC (Flannery 2004: 26) has led to increased competition for them among police forces. In addition, there has also been an increase in the number of private companies offering investigative services such as surveillance, major incident management, review services and investigator training. This may lead to a blurring of the boundaries between public service investigators and those provided by private companies. If this does occur, the police service may find itself competing for the services of registered investigators with private providers who are able to offer greater rewards and status. This has occurred in the NHS, where a shortage of qualified nurses wishing to be employed directly by the NHS has made it heavily reliant on obtaining them from private agencies. This has had a huge financial impact. In England and Wales, NHS expenditure on agency nurses almost tripled from £216 million in 1997/1998 to £628 million in 2002/2003 (Royal College of Nursing 2003: 12). Even if the service can avoid this type of situation, it seems highly likely that the competition between forces for investigators that has already started will increase and will provide investigators with opportunities for professional advancement and development which is independent of any particular police agency.

Secrecy in police service

It seems highly likely that if the first three of Steinman and Eskridge's outcomes do occur, then the fourth, reduced secrecy within the police service, is almost certain. That is because the increased functional autonomy of investigators, the independence of their role definition and their loyalty to career rather than the police organization mean that traditional constraints on the disclosure of internal (but non-confidential) information that are imposed by police culture are hardly likely to survive. That would be no bad thing and may even be occurring anyway as a consequence of a more open police culture which has developed in recent years. But are chief constables likely to tolerate a situation such as exists in the NHS where doctors have the right to make comment on and to criticize the organizations that employ them because this is seen as a guarantee of their professional independence (Harrison 1999: 51)? It seems unlikely at present. But in the 2005 Dimbleby Lecture, Metropolitan Police Commissioner Sir Ian Blair called for a greater public debate about the future of policing and it seems highly likely that professionally qualified investigators will want to contribute to that debate, even if it is critical of present management systems and processes.

Conclusion

The professionalization of criminal investigation presents the police service with opportunities and challenges in equal measure. On the one hand, a well trained and motivated workforce, guided by a coherent professional practice, presents the service with the opportunity of delivering a better quality of service to individuals while reducing crime overall. But this opportunity can only be realized if the challenges of professionalism are met. The first challenge is to apply PIP with sufficient rigour to ensure that those who are not able to carry out criminal investigations to the highest standard are not allowed to practise. In reality this may mean dismissing them from the service, or at least not admitting them in the first place. The second challenge is to find the will and the resources to improve the evaluation and research capacity of the service. Only if this is done can the cycle of continuously improving professional practice be achieved. Without this it seems highly likely that the momentum of the professionalizing process will stall at some point because it will not be developing to meet new challenges, changes in legislation or developments in technology. The third, and perhaps the greatest, challenge will be the view that police leaders take of the risks of professionalization. If, as occurred in the USA, they come to view professionalization as a threat to their status, they are hardly likely to make the necessary effort to rise to the first two challenges. In this case, the professionalization of criminal investigation is likely to emerge as little more than a rhetorical device. It may be useful for persuading government and the public that radical change is being made by the service, but in reality it will fail to deliver the scale of change required to make significant performance improvements in criminal investigation.

Selected further reading

The professionalization of criminal investigation is a relatively new phenomenon and so a specific literature has not yet developed in this area. As mentioned in the text, investigative interviewing is an exception to this general pattern and Williamson's *Investigative Interviewing: Rights, Research and Regulation* (2006) together with Milne and Bull's *Investigative Interviewing: Psychology and Practice* (1999) provide authoritative information for practitioners. Reiner's *The Politics of the Police* (2000) provides a sociological analysis of the development of policing generally while Emsley's *The English Police: A Political and Social History* (2nd edn) (1996) provides a historian's perspective on the same developments. Although a great deal of the professional practice written for investigators is not available outside of the police service, the Home Office Research Development and Statistics Directorate and the National Centre for Policing Excellence both have websites that contain useful material that is relevant to this area (*http://www. homeoffice.gov.uk/police/* and *http://www.centrex.police.uk*).

Notes

1 Within the United Kingdom, Scotland is a separate jurisdiction and has its own policing arrangements under the leadership of the Association of Chief Police Officers of Scotland (ACPOS).
2 Personal communication from Gary Shaw and Danny McGrory, members of the ACPO National Investigative Interviewing Strategic Steering Group.

References

Adhami, E. and Browne, D.P. (1996) *Major Crime Enquiries: Improving Expert Support for Detectives*, Home Office Police Research Group Special Interest Series Paper 9. London: Home Office.

Alison, L.J. and Barrett, E.C. (2004) 'The interpretation and utilization of offender profiles', in J.R. Adler (ed.) *Forensic Psychology: Concepts, Debates and Practice*. Cullompton: Willan Publishing.

Allgood, J. (1984) 'A degree of professionalism', *Police Review*, 6 April: 676–7.

Association of Chief Police Officers (1998) *The Murder Investigation Manual* (unpublished outside the police service).

Association of Chief Police Officers (2000) *ACPO Investigative Interview Strategy* (unpublished outside the police service).

Association of Chief Police Officers (2003) *Practical Guide to Investigative Interviewing* (unpublished outside the police service).

Banton, M. (1985) *Investigating Robbery*. Aldershot: Gower.

Beckley, A. (2004) 'Professionalisation of the police service', *Police Research and Management*, 6: 89–100.

Benner, P.E. (1984) *From Novice to Expert: Excellence and Power in Clinical Nursing Practice*. London: Addison-Wesley.

Bernhard, L.A. and Walsh, M. (1995) *Leadership: The Key to the Professionalization of Nursing*. St Louis, MO: Mosby.

Bottomley, K. and Coleman, C. (1981) *Understanding Crime Rates*. Farnborough: Gower.

Bowling, B. and Phillips, C. (2002) *Racism, Crime and Justice*. London: Longman.

Bull, R. and Milne, R. (2004) 'Attempts to improve police interviewing of suspects', in G. D. Lassiter (ed.) *Interrogation, Confessions and Entrapment*. New York: Kluwer/Plenum.

Burrows, J. and Tarling, R. (1982) *Clearing up Crime. Home Office Research Study 73*. London: HMSO.

Burrows, J. and Tarling, R. (1987) 'The investigation of crime in England and Wales', *British Journal of Criminology*, 27: 234.

Byford, L. (1981) *The Yorkshire Ripper Case: Review of the Police Investigation of the Case* (unpublished report for Her Majesty's Inspector of Constabulary).

Causer, G. and Exworthy, M. (1999) 'Professionals as managers across the public sector', in M. Exworthy and S. Halford (eds) *Professionals and the New Managerialism in the Public Sector*. Buckingham: Open University Press.

Dale, A. (1994) 'Professionalism and the police', *Police Journal*, 67: 209–18.

Davies, M. (1994) *The Essential Social Worker: An Introduction to Professional Practice in the 1990s*. Aldershot: Arena.

Davis, M. (2002) *Profession, Code and Ethics*. Aldershot: Ashgate.

Dodd, T., Nicholas, S., Povey, D. and Walker, A. (2004) *Crime in England and Wales 2003/2004. Home Office Statistical Bulletin 10/04*. London: Home Office.

Eck, E.J. (1983) *Solving Crimes: The Investigation of Burglary and Robbery*. Washington, DC. Police Executive Research Forum.

English, J. and Card, R. (2005) *Police Law*, 9th edn. Oxford: Blackstone.

Evans, R. (2002) 'Gold standards', *Police Review*, 21 June.

Exworthy, M. and Halford, S. (1999) *Professionals and the New Managerialism in the Public Sector*. Buckingham: Open University Press.

Flannery, K. (2004) 'Watching the detectives', *Police Professional*, July: 25–7.

Flynn, R. (1999) 'Managerialism, professionalism and quasi-markets', in M. Exworthy and S. Halford (ed.) *Professionals and the New Managerialism in the Public Sector*. Buckingham: Open University Press.

Greenwood, P.W., Chaiken, J. and Petersilia, J. (1977) *The Criminal Investigation Process*. Lexington, MA: D.C. Heath.

Griffiths, B. (2003) 'Investing in investigation', *Policing Today*, 9.

Harrison, S. (1999) 'Clinical autonomy and health policy: past and futures', in M. Exworthy and S. Halford (eds) *Professionals and the New Managerialism in the Public Sector*. Open University Press: Buckingham.

Her Majesty's Inspector of Constabulary (HMIC) (2000) *Policing London*. London: HMIC.

Her Majesty's Inspector of Constabulary (HMIC) (2004) *Modernising the Police Service: A Thematic Inspection of Workforce Modernisation – The Role, Management and Deployment of Police Staff in the Police Service of England and Wales*. London: HMIC.

Hitchens, P. (2003) *A Brief History of Crime*. London: Atlantic.

Home Office (2001a) *Policing a New Century: A Blueprint for Reform*. London: Home Office.

Home Office (2001b) *Vulnerable Witnesses: A Police Service Guide*. London: Home Office.

Home Office (2004a) *Building Communities, Beating Crime: A Better Police Service for the 21st Century*. London: Home Office.

Home Office (2004b) *National Policing Plan 2004–2007*. London: Home Office.

Innes, M.R. (2003) *Investigating Murder: Detective Work and the Police Response to Criminal Homicide*. Oxford: Oxford University Press.

Irvine, B. and Dunningham, C. (1993) *Human Factors in the Quality Control of CID Investigations. Royal Commission on Criminal Justice Research Study 21*. London: HMSO.

Johnston, D. and Hutton, G. (2005) *Evidence and Procedure*. Oxford: Blackstone.

Jones, J. (2004) 'Commentary', *Police Journal*, 77.

Laurenson, S. (1995) *Health Service Developments and the Scope of Professional Nursing Practice: A Survey of Developing Clinical Roles within NHS Trusts in Scotland*. Edinburgh: National Nursing, Midwifery and Health Visiting Advisory Committee.

Laycock, G. (2001) 'Research for police, who needs it?', *Issues and Trends*, 211. Canberra: Australian Institute of Criminology.

Laycock, G. (2005) 'Defining crime science', in M.J. Smith and N. Tilley (eds) *Crime Science: New Approaches to Preventing and Detecting Crime*. Cullompton: Willan Publishing.

Macpherson, Sir, W.M. (1999) *The Stephen Lawrence Inquiry: Report of an Inquiry by Sir William Macpherson of Cluny*. London: HMSO.

Maguire, M. (2003) 'Crime investigation and crime control', in T. Newburn (ed.) *Handbook of Policing*. Cullompton: Willan Publishing.

Malin, N. (ed.) (2000) *Professionalism, Boundaries and the Workplace*. London: Routledge.

Milne, R. and Bull, R. (1999) *Investigative Interviewing: Psychology and Practice*. Chichester: Wiley.

National Centre for Policing Excellence (2005a) *Core Investigative Doctrine*. Wyboston: NCPE.

National Centre for Policing Excellence (2005b) *Professionalising Investigation Programme Information Pack*. Wyboston: NCPE.

National Centre for Policing Excellence (2005c) *The Use of Immigration Powers Against Crime*. Wyboston: NCPE.

National Centre for Policing Excellence (2005d) *Part 4 of the Anti-social Behaviour Act 2003*. Wyboston: NCPE.

National Centre for Policing Excellence (2005e) *Evidence of Bad Character*. Wyboston: NCPE.

National Centre for Policing Excellence (2005f) *ACPO Guidance on Investigating Child Abuse and Safeguarding Children*. Wyboston: NCPE.

National Centre for Policing Excellence (2005g) *ACPO Guidance on Investigating Domestic Violence*. Wyboston: NCPE.

Neyroud, P.W. (2003) 'Policing and ethics', in T. Newburn (ed.) *Handbook of Policing*. Cullompton: Willan Publishing.

Neyroud, P.W. and Beckley, A. (2001) *Policing, Ethics and Human Rights*. Cullompton: Willan Publishing.

Nicol, C., Innes, M., Gee, D. and Feist, A. (2004) *Reviewing Murder Investigations: An Analysis of Progress Reviews from Six Police Forces*. London: Home Office.

Nutley, S., Davies, H. and Walter, I. (2002) *Evidence Based Policy and Practice: Cross Sector Lessons from the UK*. London: ESRC.

Ormerod, T.C., Barrett, E.C. and Taylor, P.J. (2005) 'Investigative sense-making in criminal contexts', in J.M.C. Schraagen (ed.) *Proceedings of the Seventh International NDM Conference*. Amsterdam, June.

Perrier, D.C. (1978) 'Police professionalism', *Canadian Police College Journal*, 2: 209–14.

Phillips, Sir David (2002) 'Professionalism and performance', *Policing Today*, 8: 5.

Phillips, Sir David (2003) The route to professionalism', *Policing Today*, 9: 5–6.

Policing Standards Unit (2003) *Domestic Burglary: National Good Practice and Tactical Options Guide* (unpublished outside the police service).

Potter, K. (2004) 'Standing on the shoulders of giants', *Police Professional*, August: 6–9.

Price, B.R. (1977) *Police Professionalism: Rhetoric and Action*. Lexington, MA: Lexington Books.

Price, B.R. (1979) 'Integrated professionalism: a model for controlling police practice', *Journal of Police Science and Administration*, 7: 93–7.

Reiner, R. (2000) *The Politics of the Police*. Oxford: Oxford University Press.

Royal College of Nursing (2003) *Fragile Future: A Review of the UK Nursing Labour Market 2003*. London: Royal College of Nursing.

Saunders, E. (2001) 'The decision-making processes used in operational policing and serious crime investigation'. Unpublished PhD thesis, Warwick University.

Small, M.W. (1991) 'Police professionalism: problems and issues in upgrading an occupation', *Police Journal*, 64: 314–20.

Smith, Dame J. (2003) *The Shipman Inquiry Second Report: The Police Investigation of March 1998*. London: HMSO.

Smith, N. and Flanagan, C. (2000) *The Effective Detective: Identifying the Skills of an Effective SIO. Police Research Series Paper 122*. London: Home Office.

Steer, D. (1980) *Uncovering Crime: The Police Role. Royal Commission on Criminal Procedure Research Study 7*. London: HMSO.

Steinman, M. and Eskridge, C.W. (1985) 'The rhetoric of police professionalism', *Police Chief*, February: 26–9.

Stelfox, P. (2005) 'The factors that determine outcomes in the police investigation of homicide.' Unpublished PhD thesis, Open University.

Stelfox, P. and Pease, K. (2005) 'Cognition and detection: reluctant bedfellows?', in M.J. Smith and N. Tilley (eds) *Crime Science: New Approaches to Preventing and Detecting Crime*. Cullompton: Willan Publishing.

Thomas, N. and Feist, A. (2004) 'Detection of crime', in T. Dodd, S. Nicholas, D. Povey and A. Walker (eds) *Crime in England and Wales 2003/2004*. London: Home Office.

West, A. (2001) 'A proposal for an investigative science course: any takers?', *Police Research and Management*, 5: 13–22.

Wilson, G. (2004) *The Beat Officer's Companion*. Coulsdon: Janes Police Review.

Zander, M. (1979) 'The investigation of crime: a study of cases tried at the Old Bailey', *Criminal Law Review*: 203–19.

Chapter 27

The future of investigation

Tom Williamson, Tim Newburn and Alan Wright

When the New Police were introduced in the early nineteenth century, the political climate at the time favoured a crime prevention model of policing based on patrol. The creation of a criminal investigation capability took another 50 years to emerge, even in embryonic form. It is fair to say that the development of an investigative capability by the police has been under-researched by historians – certainly in comparison with other aspects of policing. What we do know is that, over the next 50 years, there were a number of high-profile cases of corruption and indications that some areas of police investigation might be institutionally corrupt.

In the 1930s a Home Office committee examined the role played by detectives. The committee reported just before the Second World War, though the report was immediately given a very high security classification which has restricted access ever since. Two themes identified by the committee – we believe – still resonate with us today. The first was that the education and training of detectives were seen as wholly inadequate. The second conclusion was that there was vast potential to make better use of forensic science. The theme of education and training for detectives was taken up by the Commission on Criminal Procedure in 1981 and became a central recommendation. Realizing the benefits from forensic science became a government priority at the beginning of the twenty-first century, enabled by a huge investment, especially in DNA analysis. So what was the investigative paradigm that evolved in the period between the late nineteenth and late twentieth centuries, and how does it differ from current philosophy and practice?

The old investigative paradigm placed great emphasis on confession evidence. Indeed, it could be argued that the investigatory culture was over-reliant on such evidence. Interrogations that led to a confession helped achieve the intended outcome of a conviction – courts and juries generally accepting confessions as damning evidence of guilt. There were many problems with this model. It led to what has been called 'tunnel vision' in which detectives and prosecutors become focused on one suspect to the exclusion of all others, closing down opportunities to test alternative hypotheses. The result was that, in many countries around the world, there have been failures of investigation and, worse still, miscarriages of justice. Though reform efforts were initially slow, the investigatory approach that relied on confession evidence is now widely perceived to be a failed paradigm.

A sizeable shift in investigative principles and practice is apparent in the UK, Europe, Australia and parts of North America. This can best be illustrated through developments in three areas discussed at length in this Handbook: intelligence-led policing, investigative interviewing and forensics. Intelligence systems in policing were, until recently, relatively rudimentary, often bureaucratic and swamped by volume, which meant that little actionable intelligence emerged from all this industry. Crime information that was more likely to be actioned could come from informants who were recruited by police officers, and information that was obtained from these sources was seen as being private to the detective. A challenge to this way of thinking came from attempts in the 1980s to reform the intelligence system. Information was deemed to be a corporate resource. Therefore information from an informant was no longer private and should be made available to the organization. Furthermore, the relationship between officer and informant was to be registered, the real identity of the informant being kept in a secure location and a pseudonym allocated instead. During the 1990s forces began to appoint directors of intelligence and, as the philosophy of a proactive intelligence-led policing style developed (see Chapter 8), the process was given added impetus by the Human Rights Act 1998 and the Regulation of Investigatory Powers Act 2000. This put covert investigation on a legal basis. Its Code of Practice, together with the checks and balances required to satisfy the surveillance commissioners, meant it became a driver for greater professionalism in the use of intelligence – a process that enjoys the endorsement of the Association of Chief Police Officers as the National Intelligence Model.

The paradigm shift represented here is from reactive towards proactive intelligence-led investigations. Although police officers are still centrally involved, there are now many non-police actors – from civilian surveillance operatives to highly skilled analysts – without whom the system could not work. As the data from an intelligence-led operation are analysed, this may lead to evidence and to the conviction of the target of the operation but, in this new paradigm, even if it is not possible to convict, the intelligence may show how and where the criminal organization may be disrupted. Therefore another characteristic of the new paradigm is the shift away from a narrow focus on securing convictions to the broader one of managing and controlling an individual or group whose criminal activities represent a continuing threat. Increasingly this is being done by adopting a risk management approach to investigations.

A similar pattern can be seen in relation to investigative interviewing. Whereas the objective of an interrogation under the old paradigm was to obtain a confession from a suspect with a view to securing a conviction, the modern investigative interview has a different set of intended outcomes. It is viewed as being a search for the truth. The manner in which it is conducted should be conducive to the elicitation of accurate and reliable information from victims, witnesses and suspects. Psychological research (see Chapter 19) has demonstrated that the most powerful influence in a suspect's decision-making is his or her perception of the weight of evidence against him or her. Therefore developments in investigative interviewing are forcing a larger paradigm shift in investigation by encouraging investigators to conduct more thorough investigations and to gather evidence prior to questioning suspects. The need to gather more evidence draws attention to the important contributions of covert investigations and of the information obtained from victims, witnesses and even the suspect. This is forcing a reappraisal of the case construction hypothesis which considered that the police were selective in the evidence they collected and in the narrative they developed for the prosecutor and court. The new paradigm is focused on gathering accurate and reliable information and it stops short of achieving a conviction as the outcome. This can relieve officers from the burden of having to achieve a conviction. It is part of the modernizing and professionalizing of investigative competency. It has a stronger ethical foundation.

Something similar can be seen in developments in forensics. Police forces developed an early capability in fingerprints, but it was only in the 1980s that the role of civilian crime scene examiners spread to all forces. The creation of the Forensic Science Service as a 'Next Steps' agency separated laboratories from police forces and opened the door to competition and to the creation of a market for forensic services. This led most forces to appoint at a senior level their own head of forensic services as an intelligent customer to providers of forensic services and to control costs. Heavy government investment in forensic services has provided forces with a source of clearing up crimes, much of which would previously have gone undetected. Nearly all this investigative activity is being conducted by non-police officers.

From these three examples we can see that investigation is fragmenting into a number of discrete subdisciplines, each developing its own unique set of competencies and providers. The output of their activities becomes a flow of information to be assembled by other investigators into actionable intelligence or evidence. Rather like an assembly line for motor vehicles where parts are fitted that have been manufactured elsewhere and delivered just in time to the factory so, too, have modern investigations become a process of managing information (see Chapter 10). From one standpoint, investigators are viewed increasingly as 'knowledge workers'. The information and communications technology that is driving many of the changes associated with late modernity is also providing the new tools to assist investigators to manage data and information and to turn them into intelligence and knowledge (see Chapter 21).

Investigations and the subdisciplines that contribute to them are no longer restricted to 'the police' as traditionally envisaged as agents of the state. Many organizations in the public and private sector have developed sophisticated investigative capabilities (see Chapter 11). Managing the change to the new paradigm did not come easily, and the ground has been bitterly fought over. The publicity attending miscarriages of justice and inept investigations became a driver for change, and research for government inquiries provided an evidence base for new policy initiatives. New laws have provided clear legal powers instead of the murky common law grounds previously used to justify investigative action. New regulatory bodies provide independent oversight into allegations of police corruption or incompetence. Greater professionalism is likely to come from the development of investigative doctrine and from any future attempt to provide a competency-based licence-to-practise for investigators. That said, it is worth reminding ourselves that failures in criminal investigation may be failures in moral conduct and responsibility, as much as failures in technical ability or factual knowledge. Although incompetence may appear on occasions, corruption or malpractice are more devastating and much more likely to affect the integrity of criminal investigation, especially in the longer term.

It would be fair to say that the new investigative paradigm is still a work in progress. The transition from the old to the new paradigm is far from complete. Anyone working with investigators will find abundant evidence that the old practices are very much alive and remain the default paradigm for too many investigators. Though a work in progress, there is evidence of substantial change in the direction of the new investigative practices, as well as indications of the likely future direction of travel. Almost certainly this will be intelligence-led and knowledge-based. Conviction will still be one of the important outcomes, of course, but increasingly investigators will tend to work within a risk management methodology where prosecution is only one of a range of options for managing the risk. Those looking to establish the legitimacy of these risk-based approaches need only refer to the terms of reference for the Serious and Organized Crime Agency in the 2005 Act (see the Introduction) to see that risk management already has a legal basis, at least for that organization.

In the longer term?

Social, economic and political changes associated with late modernity and globalization will undoubtedly play out in the investigatory sphere just as they will in others. This is likely to see a number of related developments, most obviously involving the further spread of global private security providers with sophisticated technical investigative competences that would stand comparison with any investigation conducted by the public sector. Although the marketplace has thus far had a relatively limited impact on criminal investigation in England and Wales, there is no guarantee this will continue. Should a fully fledged market in investigation services emerge, it would require the establishment of some form of regulatory framework. One scenario for the future is that there will emerge a plurality of providers (and 'auspices') of investigative services, and that, over time, the market for these services will come to be dominated by those providers with the most cost-effective business mode. These are likely to be those that have invested most heavily in information and communications technology to enable them to collect, processes and analyse data and information to provide intelligence and knowledge that improve investigative performance. Such a future raises profound challenges for the public police and for their role in criminal investigation.

Glossary

Abductive inference

Abductive inference is the process of reasoning 'to the best explanation'. It is suggested by some commentators as the primary method through which homicide investigators assess the evidence available in their cases. It involves asking, in effect, "…what is the best, most plausible reason, given what is known at the current time, to explain how these circumstances came to be?" (*see also* Deductive inference *and* Inductive inference, *below*).

Active investigation management

Active investigation management requires detailed plans to be set for the conduct of investigations. This is intended to promote the systematic exploration of lines of enquiry and to enable the close supervision of investigator activity.

Association of Chief Police Officers (ACPO)

The association representing all officers of assistant chief constable rank and above and their equivalents in the Metropolitan Police. It is not a staff association (the separately constituted Chief Police Officers' Association fulfils that function). The work of ACPO is on behalf of the police service as a whole, rather than individual members. Every aspect of policing and its management is covered by a number of ACPO 'business areas', which are further subdivided into portfolios. In relation to the crime business-area, portfolios include forensic science, serious and organised crime, intelligence, drugs, firearms, violent crime, property crime, standards, competencies and training, technology and economic crime. A separate business area relates to matters affecting criminal justice, with portfolios covering victims and witnesses, pre-trial issues, disposal of cases, recording and disclosure, legislation and information technology.

Audit Commission

A non-departmental public body established in the 1980s to promote economy, efficiency and effectiveness in the public services. It has become increasingly influential in matters relating to criminal justice and policing. Its 1993 paper *Helping with Enquiries: Tackling Crime Effectively* was influential especially in relation to investigation of high-volume crime (http://www.audit-commission.gov.uk)

657

Behavioural Science Support
Although the term Behavioural Science Unit (BSU) is not in common use in the UK, some police forces employ people with psychological qualifications in a number of support functions. The services of Behavioural Investigative Advisors (BIAs) and a Serious Crime Analysis Section (SCAS) are available nationally through NCPE to provide psychological and other expertise to investigators, especially in cases of serious and/or serial crime. BIAs link the theoretical basis of behavioural science to its application in the investigation of serious crime. Advice available includes crime scene assessment; motivational factors; cold case review; series identification; risk assessment; DNA screening; suspect prioritisation; familial DNA; nominal pool generation; interview strategy; media strategy; offender background characteristics; and investigation strategy. The services of a consultant clinical psychologist are also available. SCAS was established in 1998 to identify the potential emergence of serial killers and serial rapists. Other crime-related services offered to police forces by NCPE Operations Centre include Regional Advisors and Crime Investigation Support Officers; National Search Advisor; National Interview Advisor; National Family Liaison Advisor; geographical profilers; and physical evidence advisors. NCPE also maintains a number of databases, including CATCHEM, which holds every case of child homicide since 1960; and the National Injuries Database (NID). (*See also* Centrex, NCPE *and* NPIA, *below*.)

Bichard Inquiry (Interim Report 2004/Final Report 2005)
The inquiry chaired by Sir Michael Bichard was set up by the Home Secretary following the conviction of Ian Huntley for the murders of Holly Wells and Jessica Chapman in Soham, Cambridgeshire. Huntley was a school caretaker at Soham Village College and had been subject to vetting for the post, including police checks. These revealed no relevant information about him. Huntley had previously lived for some time in Humberside and after the verdict, Humberside Police disclosed that between 1995 and 1999 there had been series of incidents involving allegations of sexual offences committed by Huntley. The Inquiry examined the effectiveness of Humberside and Cambridgeshire police forces' intelligence-based record keeping, vetting practice and information sharing with other agencies. The Bichard Inquiry Report recommended changes to vetting and other procedures to protect children and the vulnerable nationally. It also supported radical changes to police information technology systems to make them effective in handling preventive intelligence and other data on a national basis. It supported the setting up of a national nominal index as a step towards a fully-fledged national system (IMPACT – *see below*).

Case construction
The case construction thesis suggests that as soon as someone is suspected of an offence, the investigation becomes a search for information that will support that suspicion, rather than a continuing search for the truth which is based upon what happened. This has been widely criticised and may lead to miscarriages of justice when premature conclusions are drawn.

Centrex
Centrex is the name of the Central Police Training and Development Authority. Its role is to define, develop and promote excellence in the police service and it does so by providing a National Centre for Police Excellence (NCPE – *see below*) and by creating and implementing the means to develop competence through police careers (http://www.centrex.police.uk). These functions will be incorporated as part of the National Police Improvement Agency (NPIA), which becomes operational in April 2007 (*see also* Competency Framework; National Police Improvement Agency).

CID (officer)

The Criminal Investigation Department (CID) was the successor to the Detective Branch in the Metropolitan Police and has become the normal term for plain-clothes police detectives in the UK. CID is also a mnemonic for Core Investigative Doctrine (*see below*).

Cognitive interview

(*See* Investigative interviewing *below*)

Community Impact Assessment (CIA)

This involves the calibration of the impact that a major crime may be having upon a local community. CIA was an important consideration of the Stephen Lawrence Inquiry (*see below*) and has been incorporated in the methods of critical incident management discussed in this volume (*see* Critical incident management, *below*).

Competency framework

Investigators at each level, from patrol constables and newly-appointed dedicated investigators through to specialists and senior investigating officers (SIOs), are required to demonstrate the competencies appropriate to their role. The development of a framework of skills and competencies for each role has been the responsibility of the Police Skills and Standards Organisation (now called 'Skills for Justice'). Such competencies are to be assessed against National Occupational Standards (NOS) and are also informed by the Core Investigative Doctrine developed by NCPE. Training systems should follow the patterns set by the competency framework, as should any future system for the accreditation of professional crime investigators (*see also* Core investigative doctrine and Professionalizing Criminal Investigation Programme (PIP)).

Confession evidence

Confession evidence was often regarded by investigators (and to an extent by the courts) as the cornerstone of 'reactive policing' and of criminal prosecutions more generally. In recent decades, however, it has been shown often to be flawed. False confessions have been at the centre of a number of prominent miscarriage-of-justice cases (*see* for example, Fisher Inquiry – *below*). The provisions of the Police and Criminal Evidence Act 1984 (PACE) and procedures such as the tape- or video-recording of police questioning have tightened the systems under which such evidence may validly be obtained. As a result investigators have been encouraged to seek more objective forms of evidence, such as those afforded by technological and scientific advances; especially identification based upon analysis of DNA (*see below*). Where questioning is required, it is based upon 'investigative interviewing' principles (*see below*).

Conversation management

(*See* Investigative interviewing *below*)

Core Investigative Doctrine

The Core Investigative Doctrine has been developed by ACPO and NCPE to provide definitive national guidance on the principles of criminal investigation. The Core Investigative Doctrine is intended to encapsulate the collective knowledge of the police service into a coherent set of guidance. It is published in the form of manuals written specifically for practitioners and is often accompanied by a training programme. It also refers investigators to further sources of information and specialist techniques for investigating particular types of crime (*see also* Competency framework and Professionalizing Criminal Investigation Programme (PIP)).

Corruption

The term 'police corruption' has been used to describe many activities: bribery, violence and brutality; fabrication and destruction of evidence; racism; and favouritism and nepotism. Most typologies include a range of activities that can be analysed along five dimensions: the acts and the actors involved; the norms violated; the degree of support from the peer group; the degree of organisation of deviant practices; and the reaction of the police department. Police corruption, it is generally accepted, necessarily involves an abuse of position; what is corrupted is the special 'trust' invested in the occupation. Investigators in fields such as drugs, vice and undercover work may be particularly susceptible to temptation, because of their role at the so-called 'invitational-edge' of corrupt activities.

Council for the Registration of Forensic Practitioners (CRFP)

CRFP is the professional regulatory body for forensic practitioners. Although it is non-profit-making limited company, it is funded by the Home Office by means of a grant. Those registered by CRFP are assessed by current practitioners and accreditation is based upon a review of their recent cases.

Covert Human Intelligence Source (CHIS)

A 'Covert Human Intelligence Source' (CHIS) is the now preferred term in policing for 'informant'. These are now often handled by Dedicated Source Units (DSUs) through which integrity and confidentiality are preserved.

Covert methods

Advances in technology and the need to combat serious crime have had a significant impact on British policing. Covert investigative methods, such as the use of surveillance devices, informants (CHIS) and undercover operations, backed by extensive databases of criminal intelligence information, are now widely employed. Increasingly, attention is being paid to the need to regulate and control covert policing. Both the Human Rights Act 1998 (HRA) and the Regulation of Investigatory Powers Act 2000 (RIPA) are relevant in this regard (*see below*).

Crime analysis

The synthesis of police and other relevant data to identify and interpret patterns and trends in crime (among offenders, offences, victims, spaces and places) in order to inform policing, investigation and criminal justice practice. A number of more specific terms may also be identified:

Analytical process – a series of stages including, inter alia, collection of data, representation of data, recommendations, evaluation
Tactical analysis – aims to maximise the impact of enforcement by reviewing current crime problems and prolific offenders to inform investigations and operations.
Analytical techniques - these may include crime pattern analysis, time series analysis and risk analysis.

Crime management

The idea that investigations can be managed proactively, with resource deployment according to their seriousness and likelihood of clear-up. (*See also* Triage.)

Crime Mapping Analysis (CMA)
Crime is unevenly spatially and temporally distributed. It is possible, therefore, to 'map' crime according to where and when it occurred (and by type of offence). Such mapping can help in their targeting, deployment and allocation of crime prevention and investigative resources to areas of vulnerability. Maps showing patterns or hotspots of crime can present effective visual images that help people to understand their distribution and to explore possible reasons behind certain types of criminal activity. Such explorations of crime data are increasingly being complemented by the use of socio-demographic data to help understand the distribution of crime. (*See also* crime analysis, hotspots.)

Crime Scene Investigation (CSI)
Also known as crime scene examination, this is carried out through the preservation and construction of a series of physical artefacts alongside a contemporaneous written record of observations made and actions taken during the examination. This work is carried out by Crime Scene Investigators, which is the term now commonly in use to replace the previously entitled Scenes of Crime Officers (SOCO – *see below*). Subsequent examination and questioning of these artefacts are undertaken by other forensic experts. This, together with witness accounts, provides an opportunity for reconstructing and interpreting the events that took place before, during and after the commission of the crime.

Criminalistics
Criminalistics is another name for forensic identification science. Logically speaking, criminalistics is the science of individualisation or source attribution; properly understood as the systematic process of associating every trace with its source (*see* individualisation *below*). Criminalistics is also a term sometimes used (perhaps more generally) to refer to the whole process of forensic crime-scene investigation.

Critical incident management
A 'critical incident' can be defined as any event where the effectiveness of the policing response is likely to have a significant impact of the confidence of the victim, their family or the community. They include such things as a racist or sectarian murder or other hate-crimes (*see* Stephen Lawrence Inquiry, *below*). The management of critical incidents requires a systematic and sensitive approach. It includes the provision of family liaison officers; carrying out community impact and other risk assessments; providing management structures with minimum standards for supervision; the involvement of lay advisors; keeping logs of decisions taken and the reasons for taking them; and systematic debriefing.

Deductive inference
Deductive inference is the process of reasoning from a set of valid premises to a logically compelling conclusion. Although it is the method apparently favoured by the fictional Sherlock Holmes and his followers, the ambiguities of information and the probabilistic nature of evidence mean that it is of very limited utility when set against the real-world problems of modern criminal investigation. For comparison with other forms of reasoning of relevance to criminal investigation, *see* Abductive inference and Inductive inference *above*.

Detection rate
Detection rates (the offences 'cleared up' by the police) are an important indicator of performance. The detection rate is expressed as the percentage of the number

of detections against total number of recorded offences under each category of recorded crime. The detection statistics published by the Home Office distinguish between 'sanction' detections and 'non-sanction' detections. The former (as 'offences brought to justice' (OBTJ)), involve crimes where the suspect is charged, cautioned or where offences are 'taken into consideration' (TIC). The latter are offences which are regarded as detected for administrative reasons, or where no further action is taken.

DNA evidence
DNA (Deoxyribonucleic acid) is found in the cells of the body and contains genetic information that helps determine a person's physical characteristics. Each person's DNA is unique (with the exception of identical twins). DNA profiling is used to examine samples such as semen, saliva and blood and to establish how much one person's DNA differs from that of another. Samples taken from suspects detained for recordable offences may be compared with others found at a scene of crime and with information held on the National DNA database (NDNAD – *see below*).

Due process and crime control
An ideal typical formulation of contrasting models of criminal justice outlined by Herbert Packer (a distinguished American academic lawyer). The ideal types are designed to contrast differing emphases on procedure and outcome. Thus the values inherent in 'due process' give greater prominence to civil liberties in order to maximise the likelihood that the innocent will be acquitted. By contrast the values inherent in the 'crime control' model give much greater prominence to the goal of convicting the guilty.

Europol
Europol is the European Union law enforcement organisation that handles criminal intelligence. Its mission is to assist the law enforcement authorities of member states in their fight against serious forms of organised crime. It was established in the Maastricht Treaty in 1992 and is based in The Hague (http://www.europol.eu.int).

Evidence-based practice
Evidence-based practice encapsulates the idea that whatever an organisation does should be underpinned by evidence of 'what works'. Thus, just as the National Institute for Clinical Excellence was established in the Health Service in 1999, so similar developments are being encouraged in policing, including the establishment of the National Centre for Policing Excellence (NCPE) (*see also* Centrex, National Centre for Policing Excellence, National Police Improvement Agency (NPIA), Competency framework).

Family liaison officer (FLO)
The deployment of a Family Liaison Officer is now a fairly standard procedure in relation to the investigation of homicide and some other serious crimes. Although the role of the FLO is primarily to provide emotional and practical support for a bereaved family, they can also make an important contribution to the investigation itself. Because they are close to the victim's relatives they are well placed to identify any indications of suspicion which might help to progress the investigation (*see also* Critical incident management).

Fingerprint evidence
Dactyloscopy, or the comparative examination of fingerprints (friction ridge patterns), is an important part of the identification process. Fingerprint evidence uses categorical

conclusions, in the sense that fingerprint practitioners have long relied upon the assumption that each individual carries unique fingerprints; something which they regard as setting it apart from other forms of probabilistic identification (*see* Probability, *below*). The collection of fingerprint evidence at scenes of crime is the responsibility of Crime Scene Investigators (CSIs). Marks at scenes are then compared with those previously obtained, either from criminal records or from other scenes of crime. The process of identification has been enhanced by the introduction (in 2001) of records held by the National Automated Fingerprint Identification Service (NAFIS), which processes the prints of arrestees and allows computerised comparison of crime-scene marks. The increasing provision of the digital 'livescan' technology allows scans and comparisons to be made directly from individuals or deceased persons rather than through paper records.

Fisher Inquiry (1977)
An official inquiry under Sir Henry Fisher (a High Court Judge), who examined failures in police questioning in the case relating to the murder of Maxwell Confait. In this case, three teenage boys had been convicted on the basis of false confessions, which they had provided because of their suggestibility. Fisher's recommendations were an import element in the deliberations of the Royal Commission on Criminal Procedure 1981 and subsequently influenced the Police and Criminal Evidence Act 1984. (*See* Confession Evidence; Investigative Interviewing; Police and Criminal Evidence Act 1984.)

Forensic reconstruction
A significant element of the forensic process at a crime-scene and thereafter involves the attempt to reconstruct the sequence of events being investigated.

Forensic Science Service (FSS)
Until the late 1980s, forensic science was within the full remit of the Home Office. Thereafter, the FSS became an independent supplier, as an 'executive agency' of the Home Office, charging police forces and other agencies for their services. In fact, other companies also now provide forensic science services and some police forces do not use FSS at all. In the future, the FSS may become a private company. However, the primary responsibility for crime-scene assessment remains with police forces, through Crime Scene Investigators (CSIs), coordinated by Scientific Support Units (SSUs) (*see below*).

'Golden hour' principle
The principle that quick and effective response to the scene of a crime is imperative in terms of being able to identify and acquire correctly those materials necessary for conducting a successful investigation. This is especially important in serious crime cases such as homicide but could be applied to all crimes.

Her Majesty's Inspectorate of Constabulary (HMIC)
For well over a century, HM Inspectors of Constabulary have been charged with examining and improving the efficiency of the police service in England and Wales, with the first HMIs appointed under the provisions of the County and Borough Police Act 1856. In 1962, the Royal Commission on the Police formally acknowledged their contribution to policing. The statutory duties of HMIs are described in the Police Act 1996 (http://www.homeoffice.gov.uk/hmic/hmic.htm).

Home Office

The government department currently responsible for internal affairs in England and Wales and therefore for police and policing policy. Recent proposals suggest that this large department may be divided into a separate Ministry of Justice responsible for penal and criminal justice matters and another responsible for public security. (http://www.homeoffice.gov.uk).

Home Office Large Major Enquiry System (HOLMES)

Introduced in its earlier form after the failures of information management in the Yorkshire Ripper Inquiry (*see below*), HOLMES is a computerised investigation database which is routinely used in major investigations, especially homicide inquiries. It enables the comprehensive storage and retrieval of information collected during a major crime investigation (now updated to HOLMES 2).

Hot products

So-called 'hot products' are those that are most likely to be taken by thieves. Following insights from research on hotspots and repeat victimisation, the theory is that a better understanding of which products are 'hot', and why, could help to reduce certain forms of crime. This is as relevant to the investigation of high volume crime as it is to prevention methodologies (*see also* hotspot, repeat victimisation) (http://crimereduction.gov.uk/stolengoods1.htm).

Hotspots

Arising from the finding that crime is highly concentrated geographically and socially. Some communities have crime rates 10–20 times higher than others and in both crime prevention and investigation terms, focusing resources where crime is highest – 'hotspots' – is likely to yield the greatest results. To do this accurately, information and analysis of crime data are required, usually referred to as crime mapping (*see also* crime analysis) (http://www.crimereduction.gov.uk/toolkits/p031309.htm).

Human Rights Act 1998 (HRA)

This Act gives legal effect in England and Wales to the substantive rights guaranteed by the European Convention on Human Rights (ECHR) and the decisions of the European Court of Human Rights (ECtHR) in Strasbourg. ECHR guarantees (amongst other rights) the right to life; freedom from torture or degrading treatment or punishment; the freedom from slavery; the right to liberty and security of the person; the right to a fair trial; the right to respect for private and family life, home and correspondence; right to freedom of thought, conscience and religion; freedom of expression; and freedom of assembly and association. As 'public authorities' under the Act, the public police and other investigative bodies have an obligation to respect these rights. The courts in England and Wales can now directly take account of the Articles of the convention and redress may be sought initially in the domestic jurisdiction. However, it remains open for an applicant to take the case to ECtHR where it is thought that the domestic court has misinterpreted the ECHR or failed to take account of an applicant's rights.

Identification evidence

This usually refers to identification of suspects by eye-witnesses; something which has been subject to critical examination in recent years and which is now regulated by PACE. Due to psychological limitations of eye-witness evidence, there are dangers in uncritical reliance on evidence of this kind. Other forms of identification, including fingerprints and DNA, are regarded as having more objectivity.

IMPACT

IMPACT is a national police database that will link up police information and intelligence across England and Wales. It paves the way for a new technology-based system designed to connect information held locally and nationally by police systems, as well as on the Police National Computer. It is intended to provide investigating officers, for the first time, with a single point of inquiry and access to operational information held by forces anywhere in the country. It provides a nominal index, and a police national database linking information held on both local and national systems. This will include replacing the Police National Computer by 2010.

Independent Police Complaints Commission (IPCC)

The Independent Police Complaints Commission (IPCC) was created by the Police Reform Act 2002 and became operational on 1 April 2004. It is a non-departmental public body funded by the Home Office, but independent of the police, interest groups and political parties. IPCC has a legal duty to oversee the whole of the police complaints system but also carries out investigations into serious or contentious cases, including those where suspects are shot by police. In Northern Ireland, the Police Ombudsman has similar responsibilities.

Individualisation

In forensic science, individualisation is the establishment of an association between a trace and single unique source of that trace. 'Criminalistics' is the science of individualisation (*see above*).

Inductive inference

Inductive inference is the process of reasoning from observed particular instances to a probable conclusion. Although the combination of observations may not lead to the conclusion in a strictly logical sense, if they have enough weight (or a high probability) we can legitimately draw conclusions from them, or at least use them to test our hypotheses. Although inductive inference may not often explicitly be used as a model for criminal investigation, it may provide a better explanation for the claim that some investigations have followed 'scientific' principles than other approaches (*see also* Abductive inference *and* Deductive inference).

Intelligence

Information derived from informants (CHIS) and other sources. However, intelligence is not simply the raw data from such sources. The intelligence cycle includes the collection, evaluation, analysis and dissemination/actioning of criminal intelligence at the relevant levels in police and other investigative agencies. Police forces now employ many (mainly civilian) intelligence and crime analysts, whose principal job is to create intelligence products for both strategic and tactical use (*see also* Crime analysis, Covert human intelligence sources (CHIS), National Intelligence Model (NIM)).

Intelligence analysis tools

These include systems such as I2 and WATSON which allow flexible manipulation of intelligence data and its pictorial representation, enabling the development of investigative themes and association charting.

Intelligence-led policing

Essentially, a model which seeks to increase the effectiveness of policing through greater emphasis on the collection and analysis of intelligence and the development of targeted responses to that analysis (*see also* Crime analysis, National Intelligence Model, problem-oriented policing).

International Criminal Police Organisation (ICPO-Interpol)
'Interpol' was officially adopted as the International Criminal Police Organisation (abbreviated to ICPO-Interpol) in 1956. Interpol was set up to enhance and facilitate cross border criminal police cooperation. Today it is the second biggest international organisation after the United Nations, with 181 member countries spread over five continents (http://www.interpol.int/default.asp).

Investigative interviewing
The term introduced during the 1990s to represent the shift in focus in police interviewing away from the traditional process of questioning (interrogation) aimed at obtaining confessions towards more generalised evidence gathering (*see* Confession evidence *above*). In England and Wales, investigative interviewing as a 'search for truth' is based upon five distinct parts, represented by the mnemonic PEACE (*see below*). The two methods taught for eliciting an account from the interviewee are the 'cognitive interview' and 'conversation management'. The cognitive interview involves a memory-facilitating process based on psychological principles and is commonly used with cooperative witnesses and suspects. Conversation management is recommended when cooperation from a suspect is not forthcoming. (*See also* Reid Technique *below*.)

Laming Inquiry 2003
A public inquiry into the death of eight-year-old Victoria Climbié was set up after an Old Bailey jury found her carers, Marie-Therese Kouao and Carl Manning, guilty of murder and child abuse in 2001. Chaired by Lord Laming, the former Chief Inspector of the Social Services Inspectorate, the inquiry finally reported in January 2003. The inquiry severely criticised the agencies who could have taken more effective action, including local social services and police. The failure of child protection arrangements in this case led to an overhaul of the child protection system, including a new Children Act, and to changes to procedures and resources in local police child protection.

Major Incident Room Standardised Administrative Procedures (MIRSAP)
A major incident room is set up at a very early stage during enquiries into serious crime. It is the coordinating hub of investigative activity, with roles covering both investigative management and information management. The former includes co-ordinating lines of enquiry and allocating 'actions' and the latter processing and analysing incoming data and establishing further lines of enquiry based upon this analysis. The processes of gathering and collating evidence in such enquiries are managed to national standards through agreed Major Incident Room Standardised Administrative Procedures (MIRSAP). (*See also* Home Office Large Major Enquiry system (HOLMES) – *above*.)

Media liaison
This is an important function in the investigation of serious crime. It includes devising strategies and working with the local and national media to provide appropriate information on such things as progress of the case, appeals for witnesses and public reassurance.

Murder Investigation Manual (MIM)
This was first published by ACPO in 1998, to set out guidance to investigators

on the investigation of homicide. It complements MIRSAP (*see above*). The most recent (2006) edition produced by NCPE for ACPO covers the role of the senior investigating officer; the strategic management of homicide and major incident investigations; the role of chief officers; major crime reviews; working with other agencies; investigative support; coroners and inquests, inter-jurisdictional homicide investigations; crime-scene management; forensic strategy and pathology; searches; house-to-house enquiries; witness management; family liaison; communication; community involvement; elimination enquiries; suspect management; surveillance and covert human intelligence sources; and reconstructions.

National Automated Fingerprint Identification Service (NAFIS)
See Fingerprint evidence, *above*.

National Centre for Policing Excellence (NCPE)
The concept of the National Centre for Policing Excellence was introduced in the government's 2001 white paper, *Policing a New Century: A Blueprint for Reform.* (http//www.archive.official-documents.co.uk/document/cm53/5326/cm5326.htm). The work programme of NCPE reflects the requirements of the National Policing Plan, especially its intention to tackle and reduce crime by reversing the fall in detection and conviction rates (http://www.centrex.police.uk). (*See also* National Police Improvement agency (NPIA).)

National Crime Squad (NCS)
National Crime Squad (NCS) was established in April 1998 as a result of the 1995 report by the Home Affairs Select Committee on the threat of organised crime and its impact on the UK. This report argued for the replacement of the existing structure of separate regional crime squads (RCS) by a more nationally coordinated structure. NCS was responsible for the investigation of serious organised crime at the national level until the formation in April 2006 of the Serious Organised Crime Agency (SOCA – *see below*), into which it was incorporated.

National Criminal Intelligence Service (NCIS)
NCIS was responsible for providing strategic and tactical intelligence on serious and organised crime, nationally and internationally and for providing the gateway for UK law enforcement enquiries overseas via Interpol, Europol and its overseas liaison officers. It also provided the coordinating authority on behalf of UK police forces for the tasking of the Security Service, in accordance with the Security Service Act 1996. These functions were incorporated into the Serious Organised Crime Agency (SOCA – *see below*) when it was formed in April 2006.

National DNA Database (NDNAD)
NDNAD was established in England and Wales in 1995. Scotland and Northern Ireland have their own databases and submit profiles to NDNAD. DNA profiles of persons arrested and detained in police custody for a recordable offence are held in the database, together with crime-scene samples and samples taken from volunteers.

National Intelligence Model (NIM)
It has been argued that intelligence has lagged behind investigation in the codification of best practice, professional knowledge and in the identification of selection and training requirements of police service staff. As a consequence, a model, namely the National Intelligence Model (NIM), encapsulating best practice in intelligence-

led policing and law enforcement, was developed. NIM recognises the important function of police (especially investigators) as information-brokers and managers at the strategic and tactical levels. It sets out the 'business processes' required at each of three levels, namely national/international; force/regional; and basic command unit (BCU), which enable intelligence to be gathered and used in a structured way. The tasking and co-ordinating processes of NIM allow resources to be allocated in a more rational and cost-effective manner. Specific NIM intelligence products are based upon nine analytical techniques including: crime pattern analysis; market profile analysis; demographic/social trend analysis; criminal business profile; network analysis; risk analysis; target profile analysis; operational intelligence assessment; and results analysis.

National Police Improvement Agency (NPIA)
This agency will replace the existing national policing organisations such as the Police Information Technology Organisation (PITO) and Centrex (including NCPE) and will also take on new work needed to support national police development. It will support local implementation of the government's policing priorities, including the recommendations of the Bichard inquiry (*see above*).

Offender profiling
Although there is no universally accepted definition, offender profiling is the name given to various scientific and psychological theories and techniques that attempt to draw inferences about an offender's characteristics by examining behaviour exhibited at a crime scene. There has been a rapidly growing interest in this subject over recent years both within the police service and in the media through films like *Silence of the Lambs* and television programmes such as *Cracker*.

Organised crime
Organised criminal groups often use violence, coercion or corruption to maintain discipline; to influence victims and competitors; and to deter law enforcement. Their activities include protection rackets, trafficking in drugs and people, fraud, corporate crime and money laundering. Measures for investigating organised crime operate at the national, international and local levels. In addition to the role of individual police forces, the Serious and Organised Crime Agency (SOCA - *see below*) brings together police, customs and intelligence officers to deal with serious cases and to form links with agencies abroad. The Security Services have increasingly become involved in this field, especially where there are links with terrorism. The expansion of the Europol mission provides a means of combating organised crime across Europe. International conventions, especially those relating to drugs and to the seizure of criminal assets, help to tackle the problems of organised crime internationally. It is important to remember, however, that in numerical terms, the overwhelming number of operations against organised crime are mounted by, and occur within, police forces. The numbers mounted by national and international agencies are very small by comparison.

Outside inquiry team
The outside inquiry team is an important part of the investigation of serious crime. Its role is to interview witnesses, to gather evidence and to take systematic action to follow up and resolve outstanding issues generated by the major incident room team.

PEACE
The mnemonic which represents the five distinct parts required in investigative interviewing, namely;
P – Preparation and planning
E – Engage and explain
A – Account
C – Closure
E – Evaluate

Police and Criminal Evidence Act 1984 (PACE)
This Act was the outcome of the deliberations of the Royal Commission on Criminal Procedure 1981 – RCCP, *see below*) The Act and its associated guidelines control the ways in which the public police and other investigative agencies deal with suspected offenders in respect of their arrest, detention, questioning and the obtaining of samples for forensic examination. It also deals with stop, search and seizure of property, entry to premises and procedures for identification of suspects. Although amended in some aspects by subsequent legislation and not without its critics, PACE remains the most important vehicle through which the powers of investigators are codified and the rights of suspects are ensured.

Police Information Technology Organisation (PITO)
PITO is the organisation responsible for the development and commissioning of information technology for the police service and other agencies in the criminal justice system. Its work falls under six main headings: communications; identification; police national computer; criminal justice; intelligence and investigation; and police support services. These functions will be incorporated as part of the National Police Improvement Agency (NPIA), which becomes operational in April 2007 (*see also* National Police Improvement Agency).

Proactive model of investigation
Proactive methods of investigation (in contrast to 'reactive' methods, *see below*) entail initiation of the investigative process by the police or other agency rather than by victims or witnesses. In proactive investigation, the attention of the investigating agency is primarily upon the criminal, rather than upon the crime. This may be through the process of intelligence gathering, where the agency becomes aware that a crime or crimes (such as a series of robberies or a terrorist event) may be committed. It may be in relation to so-called consensual or victimless crimes, such as drug trafficking, people trafficking or money laundering. Proactive investigation often uses covert methods, including surveillance, covert human intelligence sources (CHIS – *see above*) and interception of communications to gather further intelligence and evidence prior to arrest.

Probability
In forensic science, all evidence is regarded as probabilistic. Strictly speaking, nothing is incontrovertible, even DNA evidence. The logically correct way to express the value of the findings of a source-attribution examination of trace material is in the form of a likelihood ratio. However, fingerprint practitioners have long relied upon the assumption that each individual carries unique fingerprints (*see* DNA evidence and Fingerprint evidence, *above*).

Problem-oriented policing (POP)
The brainchild of US academic lawyer and police scientist Herman Goldstein, POP

begins from a critique of incident-driven policing and suggests that policing at heart should be about solving the underlying problems within communities. At its most radical it involves empowerment of the local beat officer who is given responsibility for imaginative local problem solving. On the grand scale, it has also been an important principle in the development of more holistic approaches to policing in the UK, such as the National Intelligence Model (NIM – *see above*).

Prolific offender
Considerable criminological evidence points to the uneven distribution of offending. Put crudely, a small number of offenders are responsible for a disproportionate amount of crime. These are variously referred to as 'prolific', 'persistent', or 'volume' offenders. They have been the subject of a considerable amount of legislative attention, and are also often a particular focus of police intelligence gathering, enforcement and targeted rehabilitation programmes.

Professionalising Criminal Investigation Programme (PIP)
PIP is a tripartite ACPO, Home Office and Police Skills and Standards Organisation (PSSO) project, aimed at improving investigative standards in the public police. It was launched in September 2005 and is a core part of the government's police reform programme. When completed, PIP will provide the basis for the professional practice of criminal investigation, setting out the expert knowledge and competencies required of an investigator; alongside agreed training and accreditation procedures (*see also* Competency framework and Core investigative doctrine, *above*).

Reactive model of investigation
Despite the growth of proactive methods (*see above*), most investigation is reactive (*ex post facto*), in the sense that investigators respond to complaints from a victim or witness or react to the discovery of a crime that has already been committed; for example in a case of homicide, by the discovery of a body. The pattern of activity in reactive investigation includes crime-scene preservation and examination; the search for witnesses; and information evaluation. The purpose of such investigations is to establish who did what to whom, when, where, how and why? In recent years, the inadequacy of purely reactive investigation in dealing with high-volume crime has resulted in the development of more holistic methods of crime management. In contrast to investigation on a simple incident-by-incident basis, multiple crimes are assessed together to identify and catch offenders, and covert methods are often added to the pattern of investigative activity.

Regulation of Investigatory Powers Act 2000 (RIPA)
Introduced following a number of adverse decisions in the European Court of Human Rights, this legislation regulates the interception of communications, intrusive surveillance and the use of covert human intelligence sources (CHIS – *see above*). Constraints and safeguards are set out in a Code of Practice pursuant to the Act. The system is overseen by an Interception of Communications Commissioner and there is an Investigatory Powers Tribunal to adjudicate on abuses.

Reid Technique
An interrogation technique which is widely practised in the US, intended to break down the resistance of reluctant suspects and to make them confess. This approach is widely criticised in the UK because of its psychologically manipulative nature and its failure to address risks associated with false confessions. Evidence obtained using the Reid technique would not be admissible in the courts in England and Wales.

Royal Commission on Criminal Justice 1991-1993 (RCCJ)
In March 1991, the then Home Secretary announced the establishment of a Royal Commission on Criminal Justice to be chaired by Viscount Runciman of Doxford.
This followed growing concern about a succession of miscarriages of justice which had undermined public confidence, including the Birmingham Six case, which was specifically referred to by the Home Secretary in announcing the commission. The Royal Commission was charged with examining the effectiveness of the Criminal Justice System in securing the convictions of the guilty and the acquittal of the innocent. The commission reported in July 1993 and recommended the establishment of an independent body to consider suspected miscarriages of justice; to arrange for investigation where appropriate; and to refer cases to the Court of Appeal where matters needed further consideration. The Criminal Appeal Act 1995 was subsequently passed, enabling the establishment of the Criminal Cases Review Commission as an executive non-departmental public body.

Royal Commission on Criminal Procedure 1981 (RCCP)
The Royal Commission on Criminal Procedure (chaired by Sir Cyril Phillips) focused extensively on the rights of suspects and other matters of growing concern about police powers in investigations, especially the questioning of suspects and the use of confession evidence. Their recommendations for far-ranging changes to the law under which investigators operate led to the Police and Criminal Evidence Act 1984 (PACE – *see above*).

Scenes of Crime Officer (SOCO)
These investigators carry out examination of crime scenes for contact trace materials, including fingerprints, DNA traces, shoe-marks and other evidence. They are now usually referred to as Crime Scene Investigators or, in the case of local, high volume crime, as Volume Crime Scene Examiners (VCSEs).

Scientific Support Units/Departments (SSUs/SSDs)
Scientific Support Units or Departments exist within police forces to coordinate the work of Crime Scene Investigators, and to provide fingerprint, photographic and other expertise and overall management of the organisation's forensic efforts. The title of the unit and its internal structure may vary, depending on the organisation.

Senior Investigating Officer (SIO)
The SIO is the officer responsible for leading an investigation; for setting the strategic direction to be followed by the inquiry team; and for taking the key decisions.

Serious Organised Crime Agency (SOCA)
SOCA was created by the Serious and Organised Crime Act 2005 and became operational in April 2006. It is an executive Non-Departmental Public Body sponsored by, but operationally independent from, the Home Office. It was formed from the amalgamation of the National Crime Squad (NCS), National Criminal Intelligence Service (NCIS), that part of HM Revenue and Customs (HMRC) dealing with drug trafficking and associated criminal finance and a part of UK Immigration dealing with organised immigration crime (UKIS). It is an intelligence-led agency with law enforcement powers and responsibility for the reduction of the harm caused to people and communities by serious organised crime.

Signal crimes
A signal crime is an incident that, because of how it is interpreted, functions as a

warning signal to people about the distribution of risk throughout social space. This way of understanding the public effect of certain crimes, perhaps most particularly crimes of violence, is preferable to the somewhat amorphous concept of 'fear of crime', which has proved difficult to evaluate in terms of its distribution across affected populations.

Special Branch (SB)

With origins in the Metropolitan Police 'Irish Branch' in the nineteenth century, special branch became the policing body with primary responsibility initially for investigating espionage, and in more recent times, terrorism. Special Branch officers are involved in risk assessment in relation to terrorist threats and provide armed personal protection for people judged to be at risk. Because of their anti-terrorist role, Special Branch officers are permanently stationed at ports and airports to gather intelligence, identify suspects and to provide support to other anti-terrorist activity. On 2 October 2006, the Metropolitan Police Special Branch and the Anti-terrorist Branch were restructured to form a new Counter-terrorism Command. The protection arm of SB now forms part of the Protection Command of Metropolitan Police Specialist Operations Directorate.

Stephen Lawrence Inquiry 1999

This inquiry was established to inquire into the murder in April 1993 of Stephen Lawrence in Eltham, South East London, and the police investigation that followed. The inquiry, chaired by Sir William Macpherson (later Lord Macpherson of Cluny) was set up by Jack Straw in 1997 and reported in February 1999. It made 70 recommendations, and famously concluded that 'the police investigation was marred by a combination of professional incompetence, institutional racism and a failure of leadership by senior officers'.

Terrorism

This term is highly problematic to define but in shorthand, it is often referred to simply as 'political violence'. The definition of terrorism in s.1 of the Terrorism Act 2000 includes actual or threatened acts of violence against people and/or property designed to influence the government, to intimidate the public, or to advance a political, religious or ideological cause.

Transfer principle

Locard's principle that 'every contact leaves a trace' is one of the underlying principles of criminalistics (*see above*). Also known as the 'exchange principle', the transference may go either way – i.e., from crime-scene to person and *vice versa*. However, the transfer principle may sometimes appear to be in contradiction of another principle of criminalistics, namely, that 'absence of evidence is not evidence of absence'. Absence of evidence may of course, be due to human limitations or to a lack of 'technically detectable' traces.

Triage

Triage is the crime-management process and set of protocols through which decisions are made as to what action should be taken on cases of reported crime. Also known as case-screening, this was introduced into the UK during the 1980s and has been further refined since then. The crime-desk takes the initial report and screening is carried out within the local crime management unit where further decisions for action and resource deployment are made.

Vulnerable and Intimidated Witnesses (VIWs)

The Youth Justice and Criminal Evidence Act (1999) and the Vulnerable Witnesses (Scotland) Act (2004) identified five categories of vulnerable and intimidated witness, namely: children; adults with learning disabilities; adults with a physical disability or disorder; adults with a mental disorder; adult suffering from fear or distress as a result of crime or intimidation. Such witnesses are entitled to special measures in courts when required to give evidence although an investigating officer also has a clear responsibility for identifying such people early in an investigation and providing pre-trial support.

Yorkshire Ripper Inquiry

This refers to the investigation of a series of at least 13 murders committed by Peter Sutcliffe during the late 1970s and early 1980s against women in the north of England. Misjudgements by the inquiry team, including the failure to identify Sutcliffe from the huge volume of material generated by the inquiry, led to public and official condemnation. The failures in this case were subject to inquiry by Sir Lawrence Byford, then Chief HMI. The Byford Report (1981) was a spur to the introduction of the HOLMES computer system (*see above*), although his full findings have only recently reached the public domain.

Index

Muir, Richard 30
Municipal Corporations Act 1835 16
murder
  critical incidents 572, 575, 582
  ethics and corruption 46, 600
  forensic science 305–7, 389–91, 397–9
  history of criminal investigation 25,
    26, 33
  investigative interviewing 472, 482,
    485
  major crime inquiries 256–7, 259–65,
    269–70, 272–3
  management, supervision and
    oversight 549, 565
  media 153, 160
  miscarriages of justice 613, 618, 623
  models of investigation 408, 409, 410,
    418
  police powers 99
  private investigation 287, 288
  professionalization 632, 633, 644
  profiling places 533, 542
  profiling suspects 495, 499
  trace biometrics 369
  witnesses 451
Murder Blues 154
Murder Investigation Manual 391, 397–8,
  552, 623, 635, 640, 666–7
The Murder of Stephen Lawrence 153
Murder Prevention 152, 153, 157
Murray, Dr Henry 494
mutual judicial assistance 184–7

narrative reasoning 264–9, 616, 654
National Automated Fingerprint
  Identification Service (NAFIS) 244,
  369, 375, 389, 667
National Centre for Policing Excellence
  (NCPE)
  definition 667
  forensic science 391
  management, supervision and
    oversight 57, 552
  models of investigation 420
  professionalization 7, 634, 635, 636,
    640
  profiling places 542
  profiling suspects 502, 506
National Crime Recording Standard 232
National Crime Squad (NCS) 32, 59,
  203, 432, 435, 667
National Criminal Intelligence Service

(NCIS)
  centralization 58, 59
  covert surveillance 433, 435
  criminal intelligence 201, 203, 210
  definition 667
  history of criminal investigation 32
  organized crime 192
National DNA Database (NDNAD)
  definition 667
  forensic science 34, 343, 382, 385, 386,
    399
  high-volume crime 244, 343
  law 131
  trace biometrics 368
National Drugs Intelligence Unit (NDIU)
  59
National Intelligence Model (NIM)
  criminal intelligence 201, 203, 207–9,
    210–16, 218–21
  definition 667–8
  forensic science 352
  future of investigation 653
  high-volume crime 249
  management, supervision and
    oversight 58, 553
  private investigation 290, 291
  understanding investigation 4–5, 8
National Occupational Standards (NOS)
  642, 643
National Policing Board 33
National Policing Improvement Agency
  (NPIA)
  definition 668
  forensic science 392
  history of criminal investigation 28, 33
  management, supervision and
    oversight 548, 552, 556
  professionalization 7, 635, 642
National Policing Plan 4, 33, 58, 210,
  564, 628
national security 61, 62, 194, 440
National Security Advice Centre (NSAC)
  194
National Statistics Area Classification
  536
National Technical Assistance Centre
  (NTAC) 192
National Training Centre for Scientific
  Support to Crime Investigation
  (NTC) 390, 400
NCIS *see* National Criminal Intelligence
  Service